Pro Azure Governance and Security

A Comprehensive Guide to Safeguarding Your Cloud Computing

Second Edition

Rezwanur Rahman

Apress®

Pro Azure Governance and Security: A Comprehensive Guide to Safeguarding Your Cloud Computing, Second Edition

Rezwanur Rahman
Innsbruck, Austria

ISBN-13 (pbk): 979-8-8688-1526-3				ISBN-13 (electronic): 979-8-8688-1527-0
https://doi.org/10.1007/979-8-8688-1527-0

Copyright © 2025 by Rezwanur Rahman

This work is subject to copyright. All rights are reserved by the Publisher, whether the whole or part of the material is concerned, specifically the rights of translation, reprinting, reuse of illustrations, recitation, broadcasting, reproduction on microfilms or in any other physical way, and transmission or information storage and retrieval, electronic adaptation, computer software, or by similar or dissimilar methodology now known or hereafter developed.

Trademarked names, logos, and images may appear in this book. Rather than use a trademark symbol with every occurrence of a trademarked name, logo, or image we use the names, logos, and images only in an editorial fashion and to the benefit of the trademark owner, with no intention of infringement of the trademark.

The use in this publication of trade names, trademarks, service marks, and similar terms, even if they are not identified as such, is not to be taken as an expression of opinion as to whether or not they are subject to proprietary rights.

While the advice and information in this book are believed to be true and accurate at the date of publication, neither the authors nor the editors nor the publisher can accept any legal responsibility for any errors or omissions that may be made. The publisher makes no warranty, express or implied, with respect to the material contained herein.

    Managing Director, Apress Media LLC: Welmoed Spahr
    Acquisitions Editor: Ryan Byrnes
    Editorial Assistant: Gryffin Winkler

Cover designed by eStudioCalamar

Cover image designed by Photoangel on freepik

Distributed to the book trade worldwide by Springer Science+Business Media New York, 1 New York Plaza, New York, NY 10004. Phone 1-800-SPRINGER, fax (201) 348-4505, e-mail orders-ny@springer-sbm.com, or visit www.springeronline.com. Apress Media, LLC is a Delaware LLC and the sole member (owner) is Springer Science + Business Media Finance Inc (SSBM Finance Inc). SSBM Finance Inc is a **Delaware** corporation.

For information on translations, please e-mail booktranslations@springernature.com; for reprint, paperback, or audio rights, please e-mail bookpermissions@springernature.com.

Apress titles may be purchased in bulk for academic, corporate, or promotional use. eBook versions and licenses are also available for most titles. For more information, reference our Print and eBook Bulk Sales web page at http://www.apress.com/bulk-sales.

Any source code or other supplementary material referenced by the author in this book is available to readers on GitHub. For more detailed information, please visit https://www.apress.com/gp/services/source-code.

If disposing of this product, please recycle the paper

*Dedicated to my parents, sister, and radiant wife —
the stars in my sky, the ink in my life.*

Table of Contents

About the Author xvii

About the Technical Reviewer xix

Acknowledgments xxi

Introduction xxiii

Chapter 1: Modern Governance in the Cloud 1

Evolution of Cloud Governance 1

    Governance in Cloud Provider 2

    Governance in Cloud Consumer 3

Key Principle of Cloud Governance 4

    Core Principles of Cloud Governance 4

    Tools for Enforcement 5

Overview of Azure Governance Services 9

    Tenants 10

    Subscriptions 11

    Management Group 13

    Resources and Resource Group 16

    Blueprints 18

Role of Cloud Governance in Digital Transformation 20

    How Governance Facilitates Digital Transformation 20

    Strategic Importance of Governance Planning and Implementation 21

Summary 31

TABLE OF CONTENTS

Chapter 2: Advanced Azure Scaffold for Enterprise Architecture 33
Designing an Effective Azure Scaffold 33
Governance and Security Best Practices 35
Management Group Strategies 38
Subscription Models and Scalability 41
Summary 42

Chapter 3: Contemporary Azure Naming Conventions and Standards 43
Importance of Consistent Naming Conventions 43
    General Recommendations and Standards 44
    Azure Governance Naming Categories 45
Advanced Tagging Strategies 47
    Tags for Governance and Compliance 49
Automation of Naming Standards 50
    Naming at Scale with Automation 50
Naming Standards in Action 55
    Subscriptions 56
    Resource Groups 59
    Management Groups 60
    Policies 63
    Initiatives 67
    Blueprints 69
Summary 74

Chapter 4: Comprehensive Azure Policy Implementation 75
Introduction to Azure Policy 75
    Azure Policy Planning 76
    Azure Policy Terminology 76
    Policy Basics 78
    Policy Location 81
Creating and Managing Policy Definitions 83
    Creating Policy Definitions 83

Assigning Policies	89
Updating Policies and Assignments	96
Policy Initiatives and Scoping	102
Creating Initiatives	103
Assigning Initiatives	108
Updating Initiatives	113
Policy Assignment Scope and Exclusions	115
Compliance Management and Reporting	116
Taking Action on Policy Results	117
Real-Time Policy Enforcement	121
Remediation Options	122
Manual Remediation	122
Automatic Remediation	122
Summary	123

Chapter 5: Enhanced Security with Microsoft Defender for Cloud 125

Overview of Microsoft Defender for Cloud and Its Capabilities	125
A Changing World of Cloud Security	126
Cloud Security Is Still a Shared Responsibility	128
Addressing Modern Security Challenges	129
Key Features of Microsoft Defender for Cloud	131
Real-Time Threat Protection	137
Defender for DevOps: Security from Code to Cloud	138
Compliance, Automation, and Playbooks	140
Pricing: Free vs. Paid Defender Plans	143
Configuring Microsoft Defender for Cloud for Enterprises	146
Enabling Free Tier	147
Managing Microsoft Defender for Cloud Using PowerShell	148
Enabling Paid Defender Plans	151
Switching Between Editions	156
Collecting Data in Microsoft Defender for Cloud	157

TABLE OF CONTENTS

Advanced Threat Protection and Detection 159
    Just-in-Time VM Access 160
    File Integrity Monitoring 166
    Threat Detection and Response 168
    Simulating Attacks 170
    Microsoft Defender for Cloud Threat Intelligence Report 171

Security Automation and Orchestration 179
    What Are Security Playbooks? 179
    Building Automated Workflow Using Logic Apps 180
    Configuring Playbook Triggers 195

Continuous Security Monitoring 198
    Fixing Security Recommendations 198
    Monitoring Resource Health 200
    Hardening Network Resources 201

Firewall Management 206
    Azure Firewall Manager 206

Conclusion 211

Chapter 6: Leveraging Azure Monitor and Log Analytics for Operations 213

Comprehensive Monitoring Strategies 214
    Defining a Monitoring Strategy Aligned with Governance Goals 214
    Differences Between Observability, Monitoring, and Alerting 217
    Monitoring in Hybrid vs. Cloud-Native Environment 218
    Hybrid Monitoring: Bridging Two Worlds 218
    Cloud-Native Monitoring: Born in the Cloud 219

Understanding Core Concept of Azure Monitor 221
    Metrics: Real-Time Numerical Data 221
    Logs: Detailed Event and Diagnostic Data 223
    Workbooks: Interactive Data Visualization and Reporting 226

Exploring Log Analytics Workspace 227
    What Is a Log Analytics Workspace 227

    Creating and Adding Resources in Log Analytics Workspace 228

    Writing Basic Kusto Query Language (KQL) 233

    Real-World Use Cases 237

    Demo: Try KQL Using Microsoft Demo Environment 239

Automated Alerting and Response 246

    Setting Up Alerting in Azure Monitor 247

Summary 256

Chapter 7: Scaling Governance with Azure Blueprints 257

Introduction to Azure Blueprints 257

    What Are Azure Blueprints? 258

    Key Concepts: Definitions, Artifacts, Assignments 259

    Why Organizations Need Blueprints for Governance at Scale 261

    Blueprints vs. ARM Template vs. Azure Policy 263

    Supported Artifact Types 265

    Use Cases: Greenfield vs. Brownfield Environments 268

Creating and Assigning Blueprints 269

    Designing Blueprint Structure for Standardized Environment 270

    Creating Blueprint Definitions in Azure Portal 274

    Specifying Artifacts: Best Practices for Each Artifact Type 286

    Publishing Azure Blueprints with Versioning 294

    Assigning Blueprint to Subscriptions 298

    Parameterization and Dynamic Assignment 302

    Blueprint Assignment Modes: Locking Options (ReadOnly, DoNotDelete, Don't Lock) 304

    Troubleshooting Assignment Failures 305

Lifecycle Management of Blueprints 308

    Understanding the Blueprint Lifecycle 308

    Blueprint Lifecycle Stages 309

    Updating Blueprints Without Impacting Assignments 311

Infrastructure As Code (IaC) with ARM Templates 313

    What Is Infrastructure As Code in Azure? 314

    Core Concepts of ARM Template Design 316

TABLE OF CONTENTS

    Validation and Testing of ARM Templates 329

    Integration with Source Control Systems 331

    Real-World Scenarios: Automating Environment Deployments 335

Summary.. 336

Chapter 8: Azure Sentinel: Next-Generation SIEM 339

Introduction to Azure Sentinel.. 339

    What Is Azure Sentinel?... 340

    Why Cloud-Native SIEM? 341

    Comparison: Traditional SIEM vs. Azure Sentinel 343

    Positioning Sentinel Within Microsoft Security Ecosystem 344

Key Features and Benefits of Azure Sentinel 346

    Scalability and Cloud-Native Architecture 346

    Native Integration with Microsoft 365, Defender, and Other Services............. 348

    Machine Learning and AI for Threat Detection 349

    Integration with MITRE ATT&CK Framework.. 351

    Custom Workbooks and Dashboards 352

Deploying and Configuring Azure Sentinel 354

    Prerequisites and Initial Planning... 355

    Step by Step: Onboarding Azure Sentinel 357

    Connecting Data Sources 361

Automating Incident Response with Playbooks 368

    What Are Playbooks (Based on Logic Apps)?... 368

    Common Use Cases: Email Alerts, Ticketing Integration, Containment 369

    1. Email Alerts and Notifications 369

    2. Ticketing System Integration 370

    3. Threat Containment and Remediation 371

    Creating Playbooks from Templates 371

    1. Accessing Templates via Content Hub... 371

    2. Using Logic App Designer for Customization 372

    3. Trigger Types and Automation Rules... 373

Triggering Playbooks via Analytics Rules 374
1. Linking Playbooks to Analytics Rules 374
Advanced Threat Hunting Techniques 381
What Is Threat Hunting? 381
Importance of Threat Hunting in Azure Governance 382
Demo: Use Threat Hunting Query in Microsoft Sentinel 382
Using Hunting Bookmarks and Annotations 385
Leveraging Machine Learning in Azure Sentinel 386
UEBA (User and Entity Behavior Analytics) 387
Fusion Rules and Correlation 390
Microsoft Security Graph 396
Building Custom ML Models with Azure ML and Notebooks 397
Summary 408

Chapter 9: AI and Machine Learning in Cloud Security 411

AI and ML for Threat Detection 411
Gaps in Rule-Based Detection: Why Custom ML Is Now Necessary 412
Using Azure Machine Learning to Classify Suspicious Logins or Resource Changes 414
Creating Custom Models with Historical Incident Labels (True/False Positive) 424
Automating Security Responses 429
AI-Driven Decision Logic in Playbooks: Confidence-Based Branching in Logic Apps 429
Using Enrichment Data to Escalate, Isolate, or Log 437
Predictive Analytics for Security 441
What Is Predictive Security? 441
Forecasting Future Threats 442
Prioritizing Risks with AI Models 443
What Is Risk Prioritization? 443
Proactive Responses Based on Predictions 444

TABLE OF CONTENTS

Real-World Applications and Case Studies 445

    Enterprise Use Case: Reducing Alert Fatigue Using Supervised ML to Rank Alerts 445

    Cross-Cloud Risk Detection: Azure ML Model Consuming AWS IAM and
Microsoft Entra ID Login Anomalies 446

    Financial Sector: Predicting Fraudulent Resource Creation Using Correlation Graphs 447

Summary 448

Chapter 10: Implementing Zero Trust Architecture in Azure 449

Principles of Zero Trust 449

    What Is Zero Trust? 450

    Core Tenets of Zero Trust 450

    Why Zero Trust in the Cloud Era 452

    Zero Trust vs. Traditional Perimeter Security Models 453

Zero Trust Model in Azure 454

    Zero Trust Architecture for Microsoft Azure 455

    Mapping Zero Trust Pillars to Azure Services 458

    Zero Trust Maturity Model (Basic to Optimal) 462

Identity and Access Management 464

    Microsoft Entra ID as the Identity Control Plane 464

    Privileged Identity Management (PIM) 465

    Entitlement Management and Access Reviews 468

    Securing Machine Identities and Service Principals 480

Network Segmentation and Micro-segmentation 482

    The Role of Network Isolation in Zero Trust 482

    Hub-and-Spoke Network Topology in Azure 483

    NSGs, ASGs, and Route Tables 485

    Private Endpoints and Service Endpoints 486

    Micro-segmentation with Azure Application Gateway and WAF 495

Summary 496

Chapter 11: Multi-Cloud Environment 499

Governance Challenges in Multi-cloud Environments 499
- What Is Multi-cloud? 500
- Why Companies Use More Than One Cloud 500
- Common Problems in Multi-cloud: Visibility, Control, and Costs 502
- Real-World Example: Inconsistent Tagging Across Clouds 503

Tools and Strategies for Multi-cloud Governance 505
- Introduction to Governance Tools 505
- Organizing Resources with Tags and Naming Rules 506
- Tracking Cloud Costs with Microsoft Cost Management + GCP Billing 512

Integrating Azure with Other Cloud Providers 520
- Connecting Azure and AWS Using Azure Arc 520

Summary 529

Chapter 12: Future Directions in Cloud Governance and Security 531

Emerging Trends and Technologies 531
- The Expansion of Zero Trust into AI, IoT, and Edge Workloads 532
- Rise of AI-Powered Governance and Security Tools 535
- Shift Toward Multi-cloud Governance Standards 540

The Role of Quantum Computing in Cloud Security 541
- Understanding Post-Quantum Cryptography (PQC) 542
- Quantum Threat Modeling for Cloud Systems 544
- Quantum-Resistant Key Management in Azure 545
- Microsoft's Quantum Initiatives in Cloud Security 547

Enhanced Compliance and Regulatory Requirements 550
- Anticipating Changes in Global Data Privacy Laws 550
- Industry-Specific Compliance Trends 553

The Future of Cloud Governance Frameworks 557
- From Blueprints to Azure Landing Zones 3.0 557
- Sustainability and ESG Integration in Governance Strategies 561
- Looking Ahead: A Cloud Governance Vision for 2030 563

Summary 566

Chapter 13: Harnessing Azure AI and Copilot for Governance and Security 569

Overview of Azure AI Capabilities 569
    Evolution of AI in Microsoft Azure 570
    Key Azure AI Services 571
    Role of AI in Enterprise Governance and Security 577

Implementing Azure AI for Security and Compliance 579
    AI-Driven Threat Detection with Microsoft Defender for Cloud 579
    Using AI in Risk Analysis and Regulatory Compliance 581
    Demo: Automating Compliance Reports with AI 583

Introduction to Azure Copilot 590
    What Is Azure Copilot? 590
    Architecture and Deployment Overview 591
    Comparison with Other Microsoft Copilots 593

Using Copilot for Governance and Automation 597
    Copilot Scenarios for Resource Governance 597
    Automating Azure Policy Creation and Management with Copilot 602
    Enhancing Cost Management and Budget Forecasting 605

Real-World Use Cases and Best Practices 607
    AI for Large-Scale Policy Enforcement 608
    Copilot for Incident Response in Zero Trust Architectures 608
    Lessons from Early Adopters 609
    Ethical Considerations and Data Residency Concerns 610

Summary 611

Chapter 14: Elevating skills in Azure Governance and Security 613

Evolving As a Governance and Security Practitioner 613
    The Mindset of Lifelong Learning in the Azure Ecosystem 614
    Adapting to Continuous Change in Cloud Platforms 616
    The Shift from Reactive Management to Proactive Governance 618

Building a Personal Azure Governance Lab 619
    Setting Up a Free-Tier or Sandbox Environment Safely 620

Mastering Microsoft Learn for Governance and Security 625
    Targeted Learning Paths and Modules 625
    Maximizing Sandbox Labs and Assessments 627
Leveraging Open Source and Community Projects 628
    Essential GitHub Repositories Every Architect Should Follow 628
    Reusable Templates and Automation Tools 630
    Community Contributions and Collaboration 630
Certifications for Strategic Advancement 631
    SC-100, AZ-500, AZ-305: What to Pursue and Why 632
    Study Strategies, Labs, and Learn Integration 634
    Mapping Certifications to Job Roles 635
Staying Current in the Azure Ecosystem 636
    Monitoring Updates, Blogs, and Release Notes 637
    Tools for Tracking Road Map and Platform Changes 638
Summary 639

Index 641

About the Author

Rezwanur Rahman is a globally recognized cloud solution architect, Microsoft Most Valuable Professional (MVP) in Microsoft Copilot and Microsoft 365 Development, and Microsoft Certified Trainer (MCT). He currently serves as the CEO and managing director of Backend Emerging Business Limited (Backend EBL), where he spearheads digital transformation projects and champions secure, scalable cloud strategies across industries. With deep-rooted expertise in Azure governance and enterprise security, Rezwanur is widely known for architecting modern, compliant, and intelligent cloud solutions that align with business-critical requirements.

Rezwanur began his academic journey at the American International University-Bangladesh (AIUB), specializing in software engineering. His career path includes notable roles such as senior technical lead (escalation engineer) for Microsoft 365 Global Support at Microsoft and technical evangelist intern at Microsoft Bangladesh, where he developed a strong foundation in cloud-native technologies and enterprise systems.

In 2018, Rezwanur became the first Bangladeshi recipient of the Windows Insider MVP Award, a landmark achievement that underscored his leadership in emerging technologies. He later received the prestigious Microsoft MVP Award in Microsoft 365 Development in 2021, recognizing his continued contribution to Microsoft ecosystems and developer communities.

Rezwanur is an accomplished international speaker, having shared his insights at premier global conferences such as Microsoft Ignite, Microsoft AI Tour, GraphDevDay, TeamsNations, Global AI Bootcamps, M365 Developer Conferences, Global Power Platform Bootcamp, and Azure Developer Community Day. His engagements reflect a broad influence on the tech community, particularly in the fields of AI-driven development, cloud governance, and secure DevOps practices.

ABOUT THE AUTHOR

His professional portfolio is further strengthened by his active involvement in cybersecurity initiatives. Rezwanur has collaborated with leading ethical hacking and cyber awareness communities, including the Bangladesh Grey Hat Hackers and the Cybersecurity Alliance-Bangladesh, promoting secure coding practices, cyber resilience, and responsible technology use. These collaborations underscore his commitment to fostering a safer digital ecosystem both locally and globally.

His previous book, *Microsoft Copilot for Power Apps: Transforming App Development with AI Assistance*, was published by Apress in November 2024. The book serves as a comprehensive guide to leveraging AI and Copilot within the Microsoft Power Platform, bridging the gap between AI innovation and practical app development.

Beyond technology, Rezwanur's leadership has also been internationally recognized. He was nominated as the National Youth Delegate for the Commonwealth Heads of Government Meeting (CHOGM) 2018, held in London, United Kingdom. In this role, he represented Bangladesh in critical dialogues on youth empowerment, digital innovation, and sustainable development, collaborating with policymakers and heads of government from across the Commonwealth nations. Rezwanur also served as the Asian Regional Committee Member of the Commonwealth Youth Council (CYC) for the 2018–2020 term. As part of the CYC executive, he contributed to shaping regional youth policies and supporting initiatives focused on civic engagement, capacity building, and inclusive participation of young people across Asia.

Currently based in Tirol, Austria, Rezwanur continues to blend strategic vision with deep technical expertise, remaining at the forefront of Azure cloud innovation, governance, and cybersecurity. With *Pro Azure Governance and Security*, he aims to empower professionals, architects, and decision-makers with a thorough understanding of Azure's governance and security landscape, equipping them to design resilient architectures, enforce compliance at scale, and implement robust security frameworks across modern cloud environments.

About the Technical Reviewer

As an IT solutions architect with 18 years of experience, **Amit Prasad** played a pivotal role in defining and executing IT strategies that aligned with organizational objectives. This involved steering technology initiatives across the enterprise to foster innovation, improve operational efficiency, and drive measurable business outcomes. A strong focus on collaboration, technical excellence, and leadership enabled Amit to build scalable, secure, and high-performance IT solutions tailored to the specific needs of the organization.

Acknowledgments

I am deeply grateful to my father and mother for their unwavering love and steadfast support. Their encouragement has been a pillar of strength throughout this journey. My heartfelt thanks also go to my younger sister, Zarin Tasnim, and to my loving wife, Mobaswira Farzana Munia, whose patience, understanding, and belief in me have meant more than words can express.

A special note of appreciation goes to my beloved aunt, Farida Khanam. Her warmth, wisdom, and quiet confidence in me have been a guiding force and a source of enduring motivation.

I would also like to thank my technical reviewer, Amit Prasad, for his meticulous insights and valuable feedback that significantly enhanced the quality of this work. My sincere thanks to Apress and Springer Nature, especially Ryan Byrnes, for entrusting me with this second edition and for their continued support throughout the publishing process.

A heartfelt acknowledgment goes to the authors of the first edition of this book—Peter De Tender, David Rendon, and Samuel Erskine. Your foundational work laid the path for this updated edition, and I am honored to build upon your contributions.

To the incredible teams at Microsoft Bangladesh, Microsoft Austria, Microsoft Deutschland, and the Microsoft Global Headquarters—thank you for your trust and collaboration. Special thanks to Alice Piras, EMEA Lead for Community Program Management, for her generous support and guidance. I am also grateful to the Microsoft Product Groups for their partnership and to Fabian Williams, Senior Product Manager for Microsoft 365 Copilot and Microsoft Graph, for his exemplary leadership.

To my fellow Microsoft MVPs, your encouragement and open sharing of knowledge have made this experience more enriching. Lastly, I owe sincere thanks to my friend and legal advisor, Mag. Stefan Gamsjäger, whose wise counsel and dependable support were instrumental in navigating key decisions along the way.

Thank you all for being part of this meaningful journey.

Introduction

As cloud adoption accelerates, so does the need for robust governance and security practices. Azure offers a wide range of tools and frameworks—but knowing how to use them effectively is key. This book is designed to help you build a secure, compliant, and well-structured Azure environment, whether you're starting fresh or scaling an existing deployment.

What This Book Is About

Pro Azure Governance and Security is your practical companion to mastering security, compliance, and governance in Microsoft Azure. As enterprises scale their cloud presence, maintaining control, visibility, and policy consistency becomes both critical and complex. This book helps you navigate that complexity by blending strategic principles with hands-on implementation of Azure-native tools. Covering everything from naming conventions to Zero Trust and AI-driven threat detection, it prepares you to govern at scale and build resilient, compliant Azure environments.

Who This Book Is For

This book is for cloud architects, security engineers, compliance teams, and technical leaders responsible for managing secure and well-governed Azure environments. It also supports advanced learners and certification candidates seeking deeper expertise. A basic understanding of core Azure services is recommended, though intermediate readers will find ample guidance throughout.

INTRODUCTION

Structure of the Book

This book comprises 14 chapters. Here's a brief overview of what each chapter covers:

- **Chapter 1: Modern Governance in the Cloud**

    Introduces cloud-native governance principles, the shared responsibility model, and Microsoft's approach to building trust, privacy, and compliance

- **Chapter 2: Advanced Azure Scaffold for Enterprise Architecture**

    Covers how to organize tenants, management groups, subscriptions, and resource groups—laying the foundation for enterprise-scale governance

- **Chapter 3: Contemporary Azure Naming Conventions and Standards**

    Establishes consistent naming rules, tagging standards, and automation techniques to streamline resource management and policy application

- **Chapter 4: Comprehensive Azure Policy Implementation**

    Guides you in creating, assigning, and managing Azure Policy and Initiatives to implement compliance controls and define organizational standards

- **Chapter 5: Enhanced Security with Microsoft Defender for Cloud**

    Explains how to monitor and protect your cloud workloads using Defender for Cloud, Secure Score, and integration with Azure Policy

- **Chapter 6: Leveraging Azure Monitor and Log Analytics for Operations**

    Delivers in-depth guidance on managing user access, privileges, Conditional Access, and just-in-time elevation through PIM

- **Chapter 7: Scaling Governance with Azure Blueprints**

  Teaches how to build end-to-end monitoring, detect threats, and respond to incidents using Azure Monitor, KQL, and Microsoft Sentinel

- **Chapter 8: Azure Sentinel: Next-Generation SIEM**

  Focuses on automating compliance enforcement, configuring remediation tasks, and using policy effects to drive governance at scale

- **Chapter 9: AI and Machine Learning in Cloud Security**

  Shows how to apply AI and ML for anomaly detection, threat prediction, and intelligent security operations using Azure-native tools

- **Chapter 10: Implementing Zero Trust Architecture in Azure**

  Provides a comprehensive guide to adopting Zero Trust in Azure, focusing on identity, access control, segmentation, and continuous validation

- **Chapter 11: Multi-cloud Environment**

  Introduces foundational concepts of multi-cloud governance, highlighting basic strategies for visibility, cost control, and policy consistency across non-Azure platforms

- **Chapter 12: Future Directions in Cloud Governance and Security**

  Explains how to use built-in compliance tools like Microsoft Compliance Manager and Azure Policy to track and report regulatory conformance

- **Chapter 13: Harnessing Azure AI and Copilot for Governance and Security**

  Explores how Microsoft Copilot and AI-driven tools assist in policy management, compliance monitoring, and intelligent threat response

- **Chapter 14: Elevating Skills in Azure Governance and Security**

  Wraps up the book by helping readers plan their skill development through certifications, labs, learning paths, and community engagement

CHAPTER 1

Modern Governance in the Cloud

In today's rapidly evolving technological landscape, the cloud represents a pivotal shift in how businesses operate and manage their IT resources. Modern governance in the cloud is no longer an optional luxury but a crucial necessity for organizations striving to maintain security, compliance, and operational efficiency.

This chapter explores the intricate landscape of cloud governance, examining how organizations can leverage advanced technologies and methodologies to create robust governance frameworks. As businesses increasingly adopt cloud platforms like Microsoft Azure, understanding the nuances of governance becomes imperative to ensure that cloud environments are secure, compliant, and aligned with organizational goals.

Through detailed insights and practical guidance, this chapter aims to equip you with the knowledge to navigate the complexities of modern cloud governance, setting the stage for successful implementation and management in your organization.

In this chapter, we will learn about modern cloud governance, key principles of modern cloud governance, and best practices.

Evolution of Cloud Governance

The evolution of cloud governance has been a journey from adapting traditional IT governance models to developing specialized frameworks that leverage the unique capabilities of cloud environments. Initially, organizations tried to apply their existing governance practices to the cloud, focusing on replicating on-premises controls. However, the dynamic and scalable nature of cloud computing quickly revealed the limitations of this approach.

CHAPTER 1   MODERN GOVERNANCE IN THE CLOUD

As cloud adoption grew, organizations began embracing cloud-native governance, which emphasized automation, real-time monitoring, and the use of Infrastructure as Code (IaC) to enforce policies. This shift allowed for more agile and scalable governance, aligning better with the cloud's inherent flexibility.

With the rise of multi-cloud and hybrid environments, governance frameworks had to evolve further to manage resources across different platforms seamlessly. Tools like Azure Arc enabled centralized governance, extending Azure's capabilities to other cloud platforms and on-premises data centers.

Today, the role of AI and automation is central to cloud governance. AI-driven insights help organizations proactively manage compliance and optimize resource usage, while automation ensures policies are consistently enforced across all environments.

Governance in Cloud Provider

Cloud providers are obligated to implement stringent controls and procedures that go beyond standard industry requirements, offering customers governance frameworks they can rely on. For example, Microsoft provides the option for customers to select from a global network of data centers, ensuring compliance with regional data privacy and sovereignty regulations.

The Microsoft Trust Center (www.microsoft.com/en-us/trustcenter/cloudservices/Azure) outlines the key aspects that organizations prioritize and inherit from their cloud provider.

- **Compliance**: Certification of adherence to industry standards
- **Privacy**: Conformance with privacy legislation
- **Transparency**: Clear visibility into your data within the cloud environment
- **Government Regulations**: Specialized cloud instances for government-related workloads
- **Industry Regulations**: Compliance with regulations tailored to specific industries

Governance in Cloud Consumer

When cloud consumers utilize a cloud provider's services, they inherit the governance structures established by the provider. However, they must also apply their organization's specific governance frameworks and policies within this shared environment. This is akin to moving into a managed apartment complex, where the building owner (the provider) ensures that common services adhere to necessary regulations and standards. Meanwhile, each tenant (the consumer) is responsible for enforcing their own rules and policies within their individual apartments—such as managing their furniture, cleanliness, and internal security. Similarly, cloud consumers retain responsibility for internal configurations, access controls, and compliance within their allocated environment. Below are key areas where cloud consumers must focus their governance efforts:

- **Departmental Governance**: Management of cost centers, geographic locations, and other internal organizational structures

- **Architectural Governance**: Customization and control over the internal architecture specific to the organization's needs

- **Technology Standards**: Implementation of specific standards and practices for technological components and solutions

- **Role-Based Access Controls**: Management of resource access, ensuring alignment with operational procedures and thorough auditing

- **Business Continuity**: Strategies for recovery, resilience, and contingency planning to maintain operations during disruptions

- **Security Measures**: Implementation of security protocols, such as antivirus protection and perimeter defenses

- **Monitoring and IT Auditing**: Collection of logs, intrusion detection, and other mechanisms to ensure oversight and compliance

Figure 1-1 provides a pictorial representation of the two core layers of governance in the Microsoft Azure cloud environment and the cloud resources inheritance.

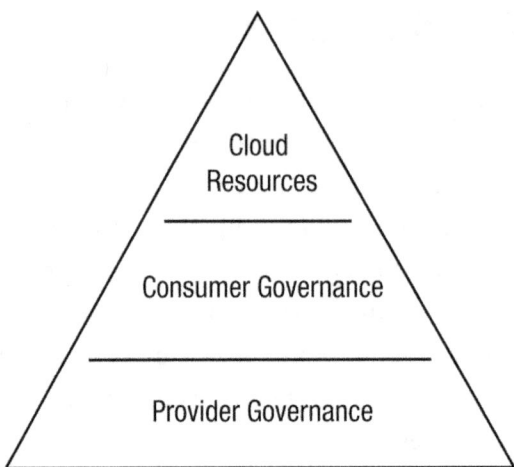

Figure 1-1. *A pictorial representation of the two core layers of governance in the Microsoft Azure cloud environment and the cloud resources inheritance*

Key Principle of Cloud Governance

Having explored the evolution of cloud governance and the shared responsibilities between cloud providers and consumers, it's essential to delve into the foundational principles that underpin effective governance frameworks. These key principles—compliance, privacy, transparency, and regulation—are not just theoretical concepts but practical guidelines that help organizations navigate the complexities of cloud environments. Understanding these principles is crucial for maintaining a secure, compliant, and well-managed cloud infrastructure. Let's now examine each of these core principles and their role in shaping robust cloud governance strategies.

Core Principles of Cloud Governance

At the heart of an effective cloud governance framework are the core principles of compliance, privacy, transparency, and regulation. These principles ensure that cloud environments are not only secure and efficient but also aligned with industry standards and legal requirements.

- **Compliance** involves adhering to various industry standards, certifications, and regulations. Organizations must ensure that their cloud infrastructure meets the necessary guidelines, whether it be ISO standards, GDPR, HIPAA, or other regulatory frameworks. Compliance helps mitigate risks, avoid legal penalties, and maintain trust with stakeholders.

- **Privacy** focuses on protecting sensitive data within cloud environments. It's vital to ensure that personal and organizational data is handled in accordance with laws like GDPR and that privacy is preserved throughout data collection, storage, and processing. Organizations must implement privacy controls to safeguard data from unauthorized access and misuse.

- **Transparency** is critical for providing visibility into how data is managed and secured in the cloud. Cloud providers offer transparency through clear service agreements, audit logs, and monitoring tools, allowing organizations to track their data and infrastructure. This helps in maintaining control over resources and ensures that governance policies are followed across the cloud environment.

- **Regulation** entails adhering to specific governmental and industry regulations that govern cloud usage. From financial services to healthcare, different sectors have unique compliance needs. Cloud governance must ensure that all services and applications meet these sector-specific legal requirements, safeguarding the organization from regulatory breaches.

Tools for Enforcement

Cloud governance relies on a set of tools to ensure that organizational policies, compliance requirements, and security standards are consistently applied across the cloud environment. In Azure, key enforcement mechanisms include **Policies**, **Initiatives**, and **Role-Based Access Control (RBAC)**. These tools help automate compliance checks, enforce resource tagging, control access, and ensure that the environment adheres to both internal and external regulations. By using these tools, organizations can maintain a secure and compliant cloud infrastructure while minimizing manual intervention.

Table 1-1 shows the common Azure RBAC roles with description.

Table 1-1. Common Azure RBAC roles with description

Role	Description
Owner	Full access to all resources, including permission to delegate access to others
Contributor	Can create and manage all types of Azure resources but cannot assign roles
Reader	Can view existing Azure resources but cannot make any changes
User Access Administrator	Can manage user access to Azure resources, including assigning roles

Policies

Azure Policy is a service that enables you to audit and enforce your organization's rules and standards across resources created and managed within Azure. It ensures that resources remain compliant with organizational requirements throughout their lifecycle. For instance, policies can enforce tagging of all resources with a cost center value or restrict the creation of resources for specific regions, such as ensuring that resources for the European branch are only deployed in European Azure locations to maintain data sovereignty.

Azure offers numerous prebuilt policies that any subscribed tenant can use. These built-in policies cover common organizational needs, making it easier to apply governance rules. You can view and assign these policies either through the Azure portal or programmatically.

In the Azure portal, you can search for "policy," and under the Authoring section, select Definitions to explore the available built-in policies, as shown in Figure 1-2.

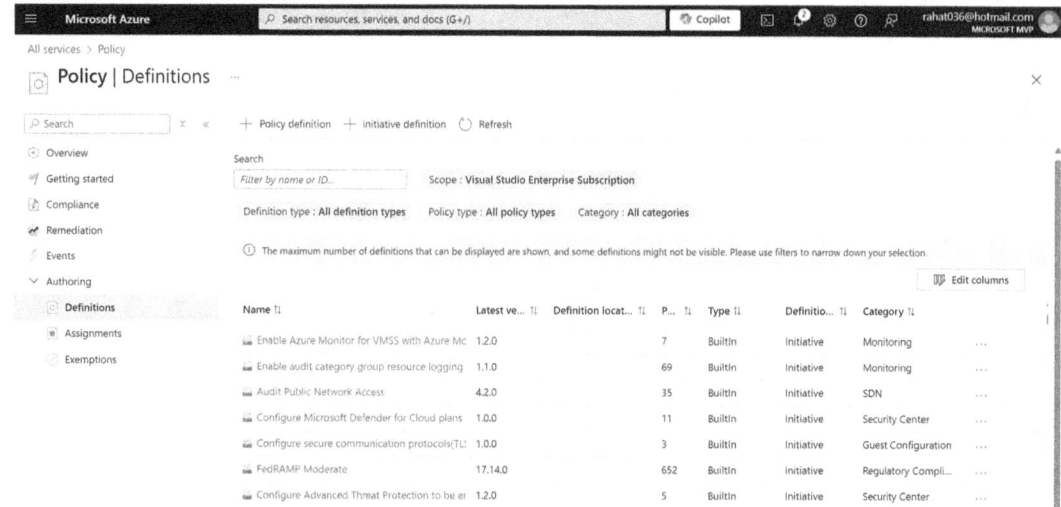

Figure 1-2. Azure Policy definition mode

Policies are applied at multiple levels, known as scopes, which can include management groups, subscriptions, or resource groups, ensuring governance is consistently enforced across different parts of your Azure environment.

Initiatives

Initiatives are a collection of one or more Azure Policies grouped together to enforce and audit an organization's governance rules. They allow you to manage multiple policies as a single entity, simplifying the application of comprehensive governance frameworks. Azure offers several prebuilt initiatives that can be leveraged, which typically include templates that you can duplicate and customize according to your organization's specific needs. Alternatively, you can use the default configurations if they meet your requirements.

Initiatives help streamline policy management by consolidating related policies into a single assignment, making it easier to ensure compliance across various aspects of your cloud environment. You can view and manage these initiatives through the Azure portal, where you can explore their relationships with individual policies and understand the scope options for applying them (as illustrated in Figure 1-3).

CHAPTER 1 MODERN GOVERNANCE IN THE CLOUD

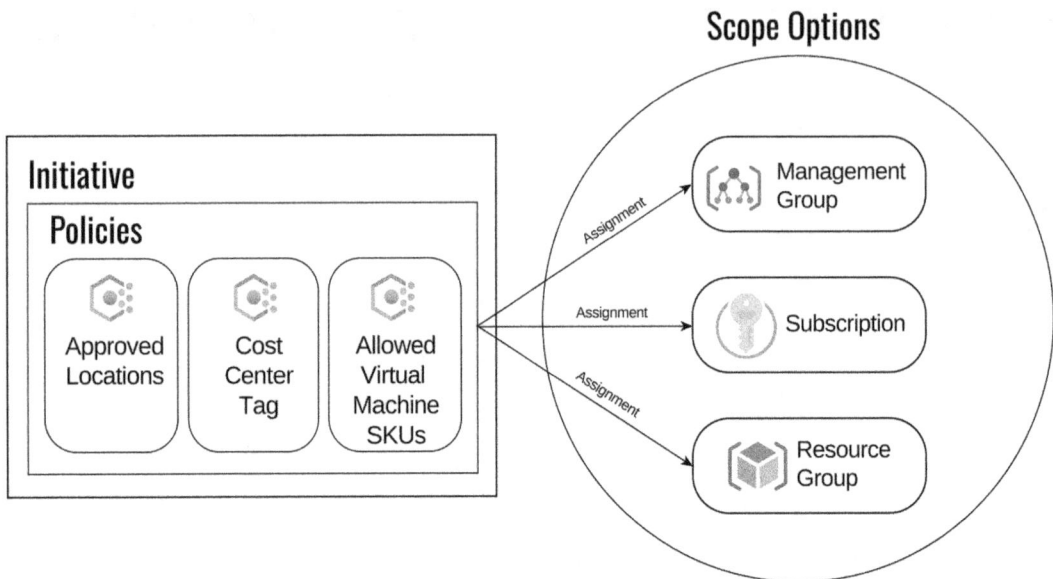

Figure 1-3. Relationship between policies and an initiative and assignment scope options

Role-Based Access Control (RBAC)

Role-Based Access Control (RBAC) is a crucial element of an organization's governance framework, designed to regulate who can access resources and what actions they can perform. While Azure Policies and Initiatives set and enforce compliance rules, RBAC ensures that these rules are applied by controlling user permissions effectively. RBAC in Microsoft Azure operates with predefined roles that you can use to manage access at various levels—subscription, resource group, or individual resource.

Each predefined role has specific permissions associated with it, such as the ability to read, write, or delete resources. This setup ensures that only authorized users can perform actions within their assigned scopes. Additionally, Azure allows you to create custom roles if the predefined ones do not meet your organization's specific needs. Custom roles offer flexibility to tailor permissions to precise requirements, enhancing security and operational control.

RBAC helps to minimize the risk of unauthorized access and ensures that users have the appropriate level of access needed for their roles. This structured approach to access management supports the enforcement of governance policies and helps maintain a secure and compliant cloud environment. For a visual representation of how RBAC is structured, refer to Figure 1-4.

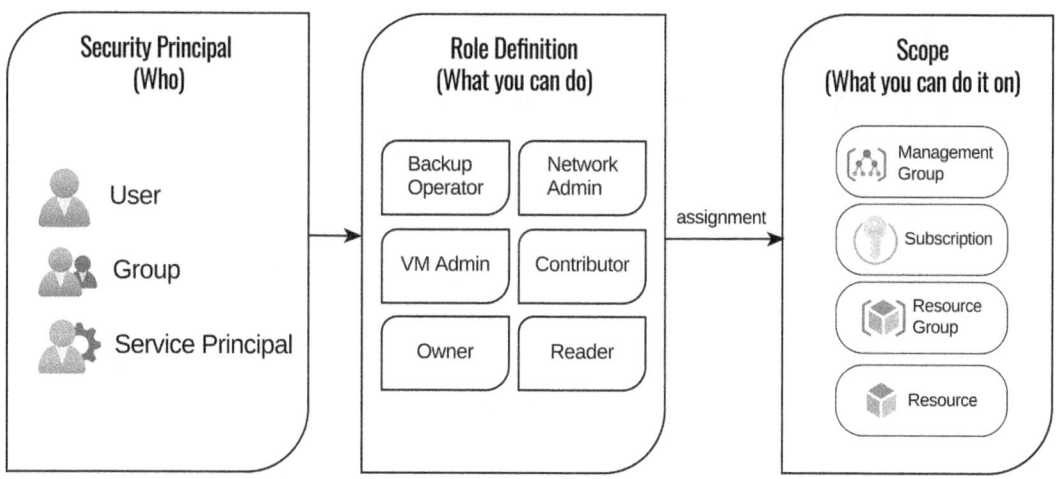

Figure 1-4. *RBAC structure and usage*

Overview of Azure Governance Services

Azure Governance Services are fundamental to organizing, managing, and controlling your cloud environment. Key components of Azure governance include **tenants**, **subscriptions**, **management groups**, **resources and resource groups**, and **blueprints**. Each of these services plays a crucial role in the overall governance framework, providing the tools and structure needed to ensure effective management, compliance, and security within your Azure environment. I will introduce these core Azure governance services, setting the stage for a detailed exploration of how they function and interact to support robust cloud governance.

> **Note** Azure Blueprints will be **deprecated on July 11, 2026**. Organizations currently using Blueprints should begin planning their migration to alternative solutions such as **Azure Landing Zones**, **ARM templates**, or **Bicep**. These tools provide robust Infrastructure-as-Code capabilities and support governance and compliance automation more effectively in the evolving Azure ecosystem.

CHAPTER 1   MODERN GOVERNANCE IN THE CLOUD

Tenants

A tenant is the highest level of organization in your Microsoft Azure environment. When you first sign up for any Azure service, a tenant is automatically created for you. Each Azure tenant is unique and represents your organization, whether you're an individual or an enterprise. You can think of your organization as the tenant.

To illustrate this concept, imagine your organization has rented space in an office building alongside other companies. Each company (tenant) has its own separate office space with access controls and the ability to customize as needed. While each tenant is distinct, they all consume services from the building owner (provider), which in this case is Microsoft.

The fundamental component of a tenant is Microsoft Entra ID (formerly Azure Active Directory), which can be likened to creating your identity and access management system in the cloud. Figure 1-5 depicts the tenant representation in Microsoft Azure.

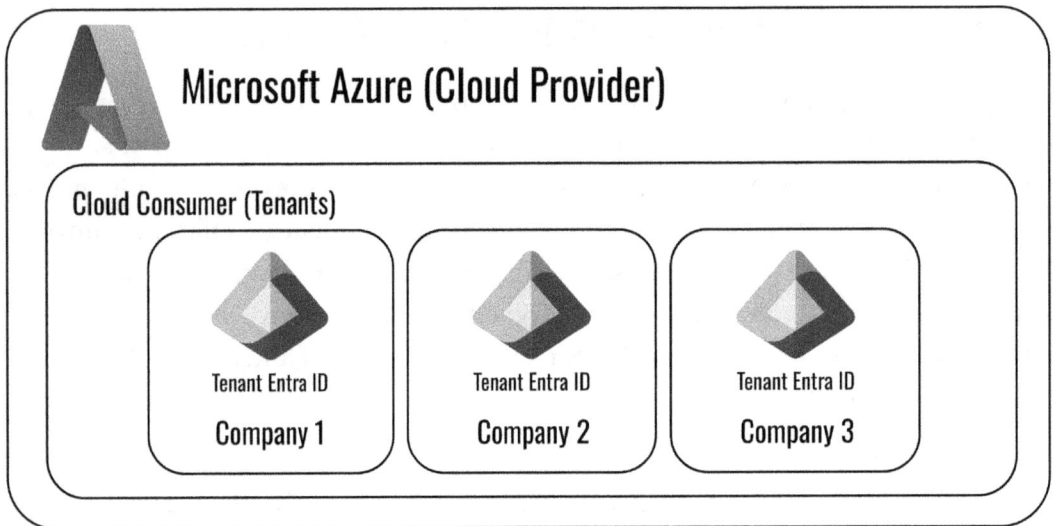

Figure 1-5. *Tenant representation in Microsoft Azure*

You don't necessarily need to sign up for an Azure service to obtain an Azure tenant. However, you must have at least one Azure tenant before you can use a paid service like Microsoft 365. It's also worth noting that a company has the option to create multiple unique tenants if required.

Key Points About Azure Tenants

- **Uniqueness**: Each tenant is separate and distinct from others.
- **Representation**: A tenant represents your entire organization in the Azure ecosystem.
- **Core Component**: Microsoft Entra ID serves as the foundation for identity and access management within a tenant.
- **Multiple Tenants**: Organizations can create and manage multiple tenants if needed.
- **Service Prerequisites**: While not required for tenant creation, at least one tenant is necessary for using paid Azure services.

Subscriptions

The creation and use of an Azure tenant is free and comes with basic capabilities available to all registered Azure consumers. However, to utilize Azure's core cloud service categories, an Azure subscription is required. These categories include the following.

Core Cloud Service Categories

- **Infrastructure as a Service (IaaS)**
  - **Example**: Building and running virtual machines, including traditional infrastructure components like domain controllers or database servers
- **Platform as a Service (PaaS)**
  - **Example**: Database as a Service
- **Software as a Service (SaaS)**
  - **Example**: Microsoft 365 (formerly Office 365)

An Azure subscription is essential for enabling and using these SaaS, PaaS, and IaaS capabilities in Azure. It's important to note that a single organization can have multiple subscriptions linked to one tenant, as illustrated in Figure 1-6.

CHAPTER 1 MODERN GOVERNANCE IN THE CLOUD

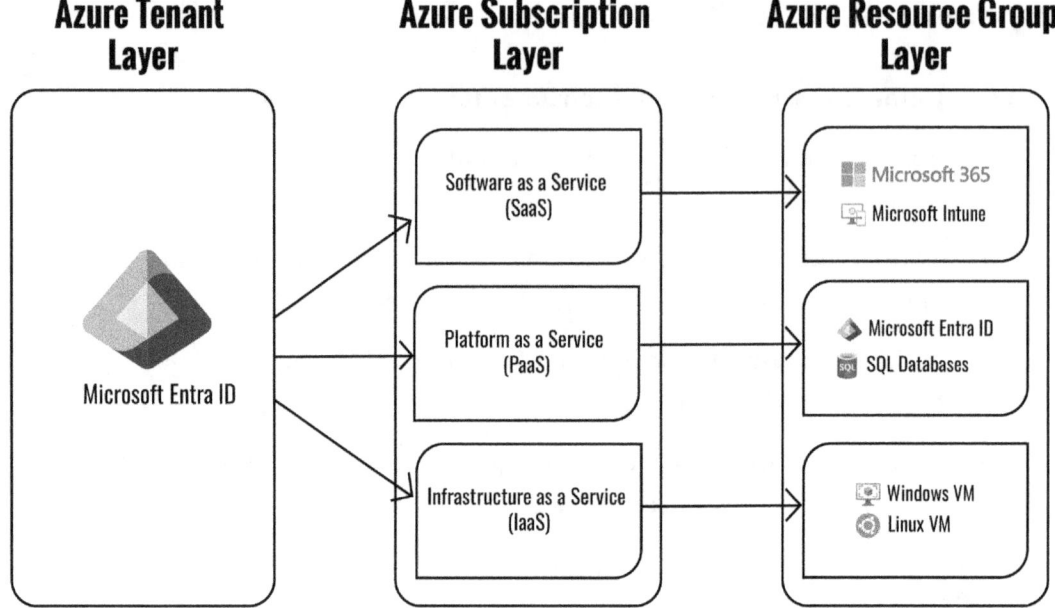

Figure 1-6. Subscriptions and the relationship to the tenant in Azure

Tenant and Subscription Relationship

- A tenant represents your organization in the Azure ecosystem.
- The tenant is managed through Microsoft Entra ID (formerly Azure Active Directory).
- Multiple subscriptions can be associated with a single tenant.
- Each subscription enables access to different Azure services and resources.

Key Points

- **Tenant Creation**: Free and provides basic Azure capabilities.
- **Subscription Purpose**: Required to consume specific Azure services.
- **Flexibility**: Organizations can have multiple subscriptions under one tenant.
- **Service Access**: Subscriptions enable the use of IaaS, PaaS, and SaaS offerings.

Management Group

Management groups in Azure are used to group multiple subscriptions linked to one Microsoft Entra ID tenant. They allow organizations to create a logical hierarchy for subscriptions, enabling more efficient governance and resource management.

Key Aspects of Management Groups

- Each Microsoft Entra ID tenant has a root management group that sits at the top of the hierarchy.
- The root management group cannot be deleted but its display name can be changed to reflect the organization (e.g., company name).
- Management groups are used to implement and scope governance policies and initiatives.
- Policies applied at the management group level are inherited by assigned subscriptions, their child management groups, resource groups, and resources.

Creating a Management Group Structure

Organizations typically create management groups to represent their organizational structure. This structure may align with

- Lifecycle environments
- Departments
- Other logical representations

Example Organization Structure

Let's consider an example for **Backend Emerging Business Limited**:

1. Sales
   - Local Sales
   - International Sales

2. Marketing
   - Events
   - Corporate Branding
3. Information Technology
   - Compute Management
   - Network Management

In this example, subscriptions can be associated with each department and subdepartment. The management group hierarchy is then used to apply the organization's governance framework.

Benefits of Management Group Hierarchy

- **Consistent Policy Application**: Ensures uniform governance across multiple subscriptions.
- **Inheritance**: Child subscriptions inherit policies from parent management groups.
- **Flexibility**: Allows for easy reorganization as the company structure evolves.
- **Granular Control**: Enables specific policies for different departments or projects.

Figure 1-7 illustrates the management group's structure used for this logical organization structure, showcasing how subscriptions can be organized to reflect the company's departmental hierarchy.

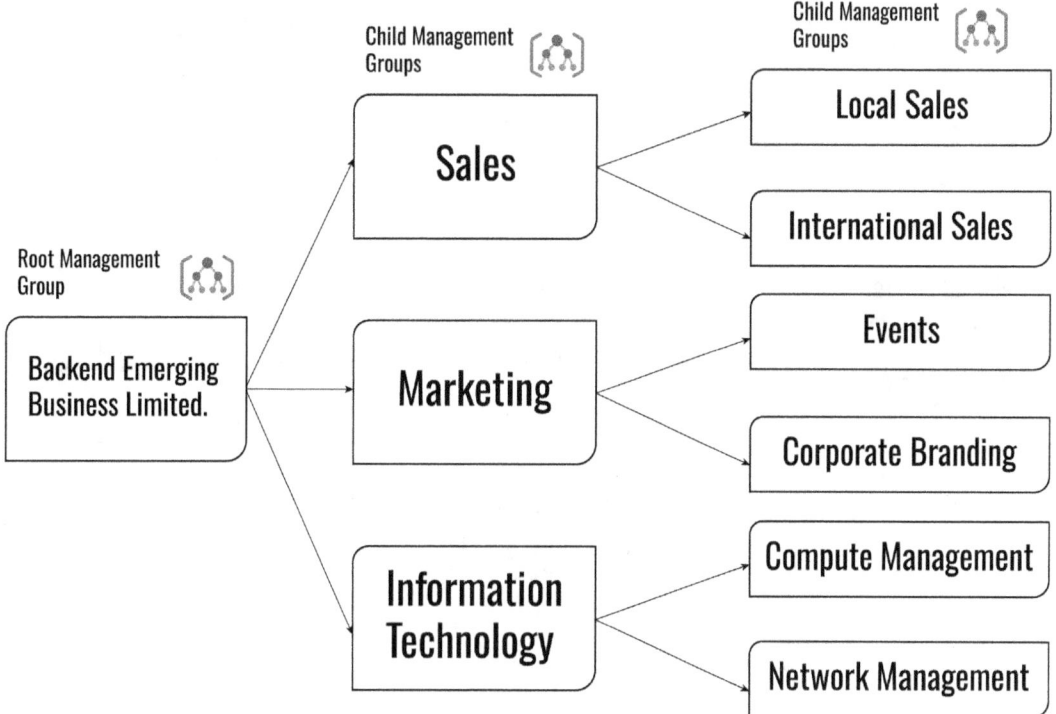

Figure 1-7. *Example management group structure by departments*

Figure 1-8 shows how subscriptions can be assigned to child management group.

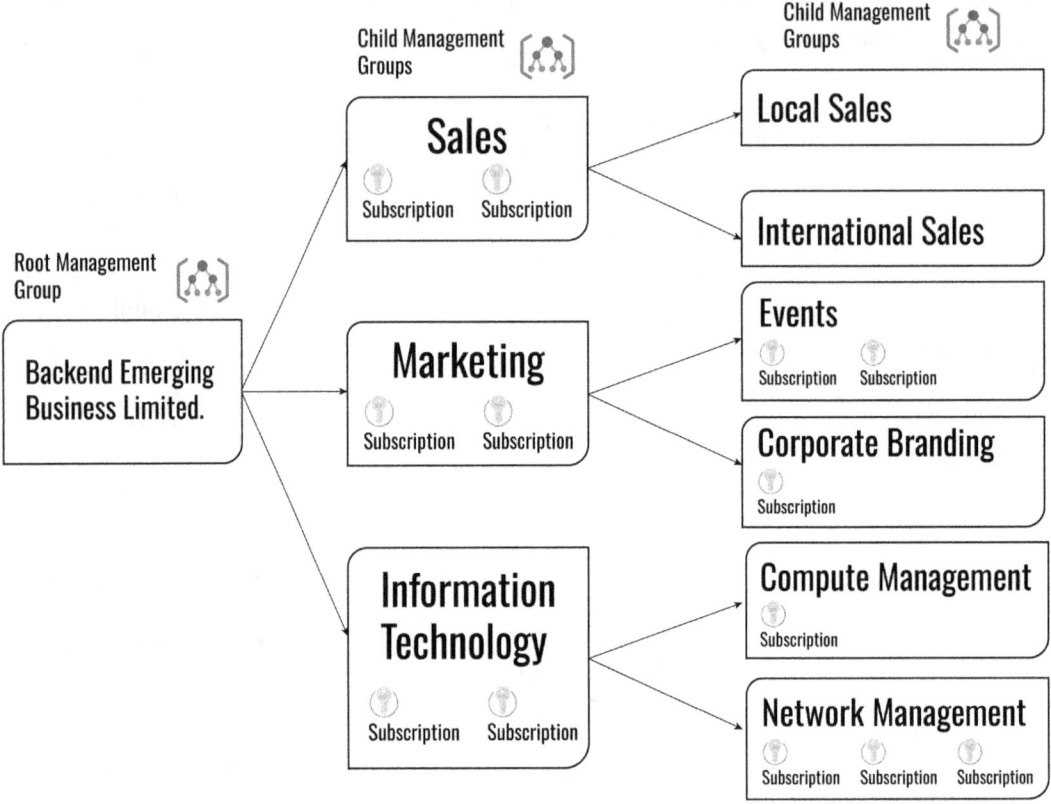

Figure 1-8. *Subscription assignment to child management groups*

Resources and Resource Group

In Azure, resources and resource groups are fundamental concepts for organizing and managing your cloud infrastructure.

Resources

Resources in Azure represent the individual entities or objects that you can create, configure, and manage. These include

- Virtual machines
- Storage accounts
- Virtual networks

- Virtual subnets
- Databases
- Web apps
- And many other Azure services

Each resource is a specific instance of a service that you can deploy and utilize within your Azure environment.

Resource Groups

Resource groups serve as logical containers for organizing related Azure resources. They offer several key benefits:

- **Unified Management**: Resources within a group can be managed as a single unit.
- **Inherited Properties**: All resources in a group inherit common properties and controls.
- **Access Control**: Microsoft Entra ID (formerly Azure AD) role-based access controls can be applied at the resource group level.
- **Tagging**: Resources can be tagged collectively for easier categorization and billing.
- **Lifecycle Management**: You can deploy, update, or delete all resources in a group together.

Relationship Structure

Figure 1-9 illustrates the hierarchical relationship between an Azure subscription, resource groups, and individual resources:

- At the top level is the Azure subscription.
- Within the subscription, you can create multiple resource groups.
- Each resource group contains one or more related resources.

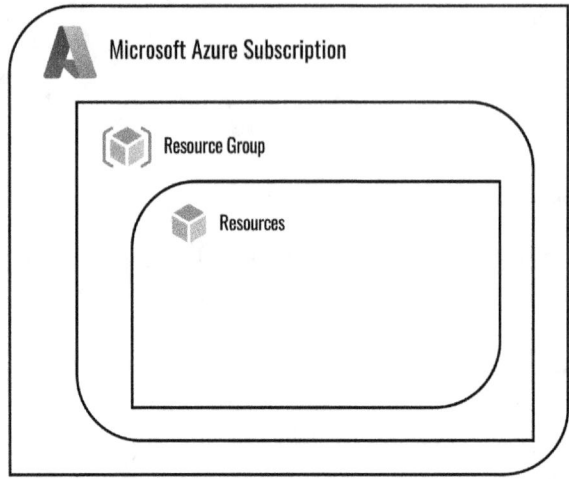

Figure 1-9. *Resource group structure and relationship to Azure subscription*

This structure allows for efficient organization and management of your Azure assets, enabling you to

- Group resources by project, department, or application
- Apply consistent policies and access controls
- Simplify billing and cost management
- Streamline deployment and maintenance processes

Blueprints

Cloud adoption often follows a familiar pattern:

1. **Trial**
2. **Proof of Concept (POC)**
3. **Limited Usage**
4. **Full Cloud Migration**

Organizations typically start with limited trials, move to a proof of concept (POC) with controlled usage, and eventually transition to a full-scale cloud adoption or migration program. Historically, this phased approach has had a downside: early

CHAPTER 1 MODERN GOVERNANCE IN THE CLOUD

initiatives often do not fully adhere to organizational rules or governance frameworks. This has resulted in several "brownfield" deployments—live environments that do not conform to recommended practices or organizational governance standards.

Azure Policy and initiatives offer a way to audit these existing environments retrospectively and help organizations gradually correct non-compliances and governance drifts. However, to avoid such governance issues from the beginning, Microsoft introduced **Azure Blueprints**. While still in preview at the time of writing, Azure Blueprints provide a comprehensive framework for organizations to "build it right from the start." They allow for the configuration of a governance template that includes policy assignments, role assignments, resource groups, and Azure Resource Manager (ARM) templates, as shown in Figure 1-10.

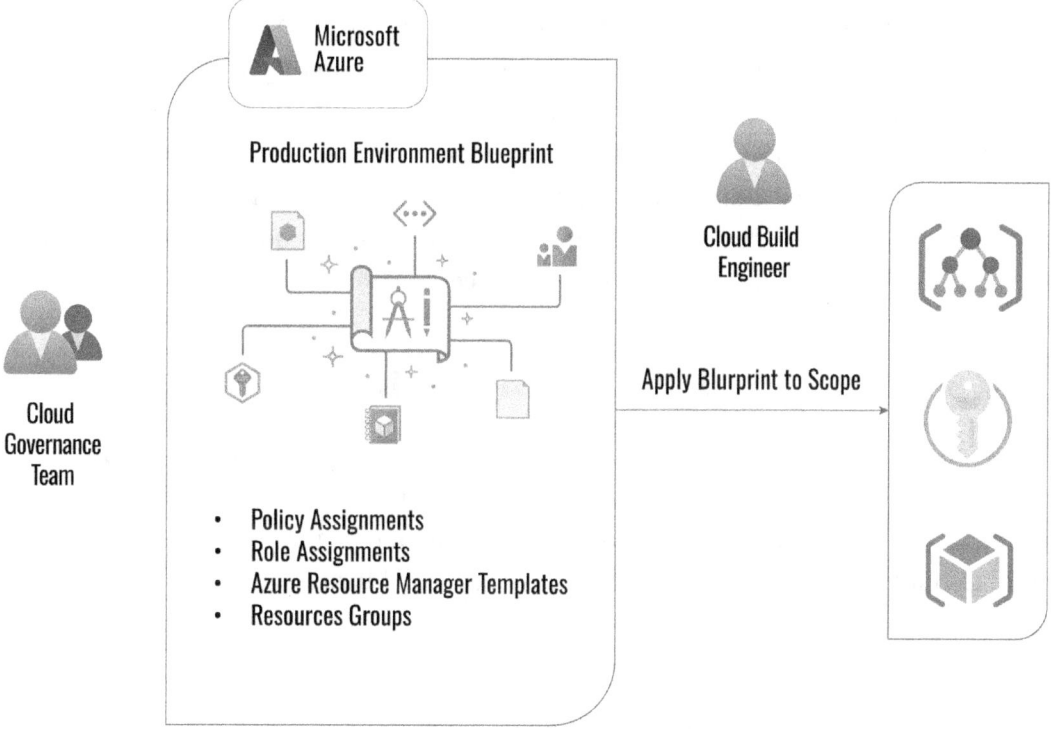

Figure 1-10. *Blueprint illustration with the supported artifact types*

Once a blueprint is created and published, cloud deployment engineers or developers inherit the governance framework automatically when the blueprint is assigned to a subscription. Essentially, Azure Blueprints allow organizations to not only *build it right* but also *run it right* by embedding governance principles into the cloud infrastructure from the very beginning.

> **Note** On July 11, 2026, Blueprints (Preview) will be deprecated. You can find more information here: https://aka.ms/AzureBlueprintNotice.

Role of Cloud Governance in Digital Transformation

Cloud governance is instrumental in guiding organizations through their digital transformation journey, ensuring that cloud adoption aligns with strategic business objectives and regulatory requirements. As organizations transition from traditional IT systems to cloud-based environments, effective governance frameworks become essential for managing and securing cloud resources. These frameworks provide the necessary oversight to maintain compliance, control costs, and optimize resource utilization while supporting the seamless integration of new technologies. By establishing robust governance practices, organizations can drive their digital transformation initiatives with confidence, leveraging the cloud's scalability and agility to innovate and achieve their business goals effectively. This section explores how cloud governance facilitates digital transformation, emphasizing the importance of strategic planning and implementation in achieving a successful transition.

How Governance Facilitates Digital Transformation

Governance plays a critical role in facilitating digital transformation by providing a structured framework that ensures the effective and secure use of cloud resources. As organizations embark on their digital transformation journey, they need to adopt cloud technologies that can scale and adapt to evolving business needs. Governance frameworks help manage this transition by establishing clear policies, controls, and processes that guide the deployment and management of cloud services.

- **Ensuring Compliance and Security**: Effective governance frameworks enforce compliance with industry standards and regulatory requirements, mitigating risks associated with data privacy and security. By implementing governance policies that monitor and audit cloud activities, organizations can maintain data integrity and protect sensitive information, which is crucial for maintaining trust and avoiding legal issues.

- **Optimizing Resource Management**: Governance tools help organizations efficiently manage and allocate cloud resources, ensuring that they are used effectively and cost-efficiently. Policies and initiatives can automate the provisioning of resources, enforce tagging practices for better cost tracking, and optimize resource allocation based on demand, thereby reducing waste and controlling expenses.

- **Enhancing Operational Efficiency**: By defining clear governance structures and roles, organizations can streamline operations and improve collaboration. Governance frameworks provide guidelines for resource management, access control, and operational procedures, enabling teams to work together more efficiently and reduce the risk of errors.

- **Driving Innovation**: With a solid governance foundation, organizations can confidently experiment with new technologies and services. Governance frameworks offer the flexibility to adopt and integrate emerging technologies while ensuring that they align with the organization's strategic goals and compliance requirements. Innovation fosters an environment where innovation can thrive without compromising security or efficiency.

- **Supporting Scalability**: Governance frameworks facilitate the management of scaling cloud environments by establishing standards and practices that can be applied consistently across different regions and services. This ensures that as organizations grow and their cloud footprint expands, they can maintain control and oversight without sacrificing agility.

Strategic Importance of Governance Planning and Implementation

Governance planning and implementation are critical for effective cloud management, ensuring that organizational goals are met while maintaining compliance and security. A strategic approach to governance provides the framework needed to manage resources, enforce policies, and adapt to evolving needs. In the context of Azure, this strategic importance becomes even more pronounced due to the cloud's complexity and scale.

CHAPTER 1   MODERN GOVERNANCE IN THE CLOUD

Effective Azure Governance Planning is essential for creating a structured, compliant, and efficient cloud environment. By focusing on Azure-specific strategies for policy implementation, resource management, and access controls, organizations can ensure their cloud infrastructure aligns with both operational and regulatory requirements. Here, I will provide a detailed exploration of Azure Governance Planning, offering insights into setting up and optimizing your Azure environment to meet governance objectives effectively.

Azure Governance Planning

The principle of "Measure twice, cut once," often used in carpentry, underscores the importance of careful planning before taking action. Just as precise measurements are crucial for building a sturdy table, thorough planning is essential for effective Azure governance implementation. Inadequate planning can lead to structural weaknesses, just as cutting wood incorrectly can compromise the strength of a piece of furniture. This principle is equally applicable to Azure governance, where meticulous preparation ensures that governance frameworks are robust and effective.

This section will outline the key planning activities required before configuring and implementing your Azure governance artifacts. These activities are categorized into two main areas:

- **Azure Foundational Artifacts**
- **Governance Artifacts**

Azure Foundational Artifacts

Implementing Azure governance effectively requires careful planning and a deep understanding of several key components. The cloud custodian must be well-versed in the following elements:

- **Tenants**: The foundational structure of your Azure environment, representing the organization's overall cloud space
- **Subscriptions**: Agreements with Microsoft that define the scope of cloud service usage and billing

CHAPTER 1 MODERN GOVERNANCE IN THE CLOUD

- **Resource Groups**: Logical containers for managing and organizing Azure resources

- **Management Groups**: Hierarchical structures used to manage and apply governance policies across multiple subscriptions

Thorough planning for these components ensures a well-organized and compliant Azure environment, facilitating efficient governance and management.

Planning for Tenants

Planning for your Azure tenant is a critical first step in setting up your cloud environment. The tenant forms the **root of your security, identity, and governance architecture** and affects how resources are managed across environments. Proper tenant planning supports organizational structure, security boundaries, billing separation, and scalability. Here are the key considerations:

- **Tenant Registration and Management**

    Ensure that tenant registration is linked to your **organization's official credentials** and **not to personal accounts or individual credit cards**. Avoid using default domains like *.onmicrosoft.com in production environments. This approach centralizes governance and simplifies auditing, billing, and lifecycle management.

- **Assign Roles and Responsibilities**

    Assign appropriate **RBAC roles** (e.g., Owner, Contributor, Reader) to align access with job responsibilities. Senior personnel or security administrators should manage governance and security policies at the tenant level. This is vital for managing **subscriptions, resource groups, and resource access** in accordance with your security and procurement practices.

- **Environment Isolation**

    If your organization requires complete separation between environments—such as **development, testing, production**, or **subsidiary operations**—you should consider using **separate Azure tenants**. This ensures strong isolation in terms of identity, access, and compliance enforcement.

Example: A financial institution may isolate its internal IT operations from customer-facing applications by using different tenants, allowing separate policies, billing, and compliance boundaries.

Note When integrating **on-premises Active Directory** with **Azure AD** using **Azure AD Connect, only one Azure AD tenant can be linked to a single on-premises AD forest**. Organizations planning hybrid identity strategies should consider this limitation. If multiple Azure AD tenants are required, you may need to implement **AD forest trusts** or **external identity providers** to enable integration across tenants.

- **Domain Name Assignment**

    Decide on and register your **external DNS domain name** (e.g., yourcompany.com) early in the process. This domain will be used for user accounts, application URLs, and email identities. Proper domain setup ensures **consistency**, simplifies user onboarding, and supports branding and policy enforcement.

- **Service Enrollment and Budgeting**

    Evaluate which Azure services your tenant will use and **identify those requiring premium licensing** (e.g., Azure AD Premium, Microsoft Defender for Cloud). Collaborate with stakeholders to define a **service enrollment plan and budget** accordingly. Ensuring that budgeting is aligned with governance and security goals is key for long-term sustainability.

For detailed instructions on setting up your Azure tenant, refer to the Microsoft documentation at https://learn.microsoft.com/en-us/entra/identity-platform/quickstart-create-new-tenant.

Planning for Subscriptions

After setting up your organization's tenant(s), the next crucial step is planning for subscriptions. Subscriptions are agreements with Microsoft that define how you pay for the consumption of cloud services. These can be categorized into two main types, corresponding to the core categories of cloud services:

- **Microsoft Software-as-a-Service (SaaS) Subscriptions**: These subscriptions include services like Office 365, Intune/EMS, and Dynamics 365. They are integrated into the SaaS offering and require linking to the authoritative tenant for your organization. This tenant acts as the central identity and security layer, aligning with user accounts and devices for licensing and service charges.

- **Microsoft Platform-as-a-Service (PaaS) and Infrastructure-as-a-Service (IaaS) Subscriptions**: Unlike SaaS, PaaS and IaaS subscriptions are based on resource consumption rather than specific user accounts. These subscriptions involve managing and creating all necessary artifacts within the subscription itself.

For SaaS offerings, consider the following:

- **Licensing Authority**: Identify the department or individuals responsible for purchasing licenses, typically the procurement department. They must understand the legal aspects of the agreements to ensure compliance with purchasing rules and usage rights.

- **Identity Authority**: SaaS services require linking to a tenant to provide a trusted identity source. When signing up for these services, you can link to a generic Microsoft Entra ID tenant or an existing tenant if available. Optionally, you can synchronize with an on-premises Active Directory to manage identities centrally and offer a single sign-on experience. Figure 1-11 shows the cloud usage options and the link between Microsoft Entra ID and the on-premises AD.

CHAPTER 1 MODERN GOVERNANCE IN THE CLOUD

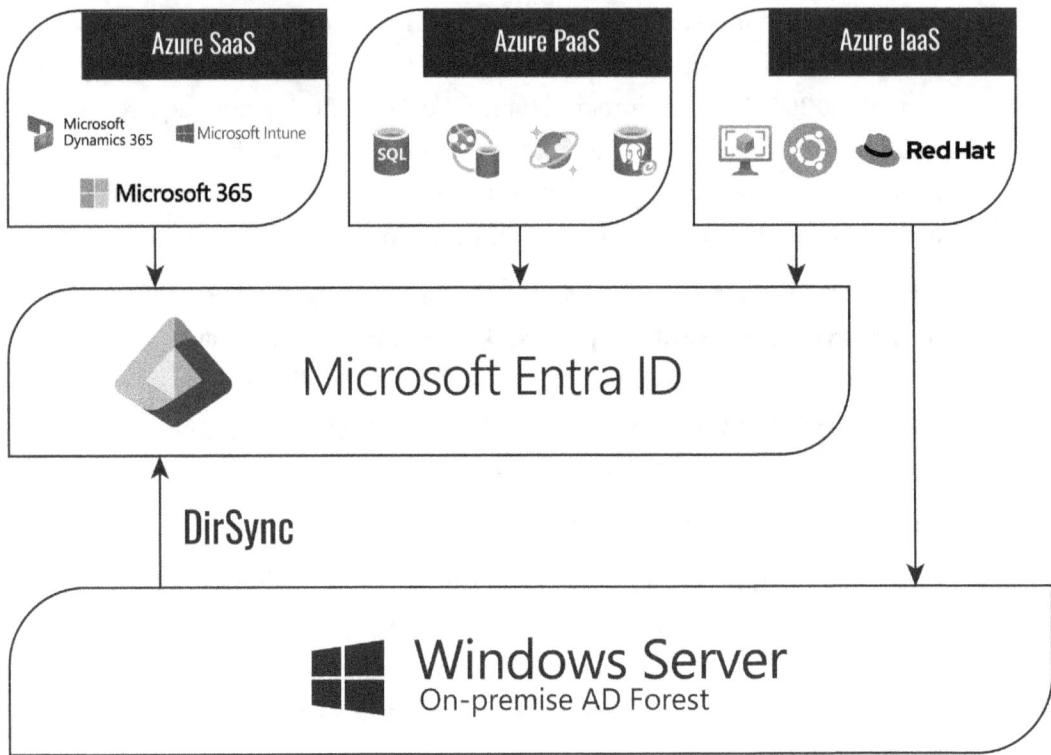

Figure 1-11. *Subscription options and the link to Microsoft Entra ID and on-premises AD*

For PaaS and IaaS offerings, planning should include:

- **Licensing Authority**: Similar to SaaS, ensure the procurement department understands the legal aspects and compliance requirements for licensing.

- **Policy and Security**: Unlike SaaS, where the provider manages policies and security, PaaS and IaaS require you to establish and manage your own policies and security frameworks. This involves setting up controls and compliance measures tailored to the resources you manage.

- **Planning Lifecycle Management**: Plan for the adoption and deprecation of features as cloud services evolve. For instance, in IaaS, changes to virtual machine SKUs require monitoring and adjustment to maintain alignment with organizational needs. Effective lifecycle management ensures you leverage the elasticity of cloud services and adapt to new features and changes.

CHAPTER 1 MODERN GOVERNANCE IN THE CLOUD

Chapter 2 will provide further details on planning, purchasing, and consuming SaaS, PaaS, and IaaS subscriptions.

Planning for Resource Groups

Below subscriptions, the next layers are resource groups and individual resources. Effective planning for resource groups is essential to ensure that resources are appropriately placed and managed. Proper organization of resource groups helps in applying governance policies consistently and effectively.

Resource groups should be planned with consideration for both geographical location and organizational needs. For example, creating resource groups based on geographic locations can help meet data sovereignty requirements for a global organization, as illustrated in Figure 1-12. Alternatively, resource groups can be organized by lifecycle environments (such as development, preproduction, and production) and business application types, as shown in Figure 1-13. This approach facilitates management and policy application according to the stage of the resource lifecycle and the specific needs of different business applications.

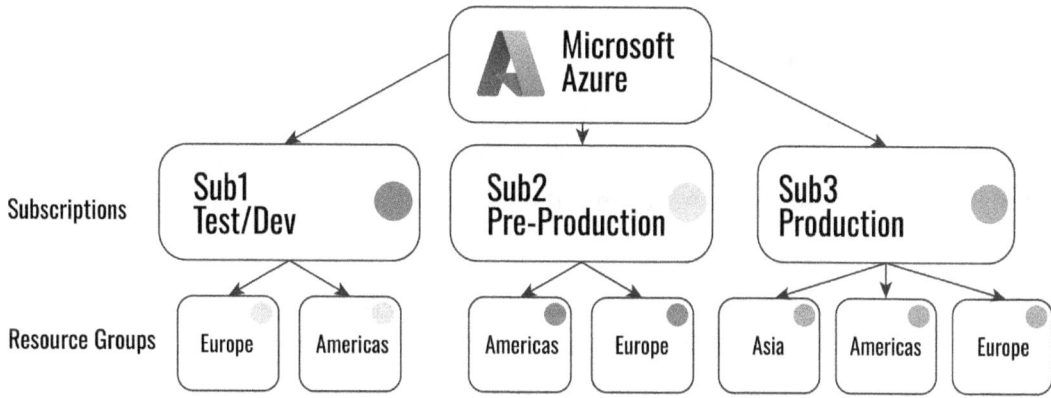

Figure 1-12. *Resource group structure by geographic location*

CHAPTER 1 MODERN GOVERNANCE IN THE CLOUD

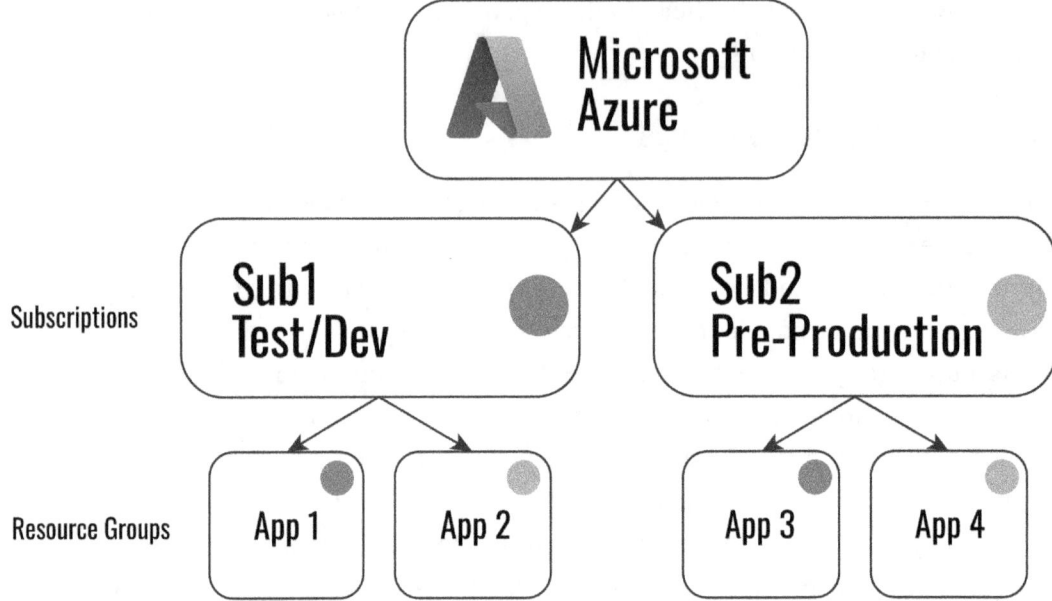

Figure 1-13. Resource group structure by environment and application type

Planning for Management Groups

In the context of Azure governance, management groups are essential for organizing and applying governance artifacts effectively. This section focuses on the strategic planning required before creating your management group hierarchy.

- **Governance Artifact Placement**: When setting up Azure artifacts such as policies, initiatives, and blueprints, you must select an appropriate storage location. This choice impacts the scope of assignment options available. For example, as shown in Figure 1-14, you might create a management group to manage subscriptions that are not yet assigned and another for active subscriptions. These management groups should be placed at the highest level of your hierarchy, typically as child management groups under the root management group.

CHAPTER 1   MODERN GOVERNANCE IN THE CLOUD

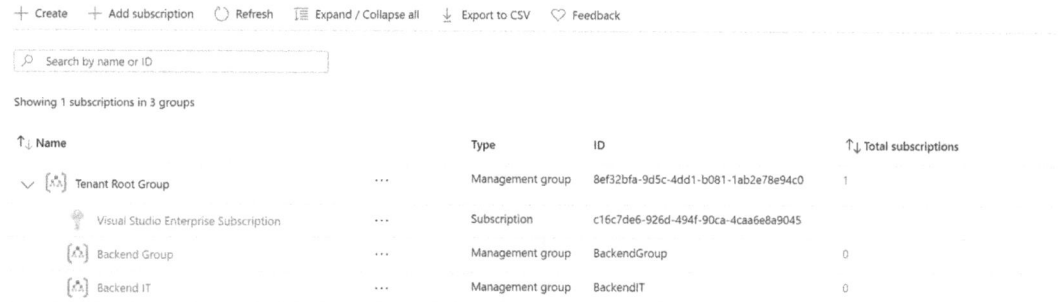

Figure 1-14. *Example management group structure with subscriptions*

- **Governance Artifact Assignment**: Planning for the assignment of policies, initiatives, and blueprints is crucial. Assignments should be made at the highest level in the management hierarchy to ensure maximum flexibility and minimize complexity. A well-structured management group hierarchy, as illustrated in Figure 1-15, allows for consistent and effective application of governance artifacts across the organization, aligning with your compliance objectives.

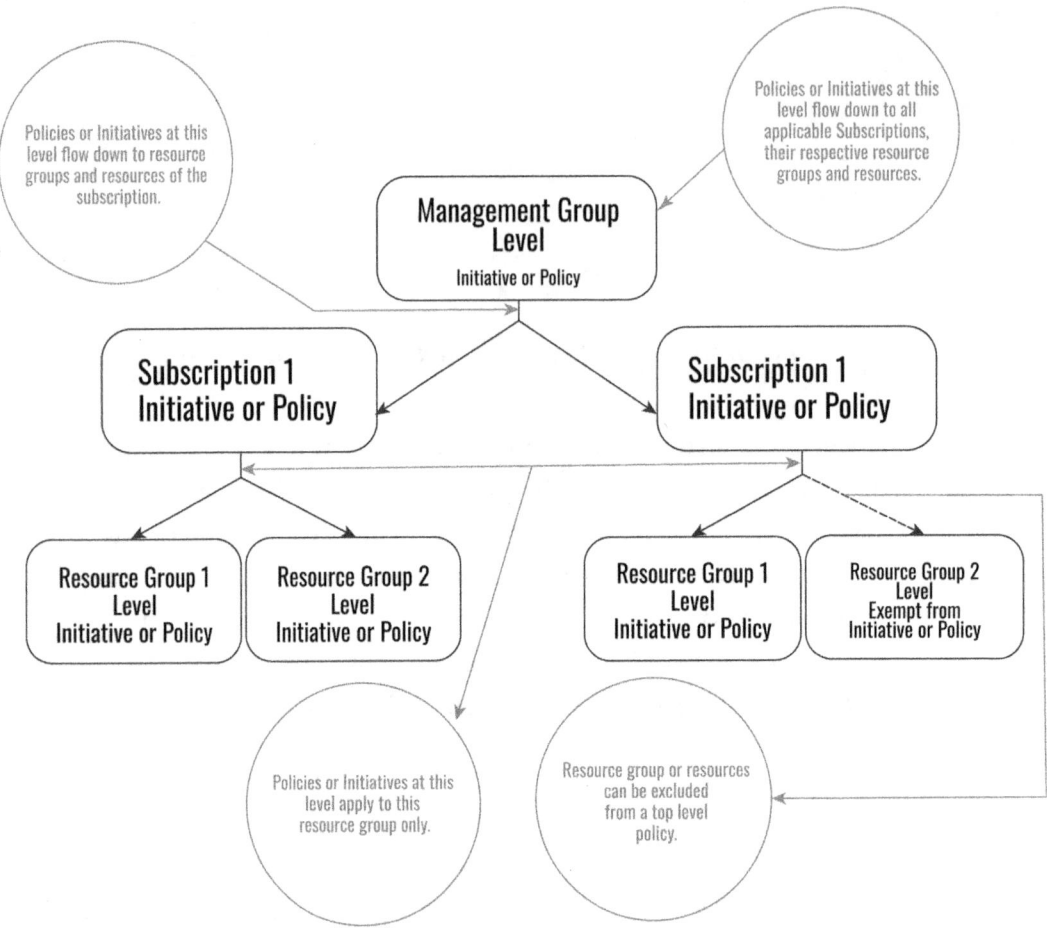

Figure 1-15. *Planning for policy exclusions*

- **Managing Exclusions**: Another important aspect to consider is the use of exclusions. While exclusions can be useful for specific scenarios, they can also introduce conflicts or unintended consequences if not managed carefully. It is advisable to design your management group structure to minimize the need for exclusions and reduce potential governance issues. Figure 1-15 demonstrates an example of how exclusions are applied within a management group structure, highlighting the need for thoughtful planning to prevent complications.

Planning for Azure Governance Artifacts

When planning Azure governance, there are several core artifacts to consider:

- **Policies**
- **Initiatives**
- **Blueprints**

Effective planning for these artifacts involves addressing key areas such as naming conventions, testing, and lifecycle management:

- **Naming Conventions**: Establish and maintain consistent naming conventions for all governance artifacts. Document these conventions and ensure they are communicated across the organization. Consistent naming helps maintain clarity and organization in managing and applying these artifacts.

- **Testing**: Proper testing of governance enforcement is crucial to prevent potential issues. For example, implementing deny policies without adequate testing can lead to unintended disruptions or downtime. If a policy is designed to deny resource creation, ensure that it does not interfere with self-service options and that user expectations are properly set and communicated.

- **Lifecycle Management**: Change is inevitable, and governance artifacts will need to be updated as organizational needs and compliance requirements evolve. Plan for lifecycle management by using versioning and other controlled approaches to handle changes in governance artifacts. This ensures that updates are managed systematically, minimizing disruption and maintaining compliance.

Summary

This chapter explored the evolution of cloud governance from traditional IT models to frameworks tailored for cloud environments like Microsoft Azure. It highlighted the transition to automation, real-time monitoring, and Infrastructure as Code (IaC) for effective policy enforcement and resource management.

I covered the shared responsibilities between cloud providers and consumers, focusing on core principles such as compliance, privacy, transparency, and regulation. Azure's governance tools—Policies, Initiatives, and Role-Based Access Control (RBAC)—are key to automating and enforcing these principles.

Additionally, key Azure governance services—tenants, subscriptions, management groups, resource groups, and blueprints—are introduced as fundamental components for organizing and managing cloud resources.

In Chapter 2, I will discuss advanced topics, including designing an Azure scaffold, governance and security best practices, management group strategies, subscription models, and resource group organization.

CHAPTER 2

Advanced Azure Scaffold for Enterprise Architecture

The previous chapter laid the groundwork for modern cloud governance, focusing on the principles of compliance, privacy, and transparency, as well as the shared responsibilities between cloud providers and consumers. I also covered essential governance tools like Policies, Initiatives, and RBAC, along with core services such as tenants, subscriptions, and resource groups, which form the foundation for managing cloud resources effectively.

Now, I will move forward to more advanced topics. This chapter focuses on building an Azure scaffold that ensures governance and security best practices are in place from the start. I will guide you through strategies for organizing management groups, selecting scalable subscription models, and structuring resource groups for optimal efficiency and control within your enterprise architecture.

Designing an Effective Azure Scaffold

When moving from a traditional IT setup to a cloud-based model, Azure scaffolding is a crucial framework for managing the key areas impacted by cloud adoption, such as DevOps, automation, data analytics, solution architecture, and R&D.

Figure 2-1 showcases the main components of Azure scaffolding, providing a simple guide to understanding how resources are managed in the cloud. This framework acts as a road map for structuring and organizing these resources effectively.

CHAPTER 2   ADVANCED AZURE SCAFFOLD FOR ENTERPRISE ARCHITECTURE

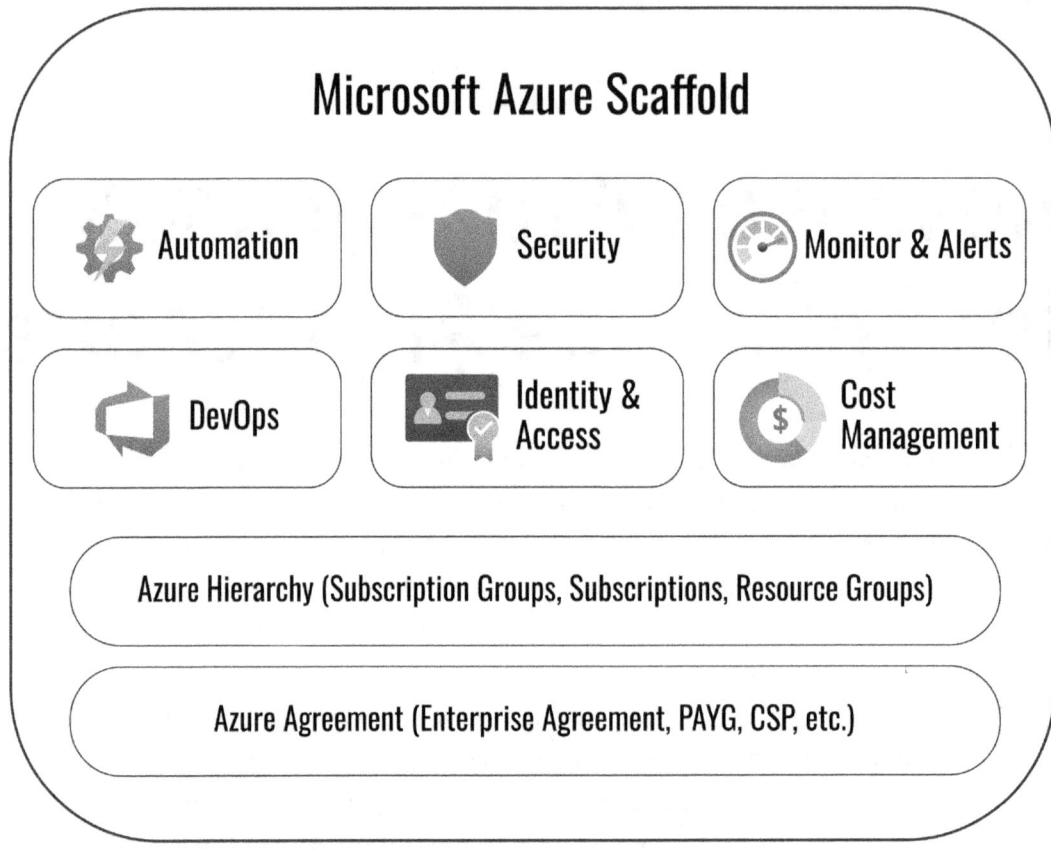

Figure 2-1. *Core components within the Azure scaffold*

A major focus within this model is the creation and management of multiple subscriptions. These subscriptions act like containers for your resources, and controlling access to them is vital for efficient resource management. A robust governance model is essential to ensure that your cloud transition is both successful and sustainable.

In this Azure scaffolding governance framework, the type of agreement you have with your cloud provider plays a foundational role. Whether you have an Azure Enterprise Agreement, a pay-as-you-go model, or any other contract type, these agreements determine how you set up your cloud environment. Through these agreements, you create various subscriptions to host the core components of your applications. Designing a clear and organized hierarchy of subscriptions is key to maintaining control and governance over your cloud resources, helping you monitor key metrics and ensure everything is running smoothly as you scale in the cloud.

Table 2-1 shows the comparison of different agreement types in Microsoft Azure.

Table 2-1. Comparison between Azure EA, MCA, and CSP

Agreement Type	Who It's For	Subscription Creation and Management	Billing Model
Enterprise Agreement (EA)	Large enterprises with high-volume usage	Centralized via EA portal; linked to enrollment	Prepaid, with discount tiers
Microsoft Customer Agreement (MCA)	Mid-sized to large orgs; direct with Microsoft	Managed via Azure portal	Pay-as-you-go or Azure Prepayment
Cloud Solution Provider (CSP)	SMBs or orgs working with Microsoft partners	Partner-managed subscriptions	Partner bills customer

Governance and Security Best Practices

When managing resources in Azure, establishing a strong governance framework is essential for ensuring both security and operational efficiency. The following are key areas to focus on when setting up an initial governance hierarchy in Azure:

- **Management Groups**
- **Subscriptions**
- **Resource Groups**

A major concern for organizations is ensuring their operations teams have the necessary controls to safely use the cloud. Common issues arise when policy, auditing, and compliance controls are either insufficient or absent in cloud environments. Without these controls, teams often face the challenge of manually reviewing access permissions before DevOps teams can provision cloud resources.

Note For a more detailed discussion on access governance, role assignments, and policy-based controls, refer to Chapter 1, "Modern Governance in the Cloud."

Azure addresses these concerns by offering cloud-native governance solutions, ensuring consistent control across all Azure platforms. This built-in governance model allows organizations to maintain better oversight of their resources and access management.

Figure 2-2 outlines a general hierarchy for managing resources in Azure, demonstrating the logical steps involved in setting up this governance structure.

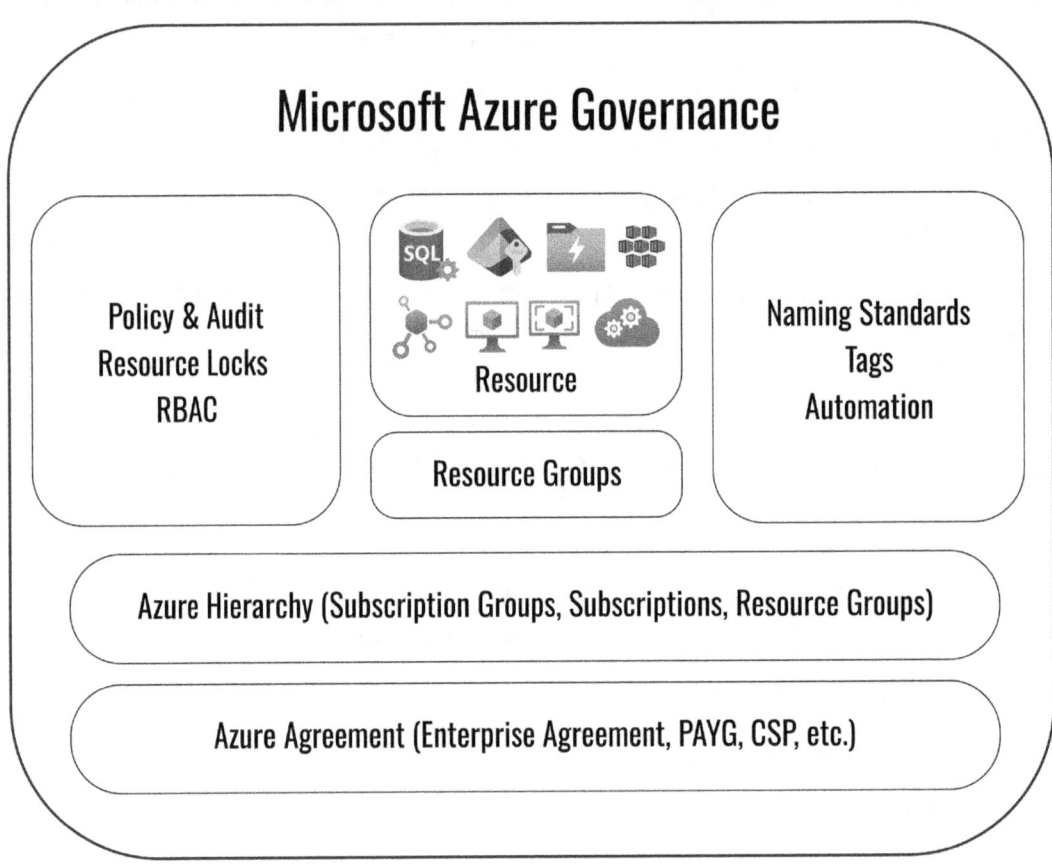

Figure 2-2. *Initial hierarchy for the administration of Azure resources*

At this level of governance, there are two critical elements to consider:

1. **Access Management**: You need to ensure the correct permissions are applied within subscriptions. **Azure Role-Based Access Control (RBAC)** enables fine-grained control over what users can and cannot do with specific resources, known as resource actions (e.g., `Microsoft.Compute/virtualMachines/read` or `Microsoft.Storage/storageAccounts/write`). This ensures only authorized users can perform sensitive operations. For a complete list of actions, refer to the Azure RBAC permissions documentation (`https://learn.microsoft.com/en-us/azure/role-based-access-control/resource-provider-operations`).

2. **Naming Conventions and Labels**: Consistent naming standards and labels are essential for maintaining order and improving resource tracking. Proper naming conventions allow for easier management and better identification of resources across teams and projects.

For example, the fictional company named Backend might implement governance by ensuring that all users with access to their subscription are only able to create virtual machines in data centers within the United States. Additionally, Backend would enforce strict naming conventions for these Azure resources to ensure uniformity throughout the organization.

Figure 2-3 illustrates how an organization could implement Azure Governance, demonstrating how policies and naming standards can be applied for better control.

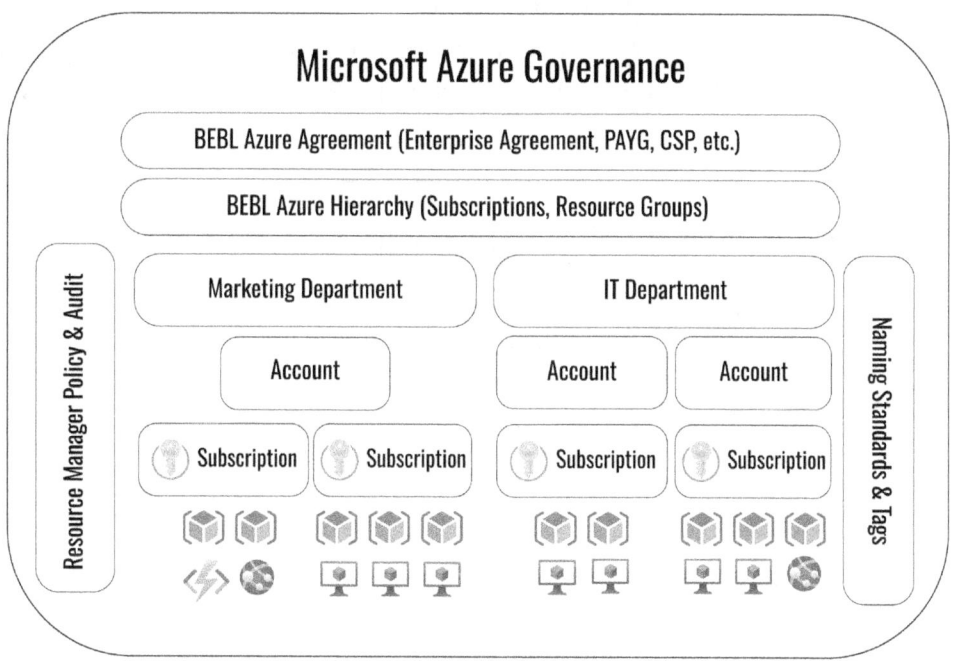

Figure 2-3. *Example of how an organization could implement Azure Governance*

For a clearer understanding, consider an Azure subscription as a basic logical unit that contains one or more resource groups. Governance is applied both at the subscription and resource group levels to provide an organized structure for provisioning and managing cloud resources. This ensures that security, compliance, and resource management practices align with the organization's operational goals while also simplifying auditing and reporting efforts.

CHAPTER 2 ADVANCED AZURE SCAFFOLD FOR ENTERPRISE ARCHITECTURE

Management Group Strategies

Management groups provide a versatile way to manage and access Azure resources through the Azure portal, CLI, or REST API. When you first explore management groups in the Azure portal, you'll notice that a top-level management group is automatically created within each tenant. This group, also known as the root management group, serves as the highest node in a hierarchical structure. Like a tree, the root management group forms the central node, with all other management groups and resources in the tenant branching up to this top-level entity.

> **Note** Although the root management group is created automatically, access to it is **not granted by default**. A **Global Administrator** must **elevate access** via the Azure portal to manage this group and assign policies or RBAC roles at this level. This ensures that only privileged users can control governance settings across the entire tenant.

Figure 2-4 shows the top management group view.

Figure 2-4. Top management group view

Once you begin utilizing management groups, you'll gain visibility into all the subscriptions or child management groups that reside within the tenant, organized under the root management group (as illustrated in Figure 2-5).

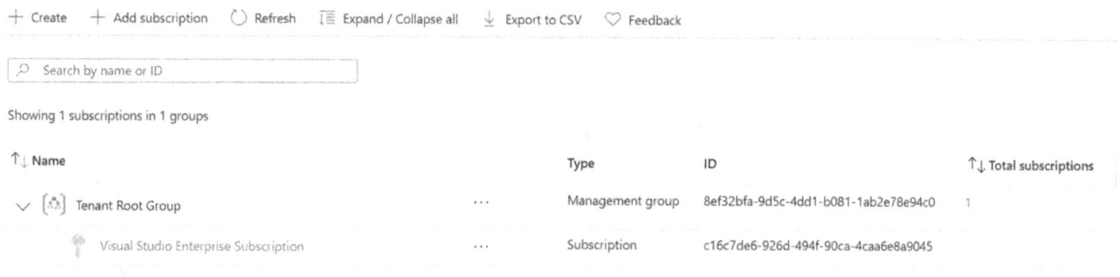

CHAPTER 2   ADVANCED AZURE SCAFFOLD FOR ENTERPRISE ARCHITECTURE

Figure 2-5. Azure subscription organized beneath the Tenant Root Group

The primary purpose of the root management group is to enable your organization to implement policies and Role-Based Access Control (RBAC) on a broad, organization-wide level. This allows for governance at the highest scale when required. Figure 2-6 shows the functional hierarchy in Azure governance.

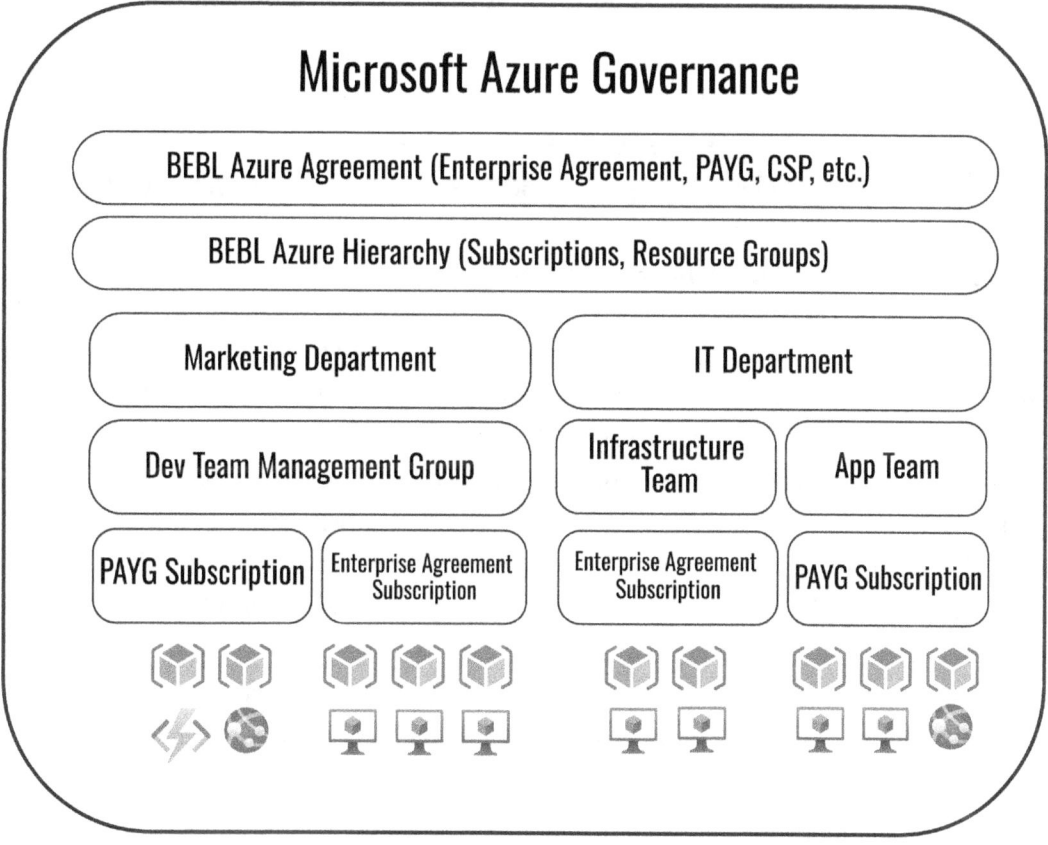

Figure 2-6. Example of a functional hierarchy in Azure Governance

39

Only the tenant administrator role grants access to the root management group level. To simplify the governance of management groups, it's best practice to follow naming conventions. For example, you might structure your hierarchy like this: Root Management Group ➤ Backend ➤ Marketing ➤ internal website ➤ production. You can establish up to 10,000 management groups within a single tenant. You can learn more about Root Management hierarchy from the official Microsoft documentation: `https://learn.microsoft.com/en-us/azure/governance/management-groups/overview`.

When managing subscriptions, it is important to consider the hierarchy model of the subscriptions tied to your tenant. These hierarchies help in standardizing nomenclature, which leads to more effective governance in your cloud environment. Using a functional pattern, you can apply a consistent naming system to a subscription, as illustrated in Figure 2-7.

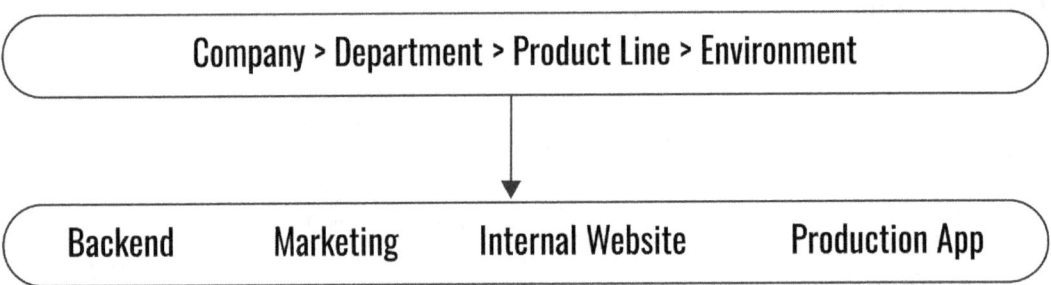

Figure 2-7. *Standard nomenclature across an organization*

For organizations with multiple environments, adhering to a structured naming convention provides greater control over subscription costs and offers enhanced visibility into who is managing resources within the subscription.

When designing a governance model for Azure resources that supports multiple teams, workloads, or environments, the complexity increases, particularly as administrators delegate responsibilities for different subscriptions through resource groups. This is further enhanced using Azure Policy and Role-Based Access Control (RBAC).

Resource groups serve as a logical boundary, defining the limits and scope of Azure components, including storage accounts, virtual networks, cores, and more. It is recommended to use resource groups as primary containers for resources that share a common function or purpose. Assigning names that reflect the workload or resource type helps streamline management.

CHAPTER 2 ADVANCED AZURE SCAFFOLD FOR ENTERPRISE ARCHITECTURE

Subscription Models and Scalability

One of the foundational aspects of Azure governance is the consistent and standardized naming of resources, starting at the subscription level. In many organizations, managing multiple subscriptions can become complex and cumbersome. To streamline this, Azure provides a powerful feature known as management groups. These groups enable you to manage multiple subscriptions efficiently within an organization.

Think of management groups as containers that hold one or more subscriptions. Each subscription, in turn, contains its respective resource groups and resources. This hierarchical organization simplifies large-scale management by allowing subscriptions to be grouped logically, making it easier to apply governance policies. For example, Figure 2-8 illustrates the management groups previously introduced in Chapter 1.

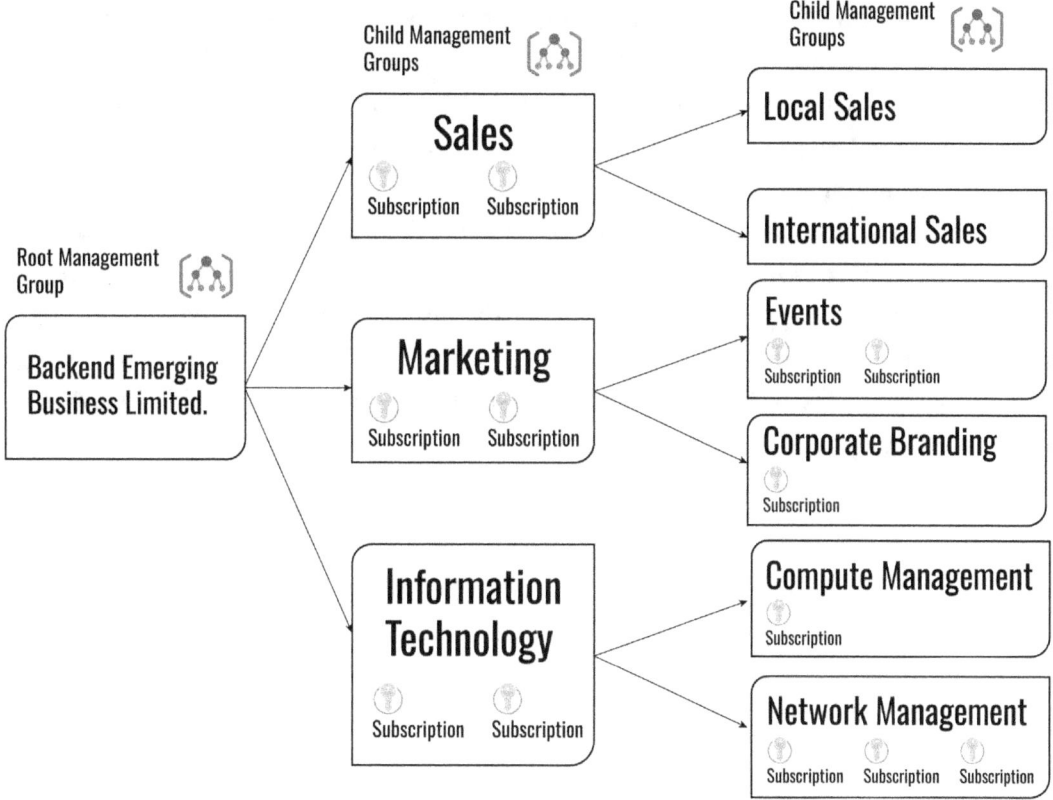

Figure 2-8. *Example of a management group hierarchy organized by departments*

In the broader context of Azure governance, management groups sit at a level above subscriptions, facilitating organization-wide governance. They are particularly useful for large-scale operations and centralized management. With management groups, you can define custom hierarchies and apply specific policies or Role-Based Access Control (RBAC) across different subscriptions and resource groups, enhancing both security and operational efficiency.

Summary

In this chapter, I focused on the fundamentals of building an **Azure scaffold** for enterprise architecture, laying out the governance and security best practices required from the outset. I walked you through the essential components like **management groups**, **subscriptions**, and **resource groups**, showing how organizing these elements effectively is key to achieving both governance and operational efficiency. Additionally, I explained how structuring a clear hierarchy in Azure helps manage resources, control access, and maintain scalability within a cloud environment, ensuring long-term security and compliance.

As we move into Chapter 3, I will shift the focus to the critical role that **naming conventions and standards** play in cloud management. I will guide you through the importance of **consistent naming**, introduce advanced **tagging strategies**, and explore ways to automate naming standards for ease of governance. Furthermore, by reviewing **real-world examples** and case studies, I will illustrate how these principles are applied in practice to keep your cloud infrastructure well organized, scalable, and efficient.

CHAPTER 3

Contemporary Azure Naming Conventions and Standards

In Chapter 2, I introduced the essential elements of building an Azure scaffold for enterprise architecture, emphasizing governance, security, and effective resource management. This included structuring Management Groups, Subscriptions, and Resource Groups to ensure scalable, secure operations. Additionally, I outlined best practices for access control and the importance of a clear hierarchy for efficient governance.

Moving forward to Chapter 3, the focus will shift to the critical role of consistent naming conventions and standards. I will explore advanced tagging strategies that enhance resource visibility and organization, as well as automation techniques to enforce naming rules across your cloud environment. These practices are vital for maintaining clarity, ensuring compliance, and streamlining management as your infrastructure expands.

Importance of Consistent Naming Conventions

Clear and consistent naming conventions are essential in Azure for effective resource management, automation, and governance. They minimize confusion, streamline operations, and ensure compliance, especially when using tools like Terraform or Bicep. A standardized approach simplifies identifying resources, enforcing policies, and scaling cloud environments. Without clear naming, resource tracking becomes inefficient, leading to errors and miscommunication. Establishing these conventions early is crucial for maintaining an organized and scalable infrastructure. For example, in one case, a team used inconsistent naming across environments (e.g., `web-prod-eastus` vs. `prod-web-eus`), which caused automated scripts to fail during deployment and led to delays in production rollout. Clear conventions help avoid such issues.

General Recommendations and Standards

The two core objectives of naming standards are clarity and consistency. While this sounds simple, implementing it can be complex, as different people may interpret clarity differently. The first step is to define what is not allowed when naming resources in Azure.

This book is focused on Azure governance, so understanding Azure's restrictions is essential. Microsoft Azure provides detailed rules for naming conventions, available in this link (`https://learn.microsoft.com/en-us/azure/cloud-adoption-framework/ready/azure-best-practices/naming-and-tagging`).

Example In one project, teams used inconsistent naming patterns like `webApp-prod`, `ProdWebApp`, and `web_app_prd`. This caused confusion during resource identification and led to failures in automation scripts. A well-documented and enforced naming standard would have prevented these operational issues.

These restrictions are foundational in creating scalable and efficient resource management. Table 3-1 summarizes the rules for common Azure resources.

Table 3-1. Examples of naming convention rules in Azure

Azure Entity	Length	Casing	Valid Characters
Resource Group	1–90	Case insensitive	Alphanumeric, underscore, parentheses, hyphen, period (but not at the end), and Unicode characters that adhere to regex
Tag	512 (name), 256 (value)	Case insensitive	Alphanumeric
Virtual Machine	1–15 (Windows), 1–64 (Linux)	Case insensitive	Alphanumeric and hyphen
Storage Account Name (Disk)	3–24	Lowercase	Alphanumeric
Virtual Network (VNet)	2–64	Case insensitive	Alphanumeric, hyphen, underscore, period
Subnet	2–80	Case insensitive	Alphanumeric, hyphen, underscore, period
Network Interface	1–80	Case insensitive	Alphanumeric, hyphen, underscore, period
Network Security Group	1–80	Case insensitive	Alphanumeric, hyphen, underscore, period

Once you've identified what is not permitted, the next crucial step is to establish a clear naming convention, create appropriate categories, and, most importantly, ensure that all of this is properly documented and effectively communicated.

Azure Governance Naming Categories

In Azure Governance, the primary naming categories include

- Resources governed by policies
- Resources and artifacts used to enforce governance

CHAPTER 3   CONTEMPORARY AZURE NAMING CONVENTIONS AND STANDARDS

To begin categorizing resources within Azure's governance framework, it is helpful to leverage the predefined categories available in Azure Policy ➤ Authoring ➤ Definitions section as illustrated in Figure 3-1.

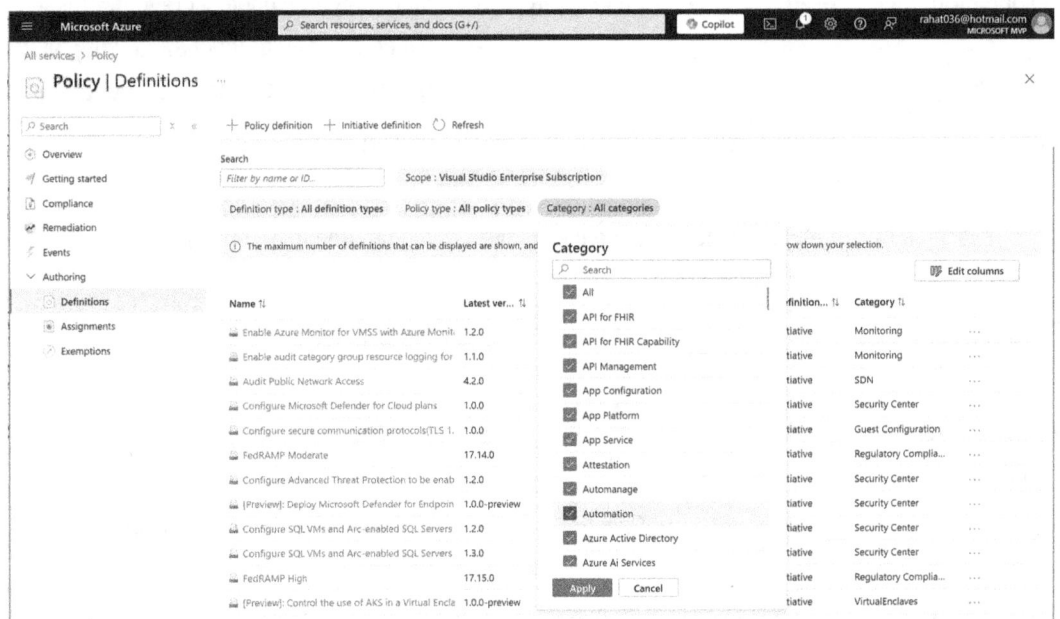

Figure 3-1. Predefined policy categories in Azure

The governance team may not always have direct control over implementing or enforcing the naming convention for resources within their governance scope. In such cases, it is essential for the governance team to first gather information about the existing naming conventions before assigning policies.

However, the naming of resources and artifacts used specifically for Azure Governance falls under the governance team's responsibility. The key principle is to establish, document, and standardize naming conventions that are both logical and conducive to automation and reporting. Additionally, it is critical to define and maintain naming standards from the outset in cloud environments. Attempting to modify naming conventions retrospectively can be complex and, in some cases, may require deleting and recreating resources, particularly with the rise of **Infrastructure-as-Code (IaC)** tools like Terraform or Bicep, which further emphasize the importance of consistency from day one.

Advanced Tagging Strategies

Tags in Azure offer a versatile way to apply additional metadata to your resources, playing a critical role in governance, cost management, automation, and operational monitoring. By applying tags, you introduce a new layer of organization that complements existing naming conventions, making it easier to classify and manage resources according to your organizational needs.

In terms of governance, carefully planned tag naming standards are essential to ensure that resources are categorized effectively. Common tags such as **CostCenter**, **Department**, **Location**, and **Environment** can enhance visibility, enabling more structured management and compliance with governance policies. These tags help streamline tasks like cost tracking, operational segmentation, and reporting, making it easier to manage large-scale Azure environments.

Consider a scenario where you manage several resource groups for different departments and environments, and you need to ensure that each resource group is tagged appropriately. For example, the Finance department has a resource group called **Finance-RG** that is tagged with the following attributes:

CostCenter: CC036-Finance
Department: Finance
Environment: Production
Location: East US
Owner: Rezwanur Rahman

To support consistent tagging practices, Table 3-2 outlines commonly used tags and their intended purpose.

CHAPTER 3   CONTEMPORARY AZURE NAMING CONVENTIONS AND STANDARDS

Table 3-2. *Commonly recommended Azure tags*

Tag Name	Purpose	Example Value
Owner	Identify the person or team responsible	Rezwanur Rahman
Department	Maps resource to a business unit	Finance
CostCenter	Supports chargeback or financial reporting	CC036-Finance
Environment	Differentiates between Dev, Test, Prod	Production
Location	Indicates deployment region	East US
Project	Groups resources by initiative or project	AzureMigration2025
Criticality	Priorities based on business impact	High

By applying these tags to the resource group, you can effectively manage governance policies, ensuring that the resources within this group are easily identifiable and categorized. These tags help with cost allocation, tracking the resources' ownership, and separating environments like Production, Development, or Testing.

Figure 3-2 shows the tags assigned in Resource Group named **Finance-RG**.

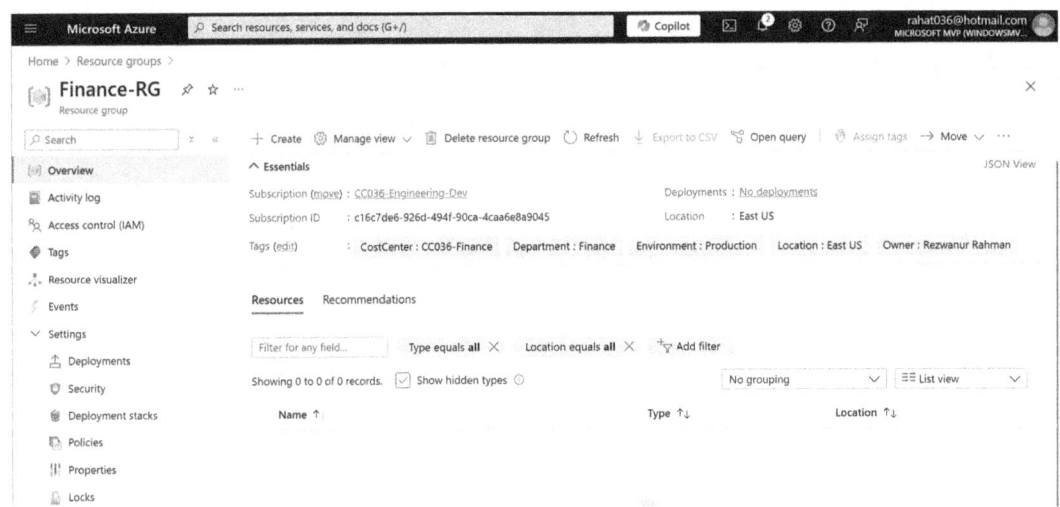

Figure 3-2. *Tag example for resource group*

Before implementing tags, you must ensure that **naming standards for tags are well defined**. If your organization already uses specific conventions for cost centers, departments, or environments, decide whether to maintain those standards in Azure or

CHAPTER 3 CONTEMPORARY AZURE NAMING CONVENTIONS AND STANDARDS

introduce Azure-specific prefixes (e.g., "AZ-"). Documenting these naming conventions ensures consistency across your organization, preventing misalignment when policies are applied to enforce or monitor tags.

Tags for Governance and Compliance

Tags contribute to governance by improving resource visibility and control. For example, using a **CostCenter** tag enables cost reporting and tracking for each department, allowing financial teams to understand resource expenditures more clearly. Similarly, the **Environment** tag helps categorize resources by their usage, ensuring that production environments are managed separately from development or testing environments.

- **Automating Tagging**: Tools like **Azure Blueprints** and **Azure Policy** can help automate the application of tags to resource groups. By defining governance rules centrally, you can ensure that all resources in a management group or subscription are consistently tagged, reducing manual effort and enforcing compliance automatically.

Common Pitfall One frequent issue is the inconsistent application of tags—for instance, some resources might be tagged as Prod, while others use Production, or some might be missing tags entirely. This inconsistency can lead to reporting errors, broken automation scripts, or audit failures. To avoid this, organizations should establish a set of **approved tag keys and values**, enforce them using **Azure Policy**, and regularly audit tag compliance using tools like **Azure Resource Graph**.

- **Scaling Tagging**: As your Azure environment grows, scalability becomes essential. **Azure Resource Graph** provides the ability to query and monitor tag compliance across thousands of resources, ensuring that all required tags are in place and governance policies are adhered to.

CHAPTER 3   CONTEMPORARY AZURE NAMING CONVENTIONS AND STANDARDS

Automation of Naming Standards

As organizations scale their cloud infrastructure, managing resources manually becomes impractical and inefficient. A well-implemented naming standard is critical for clarity, consistency, and governance, but when deployed at scale, manual processes can lead to errors and inconsistency. Automating the enforcement of these naming conventions not only saves time but also ensures that every resource adheres to organizational policies, streamlining operations and minimizing the risk of oversight.

For example, in a large enterprise, inconsistent naming of virtual machines—such as `vm-prod-eastus-01`, `eastus01-prod-vm`, and `vm01eus-prod`—led to confusion during audits and challenges in applying automation policies. These inconsistencies also made it difficult to track usage and decommission stale resources. Automation could have prevented these issues by enforcing a consistent naming pattern across all teams.

Naming at Scale with Automation

Managing naming conventions at scale presents several challenges, especially when handling vast numbers of cloud resources. Human errors can easily arise when naming resources manually, leading to inconsistencies and confusion across teams and environments. As cloud deployments expand globally, maintaining uniform naming standards becomes increasingly complex. Without automation, organizations may face issues like duplicated names, difficulty in searching for resources, and challenges in meeting compliance requirements.

Benefits of Automation in Naming

Automating the naming process in Azure not only enhances consistency and efficiency but also ensures that governance and compliance standards are met across all resources, reducing manual oversight.

1. **Consistency:** Automated naming ensures that the same naming rules are applied across all resources, minimizing discrepancies that can occur with manual processes.

2. **Efficiency:** Automation significantly reduces the time and resources required to name assets appropriately. For example, provisioning hundreds of resources can be streamlined through scripts or templates that follow predefined naming patterns.

3. **Governance and Compliance:** Automated naming integrates well with governance policies, ensuring resources adhere to organizational standards. Azure Policies can enforce these naming standards automatically, ensuring compliance even as environment scale.

4. **Simplified Auditing:** Automated, consistent naming conventions improve the ability to audit environments. When every resource follows a set pattern, searching, reporting, and auditing become far easier.

Automation Methods

Azure offers several automation tools, such as ARM templates, PowerShell, and Azure Policies, to streamline the naming process and enforce conventions at scale, improving management in large, complex environments.

1. **Infrastructure-as-Code (IaC) Templates**: Using Azure Resource Manager (ARM) templates, Terraform, or Bicep, you can define dynamic naming conventions within your deployment templates. For example, a common pattern is [Environment]-[Service]-[Region]-[Identifier], ensuring that every resource has a unique and traceable name based on its location, environment, and type.

   Here is an example of an ARM template-based naming convention:

   ```
   {
       "type": "Microsoft.Storage/storageAccounts",
       "name": "[concat(parameters('environment'), '-st-', parameters('location'), uniqueString(resourceGroup().id))]",
       "location": "[parameters('location')]",
       ...
   }
   ```

CHAPTER 3   CONTEMPORARY AZURE NAMING CONVENTIONS AND STANDARDS

2. **PowerShell and Azure CLI Scripts**: Scripting allows you to define and automate naming conventions dynamically during resource creation. These scripts can be embedded into deployment pipelines for continuous integration/continuous delivery (CI/CD). For example, using PowerShell:

```powershell
$env = "Prod"
$location = "EastUS"
$name = "$env-RG-$location"
New-AzResourceGroup -Name $name -Location $location
```

This script ensures that every resource group follows the pattern [Environment]-RG-[Location].

3. **Azure Policies for Naming Enforcement:** Azure Policies provide a robust method for enforcing naming conventions across the entire organization. By defining policy rules, you can ensure that only resources adhering to specific naming patterns are allowed. Here is an example of a policy definition to enforce naming standards using JSON:

```json
{
  "if": {
    "not": {
      "field": "name",
      "like": "prod-%"
    }
  },
  "then": {
    "effect": "deny"
  }
}
```

This policy denies the creation of any resource whose name does not start with "prod," ensuring that naming conventions are followed.

4. **Automation with Tags:** As we discussed in this chapter, tags are an additional layer of metadata that can complement naming conventions, especially in large-scale environments. Tags such as `CostCenter`, `Environment`, and `Owner` can be automatically applied to resources during deployment, further simplifying management and governance.

Tags provide flexibility when used alongside automated naming, ensuring that information like cost allocation or business unit ownership is embedded within the resource metadata, regardless of naming.

Different automation tools offer different strengths for enforcing naming standards:

- **ARM Templates/Bicep**

  Ideal for embedding naming patterns into deployment workflows

  - *Best for*: Standardizing names during large-scale, repeatable deployments

  - *Limitation*: Does not enforce or correct naming outside of template use

- **PowerShell/CLI Scripts**

  Useful for scripting custom naming logic or retroactively fixing inconsistent names

  - *Best for*: Bulk renaming or custom tasks

  - *Limitation*: Requires manual execution or scheduling and ongoing maintenance

- **Azure Policy**

  Enforces naming rules automatically by auditing or denying non-compliant resource names

  - *Best for*: Preventing bad names during resource creation

  - *Limitation*: Does not rename existing resources and may require advanced policy definitions

Scaling Naming in Multi-region and Multi-team Scenarios

As organizations expand their cloud presence across multiple regions and teams, maintaining consistency in naming becomes critical for smooth operations. Automation helps scale naming across different regions by dynamically appending region codes to resource names. For example, using a template that appends the appropriate region (**usw** for West US, **euw** for Western Europe) ensures that resources across multiple geographic locations are easily identifiable.

Similarly, for teams, unique team identifiers can be incorporated into the naming convention, ensuring that resources are traceable back to specific departments or business units. Automation ensures this naming logic is applied consistently, regardless of the number of resources being deployed.

Here I would like to share an example. In a large enterprise, managing hundreds of Azure resources across several subscriptions, automated naming conventions were applied using ARM templates and Azure Policies. By embedding naming logic directly into deployment templates and enforcing them via Azure Policies, the organization eliminated the need for manual naming oversight. Resources such as virtual machines, storage accounts, and network components were automatically named according to the predefined structure, for example, **Prod-App-WestUS-VM01**. This automation not only improved governance and compliance but also reduced errors, accelerated deployments, and simplified auditing. Table 3-3 demonstrates how naming conventions can scale across regions and teams using structured patterns.

Table 3-3. Sample naming patterns for multi-region and multi-team scenarios

Environment	Team	Region Code	Resource Type	Example Name
Prod	App	usw (West US)	VM	Prod-App-usw-VM01
Dev	Network	euw (West Europe)	VNet	Dev-Network-euw-VNet01
Test	Data	use (East US)	Storage Account	Test-Data-use-Stor01

Additional Resources and Examples

There are great examples of Azure naming conventions in the official Microsoft online documentation:

- `https://docs.microsoft.com/en-us/azure/architecture/best-practices/naming-conventions` offers recommended patterns as well as rules and constraints for naming resource types.

- `https://docs.microsoft.com/en-us/rest/api/storageservices/naming-and-referencing-containers--blobs--and-metadata` provides examples of naming of containers, blobs, and metadata.

- `https://docs.microsoft.com/en-us/azure/virtual-machines/windows/infrastructure-example` uses an application workload to demonstrate naming for virtual machines (VM) and the associated resources. The extracts highlight the sections showing the example naming conventions.

- Sample of enforcing naming standards with Azure policies (`https://github.com/Azure/azure-policy/tree/master/samples/TextPatterns/enforce-match-pattern`).

- Sample of enforcing naming standards with ARM templates (`https://github.com/Azure/azure-quickstart-templates/blob/master/1-CONTRIBUTION-GUIDE/README.md`).

Naming Standards in Action

Here I will discuss a detailed explanation of naming conventions for governance artifacts in an organization. It covers best practices and examples for the following key categories:

- Subscriptions
- Resource Groups
- Management Groups
- Policies
- Initiatives
- Blueprints

Each category is discussed in depth to promote clarity and consistency in managing cloud resources effectively.

Subscriptions

Each Azure subscription comes with a unique ID and a default friendly name. It is advisable to rename the friendly name to align with a naming standard that fits your organizational needs and environment. This ensures clarity and consistency across your subscription management.

Many organizations overlook the importance of renaming their subscriptions, often keeping default names like "Pay-As-You-Go" or using inconsistent formats across departments. This can lead to confusion in cost reporting, unclear ownership, and errors in resource provisioning. A clear, standardized naming convention helps mitigate these issues. For example, using a format like `[Environment]-[Department]-[Region]` (e.g., `Prod-Finance-EastUS`) ensures that each subscription is easily identifiable and aligned with its purpose. Avoid using vague terms such as "Test" or personal names and instead focus on descriptive but concise labels that reflect lifecycle stage, function, and geography.

The default name is usually determined by the type of subscription you choose during sign-up. For example, options like Pay-As-You-Go or MSDN Visual Studio set the initial subscription name.

You can modify subscription names to reflect their specific usage and departmental ownership. Use the following steps to update the subscription name to follow a naming standard that incorporates elements like cost center, department, and lifecycle environment:

1. Using a supported browser, log in into the Azure portal at `https://portal.azure.com`.

2. In the search, type **subscriptions**, and click the subscriptions from the search result as shown in Figure 3-3.

CHAPTER 3   CONTEMPORARY AZURE NAMING CONVENTIONS AND STANDARDS

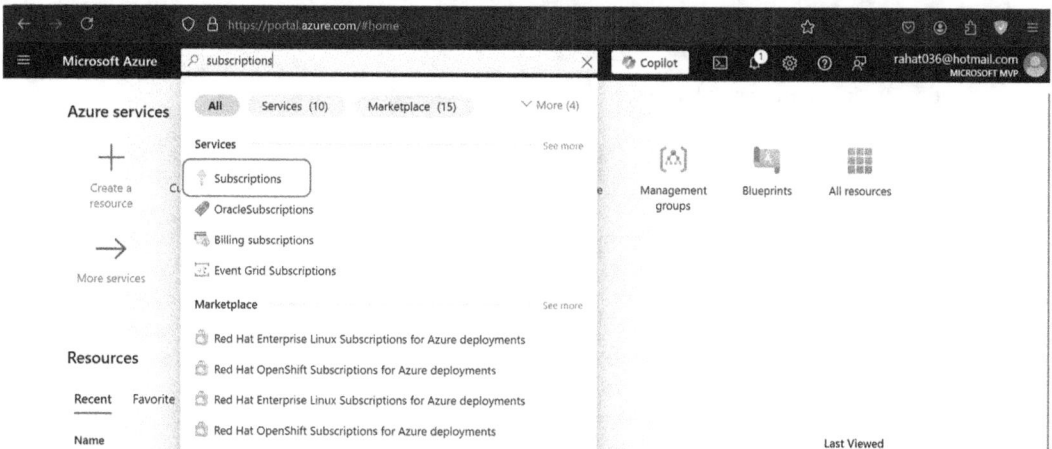

Figure 3-3. *Subscriptions option in Azure search result*

3. You can see the list of subscriptions as shown in Figure 3-4.

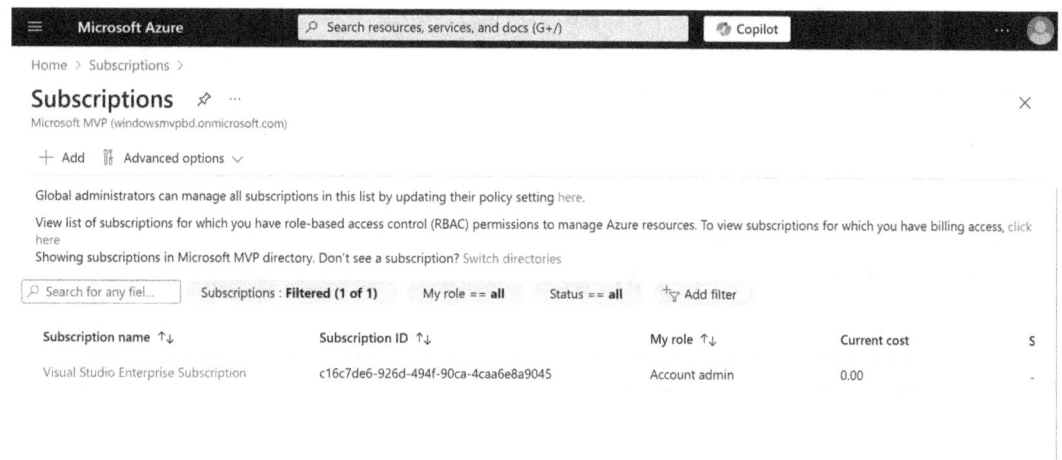

Figure 3-4. *List of subscriptions*

4. Click the Subscription that you want to rename. After that you can see the option named Rename as shown in Figure 3-5.

57

CHAPTER 3   CONTEMPORARY AZURE NAMING CONVENTIONS AND STANDARDS

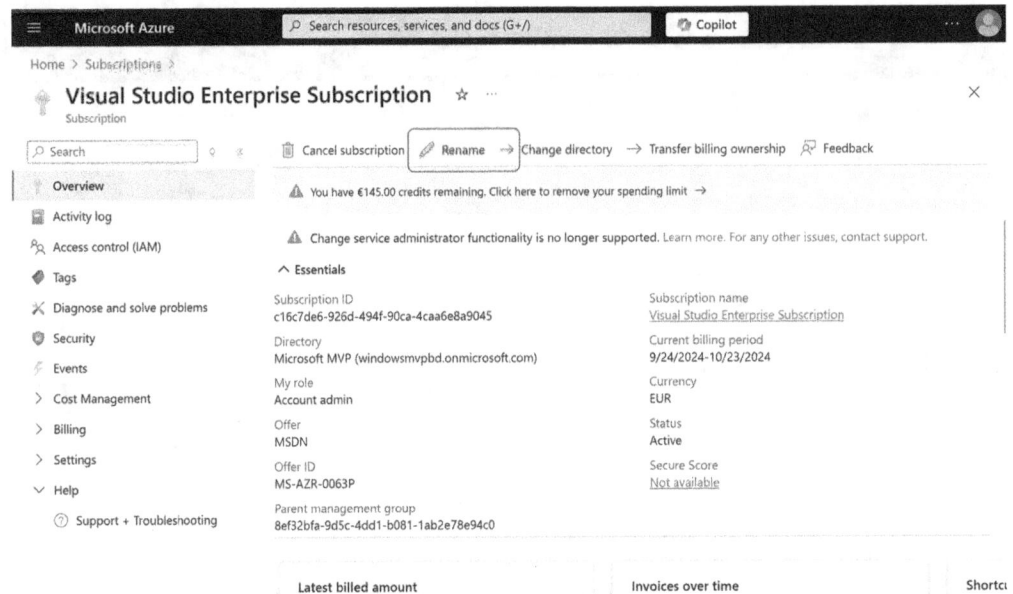

Figure 3-5. *Option to rename the Subscription name*

5. After clicking the Rename, you will have the option to change the name. Type the new name and click Save as shown in Figure 3-6. Please note it will take ten minutes to reflect the new name.

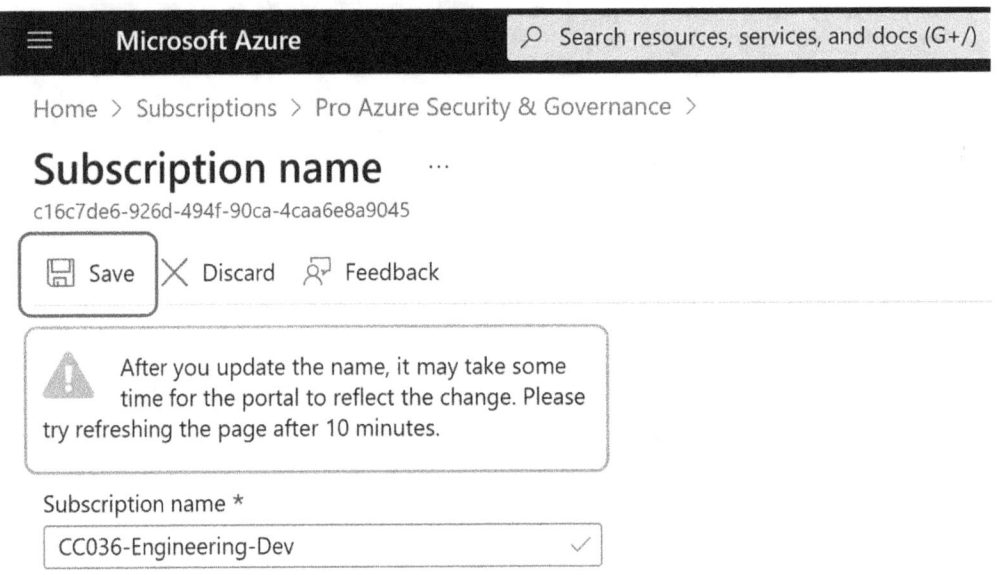

Figure 3-6. *Changing the Subscription name*

6. After a few minutes, refresh the browser to see the effect of the change as shown in Figure 3-7.

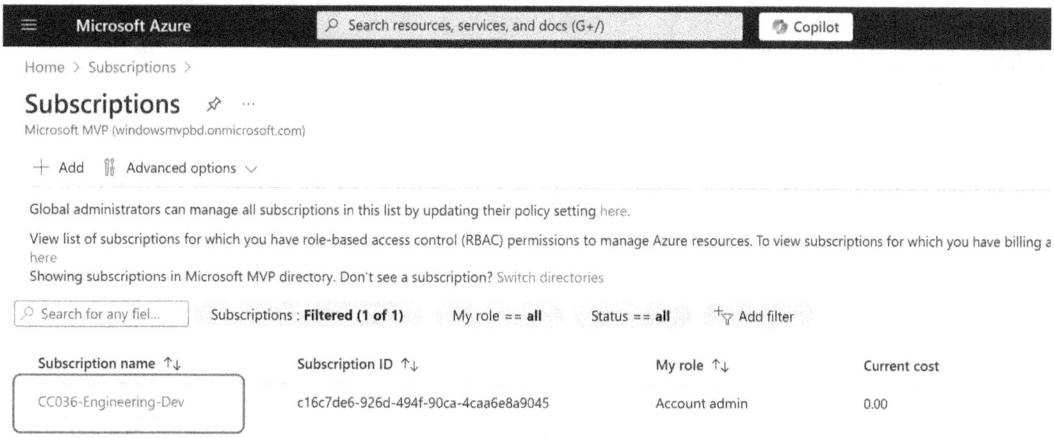

Figure 3-7. Updated name of the subscription

In this example, we applied a logical naming convention based on `<Cost Center>-<Department>-<Environment>`.

Resource Groups

In Azure, resource groups serve as an essential organizational tool for managing all resources that form a particular solution. This solution could range from something simple like a single virtual machine to a more complex, multitier application with virtual networks, virtual machines, databases, and other interconnected Azure services. Resource groups represent the layer directly beneath subscriptions in Azure's hierarchical structure. In this governance model, management groups sit at the top, encompassing one or more subscriptions, while each subscription contains multiple resource groups.

Resource groups play a pivotal role not only in organizing resources but also in defining the scope for applying Azure policies or initiatives. For effective governance, it's highly recommended to implement a consistent naming convention for resource groups as part of a broader Azure naming strategy.

While Azure offers flexibility in naming, it's critical to follow Azure's naming rules for resource groups to maintain order and ensure clarity across environments. A well-defined naming convention improves resource management, monitoring, and automation.

CHAPTER 3 CONTEMPORARY AZURE NAMING CONVENTIONS AND STANDARDS

Table 3-4 provides examples of standard naming conventions for resource groups, illustrating how different strategies can be applied based on your organization's requirements.

Table 3-4. *Example of Resource Groups naming*

Standard	Example
<CC>-<ResourceTypes>-RG	CC036-Netw-RG
<CC>-<Environment>-RG	CC036-Dev-RG
<CC>-<AppName>-RG	CC036-App1-RG
<CC>-<Environment>-<AppName>-RG	CC036-Dev-App3-RG
<CC>-<Environment>-< ResourceTypes >-RG	CC036-Dev-Netw-RG

Figure 3-8 is a graphical representation of the examples in the table, showing resource groups created under a subscription called **CC036-Engineering-Dev**.

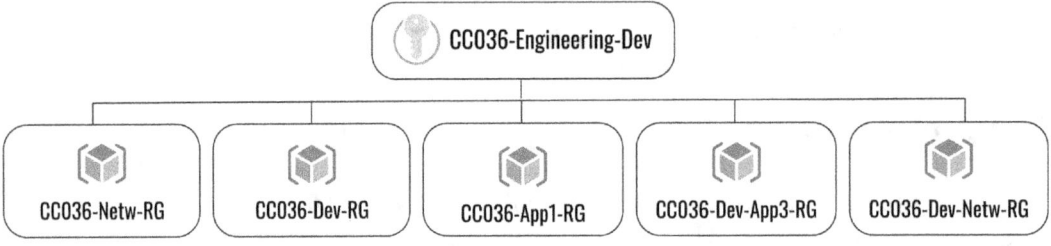

Figure 3-8. *Graphical representation of the resource groups naming*

Management Groups

Management groups offer a powerful way to organize your Azure subscriptions, enhancing your governance capabilities, as introduced in Chapter 1. It is essential to apply an appropriate naming convention to management groups to streamline operations while maintaining flexibility. When planning the structure of management groups, it's crucial to adopt a logical approach that aligns with your organizational structure, subscription management, role-based access control, and governance artifacts.

CHAPTER 3 CONTEMPORARY AZURE NAMING CONVENTIONS AND STANDARDS

Since management groups are hierarchical, careful planning of their naming is necessary to ensure clarity and adaptability. You can create up to six hierarchical levels of management groups, in addition to the root management group, resulting in a total of seven layers. Although Azure allows for up to 10,000 management groups, it's important to treat this as a limit rather than a target. Minimizing the number of management groups will help avoid overly complex structures.

Figure 3-9 illustrates a five-layer management group structure following a naming convention. This structure starts with a top-level division of assigned or unassigned subscriptions, branching into the organization's primary structure (such as Research and Development and the main company). From there, it's further divided into environments and sub-departments, ensuring both clarity and scalability for future growth.

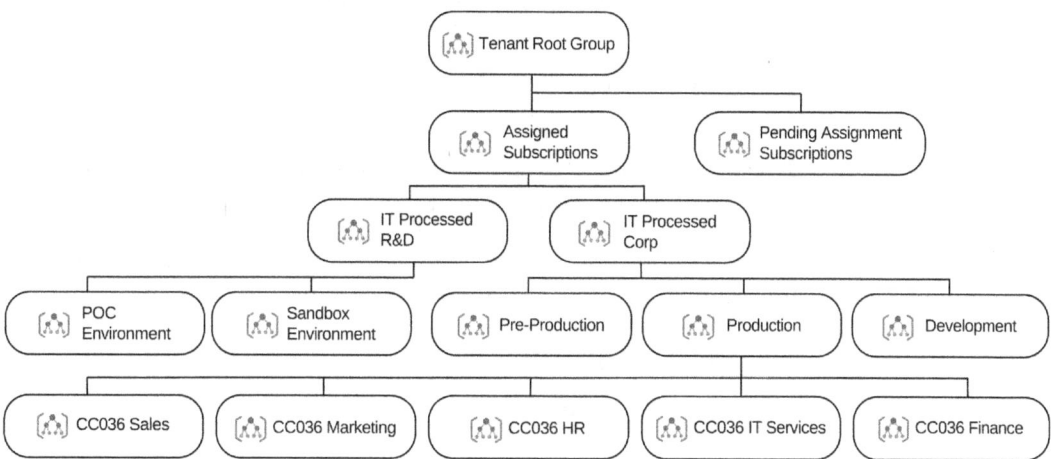

Figure 3-9. *Management groups structure planning*

Here, you will see a visual representation of the management group hierarchy, providing an overview of how your policies are applied across the organization, as illustrated in Figure 3-10.

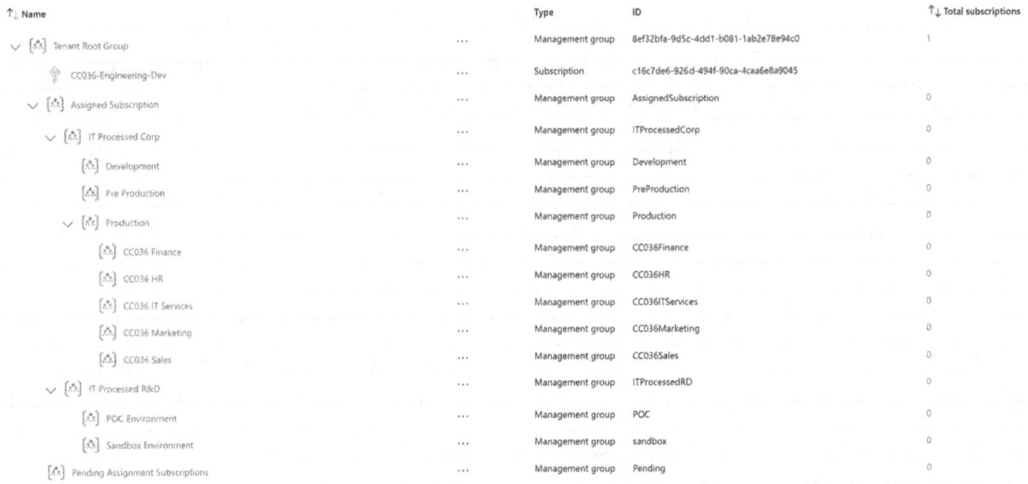

CHAPTER 3   CONTEMPORARY AZURE NAMING CONVENTIONS AND STANDARDS

Name		Type	ID	Total subscriptions
∨ Tenant Root Group	...	Management group	8ef32bfa-9d5c-4dd1-b081-1ab2e78e94c0	1
CC036-Engineering-Dev	...	Subscription	c16c7de6-926d-494f-90ca-4caa6e8a9045	
∨ Assigned Subscription	...	Management group	AssignedSubscription	0
∨ IT Processed Corp	...	Management group	ITProcessedCorp	0
Development	...	Management group	Development	0
Pre Production	...	Management group	PreProduction	0
∨ Production	...	Management group	Production	0
CC036 Finance	...	Management group	CC036Finance	0
CC036 HR	...	Management group	CC036HR	0
CC036 IT Services	...	Management group	CC036ITServices	0
CC036 Marketing	...	Management group	CCD36Marketing	0
CC036 Sales	...	Management group	CC036Sales	0
∨ IT Processed R&D	...	Management group	ITProcessedRD	0
POC Environment	...	Management group	POC	0
Sandbox Environment	...	Management group	sandbox	0
Pending Assignment Subscriptions	...	Management group	Pending	0

Figure 3-10. *Management group structure hierarchy in the Azure portal*

When setting up management groups, you must specify both an ID and a display name. While the display name can be modified at any time, the ID is permanent and cannot be changed unless the management group is deleted. Therefore, it's important to establish a logical naming convention for the management group ID, as it may be utilized in automation processes. Figure 3-11 illustrates the creation dialog box for a management group, where you input both the display name and the ID.

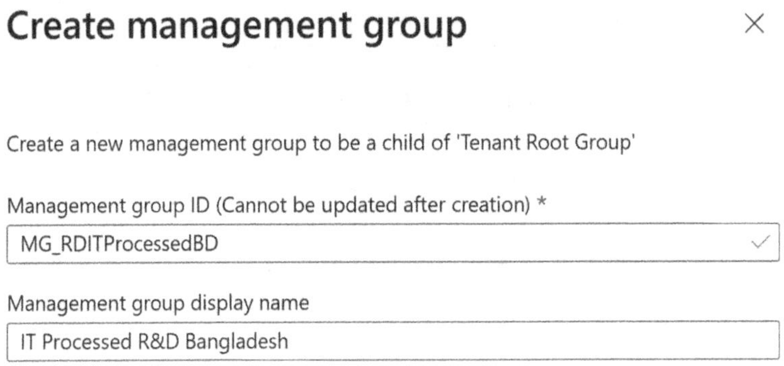

Create management group ✕

Create a new management group to be a child of 'Tenant Root Group'

Management group ID (Cannot be updated after creation) *

MG_RDITProcessedBD

Management group display name

IT Processed R&D Bangladesh

Figure 3-11. *Management group naming example showing ID and display name*

Management groups can be created using the Azure portal, PowerShell, or the Azure CLI. When using PowerShell, the following syntax creates a new management group:

```
New-AzManagementGroup -GroupName '<New Management Group ID>' -DisplayName
'<New Management Group Display Name>' -ParentId '<Management Group Parent ID>'
```

After the management group is created, while the display name can be updated at any time via either the Azure portal or PowerShell, the management group ID is permanent and cannot be modified without deleting and recreating the group.

To update the display name of an existing management group using PowerShell, you can use the following syntax:

```
Update-AzManagementGroup -GroupName '<Existing Management Group ID>'
-DisplayName '<New Management Group Display Name>'
```

Ensure you're using the updated **Az** module, as Azure continues to replace older cmdlets like **AzureRm** with the latest **Az** equivalents to support the most current Azure features.

Policies

Azure policies are organized into three key naming categories:

- **Policy Definition Name**
- **Policy Assignment Name**
- **Policy Category**

Microsoft offers a wide range of built-in policies, grouped under various default categories. These built-in policies are not assigned by default, so when you assign them, your primary focus is on the policy assignment name. The best practice is to create your own policy categories and custom policies before assigning them. This allows you to establish a consistent naming convention and maintain control over any customizations, while keeping the default policies as template artifacts for reference.

An effective approach, as illustrated in Table 3-5, is to use a prefix to clearly identify custom policies and create distinct categories. For example, you could create separate categories for production policies and policies under review. This method provides flexibility in managing policies while maintaining clarity across your governance structure.

Table 3-5. Custom policy category example

Policy Prefix	Category Name
POL-	ITP Under Review|ITP Production

CHAPTER 3 CONTEMPORARY AZURE NAMING CONVENTIONS AND STANDARDS

This implements a standard of naming that gives a clear view of the purpose of the policies. Figure 3-12 shows the Azure policy definition node listing custom policies with the category and naming standards.

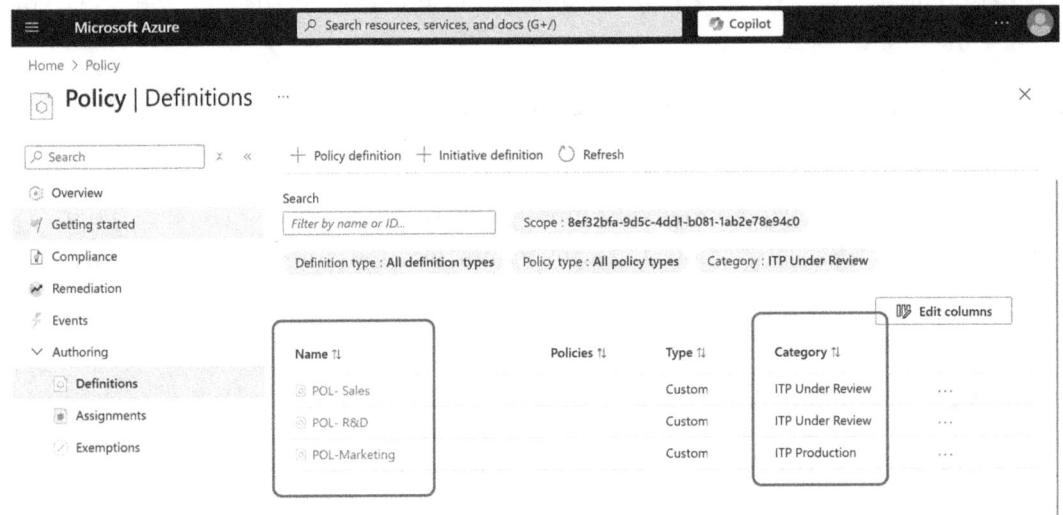

Figure 3-12. *Implementation of policy categories in the Azure portal*

When creating a custom policy, the process of assigning a custom name and category is done during the policy creation itself. If needed, you can later modify the name or category of the policy by using the edit option. Figure 3-13 highlights these sections where you can adjust. This flexibility allows you to maintain and update your naming conventions and categories as your governance needs evolve.

64

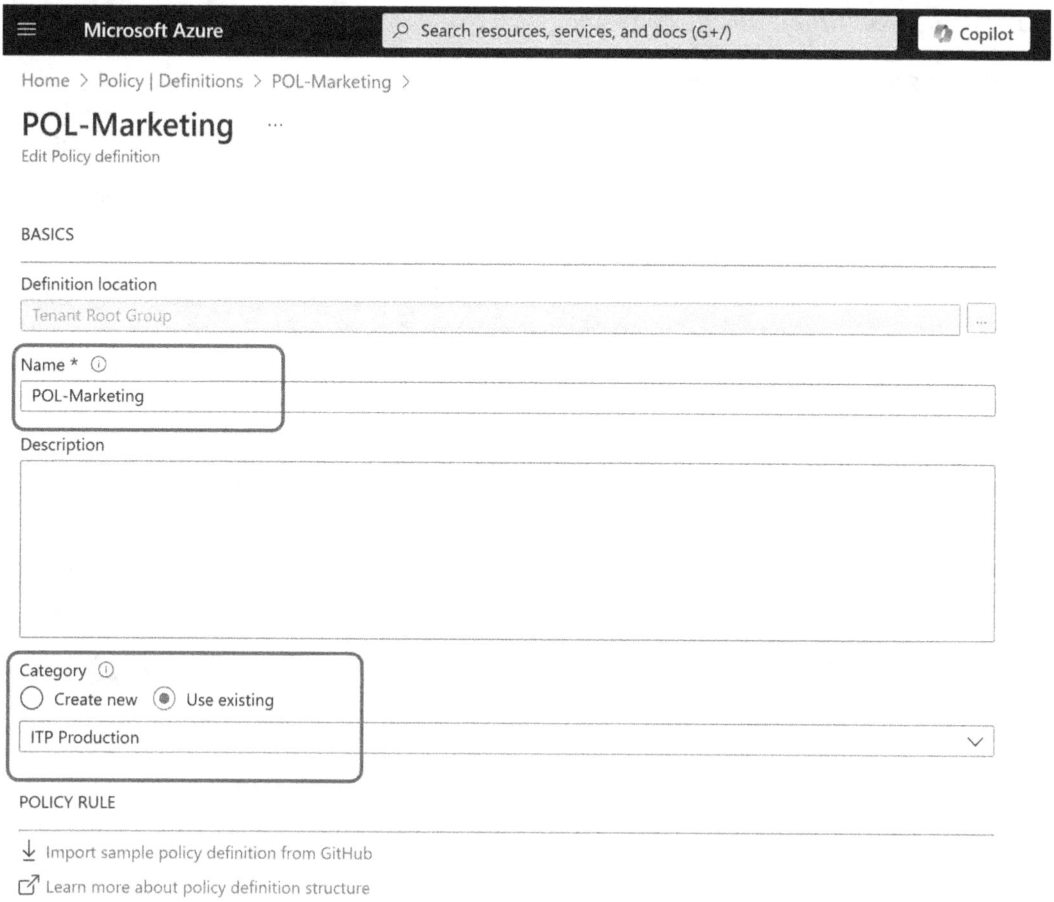

CHAPTER 3   CONTEMPORARY AZURE NAMING CONVENTIONS AND STANDARDS

Figure 3-13. Editing the policy names and categories in Azure

Once a category is created, you can choose the **Use existing** option to select from a previously established category, whether it's a built-in or custom category. This feature simplifies policy management by allowing you to consistently apply categories across policies. Additionally, applying naming standards to policy assignments further enhances the organization of your governance environment. Table 3-6 illustrates examples of assignment naming conventions that help maintain a clear and consistent structure within your Azure governance framework.

CHAPTER 3 CONTEMPORARY AZURE NAMING CONVENTIONS AND STANDARDS

Table 3-6. *Assignment name example*

Assignment Prefix	Description
Enforce	Used for policies that actively enforce a specific standard or requirement
Auditing	Applied to policies that are set to audit-only mode, tracking compliance without enforcing actions
ASC	A prefix automatically added to policies that are assigned through Microsoft Defender for Cloud (formerly Azure Security Center)

Figure 3-14 demonstrates the assignment naming in practice. The applied naming convention is intuitive and clearly understandable for portal users, making it easy to identify the purpose and type of each policy assignment within the Azure portal. This approach enhances user experience by providing clear, descriptive names that align with your governance standards.

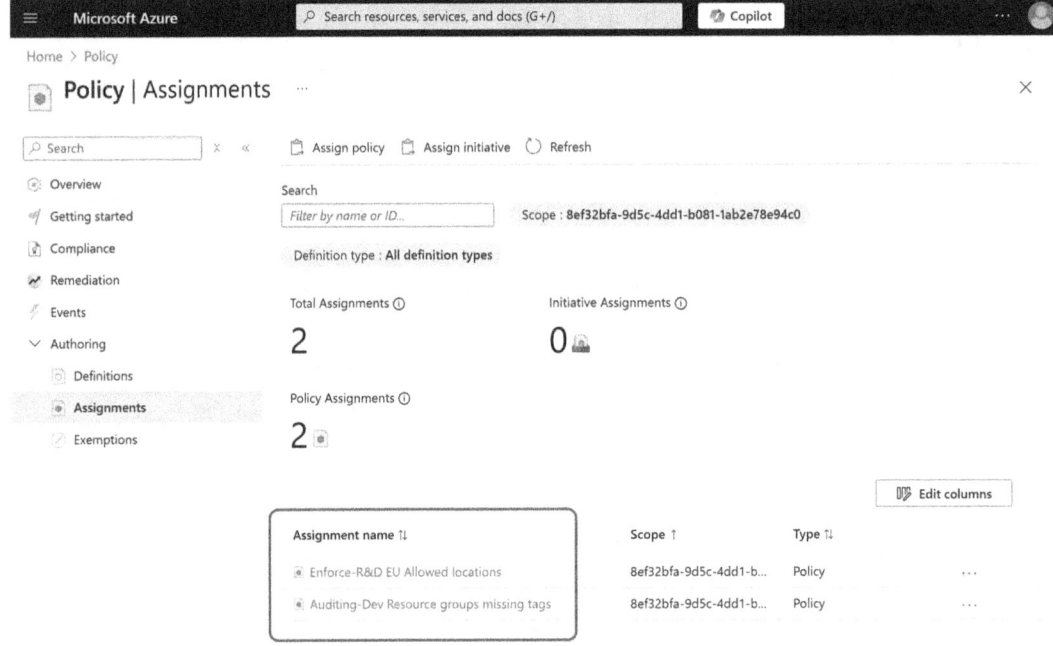

Figure 3-14. *Assignment naming examples*

Initiatives

As introduced in Chapter 1, **initiatives** allow you to group multiple policies together to achieve consistent compliance with specific governance and compliance objectives. Similar to policies, initiatives have three key naming categories:

- **Initiative Definition Name**
- **Initiative Assignment Name**
- **Initiative Category**

Microsoft Azure provides built-in initiatives across several default categories, but these are not assigned by default. The best practice is to create custom categories and initiatives that are tailored to your environment's governance objectives. These initiatives should be carefully planned, scoped, and assigned to meet your specific compliance needs.

Table 3-7 provides an example of initiative naming, where a prefix is used to clearly identify custom initiatives. Additionally, the categories you establish for initiatives can mirror those used for policies, ensuring consistency across your governance framework.

Table 3-7. Custom initiative category examples

Initiative Prefix	Category Name
INI-	ITP Under Review|ITP Production|ITP POC

The naming convention ensures that the purpose of the initiatives you create and assign is immediately clear. Figure 3-15 shows the Azure policy definition node, where custom initiatives are listed, displaying their categories and naming standards. This clear structure allows for easy identification of the intent and role of each initiative, enhancing organization and governance efficiency in Azure.

CHAPTER 3   CONTEMPORARY AZURE NAMING CONVENTIONS AND STANDARDS

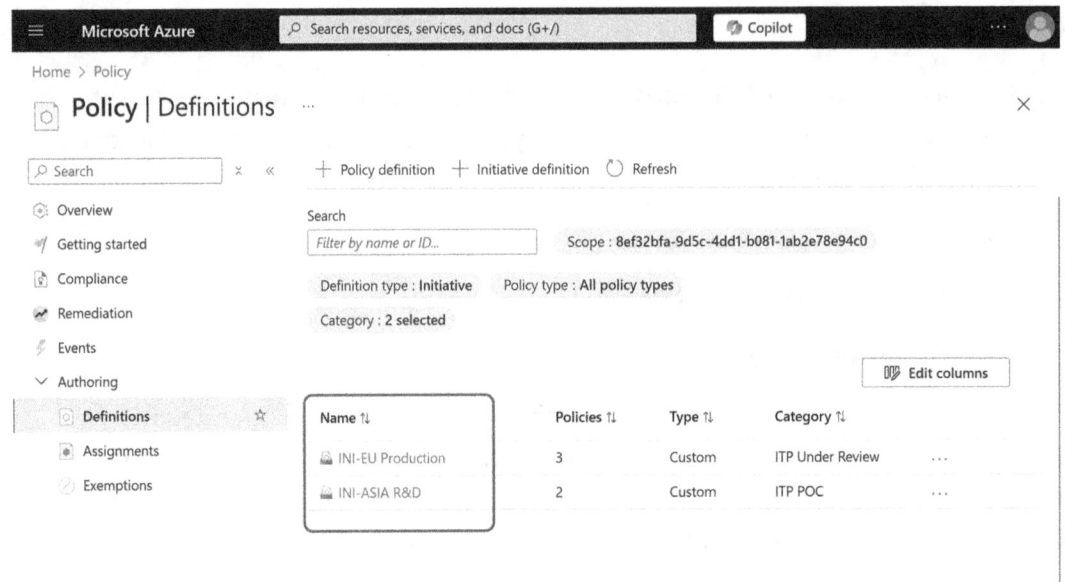

Figure 3-15. *Initiative naming with a custom category*

When creating an initiative, the steps for assigning custom names and categories are completed during the initiative creation process. You can later modify both the name and category by using the edit option. After a category is created, you can select the Use existing option to choose a previously established category, whether it's built in or custom.

However, it's important to note that the availability of categories depends on the scope you select. The scope option will only display categories created and stored at that level during the creation of a policy or initiative.

In addition to categories, assignment naming standards can be applied to further enhance the organization of your governance environment. By default, the assignment name for initiatives will match the initiative name, but you can modify this name to adhere to your specific naming conventions. Figure 3-16 illustrates the required initiative assignment naming field, which allows you to customize the name as needed.

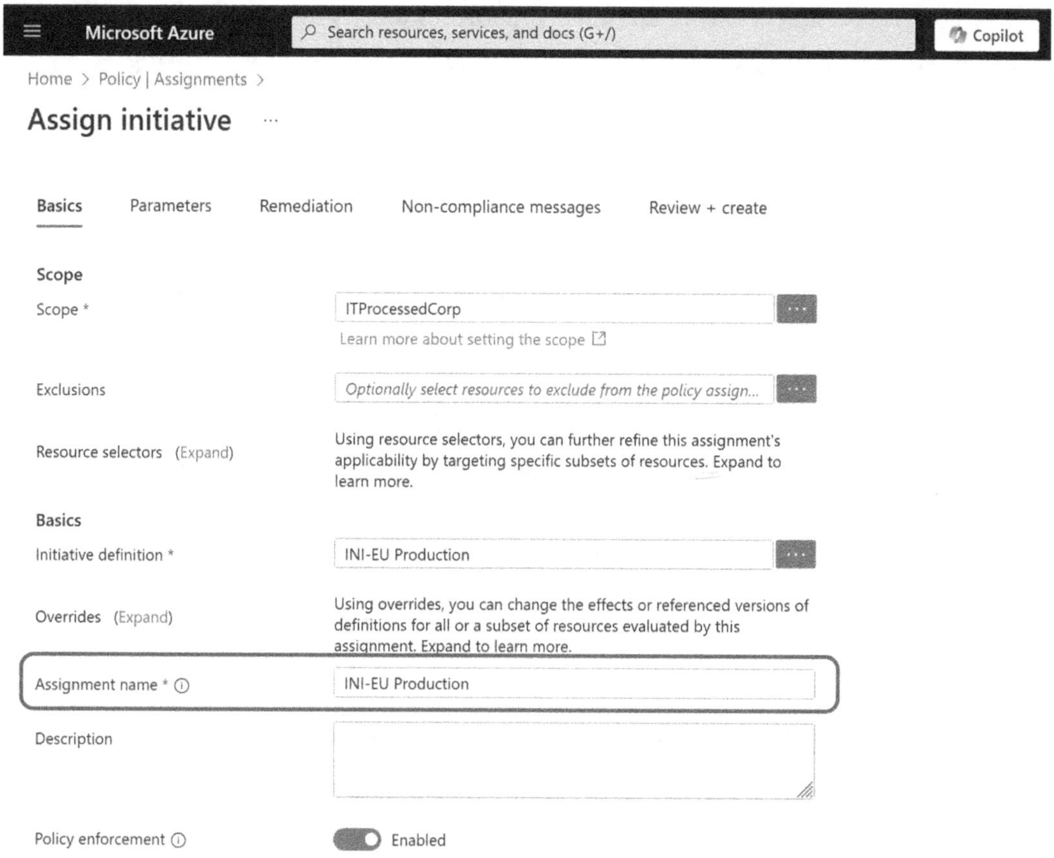

CHAPTER 3   CONTEMPORARY AZURE NAMING CONVENTIONS AND STANDARDS

Figure 3-16. Initiative assignment naming in Azure portal. You can change this value to your custom assignment naming standard.

Blueprints

Azure Blueprints offer a way to establish standardized patterns for your Azure environments, ensuring that they align with your organization's requirements and compliance frameworks from the start. Blueprints are applied at the subscription level and, at the time of writing, can include the following elements:

- Role assignments
- Policy assignments
- Azure Resource Manager templates
- Resource groups

69

CHAPTER 3 CONTEMPORARY AZURE NAMING CONVENTIONS AND STANDARDS

Each of these artifacts within an Azure Blueprint inherits the naming convention you establish. The key naming considerations for Blueprints include the following:

- Blueprint name
- Blueprint version
- Blueprint assignment name

These naming conventions correspond to the different lifecycle stages of a blueprint: creation and assignment. While blueprints can be edited after creation, the blueprint name itself cannot be changed once it's set.

It is recommended to use a naming convention for blueprints that follow a similar pattern to the one used for subscriptions. Blueprint names can include up to 48 characters (letters and numbers) without spaces or special characters. Table 3-8 provides examples of blueprint naming conventions to guide your practice.

Table 3-8. Azure blueprint naming examples

Blueprint Standard	Example
<Lifecycle stage>SubBP	DevSubBP
<Application><Lifecycle stage>SubBP	MyBusinessAppProdSub

When starting the process of creating a blueprint, you will be prompted to provide a **blueprint name** and a **description** as shown in Figure 3-17. It's crucial to not only choose a clear and concise name but also include a detailed description that explains the intended use and purpose of the blueprint. This description helps ensure that the blueprint's role within your organization's governance and compliance structure is easily understood.

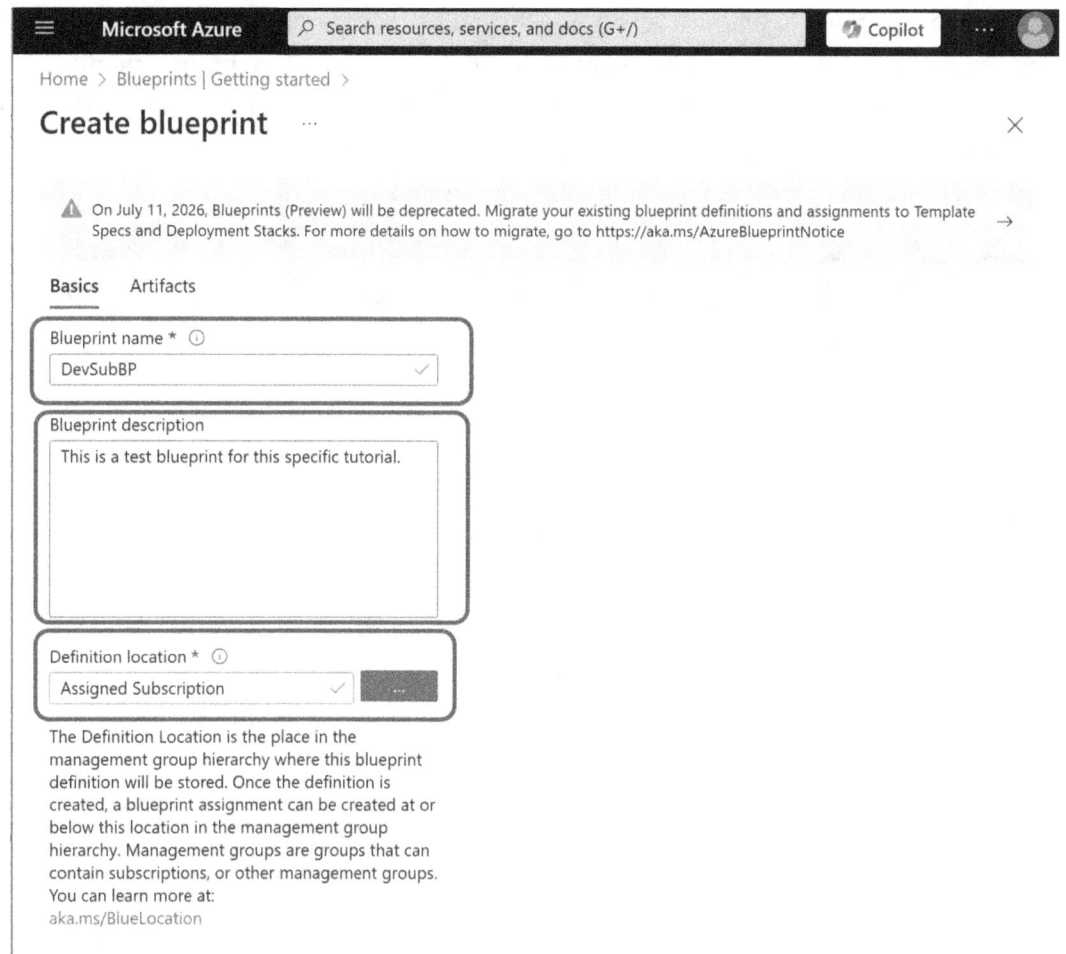

Figure 3-17. *Blueprint name, description, and definition location in the Azure portal*

> **Note** Blueprint (Preview) will be deprecated on July 11, 2026. For more information, please visit `https://aka.ms/AzureBlueprintNotice`.

The next step in naming a blueprint is assigning a version. By default, blueprints are saved as drafts and cannot be used until they are published. Once you're ready to use the blueprint in assignments, you must publish it. During the publishing process, assigning a version is mandatory, and you can also include optional change notes. The version can contain letters, numbers, and hyphens, with a maximum length of 20 characters.

CHAPTER 3 CONTEMPORARY AZURE NAMING CONVENTIONS AND STANDARDS

It's recommended to follow a versioning format like software, where the first number represents a major version, and subsequent numbers indicate minor or incremental updates. For example, 1.0 would be the initial version, 1.1 for a minor update, and 2.0 for a major revision of the same blueprint. Figures 3-18 and 3-19 show how this versioning is displayed in the Azure portal, following this recommended notation.

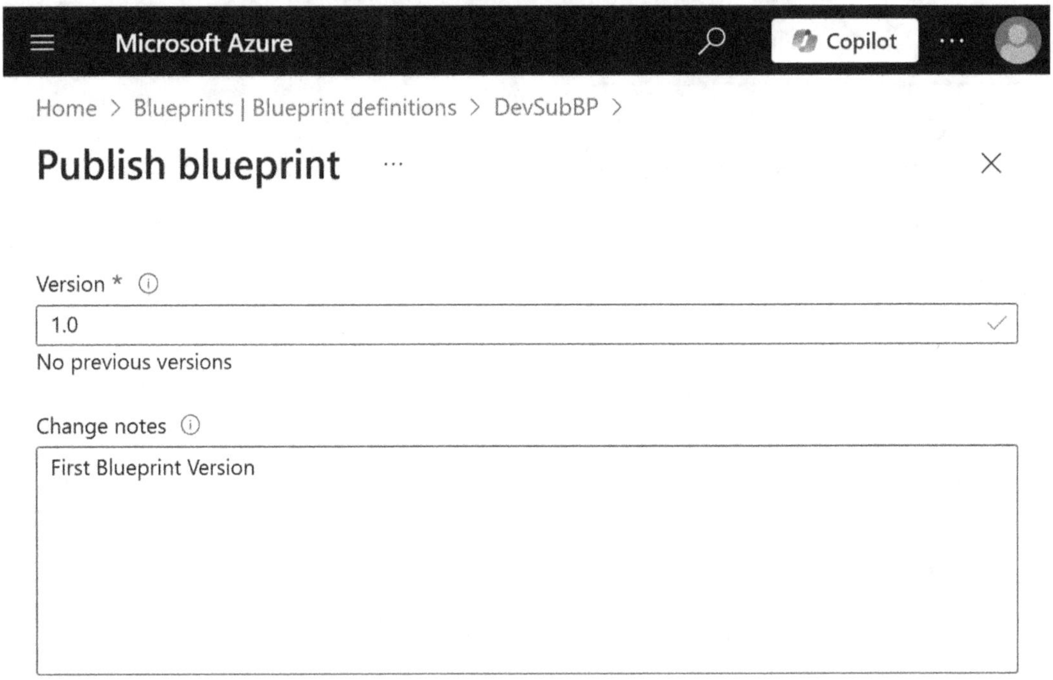

Figure 3-18. Blueprint version and change notes

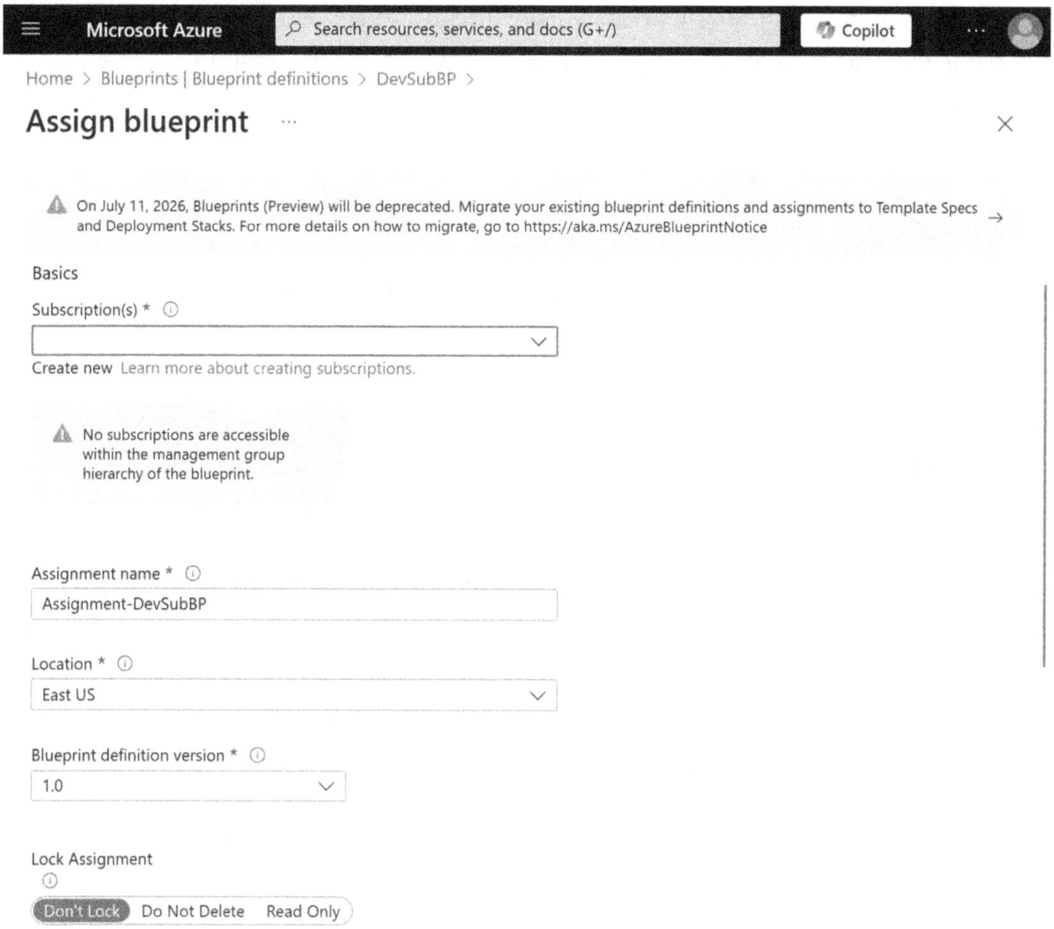

CHAPTER 3   CONTEMPORARY AZURE NAMING CONVENTIONS AND STANDARDS

Figure 3-19. Blueprint version changes as seen in the Azure portal. The latest version of the blueprint is what you will see in the blueprint definitions node. The previous versions are visible and available when you initiate the assignment process.

By default, the assignment name for a blueprint is typically the blueprint name prefixed with "assignment," though you have the flexibility to use your own custom naming convention if needed.

One important consideration regarding blueprint names is that, while renaming through the Azure portal is not supported, you can achieve this by using an export/import process. A solution available in the PowerShell Gallery, located at www.powershellgallery.com/packages/Manage-AzureRMBlueprint/2.2, allows you to export or import an existing blueprint. During the import process, you have the option to rename the blueprint, providing a workaround for renaming constraints within the portal.

Summary

In Chapter 3, we focused on the importance of Azure Naming Conventions and Standards for maintaining clear, consistent resource management and governance. Consistent naming, combined with automation, ensures efficiency and compliance across cloud environments, reducing the risk of errors and confusion. The chapter also covered tagging strategies and how proper naming conventions enhance cost management and operational control, particularly when dealing with policies, resource groups, and management groups.

Moving into Chapter 4, the focus shifts to Azure Policy Implementation, where policy definitions, initiatives, and compliance reporting take center stage. This chapter will explore how to enforce governance policies in real time, manage compliance, and automate policy deployment, ensuring that governance remains scalable and efficient as environments grow.

CHAPTER 4

Comprehensive Azure Policy Implementation

In Chapter 3, we explored how consistent **naming conventions** and **tagging strategies** are essential for managing Azure environments on a scale. We looked at how automation and Azure Policies can help enforce these standards across subscriptions, resource groups, and management groups.

Now in Chapter 4, we move from defining standards to **enforcing them** through **Azure Policy**. This chapter covers how to plan, create, assign, and manage policies and initiatives to ensure compliance and governance. You'll learn how to apply policies at different scopes, handle exclusions, use real-time enforcement, and set up remediation workflows.

By the end, you'll be equipped to implement governance that's not only structured but also automated and scalable.

Introduction to Azure Policy

Maintaining control over an expanding digital landscape can be challenging in today's cloud-first world. Azure Policy serves as a centralized way to define, enforce, and manage rules across your Azure environment, ensuring that every resource aligns with your organizational standards and compliance requirements. Rather than relying on reactive governance, Azure Policy empowers you to be proactive—automatically auditing, preventing, or remediating non-compliant resources before they become issues. Whether you're aiming to control costs, enforce security practices, or support regulatory frameworks, Azure Policy provides the structure and automation needed to embed governance into the very foundation of your cloud operations.

CHAPTER 4 COMPREHENSIVE AZURE POLICY IMPLEMENTATION

Azure Policy Planning

In the world of technology, it's easy to overlook the importance of proper planning. Unlike many other industries, technology often allows us to dive deep into action without encountering immediate obstacles. However, this leads to a common pitfall: just because we can, doesn't mean we should. Careful consideration and planning are essential, especially when it comes to creating and deploying policies. Before moving forward, keep these key building blocks in mind:

- **Understanding Azure Policy Terminology**
- **Defining the Scope of Your Policy**
- **Managing the Policy Lifecycle**

Azure Policy Terminology

In today's fast-paced technology landscape, mastering new terminology is crucial to fully leveraging products and services. Much like navigating a restaurant menu where each dish requires interpretation, technology terms can vary in meaning depending on the context. In the case of Azure Policy, understanding these terms ensures you can effectively implement governance strategies. Table 4-1 presents a curated list of key Azure Policy terms along with their concise definitions to help you get started. For in-depth and real-time updates, refer to the official Azure policy website: `https://learn.microsoft.com/en-us/azure/governance/policy/overview`.

Table 4-1. *Azure Policy Terminology with policy description*

Azure Terminology	Policy Description	Example
Policy	A **Policy** in Azure defines rules that govern the compliance of resources within your environment, ensuring they meet specific organizational or regulatory standards. Policies can enforce actions like auditing, denying, or modifying non-compliant resources. They are essential for maintaining consistency, security, and control across your Azure infrastructure	A policy that restricts VM deployment to specific regions like East US or West Europe
Initiative	An **Initiative** in Azure Policy is a collection of multiple policy definitions aimed at achieving broader compliance objectives. It simplifies policy management by applying a unified set of rules across resources or environments. Initiatives also offer enhanced tracking and reporting capabilities through **Policy Insights**, making governance more efficient and scalable	An initiative enforcing ISO 27001 compliance by grouping several security-related policies
Scope	**Scope** defines the boundaries where policies are applied, such as management groups, subscriptions, resource groups, or individual resources. It helps you target specific areas for governance, ensuring that policies are enforced only where necessary. This flexibility allows for fine-tuned control over resource compliance across different levels of the organization	A policy scoped at the subscription level to enforce tag requirements for all resources

(continued)

Table 4-1. *(continued)*

Azure Terminology	Policy Description	Example
Exclusion	**Exclusions** in Azure Policy allow you to exempt specific resources from the enforcement of a policy within a defined scope. This flexibility enables certain resources to bypass compliance checks while the policy remains applied to the rest of the environment. It helps manage exceptions without compromising overall governance objectives	Excluding a test resource group from the "Allowed Locations" policy
Policy Location	**Policy Location** in Azure Policy refers to where a policy or initiative is assigned within the Azure hierarchy, such as at the management group, subscription, resource group, or resource level. This defines the scope at which the policy is enforced, ensuring that it applies to the correct segment of your environment. Properly assigning the policy location is crucial for effective governance and compliance	A policy definition stored at the management group level, assigned to a subscription
Assignment	An **Assignment** in Azure Policy refers to the application of a specific policy or initiative to a defined scope, such as a management group, subscription, or resource group. Assignments enforce the rules of the policy at that level, ensuring resources within the scope adhere to the set compliance standards. It's through assignments that policies take effect and govern resources	Assigning a tag-enforcement policy to a resource group to ensure all resources include a CostCenter tag

Policy Basics

While creating a policy may seem straightforward, it's essential to understand a few fundamental principles before drafting one or applying a built-in policy. A policy definition follows a structured format in JSON like below:

```json
{
  "properties": {
    "displayName": "Allowed locations",
    "description": "This policy enables you to restrict the locations your
    organization can specify when deploying resources.",
    "mode": "Indexed",
    "metadata": {
      "version": "1.0.0",
      "category": "Locations"
    },
    "parameters": {
      "allowedLocations": {
        "type": "array",
        "metadata": {
          "description": "The list of locations that can be specified when
          deploying resources",
          "strongType": "location",
          "displayName": "Allowed locations"
        },
        "defaultValue": [
          "westus2"
        ]
      }
    },
    "policyRule": {
      "if": {
        "not": {
          "field": "location",
          "in": "[parameters('allowedLocations')]"
        }
      },
```

```
      "then": {
        "effect": "deny"
      }
    }
  }
}
```

Tips Instead of creating a policy from scratch, you can export existing built-in policies from the Azure Portal or use the Azure CLI (az policy definition list) as templates. This helps reduce JSON syntax errors and speeds up policy creation.

Let's review the contents within the JSON structure:

- **Display Name:** This is the name displayed for the policy, in this case, "Allowed locations."

- **Description:** Provides an overview of the policy's purpose, which is to restrict the locations that can be specified when deploying resources within the organization.

- **Mode**: Specifies the types of resources evaluated by the policy. In this instance, the mode is set to Indexed, typically used for policies relevant to tags and location-based restrictions.

- **Version:** Indicates the version of the policy, set here as "1.0.0."

- **Metadata:** Contains additional details that categorize the policy, such as its category (set as "Locations") and version for version tracking and organization.

- **Parameters:** Enables flexibility by allowing placeholders that can be set during policy assignment. This policy defines an allowedLocations parameter:

  - **allowedLocations**: An array parameter, with a strong type of "location," which specifies the locations permitted for resource deployment. The default value here is "westus2," meaning resources are restricted to the West US 2 region unless altered during assignment.

- **Policy Rule:** This is the engine of your policy. It has a logical evaluation part to test for conditions and an effect part to action rules. The full details of the policy definition structure can be found at https://learn.microsoft.com/en-us/azure/governance/policy/concepts/definition-structure-basics. Figure 4-1 is a summarized view of the policy rules.

- **Logical Evaluations (If Clause):** Checks if a resource's location is not within the allowed locations specified by the parameter.

- **Effect (Then Clause):** Defines the action to take when the condition is met, which in this case is "deny." This prevents resource deployment in any location outside the allowed list.

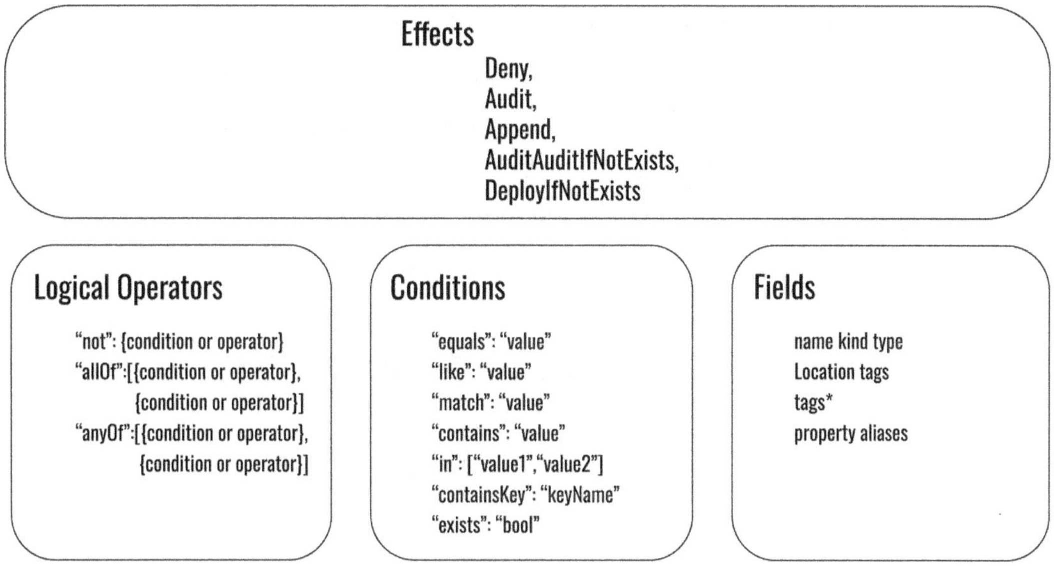

Effects
Deny,
Audit,
Append,
AuditAuditIfNotExists,
DeployIfNotExists

Logical Operators
"not": {condition or operator}
"allOf":[{condition or operator}, {condition or operator}]
"anyOf":[{condition or operator}, {condition or operator}]

Conditions
"equals": "value"
"like": "value"
"match": "value"
"contains": "value"
"in": ["value1","value2"]
"containsKey": "keyName"
"exists": "bool"

Fields
name kind type
Location tags
tags*
property aliases

Figure 4-1. Logical view of Azure Policies and their different operations, conditions, and fields

Policy Location

When defining and managing policies and initiatives in Azure, selecting an appropriate storage location is crucial. Policy and initiative definitions must be stored either at a **management group** or a **subscription** level. The chosen location dictates the scope of applicability for the policy, as policies stored at lower hierarchical levels cannot

CHAPTER 4   COMPREHENSIVE AZURE POLICY IMPLEMENTATION

be assigned to resources at higher levels or parallel branches within the hierarchy. Additionally, once a definition's storage location is configured and saved, it cannot be altered.

Referring to Figure 4-2, different policy definitions (POL) demonstrate distinct scopes based on their designated storage location:

- **POL-A** is stored at a higher level, enabling assignments across all management groups, their respective child groups, and all underlying subscriptions and resource groups.

- **POL-B**, stored under MG-Production, applies to MG-Production, its child management groups, and all associated resources within that scope. However, it cannot be assigned to MG-Pre-Production or MG-Development nor to their respective child resources. Additionally, it cannot be assigned at levels above MG-Production.

- **POL-C**, defined at the CC001-Sales-Sub subscription level, has the narrowest scope. It can only be applied within this specific subscription and its resource groups.

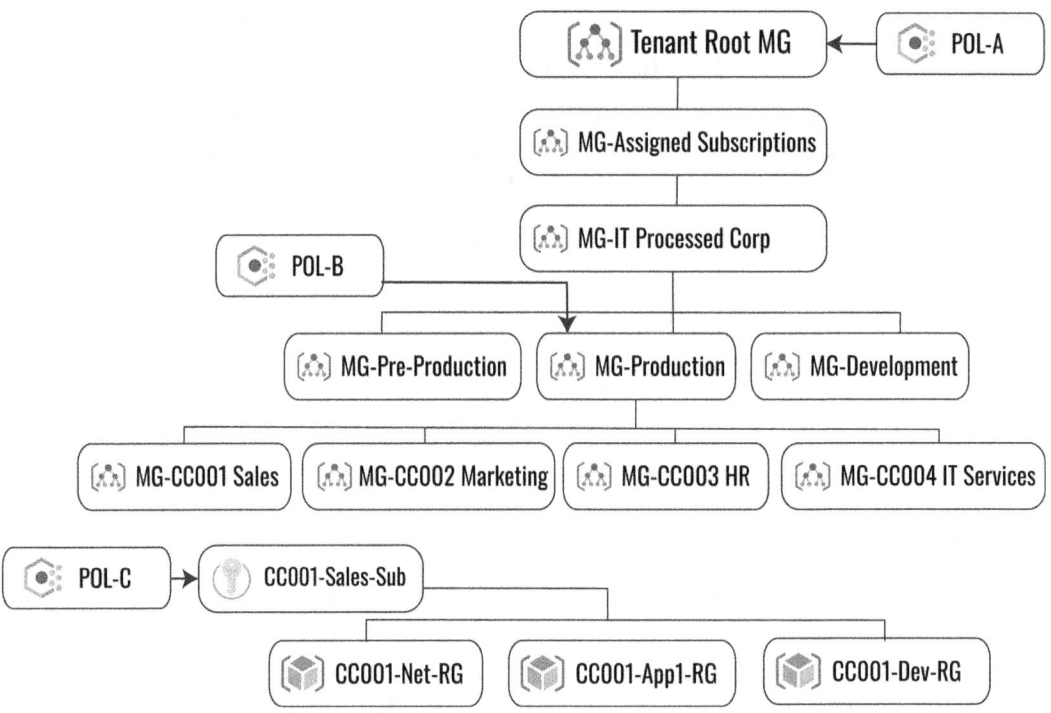

Figure 4-2. *Policy location planning*

In environments where multiple teams collaborate on policy development, it's vital to manage updates systematically. Leveraging version control systems (e.g., Git) helps track changes, authorship, and revision history for JSON-based policy definitions. Additionally, embedding **metadata tags** inside the policy (such as version, author, or description) can provide at-a-glance context for administrators. These practices promote collaboration, minimize errors, and ensure compliance with governance standards across shared environments.

Creating and Managing Policy Definitions

Creating and managing policy definitions is a key part of working with Azure Policy. A policy definition is simply a rule that describes what is allowed or not allowed in your Azure environment. You can use built-in definitions provided by Microsoft or create your own to meet specific needs. Once a policy is defined, it can be assigned to a specific scope—such as a subscription, resource group, or management group. Over time, as requirements change, managing and updating these policies ensures your environment stays aligned with your organization's standards. This process helps automate compliance and reduce the need for manual checks.

Creating Policy Definitions

There are two methods for creating policy definitions: either by creating a new policy or duplicating an existing built-in or custom policy. The simplest approach is to utilize the duplicate option on a built-in policy. The following steps will guide you through the process of duplicating a built-in policy to audit permitted virtual machine (VM) SKUs.

1. Login to Azure portal from `https://portal.azure.com`.

2. Search **Policy** from the search bar and select **Policy** as shown in Figure 4-3.

CHAPTER 4   COMPREHENSIVE AZURE POLICY IMPLEMENTATION

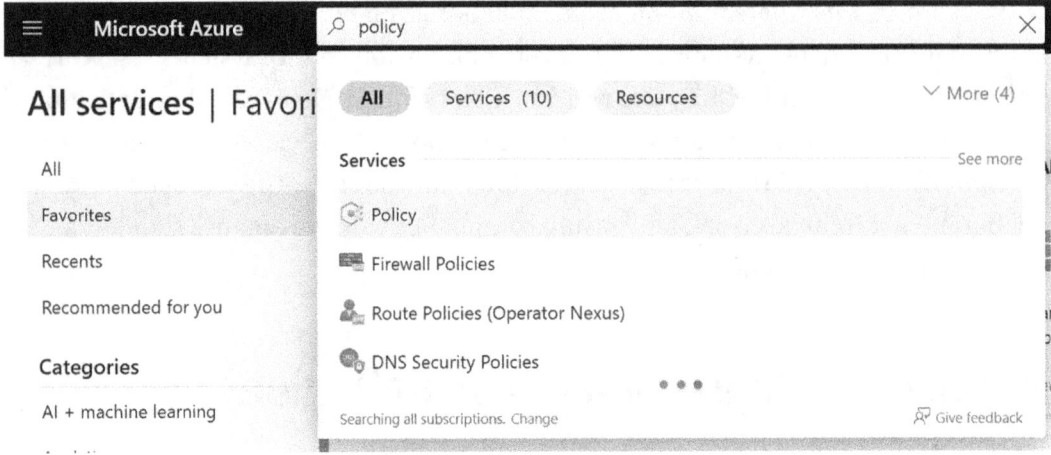

Figure 4-3. *Searching and selecting policy from Azure portal*

3. From the policy blade, select **Definitions** as shown in Figure 4-4.

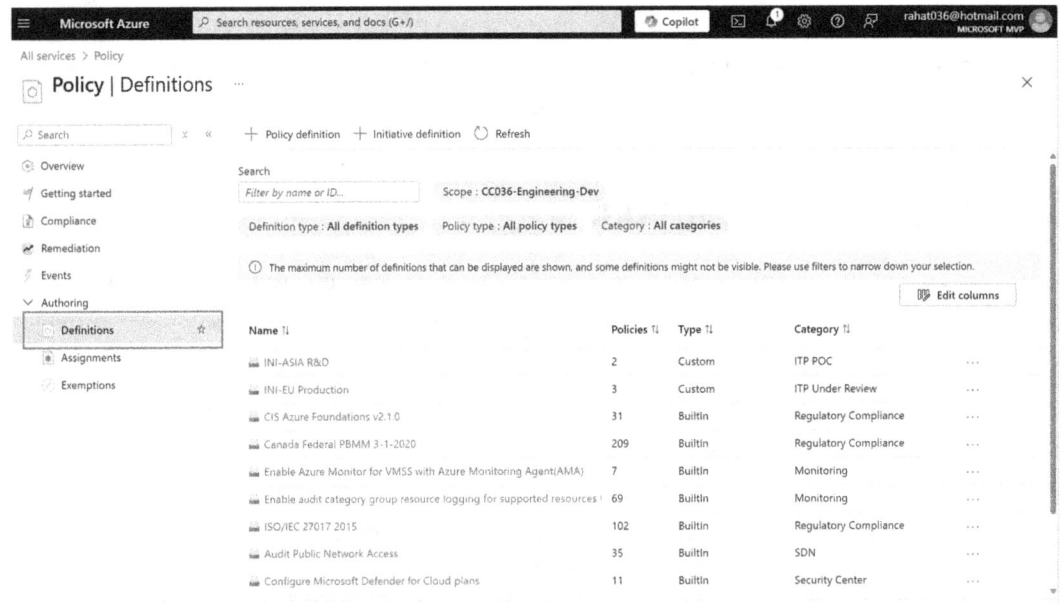

Figure 4-4. *Selecting Definitions from Policy blade*

4. In the search bar, type **SKU** and select **Allowed virtual machine size SKUs** as shown in Figure 4-5.

84

CHAPTER 4   COMPREHENSIVE AZURE POLICY IMPLEMENTATION

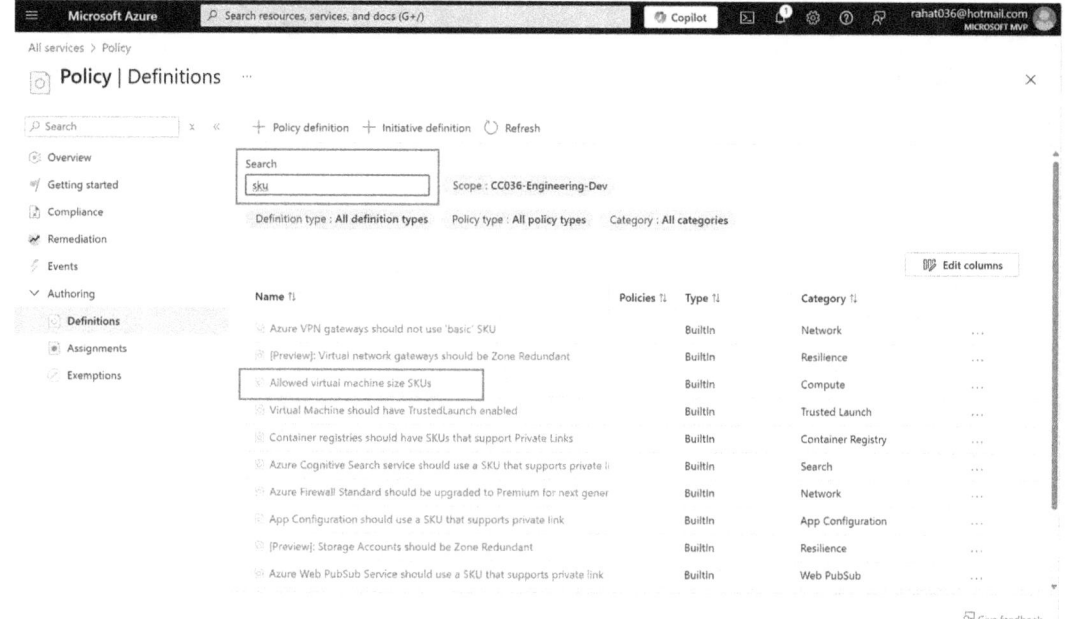

Figure 4-5. *Searching SKU and selecting Allowed virtual machine size SKUs*

5. You are presented with the built-in policy definition. Click **Duplicate definition** as shown in Figure 4-6. Please be aware that the default effect is configured to **Deny**.

85

CHAPTER 4   COMPREHENSIVE AZURE POLICY IMPLEMENTATION

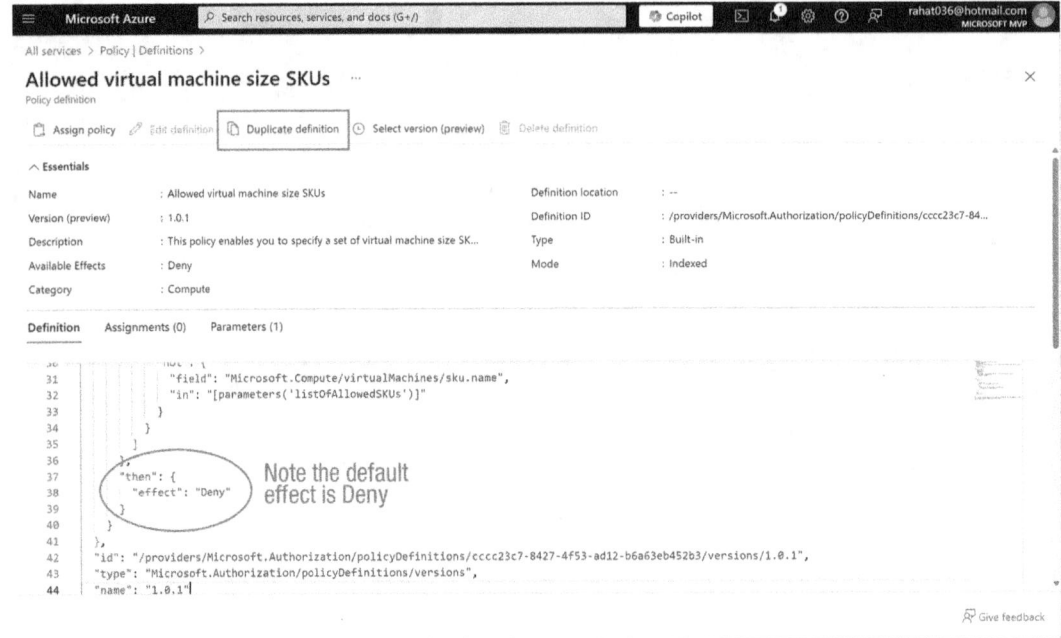

Figure 4-6. Duplicating the policy definition

6. Make the following changes:

    a. **Definition location**: Click **…** and select **Assigned Subscriptions**, and then click **Select** as shown in Figure 4-7.

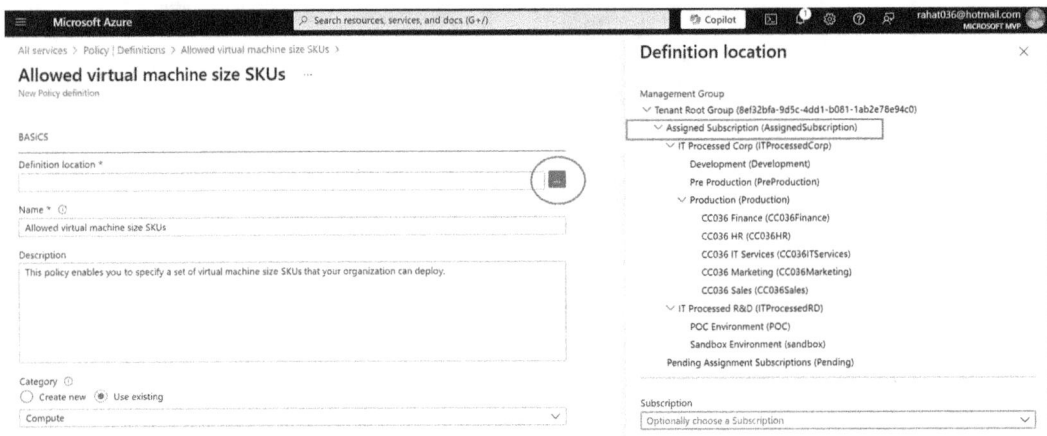

Figure 4-7. Selecting definition location

CHAPTER 4   COMPREHENSIVE AZURE POLICY IMPLEMENTATION

b. Add the following information there as well as shown in Figures 4-8 and 4-9:

   i. **Name: POL-Audit Allowed virtual machine SKUs**.

   ii. **Description: This audit only policy enables you to check for compliance against a set of virtual machine SKUs that your organization can deploy**.

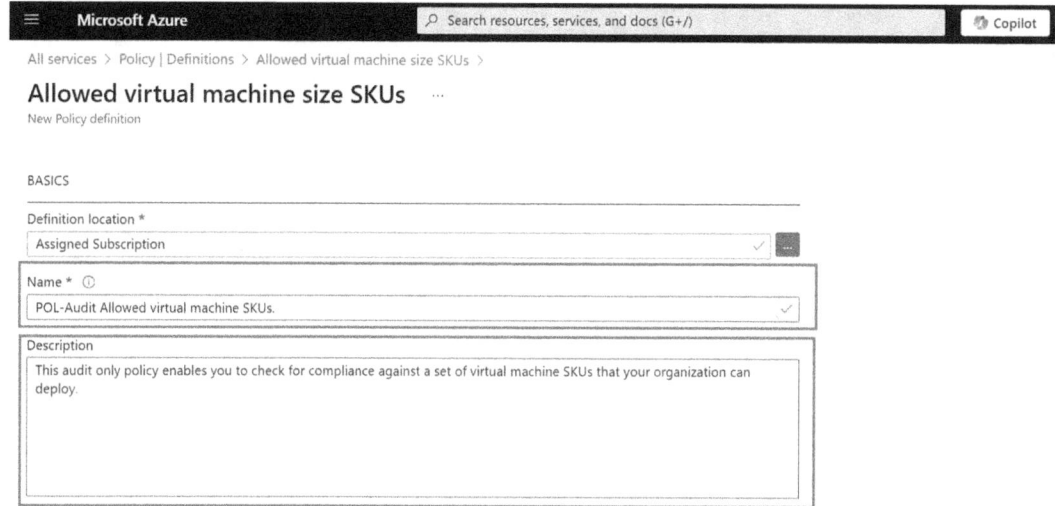

Figure 4-8. Assigning Name and Description in definitions

   iii. **Category**: Ensure that **Create new** is selected and type **Under Review**.

   iv. Change the "effect" value to "Audit".

CHAPTER 4 COMPREHENSIVE AZURE POLICY IMPLEMENTATION

Figure 4-9. *Changing the category and effect value*

7. Click Save.

8. Verify that the custom policy has been created by selecting **Definitions** and set the Policy type to **Custom** as shown in Figure 4-10.

CHAPTER 4   COMPREHENSIVE AZURE POLICY IMPLEMENTATION

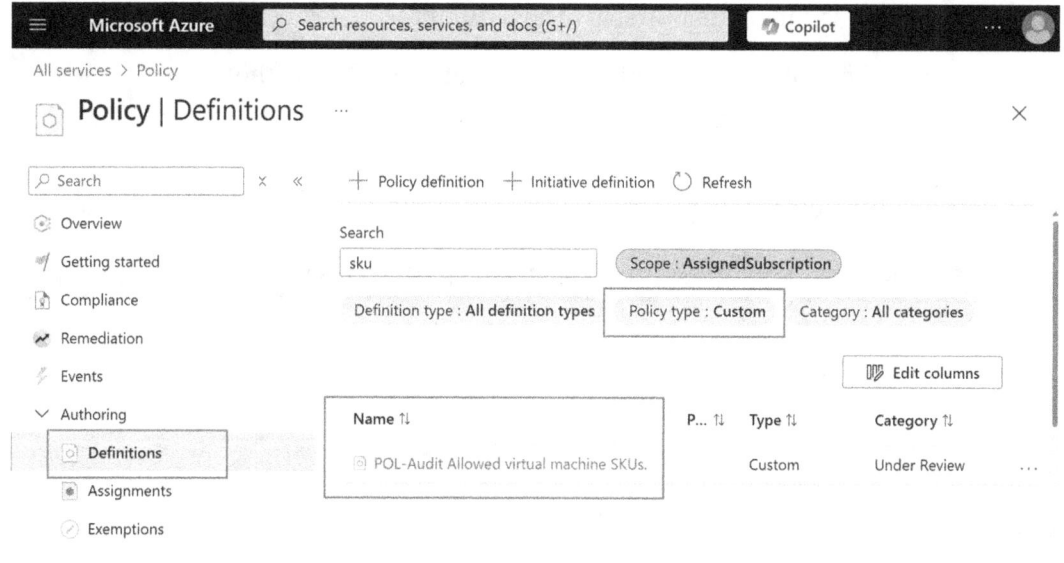

Figure 4-10. *Verifying the newly created custom definition*

Please note that the name, definition location, and category values are set according to your selections. This completes the custom policy creation using the Duplicate option. The other available options allow you to create the policy using an appropriate editor that follows JSON syntax and utilizes templates from resources available on Microsoft's websites and Git repositories.

Assigning Policies

In the previous section, you completed the steps to create a policy definition. The next step is to assign this definition to a management group, subscription, or resource group. In the following example, I will show you how to assign the policy to a management group to audit the compliance status of virtual machines within that management group.

In the current environment designed for capturing these steps, a virtual machine has been deployed within the CC036-Dev-RG resource group. This machine is provisioned with the B1s SKU, which deviates from the organization's standard of utilizing the **Standard_DS2_v3** and **Standard_DS2_v2** SKUs. Previously, the organization employed the now-unsupported Standard_D1_v2 and Standard_D2_v2 SKUs. This assignment aims to facilitate an audit of the existing virtual machines.

CHAPTER 4   COMPREHENSIVE AZURE POLICY IMPLEMENTATION

1. Connect to the Azure portal at https://portal.azure.com.

2. Go to the **Policy** option (this assumes that you followed the previous steps in this chapter).

3. In the **Policy** blade, click **Assignments** and then **Assign policy** as shown in Figure 4-11.

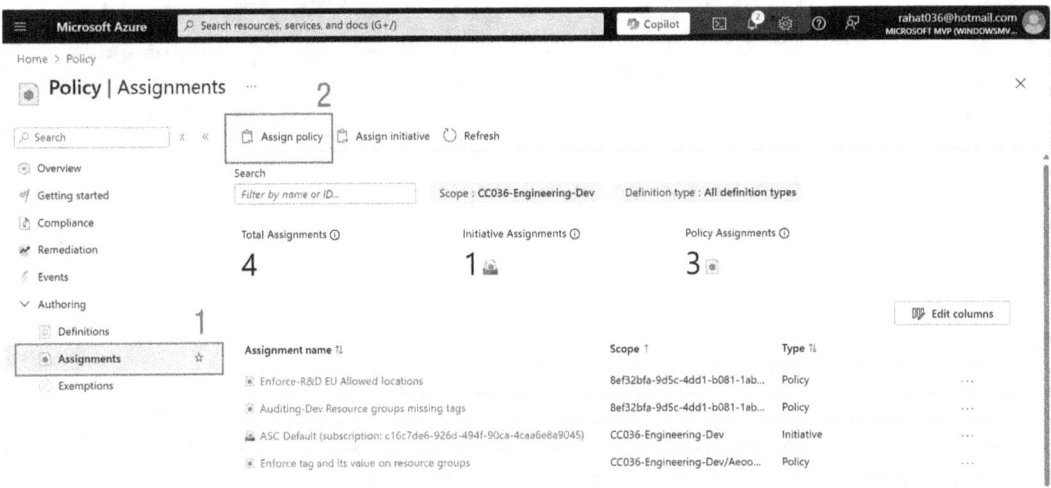

Figure 4-11. *Assignments option in Policy option*

4. Use the following to fill in the details of the assignment page.

   a. **Scope:** Click the ... button, and select **Production** from the management group as shown in Figure 4-12.

CHAPTER 4   COMPREHENSIVE AZURE POLICY IMPLEMENTATION

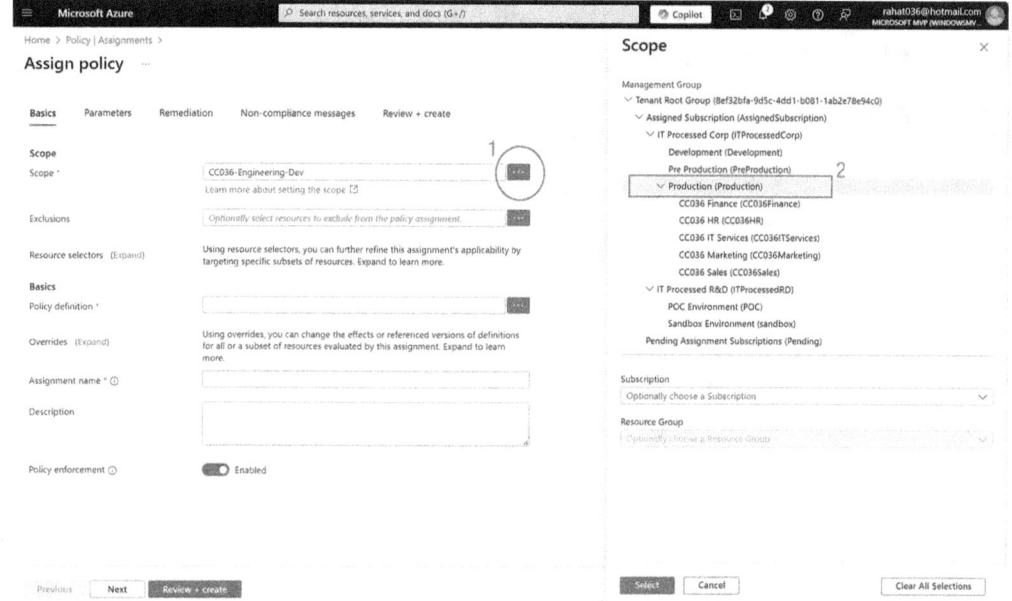

Figure 4-12. *Selecting the subscription and Resource Group in Scope option*

b. **Policy Definition:** Click the ... button and change the filter type to **Custom**.

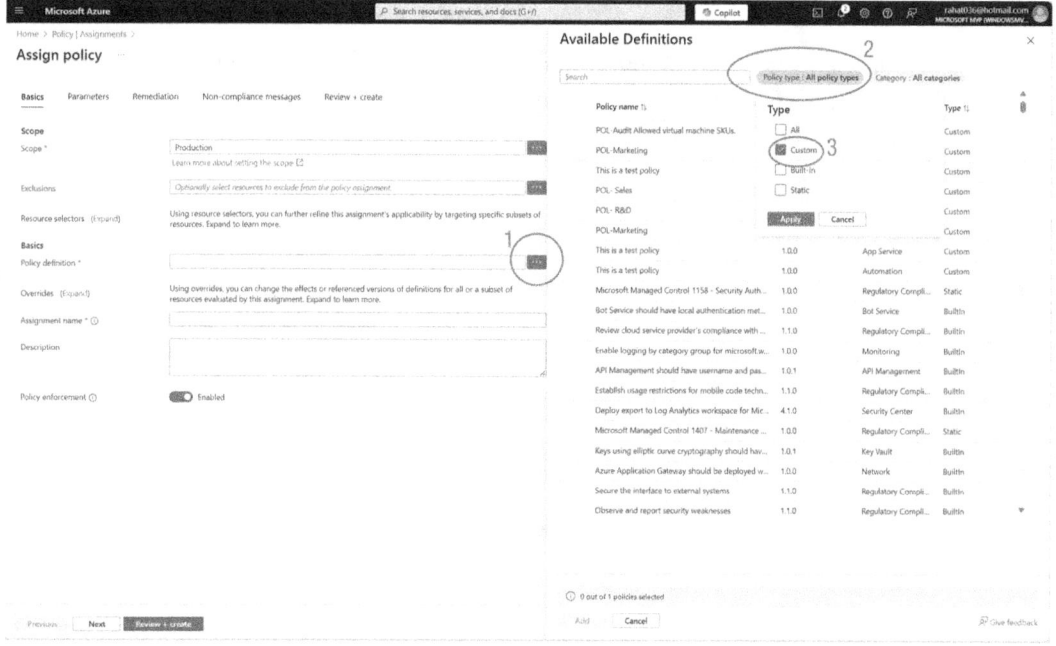

Figure 4-13. *Filtering the policy definitions*

91

CHAPTER 4   COMPREHENSIVE AZURE POLICY IMPLEMENTATION

c. Select the custom policy **POL-Audit Allowed virtual machine SKUs** as shown in Figure 4-14.

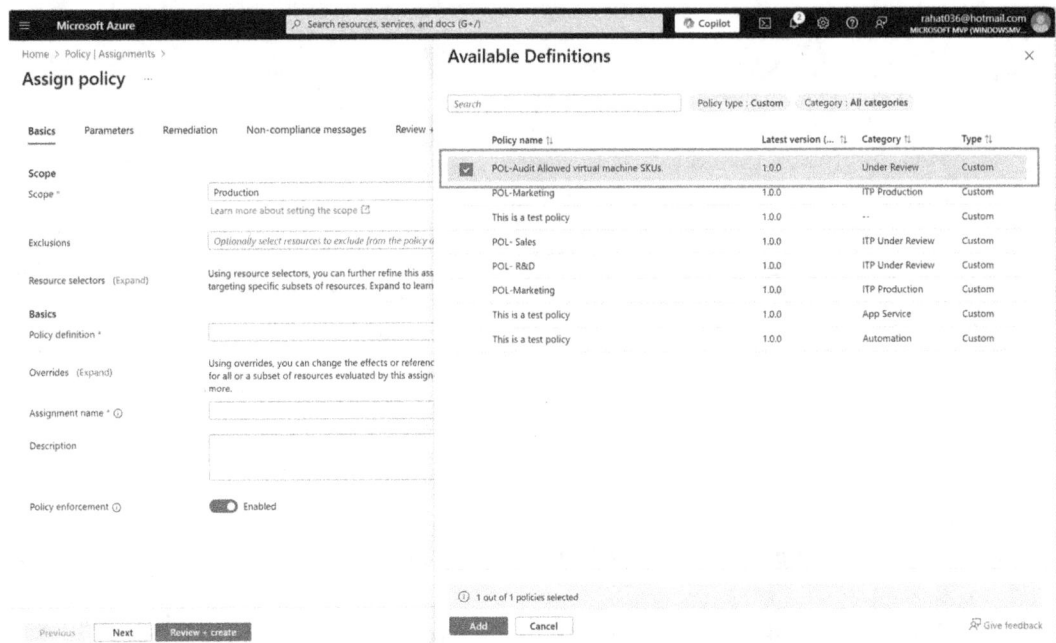

Figure 4-14. *Selecting custom policy definition created in the previous step*

d. Change the assignment name to **Auditing-POL-Audit Allowed virtual machine SKUs** and provide a description as shown in Figure 4-15.

CHAPTER 4　COMPREHENSIVE AZURE POLICY IMPLEMENTATION

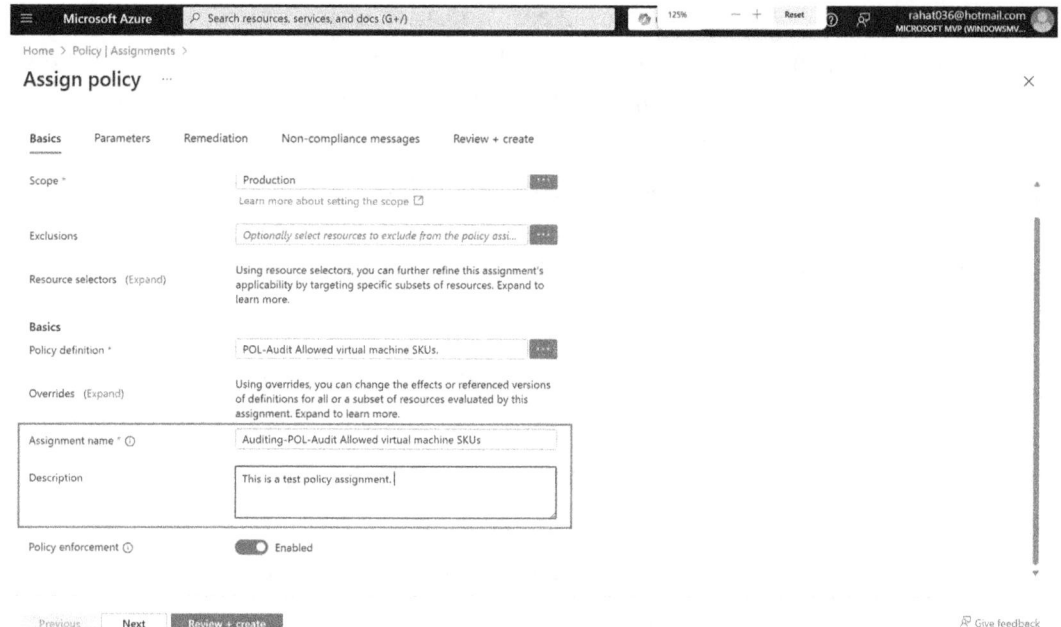

Figure 4-15. *Changing assignment name and adding description*

　　e.　In the **Parameters** section, click the **Azure VM SKU** option, and select **Standard_D1_v2 and Standard_D2_v2** from the list, and click Review + Create as shown in Figure 4-16.

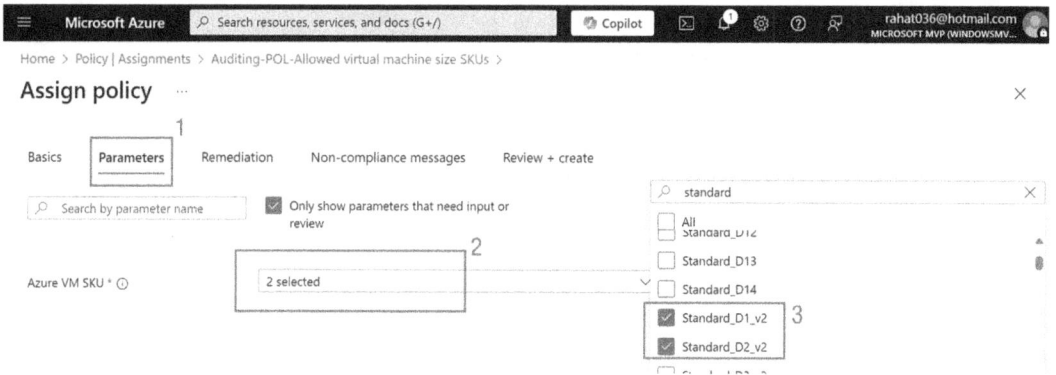

Figure 4-16. *Selecting parameters for assigning the policy*

93

This concludes the assignment steps. Please note that in your environment, the names of the management group and subscription may differ, so make sure to adjust the instructions accordingly. Additionally, for the SKU parameters, we selected a subscription scope since these values are based on what is available within that subscription.

The status of all assignments can be viewed in the Overview pane under the Policy node. Upon initially assigning a policy, its compliance state will be marked as "Not started". Policies have an evaluation schedule on creation, update, and recurring evaluation. The schedule summary is as follows:

- **New Policy/Initiative Assignment Applied to Scope:** 30 minutes from assignment

- **Update Policy/Initiative Assignment Applied to Scope:** 30 minutes from assignment

- **New Resource Deployment in Scope of Policy/Initiative Assignment:** 15 minutes from assignment

- **Normal Evaluation:** Every 24 hours

After 30 minutes, you can see the compliance status "Compliant" as shown in Figure 4-17.

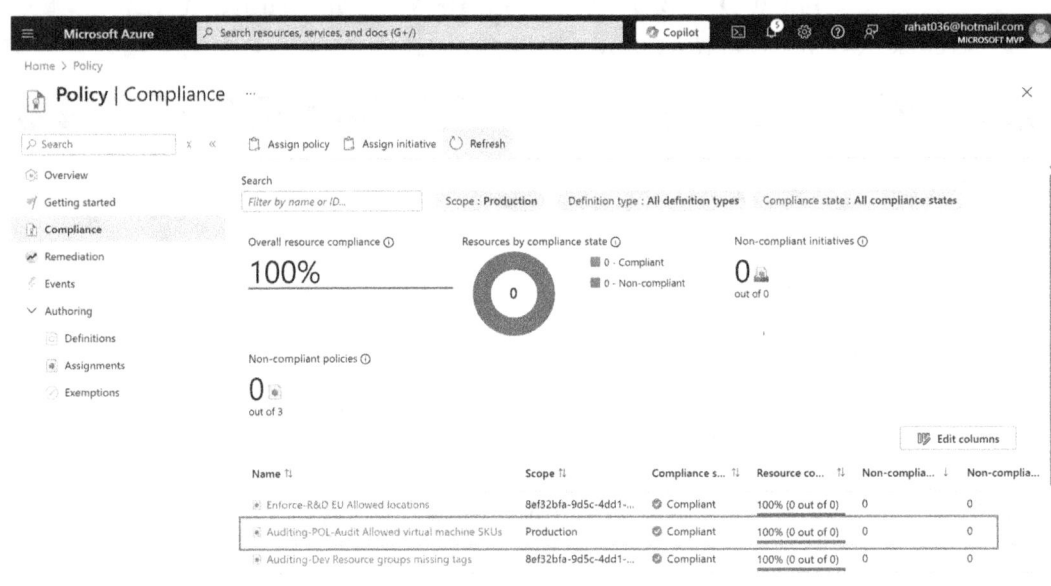

Figure 4-17. Checking the compliance status after assigning the policy

For comprehensive details on evaluation and the different conditions being assessed, refer to the official documentation at https://learn.microsoft.com/en-us/azure/governance/policy/how-to/get-compliance-data. Below is an excerpt of the information, along with the recommendation to regularly check the Microsoft website for updates and improvements. As Azure Policy is a continuously evolving cloud service, changes are to be expected.

"Evaluations of assigned policies and initiatives happen as the result of various events:

- *A policy or initiative is newly assigned to a scope. It takes around 30 minutes for the assignment to be applied to the defined scope. Once it's applied, the evaluation cycle begins for resources within that scope against the newly assigned policy or initiative and depending on the effects used by the policy or initiative, resources are marked as compliant or non-compliant. A large policy or initiative evaluated against a large scope of resources can take time. As such, there's no pre-defined expectation of when the evaluation cycle will complete. Once it completes, updated compliance results are available in the portal and SDKs.*

- *A policy or initiative already assigned to a scope is updated. The evaluation cycle and timing for this scenario is the same as for a new assignment to a scope.*

- *A resource is deployed to a scope with an assignment via Resource Manager, REST, Azure CLI, or Azure PowerShell. In this scenario, the effect event (append, audit, deny, deploy) and compliant status information for the individual resource becomes available in the portal and SDKs around 15 minutes later. This event doesn't cause an evaluation of other resources.*

- *Standard compliance evaluation cycle. Once every 24 hours, assignments are automatically reevaluated. A large policy or initiative of many resources can take time, so there's no pre-defined expectation of when the evaluation cycle will complete. Once it completes, updated compliance results are available in the portal and SDKs."*

Updating Policies and Assignments

Ensuring compliance within an organization is an evolving process influenced by regulatory shifts and technological advancements. Consequently, Azure policies used to audit or enforce these standards must be regularly adjusted to remain aligned. These adjustments can range from minor updates, such as renaming policies or modifying audit criteria, to significant changes involving rule effects and scope adjustments.

Let's illustrate this with our previous example focusing on the SKU type policy:

- **Minor Update**: Adjust the policy category to "production" and revise the description to specify the applicable SKUs. Enhancing the description is crucial as it improves visibility during compliance audits.

- **Major Update**: Convert the policy rule effect from "audit" to "enforce" to ensure that only authorized SKUs are permissible for creation.

Minor Objective Changes

Minor objective changes typically involve updates such as adding SKU names to the description or introducing a new category called "production." These changes help transition the policy from being under review to becoming production ready, ensuring that it is properly categorized and described for effective implementation.

1. Navigate to the **Definitions** section of the Policy node in the Azure portal.

2. Select **POL-Audit Allowed virtual machines size SKUs**, which you created in the previous steps. Click **Edit definitions** as shown in Figure 4-18.

CHAPTER 4   COMPREHENSIVE AZURE POLICY IMPLEMENTATION

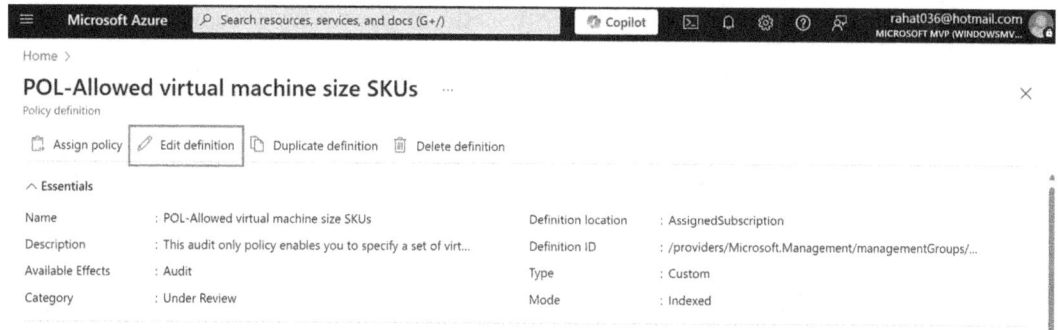

Figure 4-18. Editing option of Policy definitions

3. Add the following in the description: **The SKUs in scope of this policy are specified in the assignment. Ensure you list the SKUs in the description of the assignment**. Under the category, ensure that **Create new** is selected. Overwrite the existing value with **Production Approved** as shown in Figure 4-19. Click **Save** to complete the definition update.

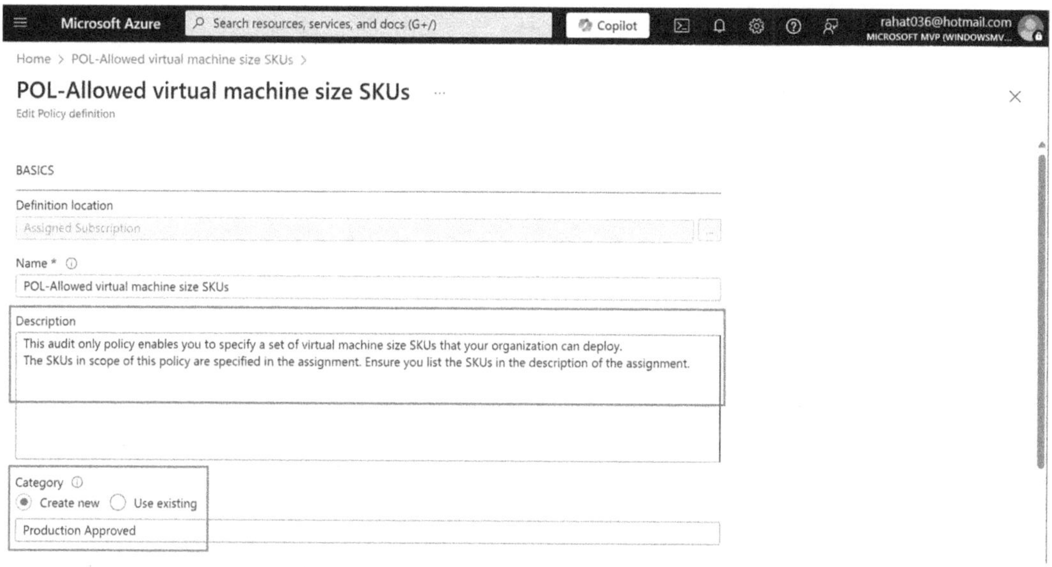

Figure 4-19. Changing Description and Category for updating the policy

CHAPTER 4 COMPREHENSIVE AZURE POLICY IMPLEMENTATION

The next steps to the minor changes involve editing the policy assignment.

1. Navigate to the Assignments section of the Policy node.

2. Select the previous assignment, **Auditing-POL-Audit Allowed virtual machine size SKUs**. Edit the assignment **Description** field to include the details of the SKUs in scope as shown in Figure 4-20.

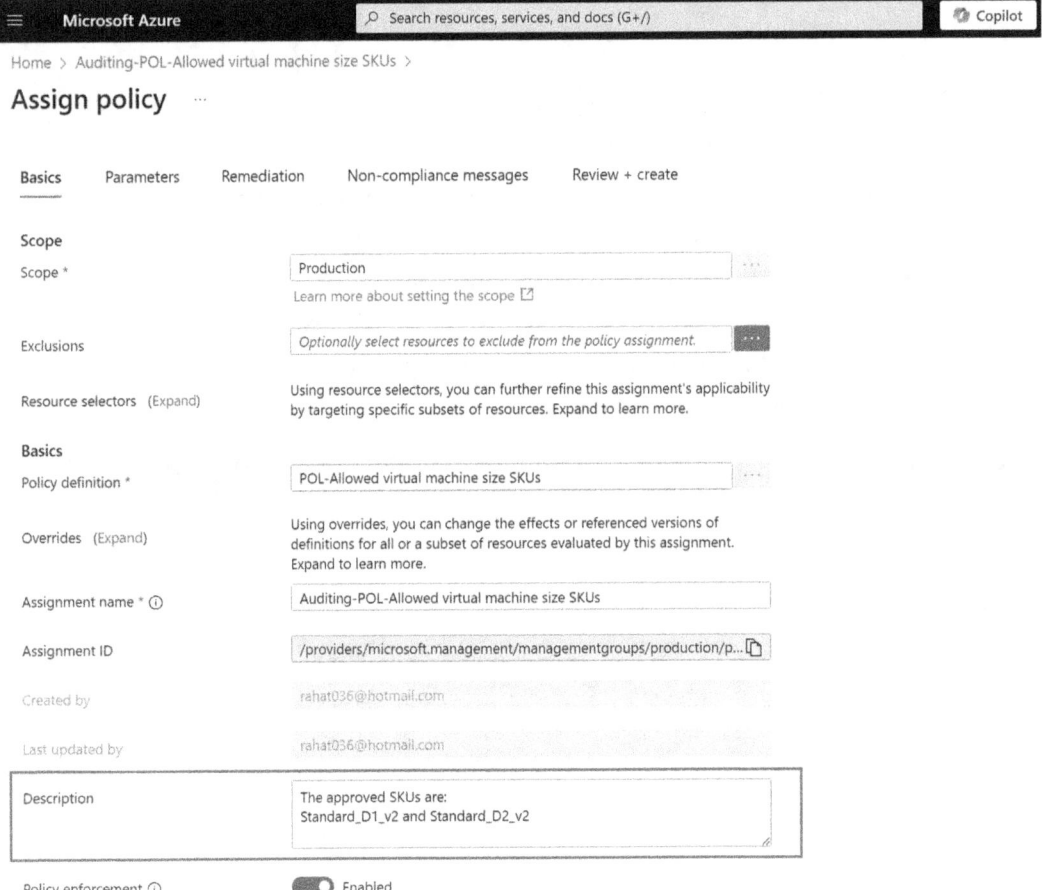

Figure 4-20. *Editing assignment description to include the SKUs information*

3. Click **Save** to complete the assignment update.

The result of the minor changes is that the policy assigner has clear instructions on the requirements, and the compliance visibility is improved as shown in Figure 4-21.

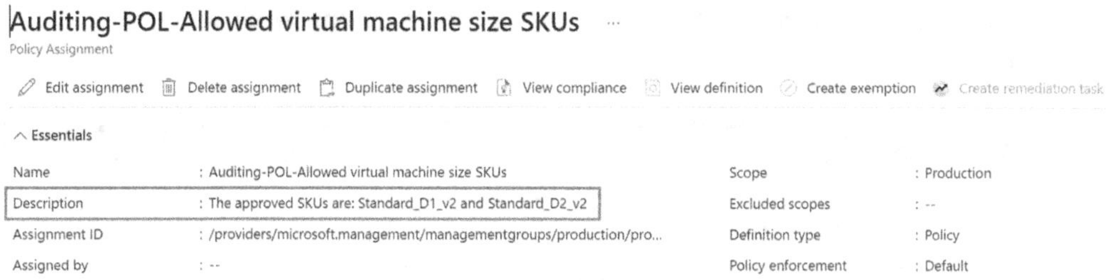

CHAPTER 4   COMPREHENSIVE AZURE POLICY IMPLEMENTATION

Figure 4-21. Policy compliance view showing updated description

Additionally, the category of the definition will show Production Approved when viewed in the definition node.

Major Objective Changes

Change the "**effect**" to "**Deny**" for policy enforcement and exclude the development resource group from the policy assignment.

1. Navigate to the Definitions section of the Policy node in the Azure portal.

2. Select **POL-Audit Allowed virtual machines SKUs**, as you created in the previous steps, and click **Duplicate definition** as shown in Figure 4-22.

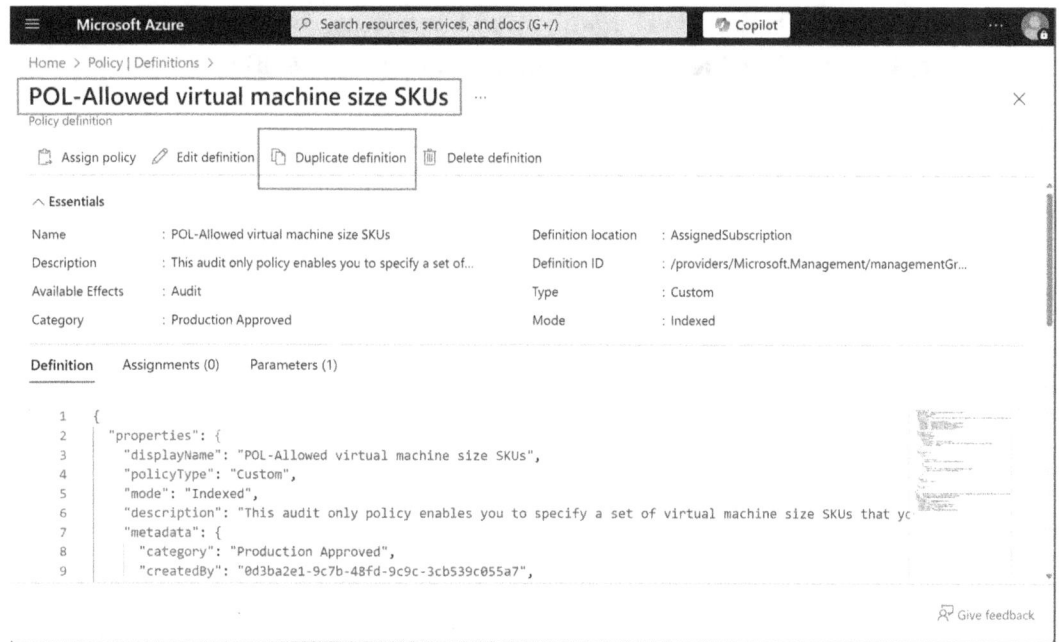

Figure 4-22. Duplicating definition

CHAPTER 4   COMPREHENSIVE AZURE POLICY IMPLEMENTATION

3. Select **Assigned Subscription** as the definition location as shown in Figure 4-23.

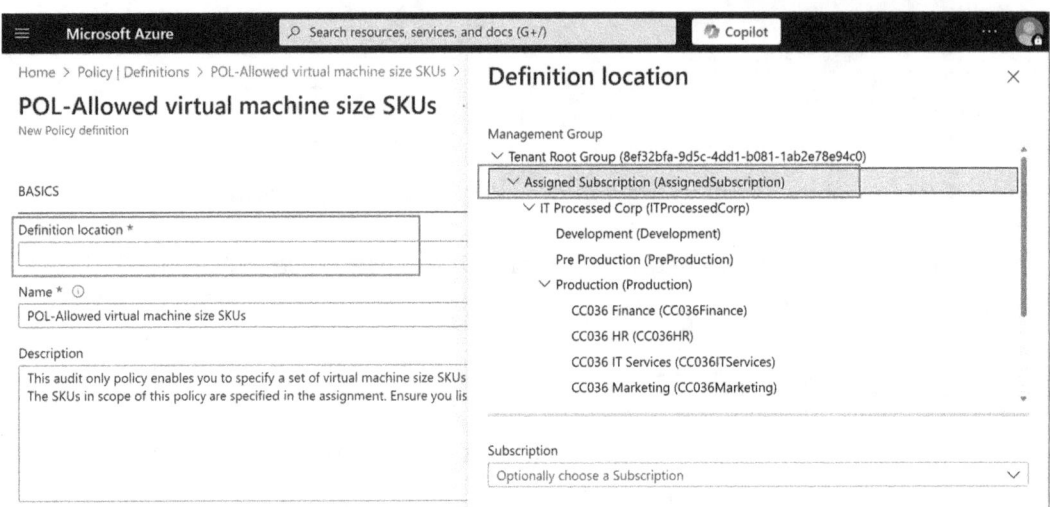

Figure 4-23. *Assigning definition location*

4. Change the policy name to **POL-Enforce Allowed virtual machine SKUs**. Update the description to the following: **This enforcement policy denies the creation of virtual machine SKUs that your organization has not approved for deployment. The SKUs in scope of this policy are specified in the assignment.** Ensure you list the SKUs in the description of the assignment and that the "effect" is "Deny" as shown in Figure 4-24.

Figure 4-24. *Changing policy name, description, and rule*

5. Click save to complete the policy update (a new policy is created).

The effect of this change is that we now have two policies. This approach ensures that you follow a process that minimizes the impact of major policy changes. In effect, we have an option to roll back our change and avoid impacting assignments using the previous policy definition.

CHAPTER 4   COMPREHENSIVE AZURE POLICY IMPLEMENTATION

Policy Initiatives and Scoping

As your environment grows, managing individual policies can become overwhelming. That's where policy initiatives and scoping come in. A *policy initiative* is a collection of related policy definitions grouped together to achieve a broader compliance goal—like enforcing security standards or regulatory requirements. Instead of assigning multiple policies one by one, you can assign an initiative and manage them as a single unit. *Scoping* allows you to apply policies or initiatives to specific levels in your Azure hierarchy, such as management groups, subscriptions, or resource groups. Together, initiatives and scoping provide a flexible way to organize and apply governance at scale, making it easier to maintain control over complex cloud environments.

To further streamline governance, policy initiatives can include **parameters** that apply across all contained policies. However, individual policies within an initiative can override these shared parameters to suit their specific compliance needs, for example,

```json
{
  "parameters": {
    "allowedLocations": {
      "value": ["westus", "eastus"]
    }
  },
  "policyDefinitions": [
    {
      "policyDefinitionId": "/providers/Microsoft.Authorization/
      policyDefinitions/allowed-locations",
      "parameters": {
        "allowedLocations": {
          "value": ["westus"]
        }
      }
    }
  ]
}
```

This JSON shows that while the initiative sets ["westus", "eastus"] as the general rule, a specific policy overrides it to only allow "westus". This flexibility ensures precise control without losing the efficiency of grouped policy management.

Creating Initiatives

Initiatives serve as a way to group multiple policies under a single assignment to achieve specific compliance objectives. It is recommended to use an initiative even when assigning a single policy, as this follows the same principle as grouping users instead of assigning roles individually in role-based security.

Azure offers a library of built-in initiatives designed for common organizational compliance needs, providing a solid starting point. These built-in initiatives can be accessed under the Policy node in the Definitions section. By setting the filter to Definition type, you can explore the available initiatives along with their respective categories. Figure 4-25 illustrates the built-in initiatives available in Azure at the time of writing.

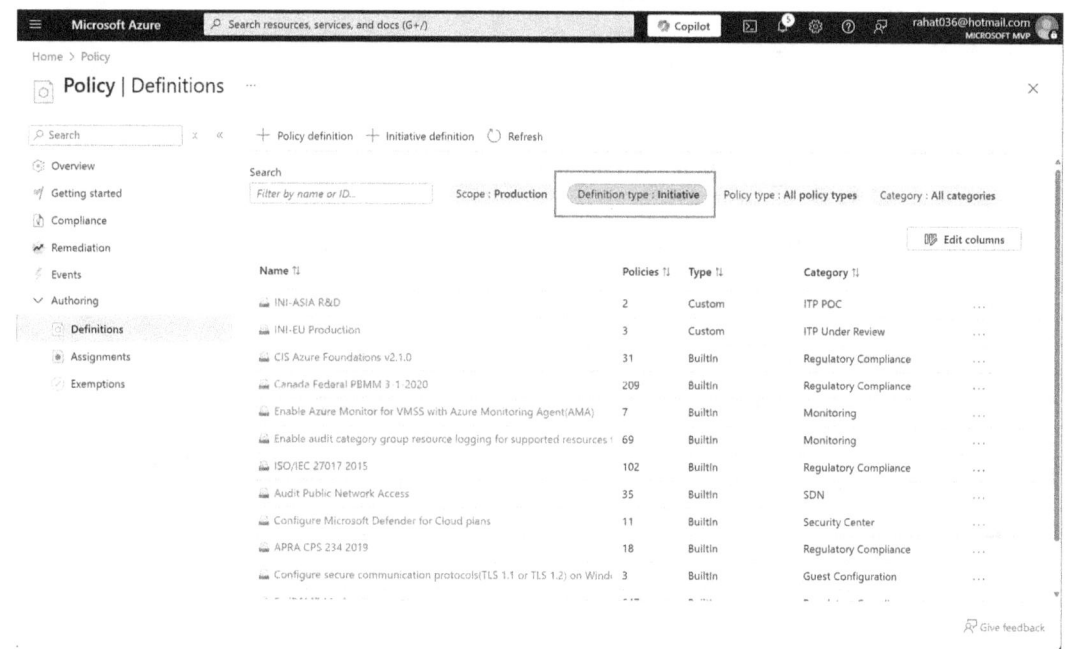

Figure 4-25. Built-in Azure initiatives

There are two ways to create an initiative definition: either by creating a new one or duplicating an existing built-in or custom initiative. The process for duplicating an initiative follows the same steps as duplicating a policy. This section focuses on creating a new initiative from scratch.

CHAPTER 4   COMPREHENSIVE AZURE POLICY IMPLEMENTATION

Before proceeding with this example, we have duplicated the Allowed Locations policy and modified the effect type to Audit. Both policies are stored in the same definition location. Figure 4-26 illustrates these policies. When following the steps in this exercise, you can create and name your initiative according to your specific requirements.

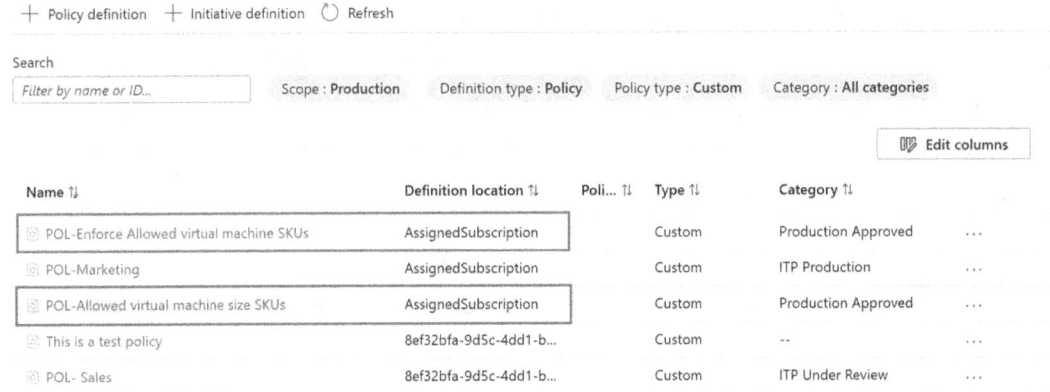

Figure 4-26. Policies in scope of initiative

Follow these steps to create a new initiative using the available policy:

1. Go to the Azure portal at `https://portal.azure.com`.

2. Go to the **Policy** section. In the policy blade, select **Definitions** and click **Initiative definition** as shown in Figure 4-27.

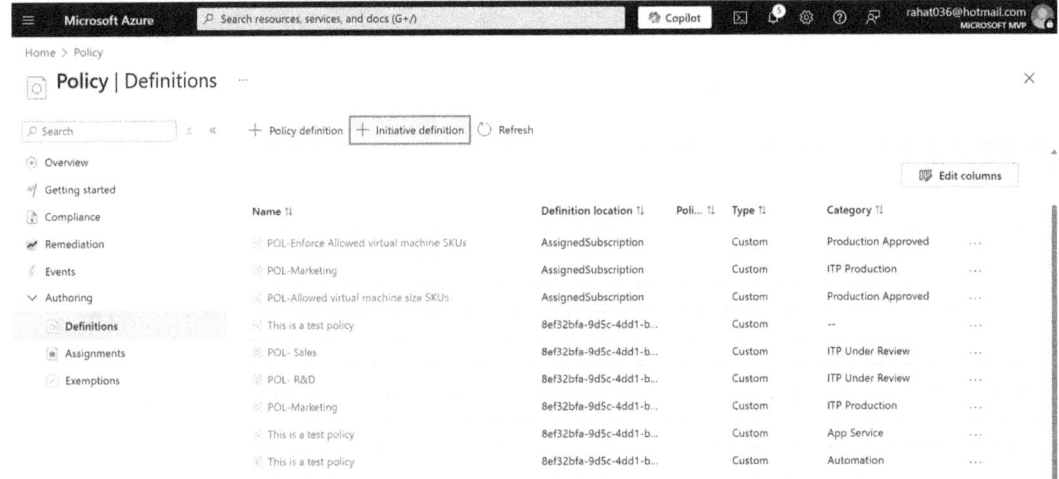

Figure 4-27. Creating new initiative definition

CHAPTER 4   COMPREHENSIVE AZURE POLICY IMPLEMENTATION

3. Select the initiative location. Provide a name and description. Either create a new category or select an existing category for the initiative.

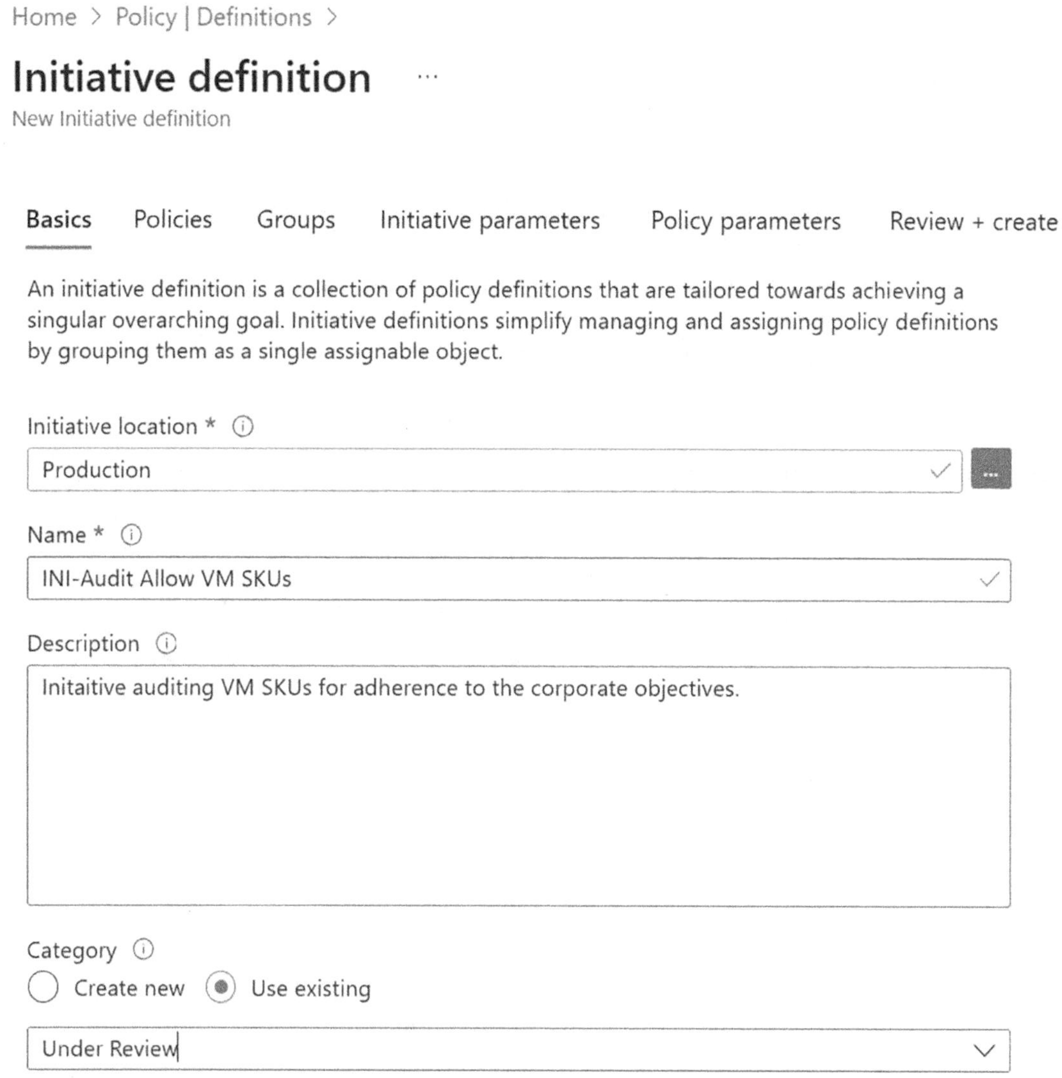

Home > Policy | Definitions >

Initiative definition
New Initiative definition

Basics   Policies   Groups   Initiative parameters   Policy parameters   Review + create

An initiative definition is a collection of policy definitions that are tailored towards achieving a singular overarching goal. Initiative definitions simplify managing and assigning policy definitions by grouping them as a single assignable object.

Initiative location *

Production

Name *

INI-Audit Allow VM SKUs

Description

Initaitive auditing VM SKUs for adherence to the corporate objectives.

Category
○ Create new   ● Use existing

Under Review

Figure 4-28. *Selecting initiative location, name, and description*

4. In Policies option, select the policy in scope of this definition by Add Policy Definition. In the example, we selected the allowed VM SKUs and the allowed locations as shown in Figure 4-29.

105

CHAPTER 4   COMPREHENSIVE AZURE POLICY IMPLEMENTATION

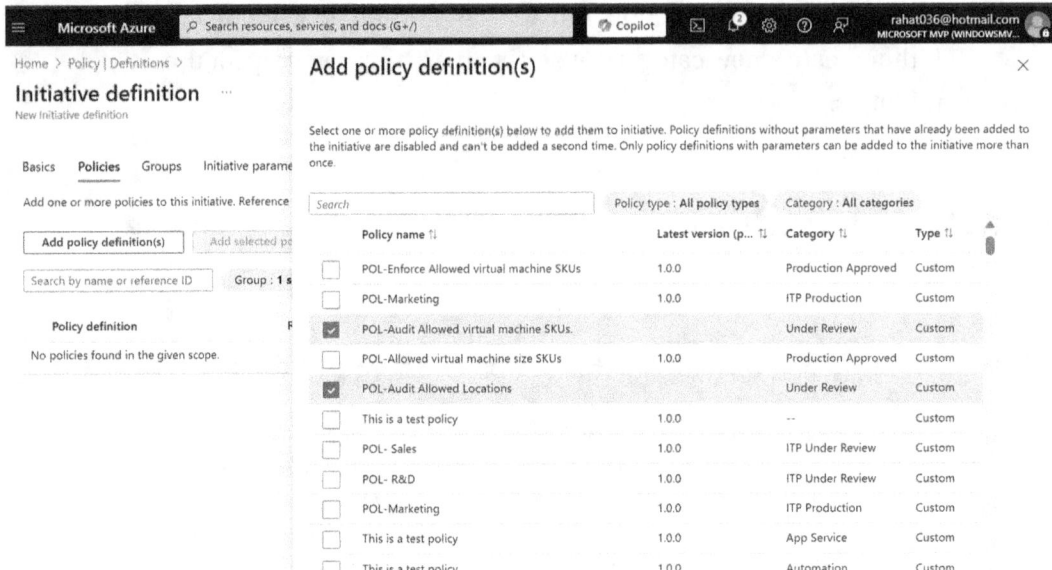

Figure 4-29. *Selecting policy definition(s)*

5. These two policies require parameter values. To create the initiative parameter, select Initiative parameters option, click Create initiative parameter, and fill up the required information as shown in Figure 4-30.

CHAPTER 4 COMPREHENSIVE AZURE POLICY IMPLEMENTATION

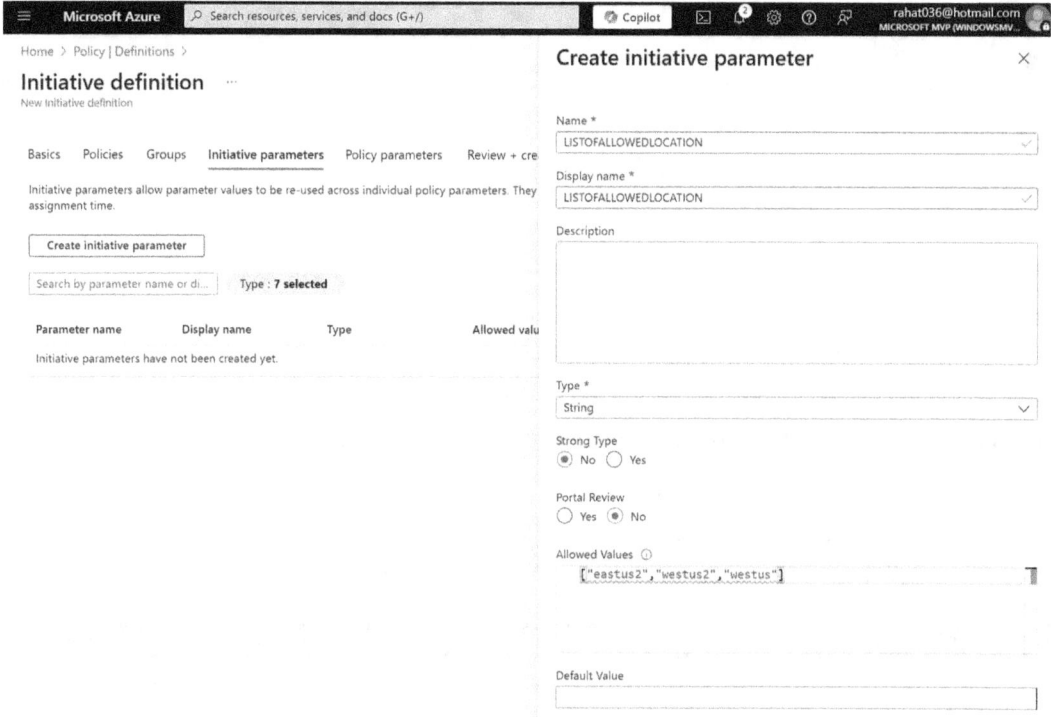

Figure 4-30. *Creating initiative parameters*

6. Create two Initiative parameters for two policies.

7. Now, select Policy parameters and set the value field for both to **Use Initiative Parameter** to allow the parameters to be set during the initiative assignment as shown in Figure 4-31. Click **Review + Create**.

CHAPTER 4 COMPREHENSIVE AZURE POLICY IMPLEMENTATION

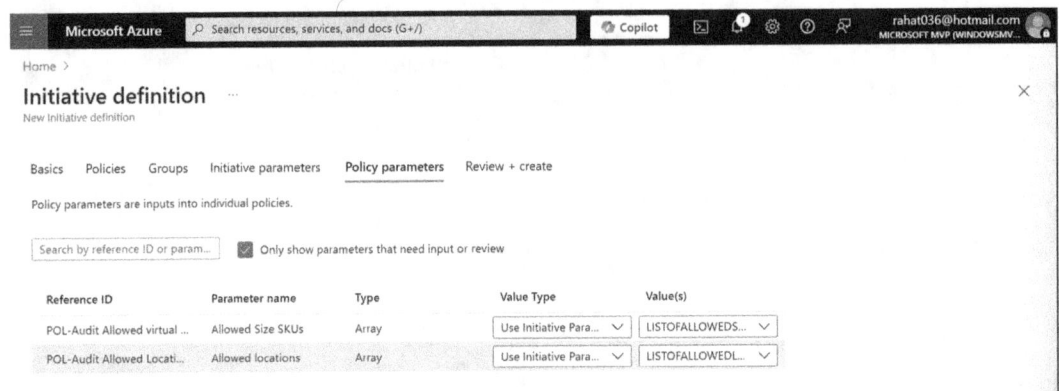

Figure 4-31. Assigning initiative parameter as value type

8. A new custom initiative containing two policies is created. It is available to you for assignment as shown in Figure 4-32.

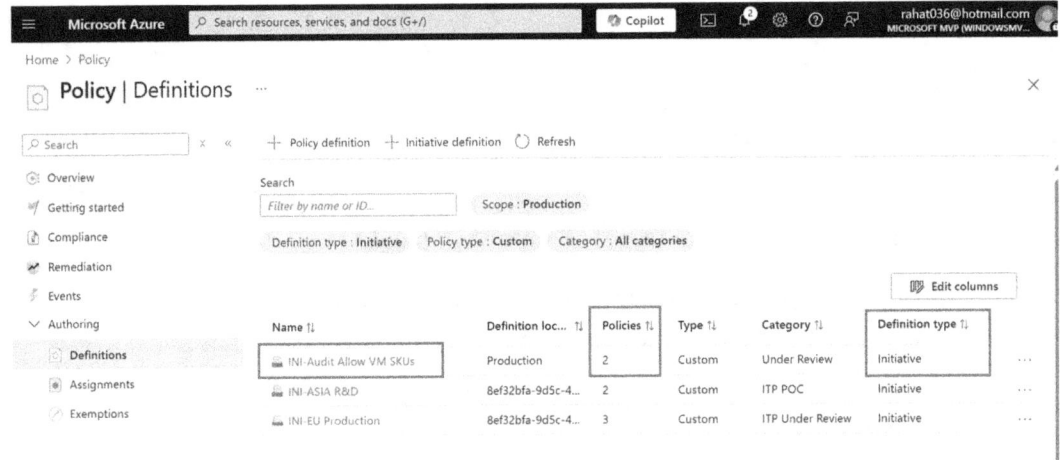

Figure 4-32. Confirmation of creating initiative

Assigning Initiatives

Once you've created a policy initiative, the next step is assigning it to the right scope within your Azure environment. Assigning initiatives allows you to enforce a set of governance rules across multiple resources in a structured and consistent way.

CHAPTER 4 COMPREHENSIVE AZURE POLICY IMPLEMENTATION

Whether you're applying security standards across an entire subscription or targeting specific resource groups for cost management, initiative assignments help streamline compliance efforts. During the assignment process, you can configure parameters, exclusions, and enforcement modes to tailor the behavior of each initiative. This ensures that policies are not only applied effectively but also remain flexible enough to meet different organizational needs.

1. Connect to the Azure portal at `https://portal.azure.com`.

2. Click Policy under the favorites section in the left navigation bar, or search Policy in the search bar.

3. In the Policy blade, click Assignment and then click Assign Initiative as shown in Figure 4-33.

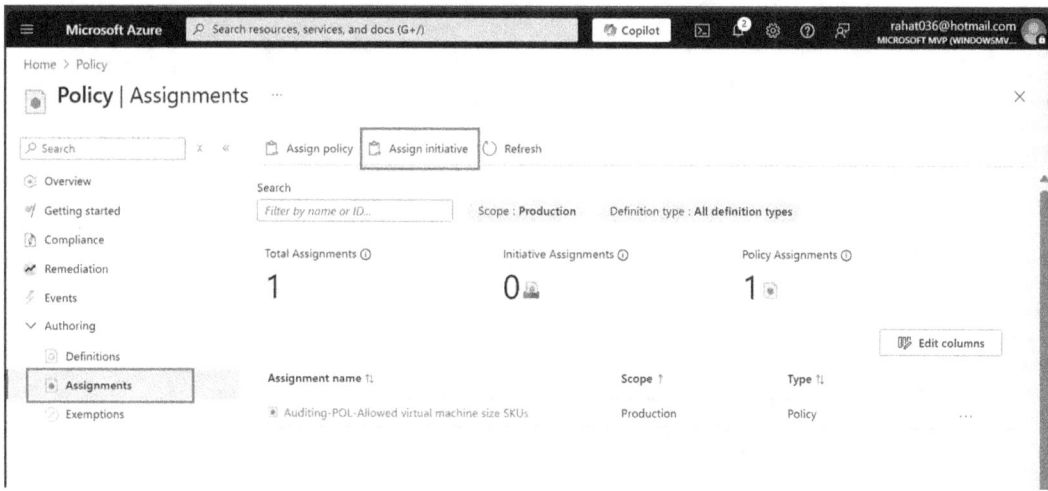

Figure 4-33. *Assigning initiative page*

109

4. Click ... button under Scope and navigate to the subscription under the CC036 IT Service child management group as shown in Figure 4-34. It may defer, so select as appropriate.

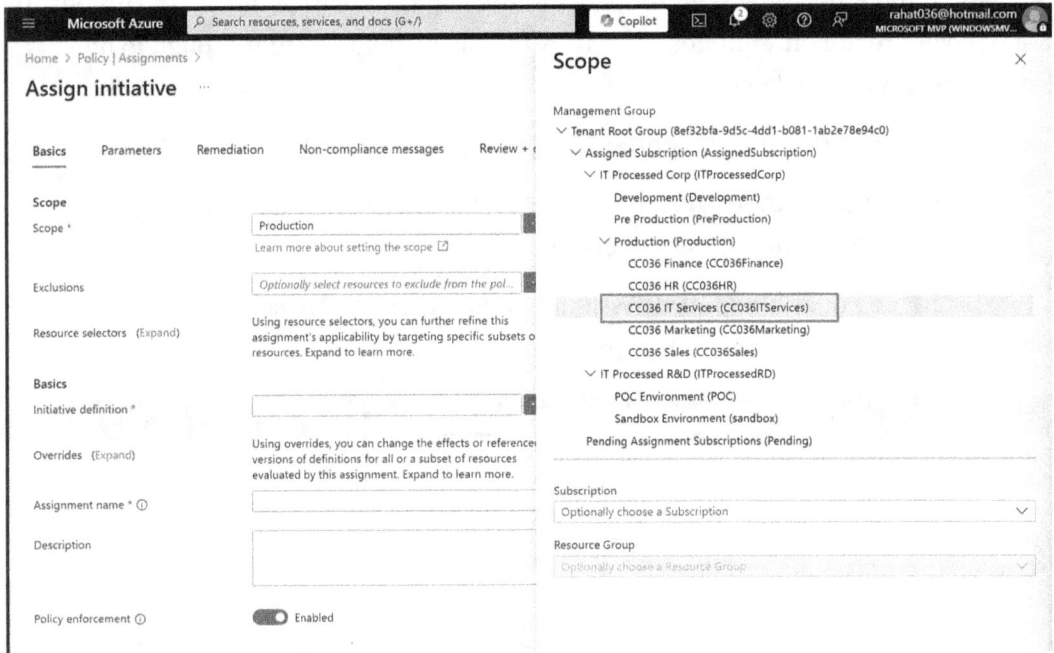

Figure 4-34. *Selecting scope*

5. Select the Initiative definition by clicking ... that we created in the previous step. Refer to Figure 4-35.

CHAPTER 4 COMPREHENSIVE AZURE POLICY IMPLEMENTATION

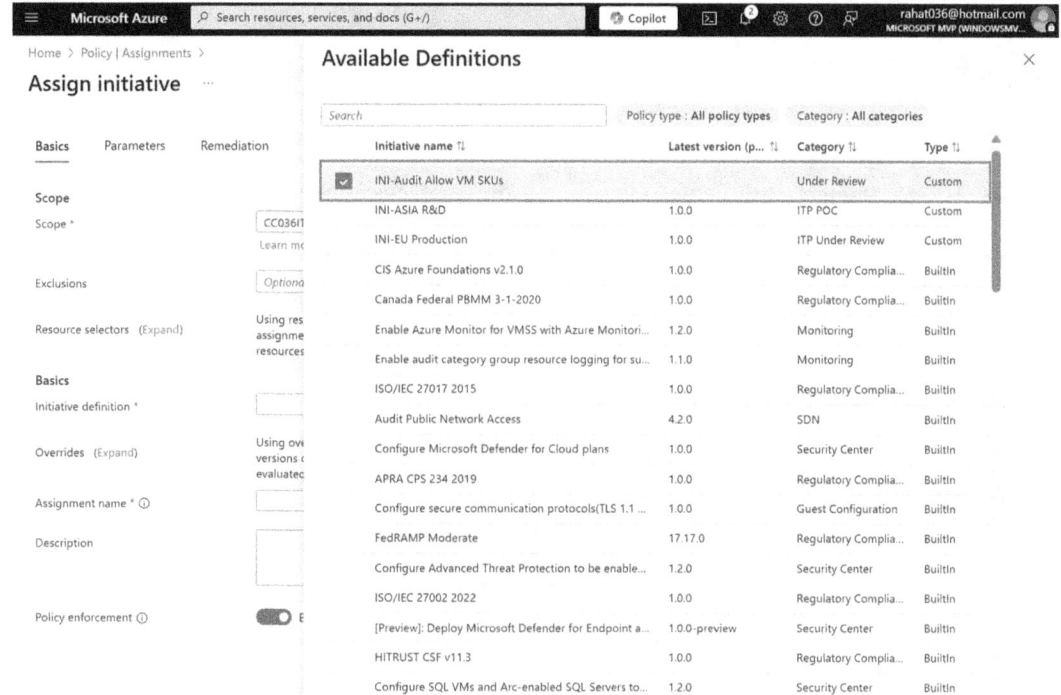

Figure 4-35. *Assigning initiative definition*

6. Provide a name and description for this assignment.

7. Select Parameters tab and assign the values of the parameters as shown in Figure 4-36.

CHAPTER 4   COMPREHENSIVE AZURE POLICY IMPLEMENTATION

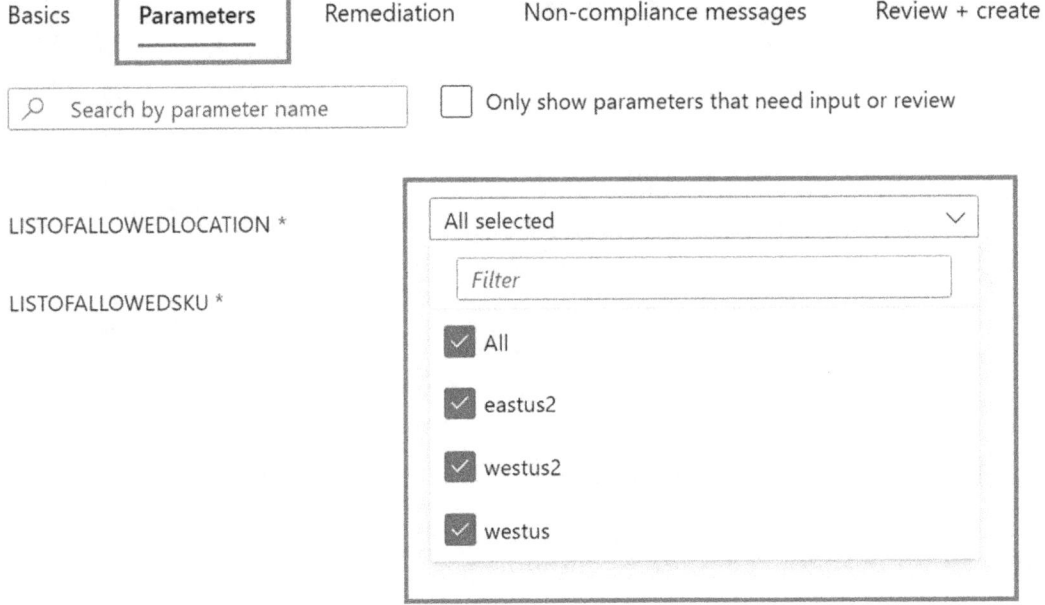

Figure 4-36. Selecting parameters value

8. You can verify that the assignment has been created by navigating to the Policy—Overview blade. The initial state will not be started. Once the evaluation cycle has been triggered, the state is updated to compliant or non-compliant based on the rules of the policies in the initiative. Figure 4-37 shows the compliant state of the initiative assigned in the example.

CHAPTER 4 COMPREHENSIVE AZURE POLICY IMPLEMENTATION

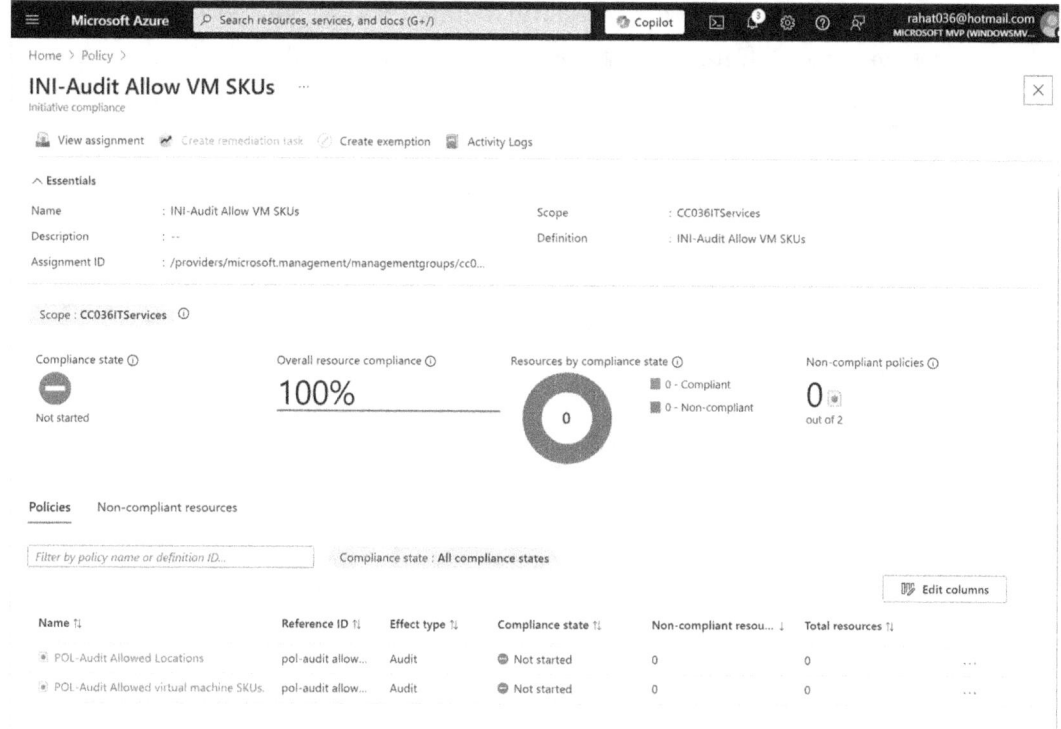

Figure 4-37. Overview page after assigning initiative

Updating Initiatives

As your organization evolves, so do your governance needs. Updating initiatives allows you to keep your policy sets aligned with changing business requirements, compliance standards, or technical environments. Whether you're adding new policy definitions, adjusting parameters, or modifying existing rules, updates ensure that your initiatives remain relevant and effective. Azure makes it easy to revise initiatives without starting from scratch—changes can be applied incrementally, minimizing disruption. Regularly reviewing and updating your initiatives is the best practice that helps maintain a healthy and compliant Azure environment over time.

1. Navigate to the Policy node and select Definitions in the Azure portal.

2. Select the initiative to be edited, and then select Edit Initiative.

CHAPTER 4 COMPREHENSIVE AZURE POLICY IMPLEMENTATION

3. To add additional policies, select the required policy/policies from the available Definitions section as shown in Figure 4-38.

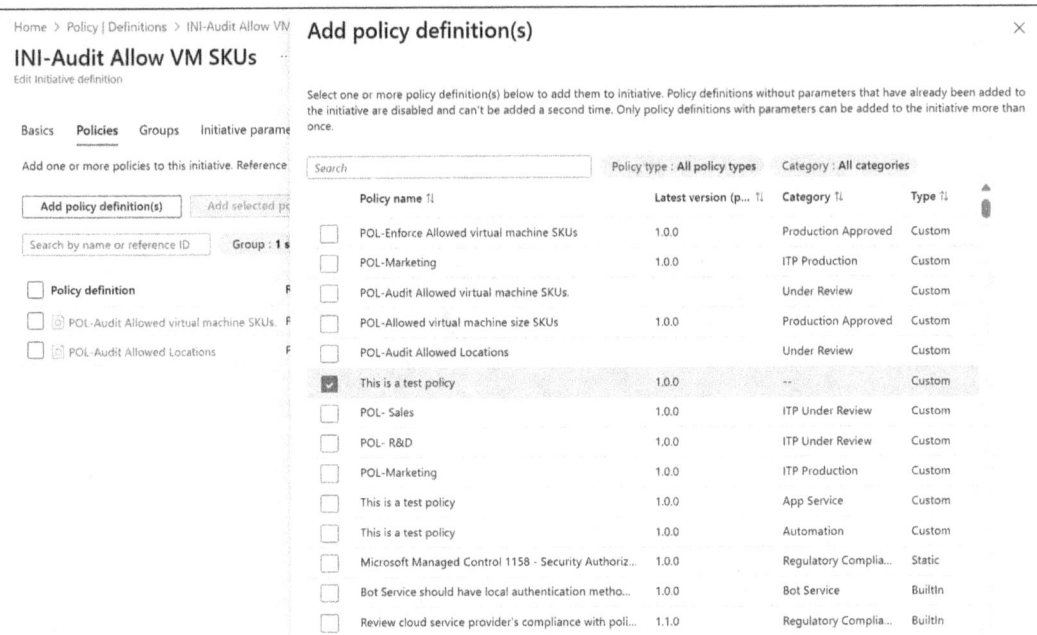

Figure 4-38. Add additional policy definition

4. You can also remove the existing policy by selecting the policy and click ... and then Remove policy as shown in Figure 4-39.

Figure 4-39. Policy definition remove option

5. You can also change the initiative's name and definition.

6. Click Save to complete the necessary update(s).

In addition to using the Azure portal for creating and updating policies/initiatives, you can also use PowerShell or Azure CLI to perform the same actions. For examples, refer to https://learn.microsoft.com/en-us/azure/governance/policy/assign-policy-powershell.

Policy Assignment Scope and Exclusions

Assigning policies in Azure is much like planning invitations for a family event—simple on the surface, but potentially tricky when certain dynamics are involved. Imagine you're hosting a celebration and plan to invite both Family A and Family B. However, there's a known issue: Munia from Family A doesn't get along with Ruhi from Family B. You now have two options. One, send the invitation to both families but include a note asking them not to bring these two ladies. Or two, send personalized invites to everyone except Munia and Ruhi. Both options achieve the same result—but which approach is more manageable?

In Azure, policy assignment scope and exclusions function in a similar way. While exclusions allow flexibility, they can introduce complexity if not handled strategically. The key to managing this complexity lies in proactive planning—specifically, by organizing your resources using management groups, subscriptions, and resource groups in a way that naturally accounts for exclusions.

If you know that certain resources need to be excluded from a policy, it's best to group them intentionally—placing them within the same management group, subscription, or resource group. This design simplifies policy management and reduces the need for scattered exclusions.

Figure 4-40 demonstrates a policy assigned at the subscription level, automatically applying to all resource groups within that subscription unless explicitly excluded.

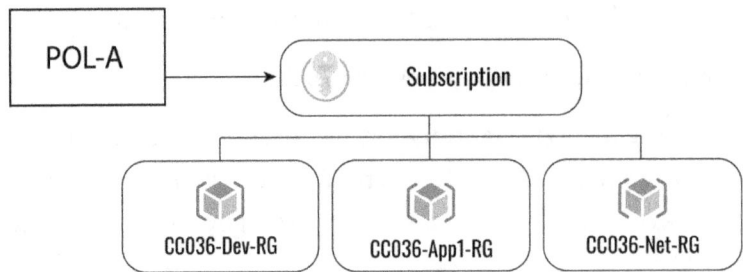

Figure 4-40. *Policy scoped with no exclusions*

Figure 4-41 shows a policy scoped at the subscription level with an exclusion of one resource group (CC001-Net-RG). This is an example of planning for exclusions using a resource group (the policy may not apply to the network resource that you store in that resource group).

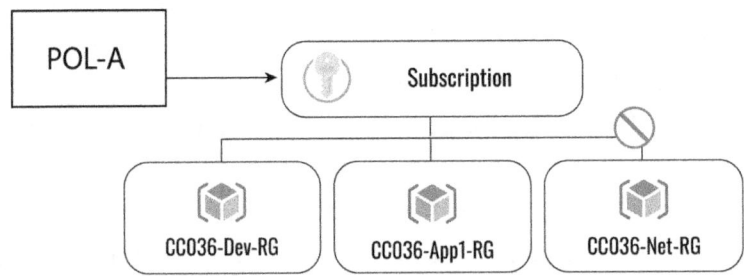

Figure 4-41. *Policy scoped with exclusions*

Compliance Management and Reporting

Compliance is a continuous process, not a one-time task—and Azure Policy helps you stay on top of it with built-in tools for tracking and reporting. Through the Azure portal, you can easily view the compliance state of your policies and initiatives, identifying which resources are compliant and which are not. This visibility is crucial for auditors, security teams, and administrators who need to ensure that organizational and regulatory standards are being met. Azure also provides detailed reporting capabilities, allowing you to drill down into non-compliant resources and take corrective action. With automated assessments and real-time insights, compliance management becomes a proactive part of your cloud governance strategy.

Taking Action on Policy Results

The follow-up actions that you can take on policy results depend on the rules, conditions, and effect specified in the policy. There are eight policy effects available:

- AddToNetworkGroup
- Append
- Audit
- AuditIfNotExists
- Deny
- DenyAction
- DeployIfNotExists
- Disabled

AddToNetworkGroup

The AddToNetworkGroup effect in Azure Policy is used to automatically add resources to a specified network group when a policy assignment is evaluated. This effect is primarily used in conjunction with Azure Firewall Policy or Microsoft Defender for Cloud capabilities, such as Just-in-Time (JIT) access, adaptive network hardening, or other network-related governance scenarios. Please note this effect works only with specific Azure resource types and services that support network groups.

Append

Append adds fields to the target resource during a create or update. Examples include adding tag values, like environment resource owner. The following is an append effect JSON that specifies an environment tag (key/value pair):

```
{
   "properties": {
      "displayName": "Apply tag and its default value",
      "policyType": "BuiltIn",
      "description": "Applies a required tag and its default value if it is
      not specified by the user.",
```

CHAPTER 4   COMPREHENSIVE AZURE POLICY IMPLEMENTATION

```
      "parameters": {
         "tagName": {
            "type": "String",
            "metadata": {
               "description": "Name of the tag, such as Environment"
            }
         },
         "tagValue": {
            "type": "String",
            "metadata": {
               "description": "Value of the tag, such as Development"
            }
         }
      },
      "policyRule": {
         "if": {
            "field": "[concat('tags[', parameters('tagName'), ']')]",
            "exists": "false"
         },
         "then": {
            "effect": "append",
            "details": [
               {
                  "field": "[concat('tags[', parameters('tagName'), ']')]",
                  "value": "[parameters('tagValue')]"
               }
            ]
         }
      }
   },
   "id": "/providers/Microsoft.Authorization/policyDefinitions/2a0e14a6-
   b0a6-4fab-991a-187a4f81c498",
   "type": "Microsoft.Authorization/policyDefinitions",
   "name": "2a0e14a6-b0a6-4fab-991a-187a4f81c498"
}
```

Audit

Audit is the equivalent of a report-only mode. The rule checks for a condition and reports as compliant if true and non-compliant if false. No action is taken. It is the condition used in most of the exercises so far in this book.

AuditIfNotExists

AuditIfNotExists can be confusing to understand, but in essence, it is similar to Audit. Audit checks for the compliance of a resource to a specific condition, such as allowed VM SKUs; however, AuditIfNotExists is more aligned to checking if a resource property or artifact exists. An example is checking whether anti-malware extensions are enabled. This effect type also reports back true or false but does not have remediation (deploy instructions as part of the then portion of the definition). The following code snippet is an example of checking for the existence of anti-malware extensions on a virtual machine:

```
{
    "if": {
        "field": "type",
        "equals": "Microsoft.Compute/virtualMachines"
    },
    "then": {
        "effect": "auditIfNotExists",
        "details": {
            "type": "Microsoft.Compute/virtualMachines/extensions",
            "existenceCondition": {
                "allOf": [{
                        "field": "Microsoft.Compute/virtualMachines/
                        extensions/publisher",
                        "equals": "Microsoft.Azure.Security"
                    },
                    {
                        "field": "Microsoft.Compute/virtualMachines/
                        extensions/type",
                        "equals": "IaaSAntimalware"
                    }
```

```
                    ]
                }
            }
        }
    }
}
```

Deny

The Deny effect is used to prevent the creation of resources that do not meet a condition. In the case where a resource already exists and does not meet the condition, then a non-compliance state is reported. An example is preventing VMs from being created that do not use an approved SKU. When evaluating creation, the effect will throw an error message and prevent the creation.

DenyAction

The DenyAction effect is a specialized enforcement mechanism that blocks specific actions performed on a resource rather than denying the entire resource creation or update operation like the standard Deny effect does. This effect provides granular control by targeting particular actions (operations) in the Azure Resource Manager (ARM) request pipeline, allowing more precise governance without fully blocking resource deployment.

DeployIfNotExists

`DeployIfNotExists` is similar to `AuditIfNotExists`; the difference is that it can deploy a template for remediation based on the non-compliance condition. When non-compliant is returned for this effect type, it is not auto-remediated. You will need to create a remediation task to complete the process using the template defined in the policy.

Disabled

This effect type disables the policy and is the equivalent of not evaluating. This is a useful effect in initiatives, where one or more policies can be disabled during testing without impacting the other policies or removing the policy from the initiative assignment.

The effects' order of precedence is documented at https://docs.microsoft.com/en-us/azure/governance/policy/concepts/effects.

Requests to create or update a resource through Azure Resource Manager are evaluated by policy first. Policy creates a list of all assignments that apply to the resource and then evaluates the resource against each definition. Policy processes several of the effects before handing the request to the appropriate resource provider. Doing so prevents unnecessary processing by a resource provider when a resource doesn't meet the designed governance controls of policy.

- **Disabled** is checked first to determine if the policy rule should be evaluated.

- **Append** is then evaluated. Since append could alter the request, a change made by append may prevent an audit or deny effect from triggering.

- **Deny** is then evaluated. By evaluating deny before audit, double logging of an undesired resource is prevented.

- **Audit** is then evaluated before the request goes to the resource provider.

- After the resource provider returns a success code, `AuditIfNotExists` and `DeployIfNotExists` evaluate to determine if additional compliance logging or action is required.

Note When evaluating compliance results, it's important to allow adequate time for policy effects to take place. Some effects, especially `DeployIfNotExists`, do not produce immediate results as they rely on external triggers or resource deployment actions. Users should review compliance states over a defined time window to ensure accurate assessments and avoid premature conclusions.

Real-Time Policy Enforcement

Real-time policy enforcement in Azure ensures that governance is not just an afterthought but an active part of every deployment and configuration change. Instead of waiting for periodic audits or manual reviews, policies are evaluated the moment a resource is created or updated. This means non-compliant configurations can be stopped before they ever reach your environment. It's a proactive approach that embeds compliance into the workflow, helping teams move quickly without sacrificing control. By integrating governance directly into the resource management process, real-time enforcement minimizes risk, reduces operational overhead, and ensures that best practices are consistently followed across the cloud.

Remediation Options

The effect settings you select for the policies you assign will determine your remediation options. You have two options available for remediation: manual and automatic.

Manual Remediation

In Azure Policy, manual remediation requires administrative intervention to address non-compliant resources identified by policy evaluations. When a policy is configured with effects such as Audit or Deny, Azure will either flag or block the resource without making any automatic changes. It is then the responsibility of the administrator to investigate and manually bring the resource into compliance. This remediation method is commonly used when configurations involve business-critical systems, require approval workflows, or need a case-by-case review due to complexity or potential impact. Manual remediation provides greater control but can be time-consuming, especially in large-scale environments.

Automatic Remediation

Automatic remediation offers a way to bring non-compliant resources back into alignment without manual intervention. This can be done directly through Azure Policy's remediation feature or by using your own automation tools and scripts to target affected resources.

When using Azure Policy's built-in remediation, it's typically applied to policies that use the `DeployIfNotExists` effect. The process starts with assigning the policy to a scope, such as a subscription or resource group. Once the policy identifies non-compliant resources, a remediation task can be created to apply the required configuration.

These remediation tasks are executed using a managed identity, which is granted the necessary permissions to make changes on your behalf. This identity can be automatically created as part of the policy definition or set up manually, depending on your governance model.

For example, in the Azure portal, you can define a `DeployIfNotExists` policy, assign it to a group of resources, and then initiate a remediation task—all through a guided experience. This approach enables efficient, consistent compliance across your environment with minimal manual effort.

Summary

In this chapter, we explored how **Azure Policy** enables organizations to enforce governance at scale. From defining custom policies and grouping them into initiatives to assigning scope, managing exclusions, and configuring remediation, you learned how to build a structured and automated compliance framework. We also discussed how to monitor policy compliance, track enforcement, and adapt your policy design to evolving organizational needs.

With a strong governance foundation in place, we are now ready to move beyond compliance into **proactive security management**. In **Chapter 5**, we'll introduce **Microsoft Defender for Cloud**, Microsoft's unified security management platform. You'll learn how it integrates with policy enforcement, strengthens your cloud security posture, and helps detect, prevent, and respond to threats in real time.

CHAPTER 5

Enhanced Security with Microsoft Defender for Cloud

In Chapter 4, we established how **Azure Policy** helps enforce governance by defining and controlling the rules that shape your cloud environment. You learned how to use policies and initiatives to automate compliance, assign scope-based controls, and remediate violations across your resources.

Building on that foundation, this chapter shifts the focus from governance enforcement to **proactive security management** using **Microsoft Defender for Cloud**. In this chapter, I will guide you through the core features of Defender for Cloud, including **secure score**, **security recommendations**, **threat protection**, and **regulatory compliance management**. You'll see how Defender integrates with Azure Policy, continuously assesses your environment, and provides intelligent insights and automation to mitigate real threats.

By the end of this chapter, you will understand how to transition from a policy-driven governance model to a **security-enhanced operational posture**, ensuring your Azure environment remains both compliant and resilient against evolving threats.

Overview of Microsoft Defender for Cloud and Its Capabilities

Microsoft Defender for Cloud, previously known as Microsoft Azure Security Center, is a security service from Microsoft designed to protect cloud-based and hybrid environments—whether you are running virtual machines in Azure, containers in AWS, or databases across different platforms. But what does that really mean in practice?

CHAPTER 5   ENHANCED SECURITY WITH MICROSOFT DEFENDER FOR CLOUD

Imagine you're managing a mix of systems: some virtual machines in Azure, a Kubernetes cluster in AWS, and a set of SQL databases on-premises. How do you keep track of all the security risks across such a diverse environment? How do you know if one of your virtual machines was left exposed to the Internet with an open port or if a developer accidentally stored sensitive credentials in a public GitHub repository?

Microsoft Defender for Cloud answers these questions by continuously monitoring your resources, identifying misconfigurations, and alerting you about threats before they become incidents. It doesn't just show you a problem—it tells you why it matters, how urgent it is, and how to fix it. For instance, if a storage account is publicly accessible, Defender for Cloud won't just flag it; it will explain the risk of data leakage and guide you through the steps to restrict access.

Another example: Say an attacker is trying to brute-force a virtual machine using RDP. Would you know right away? Defender for Cloud detects this pattern of behavior, correlates it with other signals—like failed logins or strange IP locations—and sends you a high-priority alert, suggesting actions like enabling just-in-time access or blocking the IP address.

So, what is Microsoft Defender for Cloud? It's a centralized, intelligent security assistant that watches over your cloud resources, asks the right questions on your behalf—Is this secure? Who has access? What changed?—and then answers them with real-time insights and practical guidance. It's built to simplify security, not complicate it, and helps organizations stay one step ahead in a constantly evolving threat landscape.

A Changing World of Cloud Security

The way we think about IT infrastructure has changed dramatically over the past decade. Not too long ago, most organizations ran their workloads in on-premises data centers, protected by perimeter firewalls and strict access controls. But now? More and more businesses are moving to the cloud, embracing its speed, flexibility, and global reach. That shift has brought undeniable advantages—but it has also changed the way we must approach security.

Why is cloud security different from traditional IT security? In a cloud environment, the infrastructure is no longer confined to one physical location. Workloads can be spun up in seconds, accessed from anywhere, and connected to a complex network of services—many of which are public-facing by design. So instead of a static perimeter to defend, you now have a dynamic attack surface that is constantly changing.

Let's say a developer in your team deploys a new virtual machine and forgets to close port 3389 for Remote Desktop Protocol. That one misstep—small as it may seem—could expose the VM to brute-force attacks from the Internet within minutes. Would you know about it? Would your security team catch it before it's too late?

This risk isn't just theoretical. Research from security firms like Rapid7 and Palo Alto Networks has shown that newly deployed, Internet-exposed virtual machines (VMs) can be scanned or probed by malicious actors within just three to five minutes of going online. Attackers often use automated scripts and global scanning networks to identify open ports, weak configurations, or exposed endpoints across cloud providers. This means organizations have a dangerously narrow window to detect and respond before a breach can occur—especially when basic misconfigurations, like open RDP (Remote Desktop Protocol) ports, are involved. Such speed and automation highlight the urgent need for proactive cloud security measures from the very moment resources are deployed.

This is the kind of challenge that defines cloud security today. The cloud offers power and speed, but also risk if left unchecked. And it's not just about misconfigurations. Attackers have become more sophisticated. They don't just scan for open ports—they exploit weak identities, insecure APIs, and lateral movement opportunities across hybrid environments.

So how do we respond to this reality? This is exactly where tools like Microsoft Defender for Cloud step in. It continuously watches your environment, looking for signs of misconfiguration, unusual activity, or exposed services. It doesn't wait for a full-blown breach to happen—it identifies risks early and asks the questions you might not even think to ask, like *Did someone disable MFA on a critical admin account? Is your container image being deployed with known vulnerabilities? Has a virtual machine suddenly started making suspicious outbound connections?* Then, it gives you immediate answers, complete with suggested actions.

The shift to cloud has changed the speed of innovation—but it has also changed the speed at which things can go wrong. Security needs to operate at that same pace. Defender for Cloud was built with this exact purpose in mind: to adapt to the fast, flexible, and sometimes chaotic world of cloud computing and bring clarity and control where it's needed most.

CHAPTER 5   ENHANCED SECURITY WITH MICROSOFT DEFENDER FOR CLOUD

Cloud Security Is Still a Shared Responsibility

A critical concept in cloud security that is often overlooked is this: **security in the cloud is a shared responsibility**. It's a common misconception that migrating to Azure or another cloud platform means the provider handles all aspects of security. But is that truly the case? Who ensures the security of the virtual machines you create, the storage accounts you set up, or the user identities you manage? The answer lies in understanding where your responsibilities begin—and where the provider's end.

This brings us to the concept of the shared responsibility model. In the cloud, both the provider and the customer have distinct roles to play. Microsoft is responsible for securing the cloud infrastructure itself like physical data centers, networking, host machines, and the hypervisor. But once you start deploying your own resources—whether it's a Windows Server VM, a database, or a web app—you take on the responsibility for securing them.

Table 5-1 outlines the division of security responsibilities between the cloud provider and the customer, clarifying which aspects are managed by each party in a cloud environment.

Table 5-1. Shared responsibility model in cloud security

Responsibility Area	Managed by Cloud Provider	Managed by Customer
Physical Infrastructure	Yes—Data centers, servers, and networking hardware	No—Not accessible by the customer
Host and Network Security	Yes—Base host OS, physical firewalls, network routing	No—Customer does not manage this layer
Virtual Machines and OS Patching	No—Customer must install updates, configure OS	Yes—Responsible for VM setup and maintenance
Applications and Data	No—Customer owns the apps and data security	Yes—Must secure and manage all application components
User Access and Identity	No—Customer manages access control and permissions	Yes—Defines roles, MFA, and identity strategy
Compliance and Encryption	Shared—Provider ensures platform-level compliance	Shared—Customer ensures data-level compliance and encryption settings

For example, imagine you've deployed a set of virtual machines to host a customer-facing application. Microsoft ensures those VMs run on secure infrastructure, but you're the one who needs to configure the firewall rules, apply operating system patches, and protect administrative accounts. If you leave Remote Desktop access open to the Internet or forget to update critical software, that's not Microsoft's fault—that's on you.

Now, what if you're using Platform-as-a-Service (PaaS) offering like Azure SQL Database or Azure App Service? Microsoft handles even more of the stack here—including the OS and runtime environment—but you still have to define user permissions, configure data encryption, and monitor access. In other words, the more abstraction you use, the less you manage—but you never hand off all responsibilities entirely.

So how can you be sure you're holding up your end of the deal? How do you know whether your resources are securely configured, identities properly managed, and services monitored for suspicious activity?

This is where Microsoft Defender for Cloud becomes essential. It understands the shared responsibility model and helps you manage your part effectively. It continuously asks the critical questions on your behalf: *Is your data encrypted? Are your VMs running outdated software? Have your web apps been exposed without authentication?* And when the answer is "no" or "not sure," it provides clear, actionable steps to get things back on track.

The cloud gives you incredible control and flexibility—but with that control comes responsibility. Defender for Cloud ensures you're not left alone to figure it all out. It bridges the gap between what Microsoft secures and what you must secure, guiding you toward a safer, more resilient cloud environment.

Addressing Modern Security Challenges

No matter the size of your organization—whether you're a small startup or a global enterprise—security challenges are a daily reality in today's connected world. But what exactly makes modern security so challenging? Why does it seem like the threats keep evolving faster than we can respond?

Let's consider a few real-world scenarios.

Your team deploys a new application using containers in Azure Kubernetes Service (AKS). Within minutes, the cluster is live, scalable, and accessible. But who's checking whether the container images were scanned for vulnerabilities? What if an outdated base image contains a known exploit? If this detail is missed, attackers could compromise the cluster before anyone notices.

Now imagine your organization has adopted a "work from anywhere" policy. Employees are logging in from all over the world using laptops, tablets, or even personal devices. How do you ensure the right people have the right level of access, without unintentionally opening the door to attackers? What if a single compromised account gives someone the ability to laterally move across your environment?

These examples highlight the key modern security challenges organizations face:

1. **Attacks Are More Sophisticated**

   Gone are the days when attackers relied solely on viruses and basic malware. Today, they use advanced persistent threats (APTs), social engineering, and automated vulnerability scanning tools. Many of these attacks are stealthy and intelligent, capable of lying dormant or blending in with normal activity. They don't just target firewalls, they target identities, APIs, containers, and misconfigured cloud settings.

2. **Environments Change Constantly**

   Cloud enables innovation at speed. New virtual machines, functions, containers, and databases can be spun up or torn down in seconds. But with this agility comes volatility. If security isn't automated and continuous, it's easy to fall behind. How do you know if a developer accidentally exposed a database to the Internet last night? What if a newly deployed VM hasn't been patched in weeks?

3. **There Aren't Enough Security Experts**

   Many organizations are struggling to hire experienced security professionals. Even when teams are in place, they are often overwhelmed with alerts, reports, and manual tasks. Smaller companies, in particular, may rely on IT generalists who wear many hats and can't be expected to monitor security 24/7.

So how do you address these mounting challenges without slowing down innovation or exhausting your teams?

This is exactly where Microsoft Defender for Cloud comes in. It continuously scans your environment, detects vulnerabilities, highlights misconfigurations, and alerts you to suspicious activity in real time. If an exposed storage account appears, it flags it. If a brute-force attack targets your VM, it alerts you. If a container image includes a known vulnerability, it tells you before it gets deployed. Defender for Cloud doesn't just raise red flags—it explains the risks and helps you fix them quickly.

Key Features of Microsoft Defender for Cloud

Microsoft Defender for Cloud provides a broad and integrated set of security features that address the needs of modern cloud environments. When you open Microsoft Defender for Cloud for the first time, without modifications to the dashboard, it looks like what's shown in Figure 5-1.

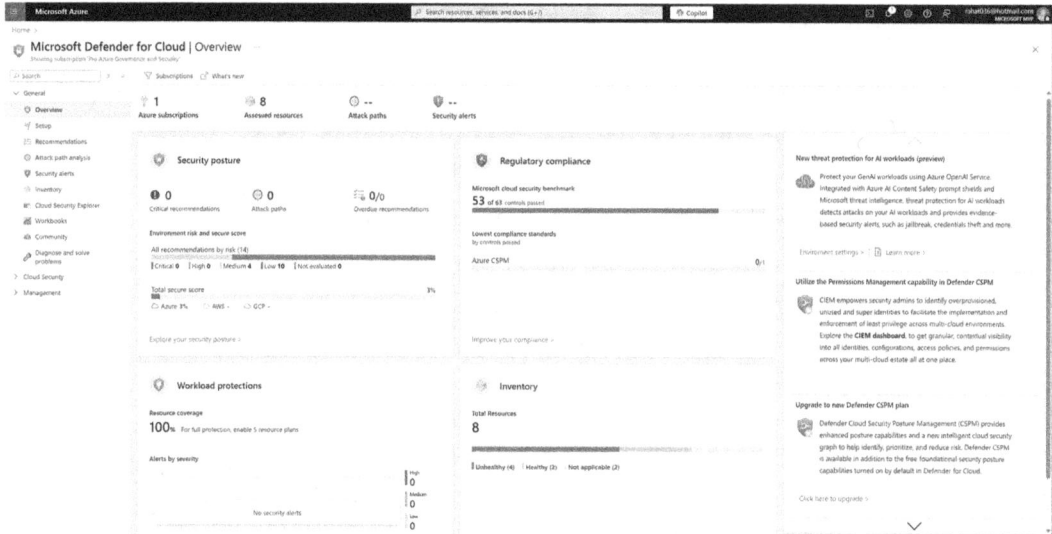

Figure 5-1. Microsoft Defender for Cloud dashboard

Its architecture is designed to deliver continuous assessment, active threat detection, compliance tracking, and workload protection across Azure, multi-cloud (AWS, GCP), and hybrid infrastructures. These features work together to give security teams deep visibility, control, and response capabilities, even in highly distributed environments.

1. **Cloud Security Posture Management (CSPM)**

    Defender for Cloud's CSPM capability is responsible for continuously evaluating the configuration of cloud resources to ensure alignment with established security best practices and organizational policies. This is achieved through automated scans that check for insecure settings, unnecessary exposure of services, overly permissive access, and other deviations from secure design principles. The findings are aggregated into a **Secure Score**, which quantifies the environment's risk level based on the number, severity, and scope of identified issues.

CSPM not only detects weaknesses but also classifies them based on categories such as identity and access, data protection, network security, and governance. These insights help organizations prioritize remediation activities according to their impact on the overall security posture.

2. **Cloud Workload Protection (CWP)**

    Cloud Workload Protection (CWP) in Microsoft Defender for Cloud offers specialized workload-aware security for a broad range of resource types deployed in cloud and hybrid environments. While Cloud Security Posture Management (CSPM) focuses on evaluating configurations and aligning environments with best practices, CWP addresses the runtime protection, behavioral monitoring, and active threat detection specific to each type of workload.

    Each supported workload is secured through an individual Defender plan, which, when enabled, activates a suite of targeted security features tailored to the unique risks and behaviors associated with that workload type. These features operate continuously, providing telemetry, analytics, and protection on a scale.

Table 5-2 outlines the currently available Defender plans and the workloads they are designed to protect:

Table 5-2. Microsoft Defender for Cloud plans with targeted workload

Defender Plan	Targeted Workload
Defender for Servers	Azure Virtual Machines, Amazon EC2 instances, and on-premises servers connected via Azure Arc
Defender for Containers	Kubernetes clusters including Azure Kubernetes Service (AKS), Amazon EKS, Google GKE, and container registries such as Azure Container Registry (ACR)
Defender for App Service	Applications and APIs hosted on Azure App Service
Defender for Storage	Azure Storage services including Blob Storage, File Shares, and Data Lake Gen2
Defender for SQL	Azure SQL Databases, SQL Server running on Azure VMs, and third party–managed instances such as AWS RDS for SQL
Defender for Key Vault	Secrets, keys, and certificates managed in Azure Key Vault

3. **Advanced Threat Detection and Alerting**

   One of the foundational features of Defender for Cloud is its threat detection engine. It uses a combination of machine learning, anomaly detection, behavioral analysis, and Microsoft's global threat intelligence to detect suspicious or malicious activity across environments.

   The platform continuously monitors telemetry from supported resources and correlates signals to identify patterns that may indicate attacks in progress, compromised identities, or misused credentials. Each alert includes detailed metadata, severity levels, and incident context.

   Alerts are enriched with mappings to the **MITRE ATT&CK framework**, allowing security analysts to understand the techniques being used and the potential attacker objectives. The alerts can be escalated to Security Information and Event Management (SIEM) platforms such as Microsoft Sentinel for further analysis and triage.

4. **Regulatory Compliance and Policy Enforcement**

    Defender for Cloud provides built-in capabilities for regulatory compliance tracking. It includes preconfigured compliance standards such as ISO/IEC 27001, NIST SP 800-53, PCI DSS, and GDPR.

    The compliance dashboard enables organizations to visualize their alignment with selected standards, highlighting passed and failed controls and identifying areas where remediation is required. Each control is linked to specific security recommendations within the platform.

    In addition to passive monitoring, organizations can enforce security policies across subscriptions and management groups using Azure Policy integrations. These policies can enforce conditions like mandatory tagging, secure encryption configurations, and approved regions for resource deployment.

5. **DevSecOps and Infrastructure-as-Code (IaC) Integration**

    Defender for Cloud includes features to integrate security into the software development lifecycle. It supports DevSecOps workflows by integrating directly with platforms like GitHub and Azure DevOps.

    It scans Infrastructure-as-Code (IaC) templates—including ARM, Bicep, Terraform, and Kubernetes manifests—for insecure configurations before resources are deployed. This early detection helps prevent misconfigurations from reaching production environments.

    It also enables continuous code-to-cloud traceability by correlating deployed resources back to their originating source code, allowing organizations to tie security issues directly to development artifacts.

6. **Automation and Response Orchestration**

   To accelerate response and reduce manual effort, Defender for Cloud supports security automation through integration with **Azure Logic Apps**. Automation workflows, also known as **security playbooks**, can be triggered in response to specific alerts or compliance failures.

   These workflows can perform a variety of tasks, such as isolating a virtual machine, revoking user access, initiating ticketing workflows, sending notifications, or collecting forensics. This capability allows organizations to standardize and scale their response processes, reduce time to containment, and ensure consistent enforcement of incident response procedures.

7. **Multi-cloud and Hybrid Security Coverage**

   Although built natively for Azure, Defender for Cloud extends its visibility and control to non-Azure environments. Support for **Amazon Web Services (AWS)** and **Google Cloud Platform (GCP)** is provided through cloud connectors and native APIs.

   Once connected, Defender for Cloud can assess configurations, monitor compliance, and detect threats across those platforms. In addition, **on-premises workloads** can be onboarded using **Azure Arc**, allowing organizations to apply Defender protections to physical or VMware-hosted machines outside of the public cloud. This cross-environment support ensures unified security management regardless of where workloads reside.

8. **Resource Inventory and Security Visibility**

   Defender for Cloud includes a centralized resource inventory feature that aggregates all discovered assets—whether in Azure, AWS, GCP, or on-prem—into a searchable interface.

   This inventory allows security teams to quickly identify unprotected resources, view associated recommendations, and understand each resource's compliance state and risk exposure.

The inventory is filterable by subscription, resource type, Defender plan status, or compliance posture, making it easier to manage large environments and ensure no critical assets are left outside of the security perimeter.

9. **Prioritized Security Recommendations with Guided Remediation**

    Every misconfiguration or risk identified by Defender for Cloud is accompanied by a detailed recommendation. These recommendations explain the issue, the potential impact, and the required remediation steps.

    Recommendations are ranked by severity and impact to the overall secure score, allowing teams to try and address the most critical issues first.

    Many recommendations include one-click remediation options or preconfigured scripts to apply changes directly, streamlining the process of bringing environments back into compliance.

10. **Native Integration with Microsoft's Security Ecosystem**

    Defender for Cloud is tightly integrated with other Microsoft security offerings. It shares telemetry, signals, and alerts with tools such as

    - **Microsoft Sentinel** for SIEM/SOAR use cases
    - **Microsoft Defender for Endpoint** for endpoint detection and response
    - **Microsoft Defender for Identity** for identity threat protection
    - **Microsoft Entra ID (formerly Azure AD)** for identity governance and Conditional Access enforcement

    This integration enables cross-domain detection, automated enrichment of incidents, and a more cohesive security operations experience across identity, endpoint, application, and infrastructure layers.

Real-Time Threat Protection

Real-time threat protection in Microsoft Defender for Cloud is designed to deliver **continuous monitoring and intelligent detection** of active threats across cloud-based and hybrid workloads. This feature plays a central role in the platform's ability to not only observe but also **analyze and respond** to potential security incidents as they unfold.

Using a combination of **machine learning models, behavioral analytics, and Microsoft's global threat intelligence**, Defender for Cloud monitors runtime activity and event patterns across supported resources. This allows the system to detect a wide variety of threat indicators, ranging from known attack signatures to subtle anomalies that suggest emerging threats or compromised systems.

The real-time detection capabilities are constantly updated and refined through Microsoft's threat intelligence network, which gathers security signals from millions of endpoints, services, and user interactions across the Microsoft ecosystem. This includes telemetry from services like Azure, Microsoft 365, Xbox, Outlook.com, and Defender for Endpoint, all of which contribute to a continuously evolving understanding of the global threat landscape.

Threat detection in Defender for Cloud operates in several ways:

- **Behavioral Monitoring**: Tracks actions and activities within cloud resources to detect suspicious usage patterns that deviate from established baselines

- **Anomaly Detection**: Identifies deviations from normal operating behavior using unsupervised learning and statistical models

- **Signature-Based Detection**: Recognizes specific threat signatures and known attack methods, enabling fast detection of common exploits or malware

- **Threat Intelligence Correlation**: Matches resource telemetry with Microsoft's internal and external threat feeds to detect the presence of high-confidence indicators of compromise (IoCs)

When a threat or suspicious event is detected, Defender for Cloud generates a **security alert**. These alerts are enriched with metadata that includes the affected resource, type of threat, confidence level, severity, attack vector, and recommended mitigation steps. Alerts are also mapped to the **MITRE ATT&CK framework**, which helps security teams understand the attacker's tactics and progression through the kill chain.

Alerts are presented through the Defender for Cloud portal and can be integrated with other tools, such as

- **Microsoft Sentinel** for advanced investigation, correlation, and incident management
- **Microsoft Defender for Endpoint**, enabling endpoint-level visibility and response
- **SIEM/SOAR platforms** through APIs or native integrations

Additionally, security alerts in Defender for Cloud can **trigger automated workflows** via Logic Apps, allowing for real-time response actions such as isolating compromised systems, revoking access tokens, notifying incident response teams, or logging the event for compliance purposes.

Real-time threat protection is available across all supported workloads, including virtual machines, containers, databases, application services, storage accounts, and more. The breadth of coverage and intelligence behind these detections enables organizations to **proactively identify and respond to threats before they escalate**, reducing risk exposure and minimizing potential impact.

Ultimately, this capability transforms Microsoft Defender for Cloud from a passive monitoring tool into an **active participant in threat defense**, providing organizations with the visibility, context, and control they need to operate securely in the cloud.

Defender for DevOps: Security from Code to Cloud

Defender for DevOps is a specialized capability within Microsoft Defender for Cloud that brings **end-to-end security visibility and enforcement** to the DevOps lifecycle. It is designed to help organizations **embed security practices into every stage of software delivery**, from Infrastructure-as-Code (IaC) authoring to deployment, ensuring that misconfigurations, vulnerabilities, and exposed secrets are identified and mitigated before they enter production environments.

Modern application development relies heavily on continuous integration and continuous delivery (CI/CD) pipelines, infrastructure automation, and version-controlled source repositories. While these practices accelerate deployment, they also introduce new attack surfaces and operational risks. Defender for DevOps addresses this challenge by integrating directly with popular development platforms and pipelines to monitor and secure the software supply chain.

Supported platforms include

- **GitHub**
- **Azure DevOps**
- **Bitbucket** (public preview support)

Once connected, Defender for DevOps performs a series of **security scans and policy evaluations**, focusing on the following areas:

- **Infrastructure-as-Code (IaC) Analysis**: IaC templates such as ARM, Bicep, Terraform, and Kubernetes manifests are scanned to detect misconfigurations and insecure design patterns. These include overly permissive access controls, exposed ports, unencrypted storage declarations, and missing identity protection mechanisms.

- **Hardcoded Secrets Detection**: The system inspects source code and pipeline variables to identify credentials, API keys, certificates, or connection strings that have been unintentionally committed to repositories. This helps prevent secret leakage and unauthorized access.

- **Pipeline-Level Visibility**: Defender for DevOps provides a comprehensive view of pipeline activity, including deployments associated with non-compliant code or infrastructure templates. It links runtime resources back to their originating repositories and pull requests, allowing for traceability and root cause analysis.

- **Policy Enforcement**: Organizations can define and apply policies that enforce secure coding and deployment practices. These policies can block non-compliant resources from being provisioned, require approval gates for certain changes, or enforce specific configurations through CI/CD checks.

- **Remediation Guidance:** Each identified issue is accompanied by detailed recommendations for resolution. This guidance includes descriptions of the risk, impacted resources, and suggested code-level or pipeline configuration changes to correct the issue.

- **Secure Development Lifecycle Support**: By embedding security assessments into version control and CI/CD processes, Defender for DevOps supports the shift-left security model, which emphasizes the identification and mitigation of issues early in the development lifecycle.

Security findings and telemetry from Defender for DevOps are integrated directly into the Microsoft Defender for Cloud experience, allowing security operations teams and developers to collaborate using a shared dashboard. This unified visibility ensures that security risks introduced at the code level are not only detected early but also contextualized within the broader cloud environment.

In addition, security insights from Defender for DevOps can be integrated into Microsoft Sentinel or external SIEM/SOAR platforms for further analysis and incident correlation.

Compliance, Automation, and Playbooks

Compliance, automation, and playbooks are foundational capabilities within Microsoft Defender for Cloud that support organizations in **governing security policies**, **meeting regulatory requirements**, and **automating incident response workflows**. These features are essential for operationalizing security at scale and ensuring consistent behavior across complex, hybrid, and multi-cloud environments.

Regulatory Compliance Monitoring and Reporting

Microsoft Defender for Cloud includes a built-in **Regulatory Compliance Dashboard** that provides visibility into how an organization's cloud environment aligns with **industry-standard regulations and cybersecurity frameworks**. This dashboard continuously evaluates the state of cloud resources against **predefined compliance templates** and surfaces control failures, gaps, and remediation needs in a centralized location.

Supported regulatory standards include, but are not limited to

- ISO/IEC 27001
- NIST SP 800-53
- PCI DSS

- SOC TSP
- HIPAA
- GDPR
- CIS Benchmarks

Each compliance framework within Defender for Cloud is composed of a structured set of controls. These controls are automatically mapped to resource configurations and compliance requirements. For every failed control, the system provides supporting details, including the affected resources, the associated policy definitions, and guidance on how to bring the environment back into compliance.

Administrators can customize compliance initiatives by

- Selecting applicable standards based on the organization's industry or geography
- Assigning policies across management groups or subscriptions
- Extending compliance assessments to hybrid and multi-cloud resources

The compliance monitoring capability ensures that security teams can proactively **track adherence, support audit preparation, and demonstrate control effectiveness** through real-time assessments and historical reporting.

Policy Management and Governance Integration

Microsoft Defender for Cloud is deeply integrated with **Azure Policy**, enabling organizations to define and enforce custom governance rules across their cloud infrastructure. These policies dictate the configuration requirements for cloud resources and help prevent non-compliant deployments.

For example, a policy might enforce encryption on all storage accounts, block deployment of public IP addresses, or require specific tag structures for resource classification. Violations of these policies are surfaced within Defender for Cloud, accompanied by Secure Score impact and remediation recommendations.

Policies can be set to

- **Audit**: Identify non-compliant resources without blocking deployments.
- **Deny**: Actively block resource creation or modification if it does not meet the policy criteria.
- **DeployIfNotExists**: Automatically deploy or configure settings to ensure compliance.

This policy-driven approach allows security and compliance requirements to be **enforced programmatically and consistently**, reducing human error and improving governance across the environment.

Security Automation and Playbooks

To support efficient incident response and reduce manual workload, Defender for Cloud provides **security automation features** through **integrated playbooks** based on **Azure Logic Apps**. Playbooks are sets of predefined workflows that can be triggered automatically in response to security alerts or compliance events.

Each playbook is composed of a series of actions that can perform tasks such as

- Sending notifications to security teams or communication platforms
- Creating incident records in ITSM tools like ServiceNow
- Enforcing remediation actions, such as isolating a virtual machine or revoking access permissions
- Collecting diagnostics or forensics for investigation

These playbooks are **event driven**, meaning they can respond to specific alert types, severity levels, or resource tags. Organizations can choose to run playbooks manually, on a schedule, or as an automated response to specific threats and compliance violations.

Playbooks help standardize incident response procedures and ensure **consistent handling of recurring issues**, regardless of environment size or complexity. By embedding security orchestration into the monitoring platform, Defender for Cloud transforms alerts into **actionable workflows**, bridging the gap between detection and resolution.

Unified Visibility and Auditability

All actions taken through compliance assessments, policy enforcement, and automated playbooks are logged and auditable. These logs contribute to the organization's security operations metrics and provide evidence for internal governance reviews and external regulatory audits.

Pricing: Free vs. Paid Defender Plans

Before we move on to configuration and deployment, it is essential to understand how Microsoft Defender for Cloud is offered from a pricing perspective. The platform follows a flexible, modular pricing model that enables organizations to adopt foundational security features at no cost and to scale into advanced, workload-specific protections as their environment grows in complexity and risk exposure.

This model includes a Free Tier and a set of individually priced Defender plans, which collectively replace the legacy "Standard Tier" once offered under Azure Security Center.

Free Tier (Plan 0)

The Free Tier, often referred to as Plan 0, is automatically enabled for all Azure subscriptions and provides core Cloud Security Posture Management (CSPM) capabilities. It delivers visibility and recommendations across Azure-native resources, with no additional licensing or setup required.

Key features of the Free Tier include

- Continuous security assessment of Azure resources
- Secure Score for posture tracking and prioritization
- Security recommendations with remediation guidance
- Inventory of unprotected or misconfigured assets
- Basic regulatory compliance dashboard for Azure subscriptions

This tier is designed for organizations looking to establish baseline visibility and control within Azure. However, it does not include threat detection, advanced workload monitoring, or support for multi-cloud (AWS, GCP) and hybrid (on-premises) scenarios. For those use cases, Microsoft offers Defender plans that extend capabilities beyond posture evaluation.

Paid Defender Plans (Modular Protection)

Microsoft Defender for Cloud's paid functionality is no longer delivered through a single "Standard Tier." Instead, it is available as a suite of modular Defender plans, each tailored to protect a specific type of workload or service. These plans activate Cloud Workload Protection (CWP) capabilities, including

- Real-time threat detection
- Behavioral analytics and anomaly detection
- File integrity monitoring
- Vulnerability scanning
- Attack path analysis
- Integration with Microsoft Sentinel and Logic Apps for response automation

Each Defender plan is billed independently and can be enabled by subscription, per resource group, or at the individual resource level, offering fine-grained control over security coverage and cost.

Each Defender plan activates protection for a particular class of resources, as outlined in Table 5-3.

Table 5-3. Microsoft Defender plan with coverage scope and pricing model

Defender Plan	Coverage Scope	Pricing Model
Defender for Servers	Azure VMs, AWS EC2, on-prem servers via Azure Arc	Per node (per server/month)
Defender for Containers	Azure Kubernetes Service (AKS), EKS, GKE, Azure Container Registry (ACR)	Per vCore/hour
Defender for App Service	Azure-hosted applications and APIs on App Service	Per app instance/month
Defender for Storage	Blob Storage, File Shares, Data Lake Gen2	Per storage account/month
Defender for SQL	Azure SQL, SQL Server on VMs, and managed instances like AWS RDS	Per SQL resource/month
Defender for Key Vault	Azure Key Vault secrets, keys, and certificates	Per Key Vault instance/month
Defender for DNS	Azure DNS query analysis and anomaly detection	Per million DNS queries
Defender for Resource Manager	Monitoring for Azure control plane operations and anomalous deployments	Per million control plane requests
Defender for Open Source DBs	PostgreSQL, MySQL, MariaDB (in preview or GA depending on region)	Per database instance/month

All Defender plans come with a 30-day free trial, giving organizations the opportunity to test features, review alert fidelity, and evaluate fit before incurring costs.

Pricing is based on usage of metrics such as compute cores, node count, storage accounts, or queries processed. Rates can vary by Azure region and should be reviewed in the official pricing documentation or calculated using the Azure Pricing Calculator.

> **Note** Prices referenced in this section reflect Microsoft Defender for Cloud rates at the time of writing. Because pricing may evolve, always consult the official pricing page for the latest information.

For the most up-to-date pricing: https://azure.microsoft.com/en-us/pricing/details/defender-for-cloud.

Multi-cloud and Hybrid Billing

When extending protection to AWS or GCP environments via multi-cloud connectors, billing is applied based on the selected Defender plans and the number of connected resources. Similarly, hybrid servers onboarded via Azure Arc and enrolled in Defender for Servers are billed in the same way as native Azure virtual machines.

Organizations with existing Microsoft licensing agreements, such as **Microsoft Defender for Endpoint**, **Microsoft 365 E5**, or **Enterprise Agreements (EA)**, may be eligible for **discounted or bundled pricing**. Licensing relationships can influence the cost structure, especially in integrated environments.

Cost Management and Estimation Tools

To support financial planning and optimization, Microsoft provides the following tools:

- **Azure Pricing Calculator**: Offers real-time cost estimation based on selected Defender plans and regional pricing
- **Cost Analysis in Azure Portal**: Provides visibility into current and forecasted Defender for Cloud expenditures
- **Budgets and Alerts**: Enables the creation of spending thresholds to proactively manage consumption

Detailed and up-to-date pricing information is published on the official Microsoft Defender for Cloud pricing page: https://azure.microsoft.com/en-us/pricing/details/defender-for-cloud.

Configuring Microsoft Defender for Cloud for Enterprises

Let's discuss the configuration for Microsoft Defender for Cloud for enterprises.

CHAPTER 5   ENHANCED SECURITY WITH MICROSOFT DEFENDER FOR CLOUD

Enabling Free Tier

Fortunately, there is no need for any additional configuration, as the service is already integrated into your Azure subscription, covering all functionalities related to the Free edition. In a later section, I will demonstrate how to enable the Standard Tier.

While there are a couple of different ways to navigate around in the Azure portal, the "easiest" path would be this one.

1. From the **Azure portal**, select **More Services** as shown in Figure 5-2.

Figure 5-2. *Azure services from the Azure portal*

2. From the list of services, search for **defender**. This brings up a list of all Azure services with the word defender in its name. Here, notice **Microsoft Defender for Cloud** as shown in Figure 5-3.

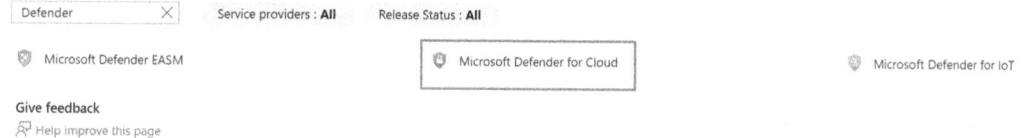

Figure 5-3. *Microsoft Defender for Cloud after searching in Azure portal*

3. If you want to add **Microsoft Defender for Cloud** to your list of favorites in the **Azure portal**, click the star icon.

4. Click **Microsoft Defender for Cloud** to open its blade in the **Azure portal** as shown in Figure 5-4.

147

CHAPTER 5   ENHANCED SECURITY WITH MICROSOFT DEFENDER FOR CLOUD

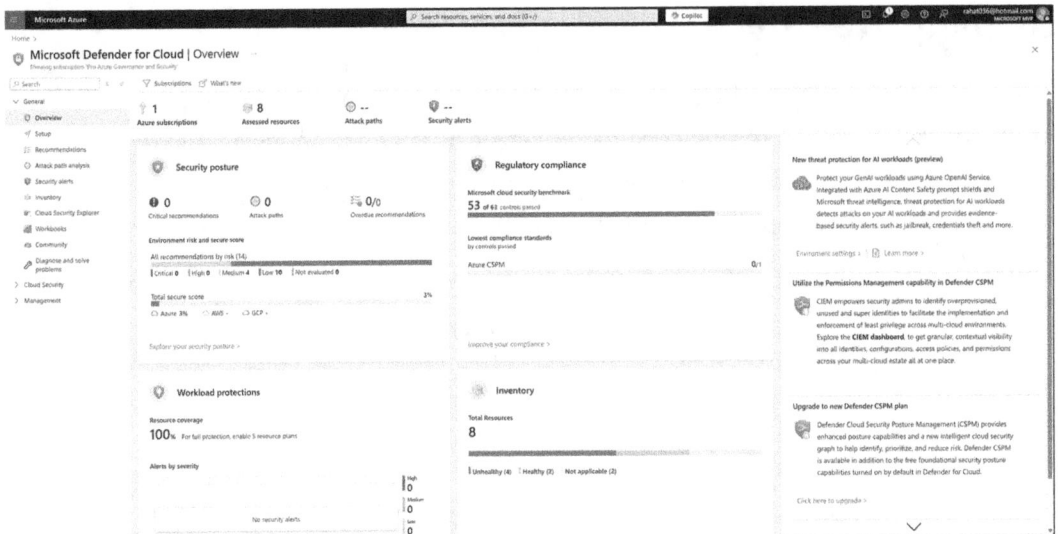

Figure 5-4. Overview page of Microsoft Defender for Cloud

Note that the content in the **Overview** pane may be different from what's shown here, depending on what you have running within your Azure subscription. If you are first enabling **Microsoft Defender for Cloud** before any other Azure resource, the Overview pane is empty. If you already have running resources, **Microsoft Defender for Cloud** reports on the security state of these resources.

Managing Microsoft Defender for Cloud Using PowerShell

In the context where you have multiple subscriptions to manage, it might be interesting to know **Microsoft Defender for Cloud** now offers management capabilities from PowerShell.

From a Microsoft Defender for Cloud perspective, the steps are mostly similar to the portal scenario and involve the following:

1. Install the latest version of PowerShell, opening the PowerShell shell with administrative rights as shown in Figure 5-5.

    ```
    install-module -name Az –allowclobber
    ```

CHAPTER 5   ENHANCED SECURITY WITH MICROSOFT DEFENDER FOR CLOUD

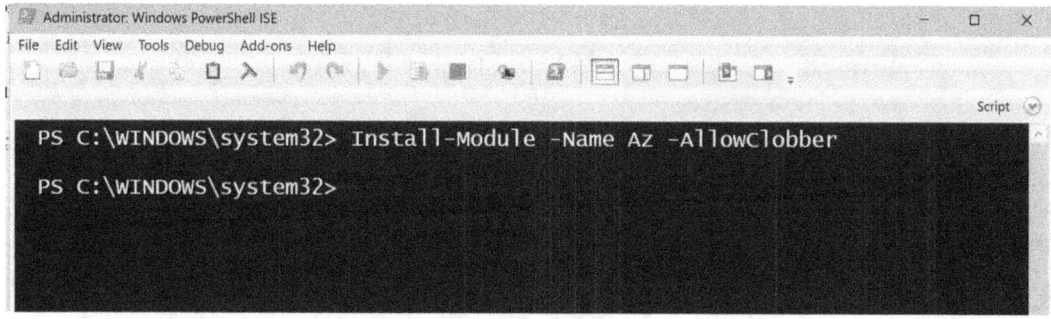

Figure 5-5. *Installing latest PowerShell using command prompt*

2. As we are running version 5.7.0 on our machine, which was recently updated with version 6.13.2, we are advised to install the latest version, by running the following cmdlet:

   `Install-module Az -allowclobber –Force`

3. The AzureRM.Security module is offered through PowerShellGet, so we have to make sure this is running in the latest available edition too.

   `Update-Module -Name PowerShellGet`

4. Next, we need to install AzureRM.Profile, requiring a specific version 5.8.4. (Again, this is preview and might have changed by the time that you read this.)

   `install-module -Name azurerm.profile -requiredversion 5.8.4`

5. Now, we can install the actual `Az.Security` module, by executing the following command:

   `Install-Module -Name az.security`

6. Once the module is installed, load it by firing off the import-cmdlet:

   `Import-Module az.security`

7. Now, log on to your Azure subscription, with an account that has administrative access (RBAC) to Microsoft Defender for Coud as shown in Figure 5-6.

```
Connect-AzAccount
```

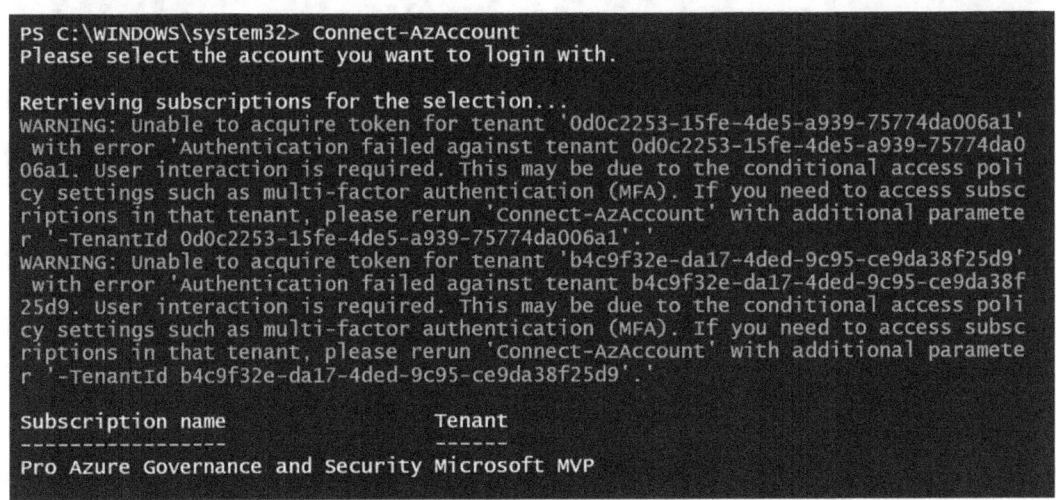

Figure 5-6. *Connecting Azure subscription using PowerShell*

8. Validate that you can read any information by running the following cmdlet as shown in Figure 5-7.

```
Get-AzSecurityLocation
```

Figure 5-7. *Validating Azure connection by checking the location cmdlet*

For your information, you can find all the available cmdlets from the following Microsoft documentation: https://learn.microsoft.com/en-us/powershell/module/az.security/.

CHAPTER 5   ENHANCED SECURITY WITH MICROSOFT DEFENDER FOR CLOUD

Enabling Paid Defender Plans

Once an organization decides to move beyond the Free Tier and adopt deeper protection through Microsoft Defender for Cloud, the next step is to enable the appropriate Defender plans. Unlike a single-tier upgrade, Defender for Cloud uses a modular approach, allowing you to selectively enable advanced protection for specific workloads based on your architecture and business priorities.

This flexibility ensures that you're only paying for what you truly need, but it also means enabling protection is a more deliberate and scoped action. Defender plans can be turned on at the subscription, management group, resource group, or individual resource level, giving security teams complete control over coverage.

Let's walk through the process:

1. In the Azure portal, select Microsoft Defender for Cloud from the favorites section or from the search bar.

2. Click Environment Settings. Click the three dots (…) of the subscriptions and click Edit Settings as shown in Figure 5-8.

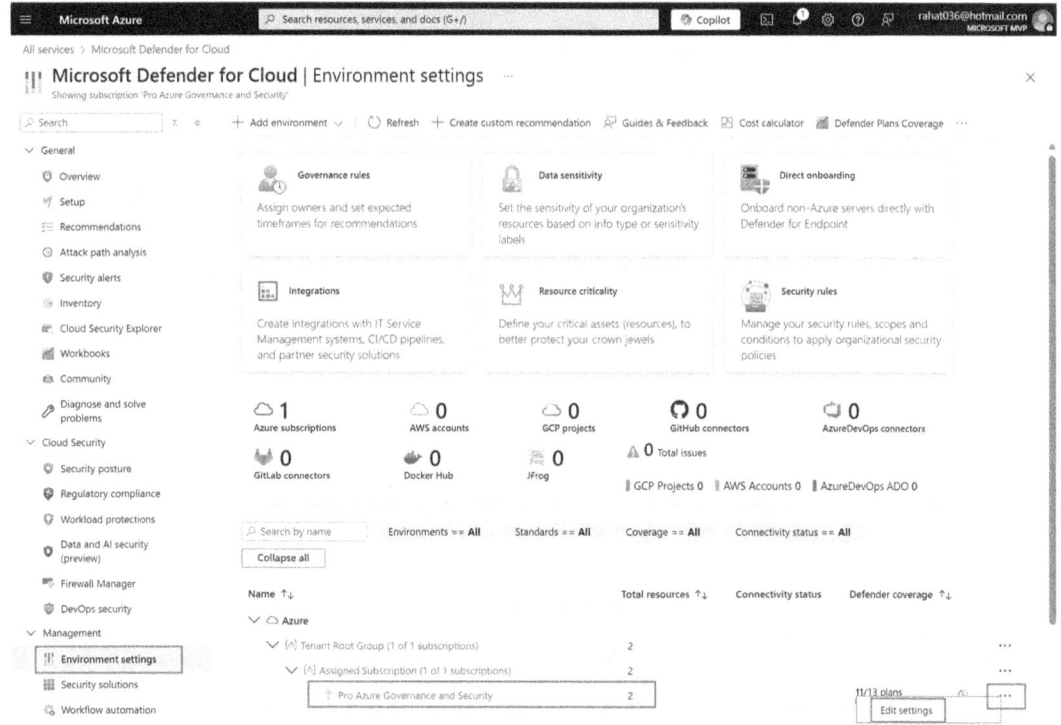

Figure 5-8. *Edit environment settings from Microsoft Defender for Cloud*

CHAPTER 5   ENHANCED SECURITY WITH MICROSOFT DEFENDER FOR CLOUD

3. After clicking Edit Settings, you can see the page shown in Figure 5-9.

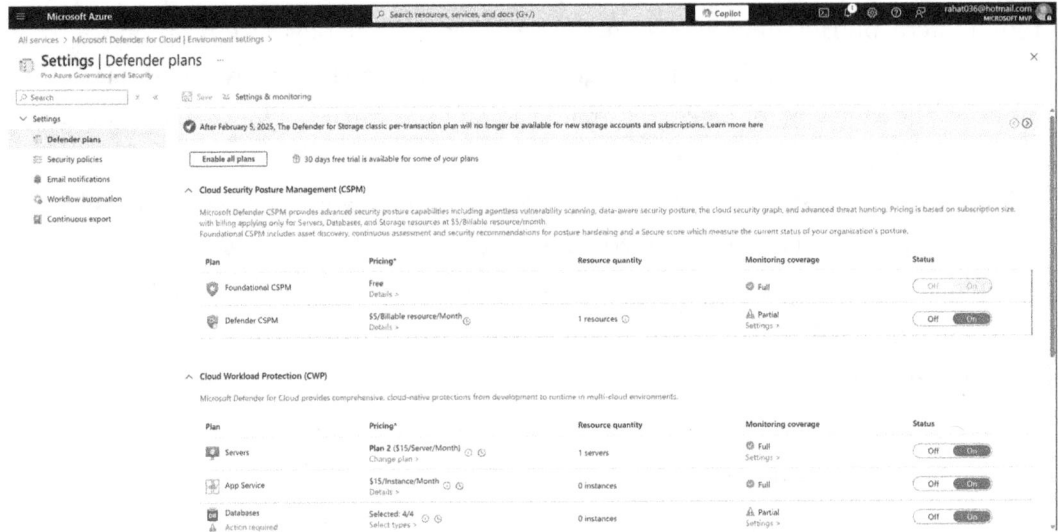

Figure 5-9. *Defender for Cloud plan settings page*

4. You can see the Defender Plan page by default. From here, you can see two sections.

   a. **Cloud Security Posture Management (CSPM)**: This section covers the posture and governance side of cloud security, helping organizations continuously assess and strengthen their security configurations across cloud environments. There are two plan options under CSPM:

      - **Foundational CSPM**: This plan is enabled by default and free for all users. It provides essential security posture capabilities, including Secure Score, regulatory compliance tracking, and basic recommendations across Azure, AWS, and GCP. (Note: This is the Free Tier, what we discussed starting to this section.)

      - **Defender CSPM**: This is a premium posture management plan, priced at $5 per billable resource per month. It unlocks advanced features such as

- Agentless vulnerability assessments
- Context-aware cloud security graph
- Data-aware risk prioritization
- Advanced threat hunting with integrated analytics
- Attack path analysis for multistep risk visualization

Defender CSPM is ideal for organizations that need proactive insights, enriched context, and deeper posture visibility across complex multi-cloud environments.

b. **Cloud Workload Protection (CWP)**: The second section focuses on protecting specific workloads, from development to runtime, using threat detection, behavioral analysis, and integrated security controls across multi-cloud and hybrid resources. This includes modular Defender plans for key workloads such as

- Servers (Azure, AWS, on-prem via Arc)
- Containers and Kubernetes clusters
- Storage accounts
- SQL databases and open source databases
- App Services
- Key Vault
- DNS and Resource Manager activity

Each plan can be enabled individually, allowing you to align security investments with actual workloads and risk exposure. These plans are billed by per resource/month or per usage metric, depending on the workload type.

CHAPTER 5 ENHANCED SECURITY WITH MICROSOFT DEFENDER FOR CLOUD

5. To enable Defender CSPM plan, toggle on the status for Defender CSPM as shown in Figure 5-10.

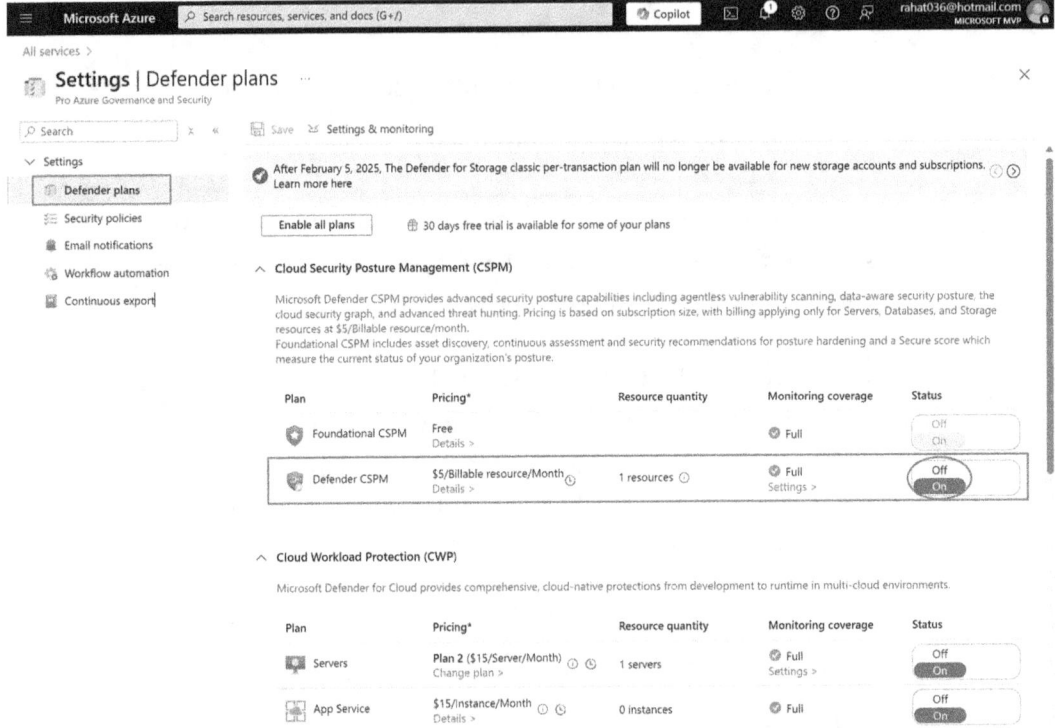

Figure 5-10. *Changing the defender plan status from Defender plan settings*

When you toggle on the status, Defender CSPM will start a 30-day trial. In my case, I already have the trial, so I cannot show it here.

6. If you want to enable specific Defender plan, you can extend the Cloud Workload Protection (CWP), choose the desire Defender plan(s), and toggle it on as shown in Figure 5-11. Please note that each Defender plan includes a **30-day free trial**, which allows you to evaluate its performance, detection quality, and operational impact before incurring charges. During the trial, you receive full functionality of the plan. Review the estimated pricing impact shown in the interface and save for applying the changes.

CHAPTER 5   ENHANCED SECURITY WITH MICROSOFT DEFENDER FOR CLOUD

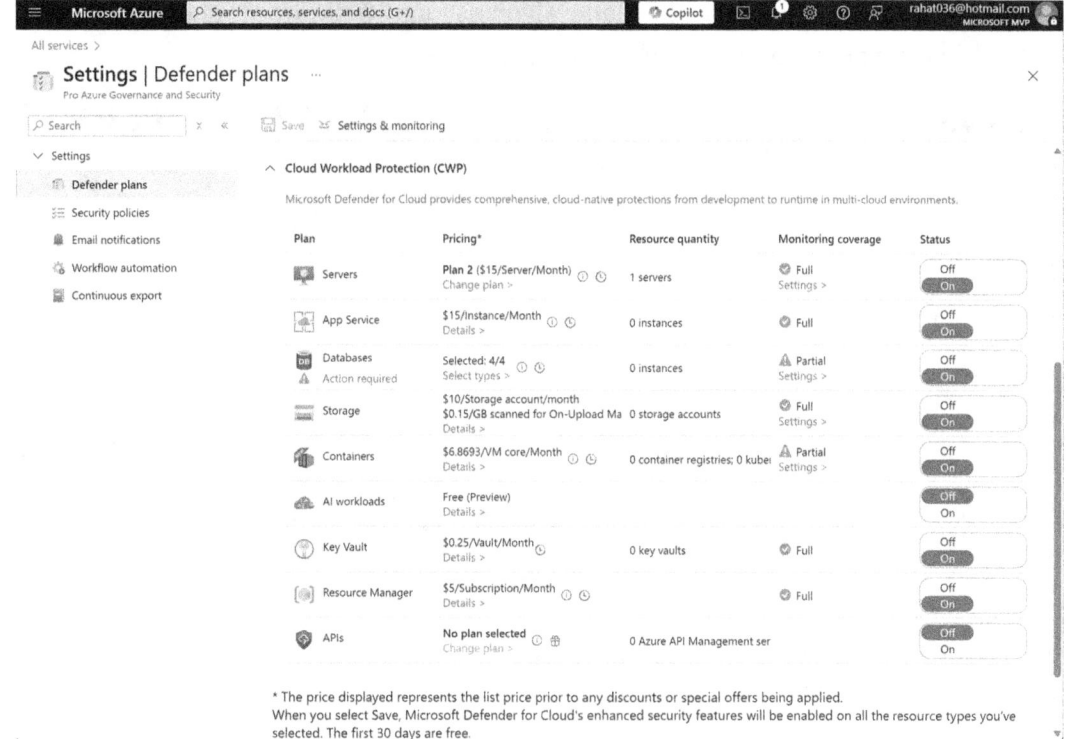

Figure 5-11. Extending the CWP under specific Defender plan

You can find the updated pricing for CWP plans from here: https://azure.microsoft.com/en-us/pricing/details/defender-for-cloud/.

7. To test the plans, you can enable all plans for a 30-day free trial by clicking Enable all plans as shown in Figure 5-12.

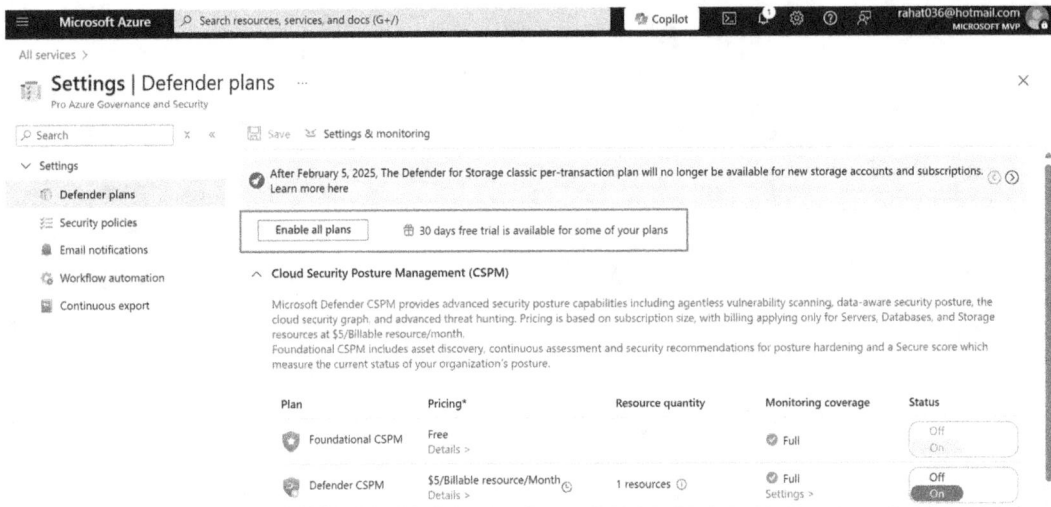

Figure 5-12. Enabling trial Defender plans

Switching Between Editions

In the previous model under Azure Security Center (ASC), organizations had the flexibility to switch between two editions: Free and Standard. This structure allowed users to either enable the full suite of security features (Standard edition) or fall back to basic visibility and recommendations (Free edition) at the subscription level.

However, Microsoft Defender for Cloud has moved away from this edition-based model and now adopts a modular, plan-driven approach. While a foundational level of security—referred to as Foundational CSPM—is always enabled and free of charge, advanced capabilities are now delivered through individual Defender plans tailored to specific workloads such as servers, containers, storage, and databases. These plans can be enabled or disabled independently at any time and at various scopes, including subscription, resource group, or individual resource level.

Although it is no longer possible to revert entirely to a "Free" or "Standard" edition as in ASC, organizations can effectively return to a foundational, no-cost state by disabling all paid Defender plans, maintaining baseline security posture management while opting out of advanced protections. This change reflects Microsoft's shift toward greater flexibility, allowing organizations to align security investments with actual workload usage and risk exposure.

Collecting Data in Microsoft Defender for Cloud

Before Microsoft Defender for Cloud can analyze, assess, and protect your resources, it must first collect relevant security data from your environment. Data collection is foundational to how Defender for Cloud operates—enabling continuous monitoring, threat detection, security recommendations, and compliance insights. The type and depth of data collected depends on which Defender plans are enabled, and the nature of the resources being protected. This includes telemetry from virtual machines, platform logs from Azure resources, vulnerability scan results, configuration metadata, and user activity across the control plane. Understanding how Defender for Cloud collects data is essential for configuring the platform effectively, managing privacy and compliance, and ensuring full visibility into your security posture across hybrid and multi-cloud environments.

Collecting Data from Azure and Non-Azure Virtual Machines

Microsoft Defender for Cloud supports data collection from both Azure-native virtual machines and non-Azure machines running in on-premises environments or other clouds like AWS and GCP. The data collected from these machines plays a critical role in enabling Defender for Cloud to assess configuration health, detect threats, monitor vulnerability exposure, and enforce security policies. However, the method of onboarding and data collection differs slightly based on where the machine is hosted.

Azure Virtual Machines

For virtual machines hosted in Azure, Defender for Cloud supports agent-based and agentless data collection, depending on the level of protection enabled.

- **Agentless Scanning**: If only Defender for Servers Plan 1 is enabled, or Defender CSPM is used with supported configurations, agentless scanning may be applied to retrieve operating system metadata, installed applications, open ports, and known vulnerabilities.

- **Agent-Based Collection**: When enabling Defender for Servers Plan 2, Microsoft recommends deploying the Log Analytics agent (deprecated), or the newer Azure Monitor Agent (AMA), for full security monitoring capabilities. This agent collects richer telemetry, including

- Security event logs
- Windows/Linux system logs
- File integrity monitoring (FIM)
- Just-in-time VM access data
- Adaptive application controls
- Behavioral and process activity for threat detection

These agents are automatically installed when enabling Defender for Servers through the Azure portal, provided the necessary permissions and extension policies are in place. Data collected from Azure VMs is securely sent to a connected Log Analytics workspace, where it's processed by Defender for Cloud.

Non-Azure Virtual Machines (Hybrid or Multi-cloud)

To collect data from machines hosted outside Azure, including on-premises servers, AWS EC2 instances, and GCP virtual machine, organizations must onboard them using Azure Arc. Azure Arc extends Azure's management and security capabilities to non-Azure resources.

Once the virtual machine is connected to Azure via Arc, Defender for Cloud treats it similarly to an Azure VM. To enable full data collection

1. Enable Azure Arc on the non-Azure machine using the Azure-connected machine agent.

2. Install Azure Monitor Agent (AMA) or Log Analytics agent, depending on your configuration and the selected Defender plan.

3. Enable Defender for Servers for the Arc-connected resource to start data ingestion.

To learn more about onboarding on-premises, AWS, or GCP VM using Azure Arc, you can check the official Microsoft documentation here: https://learn.microsoft.com/en-us/azure/azure-arc/servers/overview.

Advanced Threat Protection and Detection

Advanced cloud defense continues to be one of the strongest areas where Microsoft Defender for Cloud proves its value. It offers a tightly integrated set of powerful protections designed to actively guard your cloud workloads—especially Internet-facing resources, which are against modern and emerging threats. Whether you're securing virtual machines, databases, or containerized workloads, Defender for Cloud brings built-in intelligence and automation to detect attacks early, reduce exposure, and help you respond with confidence. These features aren't just checkboxes—they're practical, actionable defenses that work in real-world enterprise environments.

Protection and security at this level is offered by three different services:

- **Adaptive Application Controls**: Adaptive Application Controls was a feature that built upon the principles of Windows AppLocker, enabling administrators to define which applications were allowed to run on specific virtual machines. This approach helped block unauthorized software and malicious executables. However, as of August 2024, Adaptive Application Controls has been fully retired and is no longer available within Defender for Cloud. Organizations relying on this capability are now encouraged to transition to modern endpoint protection platforms or configuration management tools to maintain similar levels of application control.

- **Just-in-Time VM Access**: Just-in-Time (JIT) VM access remains a valid and effective feature within Microsoft Defender for Cloud. It operates by managing inbound access rules at the network level using a combination of Azure role-based access control (RBAC), network security groups (NSGs), and time-bound permissions. JIT Access significantly reduces the attack surface of Internet-exposed virtual machines by ensuring that even authorized administrative access is only permitted for a limited duration and under explicit request conditions.

- **File Integrity Monitoring**: File Integrity Monitoring (FIM) continues to play a crucial role in detecting unauthorized changes to operating system files, system registries, and application binaries. Defender for Cloud now relies on the Microsoft Defender for Endpoint agent to collect FIM data, phasing out the older Log Analytics agent as part of Microsoft's move toward a unified monitoring platform. FIM helps surface indicators of compromise by tracking modifications to critical components and flagging potentially malicious behavior. To learn more about FIM, refer to the official Microsoft documentation: `https://learn.microsoft.com/en-us/azure/defender-for-cloud/file-integrity-monitoring-overview`.

Just-in-Time VM Access

Configuring Just-in-Time (JIT) VM access isn't complicated at all. In fact, after enabling it for a number of high-risk, production-grade systems across different customer environments, the real question becomes this: Why isn't this turned on by default for every Internet-facing VM? Microsoft Defender for Cloud does an excellent job of guiding you toward this best practice. The moment you deploy a virtual machine that allows direct remote access (like RDP or SSH) from the Internet, Defender for Cloud automatically flags it and recommends enabling JIT access—often through a visible security warning in the Azure portal itself.

What makes the experience even more seamless is that you don't need to manually define complex network security rules before enabling it. Defender for Cloud intelligently scans your environment and classifies your VMs into three states:

- **Configured**: These are virtual machines that already have JIT access enabled. They are protected with a combination of Azure Network Security Groups (NSGs), role-based access control (RBAC), and time-limited access policies that lock down exposed management ports.

- **Recommended**: This group includes VMs that Defender for Cloud has detected with open management ports to the Internet, and for which enabling JIT would significantly reduce exposure. It's essentially a smart suggestion engine flagging high-risk machines.

- **No Recommendation**: These are virtual machines where Defender for Cloud cannot determine whether JIT access is applicable. This might be due to the VM being turned off, lacking NSG rules, or having been deployed through the older Azure Classic model. In such cases, Defender has limited visibility or control, and you'll need to assess manually.

Let's walk through the actual configuration steps for enabling Just-in-Time (JIT) VM access on a typical scenario—a standard Azure virtual machine with direct RDP access exposed to the Internet. This kind of setup is exactly what Microsoft Defender for Cloud identifies as a security risk and immediately flags as a candidate for JIT access. In fact, such a configuration is the perfect "trigger" for Defender to recommend enabling JIT as part of its built-in security recommendations. You don't have to go looking for it — the portal practically tells you that now is the time to secure that management port.

To successfully configure and use Just-in-Time (JIT) VM access in Microsoft Defender for Cloud, ensure the following prerequisites are met:

- **Microsoft Defender for Servers Plan 2** must be enabled at the subscription level. This plan includes access to JIT functionality as part of its workload protection features.

- **Supported virtual machines include**

  - Azure VMs deployed using the Azure Resource Manager (ARM) model

  - Azure VMs protected by Azure Firewalls deployed in the same virtual network as the VM

  - AWS EC2 instances, provided they are connected to Microsoft Defender for Cloud through the multi-cloud connector (currently in preview)

- **Unsupported Virtual Machines**

  - VMs deployed using the classic deployment model (pre-ARM)

  - VMs protected by Azure Firewalls managed through Azure Firewall Manager

- **AWS Integration**: To enable JIT access on AWS VMs, your AWS account must be connected to Defender for Cloud, and the instances must be fully onboarded.

- **Policy Naming Constraint**: The combined length of the JIT policy name and the VM name must not exceed 56 characters. Exceeding this limit will result in deployment failure.

CHAPTER 5   ENHANCED SECURITY WITH MICROSOFT DEFENDER FOR CLOUD

- **Permissions Requirements**

    - Users need either the Reader or Security Reader role to view JIT status and parameters.

    - For custom roles, assign only the necessary permissions. Microsoft provides a script (Set-JitLeastPrivilegedRole) to create a least-privileged role that allows users to request access without elevated rights. You can find it here: https://github.com/Azure/Microsoft-Defender-for-Cloud/tree/main/Powershell%20scripts/JIT%20Scripts/JIT%20Custom%20Role.

When Defender for Cloud detects a vulnerability, such as exposed management ports, a security alert will appear—either directly on the virtual machine blade or within the "Workload Protections" section. Enabling Just-in-Time (JIT) VM access from there is straightforward. Defender intelligently highlights high-risk ports like TCP 3389 (RDP) and TCP 22 (SSH), prefilling them in the configuration. You simply review the suggested ports, specify who can request access, and set the duration for access. In just a few clicks, you've added a powerful layer of time-based access control—without writing scripts, modifying firewalls, or making assumptions. Let's start with a demo!

1. From Microsoft Defender for Cloud Center, select Workload Protections as shown in Figure 5-13.

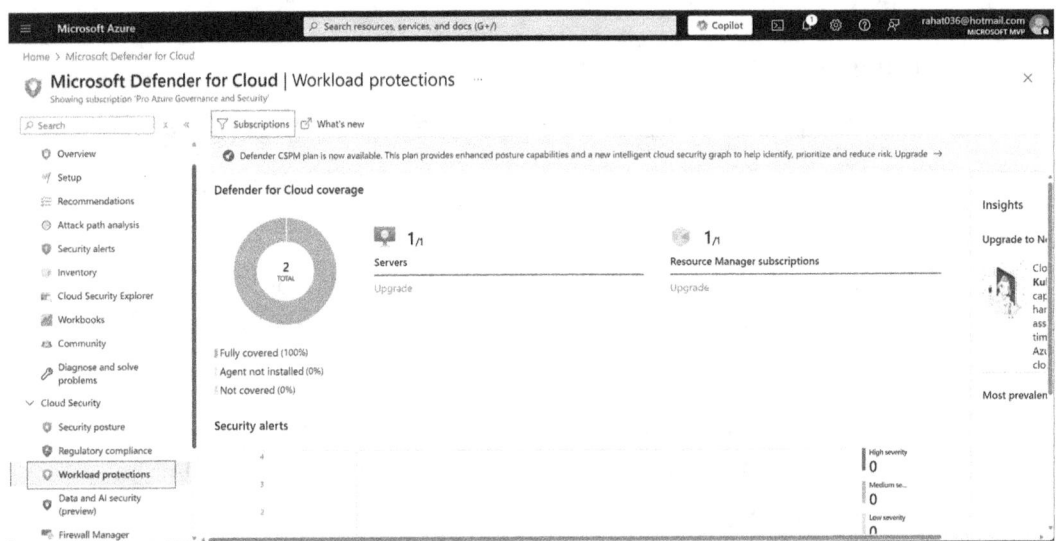

Figure 5-13. Workload Protections dashboard of Microsoft Defender for Cloud

CHAPTER 5 ENHANCED SECURITY WITH MICROSOFT DEFENDER FOR CLOUD

2. Under Advanced protection section, choose Just-in-time VM access as shown in Figure 5-14.

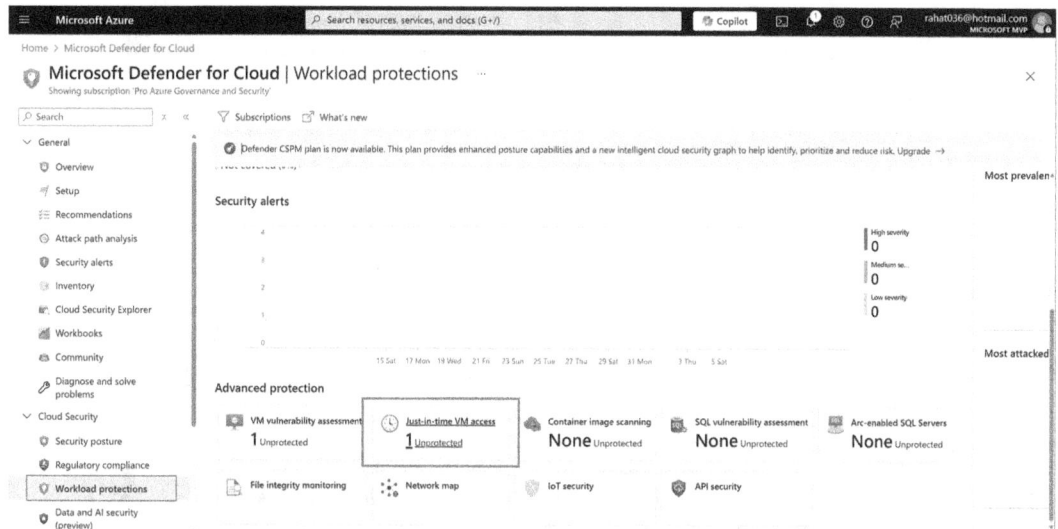

Figure 5-14. Just-in-time VM access option in Microsoft Defender for Cloud

3. To enable JIT VM access, navigate to the Not Configured option under the Virtual Machines section and choose the VM you wish to protect as shown in Figure 5-15.

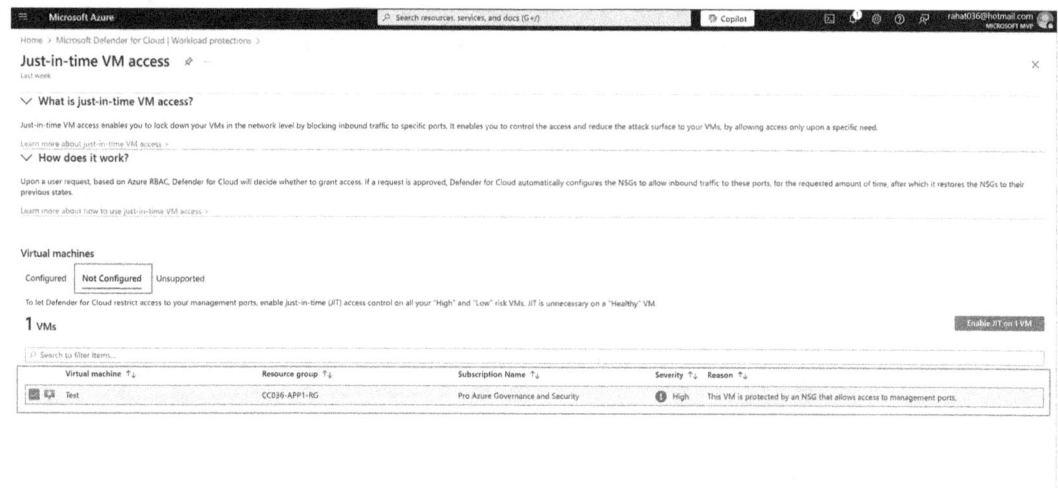

Figure 5-15. Selecting VM to enable JIT protection

163

CHAPTER 5   ENHANCED SECURITY WITH MICROSOFT DEFENDER FOR CLOUD

4. Click Enable JIT on * VM as shown in Figure 5-16.

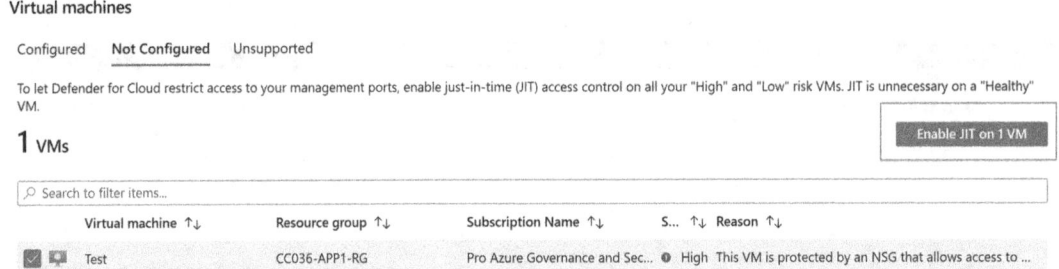

Figure 5-16. Enabling JIT for the selected VM

5. A configuration pane will display recommended ports (e.g., 22 for SSH, 3389 for RDP) as shown in Figure 5-17.

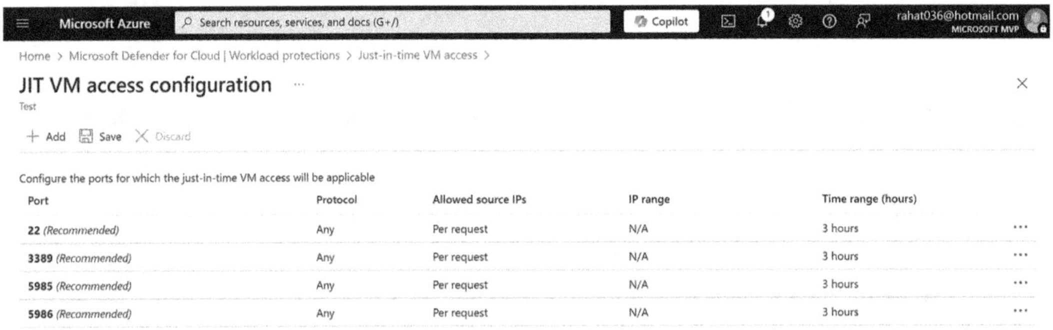

Figure 5-17. Checking and configuring the recommended ports

Note   You can remove port 22 (SSH) by clicking the ellipsis (…). SSH is typically used on a Linux machine, not on Windows, so it can be removed. You can also add any custom port if you need.

---

6. For each port, specify

    a. **Protocol:** TCP/UDP

    b. **Allowed Source IPs:** Define IP ranges permitted to access the VM.

    c. **Maximum Request Time:** Set the duration for which the port remains open.

164

CHAPTER 5   ENHANCED SECURITY WITH MICROSOFT DEFENDER FOR CLOUD

After configuring, select **Save** to apply the settings.

7. To initiate the access request, Go to **Defender for Cloud ➤ Workload protection ➤ Just-in-time VM access**, click *Configured*, and select the VM as shown in Figure 5-18.

Figure 5-18. *Initiating access request from the VM configuration*

8. Click **Request Access**.

9. Next, select the port you wish to open as shown in Figure 5-19.

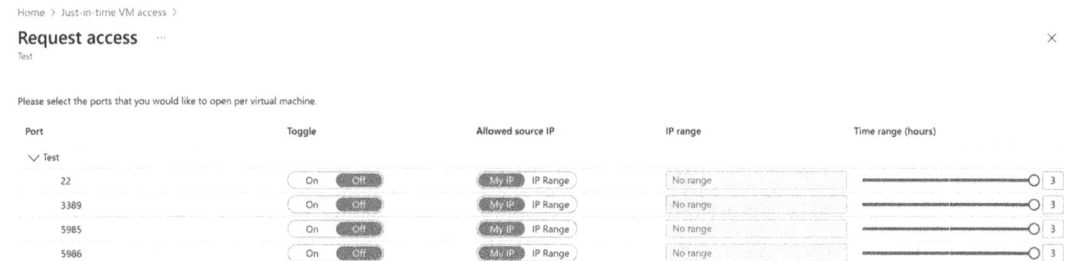

Figure 5-19. *Selecting the port to open*

10. Define the IP addresses from which the VM will be accessed. Also, set the access duration. Toggle the service on.

11. Click Open ports to activate the access request.

165

> **Note** If a user who requests access is behind a proxy, you can enter the IP address range of the proxy.

To audit the JIT access activity, Go to **Defender for Cloud** ➤ **Workload protection** ➤ **Just-in-time VM access**, click **Configured**, and select the VM. Click the ellipsis (…) and choose Activity Log to review access requests and actions taken. Refer to Figure 5-20.

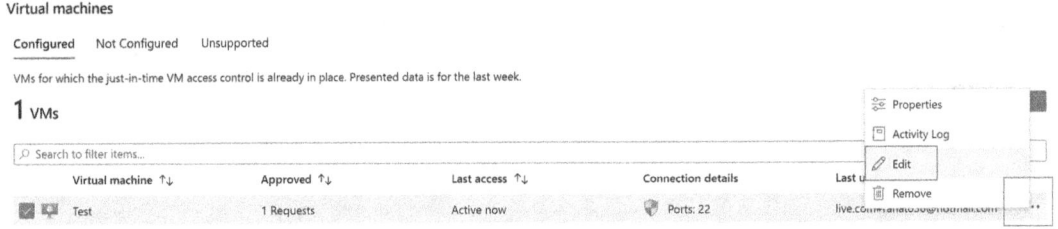

Figure 5-20. *Auditing the JIT access activity by checking activity log*

If you want to know more about JIT VM access, or other ways to work with JIT VM access, I strongly suggest to follow the official Microsoft documentation: https://learn.microsoft.com/en-us/azure/defender-for-cloud/just-in-time-access-usage.

File Integrity Monitoring

Configuring File Integrity Monitoring (FIM) is one of those tasks that feels like it should already be part of every security baseline—especially when you're dealing with production systems or critical infrastructure. After setting it up across several sensitive environments, it's honestly surprising that FIM isn't enabled by default for all supported servers. Fortunately, Microsoft Defender for Cloud makes it easy to discover this gap and helps you close it quickly. As soon as Defender is enabled for your environment, it assesses the machines under its protection and highlights those that would benefit from FIM—usually your domain controllers, application servers, or any system hosting core configuration files. With just a few clicks, you can enable monitoring for key system files and registry paths, allowing you to detect unauthorized changes that could signal tampering, privilege escalation, or malware activity. It's a lightweight addition with a heavy impact, and once in place, it becomes one of the most valuable early-warning systems in your security toolkit.

Prerequisites for File Integrity Monitoring (FIM)

To successfully enable File Integrity Monitoring (FIM) within Microsoft Defender for Cloud, the following conditions and configurations must be in place:

- **Microsoft Defender for Servers Plan 2** must be enabled on the subscription. FIM is included as a capability under Plan 2 and is not available under the Free Tier or Plan 1.

- **Supported operating systems**

    - Windows Server (2012 R2 and later)

    - Linux distributions such as Ubuntu, Debian, CentOS, Red Hat Enterprise Linux, and SUSE (specific versions only) (It's important to verify current supported distributions on Microsoft official documentation: https://learn.microsoft.com/en-us/azure/defender-for-cloud/file-integrity-monitoring-enable-defender-endpoint.)

- **Microsoft Defender for Endpoint (MDE)** must be deployed on the VM. FIM now leverages the MDE sensor to collect file integrity telemetry. Legacy methods using the Log Analytics (MMA) agent are deprecated and will be retired in November 2024.

- **Microsoft Monitoring Agent (MMA)/Log Analytics agent should not be used.** If MMA is still installed, it's recommended to migrate to the modern MDE-based solution, as the older data pipeline is no longer being updated.

- **Devices must be onboarded to Microsoft Defender for Endpoint.** For FIM to function, the VM must appear in the MDE device inventory and have reporting connectivity established.

- **File Integrity rules must be configured manually.** Although Defender for Cloud enables the core FIM capability, you must define which files, folders, or registry keys are to be monitored. This is done via the MDE console under Device Configuration ➤ File Integrity Monitoring.

- **Permissions required**
  - To view or manage FIM settings, users typically need either
  - **Security Reader** or **Security Admin** role in Azure
  - Or corresponding **Microsoft 365 Defender roles** with access to the MDE configuration portal

To learn more about FIM, you can read the official Microsoft documentation from here: https://docs.azure.cn/en-us/defender-for-cloud/file-integrity-monitoring-overview.

Threat Detection and Response

One of the most valuable and powerful components of Microsoft Defender for Cloud is its ability to deliver real-time threat detection across your cloud and hybrid environments. Whether you're running Windows or Linux workloads, hosted in Azure, AWS, GCP, or even on-premises via Azure Arc, Defender for Cloud is built to detect malicious activity that other tools may overlook.

Let's face it: every system today is a potential target. It doesn't matter whether it's Internet-facing or not. Modern cyberattacks are often subtle, multi-stage, and persistent. Many high-profile incidents in recent years—ranging from global enterprises to government institutions—have demonstrated how attackers can dwell inside a network undetected for weeks or months, often executing malicious payloads long after their initial infiltration. Traditional perimeter defenses often fail to catch these threats. Even when they do, they can create so much noise that true positives get lost in the alert fatigue.

That's where Defender for Cloud brings tangible value. Leveraging Microsoft's global threat intelligence, advanced machine learning models, and the Microsoft Threat Intelligence Center (MSTIC), it cuts through the noise and highlights what matters most. It doesn't just tell you that something might be wrong, it tells you *what, where, why*, and *how to respond*, backed by real-time analysis.

One of the core engines behind this is the Microsoft Security Graph, now known as Microsoft Threat Intelligence. This massive intelligence network aggregates signals from Microsoft's cloud ecosystem, including services like Microsoft 365, Outlook.com, Azure, Xbox, and more. These platforms continuously report on IP addresses, malicious domains, attack signatures, and emerging threat vectors. When Defender for Cloud sees a workload in your environment interacting with one of these known malicious sources, it can raise an immediate, high-confidence alert—*even before any payload is dropped.*

But threat detection doesn't stop at IP reputation. Defender for Cloud also performs deep traffic analysis of your virtual machines, containers, and PaaS workloads. It monitors runtime behaviors, access patterns, process execution, and network connections to detect anomalies and behavioral indicators of compromise. These insights are enriched through integrations with Microsoft Defender for Endpoint, Defender for Identity, and Microsoft Sentinel, allowing Defender for Cloud to participate in broader cross-domain threat correlation.

Under the hood, Microsoft Defender for Cloud leverages multiple detection engines, including

- Behavioral analytics that monitor processes, users, and system interactions
- Machine learning models trained in vast datasets of threat activity
- Statistical profiling to identify outliers or suspicious changes in usage patterns
- Malicious behavior analytics using heuristics and signature matching
- Threat intelligence feeds from Microsoft Threat Intelligence, MSTIC, and third-party partners
- Vulnerability signals from Defender Vulnerability Management and integrated scanners

These capabilities work together to detect a wide spectrum of attack types—from brute-force login attempts and port scanning to lateral movement, privilege escalation, and zero-day exploits.

Because the cloud threat landscape is dynamic, Defender for Cloud's detection mechanisms are constantly evolving. Microsoft's global security researchers regularly update detection rules, machine learning models, and behavioral baselines to adapt to the latest techniques used by adversaries.

While the full inner workings of Defender for Cloud's threat detection architecture are complex and not publicly documented in their entirety (for obvious security reasons), Microsoft provides extensive guidance and transparency around the categories of threats it detects. You can find more technical information at the official Microsoft Learn documentation: https://learn.microsoft.com/en-us/azure/defender-for-cloud/alerts-overview.

Simulating Attacks

One of the most common challenges in the world of threat protection isn't the lack of tools—it's the lack of validation. How do you know if your detection systems are truly working? How can you be confident that your security alerts are more than just theoretical? Waiting for a real attack to occur just to test your system is clearly not a good strategy. That's where controlled attack simulation becomes an essential part of your security posture validation process.

Simulated attacks serve two critical purposes: they test the detection capabilities of Microsoft Defender for Cloud, and they help verify that response processes—alerts, escalations, and automated workflows—are actually being triggered when expected. Defender for Cloud is built to recognize a wide range of threat behaviors, but without a way to trigger those behaviors safely, most organizations are left guessing whether their protection is fully operational.

To assist in this area, security professionals often rely on free, community-supported tools to simulate malicious activity in a safe and non-destructive manner. One such tool is the APT Simulator developed by Nextron Systems. Available on GitHub, APT Simulator is a lightweight framework designed to mimic tactics used in real-world Advanced Persistent Threat (APT) scenarios. Rather than exploiting actual vulnerabilities, it simulates post-compromise behaviors—like creating suspicious scheduled tasks, dropping known malware signatures, or mimicking lateral movement attempts—that trigger threat detection systems without causing harm to the underlying system.

You can find and download APT Simulator directly from its GitHub releases page: https://github.com/NextronSystems/APTSimulator/releases.

And review how it works here: https://github.com/NextronSystems/APTSimulator#advanced-solutions.

When using a tool like this, it's important to ensure it is run within a controlled and isolated test environment—ideally on a dedicated virtual machine already enrolled in Defender for Servers and connected to Log Analytics or Microsoft Sentinel. This ensures that all telemetry and alerts are captured without risking production systems or data.

Simulations like this are not just academic exercises. They help teams build confidence, validate coverage, and fine-tune alerting thresholds to reduce false positives while staying sensitive to real threats. More importantly, they expose any gaps in visibility, response automation, or incident workflows—before an actual adversary does.

Microsoft Defender for Cloud Threat Intelligence Report

Microsoft Defender for Cloud's threat detection capabilities have evolved far beyond isolated alerts. Today, when malicious activity is detected in your environment, it is surfaced not only through conventional real-time security alerts but also through comprehensive, campaign-oriented insights known as the Microsoft Defender for Cloud Threat Intelligence Report. This advanced capability combines environment-specific telemetry with Microsoft's global threat intelligence, enabling a broader and more actionable understanding of how attacker infrastructure and activity patterns intersect with your cloud workloads.

At its core, Defender for Cloud continuously monitors activity across your environment—spanning Azure, hybrid (via Azure Arc), and multi-cloud workloads (AWS and GCP)—and applies a blend of machine learning, behavior analytics, heuristics, and Microsoft Threat Intelligence correlation to detect and prioritize threats. Signals are collected from a wide range of sources, including the Azure Monitor Agent (AMA), activity logs, network flows, container runtime telemetry, and identity signals. When malicious behavior or known indicators of compromise (IoCs) are observed, Defender for Cloud generates an alert and begins associating it with known attack campaigns.

The Threat Intelligence Report aggregates multiple related detections, behaviors, and indicators into a cohesive threat narrative. Instead of treating each alert as an isolated event, Defender for Cloud contextualizes them as part of a broader attack lifecycle. These reports include

- **Campaign Overview**: The nature of the campaign, attack objectives, observed tactics, and geography of origin.

- **Threat Actor Infrastructure**: Microsoft's global threat sensors correlate your activity with infrastructure known to be used by adversaries (e.g., C2 domains, malware hashes, phishing kits).

- **Affected Resources**: Lists of your specific VMs, storage accounts, Key Vaults, or applications that have been targeted or compromised.

- **Attack Progression Mapping**: Each step of the attack is categorized using the MITRE ATT&CK framework, giving analysts insight into how far the attacker has progressed—such as from initial access to execution, persistence, or exfiltration.

- **Linked Alerts**: The report links back to all related Defender for Cloud alerts triggered during the campaign, allowing security analysts to retrace the kill chain.

- **Recommended Actions**: Step-by-step mitigations are provided for each attack stage, including isolation, credential rotation, threat hunting queries, and automated response playbooks via Logic Apps.

These Threat Intelligence Reports are automatically generated and appear in the Defender for Cloud portal when such campaigns are detected. Unlike traditional alerts that focus on resource-level activity, these reports are designed for higher-order analysis. They are especially valuable for security operations teams looking to conduct incident correlation, root cause analysis, and response orchestration at scale.

From a data access perspective, all Threat Intelligence Reports are also backed by the underlying log data in the connected Log Analytics workspace. This allows security analysts to write Kusto Query Language (KQL) queries to explore raw signals, enrich reports with additional metadata, or build dashboards within Microsoft Sentinel.

Defender for Cloud integrates with Microsoft Defender Threat Intelligence (MDTI) to enrich alerts with real-time IoC reputation data, including domain classification, threat actor attribution, and malware family associations—further enhancing the fidelity of detection and the strategic value of the response.

In essence, Microsoft Defender for Cloud no longer just detects threats—it maps how they unfold, understands who is behind them, and guides you through mitigation using intelligence that spans across the Microsoft cloud, the global threat landscape, and your own unique infrastructure. This level of visibility transforms security operations from reactive firefighting into proactive, intelligence-driven defense.

CHAPTER 5   ENHANCED SECURITY WITH MICROSOFT DEFENDER FOR CLOUD

Managing Security Alerts

1. Open Microsoft Defender for Cloud from Azure portal.

2. Navigate to the **Security Alerts** section. This page displays all active and historical security alerts detected by Microsoft Defender for Cloud across your environment. In this example, sample alerts were manually added to illustrate the interface, as no real security incidents were present at the time of writing. Refer to Figure 5-21.

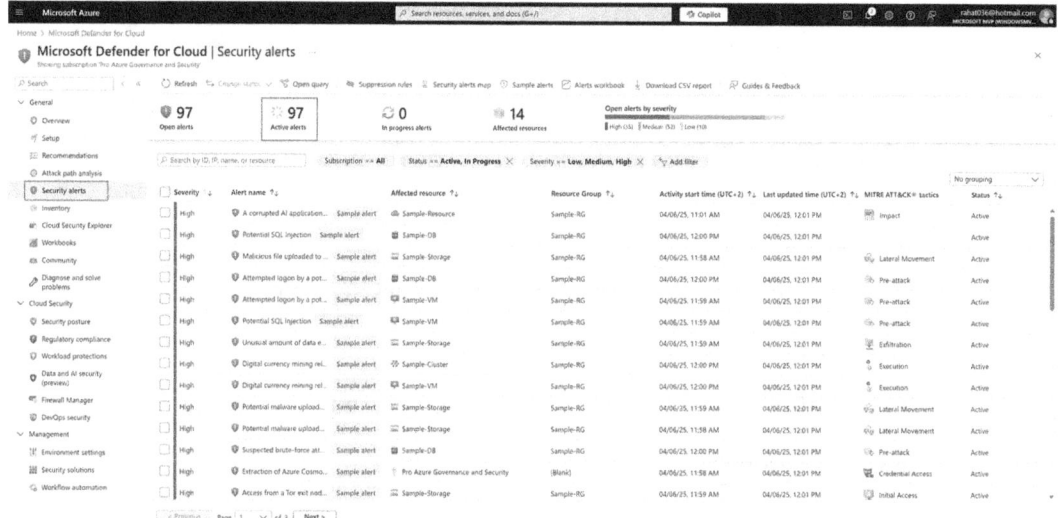

Figure 5-21. Security alert list of Microsoft Defender for Cloud

Investigate a Security Alert

Each alert contains information regarding the alert that assists you in your investigation.

1. Select an **alert**. A side pane opens and shows a description of the alert and all the affected resources as shown in Figure 5-22.

CHAPTER 5   ENHANCED SECURITY WITH MICROSOFT DEFENDER FOR CLOUD

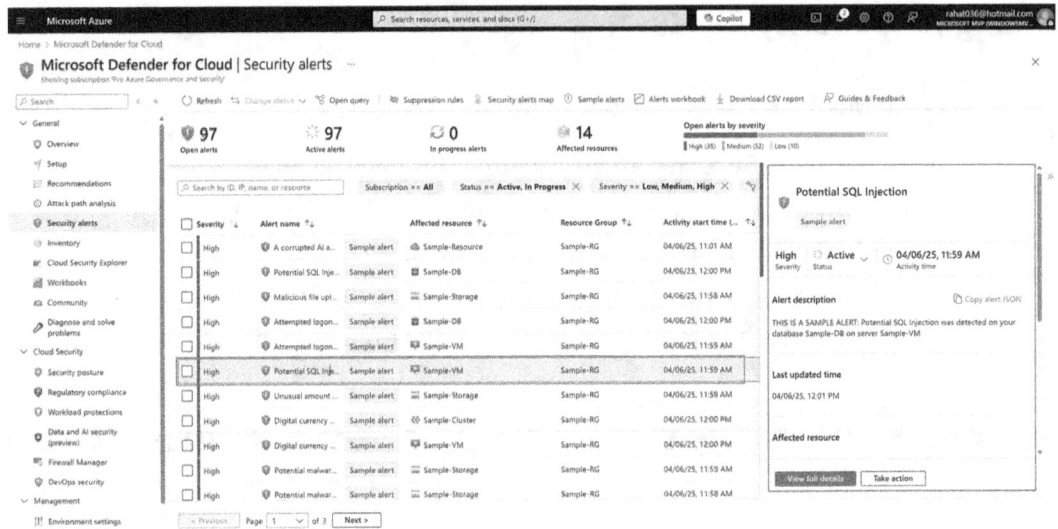

Figure 5-22. *Selecting the security alert and checking the details from the side pane*

2. Review the high-level information about the security alert:

   a. Alert severity, status, and activity time

   b. Description that explains the precise activity that was detected

   c. Affected resources

   d. Kill chain intent of the activity on the MITRE ATT&CK matrix (if applicable)

3. Click **View full details**. You can see the page as shown in Figure 5-23.

CHAPTER 5   ENHANCED SECURITY WITH MICROSOFT DEFENDER FOR CLOUD

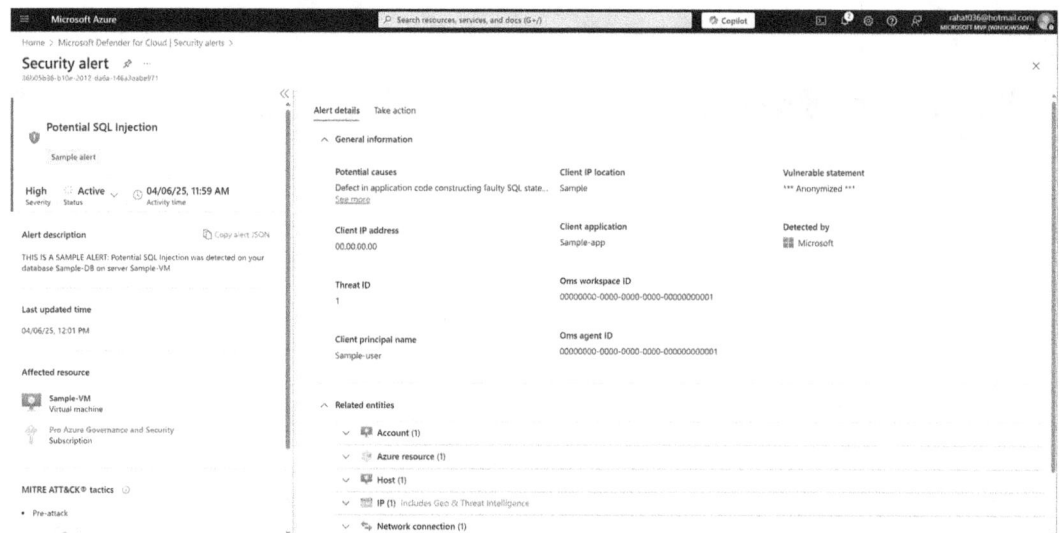

Figure 5-23. Viewing the full details of security alert

4. The right pane includes the **Alert details** tab containing further details of the alert to help you investigate the issue: IP addresses, files, processes, and more.

   Also on the right pane is the **Take action** tab. Use this tab to take further actions regarding the security alert. Actions such as

   - **Inspect Resource Context**: Sends you to the resource's activity logs that support the security alert

   - **Mitigate the Threat**: Provides manual remediation steps for this security alert

   - **Prevent Future Attacks**: Provides security recommendations to help reduce the attack surface, increase security posture, and thus prevent future attacks

   - **Trigger Automated Response**: Provides the option to trigger a logic app as a response to this security alert

   - **Suppress Similar Alerts**: Provides the option to suppress future alerts with similar characteristics if the alert isn't relevant for your organization

CHAPTER 5   ENHANCED SECURITY WITH MICROSOFT DEFENDER FOR CLOUD

Refer to Figure 5-24.

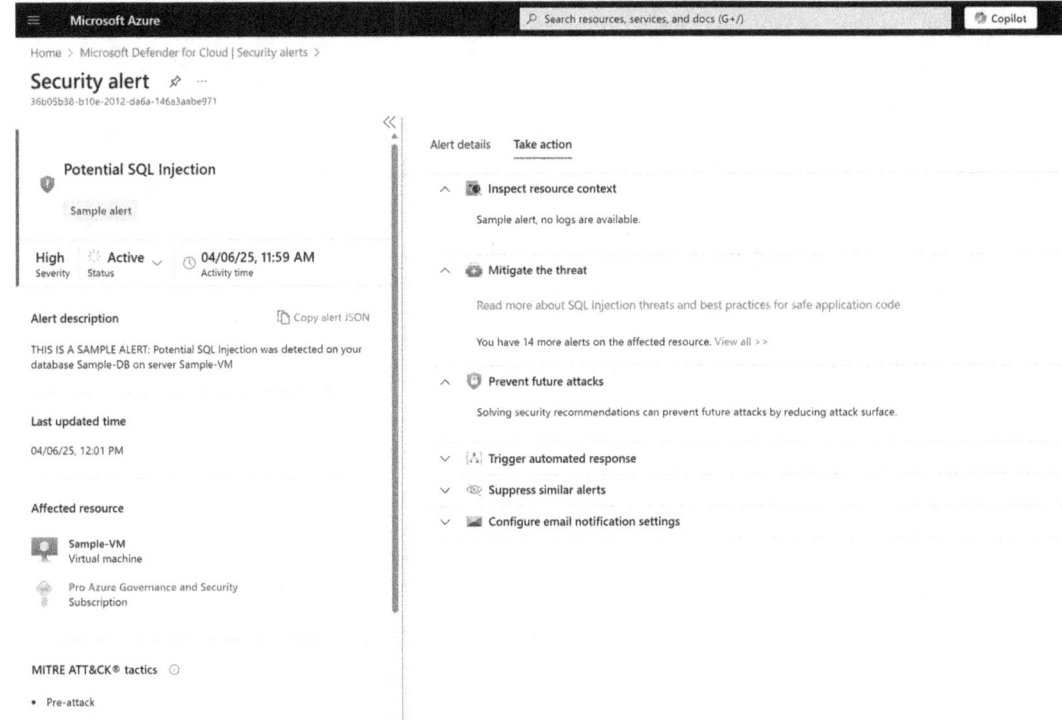

Figure 5-24. Take action page to resolve the security alert

Respond to a Security Alert

After investigating a security alert, you can respond to the alert from within Microsoft Defender for Cloud.

1. Open the **Take action** tab to see the recommended responses as shown in Figure 5-25.

CHAPTER 5   ENHANCED SECURITY WITH MICROSOFT DEFENDER FOR CLOUD

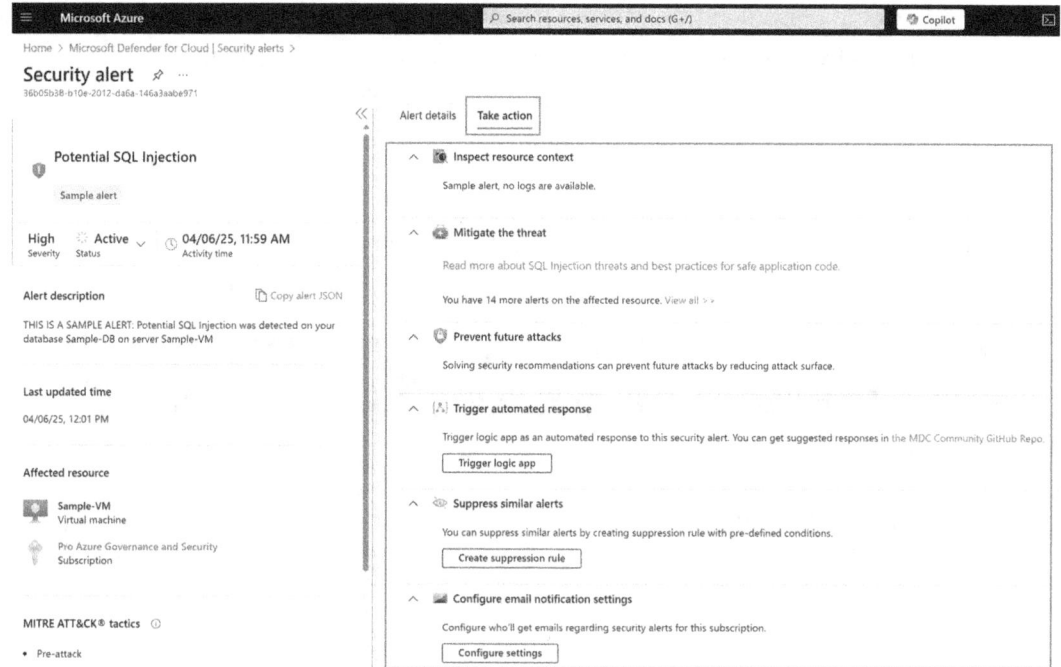

Figure 5-25. *Take action page to resolve the security alert*

2. Review the **Mitigate the threat** section to follow the manual investigation and remediation steps provided for resolving the detected issue.

3. Strengthen your environment by addressing the guidance under the **Prevent future attacks** section. This includes implementing recommended hardening actions to reduce the likelihood of similar threats occurring again.

4. Trigger an automated response by navigating to the **Trigger automated response** section. Here, you can manually execute a Logic App that initiates predefined response actions tailored to this alert type.

5. Suppress recurring false positives by opening the **Suppress similar alerts** section. Select Create suppression rule to prevent Defender for Cloud from generating alerts for this specific activity pattern in the future, if deemed non-malicious.

6. Check email notification settings by selecting **Configure email notification settings**. This shows who currently receives security alert notifications for the subscription. Contact the subscription owner to modify recipients if needed.

7. Close out the investigation by updating the alert's status to **Dismissed**, once the alert has been fully reviewed and the appropriate actions have been taken as shown in Figure 5-26.

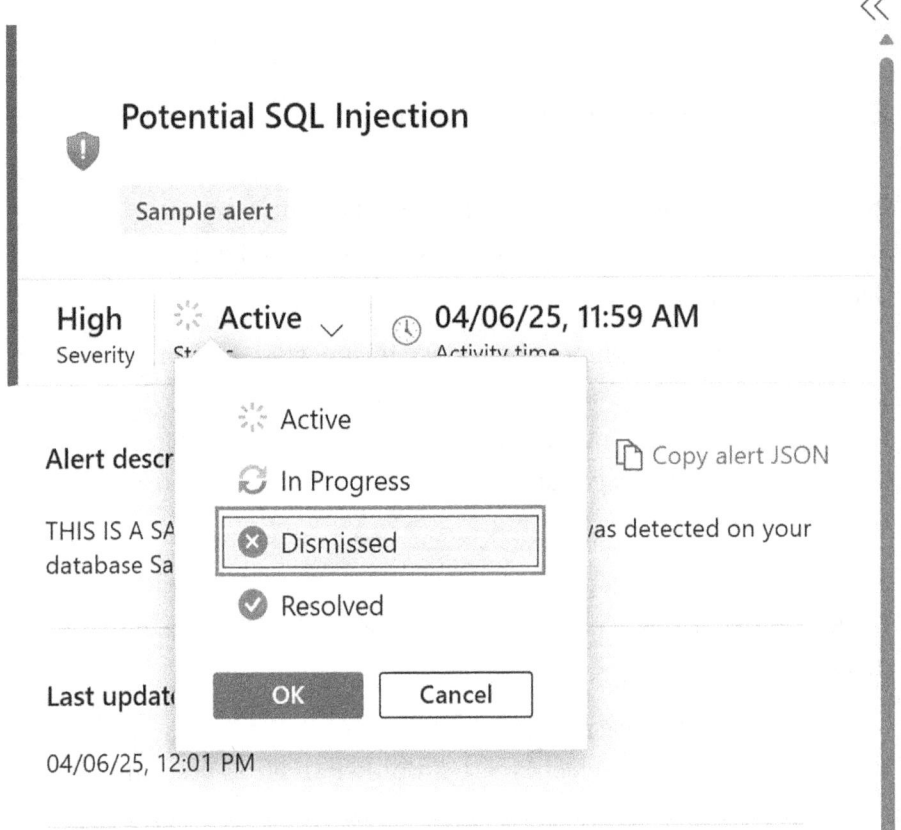

Figure 5-26. Changing the alert status

The alert is removed from the main alerts list. You can use the filter from the alerts list page to view all alerts with **Dismissed** status.

You can learn more about how it works from the official Microsoft documentation: `https://learn.microsoft.com/en-us/azure/defender-for-cloud/threat-intelligence-reports`.

Security Automation and Orchestration

As cloud environment scale and threats become more sophisticated, the need for rapid, consistent, and automated incident response has never been greater. Microsoft Defender for Cloud addresses this challenge through its built-in security automation and orchestration framework, allowing organizations to streamline their response processes, reduce manual effort, and accelerate mitigation. By integrating with Azure Logic Apps, Defender for Cloud enables the creation and execution of security playbooks—automated workflows that respond to alerts in real time or on demand. These playbooks can be used to perform a wide range of actions, such as isolating compromised resources, notifying response teams, gathering forensic evidence, or even initiating remediation steps. In this section, we will explore how Defender for Cloud leverages automation to improve operational efficiency, enforce incident response policies, and ensure a coordinated security posture across hybrid and multi-cloud environments. We'll walk through the role of playbooks, the automation engine, trigger mechanisms, and best practices for designing effective security workflows.

What Are Security Playbooks?

Security playbooks in Microsoft Defender for Cloud provide a powerful mechanism for automating incident response tasks in a structured, repeatable manner. These playbooks are built on top of Azure Logic Apps, allowing organizations to design workflows that can automatically respond to security alerts as soon as they are triggered. This is essential in high-scale environments where manual response is too slow or inconsistent to keep up with real-time threats.

A security playbook can be configured to perform a variety of actions, such as

- Sending email or Teams notifications to response teams
- Creating tickets in ITSM systems like ServiceNow

- Isolating virtual machines
- Revoking access tokens
- Collecting diagnostic logs or forensic snapshots
- Tagging resources for follow-up investigation
- Integrating with Microsoft Sentinel or other SIEM/SOAR platforms

Playbooks can be triggered automatically based on specific alert conditions—such as severity level, alert type, or affected resource—or they can be run manually by an analyst investigating an alert within the Defender for Cloud portal.

Security teams can use built-in playbook templates available in Azure or develop their own custom workflows using the visual Logic Apps designer. The playbooks framework supports conditional branching, API integrations, and parameterization, giving it the flexibility to fit into virtually any security operations workflow.

To get started with playbooks, you must grant the necessary permissions for Defender for Cloud to trigger Logic Apps within the subscription. Once configured, playbooks become a critical part of an organization's automated response and orchestration strategy.

Note Although security playbooks are part of Microsoft Defender for Cloud's response automation, the **Azure Logic Apps used to implement these playbooks are billed separately** based on the number of executions, connectors used, and runtime duration. Organizations should factor Logic Apps usage into their overall cloud cost planning. Find the pricing information here: `https://azure.microsoft.com/en-us/pricing/details/logic-apps/`.

Building Automated Workflow Using Logic Apps

Before processing to build the automated workflow, let's discuss the prerequisites:

1. You need **Security admin role** or **Owner** on the resource group.
2. You must also have write permissions for the target resource.
3. To work with Azure Logic Apps workflows, you must also have the following Logic Apps roles/permissions:

CHAPTER 5   ENHANCED SECURITY WITH MICROSOFT DEFENDER FOR CLOUD

   a. Logic App Operator permissions are required or Logic App read/
      trigger access (this role can't create or edit logic apps, only *run*
      existing ones).

   b. Logic App Contributor permissions are required for logic app
      creation and modification.

4. If you want to use Logic Apps connectors, you might need other
   credentials to sign in to their respective services (e.g., your
   Outlook/Teams/Slack instances).

Let's come back to our steps:

1. From Microsoft Defender for Cloud's sidebar, select **Workflow
   automation** as shown in Figure 5-27.

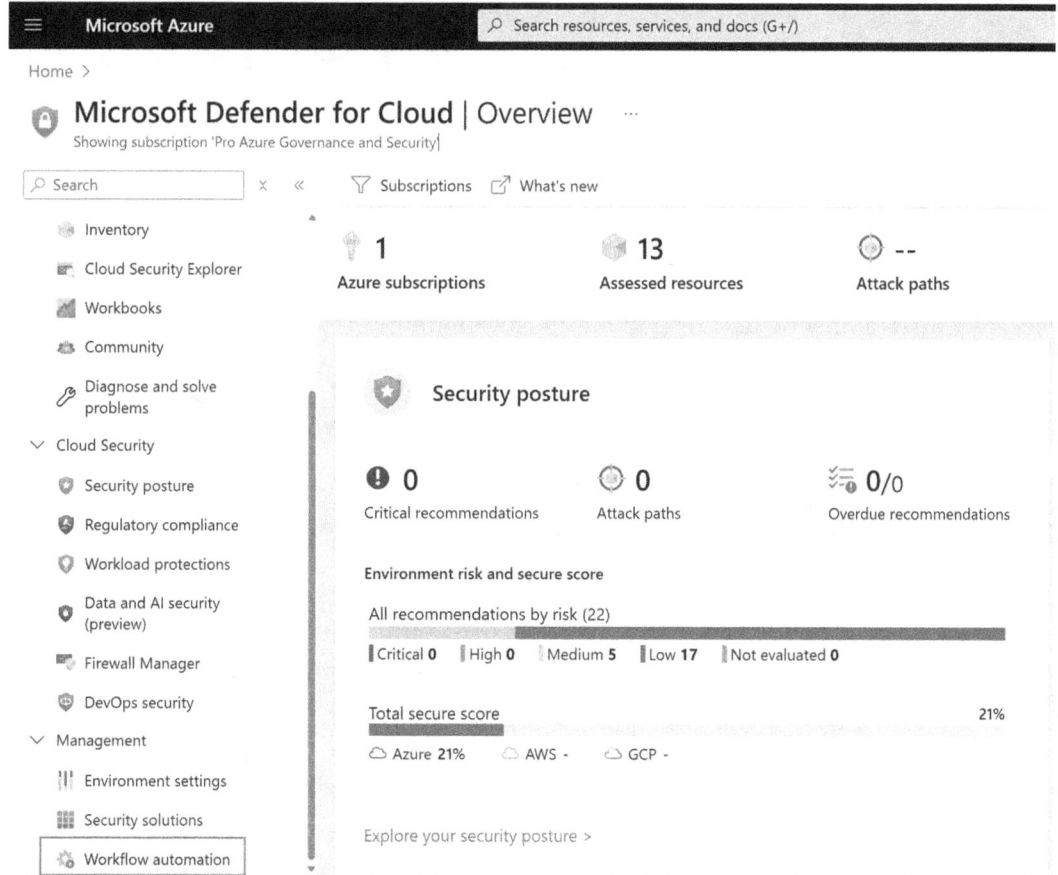

Figure 5-27. *Workflow automation dashboard in Microsoft Defender for Cloud*

181

CHAPTER 5   ENHANCED SECURITY WITH MICROSOFT DEFENDER FOR CLOUD

2. Click Add workflow automation to create a new workflow. This options pane for your new automation opens, as shown in Figure 5-28.

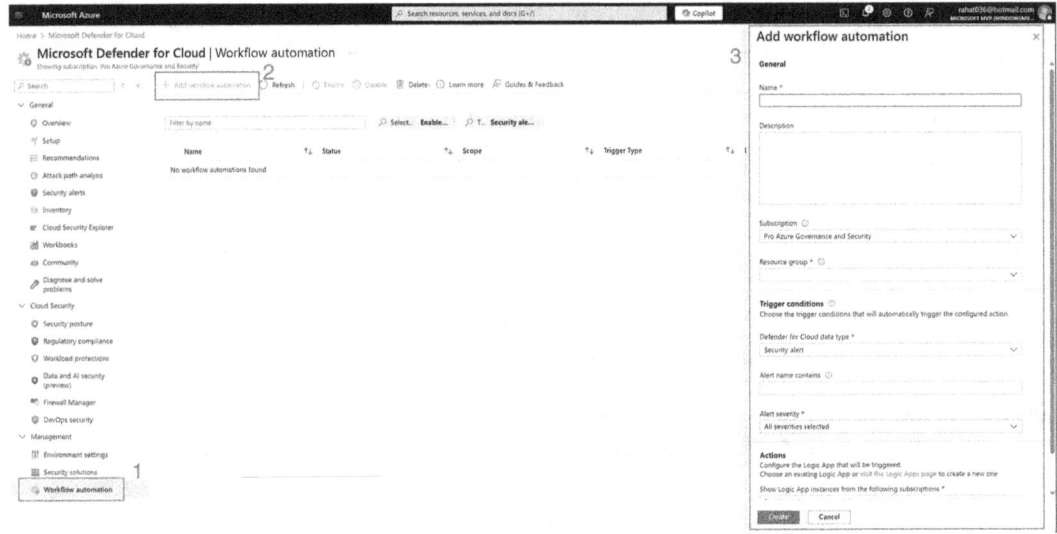

Figure 5-28. *Adding new workflow automation*

3. Enter the following:

    a. A name and description for the automation.

    b. The triggers that will initiate this automatic workflow. For example, you might want your logic app to run when a security alert that contains "SQL" is generated.

4. Specify the consumption logic app that will run when your trigger conditions are met.

5. From the Actions section, select **visit the Logic Apps page** to begin the logic app creation process as shown in Figure 5-29.

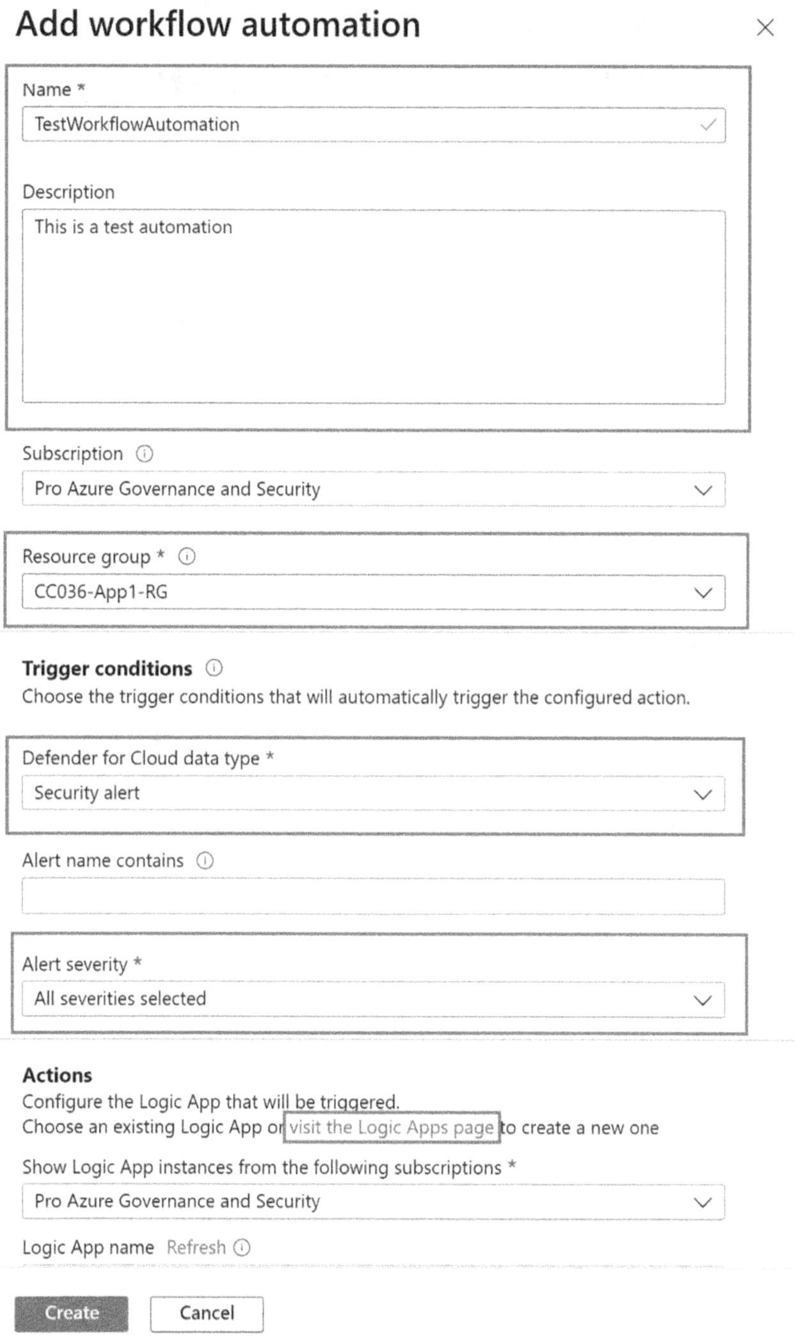

CHAPTER 5   ENHANCED SECURITY WITH MICROSOFT DEFENDER FOR CLOUD

Figure 5-29. Form to add a new workflow automation

CHAPTER 5   ENHANCED SECURITY WITH MICROSOFT DEFENDER FOR CLOUD

You will be redirected to the Azure Logic Apps page as shown in Figure 5-30.

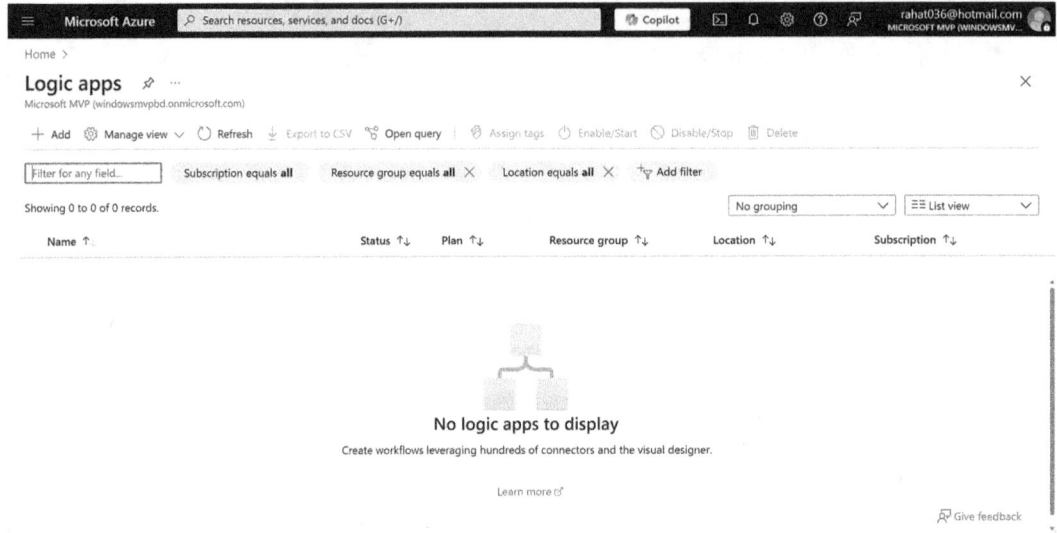

Figure 5-30. Logic apps page to create a new logic app

6. Select (+) Add. It will open the options to choose the hosting option to host the Logic app as shown in Figure 5-31. I am using the Multi-tenant Consumption Plan for this project.

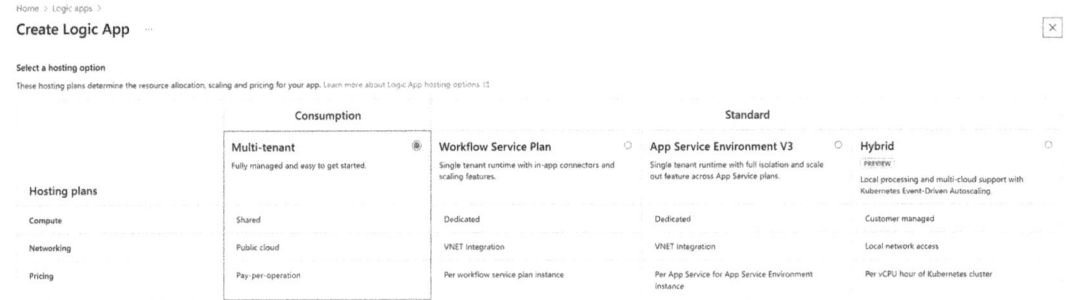

Figure 5-31. Selecting the hosting plan for the logic app

184

CHAPTER 5   ENHANCED SECURITY WITH MICROSOFT DEFENDER FOR CLOUD

7. It will open the options to create the Logic App. Fill the required fields and select **Review + Create** as shown in Figure 5-32.

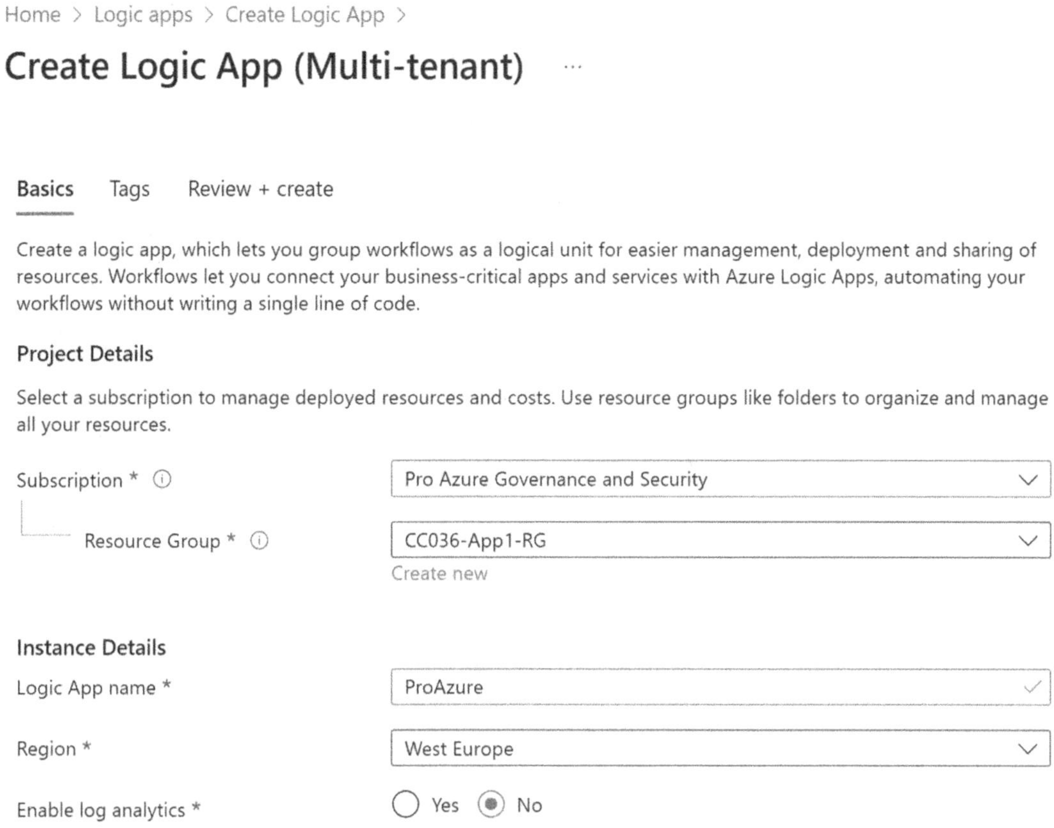

Home > Logic apps > Create Logic App >

Create Logic App (Multi-tenant)

Basics   Tags   Review + create

Create a logic app, which lets you group workflows as a logical unit for easier management, deployment and sharing of resources. Workflows let you connect your business-critical apps and services with Azure Logic Apps, automating your workflows without writing a single line of code.

Project Details

Select a subscription to manage deployed resources and costs. Use resource groups like folders to organize and manage all your resources.

Subscription * | Pro Azure Governance and Security

Resource Group * | CC036-App1-RG
Create new

Instance Details

Logic App name * | ProAzure

Region * | West Europe

Enable log analytics *   ○ Yes ● No

Figure 5-32. *Logic app creation page*

8. Review the information you entered and select **Create.** In your new logic app, you can choose from built-in, predefined templates from the security category. Or you can define a custom flow of events to occur when this process is triggered.

9. Once created, select the logic app and choose Logic app designer under the Development Tools section, as shown in Figure 5-33.

CHAPTER 5 ENHANCED SECURITY WITH MICROSOFT DEFENDER FOR CLOUD

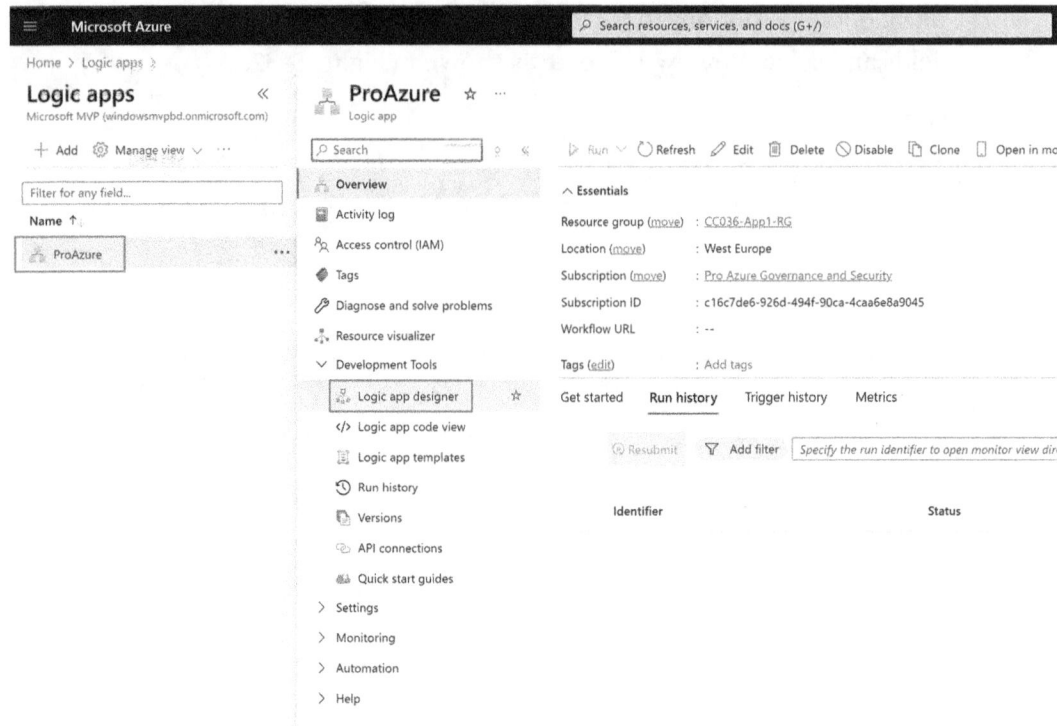

Figure 5-33. *Selecting logic app designer to design the logic app*

10. Select Add a Trigger as shown in Figure 5-34.

CHAPTER 5   ENHANCED SECURITY WITH MICROSOFT DEFENDER FOR CLOUD

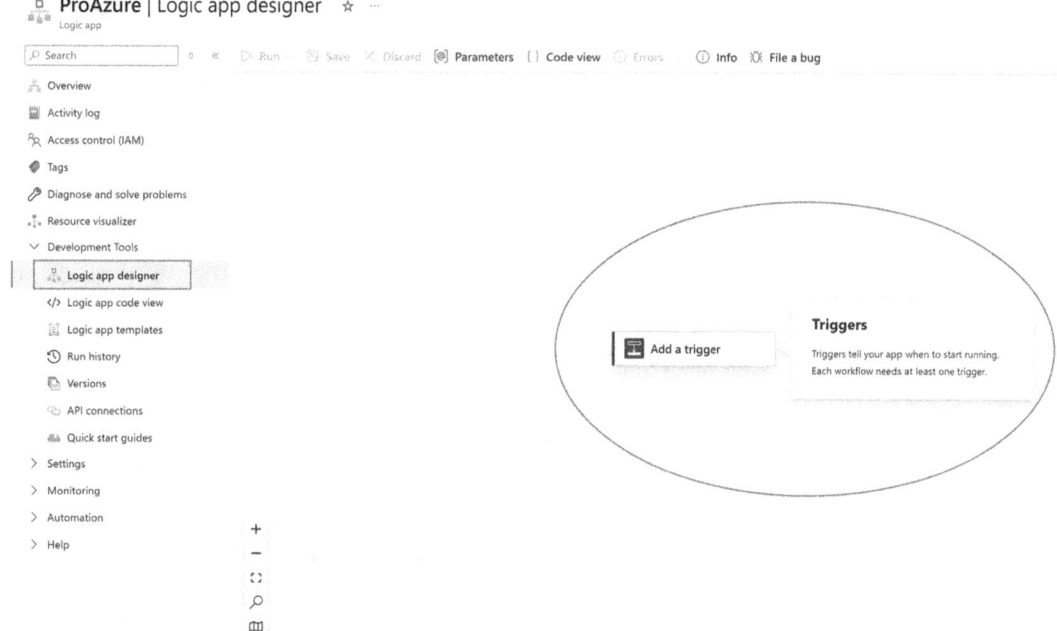

Figure 5-34. Adding trigger in logic app

11. Search Microsoft Defender for Cloud and select **When a Microsoft Defender for Cloud alert is created or triggered** as shown in Figure 5-35.

CHAPTER 5   ENHANCED SECURITY WITH MICROSOFT DEFENDER FOR CLOUD

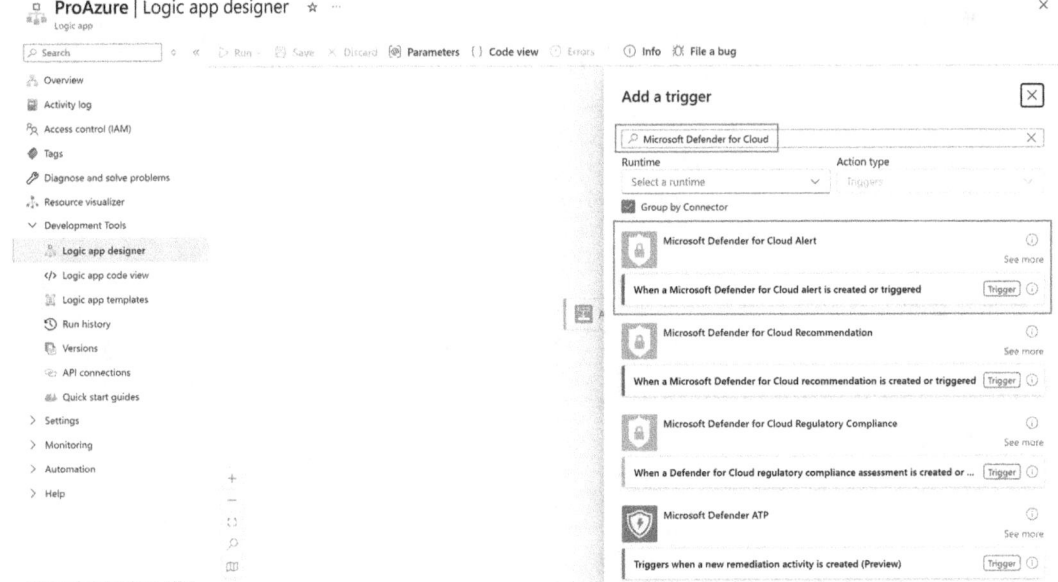

Figure 5-35. *Selecting Microsoft Defender for Cloud trigger to add it in Logic App*

12. After adding this trigger, the workflow designer opens. Here, you can add the different actions that happen as part of the workflow.

13. From here, you can integrate with about 200 connectors, from an extensive list of third-party vendors, as well as Microsoft. To keep it easy and simply introduce you to the capabilities, let's trigger the actions to

    a. Send an email

    b. Redeploy the Azure VM that's impacted, from an Azure Resource Manager template

14. Now, under the trigger **When a Microsoft Defender for Cloud alert is created or triggered,** click the + sign, and add a new action.

15. Search **Office 365 Outlook** and select **Send an email (V2)** as shown in Figure 5-36.

CHAPTER 5   ENHANCED SECURITY WITH MICROSOFT DEFENDER FOR CLOUD

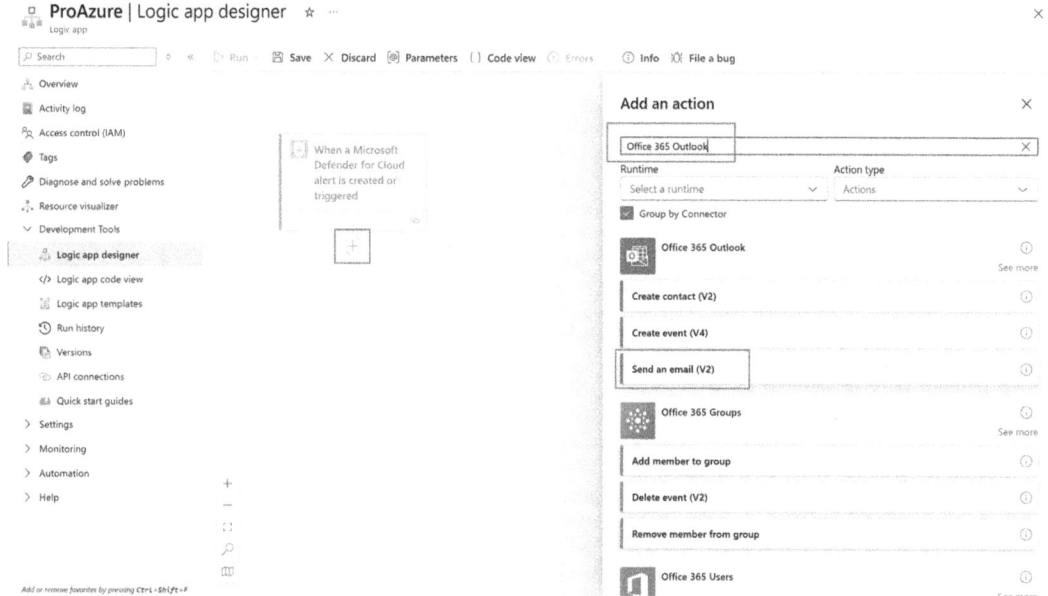

Figure 5-36. *Adding Office 365 Outlook action in Logic app*

16. When asked to sign in, provide your Office 365 credentials, which are needed to get access to the Office 365 Logic Apps connector. In a typical organization setup, I recommend using a generic account for this, for example, information@domain.com. As such, you know that the Office 365 integration is driven out of that security playbooks user account mailbox.

17. In the Send an email (V2) window, complete the required information for the email subject, as well as the body of the email as shown in Figure 5-37.

CHAPTER 5 ENHANCED SECURITY WITH MICROSOFT DEFENDER FOR CLOUD

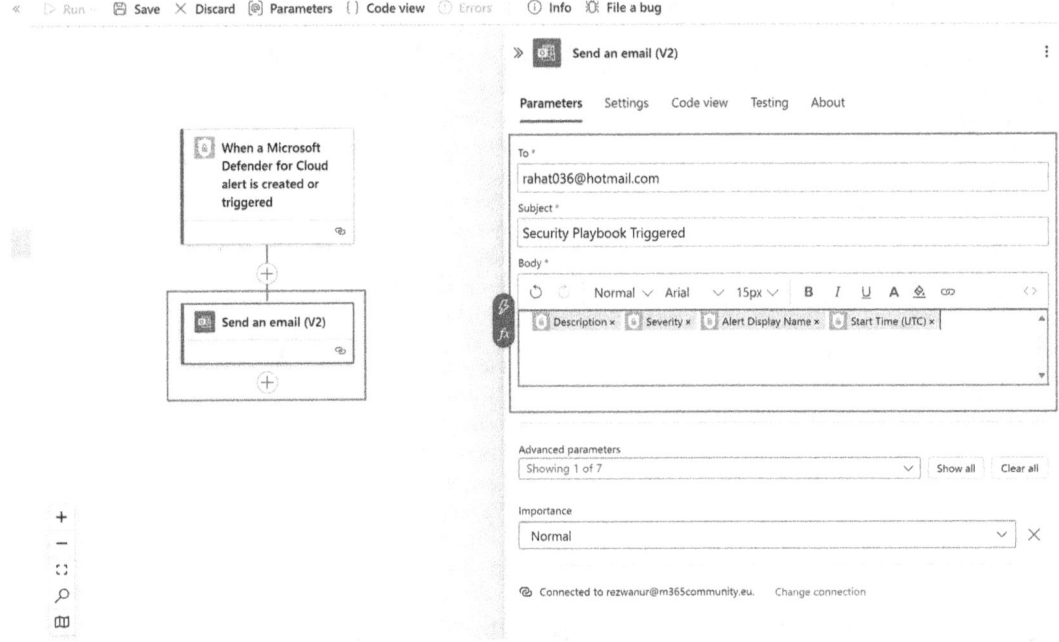

Figure 5-37. *Configuring email action to trigger in logic app*

18. Repeat the same step, click the + sign, click Add an action, and this time, search Azure Resource Manager as the action as shown in Figure 5-38.

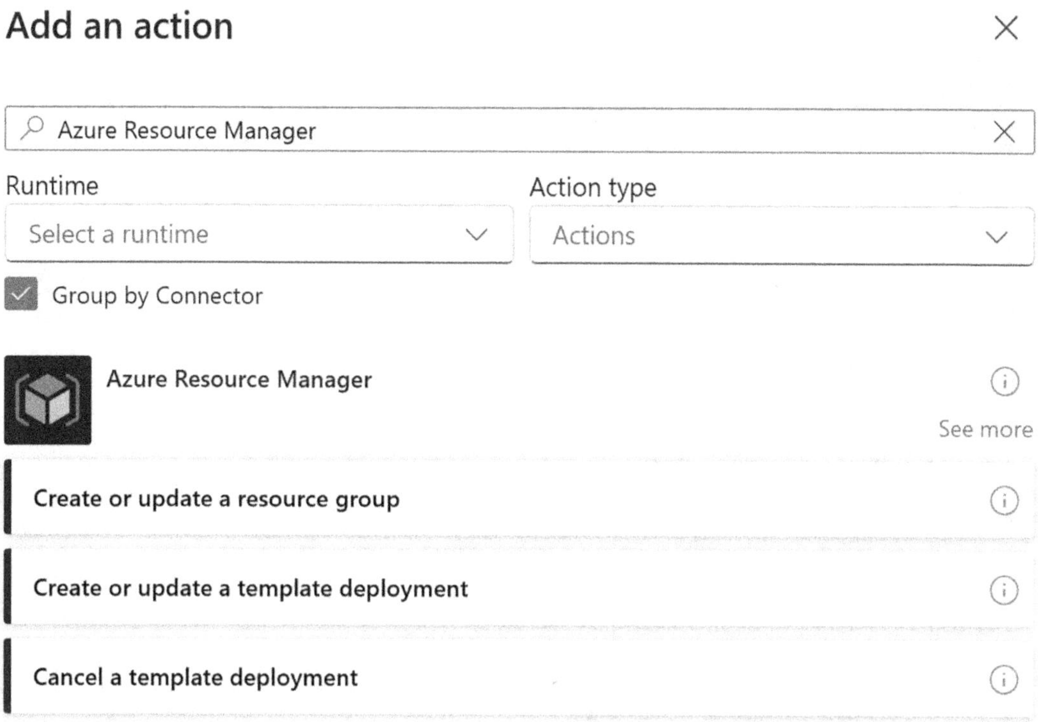

Add an action   ×

🔍 Azure Resource Manager   ×

Runtime   Action type
Select a runtime   ∨   Actions   ∨

☑ Group by Connector

    Azure Resource Manager   ⓘ
                                                                See more

    | Create or update a resource group   ⓘ

    | Create or update a template deployment   ⓘ

    | Cancel a template deployment   ⓘ

Figure 5-38. Adding Azure Resource Manager action in Logic app

19. Click **See more** and select **Create or update a template deployment** as shown in Figure 5-39.

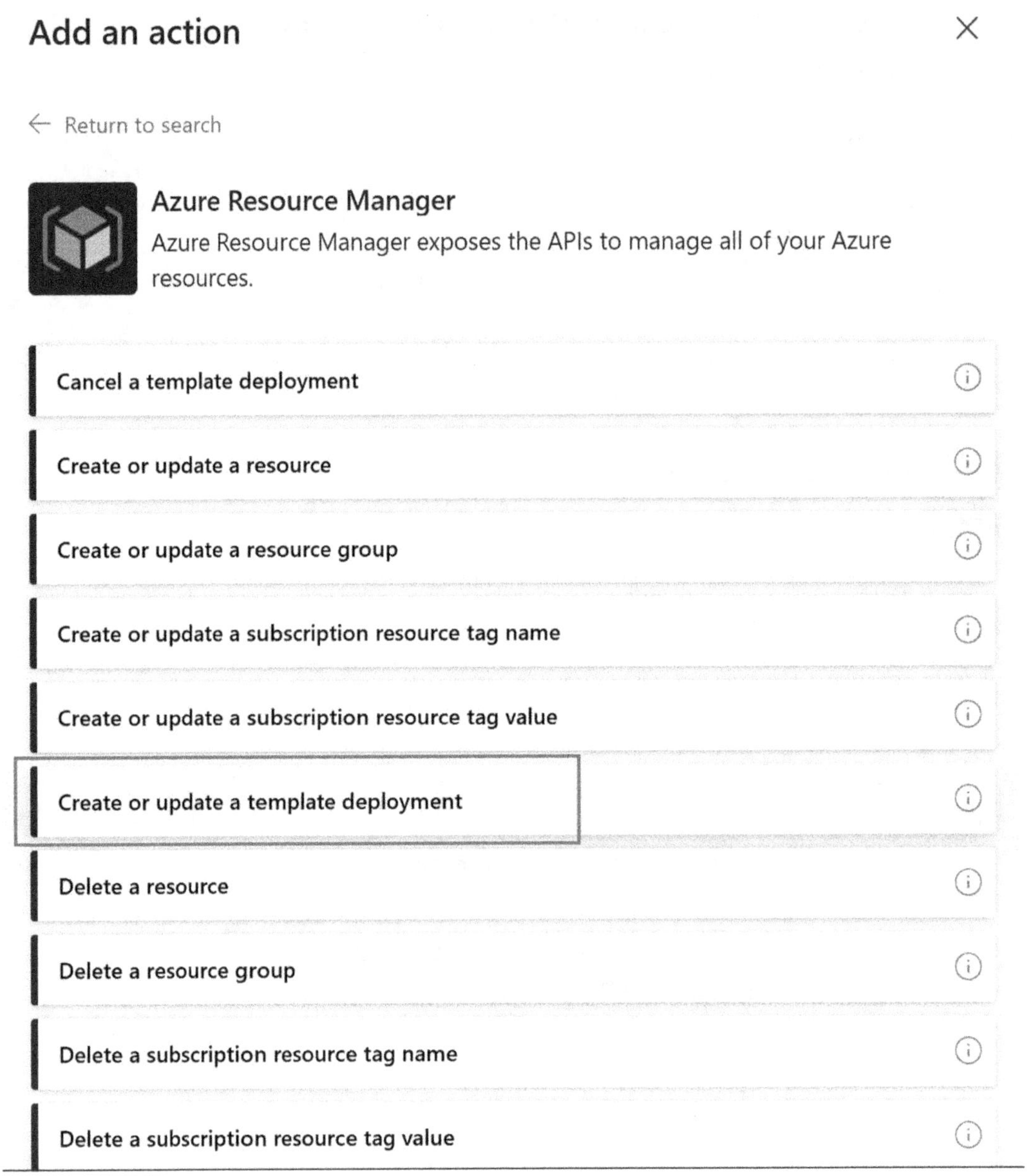

CHAPTER 5   ENHANCED SECURITY WITH MICROSOFT DEFENDER FOR CLOUD

Add an action   ✕

← Return to search

Azure Resource Manager
Azure Resource Manager exposes the APIs to manage all of your Azure resources.

| Cancel a template deployment |
| Create or update a resource |
| Create or update a resource group |
| Create or update a subscription resource tag name |
| Create or update a subscription resource tag value |
| **Create or update a template deployment** |
| Delete a resource |
| Delete a resource group |
| Delete a subscription resource tag name |
| Delete a subscription resource tag value |

Figure 5-39. Selecting the appropriate action from the Azure Resource Manager list

20. Complete the information from your Azure subscription, such as subscription ID, resource group where you want this template to run, and the link of the actual ARM template, as

CHAPTER 5   ENHANCED SECURITY WITH MICROSOFT DEFENDER FOR CLOUD

shown in Figure 5-40. You can use the following template as an example: `https://pdtitlabsstorage.blob.core.windows.net/templates/jumpvm/jumpvm.json`.

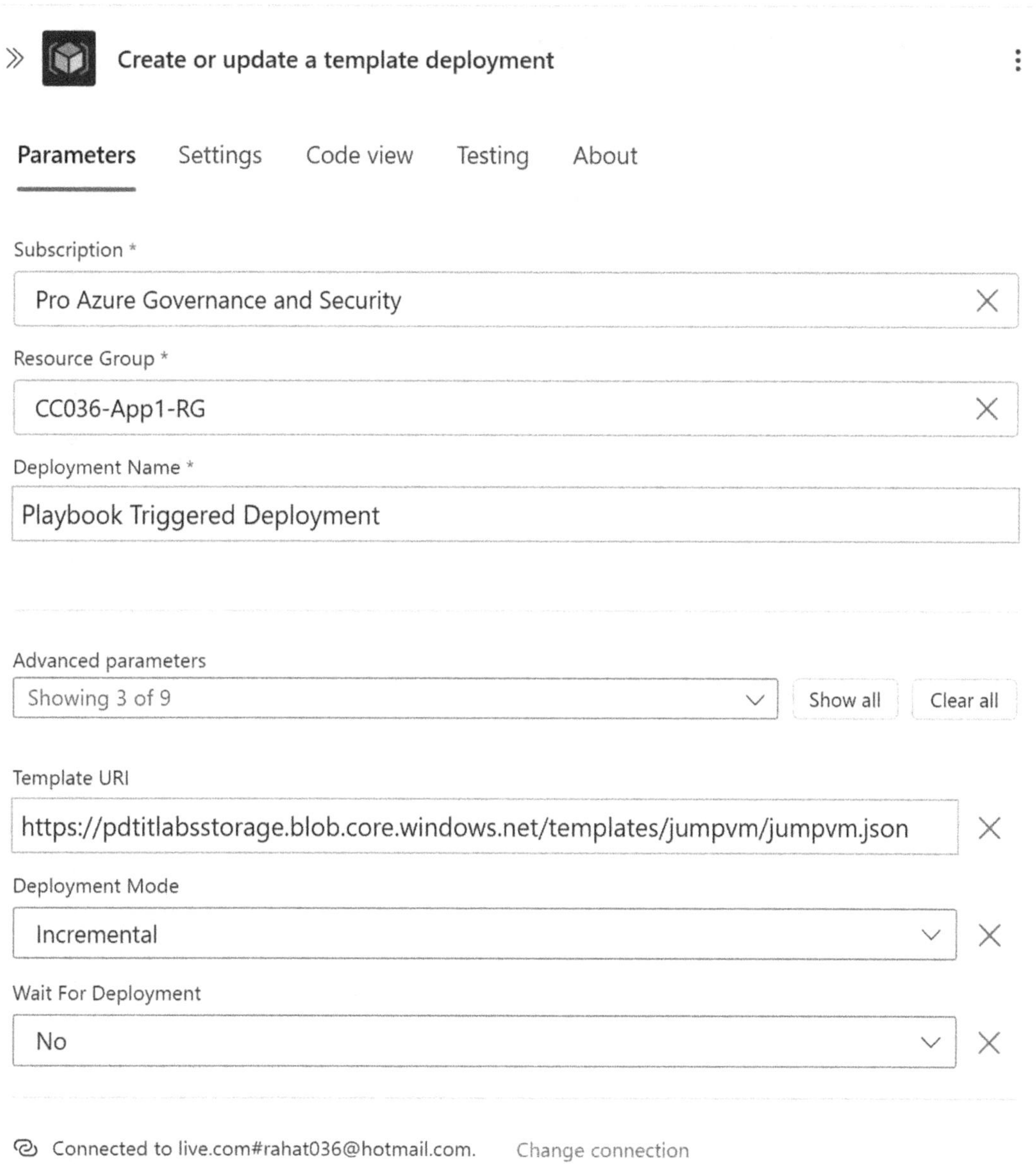

Figure 5-40. Providing the parameters information

CHAPTER 5   ENHANCED SECURITY WITH MICROSOFT DEFENDER FOR CLOUD

21. Save the workflow and go back to the Workflow automation page (where we started creating the logic app; see step 4), select the logic app that we created now, and click Create as shown in Figure 5-41.

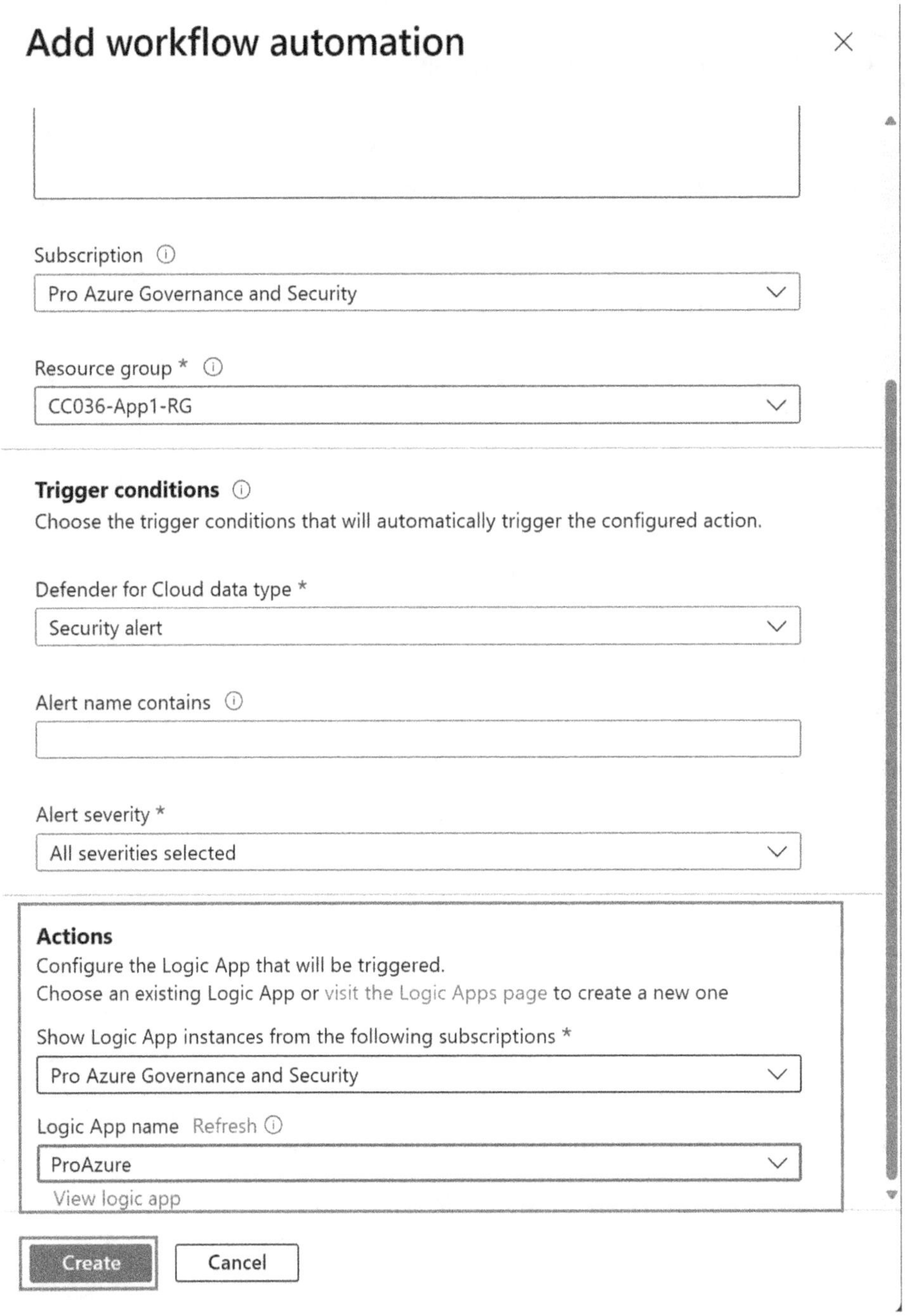

Add workflow automation

Subscription
Pro Azure Governance and Security

Resource group *
CC036-App1-RG

Trigger conditions
Choose the trigger conditions that will automatically trigger the configured action.

Defender for Cloud data type *
Security alert

Alert name contains

Alert severity *
All severities selected

Actions
Configure the Logic App that will be triggered.
Choose an existing Logic App or visit the Logic Apps page to create a new one

Show Logic App instances from the following subscriptions *
Pro Azure Governance and Security

Logic App name   Refresh
ProAzure
View logic app

[Create]   Cancel

Figure 5-41. Adding the newly created logic app

CHAPTER 5   ENHANCED SECURITY WITH MICROSOFT DEFENDER FOR CLOUD

This completes the creation process.

Configuring Playbook Triggers

As we created the automated workflow with logic app, the last thing that we need to do is integrate it into our Microsoft Defender for Cloud Security Center alerts. Meaning, setting up that whenever an alert generated for which we want to execute this playbook, it needs to get integrated.

1. From **Microsoft Defender for Cloud**, select **Security Alerts** under Overview.

2. Select the **Security Alert** for which you want to set up the security playbook. Click the **Take action** as shown in Figure 5-42.

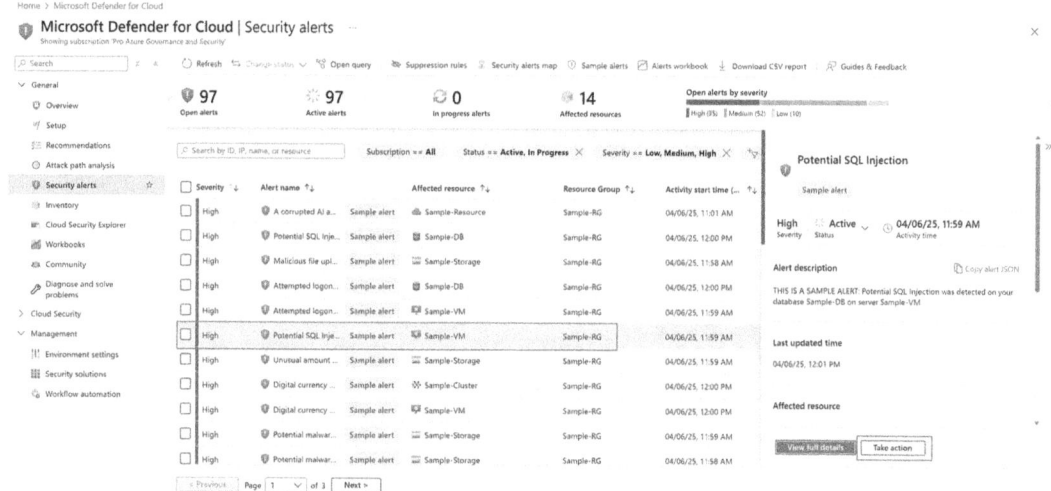

Figure 5-42. *Selecting the security alert to run the security playbook*

3. Click Trigger logic app under **Trigger automated response** as shown in Figure 5-43.

CHAPTER 5   ENHANCED SECURITY WITH MICROSOFT DEFENDER FOR CLOUD

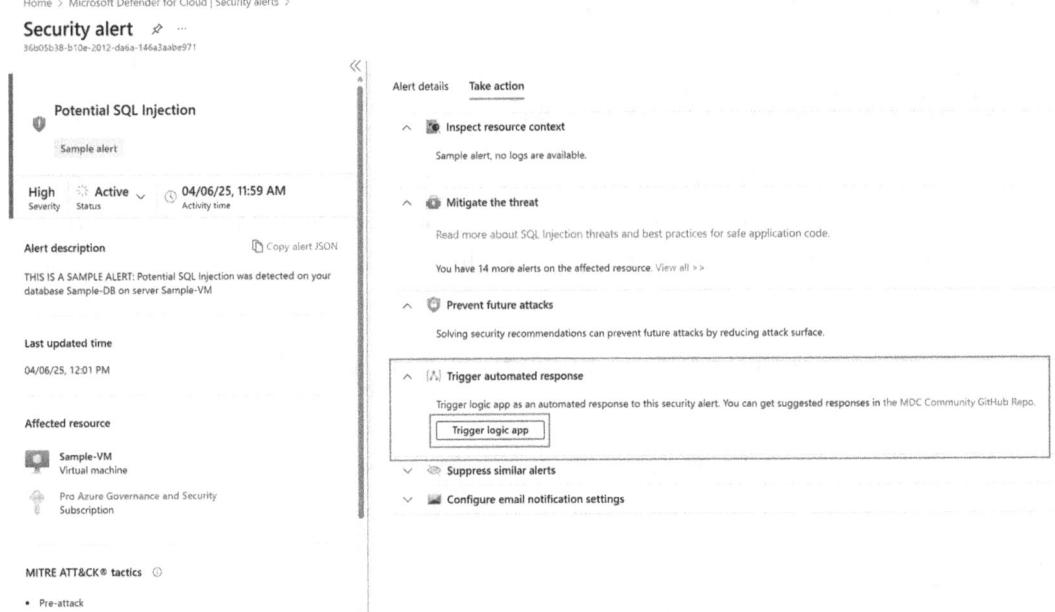

Figure 5-43. *Selecting the trigger logic app option to trigger the response automatically*

4. Select the logic app and click Trigger as shown in Figure 5-44.

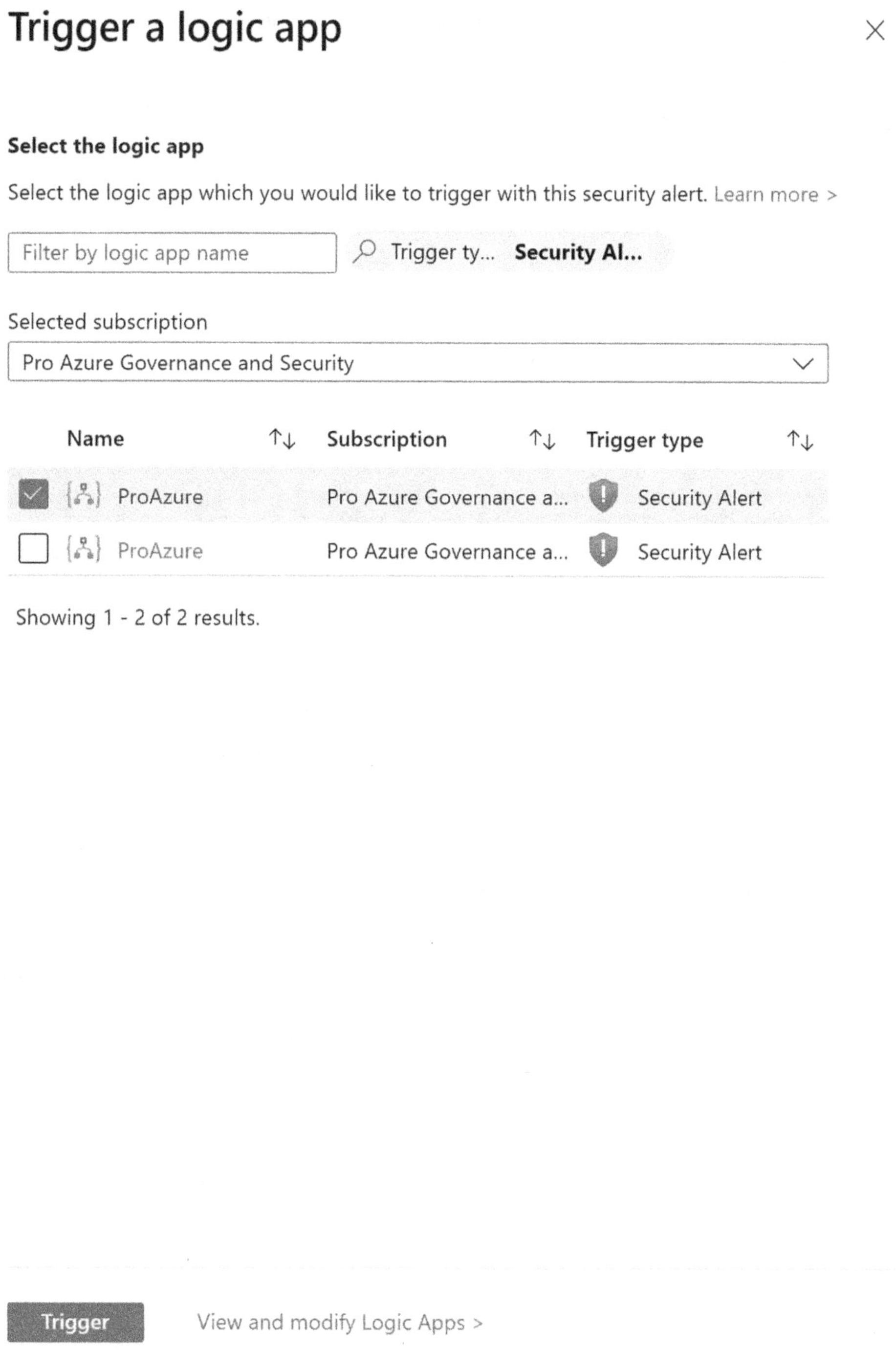

CHAPTER 5 ENHANCED SECURITY WITH MICROSOFT DEFENDER FOR CLOUD

Trigger a logic app

Select the logic app

Select the logic app which you would like to trigger with this security alert. Learn more >

Name	Subscription	Trigger type
☑ ProAzure	Pro Azure Governance a...	Security Alert
☐ ProAzure	Pro Azure Governance a...	Security Alert

Showing 1 - 2 of 2 results.

Figure 5-44. *Selecting the logic app*

5. Read the notification from Azure, which informs you about the triggered event.

6. You will receive the email as we set in the trigger as shown in Figure 5-45.

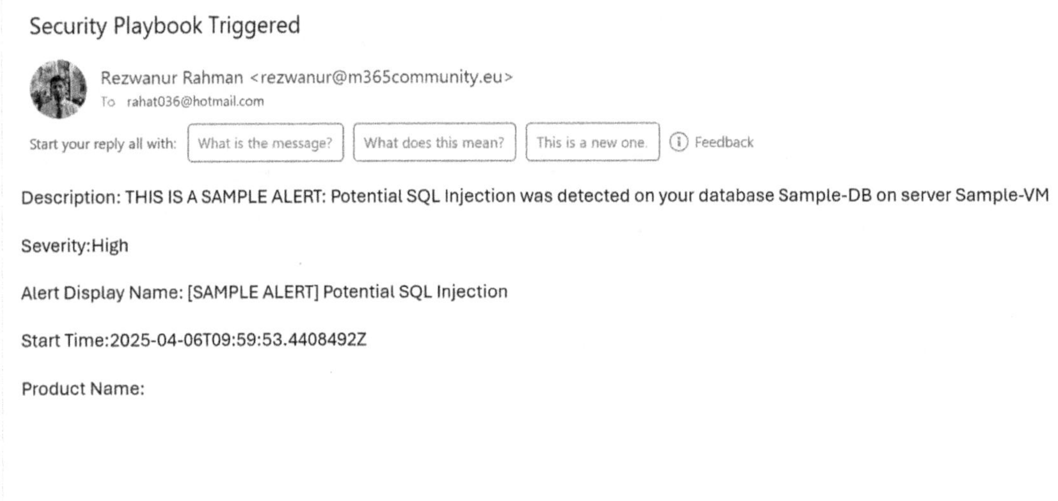

Security Playbook Triggered

Rezwanur Rahman <rezwanur@m365community.eu>
To   rahat036@hotmail.com

Start your reply all with: What is the message?   What does this mean?   This is a new one.   ⓘ Feedback

Description: THIS IS A SAMPLE ALERT: Potential SQL Injection was detected on your database Sample-DB on server Sample-VM

Severity:High

Alert Display Name: [SAMPLE ALERT] Potential SQL Injection

Start Time:2025-04-06T09:59:53.4408492Z

Product Name:

Figure 5-45. *Sample email received that was triggered from the logic app*

Continuous Security Monitoring

Microsoft Defender for Cloud enables continuous security monitoring by assessing your cloud resources in real time for misconfigurations, threats, and compliance violations. Through components like Secure Score, Cloud Security Posture Management (CSPM), and integrated recommendations, it provides ongoing visibility into your environment's security health. This allows security teams to detect issues early, prioritize remediation efforts, and maintain a strong security posture across Azure and hybrid workloads without relying on periodic audits or manual reviews.

Fixing Security Recommendations

This is the Free Tier offering, as discussed at the beginning of this section. With numerous reported vulnerabilities, prioritizing remediation efforts can be daunting. This is where Microsoft's Secure Score and Azure's Cloud Security Posture Management

CHAPTER 5　ENHANCED SECURITY WITH MICROSOFT DEFENDER FOR CLOUD

(CSPM), available through Defender for Cloud, become invaluable. Secure Score provides a consolidated metric reflecting the current security posture of your environment.

You can see all the security recommendations from **Microsoft Azure portal ➤ Microsoft Defender for Cloud ➤ Recommendations** as shown in Figure 5-46.

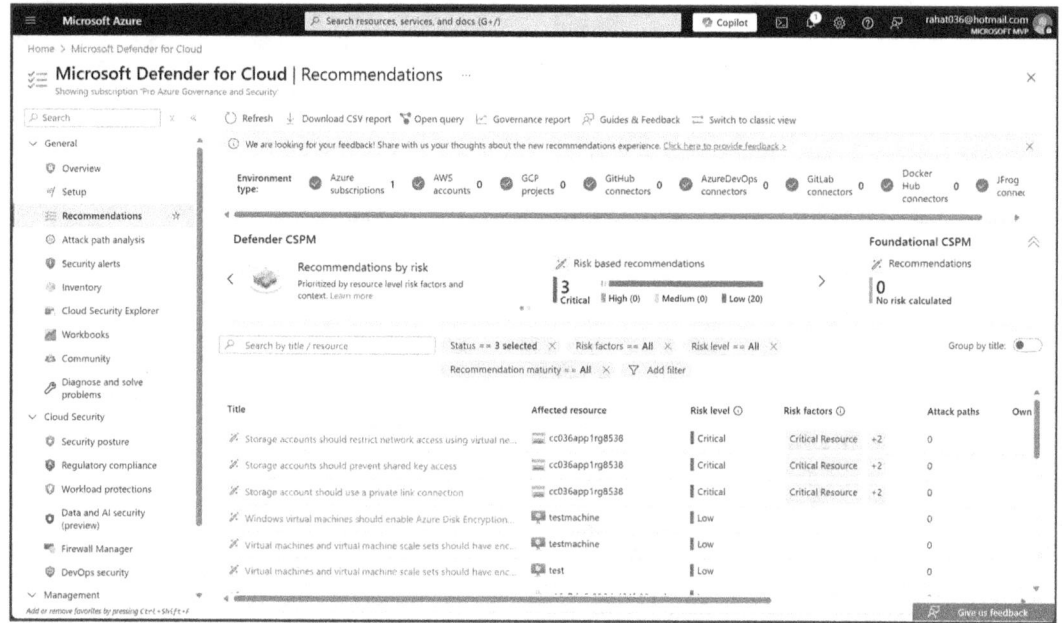

Figure 5-46. *Recommendation page of Microsoft Defender for Cloud*

Recommendations are prioritized based on the risk level of the security issue by default.

In addition to risk level, I recommend that you prioritize the security controls in the default Microsoft Cloud Security Benchmark (MCSB) standard in Defender for Cloud, since these controls affect your secure score.

1. Sign in to the Azure portal. Navigate to **Microsoft Defender for Cloud ➤ Recommendations.**

2. Select a **recommendation**.

3. Select **Take action**.

4. Locate the Remediate section and follow the remediation instructions, as shown in Figure 5-47.

199

CHAPTER 5   ENHANCED SECURITY WITH MICROSOFT DEFENDER FOR CLOUD

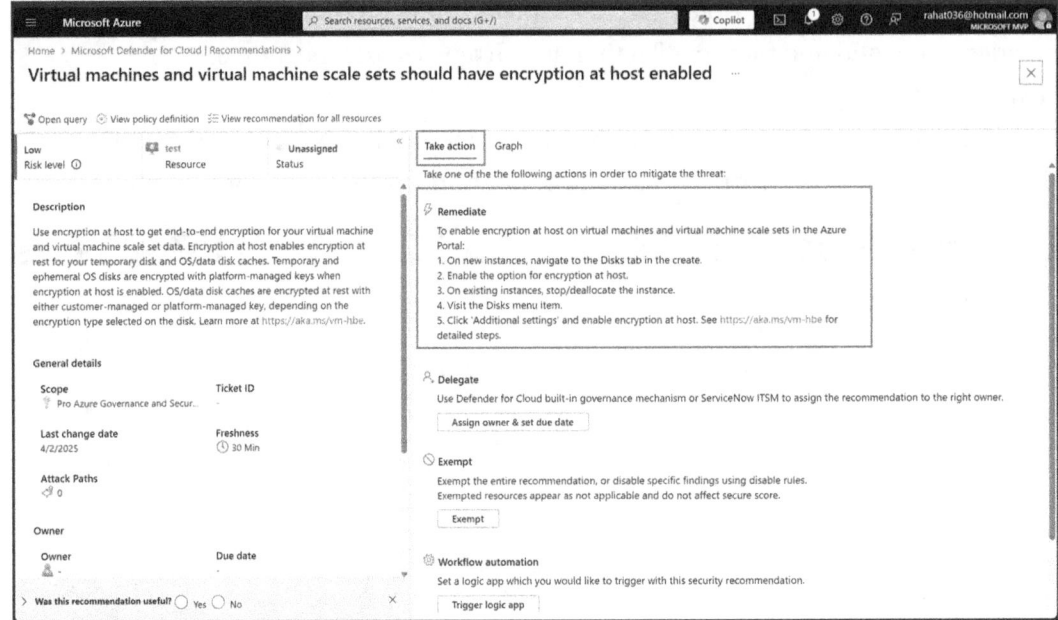

Figure 5-47. Remediate option of the security alert

Monitoring Resource Health

To monitor resource health, follow the steps:

1. Sign in to the Azure portal. Navigate to **Microsoft Defender for Cloud ➤ Inventory** as shown in Figure 5-48.

CHAPTER 5   ENHANCED SECURITY WITH MICROSOFT DEFENDER FOR CLOUD

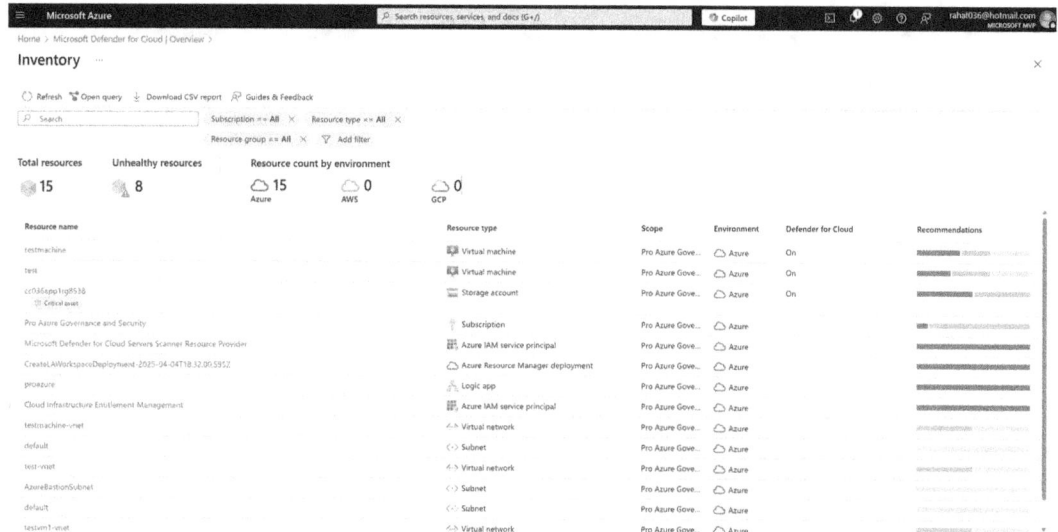

Figure 5-48. *Inventory dashboard of Microsoft Defender for Cloud*

Here, you can see the graphical overview of the secure state for Compute and apps, Networking, Data and storage, and Identity. Honestly, this is nothing more than summarized graphical view that allows you to be redirected to the detailed recommendations for each topic.

Hardening Network Resources

Microsoft Defender for Cloud also recognizes and detects security issues in the networking layer of your Azure resources. Besides listing out the different security recommendations for your networking resources, Microsoft Defender for Cloud has another pretty powerful tool to assist in detecting network security issues—Network Map. Next, it also provides another new feature called Hardening Network Security Groups.

Network Map is a graphical interface within Microsoft Defender for Cloud, highlighting any Azure Networking Resources, together with their dependencies and security issues, if any. The Network Map topology is drawn automatically by Microsoft Defender for Cloud itself. Let's walk through the core steps on how it can be used:

1. From **Microsoft Defender for Cloud**, select **Workload protections** under **Cloud Security** and select **Network Map**, as shown in Figure 5-49.

201

CHAPTER 5   ENHANCED SECURITY WITH MICROSOFT DEFENDER FOR CLOUD

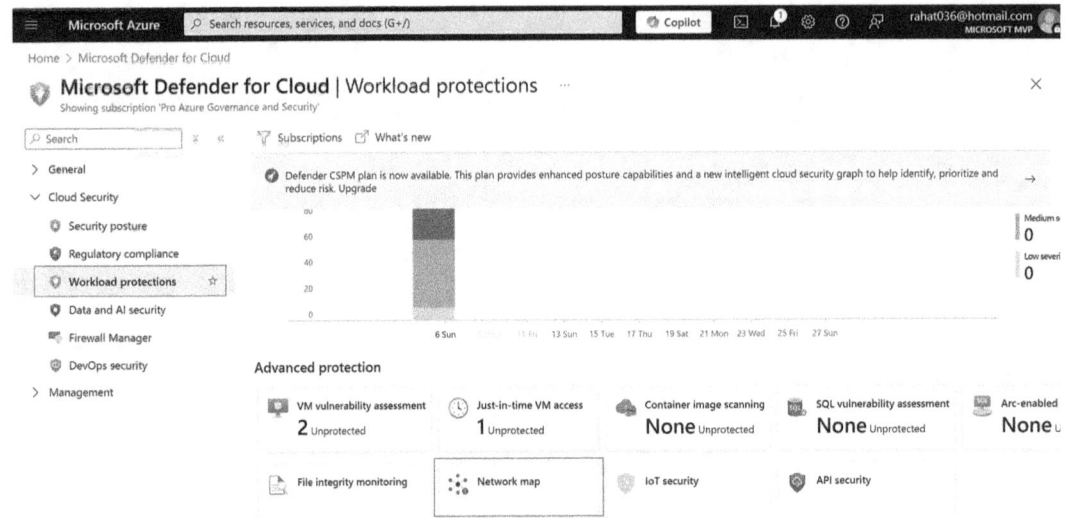

Figure 5-49. Network map option in workload protection

2. This opens a more detailed topology map of the different Azure Virtual Networks you have, together with any other Azure resources connected to it, like virtual machines and storage accounts as shown in Figure 5-50.

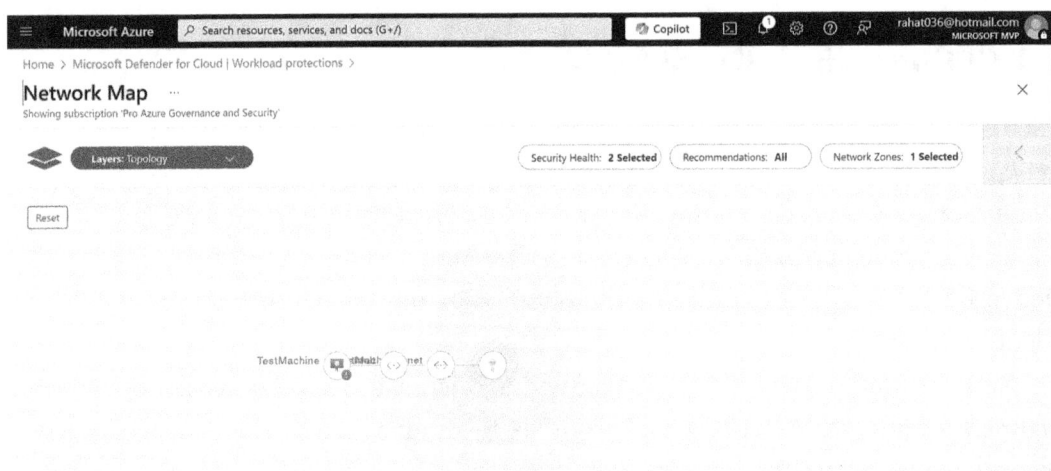

Figure 5-50. Network topology in network map

CHAPTER 5   ENHANCED SECURITY WITH MICROSOFT DEFENDER FOR CLOUD

3. Depending on the context that you want to use in Network Map, you can switch the view from Topology to Traffic. (This mainly only removes the naming of the Azure Resources in the diagram.) You can also modify the filters by selecting the Filters list box. Similarly, you can modify the recommendations that should be displayed within the topology by selecting the Recommendations list box. Lastly, you can modify the network zones, showing the Azure internal VNets only or including the Internet-facing ones.

4. By making these selections, and activating all filters, recommendations, and network zones, the diagram (for our sample scenario of Azure Resources) changes to the following topology. This shows more information in the same topology diagram as shown in Figure 5-51.

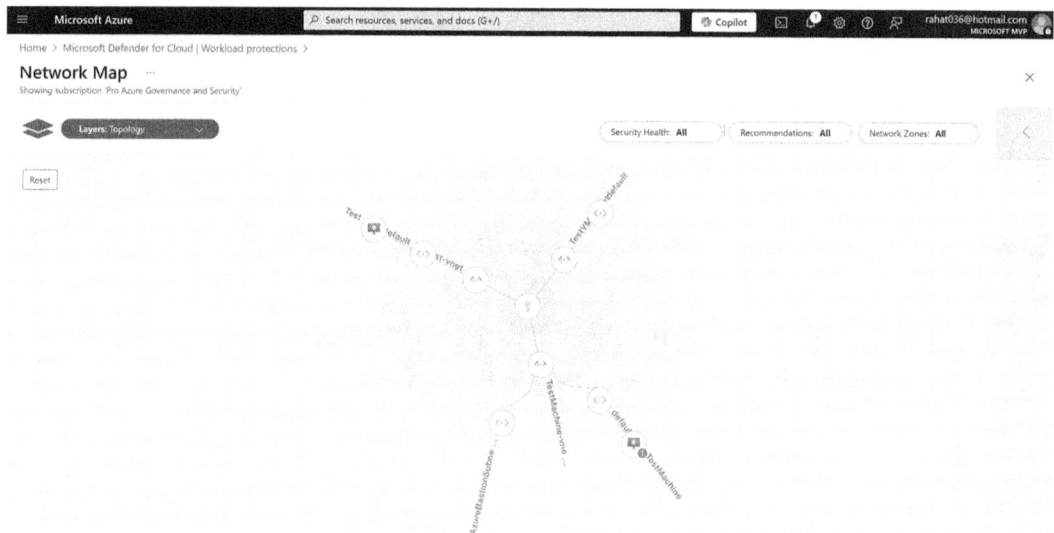

Figure 5-51. *Network topology after selecting all filters*

5. Let's drill down on some of these details listed in the diagram itself. By scrolling the mouse wheel up/down, you can zoom in/zoom out of the network map. (There is also a button for that if you don't have a wheel mouse.) Selecting any of the Azure resources in the diagram shows you more information about that specific resource as shown in Figure 5-52.

CHAPTER 5   ENHANCED SECURITY WITH MICROSOFT DEFENDER FOR CLOUD

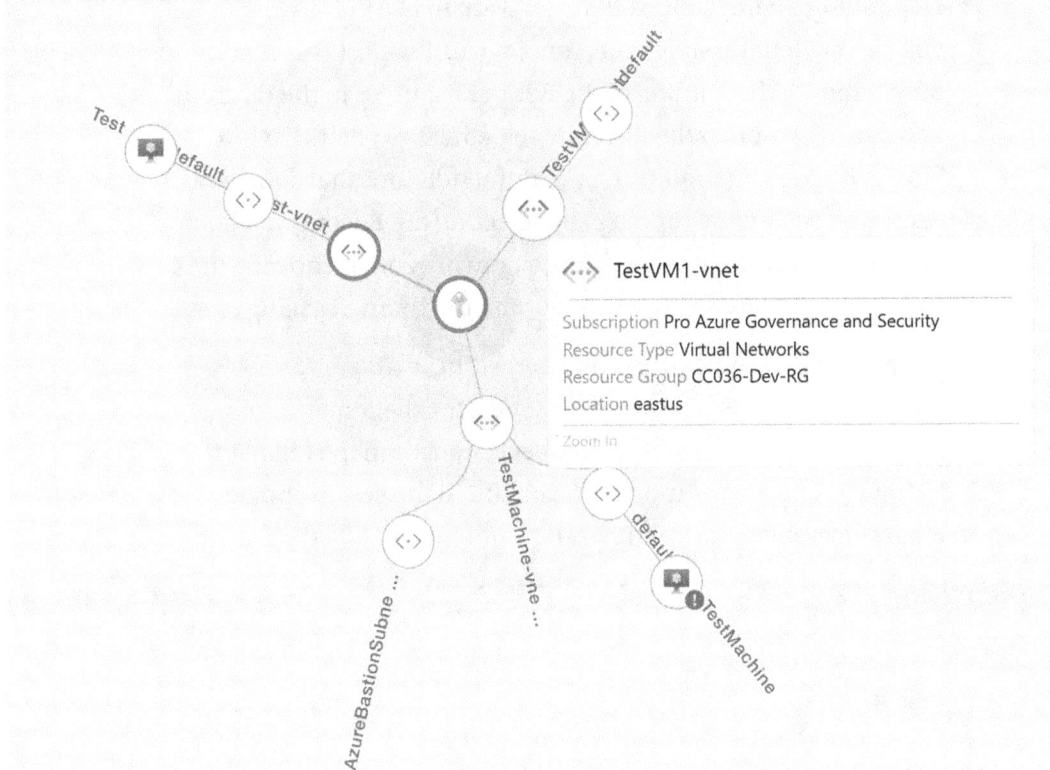

Figure 5-52. *Specific resource information in network topology*

6. It also identifies any Azure Resources for which it has security recommendations to fix, as shown in Figure 5-53.

CHAPTER 5   ENHANCED SECURITY WITH MICROSOFT DEFENDER FOR CLOUD

Figure 5-53. *Security recommendation of Azure resource in network topology*

7. As shown in Figure 5-53, notice the Info and Traffic buttons on the right. The information section lists information about the selected resources, including VNet, resource group, as well as descriptions of any recommendations to fix.

8. Now, click the Traffic button. This shows you a detailed overview of all Inbound and Outbound network traffic, including Azure Resource, as well as configured TCP and UDP ports. As I have no Outbound and Inbound traffic in my test machine, this looks empty as shown in Figure 5-54.

205

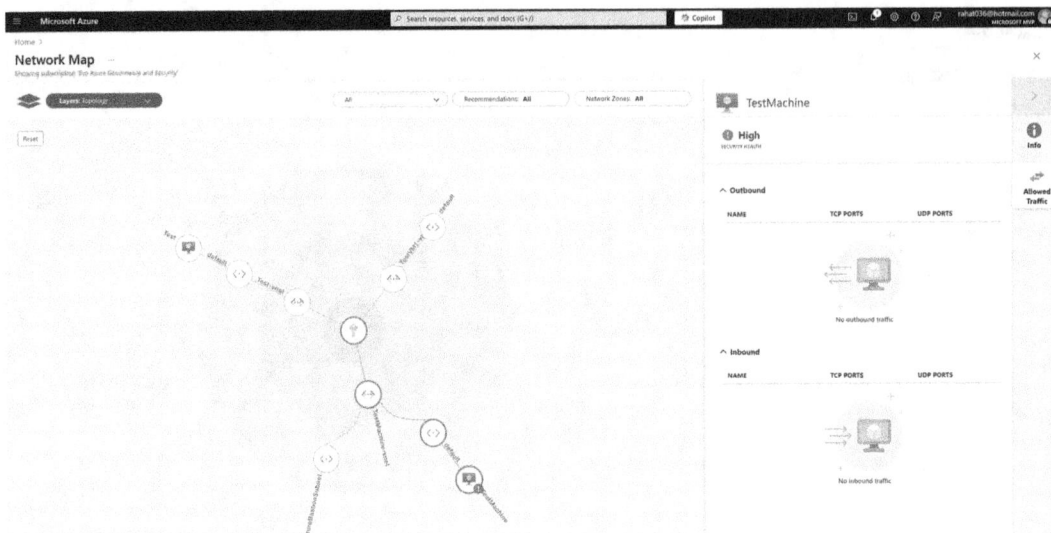

Figure 5-54. Inbound and outbound network traffic option in network topology

Firewall Management

As organizations expand their cloud presence, managing network security across multiple environments becomes increasingly complex. To address this challenge, Microsoft offers **Azure Firewall Manager**, a centralized service that streamlines the deployment and management of network security policies. With Firewall Manager, you can easily configure and govern multiple Azure Firewall instances and secure your network traffic at scale. In the following sections, I will explain Azure Firewall Manager, its architecture, and its benefits, which simplify security administration and strengthen protection across distributed cloud resources.

Azure Firewall Manager

Azure Firewall Manager is a security management service that enables centralized control and orchestration of multiple Azure Firewall instances and associated network security policies. It is specifically designed for enterprises that operate large-scale, distributed environments—such as multi-region deployments, hub-and-spoke architectures, or hybrid networks with extensive branch connectivity.

The Firewall Manager can provide security management for two network architecture types:

1. **Secured virtual hub**

   An Azure Virtual WAN Hub is a Microsoft-managed resource that lets you easily create hub-and-spoke architectures. When security and routing policies are associated with such a hub, it's referred to as a *secure virtual hub*.

2. **Hub virtual network**

   This is a standard Azure virtual network that you create and manage yourself. When security policies are associated with such a hub, it's referred to as a *hub virtual network*. At this time, only Azure Firewall Policy is supported. You can peer spoke virtual networks that contain your workload servers and services. You can also manage firewalls in standalone virtual networks that aren't peered to any spoke.

   Figure 5-55 shows the detailed comparison of *secured virtual hub* and *hub virtual network* architectures.

CHAPTER 5   ENHANCED SECURITY WITH MICROSOFT DEFENDER FOR CLOUD

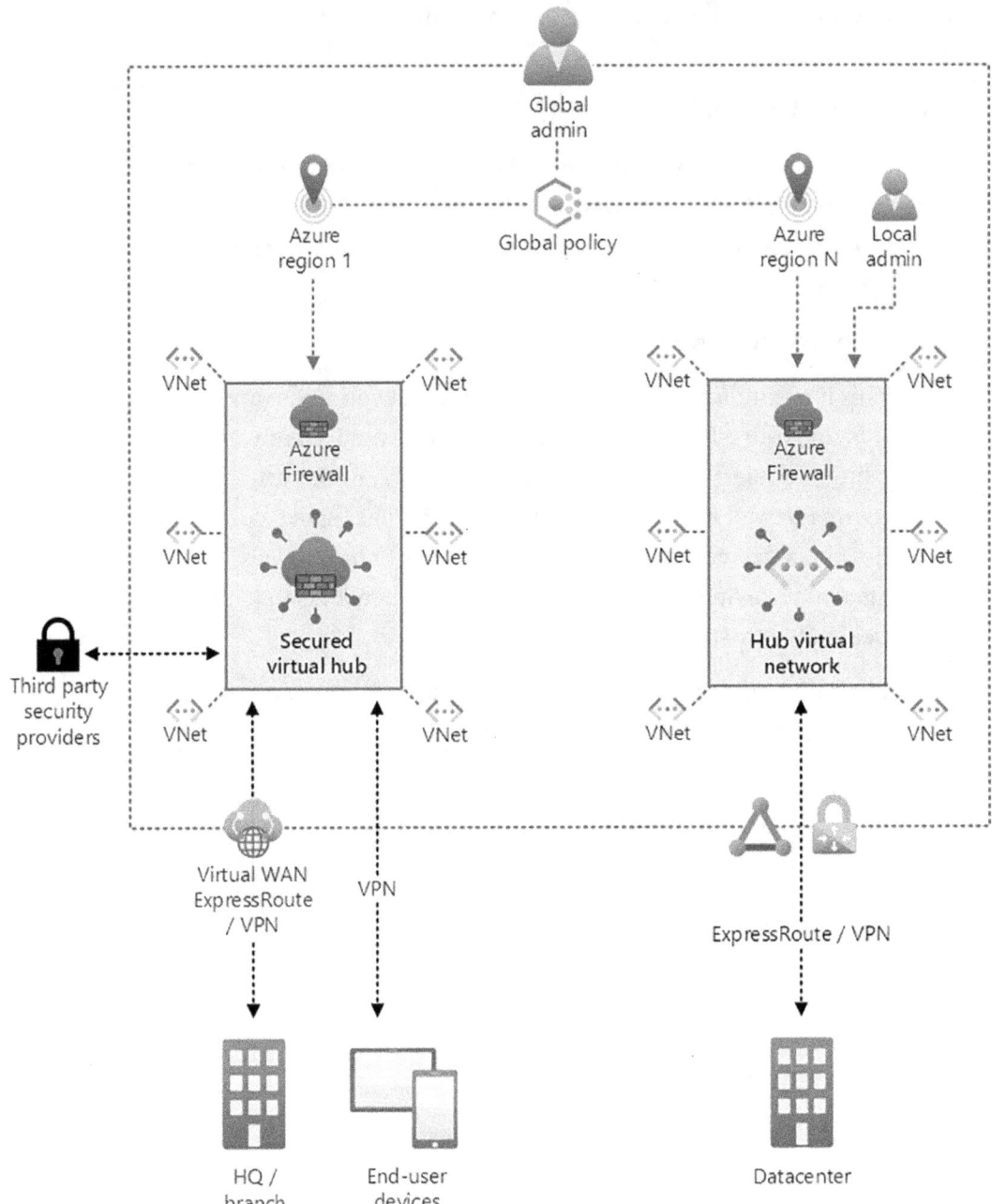

Figure 5-55. *Detailed comparison of secured virtual hub and hub virtual network architectures*

Key Features of Azure Firewall Manager

At its core, Azure Firewall Manager provides three primary capabilities:

1. **Centralized Policy Management**

    Azure Firewall Manager allows you to create and manage firewall policies centrally. These policies, which define network rules, application rules, NAT rules, threat intelligence settings, and more, can be consistently applied across multiple Azure Firewall instances, ensuring uniform protection and reducing configuration drift.

2. **Secure Virtual Hub Integration (Virtual WAN Security)**

    Firewall Manager supports Secure Virtual Hubs, where Azure Firewall instances are automatically deployed behind Azure Virtual WAN Hubs. This integration enables centralized security for large-scale, distributed environments where traffic from branches, on-premises networks, and Azure resources flow through the hub and is inspected uniformly.

3. **Policy Hierarchy and Inheritance**

    With Firewall Manager, you can design a layered policy structure:

    - Parent policies define global or corporate rules (e.g., deny access to certain regions or threat categories).

    - Child policies allow specific customizations for individual firewalls or locations. This model supports both standardization and flexibility in large enterprises.

4. **Threat Intelligence-Based Filtering**

    Firewall Manager enables centralized configuration of threat intelligence settings. Azure Firewall can alert and/or deny traffic from known malicious IP addresses and domains using threat intelligence feeds curated by Microsoft, offering proactive threat defense.

5. **Deployment Automation**

   Through Firewall Manager, you can deploy Azure Firewall instances automatically to Virtual Networks or Virtual Hubs without manually setting up each firewall. This significantly speeds up scaling and reduces operational overhead.

6. **Firewall Policy Analytics (Preview/GA in Some Regions)**

   Firewall Manager offers Policy Analytics, a feature that provides visibility into how firewall policies are used. Administrators can identify unused rules, optimize configurations, and enhance security posture by adjusting based on actual traffic patterns.

7. **Secure Internet Traffic for Branches**

   Using Secure Virtual Hubs, organizations can provide local Internet breakout for branch offices while still inspecting traffic centrally through Azure Firewall. This avoids the inefficiency of backhauling Internet traffic to a central data center.

8. **Support for Multiple Firewall SKUs**

   Firewall Manager works with both Azure Firewall Standard and Azure Firewall Premium SKUs. Premium provides advanced capabilities such as TLS inspection, IDPS (Intrusion Detection and Prevention System), and URL filtering, all manageable through Firewall Manager.

9. **Regional and Global Scalability**

   Firewall Manager is designed to manage firewall deployments across multiple Azure regions and multiple subscriptions. It supports large enterprises operating in geographically dispersed areas while maintaining a consistent security approach.

10. **Monitoring and Logging Integration**

    Firewall Manager integrates with Azure Monitor, Azure Sentinel (now Microsoft Sentinel), and Log Analytics. This provides a unified, real-time view of firewall activities, alerts, and performance metrics, empowering proactive incident response and forensic investigations.

To learn more about Azure Firewall Manager, check out the official Microsoft documentation: `https://learn.microsoft.com/en-us/azure/firewall-manager/`.

Conclusion

In this chapter, we explored the core capabilities of Microsoft Defender for Cloud, Microsoft's unified cloud-native application protection platform (CNAPP) that provides integrated tools for securing Azure, multi-cloud, and hybrid workloads. We discussed how Defender for Cloud delivers continuous security monitoring, Cloud Security Posture Management (CSPM), and Cloud Workload Protection (CWP) through modular Defender plans. You learned how features like Secure Score, Threat Intelligence Reports, security recommendations, network map, and automation playbooks guide organizations in hardening their environment, responding to threats, and achieving compliance. We also covered how to enable and manage Defender plans, simulate attacks for testing purposes, and monitor network resources and firewall policies across distributed environments.

In the next chapter, we'll shift our focus from threat protection to operational visibility by diving into Azure Monitor and Log Analytics. You will learn how to define a governance-aligned monitoring strategy; distinguish between monitoring, observability, and alerting; and explore how Azure Monitor collects telemetry from your environment. We'll walk through the core components—metrics, logs, and workbooks—as well as build Kusto Query Language (KQL) queries to analyze data and configure alerts. By the end of the chapter, you'll be equipped to design and implement a robust, intelligent, and responsive monitoring system that supports both governance and performance in your Azure ecosystem.

CHAPTER 6

Leveraging Azure Monitor and Log Analytics for Operations

In the previous chapter, we learned how Microsoft Defender for Cloud empowers organizations with threat protection, posture management, and security automation. We learned how to detect, investigate, and respond to threats using tools like Secure Score, Threat Intelligence Reports, security recommendations, and Defender playbooks. These capabilities form the reactive and proactive foundation of a secure cloud environment. However, robust cloud governance and operational resilience require more than threat defense—they demand continuous visibility into system performance, availability, and user activity.

This chapter shifts the focus to **Azure Monitor and Log Analytics**, which serve as the central observability platform for collecting, analyzing, and acting upon telemetry from Azure and hybrid resources. You'll learn how to define a monitoring strategy aligned with governance principles; understand the key differences between monitoring, logging, and alerting; and leverage tools such as **metrics**, **logs**, **workbooks**, and **alerts** to gain real-time insights. We will also explore how to build powerful queries using **Kusto Query Language (KQL)** and design intelligent alerting pipelines that support performance tuning, incident detection, and policy enforcement. Together, these tools will enable you to move from reactive monitoring to predictive operations—an essential step in mastering secure and well-governed cloud environments.

CHAPTER 6   LEVERAGING AZURE MONITOR AND LOG ANALYTICS FOR OPERATIONS

Comprehensive Monitoring Strategies

Building a strong monitoring strategy is essential for maintaining the health, performance, and security of modern IT environments. As organizations operate across on-premises, hybrid, and cloud platforms, the complexity of managing systems increases. A comprehensive monitoring approach helps create visibility across all resources, supports faster troubleshooting, ensures compliance, and aligns IT operations with business needs. It forms the foundation for proactive management and continuous improvement in dynamic environments.

Defining a Monitoring Strategy Aligned with Governance Goals

Monitoring isn't just a technical feature; it's a key part of how organizations stay compliant, secure, and operationally excellent in the cloud. But here's the truth: many Azure customers jump straight into enabling metrics and logs without asking the more strategic questions—like why they're monitoring and what they're trying to govern.

In this section, I will walk you through how to define a cloud monitoring strategy that aligns with your governance goals. We'll look at real organizational needs—not just features—and help you think through how to make monitoring purposeful and sustainable.

Step 1: Understand the Purpose of Monitoring in Governance

Monitoring is the nervous system of governance. It feeds you real-time and historical insights that answer governance-critical questions like the following:

- *Are we compliant with internal and external policies?*
- *Are we over-provisioning or overspending?*
- *Are there unapproved changes to our infrastructure?*
- *Are we exposed to any high-severity threats?*

Governance without monitoring is blind. Azure gives us tools like Azure Monitor, Policy, Defender for Cloud, and Cost Management, but we must first know *what decisions* these tools will drive.

Step 2: Define What You Want to Govern

Every monitoring strategy should begin with a list of governance focus areas. Table 6-1 shows the most common ones.

Table 6-1. List of governance with focus areas

Governance Area	Monitoring Implication
Security	Logins, role changes, firewall rules, malware alerts
Compliance	Policy compliance, audit logs, data access patterns
Cost Management	Resource usage trends, orphaned services, daily burn
Operational Health	Downtime alerts, CPU/memory spikes, service status
Data Governance	Data classifications, storage access, retention rules

Note Tie each area to a business stakeholder. For example, your finance lead may want daily burn reports, while your security officer cares about sign-in anomalies.

Step 3: Identify Who Needs What Visibility

Monitoring is not just for IT admins. Think of your organization in terms of personas:

- **CIO/CTO**: Needs executive dashboards—secure score, compliance trends, and SLAs
- **Security Team**: Wants alerts on role changes, failed logins, and threat detections
- **Finance**: Interested in forecasting costs, identifying wastage, and budgeting
- **Developers/DevOps**: Need insights into app performance and usage spikes
- **Compliance Officers**: Require evidence for audits and control effectiveness

Your monitoring strategy should define **which personas need which insights, how often, and in what format** (e.g., real-time alert vs. monthly report).

Step 4: Establish Metrics for Success

Monitoring should be measurable. Ask yourself:

- *How will we know if our monitoring is effective?*
- *What's our threshold for "normal" vs. "needs attention"?*

Define key metrics and thresholds for each governance area. I am giving some examples in Table 6-2.

Table 6-2. Example of defining key metrics and target

Governance Focus	Metric	Target
Security	Secure Score (Microsoft Defender for Cloud)	≥ 80%
Cost	Daily Spend per Sub/Resource Group	≤ $X/day
Compliance	Policy compliance rate	≥ 95%
Operations	VM availability	≥ 99.9%
Identity	MFA adoption rate	100%

Step 5: Define a Monitoring Lifecycle

Don't treat monitoring as a one-time setup. Create a lifecycle around it:

1. **Review** governance objectives quarterly.
2. **Adjust** thresholds or alerts based on new business realities.
3. **Audit** who gets reports and whether they're used.
4. **Train** teams on reading and responding to alerts.
5. **Automate** actions where appropriate (e.g., auto-remediation).

Differences Between Observability, Monitoring, and Alerting

In modern IT operations, especially within cloud-native and distributed systems, it's crucial to differentiate between observability, monitoring, and alerting. While these terms are often used interchangeably, they serve distinct purposes in system management. In Table 6-3, I tried to explain the differences between observability, monitoring, and alerting in detail.

Table 6-3. Difference between monitoring, observability, and alerting

Aspect	Monitoring	Observability	Alerting
Definition	Tracking system health by measuring predefined metrics	Understanding a system's internal state by analyzing outputs like logs, metrics, and traces	Notifying stakeholders when predefined conditions are met
Purpose	Detect known issues and system behavior deviations	Diagnose unknown or unexpected issues holistically	Trigger immediate action by notifying relevant teams
Approach	Reactive: Detects anomalies based on thresholds	Proactive: Investigates system behavior to uncover issues	Reactive: Responds when a predefined threshold is breached
Scope	Focused on predefined indicators (e.g., CPU, memory)	Comprehensive: Covers all telemetry (logs, metrics, traces)	Specific to critical conditions requiring human or automated intervention
Data Sources	Metrics (performance counters, utilization rates)	Metrics, logs, traces, events, user behavior, telemetry	Events or conditions based on monitoring and observability data
Tools Example	Azure Monitor Metrics, Azure Metrics Explorer	Azure Monitor Logs, Azure Application Insights, OpenTelemetry	Azure Monitor Alerts, Action Groups, PagerDuty

(*continued*)

Table 6-3. *(continued)*

Aspect	Monitoring	Observability	Alerting
Outcome	Know when a system is behaving outside of expected parameters	Understand *why* the system is misbehaving or deviating	Take action quickly to minimize downtime or security risks
Relation to Each Other	Foundation layer: provides raw data	Higher layer: interprets and analyzes collected data	Action mechanism: acts based on monitoring/observability findings
User Audience	Operations teams, support teams	Developers, SREs (Site Reliability Engineers), architects	Incident responders, support engineers, DevOps on call

Monitoring in Hybrid vs. Cloud-Native Environment

As cloud adoption continues to rise, many organizations find themselves operating across two worlds: hybrid environments, where legacy on-premises systems coexist with cloud services, and cloud-native environments, where applications are purpose-built to live entirely in the cloud. Each model introduces different monitoring challenges and demands distinct strategies to ensure observability, compliance, and governance.

Understanding these differences is essential for building a resilient monitoring strategy that adapts to the evolving shape of enterprise IT.

Hybrid Monitoring: Bridging Two Worlds

In a **hybrid environment**, parts of your workload remain in on-premises data centers while others are migrated to or born in Azure. For example, your finance systems may still run on traditional virtual machines in your data center, while your ecommerce portal is hosted on Azure App Service.

Monitoring in this context is about **centralization and consistency**: you want visibility across both environments with minimal fragmentation.

Key Monitoring Considerations in Hybrid Environments

- **Agent-Based Data Collection**: You often rely on the Log Analytics agent or the Azure Monitor Agent (AMA) to gather logs and performance metrics from on-premises Windows/Linux machines.

- **Integration with Legacy Tools**: Existing tools like System Center Operations Manager (SCOM) may be extended with Azure integrations to centralize monitoring.

- **Latency and Connectivity**: Network delays between on-prem and Azure resources can affect the timeliness of monitoring data and alerts.

- **Fragmented Compliance**: You need to consolidate compliance monitoring across two very different infrastructures.

Cloud-Native Monitoring: Born in the Cloud

In contrast, a cloud-native environment is built entirely on Azure's modern services—think microservices on Azure Kubernetes Service (AKS), event-driven apps on Azure Functions, and databases as a service like Cosmos DB. These systems are dynamic, distributed, and highly scalable.

Monitoring here focuses on speed, context, and depth—systems change rapidly, and monitoring must adapt just as quickly.

Key Monitoring Considerations in Cloud-Native Environments

- **Built-in Telemetry:** Azure services like App Service, AKS, and Azure SQL emit metrics and diagnostics data natively.

- **Observability by Design:** Logs, metrics, and traces are integrated from day one using Azure Monitor and Application Insights.

- **Ephemeral Resources:** Containers and functions may last seconds or make real-time collection and alerting essential.

- **High-Volume Data:** You must balance between rich insights and managing telemetry volume and cost.

Table 6-4 shows the side-by-side comparison of hybrid and cloud-native environment.

Table 6-4. Side-by-side comparison of hybrid environment and cloud-native environment

Feature/ Challenges	Hybrid Environment	Cloud-Native Environment
Infrastructure	Mix of on-premises servers and Azure resources	Entirely Azure based, using PaaS or containers
Monitoring Setup	Requires agents and connectors for on-prem systems	Built-in support via Azure Monitor and Insights
Data Sources	Event Logs, Syslog, SNMP, custom log shipping	Metrics, traces, logs via native integrations
Resource Lifespan	Static, long-lived VMs	Dynamic, short-lived containers/functions
Latency Considerations	May introduce delays due to WAN dependencies	Low-latency, native telemetry available
Tooling	SCOM, Azure Monitor, Azure Arc	Azure Monitor, Application Insights, Container Insights
Governance Complexity	Higher (two environments, different rules)	Lower (centralized policy and resource management)

Note While hybrid environments remain relevant for many organizations, this book focuses specifically on **Azure-based cloud governance and security**. For that reason, I've chosen not to include detailed demos or configurations for on-premises or hybrid monitoring scenarios. Instead, the remainder of this chapter will concentrate on **cloud-native monitoring** using Azure Monitor, Log Analytics, and Application Insights—empowering you to build scalable, secure, and observable systems fully in the cloud. If you're looking for hybrid monitoring guidance, I recommend starting with Azure Monitor for hybrid environments and Azure Arc documentation (`https://learn.microsoft.com/en-us/azure/azure-arc/overview`).

CHAPTER 6 LEVERAGING AZURE MONITOR AND LOG ANALYTICS FOR OPERATIONS

Understanding Core Concept of Azure Monitor

Before configuring Azure Monitor or analyzing data, it's essential to understand the core components that power its observability capabilities. Azure Monitor is not a single tool but a platform that collects, processes, and visualizes telemetry from across your Azure environment. At the heart of this system are three fundamental elements—**metrics**, **logs**, and **workbooks**. Each plays a distinct role: metrics offer real-time performance snapshots, logs provide detailed diagnostic and audit records, and workbooks help visualize and combine this data into actionable insights. Grasping how these elements work together is crucial for setting up effective monitoring, responding to incidents, and ensuring that your environment stays compliant, cost-efficient, and secure.

Azure Monitor also integrates seamlessly with other governance tools like Azure Policy and Microsoft Defender for Cloud, enabling organizations to correlate monitoring insights with compliance enforcement and security measures.

Metrics: Real-Time Numerical Data

Metrics are numerical values that represent the performance and health of your resources over time. They are collected at regular intervals and are ideal for identifying trends and detecting issues promptly. The fundamental characteristics of metrics are the following:

- **Time-Series Data**: Captured at consistent intervals, allowing for trend analysis.

- **Low Latency**: Available in near real time, facilitating quick detection of anomalies.

- **Pre-aggregated**: Data is aggregated to reduce storage and improve performance.

Types of Metrics

Azure Monitor provides different types of metrics depending on what you're trying to measure. The most common are **platform metrics**, which are automatically collected by Azure for services like virtual machines, storage accounts, and databases. These require no setup and give you quick insight into how your resources are performing (e.g., CPU usage or disk read/write). You can also use **custom metrics** when you need to track something specific to your application—like how long a user stays logged in or how many orders are placed per hour. These are sent to Azure Monitor using the Application Insights SDK or the Azure Monitor agent. For container-based environments like Azure Kubernetes Service (AKS), you can also collect **Prometheus metrics**, which are popular in open-source monitoring. Azure provides a managed Prometheus service to make this integration easier. Each of these metric types helps you understand different layers of your cloud environment—from the infrastructure up to the application.

Figure 6-1 shows the flowchart of Azure Monitor Metrics.

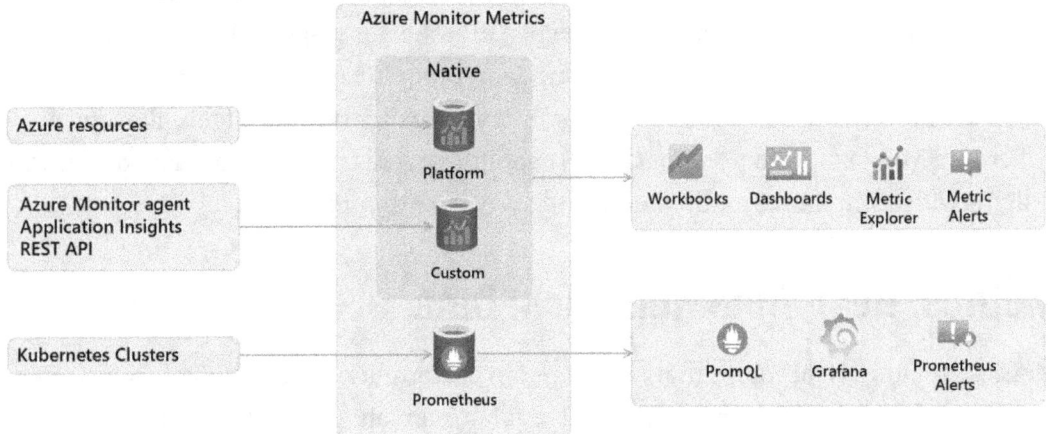

Figure 6-1. *Azure Monitor Metrics flowchart (Image: Microsoft)*

Use Case Example

I want to give an example here. Contoso Retail, an ecommerce company, uses Azure Monitor Metrics to track the performance of their shopping portal hosted on Azure App Service. During a seasonal sale, they noticed a sharp spike in **HTTP request rate** and **CPU usage**. By analyzing real-time metrics, the operations team identified that the app was hitting performance thresholds. Using autoscale rules based on these metrics, they automatically added more instances to handle the load—ensuring smooth customer experience without manual intervention. This proactive approach helped them avoid downtime and maintain service reliability during their busiest sales period.

Logs: Detailed Event and Diagnostic Data

Logs are structured records of events, providing detailed insights into the operations and diagnostics of your resources. They are stored in Log Analytics workspaces and can be queried using Kusto Query Language (KQL). The basic characteristics of Logs are the following:

- **Structured Data**: Organized in tables with defined schemas.

- **Rich Context**: Includes detailed information about events, errors, and transactions.

- **Customizable Retention**: Retention periods can be configured based on compliance and governance needs.

Types of Logs

Azure Monitor supports several types of logs, each designed to capture a specific kind of telemetry from the Azure environment. These logs are structured and stored in **Log Analytics Workspaces**, where they can be queried using Kusto Query Language (KQL). Understanding these log types is essential for designing an effective and organized monitoring setup:

- **Activity Logs** record operations at the subscription level and are automatically generated by Azure. They capture control-plane events, such as the creation, modification, or deletion of resources, and provide visibility into administrative actions across the Azure environment.

- **Resource Logs**, also known as diagnostic logs, are emitted by individual Azure resources and record internal operations. These logs are not collected by default and must be explicitly enabled using diagnostic settings. They provide detailed data-plane information, such as API requests, access events, and service-specific metrics.

- **Platform Logs** is a broader category that encompasses both activity and resource logs. These logs are generated by Azure itself and provide built-in insights into how Azure resources are behaving. They include both subscription-level and resource-level events and are a core part of platform observability.

- **Application Logs** are logs collected from the application layer, typically via Application Insights or custom logging integrations. These logs are generated by the application's runtime or code and often include trace statements, exceptions, and custom events. They help provide insights into the behavior, performance, and reliability of custom applications.

- **Security Logs** refer to telemetry related to security posture, threat detection, and compliance. These logs are collected when integrating Azure Monitor with services such as Microsoft Defender for Cloud or Microsoft Sentinel. They include information such as audit trails, security alerts, and risk assessments.

- **Custom Logs** are logs that are ingested from external sources or defined by the user. These can include logs from on-premises infrastructure, third-party tools, Syslog files, or any telemetry you define manually. Azure Monitor allows you to define custom tables to store and query this data within the Log Analytics workspace.

Each log type is stored in its own table within the workspace, with a structured schema that makes it easy to filter, search, and join with other datasets. Together, these logs provide full-spectrum visibility across applications, infrastructure, and platform services in Azure.

How Azure Monitor Logs Works

Azure Monitor Logs is a central component of Azure's observability platform, enabling you to collect, manage, and analyze log data at scale. It starts by collecting telemetry from various sources such as Azure resources, virtual machines, containers, applications, and even external systems. This data is filtered, transformed (e.g., to remove personal information or reduce volume), and then routed into structured tables within a Log Analytics workspace. Once stored, you can manage the data by customizing table schemas, configuring retention policies, selecting table plans (like Basic or Analytics), setting access controls, and monitoring log-related costs. Data is available in near real time and can be explored using Kusto Query Language (KQL) or through simplified tools like Log Analytics' Simple Mode, prebuilt Insights experiences, and ready-made queries that don't require KQL knowledge. The data can then be used across a wide range of scenarios—from troubleshooting and alerting to reporting, automation, and integration with Azure or third-party systems. Azure Monitor Logs provides the flexibility and depth needed to drive operational excellence and governance across cloud-native environments.

Figure 6-2 shows how the Azure Monitor Logs works.

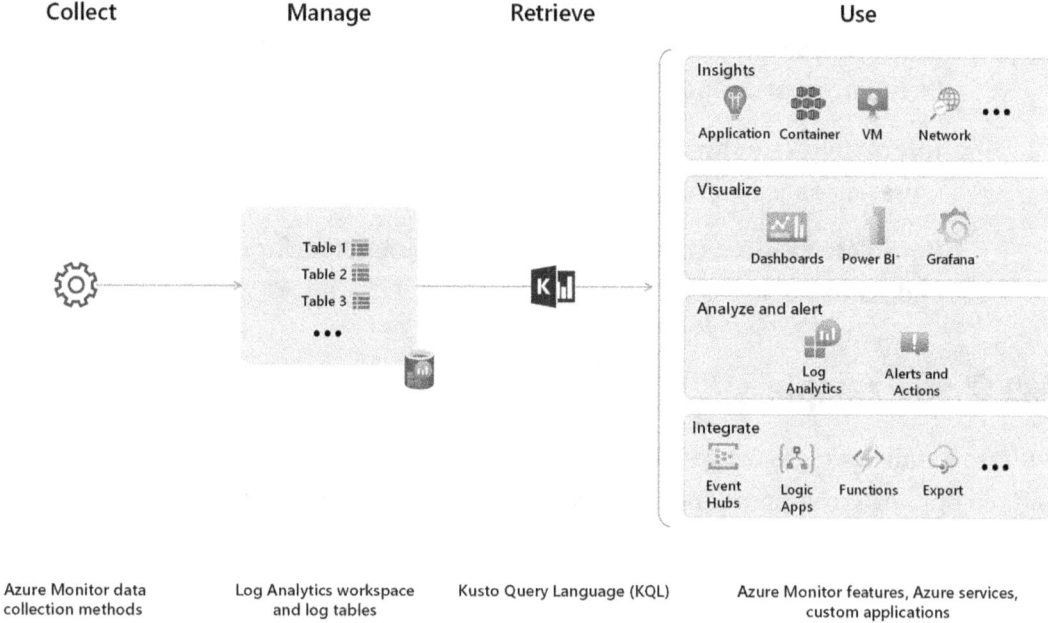

Figure 6-2. *Flowchart of how Azure monitor logs works (Image: Microsoft)*

Case Study Example

Contoso Retail also relies heavily on Azure Monitor Logs to support their security and compliance teams. After migrating their backend systems to Azure SQL Database and App Service, they configured diagnostic settings to capture detailed logs of user activity and application behavior. One evening, their security analyst noticed a spike in failed login attempts across multiple regions. Using Azure Monitor Logs and a simple KQL query, the team quickly correlated activity across resources and confirmed it was a coordinated brute-force attack. With this insight, they enforced IP restrictions and reviewed access controls. The logs not only helped them detect and respond to the threat in real time but also supported their post-incident audit and compliance documentation.

Workbooks: Interactive Data Visualization and Reporting

Workbooks are customizable reports that allow you to visualize and analyze both metrics and logs in a single pane. They provide a flexible canvas for combining text, analytics, and visuals. The key characteristics of Workbooks are the following:

- **Multi-source Integration**: Combine data from various sources, including metrics, logs, and external data.

- **Interactive Visualizations**: Use charts, graphs, and tables to represent data dynamically.

- **Parameterization**: Create templates with parameters for reusable and shareable reports.

Use Case Example

Contoso Retail leverages Azure Monitor Workbooks to create a centralized dashboard for their application support and operations teams. They built a custom workbook that combines key performance metrics like response times and server load, along with log-based insights such as failed login attempts and API error rates. By visualizing both metrics and logs in one place, the team can monitor the health of their ecommerce platform in real time. During a high-traffic Black Friday sale, the workbook helped them spot a gradual increase in failed payment transactions. With this visibility, they quickly identified a misconfigured third-party API and resolved the issue—preventing further customer impact and lost sales. The workbook now serves as their go-to operational dashboard, updated weekly to include new queries and business KPIs.

Table 6-5 shows the comparison of metrics, logs, and workbooks.

Table 6-5. Comparison of metrics, logs, and workbooks

Feature	Metrics	Logs	Workbooks
Data Type	Numerical time-series data	Structured event and diagnostic records	Combined visualizations of metrics and logs
Collection	Automatic for platform; custom via agents	Requires configuration via diagnostic settings	Manual creation combining metrics and logs

(continued)

Table 6-5. (*continued*)

Feature	Metrics	Logs	Workbooks
Storage	Azure Monitor Metrics database	Log Analytics workspace	Stored within Azure Monitor
Query Language	None (visual tools used)	Kusto Query Language (KQL)	KQL and visual configuration
Use Cases	Performance monitoring, alerting	Troubleshooting, auditing, compliance	Reporting, dashboards, interactive analysis

Exploring Log Analytics Workspace

Log Analytics Workspaces are the backbone of Azure Monitor's log data infrastructure. They serve as the central repository where telemetry—collected from virtual machines, Azure resources, applications, and diagnostics—is stored, queried, and analyzed. Whether you're tracking failed login attempts, investigating performance issues, or generating audit reports, the workspace is where all log data lives. Understanding how a workspace functions, how resources connect to it, and how you can retrieve insights using tools like Kusto Query Language (KQL) is critical for building a monitoring strategy that supports governance, compliance, and operational excellence. In this section, you'll learn what a Log Analytics Workspace is, how it fits into Azure Monitor, and how to begin working with it effectively.

What Is a Log Analytics Workspace

A **Log Analytics Workspace** is the central data environment within Azure Monitor where telemetry data is collected, stored, and analyzed. Think of it as a secure container that holds all your monitoring data—whether it comes from virtual machines, Azure resources, applications, containers, or external systems. Every log that Azure Monitor ingests—from performance metrics to security events—lands in a workspace where it can be queried and visualized.

When you enable monitoring for an Azure service, such as a virtual machine or an app service, the diagnostic logs and metrics generated by that service need to be stored somewhere. This is where the Log Analytics workspace comes into play. It serves as a backend engine for storing structured log data in tables, allowing you to retrieve and analyze it using a powerful query language called Kusto Query Language (KQL).

Unlike traditional log files, the data in a Log Analytics workspace is not raw text—it is organized into a relational format with columns and tables, making it easier to filter, join, and visualize. For example, logs related to virtual machine availability are stored in a table called Heartbeat, while logs for Azure resource activity are stored in AzureActivity. These tables are part of the workspace's internal schema and are automatically maintained by Azure based on the data sources you connect.

Each Azure subscription can have multiple workspaces, and a single workspace can be shared across many resources. This flexibility allows organizations to tailor their log storage based on team boundaries, data residency requirements, or cost optimization goals. All of this data is encrypted and can be governed using Azure Role-Based Access Control (RBAC), ensuring secure and compliant access.

In essence, a Log Analytics workspace is not just a log container—it is the analytics engine of your observability strategy. It enables centralized visibility across diverse environments, supports proactive monitoring through custom queries and dashboards, and provides the foundation for alerting, automation, and security insight across your Azure ecosystem.

You can think of it as the **"brain" of Azure Monitor Logs**, transforming raw telemetry into useful, queryable, and actionable intelligence.

Creating and Adding Resources in Log Analytics Workspace

Before you begin analyzing telemetry with Azure Monitor Logs, you must first create a **Log Analytics Workspace**—the secure, centralized location where monitoring data is collected and stored. Once created, you can connect Azure resources to this workspace so their logs and metrics flow in and become available for querying and alerting.

Let's walk through both stages: **creating** the workspace and **adding resources** to it.

CHAPTER 6   LEVERAGING AZURE MONITOR AND LOG ANALYTICS FOR OPERATIONS

Creating a Log Analytics Workspace

To create a workspace from the Azure Portal:

1. Sign in to the Azure Portal from `https://portal.azure.com`.

2. In the top search bar, type **Log Analytics workspaces** and select the service as shown in Figure 6-3.

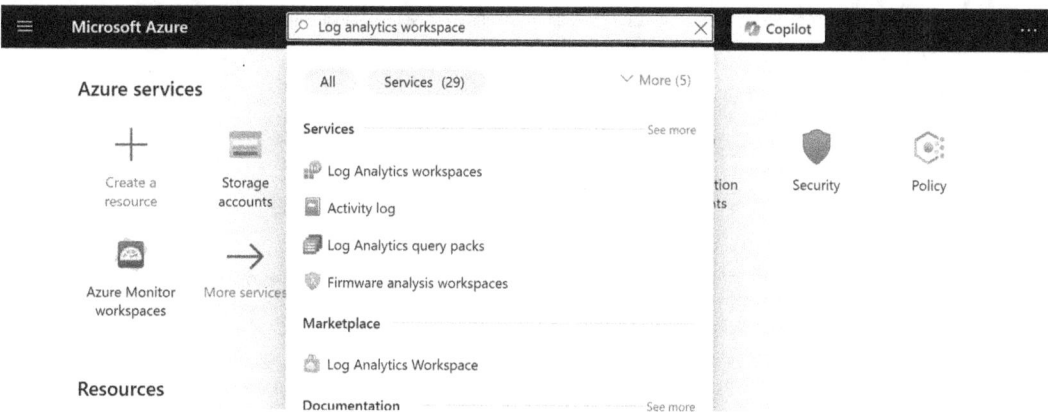

Figure 6-3. Searching Log Analytics Workspace in Azure

3. Click **+ Create** as shown in Figure 6-4.

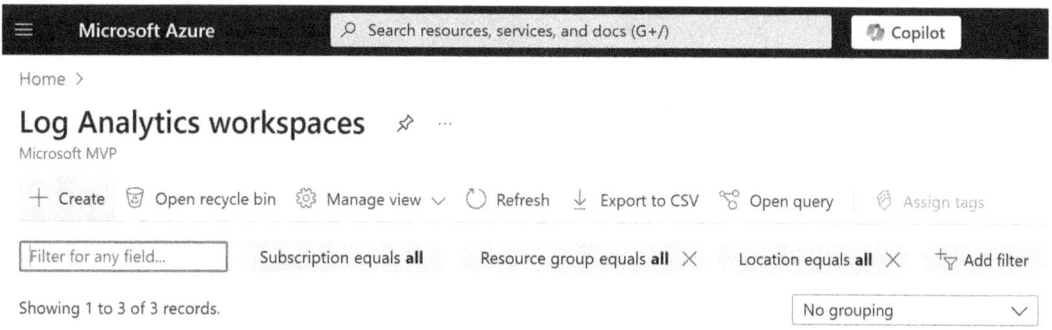

Figure 6-4. Creating Log Analytics Workspace

4. Fill in the required fields:

   - **Subscription**: Choose the correct subscription.
   - **Resource Group**: Select an existing one or create a new one.

229

CHAPTER 6 LEVERAGING AZURE MONITOR AND LOG ANALYTICS FOR OPERATIONS

- **Name**: Give your workspace a unique and descriptive name.

- **Region**: Choose the same region as the resources you plan to monitor (for performance and cost efficiency).

5. Click **Review + Create**, then click **Create** to deploy the workspace as shown in Figure 6-5.

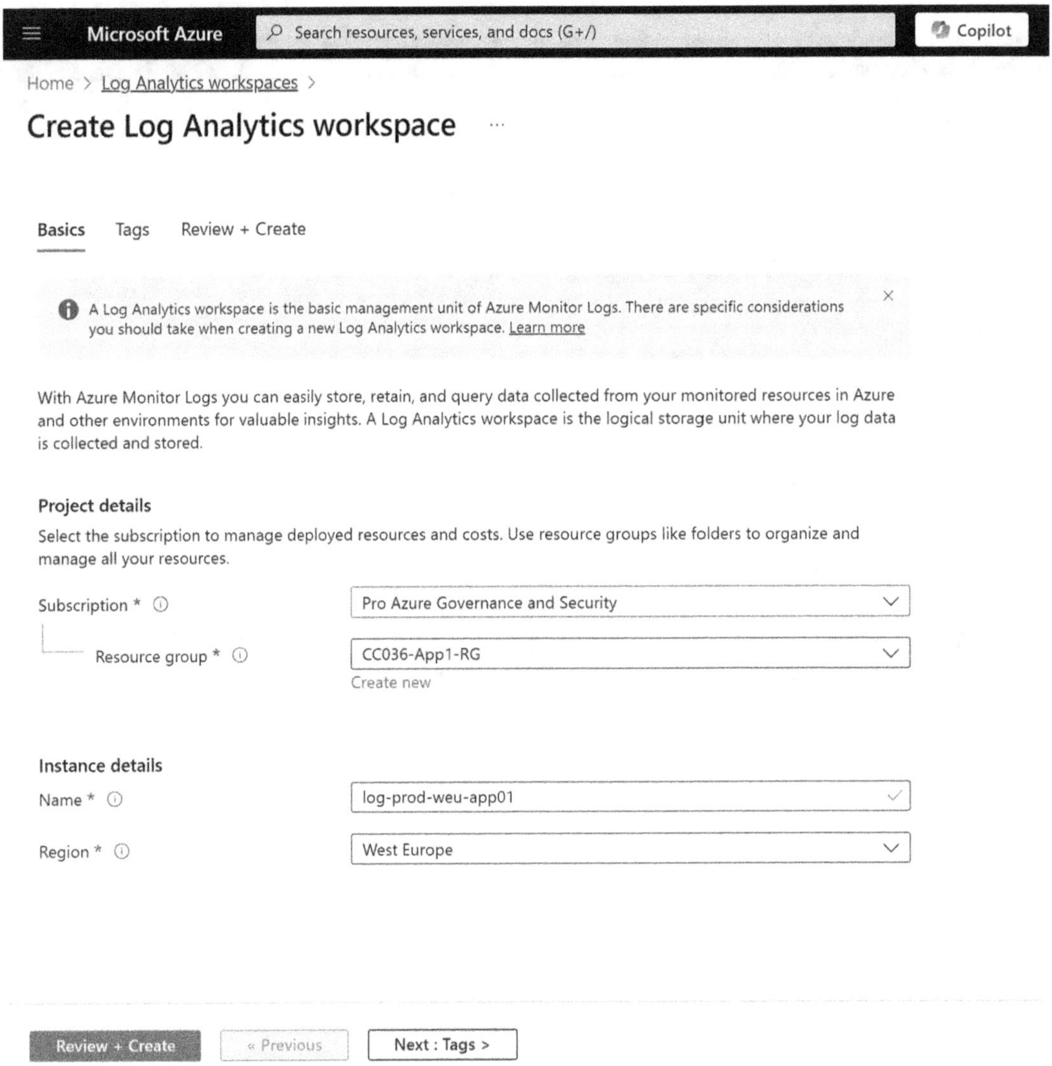

Figure 6-5. Reviewing and creating Log Analytics workspace

> **Note** Use a naming convention that reflects the scope and purpose of the workspace (e.g., log-prod-weu-app01).

Adding Resources to the Workspace

Once the workspace is deployed, you can begin connecting Azure resources to it so they can send telemetry. This step varies slightly depending on the type of resource, for example:

For Azure Services (e.g., Storage Accounts, Key Vault, SQL)

1. Open the target resource in the Azure Portal. For our case, I am selecting a storage account by searching Storage accounts and selecting the account as shown in Figure 6-6.

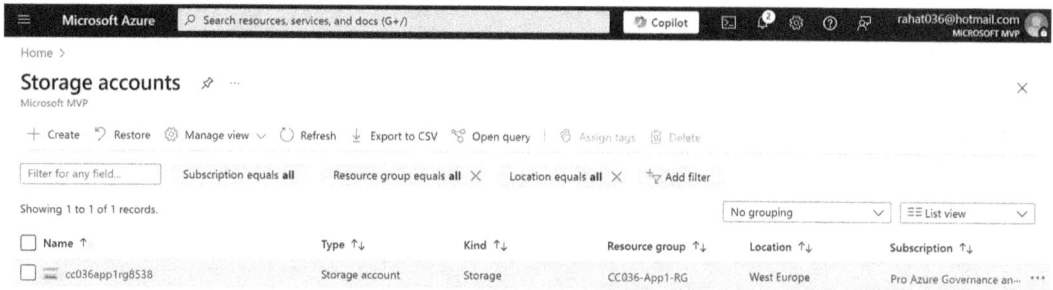

Figure 6-6. Selecting storage account

2. In the left-hand menu, go to **Monitoring ➤ Diagnostic settings** and select the resource to view the diagnostic settings as shown in Figure 6-7.

CHAPTER 6   LEVERAGING AZURE MONITOR AND LOG ANALYTICS FOR OPERATIONS

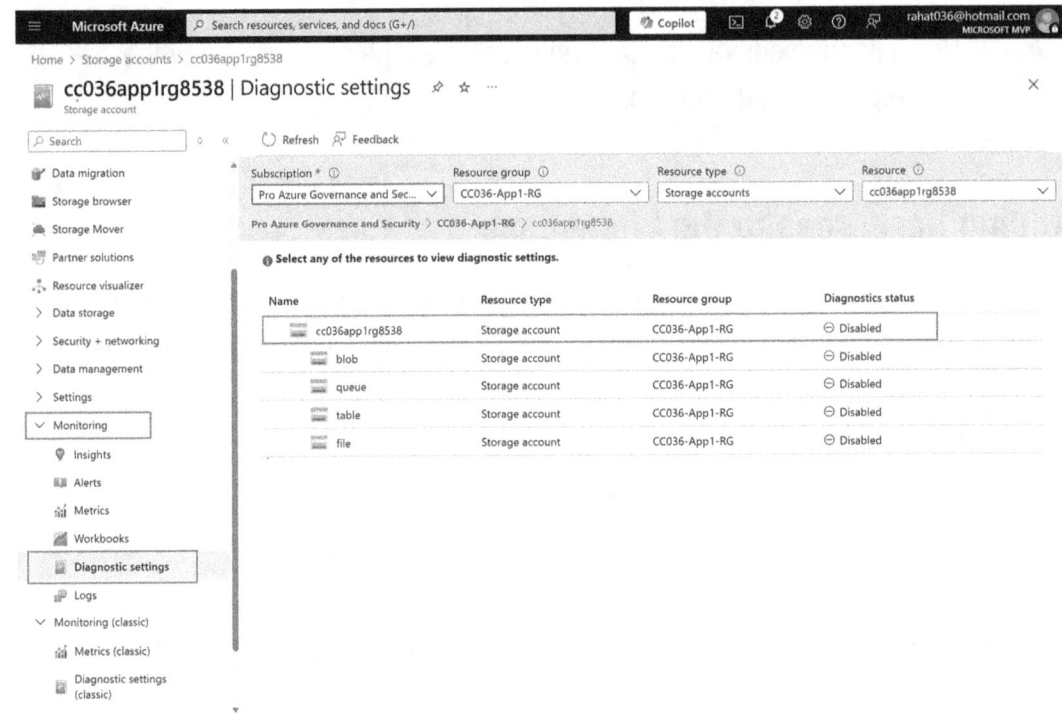

Figure 6-7. *Selecting resource for diagnostic settings*

3. Click + **Add diagnostic setting** as shown in Figure 6-8.

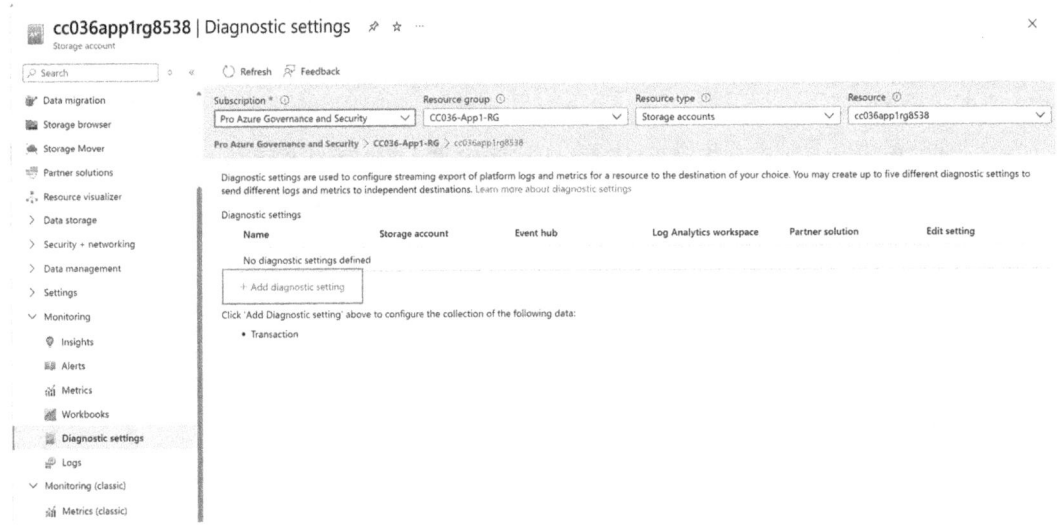

Figure 6-8. *Adding diagnostic settings*

4. Choose which **logs and metrics** you want to send. For our case, I select the Transaction under Metrics.

5. Under **Destination details**, check **Send to Log Analytics workspace** as shown in Figure 6-9.

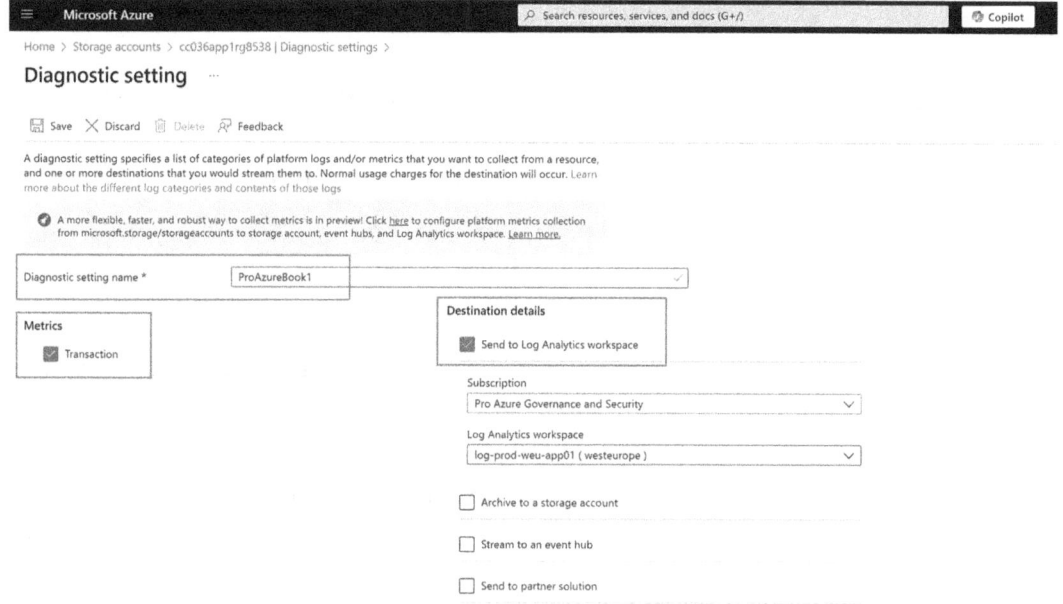

Figure 6-9. *Configuring destination details*

6. Select the workspace you created earlier in Log Analytics workspace option.

7. Save the configuration.

Writing Basic Kusto Query Language (KQL)

Kusto Query Language (KQL) is the powerful query language used to explore and analyze data in Azure Monitor Logs. It allows you to retrieve, filter, and summarize large volumes of telemetry stored in your Log Analytics Workspace using a simple, readable syntax. In this section, you'll learn how to write basic KQL queries to gain insights into your environment—even if you're completely new to query languages.

What Is Kusto Query Language (KQL)

Kusto Query Language (KQL) is a powerful, read-only language designed specifically for querying large-scale log and telemetry data in Azure. It is the primary language used to extract, transform, and analyze data stored in Log Analytics Workspaces and is shared across multiple Azure services including Azure Monitor, Microsoft Sentinel, Application Insights, and Data Explorer.

KQL is optimized for speed, flexibility, and simplicity. Even users with minimal query experience can begin writing meaningful queries in just a few lines of code.

To learn more about KQL, refer to the official Microsoft documentation at https://learn.microsoft.com/en-us/kusto/query/?view=microsoft-fabric.

What Is a Kusto Query?

A Kusto query is a sequence of operations that defines how data should be retrieved and displayed. At a minimum, a query starts with a table name and applies one or more operators (like **where**, **project**, or **summarize**) to filter, shape, or analyze the data.

You can think of a Kusto query as a pipeline: raw data flows in, passes through several stages of transformation, and exits as a refined result.

What Is a Query Statement?

In KQL, a query statement is a complete instruction that returns data from one or more tables. Each statement ends in either a visible result (like a table or chart) or feeds into another operation such as a **join**, **summarize**, or **render**.

A basic query statement has the form

```
<TableName>
| <Operator1>
| <Operator2>
...
```

for example,

```
Heartbeat
| where TimeGenerated > ago(1h)
| summarize count() by Computer
```

CHAPTER 6   LEVERAGING AZURE MONITOR AND LOG ANALYTICS FOR OPERATIONS

This statement retrieves all **Heartbeat** logs from the last hour and counts them by computer name.

Basic KQL Syntax Elements

In Table 6-6, I tried to add some core building blocks that you'll use in almost every KQL query.

Table 6-6. Example of KQL elements with purpose

Element	Purpose	Example
Where	Filters rows based on a condition	**where CPUUsage > 80**
project	Select specific columns	**project TimeGenerated, Computer**
order by	Sorts the result set	**order by TimeGenerated desc**
summarize	Groups row and calculates aggregates	**summarize avg(CPU) by bin(TimeGenerated, 5m)**
extend	Adds calculated columns	**extend LoadRatio = CPU/Cores**
limit/take	Returns only the top N rows	**take 10**

You can get the full list of KQL operator/function with description and syntax in the following Microsoft documentation: https://learn.microsoft.com/en-us/kusto/query/kql-quick-reference?view=microsoft-fabric.

Hands-On Examples

Let's now explore a set of practical KQL queries, designed to help you navigate and extract insights from your Azure monitoring data. Each query includes a short explanation, so you understand what the query does, why it's useful, and how to adapt it to your environment.

Return the Latest Log Entries

```
Heartbeat
| take 10
```

This query pulls the ten most recent entries from the **Heartbeat** table, which tracks the availability of your virtual machines. It's a simple way to verify that your VM monitoring is active and data is flowing into the workspace.

Filter Logs by a Specific Computer

```
Heartbeat
| where Computer == "vm-app-01"
```

Here, you're filtering the data to only show logs from a VM named **vm-app-01**. The **where** clause acts like a filter, helping you zoom in on logs for a particular resource without the noise from others.

Select Specific Columns

```
Heartbeat
| project TimeGenerated, Computer, Category
```

This query limits the output to only three columns: timestamp, computer name, and log category. Use **project** when you want to narrow the data view to the most relevant fields—this helps declutter the results and improves performance.

Sort Logs by Time (Most Recent First)

```
Heartbeat
| order by TimeGenerated desc
```

This orders the results from newest to oldest based on when the log entry was generated. It's particularly useful when troubleshooting recent activity or events in your system.

Count Heartbeat Entries per VM

```
Heartbeat
| summarize Count = count() by Computer
```

This groups the logs by computer name and counts how many heartbeat signals each machine has sent. It helps assess whether all VMs are reporting consistently or if one is silent—indicating a possible issue.

Measure Average CPU Usage Over Time

```
Perf
| where CounterName == "% Processor Time"
| summarize AvgCPU = avg(CounterValue) by bin(TimeGenerated, 5m), Computer
```

This query looks at performance data, specifically CPU usage, from the **Perf** table. It filters by the counter name for processor usage and then calculates the average CPU value every five minutes per machine. This is ideal for identifying CPU spikes or trends over time.

Identify Failed Login Attempts

```
SigninLogs
| where ResultType != 0
| summarize FailedLogins = count() by bin(TimeGenerated, 1h), UserPrincipalName
```

This example comes from the **SigninLogs** table (if auditing is enabled). It finds failed logins by filtering on non-zero result codes and summarizes them per user per hour. This can be a key input for security alerting or investigations.

These foundational examples give you the building blocks for more advanced KQL use. Once you're comfortable with filtering, projecting, and aggregating, you'll be ready to create dashboards, set up alerts, or automate responses—all powered by your log data.

Real-World Use Cases

Once you've learned the basics of Kusto Query Language (KQL), the next step is using it to solve actual business and operational challenges. In real-world environments, KQL is more than a technical tool—it becomes a way to enforce governance, ensure compliance, monitor performance, and respond to security events.

Below are several common, real-world scenarios where KQL becomes indispensable.

Detecting Repeated Sign-In Failures Across Users

Failed login attempts can be a sign of misconfiguration—or attempted compromise. You can use KQL to detect users with repeated failed sign-ins over a defined time window:

```
SigninLogs
| where ResultType != 0
| summarize FailedAttempts = count() by bin(TimeGenerated, 1h),
  UserPrincipalName
| where FailedAttempts > 5
```

This helps security teams detect brute-force attempts or credential issues and enables alerting through Azure Monitor.

Identifying Unauthorized Resource Deletions

To support audit requirements, you might want to monitor for when critical resources are deleted:

```
AzureActivity
| where OperationNameValue == "Microsoft.Resources/subscriptions/
  resourceGroups/delete"
| project TimeGenerated, ResourceGroup, Caller, ActivityStatusValue
```

This query shows who deleted which resource group and when, helping you enforce governance and accountability.

Tracking Cost-Intensive Operations Over Time

You can monitor operations that contribute to unexpected costs—like excessive reads from storage or high transaction volumes:

```
AzureDiagnostics
| where ResourceType == "MICROSOFT.STORAGE/STORAGEACCOUNTS"
| summarize TotalReadOps = sum(TotalRequests) by bin(TimeGenerated, 1d),
  Resource
```

This helps operations teams optimize usage patterns and control budgets.

Checking Virtual Machine Health and Reporting Gaps

To ensure all VMs are online and reporting, you can run

```
Heartbeat
| summarize LastSeen = max(TimeGenerated) by Computer
| where LastSeen < ago(30m)
```

This identifies any virtual machines that have not reported in the last 30 minutes, which may indicate downtime, misconfiguration, or a monitoring agent issue.

Monitoring Role Assignments for Compliance

Unauthorized role assignments can violate least-privileged principles. This query identifies such changes:

```
AuditLogs
| where OperationName == "Add member to role"
| project TimeGenerated, TargetResources, InitiatedBy, Result
```

This can be embedded into governance controls to detect policy violations or excessive permissions.

Demo: Try KQL Using Microsoft Demo Environment

Once you've learned the basics of Kusto Query Language (KQL), the next step is using it to solve actual business and operational challenges. In real-world environments, KQL is more than a technical tool—it becomes a way to enforce governance, ensure compliance, monitor performance, and respond to security events.

To help you build confidence with Kusto Query Language (KQL), Microsoft offers a **free interactive demo environment**. This demo simulates a real Log Analytics workspace filled with sample telemetry from virtual machines, containers, and applications—so you can practice writing and running KQL queries in a live context without touching your production resources.

This is especially useful for new learners, as it provides

- Pre-populated tables (e.g., Heartbeat, Perf, and VMConnection)
- A built-in query editor with IntelliSense
- Query templates and usage examples
- No need for an Azure subscription

CHAPTER 6   LEVERAGING AZURE MONITOR AND LOG ANALYTICS FOR OPERATIONS

For our demo, I will use the AppAvailabilityResults table that stores results from synthetic availability tests (like ping tests or URL pings). Each row represents a single test run and includes information such as success/failure status, duration, location, and error messages.

I will demonstrate various types of KQL queries that can be used in different scenarios.

Let's walk through a demo now.

1. Visit https://aka.ms/LADemo. Sign in with your Microsoft account if prompted. This takes you to the Logs view of a Log Analytics Workspace with simulated Application Insights data as shown in Figure 6-10.

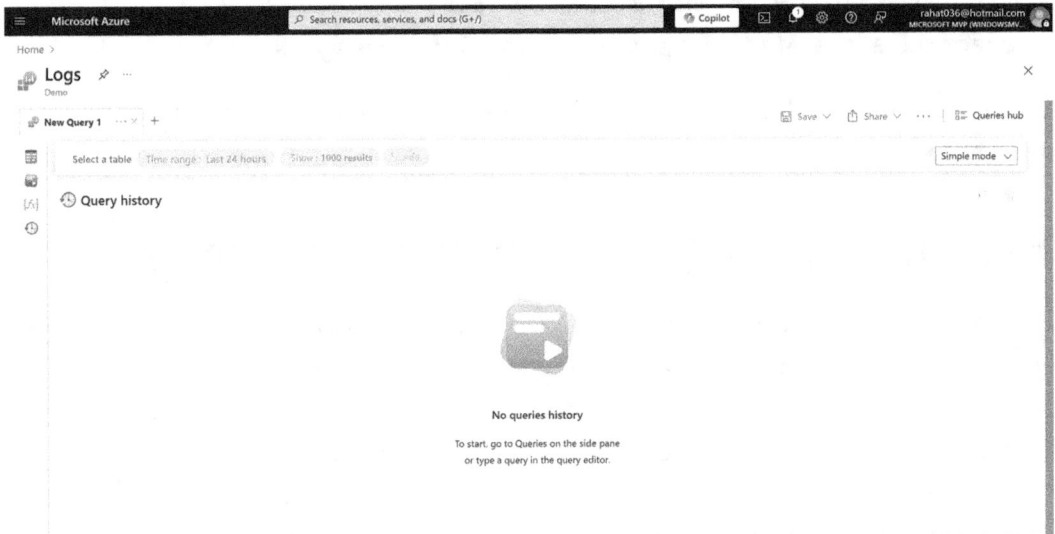

Figure 6-10.   KQL query history page

2. On the left side of the page, you will see a list of available tables like Heartbeat, Perf, VMConnection, etc. as shown in Figure 6-11. Make sure you can see and access the tables.

CHAPTER 6   LEVERAGING AZURE MONITOR AND LOG ANALYTICS FOR OPERATIONS

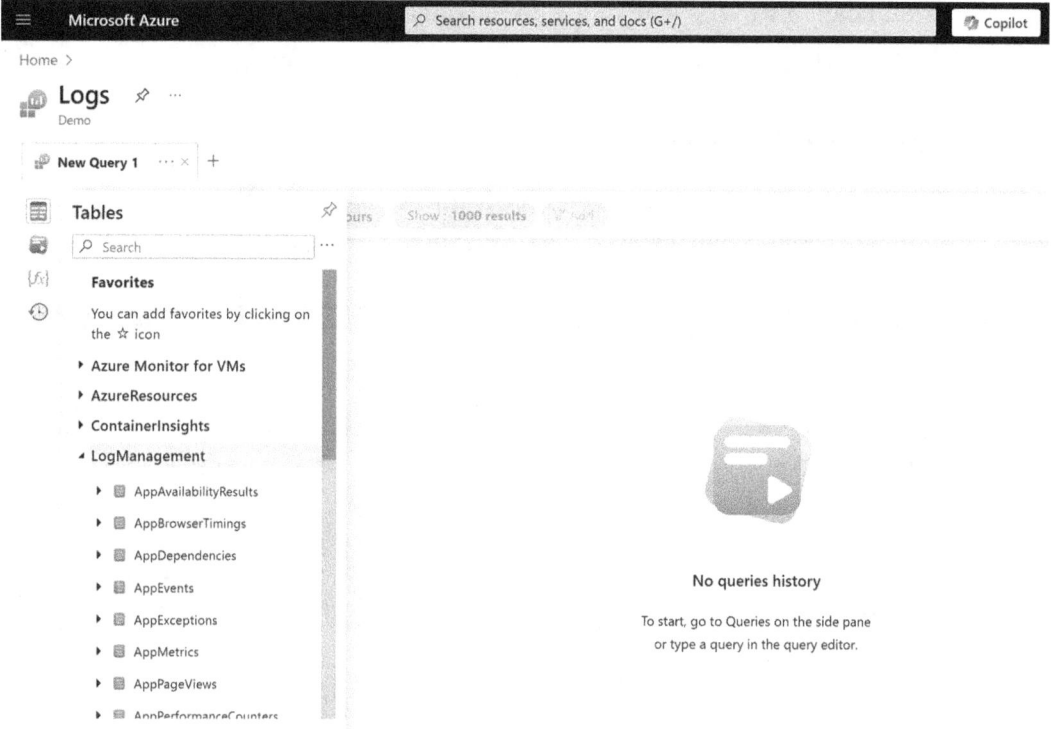

Figure 6-11.   Tables of default query in KQL

3. At the top, there is a KQL query editor where you can type and run queries. By default, you can see the Simple mode; you need to change this to KQL mode as shown in Figure 6-12.

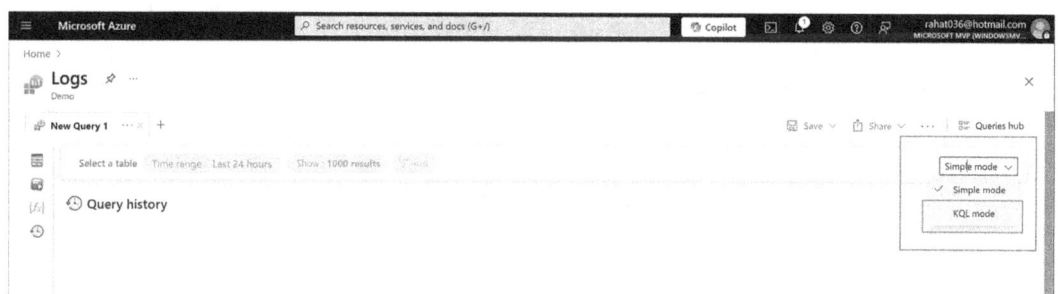

Figure 6-12.   Changing the mode to simple to KQL

CHAPTER 6   LEVERAGING AZURE MONITOR AND LOG ANALYTICS FOR OPERATIONS

4. After changing to the KQL mode, in the query section, type the following KQL query:

   `AppAvailabilityResults`

   After running the query, you can verify the table is accessible or not. If accessible, you can see the result shown in Figure 6-13.

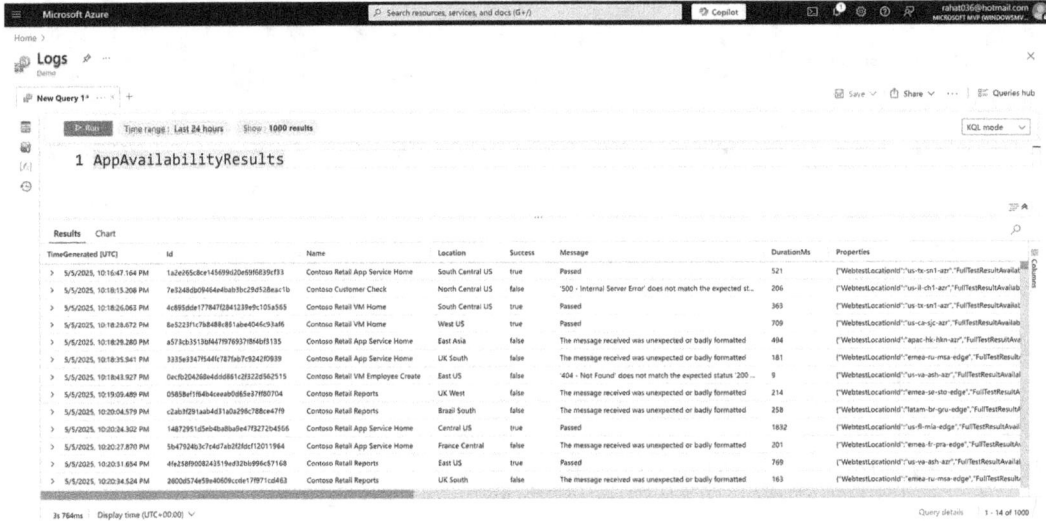

Figure 6-13. Running AppAvailabilityResults in KQL query

5. Now, fetch ten of the most recent test results across all applications and locations with the following query:

   `AppAvailabilityResults`
   `| take 10`

   You will get the ten most recent test results in the result section as shown in Figure 6-14.

CHAPTER 6 LEVERAGING AZURE MONITOR AND LOG ANALYTICS FOR OPERATIONS

Figure 6-14. *Sorting the ten most recent test results*

6. Now, I will show you how to filter the specific information from a table. For example, I will now filter the failed tests only. This will show when and where the failure happened, which test it was, and the error message. For this, run the following query in KQL query section:

AppAvailabilityResults
| where Success == false
| project TimeGenerated, Name, Location, Message

When you run this query, it will show you the result as shown in Figure 6-15.

243

CHAPTER 6   LEVERAGING AZURE MONITOR AND LOG ANALYTICS FOR OPERATIONS

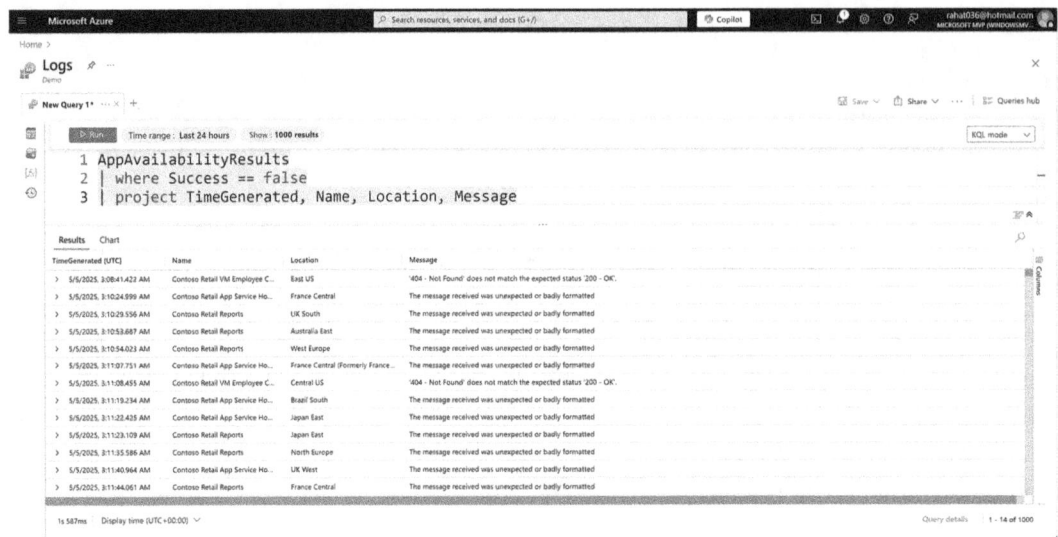

Figure 6-15. Filtering the search with specific information

7. To summarize failure count by name, run the following query in KQL query section:

AppAvailabilityResults
| where Success == false
| summarize Failures = count() by Name

When you run the query, it will show the summary list as shown in Figure 6-16.

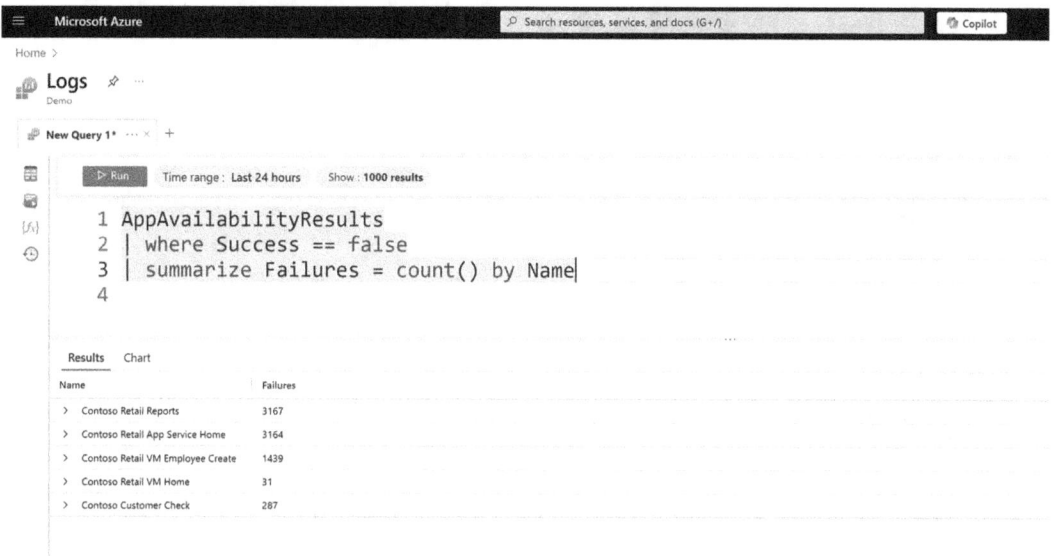

Figure 6-16. *Summarizing the search result*

8. Even you can calculate the percentage of successful test runs per hour, showing availability trends. To get the information, run the following KQL query:

**AppAvailabilityResults
| summarize SuccessRate = avg(todouble(Success)) * 100 by bin(TimeGenerated, 1h)
| order by TimeGenerated desc**

By running this query, it will show the following information as shown in Figure 6-17.

CHAPTER 6   LEVERAGING AZURE MONITOR AND LOG ANALYTICS FOR OPERATIONS

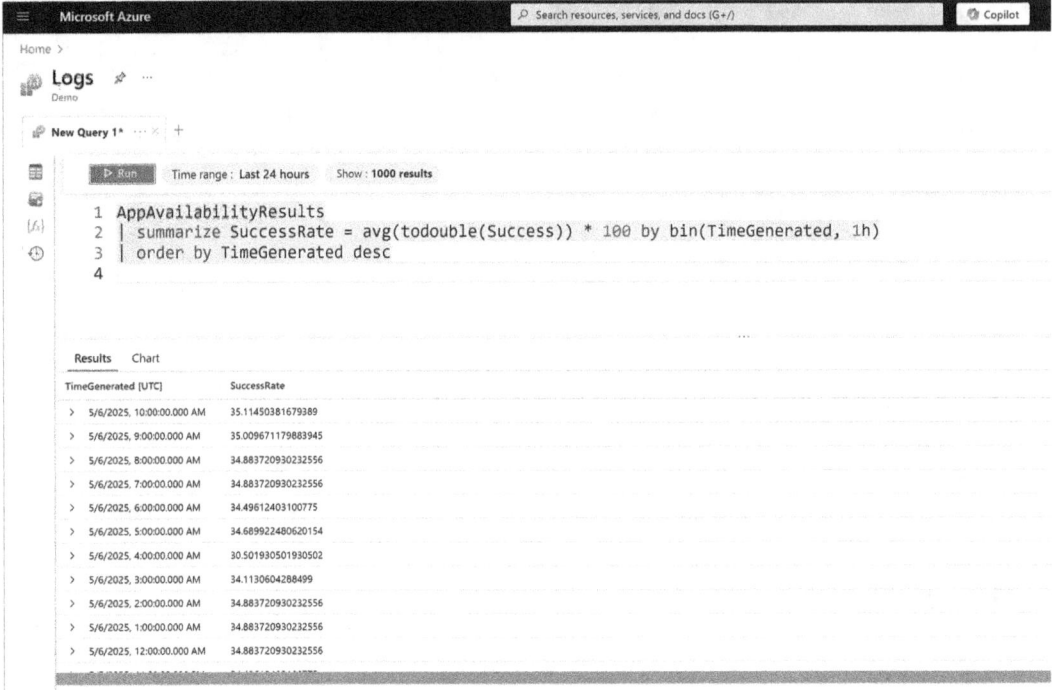

Figure 6-17. Calculating success rate percentage

Automated Alerting and Response

Collecting telemetry is only the first step in building an intelligent, governed cloud environment. The real value of monitoring comes when you can act on that data—**automatically, in real time, and with minimal manual intervention**. Azure Monitor's alerting and automation capabilities empower teams to stay ahead of issues by detecting abnormal conditions, notifying the right stakeholders, and even triggering remediation workflows without human input.

In this section, we'll explore how to create actionable alerts, route them to appropriate responders, and integrate with services like Azure Automation, Logic Apps, and Defender for Cloud to build fully automated, governance-driven response pipelines.

CHAPTER 6 LEVERAGING AZURE MONITOR AND LOG ANALYTICS FOR OPERATIONS

Setting Up Alerting in Azure Monitor

Azure Monitor alerts allow you to detect and respond to conditions in your environment proactively. Whether it's a CPU spike, unauthorized login attempt, or cost anomaly, setting up alerts ensures the right people or automation workflows are notified at the right time.

Create an Alert for High CPU Usage on a Virtual Machine

I will show you how to create an alert for high CPU usage on VM. To do this, let's walk through the steps:

1. In the Azure Portal, search for **Monitor** from the top search bar.

2. Open the **Azure Monitor** service.

3. In the Monitor blade, click Alerts from the left-hand menu as shown in Figure 6-18.

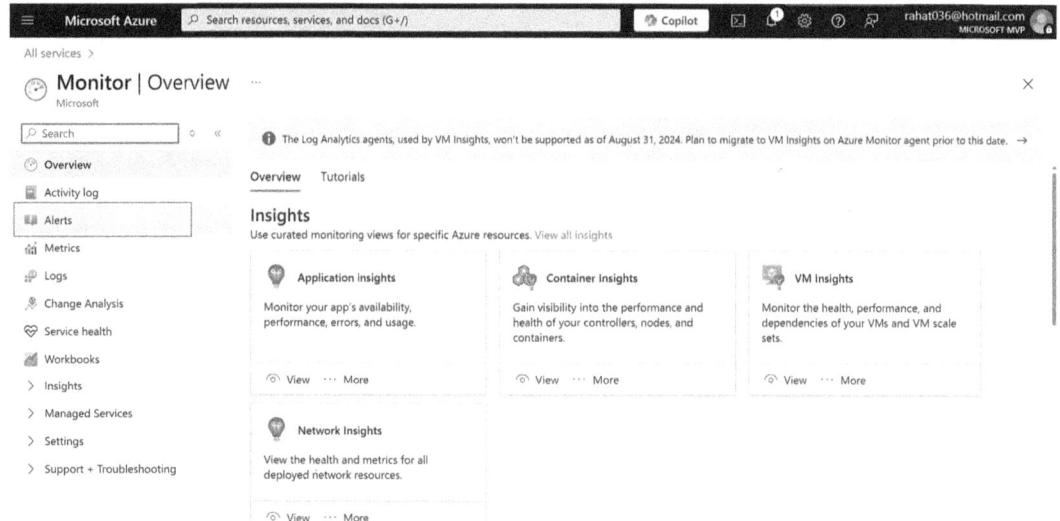

Figure 6-18. Alert page of monitor section of Azure

4. Click **+ Create** and select **Alert rule** as shown in Figure 6-19.

CHAPTER 6   LEVERAGING AZURE MONITOR AND LOG ANALYTICS FOR OPERATIONS

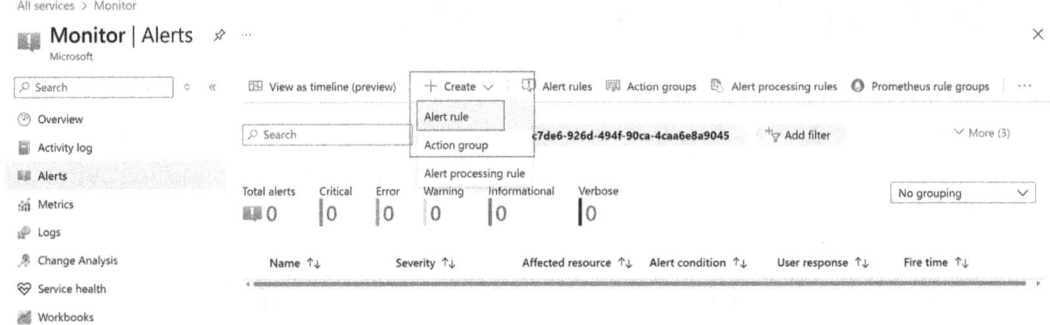

Figure 6-19. Creating a new alert rule

5. Under Scope, click Select resource.

6. Search for and choose the VM you want to monitor as shown in Figure 6-20.

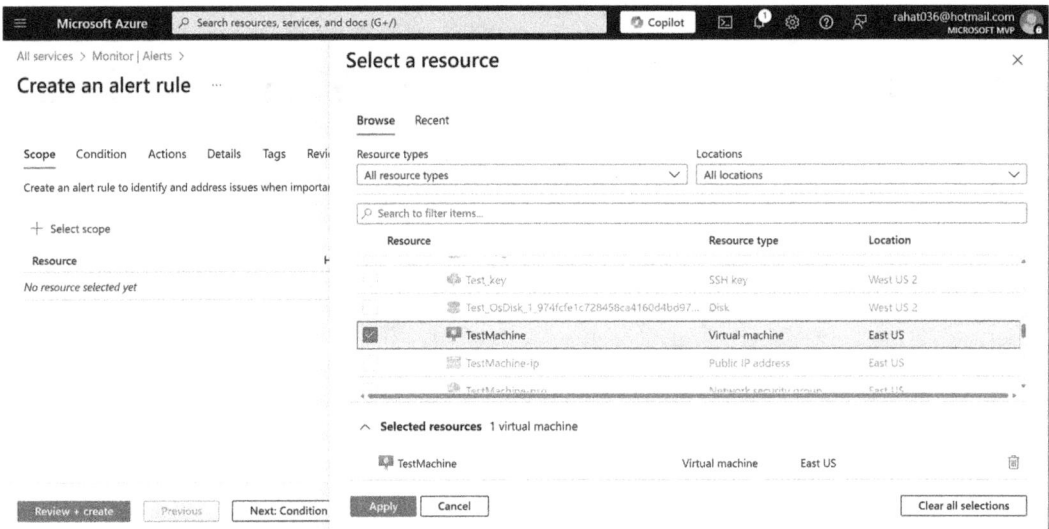

Figure 6-20. Selecting the VM for creating new alert rule

7. Click Apply to confirm.

8. Under Condition, in the Signal type, select **Percentage CPU** as shown in Figure 6-21.

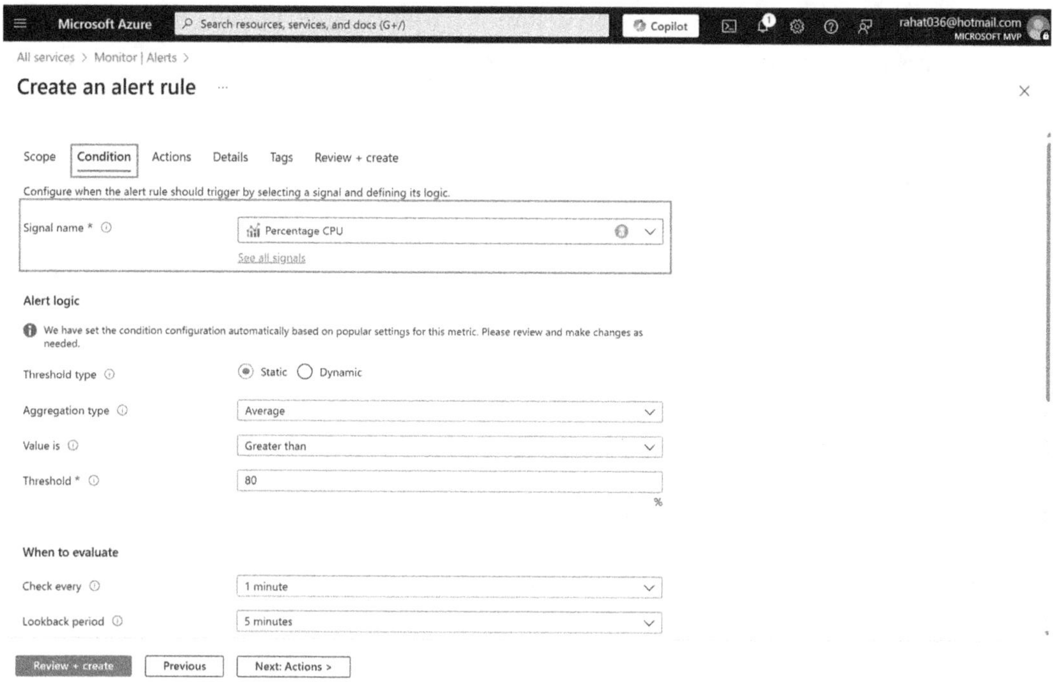

CHAPTER 6   LEVERAGING AZURE MONITOR AND LOG ANALYTICS FOR OPERATIONS

Figure 6-21. Selecting the Signal type

9. Set the Aggregation type to Average and choose greater than 80% as the threshold as shown in Figure 6-22.

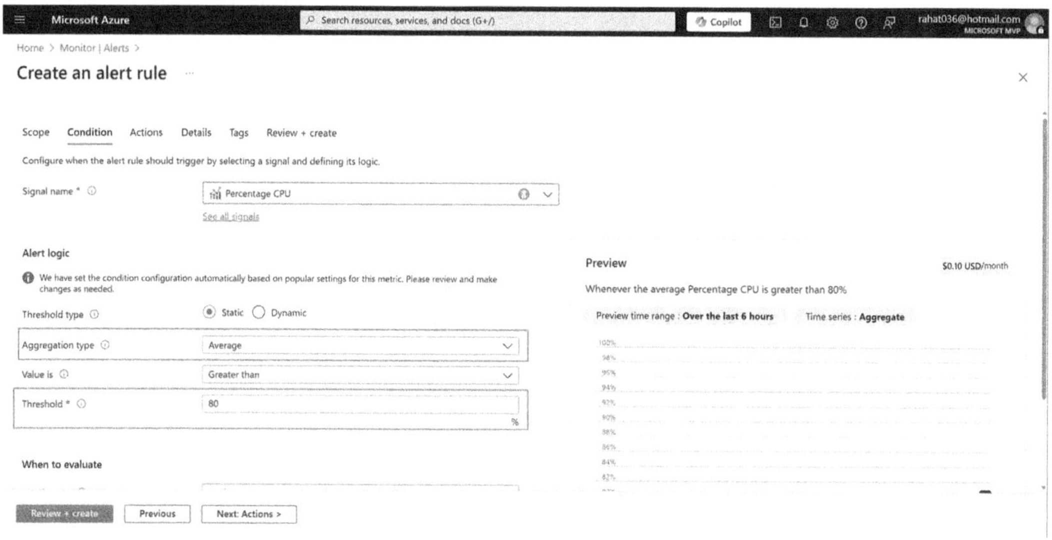

Figure 6-22. Setting up the aggregation type and threshold

CHAPTER 6 LEVERAGING AZURE MONITOR AND LOG ANALYTICS FOR OPERATIONS

10. Set the evaluation period to five minutes; for example, by default, this is set five minutes.

11. Click Next ➤ Actions.

12. Under Actions, click **Select action groups**. In Azure Monitor, an **Action Group** defines what should happen when an alert is triggered. It's the response mechanism that connects monitoring signals to human or automated actions—whether that means sending an email, calling a webhook, or executing a workflow in Logic Apps.

    Figure 6-23 shows the action groups.

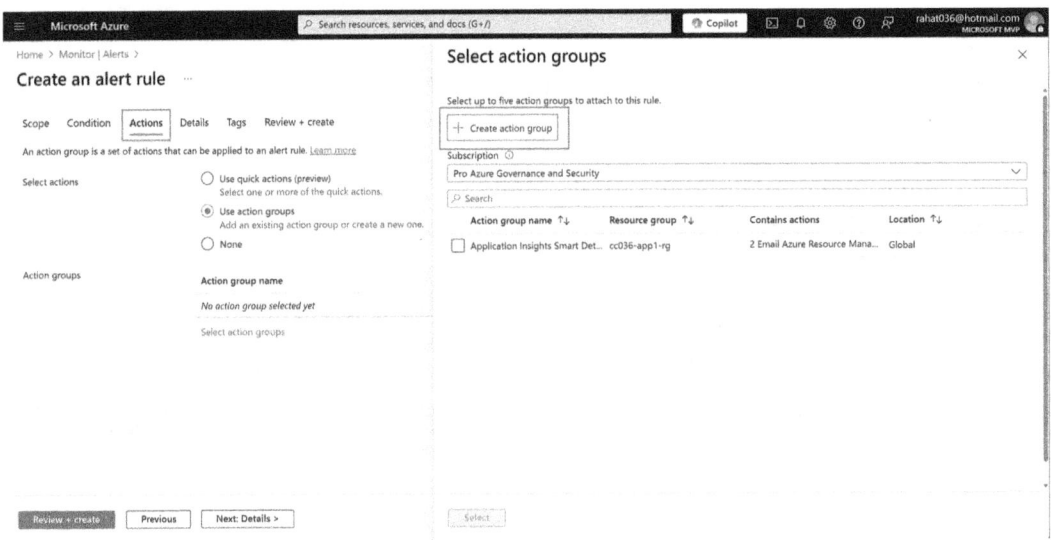

Figure 6-23. Creating new action group

13. I already have an action group in my tenant. But for this step, I am creating another one. So, I clicked + Create action group button.

14. A new page will be opened. Select the Resource group, and provide a name and a display name for this action group as shown in Figure 6-24.

250

CHAPTER 6 LEVERAGING AZURE MONITOR AND LOG ANALYTICS FOR OPERATIONS

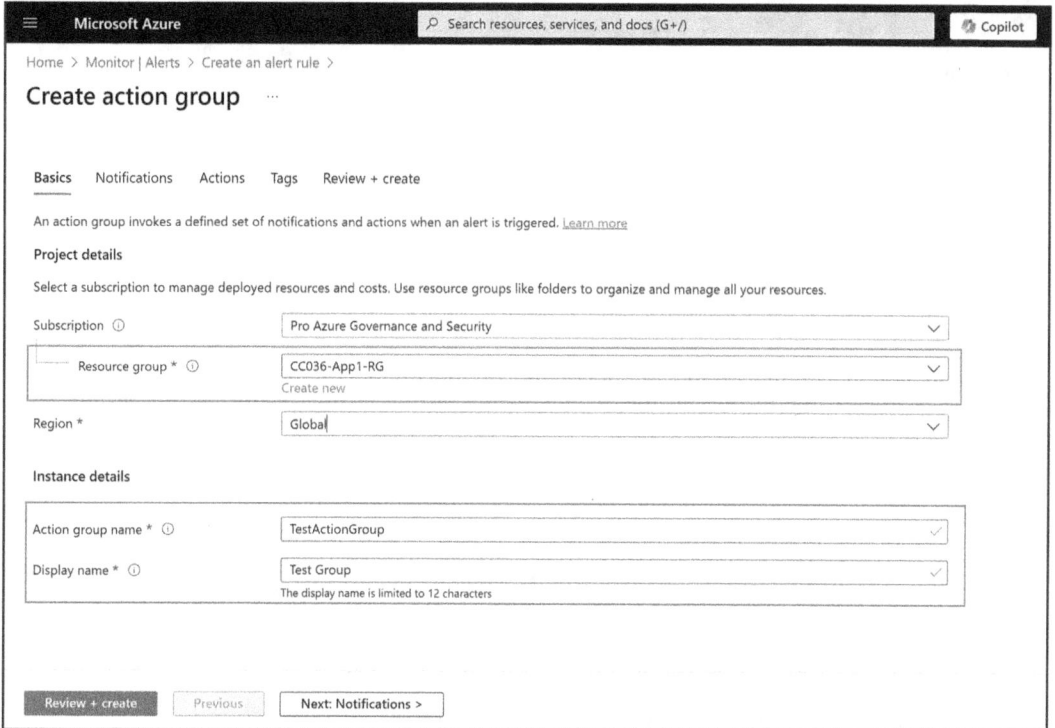

Figure 6-24. Selecting the resource group and instance details

15. Click Next ➤ Notifications.

16. In the Notifications section, click the Notifications type, select Email/SMS message/Push/Voice. A new panel will open. Select the appropriate notification field. For our case, I am only selecting Email. Refer to Figure 6-25.

CHAPTER 6   LEVERAGING AZURE MONITOR AND LOG ANALYTICS FOR OPERATIONS

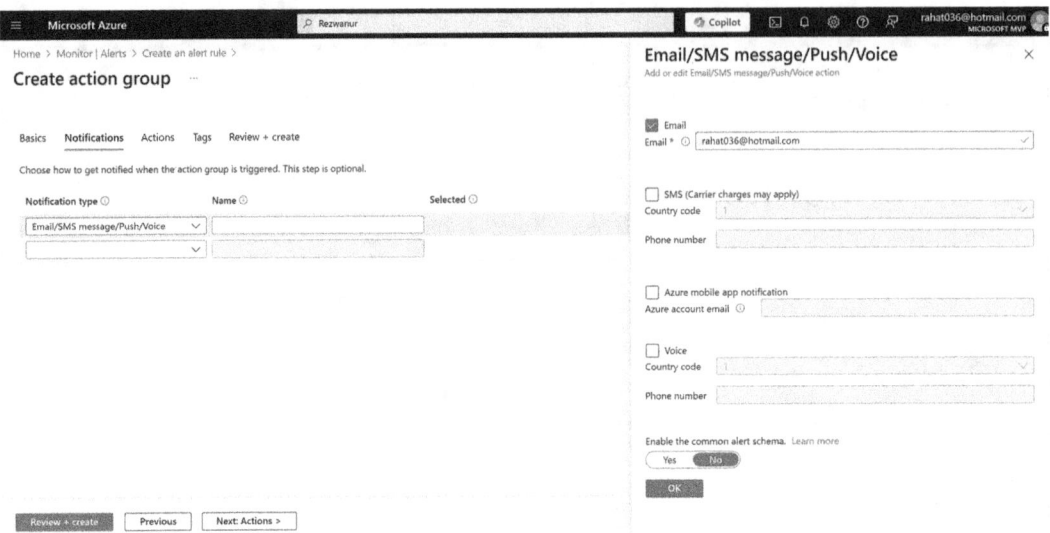

Figure 6-25. Configuring the notification section

17. Select if you want to **enable the Common alert schema**. The common alert schema is a single extensible and unified alert payload that can be used across all the alert services in Azure Monitor.

18. Add a name of the Notification.

19. Under Actions, you can also trigger an Azure Function, Runbook, or ITSM connector. This option is optional in this case.

20. Click Review + Create and then Create.

21. After creating the new action group, it will go back to the Action pages that we started (Step 12). You can see the action group is created as shown in Figure 6-26.

CHAPTER 6   LEVERAGING AZURE MONITOR AND LOG ANALYTICS FOR OPERATIONS

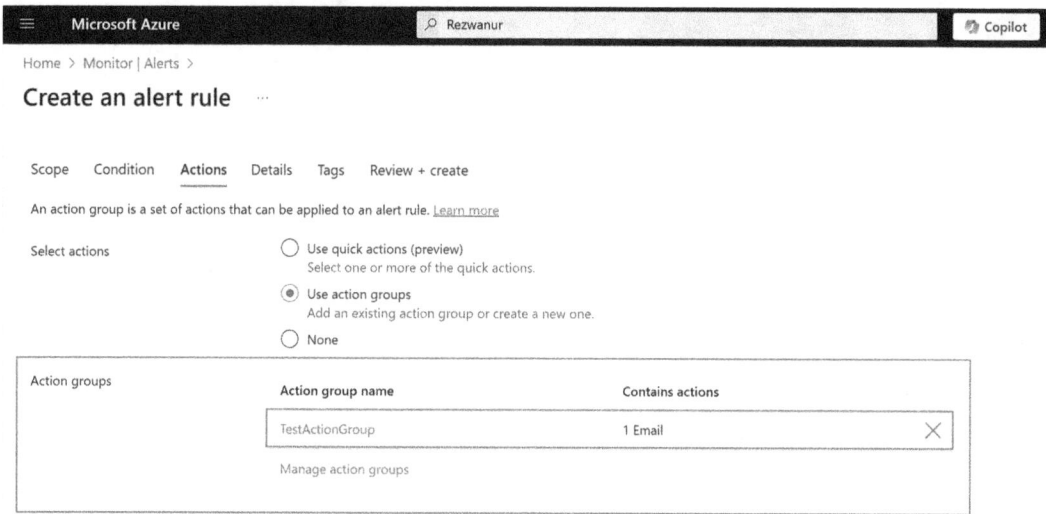

Figure 6-26. Verifying the action group that we newly created

22. Click Next ➤ Details.

23. In the Details page, set the Severity (**0–4, where 0 = Critical, 1 = Error, 2 = Warning, 3 = Informational, and 4 = Verbose**). For our case, I set it to 3—Informational.

24. Provide a name for the alert rule, for example, **HighCPU-Alert-ProdVM** as shown in Figure 6-27.

253

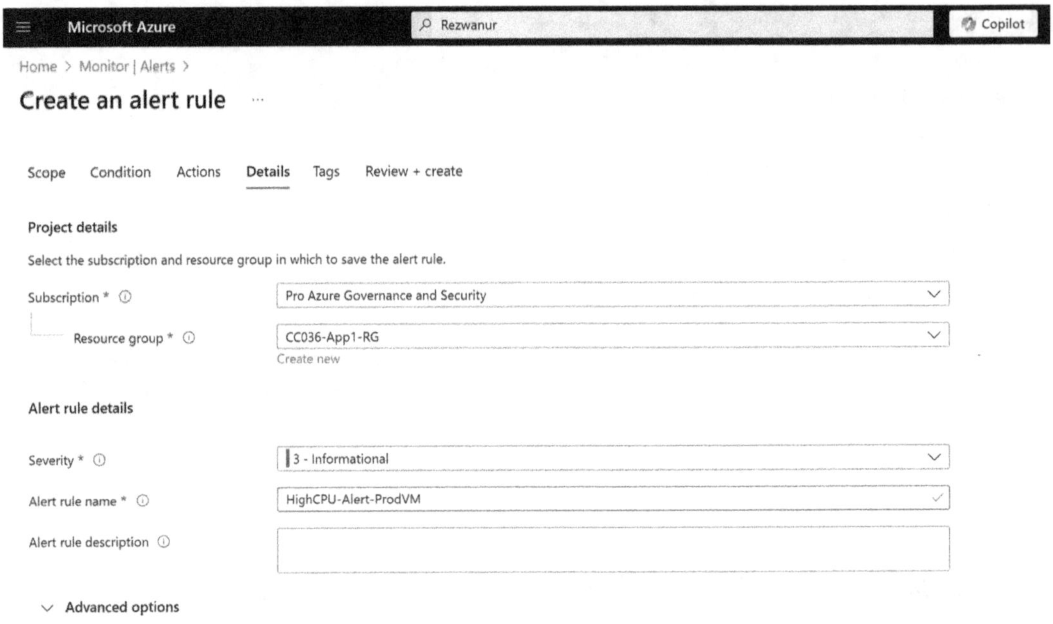

CHAPTER 6 LEVERAGING AZURE MONITOR AND LOG ANALYTICS FOR OPERATIONS

Figure 6-27. Providing alert rule name and severity

25. Then click Review + create. In the review page, you can see the product pricing. For this setting, I have to pay 0.10 USD/month. The price may vary depending on the configuration. Refer to Figure 6-28.

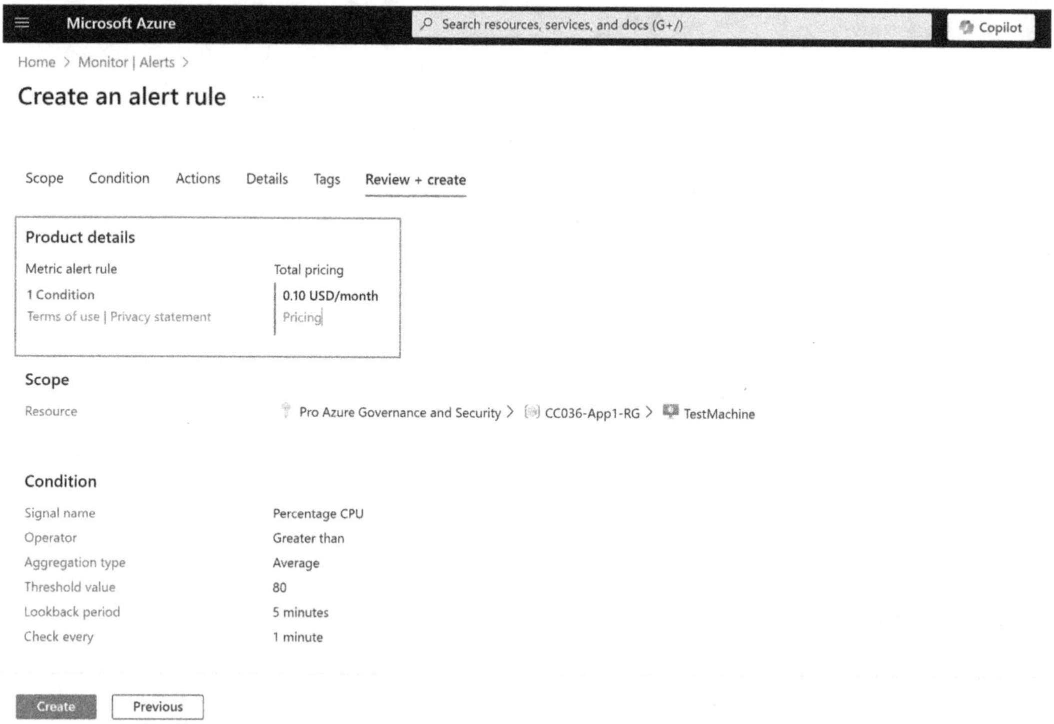

CHAPTER 6   LEVERAGING AZURE MONITOR AND LOG ANALYTICS FOR OPERATIONS

Figure 6-28. Review page that shows the total pricing per month

Once the alert is created, Azure Monitor continuously checks the metric. When the condition is met, it triggers the action group. As I added the email address, it will notify immediately via email.

You will get a confirmation email as shown in Figure 6-29.

CHAPTER 6 LEVERAGING AZURE MONITOR AND LOG ANALYTICS FOR OPERATIONS

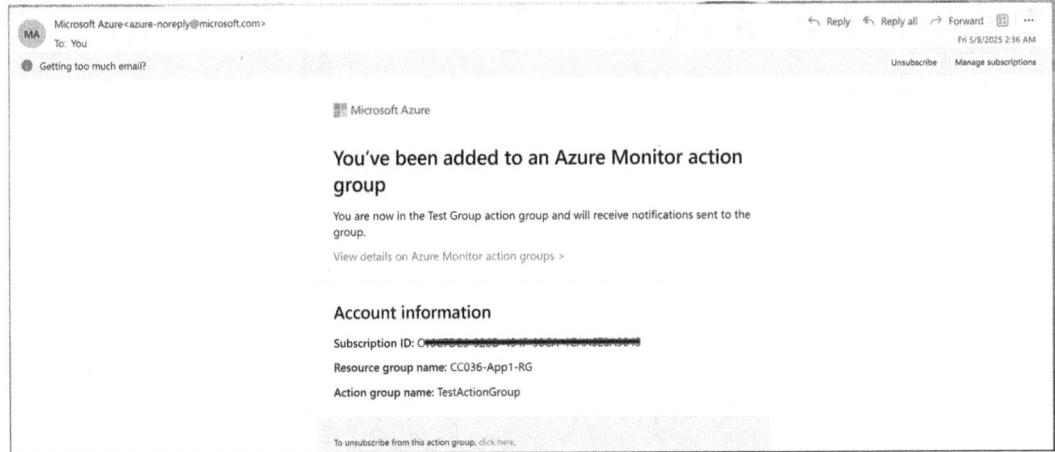

Figure 6-29. *Confirmation email that triggered the action group*

Summary

In this chapter, we focused on building a robust monitoring strategy using **Azure Monitor** and **Log Analytics**—two cornerstone services for achieving observability and operational insight in the cloud. We explored how to capture and analyze telemetry using metrics and logs, create custom queries with **Kusto Query Language (KQL)**, and configure intelligent alerts to detect anomalies in real time. We also discussed how monitoring goes beyond simple visibility—it plays a strategic role in governance, enabling proactive incident response, resource optimization, and compliance enforcement. By aligning your monitoring framework with security and operational objectives, you gain not just insights but actionable intelligence that supports long-term resilience.

In the next chapter, we'll expand this foundation by introducing **Azure Blueprints** and their role in scaling governance across large, distributed environments. Chapter 7 will show you how to package policies, role assignments, templates, and resources into repeatable governance artifacts. We'll also explore how these blueprints integrate with DevOps pipelines to ensure consistent, automated deployment of compliance standards across multiple subscriptions and management groups. If Chapter 6 was about visibility, Chapter 7 is about **control at scale**—codifying and enforcing your organization's governance principles from day one.

CHAPTER 7

Scaling Governance with Azure Blueprints

In Chapter 6, we established the importance of monitoring as a foundational pillar of governance and security. You learned how to leverage Azure Monitor and Log Analytics to capture real-time insights, detect anomalies, and respond to operational and security events using intelligent alerting and custom telemetry queries. This visibility is crucial—but on its own, it is not enough. For governance to be effective at scale, especially across enterprise-grade environments with multiple teams and subscriptions, it must be embedded into the deployment process itself.

This chapter introduces Azure Blueprints, a powerful governance framework that enables you to codify and enforce organizational standards through reusable templates. You will learn how Blueprints combine policies, role assignments, resource groups, and ARM templates into version-controlled artifacts that can be assigned and updated across multiple environments. We will also explore how integrating Blueprints with Azure DevOps brings automation and repeatability into your governance model, ensuring that every deployment adheres to security, compliance, and operational best practices by default. By the end of this chapter, you'll understand how to transform governance from a manual checkpoint into a scalable, automated, and enforceable process.

Introduction to Azure Blueprints

In enterprise-scale Azure environments, maintaining consistency, control, and compliance across multiple subscriptions can quickly become a complex challenge. Azure Blueprints are designed to solve this by enabling cloud architects and administrators to define repeatable, governed environments through a declarative model. Much like a construction blueprint ensures every building follows a predefined design, Azure Blueprints bundle key governance artifacts—such as policy assignments, role-based access controls, resource group structures, and ARM templates—into a single deployable package. This empowers organizations to deploy compliant environments at scale, whether for dev/test, production, or regulated workloads, with confidence that governance standards are enforced from the start.

What Are Azure Blueprints?

Azure Blueprints is a governance automation service in Microsoft Azure that enables organizations to standardize and enforce the configuration of Azure environments at scale. Unlike isolated deployments or loosely managed policy enforcement, Blueprints offer a centrally managed, declarative approach to defining *what an environment should look like* and ensuring that this design is reproducibly and securely applied across multiple subscriptions.

> **Note** Blueprint (Preview) will be deprecated on July 11, 2026. For more information, please visit `https://aka.ms/AzureBlueprintNotice`.

At a conceptual level, Azure Blueprints act as a *template for environments*—describing governance controls, access permissions, deployment logic, and structural design in one cohesive unit. This allows cloud platform teams to shift compliance and security left by embedding organizational standards directly into the provisioning process, rather than retrofitting controls after deployment.

What makes Blueprints particularly powerful is their integration with Azure's native management layers. Blueprint definitions can be authored once at a management group level and then versioned, published, and assigned across any child subscriptions. Once assigned, they remain *state-aware*—meaning Azure continuously monitors whether the assigned environment adheres to the blueprint's intended structure. If a deployed environment drifts from its defined state—either due to manual tampering, API-level changes, or resource reconfiguration—this can be detected and remediated through policy enforcement or reassignment.

Blueprints also provide lifecycle support for versioning and changing control. This is crucial in enterprise contexts where the evolution of governance baselines—such as new regulatory requirements or architectural standards—must be rolled out in a controlled, auditable manner. Unlike static templates or script-based deployment logic, Blueprints are designed to be maintained over time and to enforce standards even as environments grow and change.

In essence, Azure Blueprints encapsulate the principle of **Governance as Code**: empowering platform teams to define, deploy, and govern cloud environments consistently and predictably, without sacrificing agility or requiring manual oversight.

Figure 7-1 shows the overview of Azure Blueprints.

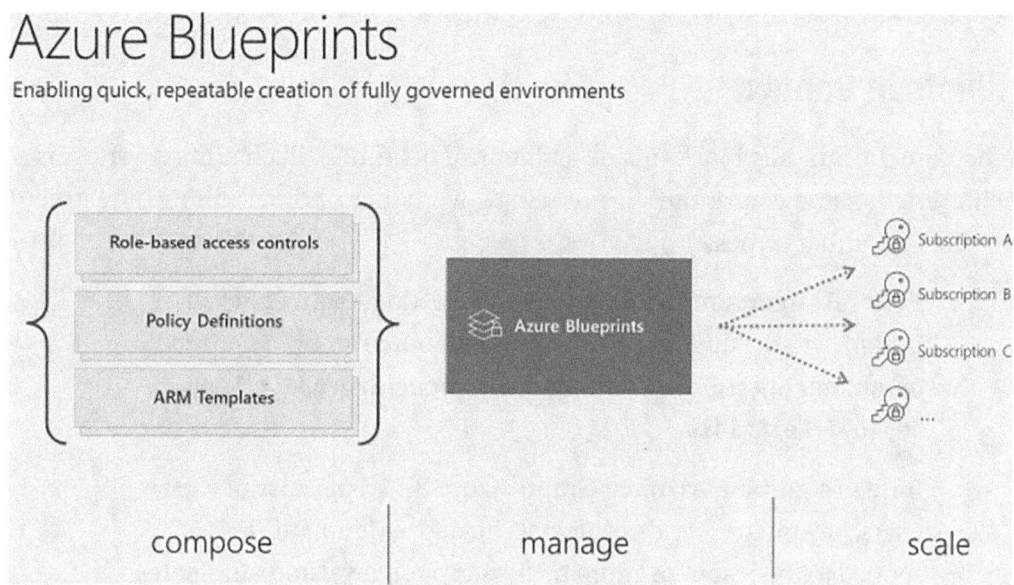

Figure 7-1. Overview of Azure Blueprints (Image: Microsoft)

Key Concepts: Definitions, Artifacts, Assignments

To operate governance through Azure Blueprints, it's essential to understand the relationship between three foundational elements: **definitions**, **artifacts**, and **assignments**. Each of these components plays a distinct role in blueprint lifecycle and enforcement logic, and they are tightly integrated with Azure Resource Manager (ARM) and Azure Policy backplanes.

Blueprint Definition

A blueprint definition is a logical, versionable container that outlines the governance intent of an environment. It is composed declaratively using JSON or managed via REST API, PowerShell, CLI, or the Azure Portal. The definition itself is metadata; it doesn't deploy resources until it's assigned.

Definitions are stored at the **management group** or **subscription** scope but can be applied across any descendant subscription. This enables central IT to define global standards—such as identity boundaries, security policies, or network configurations—once and propagate them to all consuming teams.

Blueprint definitions are **immutable once published**, enforcing a controlled release mechanism. Any modification requires the creation of a new version, which supports rollback, staging, and gradual rollout.

Artifacts in Context

Artifacts are the building blocks inside a blueprint definition. Each artifact performs a specific function and contributes to enforcing governance or provisioning infrastructure. There are four artifact types:

1. **Policy Assignment Artifact**: Links an existing Azure Policy or Initiative to the target subscription or resource group. Supports parameter injection and enforcement modes like `Audit`, `Deny`, or `DeployIfNotExists`.

2. **Role Assignment Artifact**: Grants Azure RBAC permissions to users, groups, or service principals during assignment. This is scoped to the resource group or subscription level and automates secure access provisioning.

3. **ARM Template Artifact**: Embeds an ARM template to provision Azure resources. These templates are integrated as native components within the blueprint, allowing configuration of networking, identity, monitoring, or custom resources as part of the governance package.

4. **Resource Group Artifact**: Predefines a resource group structure into which the other artifacts are deployed. This ensures logical segregation of resources and enforces naming or location standards up front.

Each artifact can optionally be parameterized, enabling blueprint definitions to be reused with dynamic inputs—such as custom naming prefixes, specific IP ranges, or environment labels.

Blueprint Assignment

An assignment is the runtime instantiation of a blueprint definition on a target subscription. It is during assignment that parameters are resolved, artifacts are deployed, and governance state is enforced.

From a deployment perspective, an assignment triggers

- **Evaluation of all policy artifacts**, including any DeployIfNotExists logic

- **Immediate application of role assignments** using Azure RBAC APIs

- **Sequential deployment of ARM templates**, executed as linked deployments under the specified resource groups

- **Optional application of resource locks**, depending on assignment configuration (ReadOnly or DoNotDelete)

Assignments are recorded as **stateful objects** in Azure. This means that the platform tracks not only that a blueprint was applied but also what version, with what parameters, and the exact state of each artifact deployment. This tracking allows for

- **Differential updates**, where only modified artifacts are redeployed

- **Drift detection**, where Azure Policy identifies deviation from enforced configurations

- **Unassignment logic**, which must handle lock removal and orphaned resource cleanup with caution

Why Organizations Need Blueprints for Governance at Scale

As enterprises expand their cloud footprint, especially across multiple Azure subscriptions, the challenge shifts from merely deploying workloads to enforcing **consistent governance, security, and compliance** across diverse environments. Manual enforcement of standards, or relying solely on documentation and tribal knowledge, is no longer tenable when hundreds of teams are provisioning infrastructure simultaneously. This is where Azure Blueprints becomes an indispensable tool.

The Scale Challenge

In most large enterprises, Azure is not used by a single team. It spans multiple departments—each with their own development, operations, and security practices. Take the example of a global financial services firm with regulatory obligations in Europe (GDPR), North America (GLBA, PCI DSS), and Asia (APPI). Each business unit might own its own subscriptions but must comply with a common security baseline.

In such environments, without centralized governance mechanisms, configuration drift is inevitable. For instance:

- A developer might deploy a virtual machine in an unapproved region, exposing the firm to data residency violations.

- A team could provision storage accounts without enforcing private endpoint integration or customer-managed keys (CMKs), violating internal encryption policies.

- Audit tags might be inconsistently applied, breaking cost reporting or compliance classification systems.

Azure Blueprints solve this by offering a mechanism to codify and enforce these standards across subscriptions automatically. Once a blueprint is defined—with all required policies, role assignments, infrastructure layouts, and compliance controls—it can be versioned, centrally maintained, and assigned across business units, ensuring every environment starts secure and compliant.

Case in Practice: HIPAA/HITRUST Compliance in Healthcare

A compelling real-world use case comes from Microsoft's release of a HIPAA/HITRUST blueprint (https://azure.microsoft.com/en-us/blog/microsoft-releases-automation-for-hipaa-hitrust-compliance/) for healthcare organizations. This blueprint includes preconfigured Azure Policy assignments, role-based access control (RBAC), logging requirements, network security rules, and encryption settings that map directly to regulatory standards.

For healthcare providers handling sensitive patient data, this blueprint dramatically reduces the complexity of setting up a compliant Azure environment. It automates enforcement of key controls—such as auditing, data protection, and access restrictions—across all resources within a subscription. As a result, teams can focus on delivering clinical or analytics solutions, knowing that foundational compliance requirements are already built into the deployment pipeline.

Strategic Advantage

By using Azure Blueprints, organizations shift from manual validation processes to a compliance-by-design model. This transition allows them to enforce standardization across all environments without limiting the autonomy of individual teams. Security is implemented at scale through consistent policy enforcement and tightly controlled role-based access, ensuring that every subscription adheres to organizational and regulatory requirements. Additionally, audit-readiness is built into each deployment by design, providing traceable, verifiable evidence of compliance and reducing the overhead typically associated with manual reviews or post-deployment corrections. For example, organizations can use Azure Blueprints to deploy standardized policy sets across subscriptions and automatically track who approved, modified, or assigned each blueprint—supporting both internal traceability and external audit readiness.

Blueprints vs. ARM Template vs. Azure Policy

While Azure Blueprints, ARM templates, and Azure Policy may appear to overlap in functionality, each plays a distinct role within the Azure governance and deployment ecosystem. Understanding how they differ—and more importantly, how they complement each other—is essential for designing scalable, automated, and compliant cloud architectures.

Azure Resource Manager (ARM) Templates: Declarative Infrastructure Deployment

ARM templates are JSON-based declarative files that define the desired state of Azure resources, ranging from simple deployments like a storage account to complex topologies such as multitier applications or enterprise-scale landing zones. Designed for Infrastructure as Code (IaC), ARM templates can be parameterized, modularized, and integrated into DevOps workflows using tools like Azure DevOps or GitHub Actions. They support linked templates, outputs, conditional logic, and dependencies—making them suitable for complex provisioning logic.

However, ARM templates are inherently stateless. Once a deployment is complete, the template does not retain any relationship with the deployed resources, nor does it track compliance over time. ARM templates are excellent for infrastructure provisioning, but they lack mechanisms for enforcing ongoing governance or responding to configuration drift.

Azure Policy: Continuous Enforcement and Compliance

As discussed in Chapter 4, Azure Policy, in contrast, operates at the control plane level and is used to enforce rules, configurations, and compliance requirements across resources—both at deployment time and throughout the resource lifecycle. It supports effects such as **Deny**, **Audit**, **Append**, and **DeployIfNotExists**, which allow organizations to implement governance checks, apply defaults, or enforce remediations.

Policy definitions are evaluated continuously by the Azure Policy engine, offering real-time compliance reporting at the management group, subscription, or resource group level. Policies can be grouped into initiatives, enabling organizations to define compliance baselines aligned with regulatory standards like ISO 27001 or NIST.

However, Azure Policy does not provision infrastructure—it evaluates and governs what's already deployed or being deployed.

Azure Blueprints: Governance Packaging and Lifecycle Management

Azure Blueprints bring ARM templates and Azure Policy together into a unified, lifecycle-managed artifact. A blueprint encapsulates policy assignments, role-based access control (RBAC) assignments, ARM templates, and resource group structures, enabling centralized governance and repeatable provisioning across multiple subscriptions.

What differentiates Blueprints is their ability to serve as a governance container. They can be defined at the management group level, versioned, and assigned with specific parameters and locking behavior. During assignment, Azure evaluates and deploys each artifact in sequence—applying policies, deploying resources via ARM templates, configuring access controls, and enforcing naming and tagging standards.

Additionally, Blueprints support assignment-level tracking, and administrators can monitor compliance drift or update definitions without disrupting deployed resources.

This lifecycle awareness—coupled with assignment history, built-in versioning, and resource locking (e.g., **ReadOnly**, **DoNotDelete**)—makes Azure Blueprints uniquely suited for organizations that need to govern at scale across distributed teams and environments.

Table 7-1 shows the difference between Blueprints, ARM templates, and Azure Policy.

Table 7-1. Difference between blueprints, ARM templates, and Azure Policy

Feature	Azure Blueprints	ARM Templates	Azure Policy
Purpose	Package and deploy governance at scale	Provision resources	Enforce rules and compliance
Format	JSON/portal-managed (composite)	JSON (ARM Schema)	JSON (Policy Definition Schema)
Enforcement Scope	Subscription-level compliance + deployment	Point-in-time deployment	Continuous evaluation
Deployment Support	Yes (via embedded ARM templates)	Yes	No
Parameterization	Yes	Yes	Yes
Version Control	Built-in versioning for definitions	Manual (via Git or templates)	Manual
Resource Locking	Yes (ReadOnly, DoNotDelete)	No	No
Assignment Tracking	Yes (assignment history + tracking)	No	Yes (compliance state only)

Supported Artifact Types

In Azure Blueprints, artifacts represent the core elements that define what gets enforced, deployed, or structured when the blueprint is assigned. Each artifact serves a distinct function and is executed in the order specified within the blueprint definition. Azure currently supports four artifact types: **Resource Group**, **Policy Assignment**, **Role Assignment**, and **ARM Template**. Together, these components allow organizations to tightly couple governance, access control, and infrastructure provisioning into a single, repeatable deployment model.

Resource Group Artifact

The Resource Group artifact instructs Azure to create one or more named resource groups at assignment time. Unlike standalone ARM templates, which often assume preexisting resource groups, this artifact ensures that the resource group structure itself is part of the blueprint's declarative intent. Each resource group can be parameterized for name and location, and it acts as a deployment boundary for the artifacts nested within it. This guarantees that infrastructure and policy enforcement occur in a consistent, predefined scope, regardless of the subscription in which the blueprint is applied.

Technically, the Resource Group artifact is not just structural—it defines the initial layout for how environment components are to be logically isolated. For example, an enterprise might define rg-networking, rg-monitoring, and rg-compute as part of a blueprint applied to all production subscriptions, ensuring standardized segmentation from the beginning.

Policy Assignment Artifact

The Policy Assignment artifact binds Azure Policy definitions or initiatives to the target subscription or resource group as part of the blueprint assignment. This integration ensures that compliance controls—such as region restrictions, allowed VM SKUs, mandatory tag policies, or encryption enforcement—are applied proactively, not reactively.

Each policy assignment artifact references either a built-in or custom policy definition by ID. Parameters required by the policy (e.g., allowed locations or required tag values) can be defined within the blueprint or provided dynamically at assignment time. The assignment supports enforcement modes (e.g., Deny, Audit, DeployIfNotExists), making it possible to block non-compliant resource deployments or trigger remediation actions post-deployment.

Internally, Azure evaluates the policy assignments immediately upon blueprint assignment and continuously thereafter. This ensures that all resources within scope remain compliant unless explicitly excluded via policy exemption or override.

Role Assignment Artifact

Role Assignment artifacts are used to define and enforce Role-Based Access Control (RBAC) during blueprint deployment. These artifacts assign Microsoft Entra ID users, groups, or service principals to specific roles (such as Reader, Contributor, or custom roles) at a defined scope—either the subscription or resource group level.

What makes blueprint-driven RBAC valuable is its consistency. For instance, if an organization wants every new subscription to have platform administrators assigned as Owners, auditors as Readers, and deployment agents as Contributors on specific resource groups, this can be embedded once in the blueprint definition. The role assignments will be applied every time the blueprint is assigned, using parameterized object IDs for identity resolution.

RBAC artifacts are evaluated and executed during the assignment phase and are stored as permanent role bindings within the Azure Resource Manager.

ARM Template Artifact

The ARM Template artifact integrates full Infrastructure-as-Code capability into the blueprint. Instead of having to manage deployments separately, ARM templates can be embedded within the blueprint to provision infrastructures such as virtual networks, NSGs, storage accounts, diagnostics settings, or custom configurations—alongside governance controls.

ARM templates within blueprints are either embedded inline (as JSON) or referenced via linked templates hosted in repositories or public URIs. Parameters within the ARM template can be mapped to blueprint-level parameters, enabling highly reusable patterns across multiple environments. These artifacts are executed after policy and RBAC assignments, ensuring that the deployed infrastructure is evaluated under the governance context from the beginning.

This combination—policies before deployment, access controls in place, and infrastructure deployed declaratively—reflects a governance-first model that goes beyond conventional infrastructure automation.

Execution and Order

Azure processes artifacts in the order defined in the blueprint. Typically, resource groups are created first, followed by role assignments, policy assignments, and finally ARM template deployments. Execution order matters: assigning a role or policy before the necessary resource group exists will fail the assignment. Administrators must carefully plan artifact sequencing to avoid dependency violations during assignment.

Use Cases: Greenfield vs. Brownfield Environments

Azure Blueprints are designed to provide value across both **greenfield** and **brownfield** scenarios, though the use cases, deployment strategies, and expected outcomes differ significantly between the two. Understanding how Blueprints interact with each context helps architects apply the tool appropriately depending on whether they're provisioning new environments or enforcing standards on existing ones.

Greenfield Deployments: Establishing Standards from the Start

In greenfield scenarios, Blueprints function as the foundation for secure-by-default and compliant-by-design infrastructure. This use case is ideal when onboarding new subscriptions, spinning up cloud environments for new business units, or launching new workloads into a fresh Azure tenant. Here, Blueprints act as a scaffolding mechanism: when assigned to a new subscription, they instantiate all required configurations, resource group structure, baseline RBAC, foundational policies, and core infrastructure—before any application workload is deployed.

This is particularly useful in organizations that apply the *landing zone* concept. For example, within a Cloud Adoption Framework–aligned enterprise, a landing zone for a production workload may include connectivity to a hub network, logging to centralized Log Analytics workspaces, diagnostic settings, cost management tags, and encryption enforcement. Rather than deploying these piecemeal or manually, the entire stack can be delivered as part of a blueprint, ensuring every new workload enters Azure through a controlled, compliant pathway.

Blueprints in greenfield cases eliminate variability at the source and reduce the risk of misconfiguration or security gaps. This model supports "governance shift-left," where compliance is not something retrofitted, but something inherently present from the first deployment.

Brownfield Environments: Retrofitting Governance at Scale

In contrast, brownfield environments represent existing Azure subscriptions or resource groups that may have been built before governance standards were established or consistently enforced. These environments typically suffer from configuration drift, inconsistent tagging, uncontrolled access, and non-standard deployment patterns. Applying Blueprints in such contexts serves to **retrofit governance**—bringing legacy or organically grown environments into alignment with current organizational standards.

While Blueprints are primarily optimized for provisioning scenarios, they can still be valuable in brownfield situations, particularly through policy assignment artifacts. When assigned to an existing subscription, a blueprint can immediately apply policy initiatives that audit for compliance, enforce tagging, restrict location or SKU usage, and trigger remediation actions. Role assignment artifacts can be used to realign access control, ensuring only approved identities have contributor or owner access. However, ARM template artifacts must be used cautiously in brownfield cases, as they may inadvertently override or conflict with existing resources unless designed to deploy nondestructively.

One challenge in brownfield scenarios is that resource locks (e.g., `ReadOnly`, `DoNotDelete`) applied through the blueprint can conflict with existing DevOps or admin practices. Organizations must plan their blueprint assignments carefully, potentially creating separate compliance blueprints tailored for audit and remediation that exclude disruptive locks or infrastructure changes.

For organizations undergoing cloud governance transformation, it is common to apply **"lightweight blueprints"**—those containing only policy and RBAC artifacts—to existing environments as an initial step. This allows the governance team to measure compliance posture without impacting existing workloads. Over time, these environments can be aligned to the full enterprise blueprint model as part of a modernization or migration initiative.

Creating and Assigning Blueprints

The process of operationalizing Azure Blueprints begins with defining the blueprint itself and culminates in its assignment to one or more subscriptions. This lifecycle—from authoring to deployment—bridges the gap between policy definition and real-world enforcement. Creating a blueprint involves assembling governance artifacts such as policies, role assignments, ARM templates, and resource group structures into a single logical definition that reflects the organization's cloud governance baseline. Once published, that definition can be versioned and consistently applied across subscriptions to instantiate secure, compliant environments. Assignment is not merely about deployment, it is a governance action that enforces structure, permissions, and configuration guardrails the moment an environment comes online. Through this workflow, Azure Blueprints empower central IT and cloud platform teams to deliver governed infrastructure with the predictability and automation expected in modern DevSecOps pipelines.

Designing Blueprint Structure for Standardized Environment

Designing the structure of an Azure Blueprint is a foundational task in governance automation. It ensures that your blueprint captures all necessary controls, compliance, access, infrastructure, and operational boundaries—before implementation. This design phase is not about creating the blueprint in the Azure Portal or CLI; rather, it's about modeling a governance standard that can be codified and reused consistently across Azure subscriptions.

A well-structured blueprint design defines

- Which **artifacts** will be used and in what sequence
- What **parameters** will be exposed for customization
- How **RBAC, policy, and infrastructure components** will interact
- What **naming conventions** and **deployment scopes** are required
- Which **environmental dependencies** must be accounted for (e.g., location, identity)

Design Scenario: Standardized Production Subscription Blueprint

Assume the goal is to create a baseline production-ready Azure environment. The blueprint must enforce resource tagging, restrict region usage, pre-provision monitoring infrastructure, and assign access controls to InfoSec and DevOps teams.

Artifact Planning

As discussed before, Azure Blueprints support four artifact types. Table 7-2 outlines the artifacts that will be included in this design:

CHAPTER 7 SCALING GOVERNANCE WITH AZURE BLUEPRINTS

Table 7-2. Four artifact types that support Azure Blueprints

Artifact Type	Target Scope	Purpose
Resource Group	Subscription	Define logical boundaries for networking, monitoring, apps
Policy Assignment	Sub/RG	Enforce region, tagging, and security policies
Role Assignment	Sub/RG	Grant Reader and Contributor roles to defined identities
ARM Template	Specific RG	Deploy a Log Analytics workspace with monitoring settings

Each artifact type will be used in this design and mapped explicitly in the next section during blueprint definition.

Resource Group Structure

Designing a clear resource group structure ensures logical separation of duties and supports future scalability. Table 7-3 shows the resource group naming structure and purpose.

Table 7-3. Resource group naming structure and purpose

Name	Purpose	Notes
`rg-networking`	For VNETs, subnets, NSGs	Foundation for connectivity
`rg-monitoring`	For diagnostics, Log Analytics	Shared monitoring layer
`rg-apps`	For hosting production application	Workload-level deployment

These groups will be created by the blueprint during assignment and must be defined **first** in the artifact execution order.

Policy Assignments

The blueprint will enforce compliance controls using Azure Policy assignments. These policies must be scoped properly and linked to parameterized values. Table 7-4 shows the scope and effect of the policy.

271

CHAPTER 7 SCALING GOVERNANCE WITH AZURE BLUEPRINTS

Table 7-4. Azure policy with scope and effect

Policy Name	Effect	Scope	Parameterized
Allowed Locations	Deny	Subscription	Yes (e.g., East US 2)
Required tag: Environment	Deny	Subscription	Yes
Required tag: CostCenter	Deny	Subscription	Yes

These will be added as policy artifacts and linked to parameters defined at the blueprint level, which allows for reuse across subscriptions with different tag values.

RBAC (Role-Based Access Control) Design

The blueprint must define least-privileged access for operations and compliance stakeholders. Table 7-5 shows what the design includes.

Table 7-5. RBAC design with scope and principle

Role	Principle	Scope	Parameterized
Reader	InfoSec Group Object ID	Subscription	Yes
Contributor	`DevOps Service Principal`	**rg-apps**	Yes

Principal IDs will be passed at assignment time as blueprint parameters. These assignments ensure that every environment built with this blueprint has secure, predefined access controls.

Infrastructure Template

The monitoring layer is a critical baseline service and will be deployed using an ARM template. The template will deploy a Log Analytics workspace with

- Custom workspace name (parameterized)
- Retention period (static: 30 days)
- Location: inherits from blueprint-level **location** parameter

The ARM template artifact will be scoped to **rg-monitoring**, and its parameters will map to corresponding blueprint parameters.

CHAPTER 7　SCALING GOVERNANCE WITH AZURE BLUEPRINTS

Parameterization Plan

Parameters increase blueprint flexibility and support variation between dev, test, and production environments. Table 7-6 shows the parameters with type and example value.

Table 7-6. Parameterization plan with example values

Name	Type	Used In	Example Value
Location	String	Resource groups, ARM	**East US 2**
environmentTag	String	Policy	**Production**
costCenterTag	String	Policy	**FIN-001**
workspaceName	String	ARM template	**prod-logs**
devOpsPrincipalId	String	RBAC	Microsoft Entra ID Object ID
infoSecPrincipalId	String	RBAC	Microsoft Entra ID Object ID

These parameters will be created during blueprint definition and exposed to users during blueprint assignment.

Execution Order Planning

Azure processes artifacts sequentially in the order defined in the blueprint. The planned order is

1. Resource Group Artifacts (**rg-networking**, **rg-monitoring**, **rg-apps**)

2. Role Assignment Artifacts (InfoSec ➤ Subscription, DevOps ➤ **rg-apps**)

3. Policy Assignment Artifacts (location, tags)

4. ARM Template Artifact (Log Analytics in rg-monitoring)

This order respects dependencies, ensuring all scopes exist before policies or templates reference them.

Naming and Versioning

To support lifecycle management, the blueprint will follow naming conventions and version metadata. For example:

- **Blueprint Name**: Enterprise-Prod-Baseline
- **Version Format**: `v1.0.0`, `v1.1.0`, etc.
- **Blueprint Description**: "Defines baseline production environment with enforced policies, logging, and access control"

Creating Blueprint Definitions in Azure Portal

With the structure of your Azure Blueprint fully designed, the next step is to implement that design by creating the blueprint definition in the Azure Portal. This section walks you through the practical creation of the blueprint—configuring each artifact, defining parameters, and publishing the final version—based entirely on the architecture from the previous discussion. BTW, in Chapter 3, I already showed how to create a basic blueprint. You can have a look there as well.

1. Sign in to the Azure portal from `https://portal.azure.com`.
2. In the search bar, type **Blueprints**; select it as shown in Figure 7-2.

CHAPTER 7   SCALING GOVERNANCE WITH AZURE BLUEPRINTS

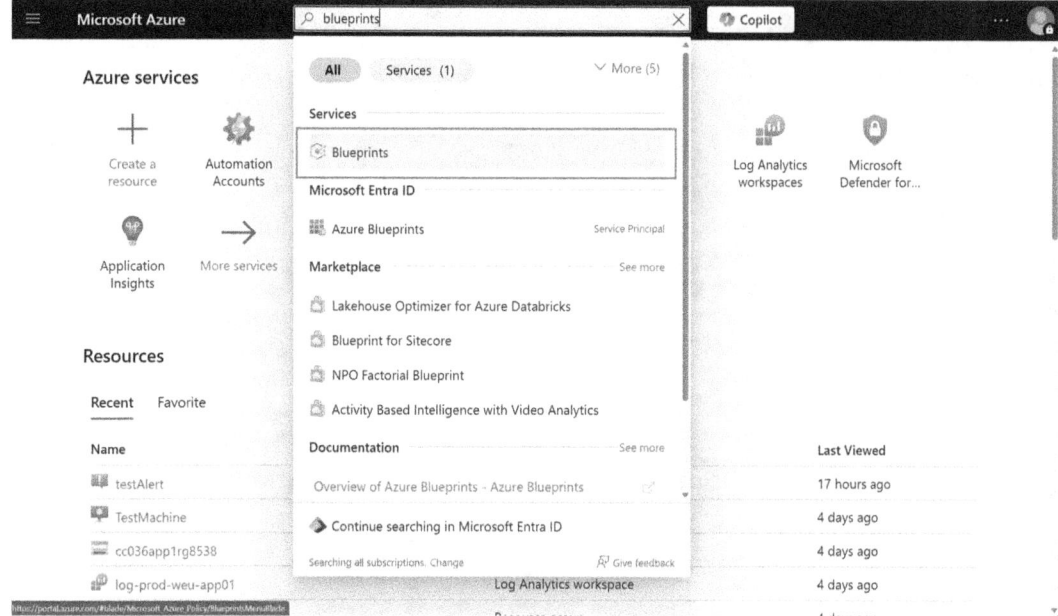

Figure 7-2. *Searching Blueprints in Azure*

3. Under Blueprints, select **Blueprint definitions** from left-side blade as shown in Figure 7-3.

CHAPTER 7 SCALING GOVERNANCE WITH AZURE BLUEPRINTS

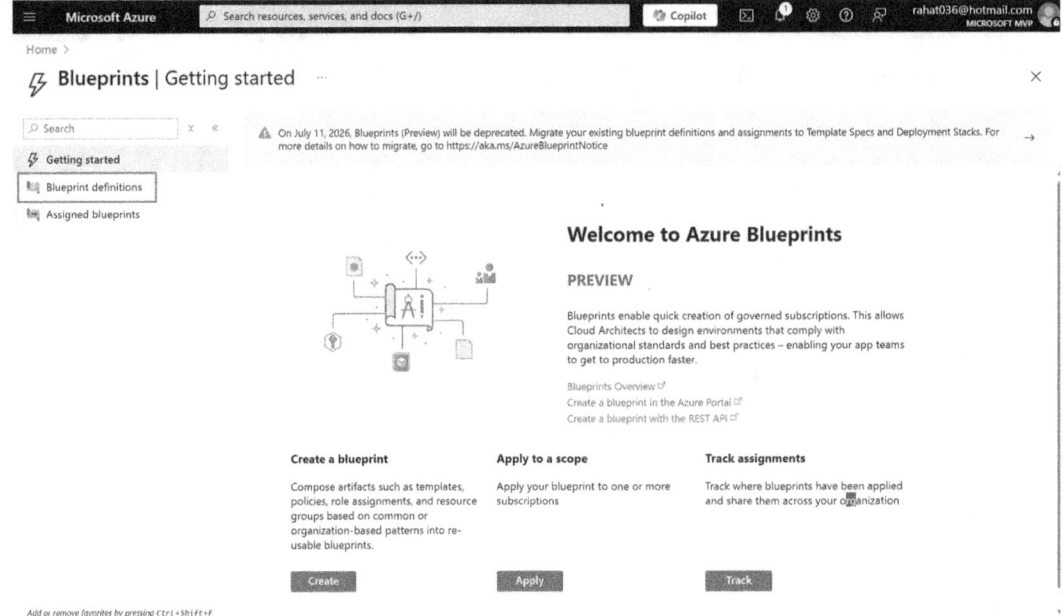

Figure 7-3. Selecting Blueprint definitions

4. Click + Create blueprint as shown in Figure 7-4.

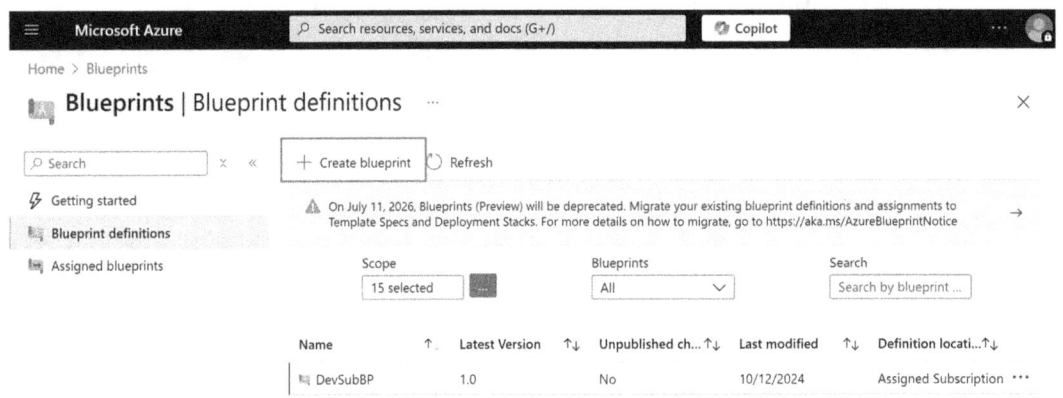

Figure 7-4. Creating blueprints

Note On July 11, 2026, Blueprints (Preview) will be deprecated. For more details on how to migrate, go to `https://aka.ms/AzureBlueprintNotice`.

CHAPTER 7   SCALING GOVERNANCE WITH AZURE BLUEPRINTS

5. Select Start with blank blueprint as shown in Figure 7-5.

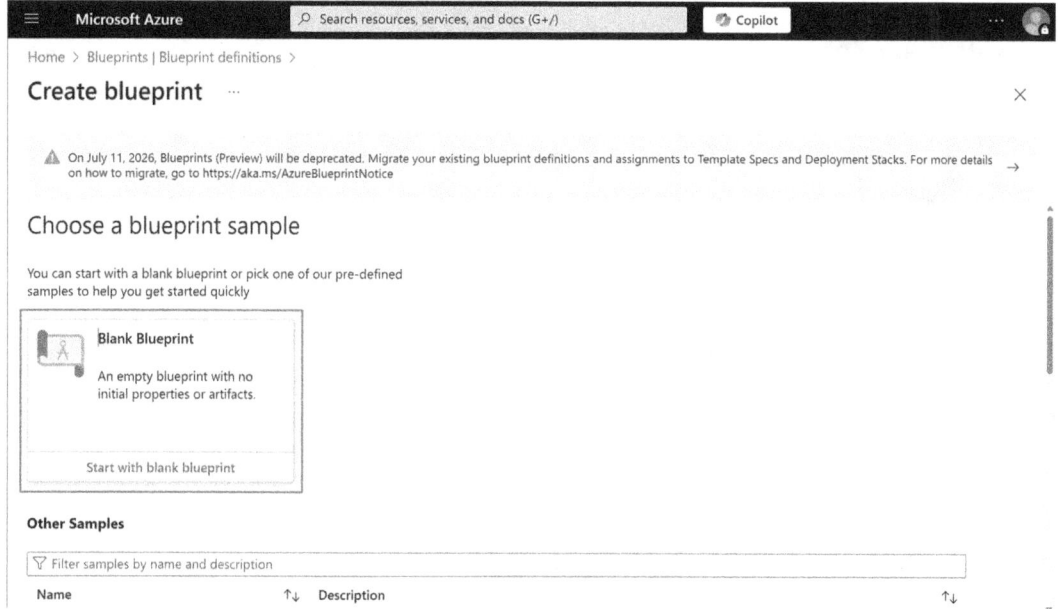

Figure 7-5.* Selecting blank blueprint*

6. In the Basic tab, add the following information:

   a. **Blueprint Name: Enterprise-Prod-Baseline**

   b. **Description**: *Defines baseline production environment with enforced policies, logging, and access control.*

   c. **Definition Location:** Choose the management group (recommended) or subscription where this blueprint will be stored and managed.

   Figure 7-6 shows the visual of the Basic tab.

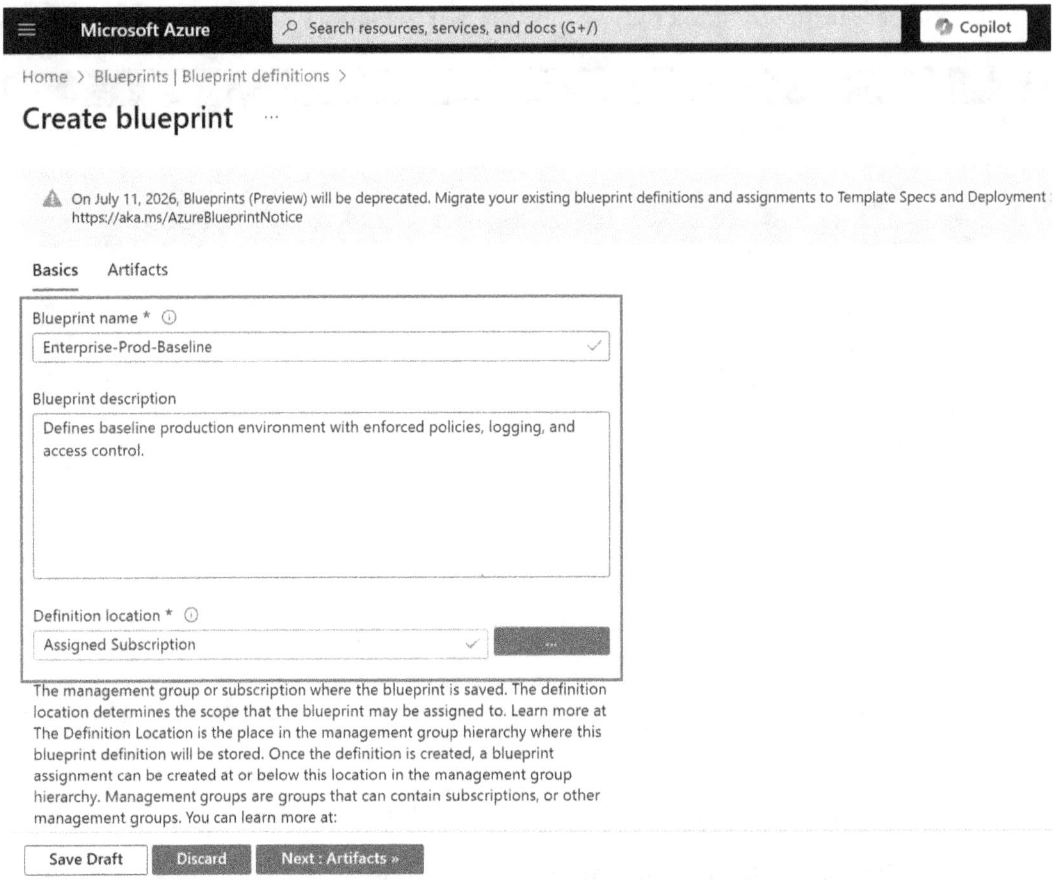

CHAPTER 7   SCALING GOVERNANCE WITH AZURE BLUEPRINTS

Figure 7-6. Providing blueprint name and description

7. Click **Next: Artifacts ➤**.

8. Here, we will begin by creating the three predefined resource groups:

   a. Click + Add artifact.

   b. When the side bar opens, click Artifact type. Select Resource group.

   c. Add the artifact display name: **rg-networking**.

   d. Add the resource group name: **rg-networking**.

   e. Set the location. For this case, I set it to Germany West Central.

   f. Click Add as shown in Figure 7-7.

CHAPTER 7 SCALING GOVERNANCE WITH AZURE BLUEPRINTS

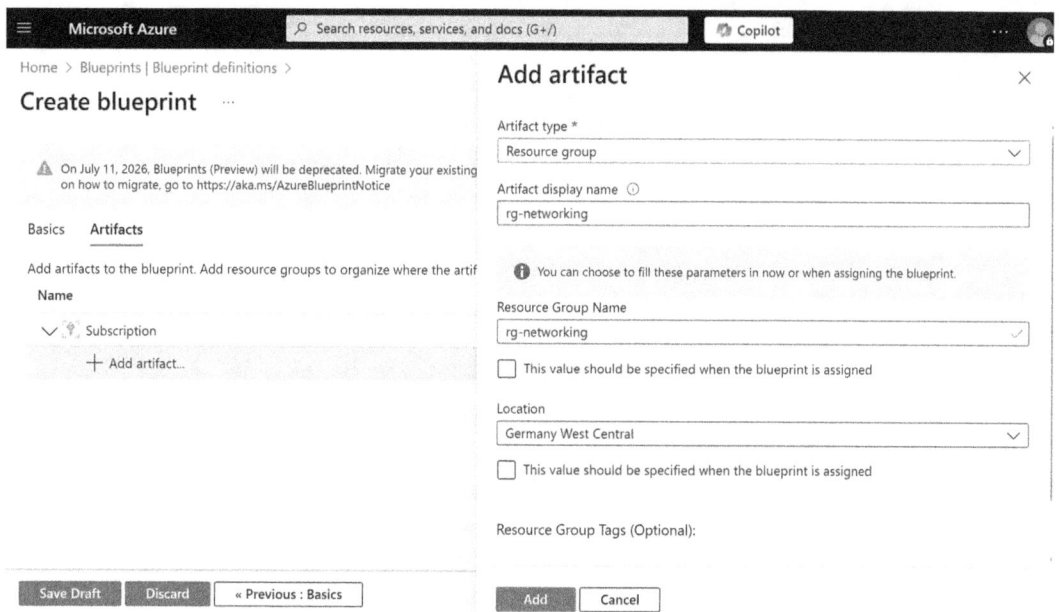

Figure 7-7. Adding artifact in blueprint

Repeat the above for **rg-monitoring, rg-apps** as well.

Note These *must be added first to ensure later artifacts (e.g., RBAC or templates) can reference them.*

---

9. Now, we will define two role assignments based on the design. The actual object ID is not defined here, only at assignment.

   Add InfoSec Reader Role at Subscription Level:

   a. Click + Add artifact.

   b. Select the artifact type: Role assignment.

   c. Role: Reader.

   d. Leave "Add user, app or group" blank.

   e. Ensure the checkbox is checked: "This value should be specified when the blueprint is assigned."

   f. Click Add; refer to Figure 7-8.

279

CHAPTER 7   SCALING GOVERNANCE WITH AZURE BLUEPRINTS

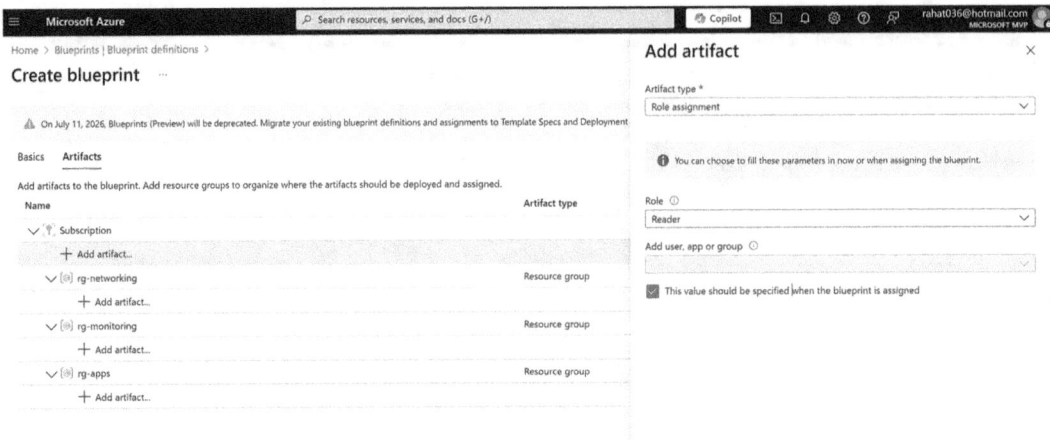

Figure 7-8. *Adding artifact type and role*

Add DevOps Contributor Role at Resource Group Scope:

   a. Expand **rg-apps**; click +Add artifact.

   b. Artifact type: Role assignment.

   c. Role: Contributor.

   d. Leave "Add user, apps, or group" blank.

   e. Confirm the checkbox is checked: "This value should be specified when the blueprint is assigned."

   f. Click Add.

   Now, you have your RBAC structure: InfoSec has read-only at subscription level; DevOps has contributor access to **rg-apps**.

10. Now, enforce compliance policies at the subscription level.

    Allowed Locations

    a. Click +Add artifact under Subscription.

    b. Artifact type: Policy assignment.

    c. Search for and select: Allowed locations.

    d. Click Add; refer to Figure 7-9.

CHAPTER 7 SCALING GOVERNANCE WITH AZURE BLUEPRINTS

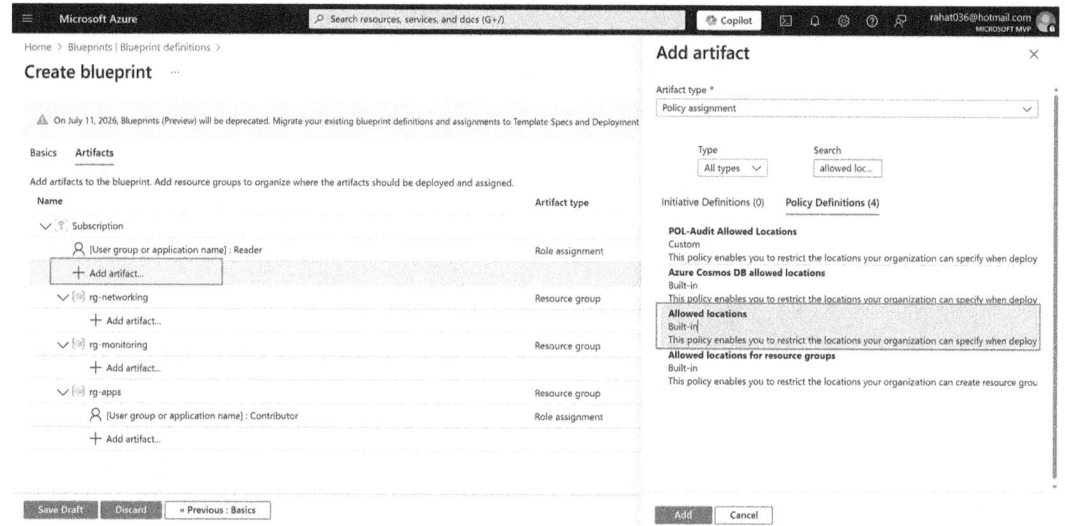

Figure 7-9. *Selecting Allowed locations policy to artifact*

Required Tag: Environment

a. Click +Add artifact under Subscription.

b. Artifact type: Policy assignment.

c. Search and select: Require a tag and its value on resources.

d. Click Add; refer to Figure 7-10.

CHAPTER 7   SCALING GOVERNANCE WITH AZURE BLUEPRINTS

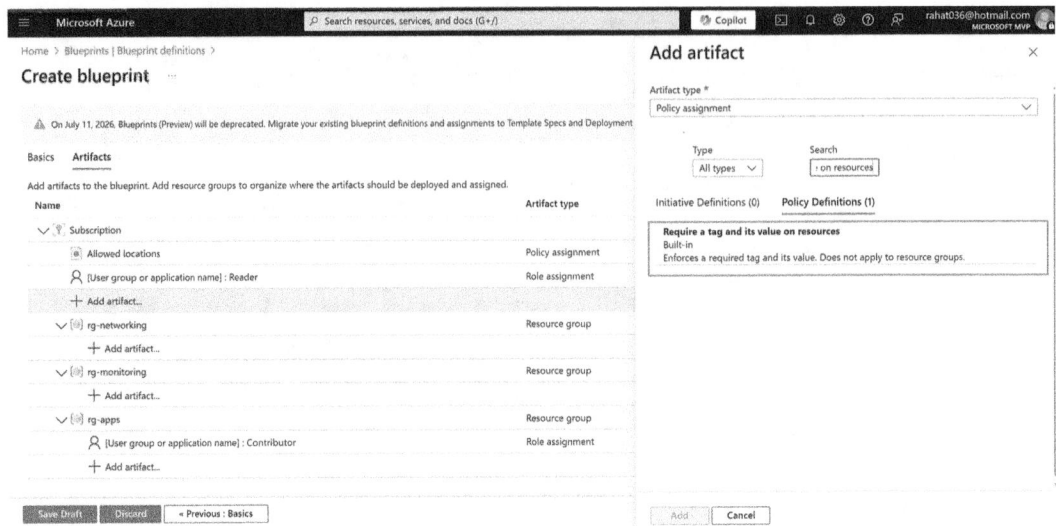

Figure 7-10. Selecting required tag policy in artifact

e. After adding the artifact, you can see it in the list of artifacts. Now click the three dots (…) and select Edit artifact as shown in Figure 7-11.

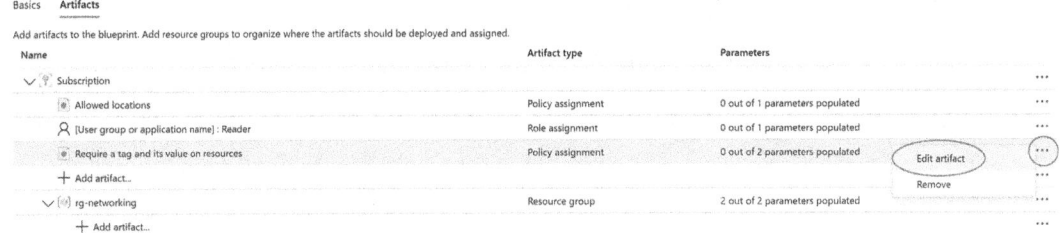

Figure 7-11. Editing artifact of required tag

f. Add the following parameters:

- Tag Name: Environment

- Tag Value: environmentTag

This is shown in Figure 7-12.

282

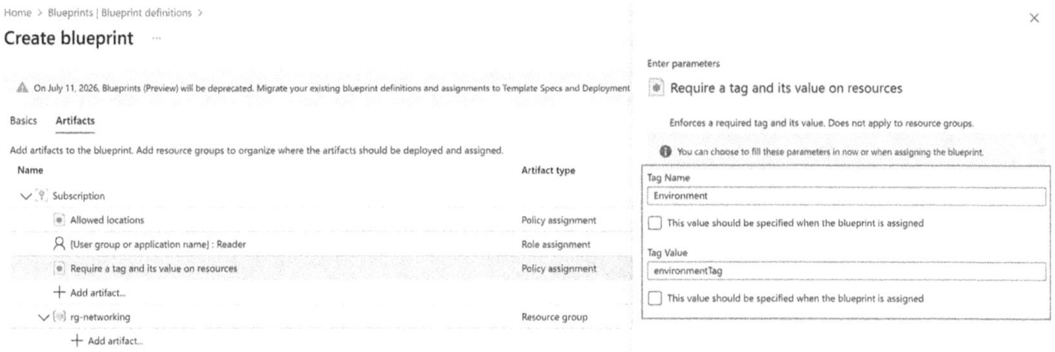

CHAPTER 7   SCALING GOVERNANCE WITH AZURE BLUEPRINTS

Figure 7-12. Adding name and value parameters

      g. Click Add.

Require Tag: CostCenter

      h. Repeat above steps again (Require a tag and its value on resources).

      i. Add the following parameters:

          a. Tag Name: CostCenter

          b. Tag Value: costCenterTag

      j. Click Add.

11. Now we will add an ARM template artifact. To do this, expand the rg-monitoring artifact.

      a. Click +Add artifact.

      b. Artifact type: ARM template.

      c. Artifact display name: Log Analytics Workspace Deployment.

      d. Under template, paste the following JSON as inline template:

```
{
  "$schema": "https://schema.management.azure.com/schemas/2019-04-01/deploymentTemplate.json#",
  "contentVersion": "1.0.0.0",
  "parameters": {
    "workspaceName": {
```

```json
          "type": "string",
          "metadata": {
            "description": "Name of the Log Analytics workspace"
          }
        },
        "location": {
          "type": "string",
          "metadata": {
            "description": "Location for the workspace"
          }
        },
        "retentionInDays": {
          "type": "int",
          "defaultValue": 30,
          "minValue": 7,
          "maxValue": 730,
          "metadata": {
            "description": "Retention period for logs in days"
          }
        }
      },
      "resources": [
        {
          "type": "Microsoft.OperationalInsights/workspaces",
          "apiVersion": "2021-06-01",
          "name": "[parameters('workspaceName')]",
          "location": "[parameters('location')]",
          "properties": {
            "sku": {
              "name": "PerGB2018"
            },
            "retentionInDays": "[parameters('retentionInDays')]"
          }
        }
      ]
    }
```

Refer to Figure 7-13.

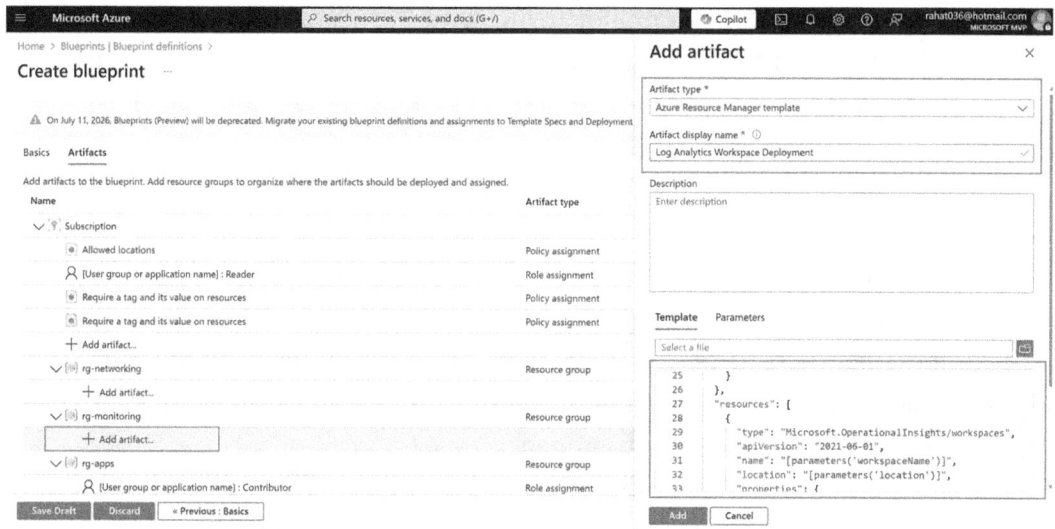

Figure 7-13. Selecting artifact type and adding template code

Now, your monitoring infrastructure is ready to be provisioned via blueprint.

Azure will auto detect used parameters, but you can conform or edit them if you want. In Table 7-7, you can see the parameters with their type and usage.

Table 7-7. Parameter name and their usages

Parameter Name	Type	Used for
Location	string	Resource groups, template
environmentTag	string	Policy assignment
costCenterTag	string	Policy assignment
workspaceName	string	ARM template
infoSecPrincipalId	string	Role assignment
devOpsPrincipalID	string	Role assignment

Next, we will see how to publish and assign blueprints.

Specifying Artifacts: Best Practices for Each Artifact Type

After completing the blueprint definition in the Azure Portal, the focus shifts to optimizing how each artifact functions at deployment and enforcement time. While the previous steps ensured that the correct components were selected and added, this section deepens the technical understanding of how to structure and configure those artifacts, effectively ensuring reliability, reusability, compliance integrity, and lifecycle manageability.

Each artifact type within a blueprint—whether a policy assignment, ARM template, role assignment, or resource group definition—carries operational implications. For example, incorrectly scoped policy assignments can unintentionally block deployments; overly complex ARM templates can fail silently; and misconfigured role assignments can violate the least privilege or cause assignment errors.

This section breaks down each artifact category individually, detailing design best practices, common pitfalls, and how to tailor artifact behavior to match enterprise requirements. Whether you're scaling governance across 10 or 100 subscriptions, the long-term success of Azure Blueprints depends on how well each artifact is specified, parameterized, and versioned.

In the following subsections, we explore how to properly define policy artifacts and initiatives, embed Infrastructure as Code via ARM templates, assign RBAC roles with flexibility and control, and structure resource groups to support workload isolation and organizational standards.

Defining Policies and Initiatives

Azure Policy and Policy Initiatives play a central role in enforcing compliance and governance across cloud environments. Since this topic has already been explored in depth in **Chapter 4**, including policy structure, lifecycle, assignment, and initiative management, this section will focus specifically on how these governance controls function when integrated into **Azure Blueprints**.

Policy Artifacts in Blueprint Context

When you add policy definitions or initiatives to a blueprint, you are not simply assigning policies, you are embedding them into a **declarative, version-controlled governance construct**. This changes their behavior in several keyways:

- **Policy assignments become part of the blueprint version.** They are not modified independently; changes require republishing the blueprint.

- **Policy parameters** can be promoted to blueprint-level parameters, allowing flexible reuse across different assignments.

- **Scope is inherited** based on where the policy artifact is placed (subscription or resource group).

- **Locking behavior** (optional) may interact with policy enforcement, further restricting what users can modify post-deployment.

This means policies within blueprints act not only as guardrails but also as **enforceable configuration contracts** for every subscription that receives a blueprint assignment.

Best Practices for Embedding Policies in Blueprints

Integrating policy definitions or initiatives into Azure Blueprints is not merely a matter of assigning rules—it's about codifying governance intent into a reusable and controllable deployment mechanism. Unlike standalone Azure Policy assignments, policy artifacts in Blueprints are version-locked, scoped declaratively, and parameterized for dynamic enforcement. Their role extends beyond prevention; they serve as embedded compliance guarantees.

One practical best practice is to assign **initiative definitions** instead of scattering individual policy definitions throughout the blueprint. Initiatives group related policies (e.g., for NIST, ISO 27001, or CIS compliance) into a single unit of control. By referencing the initiative as one artifact, you reduce maintenance overhead and ensure a coherent governance intent across all target environments.

Another critical design consideration is **parameterization**. Hardcoding values such as allowed regions or required tags make the blueprint rigid and less reusable. By promoting these values to blueprint-level parameters, you can assign the same governance package across multiple teams or geographies while adapting values as needed. This also enhances audit transparency—you know what was enforced and how it was customized per environment.

Scoping is equally important. Policies intended for enterprise-wide governance, like regional restrictions or resource type controls, should be assigned at the subscription level. In contrast, workload-specific controls—such as enforcing encryption on storage accounts or requiring cost center tags—are better scoped to the resource group level, especially if different application teams have their own deployment boundaries.

A commonly overlooked concern is **policy overlaps**. Enterprises often manage a complex mix of compliance tools, and it's easy to assign the same or conflicting policy in multiple places—for example, via a management group policy set and inside a blueprint. This can result in policy collisions or unresolvable denies. It's essential to use tools like **Azure Policy Insights** and **compliance dashboards** to evaluate the total policy surface before applying a blueprint in production.

Lastly, always validate policy behavior **prior to publishing** the blueprint. Unlike direct policy assignments, policy artifacts in Blueprints are evaluated only once—at assignment. They don't get pushed to Azure Policy until the blueprint is assigned to a subscription. As a result, syntactic or logical errors in a policy artifact won't be caught until deployment fails. Use a test subscription or development landing zone to validate policy logic, parameter values, and scoping behaviors under real-world conditions.

Embedding ARM Templates

Incorporating Azure Resource Manager (ARM) templates into Azure Blueprints allows organizations to automate the deployment of complex infrastructure components alongside governance controls. While ARM templates are extensively covered in **Chapter 5**, this section focuses on their integration within Blueprints, emphasizing best practices and considerations unique to this context.

Understanding ARM Template Artifacts in Blueprints

Within a Blueprint, ARM templates are added as artifacts, enabling the deployment of resources such as virtual networks, storage accounts, or virtual machines as part of a governed package. This integration ensures that infrastructure deployments are consistent, repeatable, and aligned with organizational standards.

Key characteristics of ARM template artifacts in Blueprints include

- **Declarative Deployment**: ARM templates define the desired state of resources, allowing for idempotent deployments.

- **Parameterization**: Templates can accept parameters, facilitating customization during Blueprint assignment.

- **Dependency Management**: Templates can specify dependencies, ensuring resources are deployed in the correct order.

Best Practices for Embedding ARM Templates in Blueprints

To effectively utilize ARM templates within Blueprints, consider the following best practices:

1. **Modularize Templates for Reusability**

   Design ARM templates to be modular, focusing on specific components or services. This approach promotes reusability across different Blueprints and simplifies maintenance.

2. **Utilize Parameters for Flexibility**

   Leverage parameters within ARM templates to allow for dynamic input during Blueprint assignment. This flexibility enables the same template to be used across various environments with differing configurations.

3. **Manage Secrets Securely**

   When ARM templates require sensitive information, such as passwords or keys, reference these values from Azure Key Vault. This practice enhances security by avoiding hardcoded secrets within templates.

4. **Validate Templates Independently**

   Before integrating an ARM template into a Blueprint, validate it independently to ensure it functions as intended. This step helps identify and resolve issues early in the deployment process.

5. **Align Template Scope with Blueprint Artifacts**

   Ensure that the scope defined within the ARM template aligns with the Blueprint's artifact scope. Misalignment can lead to deployment failures or unintended resource configurations.

Assigning RBAC Roles

Role-Based Access Control (RBAC) is foundational to securing Azure environments, ensuring that users, groups, and service principals have access only to the resources they need and only at the level required for their responsibilities. While RBAC principles and role scopes are covered earlier in the book, this section focuses on **how RBAC roles are defined, parameterized, and assigned as artifacts within an Azure Blueprint**.

RBAC in the Blueprint Context

Within Azure Blueprints, RBAC roles are added as **role assignment artifacts**. These are declarative instructions that bind Microsoft Entra ID principals (users, groups, or service principals) to specific roles (e.g., Reader, Contributor, Owner) at a chosen scope: either the **subscription level** or **resource group level**.

Unlike traditional RBAC assignments, which are created manually or scripted at runtime, blueprint-based RBAC

- Is **version-controlled** as part of the blueprint definition
- Requires **parameterized principal IDs**, which are supplied at assignment time
- Ensures **consistency** across all environments the blueprint is assigned to

This enables organizations to standardize access control across all subscriptions and resource groups created under a blueprint.

Best Practices for Role Assignments in Blueprints

When assigning RBAC roles as part of a blueprint, your goal is not just to grant access—it's to do so in a controlled, reusable, and secure manner. Below are key practices that help ensure your role assignments support scalable governance across multiple environments.

1. **Parameterize Object IDs Instead of Hardcoding Them**

   Azure Blueprints are designed for reusability. Instead of specifying a fixed user, group, or service principal in the role assignment artifact, you define the **principalId** as a **parameter**. Then, when assigning the blueprint to a subscription, you provide the actual object ID specific to that environment.

   For instance, one team might use **devOpsPrincipalId** pointing to a team in Europe, while another environment might use the same blueprint but pass in a DevOps team from the United States. This approach allows a single blueprint to support diverse access configurations without modification.

2. **Assign Roles at the Right Scope**

   Blueprints support role assignments at both the **subscription** and **resource group** level. Choose your scope intentionally:

   - If the InfoSec team needs visibility across the entire subscription, assign the **Reader** role at the **subscription level**.

   - If the DevOps team should only manage workloads in a specific resource group (e.g., **rg-apps**), assign the **Contributor** role at the **resource group level**.

   This helps maintain the principle of **least privilege**, ensuring users only have the access they truly need.

3. **Use Clear Naming and Documentation**

   Name your role assignment artifacts in a way that reflects their purpose and scope. For example:

   - **InfoSecReader_Subscription**
   - **DevOpsContributor_rgApps**

   Doing this makes it easier for others (or your future self) to understand and manage the blueprint, especially as it evolves over time.

4. **Validate Object IDs Before Assignment**

   Blueprints do not validate whether the provided `principalId` exists until assignment. If the object ID is invalid, perhaps the group was deleted, or it belongs to a different tenant, the entire assignment will fail.

   To avoid this, validate the IDs beforehand using Azure CLI or PowerShell:

   ```
   Get-AzADGroup -DisplayName "InfoSec Team"
   Get-AzADUser -UserPrincipalName "devops@yourdomain.com"
   ```

   If you're working across multiple tenants or in delegated management scenarios, make sure those identities exist in the correct Azure Active Directory tenant.

5. **Be Aware of Lock Interactions**

   If your blueprint assignment includes **resource locks** (`ReadOnly` or `DoNotDelete`), think carefully about which roles you're assigning. For example, assigning a user the **Contributor** role but locking the resource group as **ReadOnly** will prevent that user from performing actions they'd normally be allowed to do.

   This mismatch can lead to confusion or failed operations, so always align your RBAC scope with the lock behavior defined in the blueprint.

Structuring Resource Groups

Within Azure Blueprints, **Resource Group artifacts** serve as the foundational scaffolding upon which all other governance and deployment logic is applied. Structuring resource groups correctly is not just a matter of organization, it directly affects **access control**, **policy scoping**, **infrastructure automation**, **monitoring boundaries**, and **deployment reliability**.

When resource groups are defined as artifacts in a blueprint, they are declaratively provisioned at assignment time, ensuring consistent boundaries across all environments governed by that blueprint. Their order of declaration is critical: other artifacts—such as RBAC roles, ARM templates, or policy assignments—may depend on them as deployment targets.

Key Architectural Principles for Resource Group Structuring

1. **Lifecycle and Operational Cohesion**

   Resource groups should encapsulate components that share the same **lifecycle**, **availability requirements**, and **management ownership**. For instance:

   - A web application's frontend, API gateway, and app service can be grouped together in **rg-apps**.

   - Monitoring infrastructure (e.g., Log Analytics workspace, Diagnostic Settings) belongs to a centralized **rg-monitoring**.

   - Networking components such as VNETs, NSGs, and route tables should be separated into **rg-networking**.

   - This design enables safe redeployment, targeted access control, and simplified teardown processes.

2. **Scope-Based Policy Targeting**

   Policies within Blueprints can be assigned at **subscription** or **resource group** level. Resource group artifacts allow you to **narrow scope** of enforcement. For example:

   - Global tagging policies might be applied at subscription level.

   - Application-specific policies (e.g., enforce diagnostic settings or VM size restrictions) can be scoped to rg-apps only.

   - This prevents unnecessary policy propagation and reduces false-positive compliance alerts.

3. **Identity and Role Assignment Isolation**

   RBAC artifacts in Blueprints can assign roles at the same scope as the resource group artifacts. For example:

   - DevOps team gets Contributor access only to rg-apps.

   - Security audit team gets Reader access to rg-monitoring.

   This structure supports **the least privilege** and allows for **multi-team collaboration** within the same subscription without cross-boundary interference.

CHAPTER 7   SCALING GOVERNANCE WITH AZURE BLUEPRINTS

Publishing Azure Blueprints with Versioning

After completing the design and artifact configuration of your blueprint, the next step is to publish it. Publishing transitions the blueprint from an editable draft to a versioned, immutable artifact. This is a critical point in the blueprint workflow: only **published** blueprints can be assigned to subscriptions.

Publishing also enables version control, allowing you to maintain a history of changes over time and safely update blueprint definitions without impacting existing assignments. While the full lifecycle is discussed in the next part of this chapter, this section focuses solely on the technical **publishing process** and how to manage versioning effectively.

Now, I will show how to publish the Azure blueprint with correct versioning:

1. Go to **Azure portal ➤ Blueprint ➤ Blueprint definitions**. Select the blueprint which we just created, as shown in Figure 7-14.

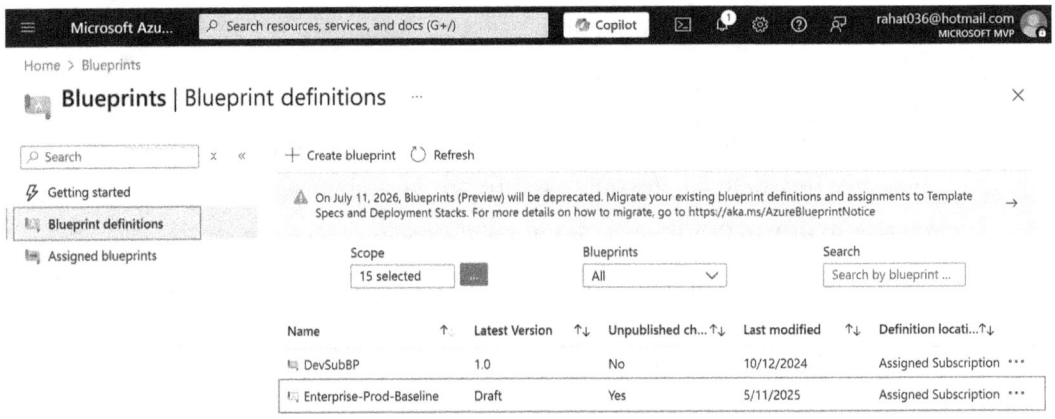

Figure 7-14. Selecting newly created blueprint definition

2. Review all the information, for example, the artifacts, mapping, and scopes, as shown in Figure 7-15.

CHAPTER 7   SCALING GOVERNANCE WITH AZURE BLUEPRINTS

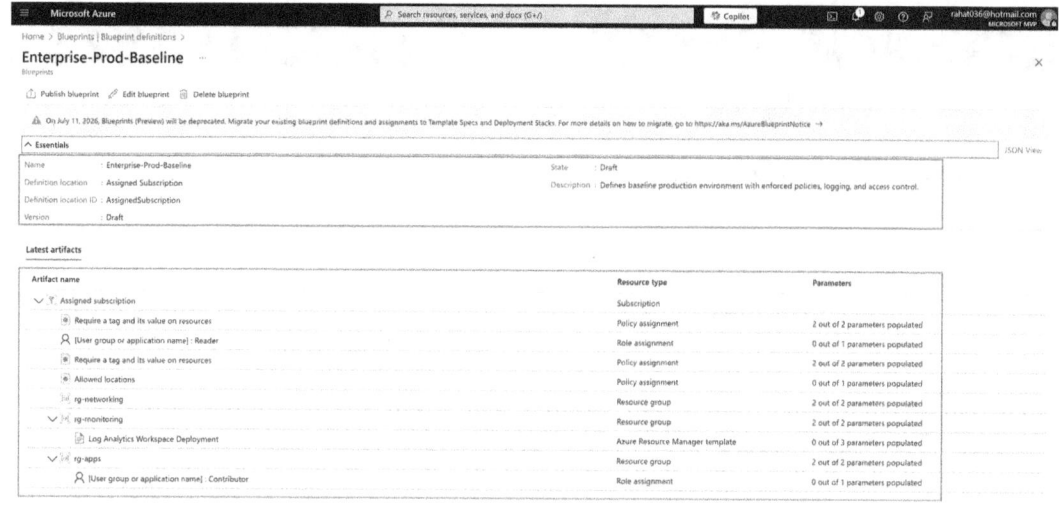

Figure 7-15. Reviewing the blueprint information

Note *Artifact execution order matters—Resource Groups must precede any artifacts that depend on them.*

3. Click the Publish blueprint button from the top menu as shown in Figure 7-16.

CHAPTER 7 SCALING GOVERNANCE WITH AZURE BLUEPRINTS

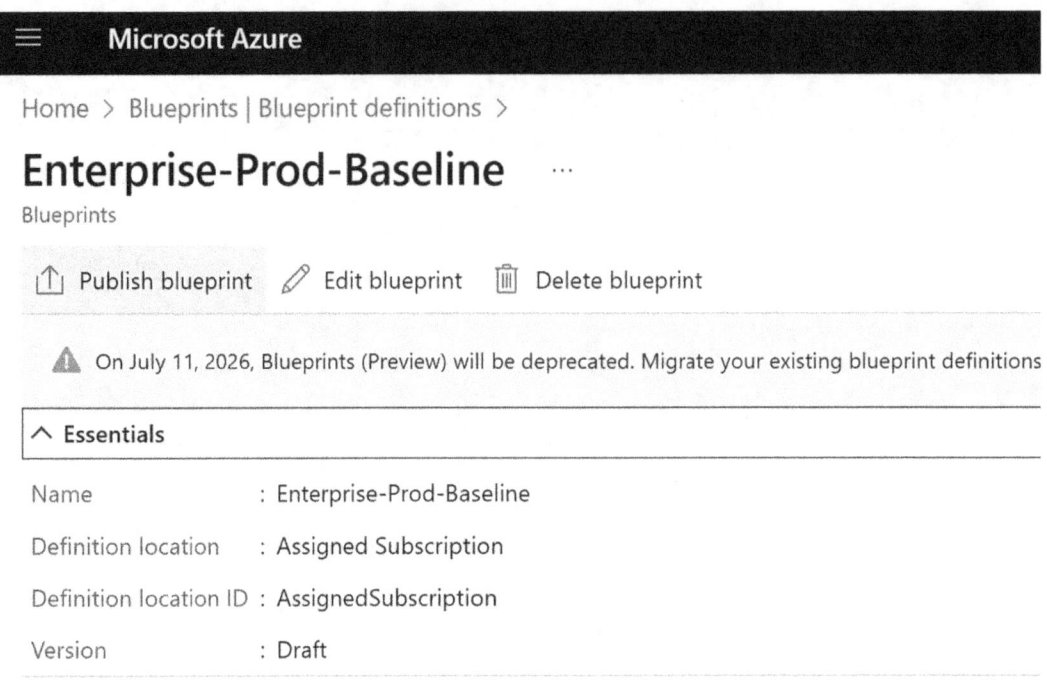

Figure 7-16. Publishing the blueprint

4. In the next page, the versioning window will open. You must specify a unique version (e.g., 1.0.0, 1.1.0, 2025-Q3, etc.), as shown in Figure 7-17.

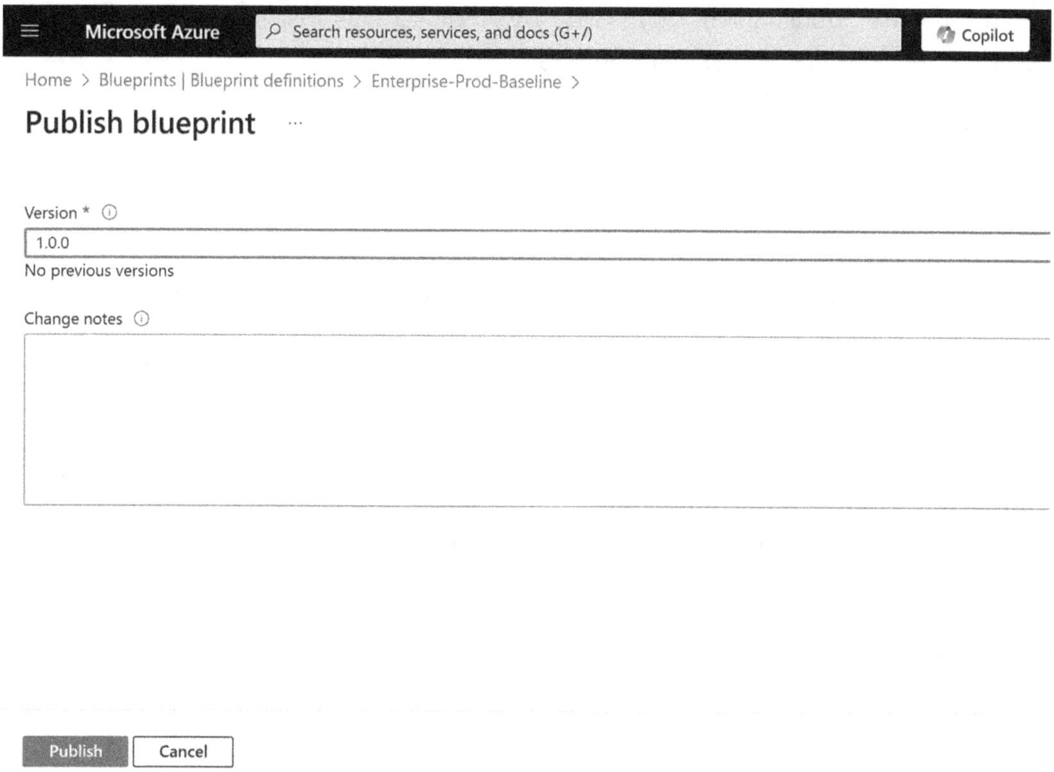

CHAPTER 7   SCALING GOVERNANCE WITH AZURE BLUEPRINTS

Figure 7-17. Versioning the blueprint

Note   Version can contain letters, numbers, and hyphens (max 20 characters). It must be unique within the same blueprint name and definition scope.

---

5. Click Publish. The blueprint is now read-only for this version.

Note   Once published, a blueprint version cannot be edited. To make changes, you must update the draft and publish a new version.

You can also publish the blueprint via PowerShell. To do this, you have to use the **Publish-AzBlueprint** cmdlet. For example:

```
Publish-AzBlueprint `
  -Name Enterprise-Prod-Baseline`
  -ManagementGroupId 'contoso-root' `
  -Version '1.0.0' `
  -ChangeNotes 'Initial baseline with network and monitoring RGs'
```

In Table 7-8, I would like to show you some versioning strategy or best practices.

Table 7-8. Versioning scenario with example

Scenario	Recommended Version	Notes
First release	1.0.0	Production-ready baseline
Minor update	1.1.0	Non-breaking improvement
Major structure change	2.0.0	Redesign or restructure
Quick fix	1.0.1	Metadata or parameter default change

Assigning Blueprint to Subscriptions

After publishing a blueprint, the next critical step is to assign it to one or more Azure subscriptions. This assignment enforces the blueprint's defined governance controls, such as policies, role-based access controls (RBAC), resource groups, and ARM templates, ensuring consistency and compliance across your Azure environment.

Understanding Blueprint Assignment

Assigning a blueprint involves specifying the target subscription(s), providing parameter values, selecting a managed identity for deployment, and configuring resource locking. Once assigned, the blueprint artifacts are deployed, and its policies and RBAC settings are enforced. I will show you step by step how to assign a blueprint to subscription:

CHAPTER 7   SCALING GOVERNANCE WITH AZURE BLUEPRINTS

1. Go to **Azure portal ➤ Blueprint ➤ Blueprint definitions**. Select the blueprint you want to assign. For example, I am selecting the blueprint that we created before. Make sure it is in a **Publish** state, as shown in Figure 7-18.

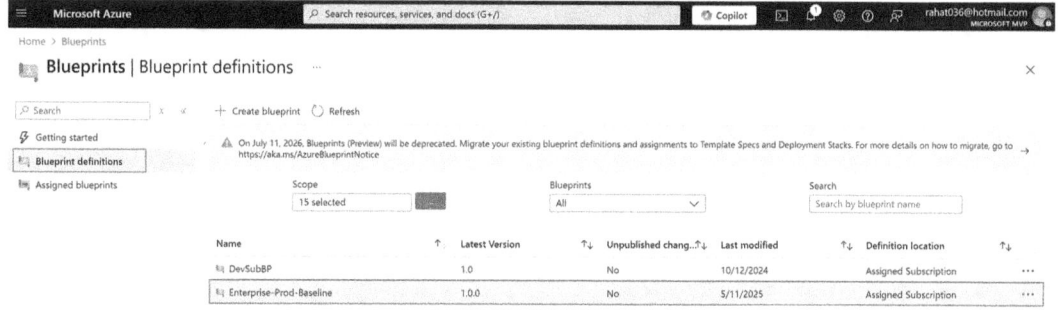

Figure 7-18. Selecting the blueprint after publishing

2. On the next page, click the Assign blueprint button as shown in Figure 7-19.

Figure 7-19. Assigning blueprint

3. Next, you need to configure the following assignment basics:

   a. **Subscriptions**: Select one or more subscriptions within the management group where the blueprint is saved.

   b. **Assignment Name**: Provide a unique name for the assignment.

   c. **Location**: Choose a region for the managed identity that will deploy the blueprint artifacts.

   d. **Blueprint Definition Version**: Select the appropriate published version of the blueprint.

299

CHAPTER 7 SCALING GOVERNANCE WITH AZURE BLUEPRINTS

Refer to Figure 7-20.

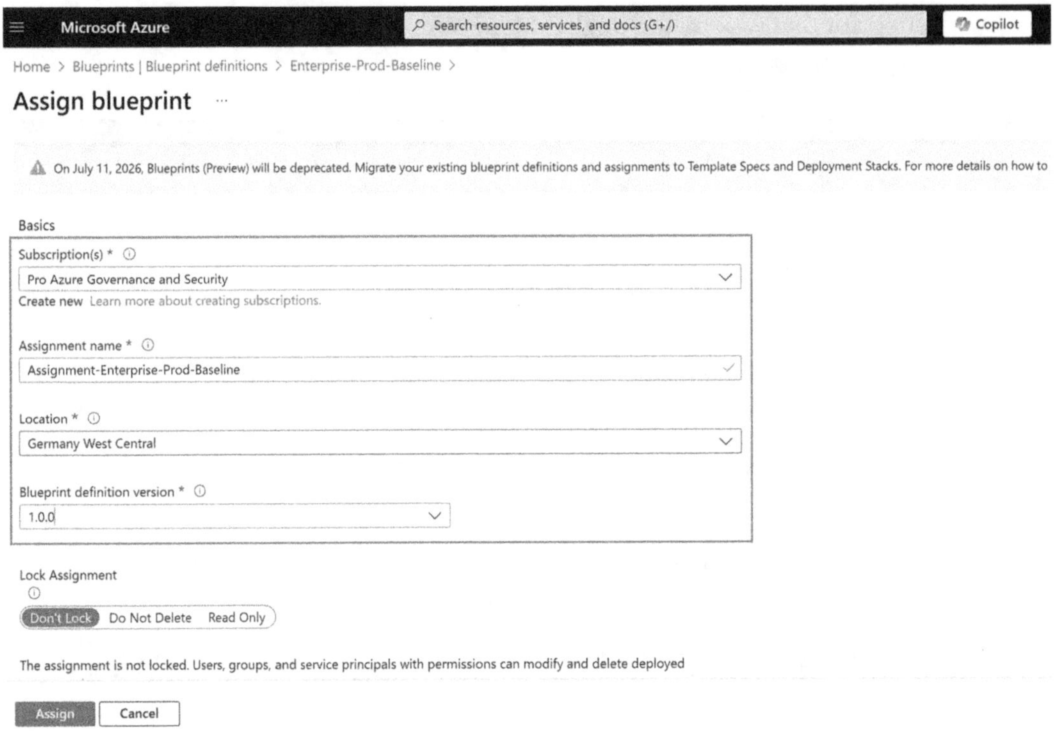

Figure 7-20. Selecting subscription, location, and version definition

4. Next, you can see the Lock Assignment option. Choose the desired lock behavior:

   a. **Don't Lock**: No locks are applied.

   b. **Read Only**: Resources can be read but not modified or deleted.

   c. **Do Not Delete**: Resources can be modified but not deleted.

Note Locks help protect critical resources from accidental changes or deletions.

5. As this is just a demo, I am choosing Don't Lock, so that I can use the resources in future.

CHAPTER 7   SCALING GOVERNANCE WITH AZURE BLUEPRINTS

6. Now, select Managed Identity. Choose between

   a. **System Assigned**: Azure creates a managed identity tied to the assignment.

   b. **User Assigned**: Use an existing managed identity.

   I am choosing system assigned in this case.

Note   System-assigned identities are suitable for most scenarios. Use user-assigned identities when you need more control over the identity lifecycle.

Refer to Figure 7-21.

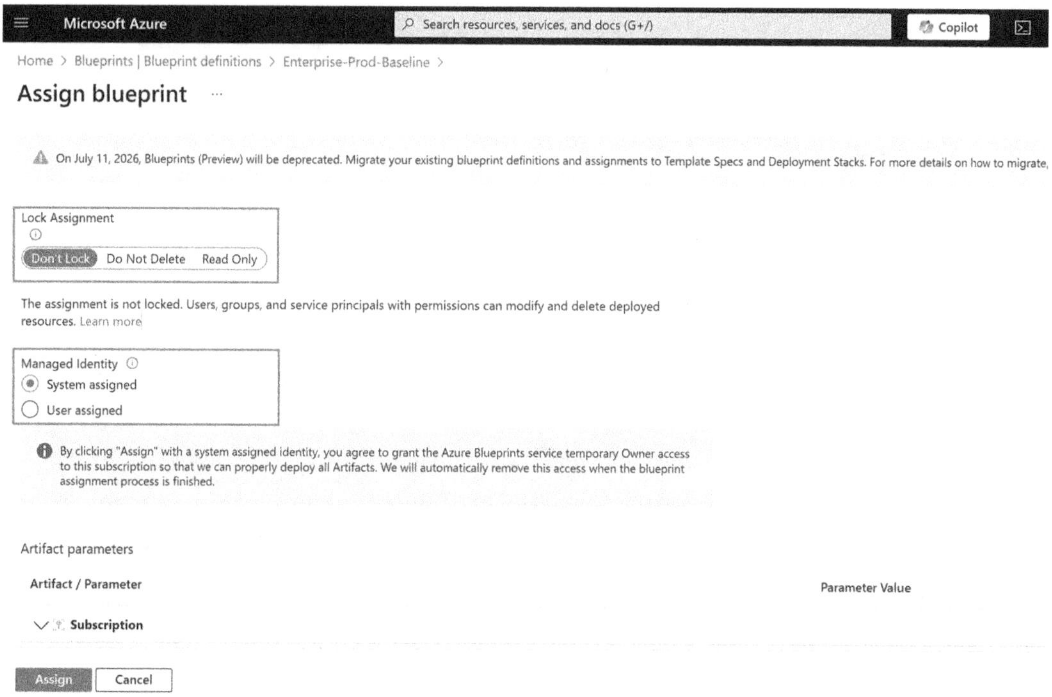

Figure 7-21.   Checking lock assignment and managed identity

7. Now, provide the artifact parameters. Do you remember when we created the artifact? I mentioned that we could add the parameters later during the blueprint assignment. We need to do it now.

301

I added the required parameter values in the artifact, as shown in Figure 7-22.

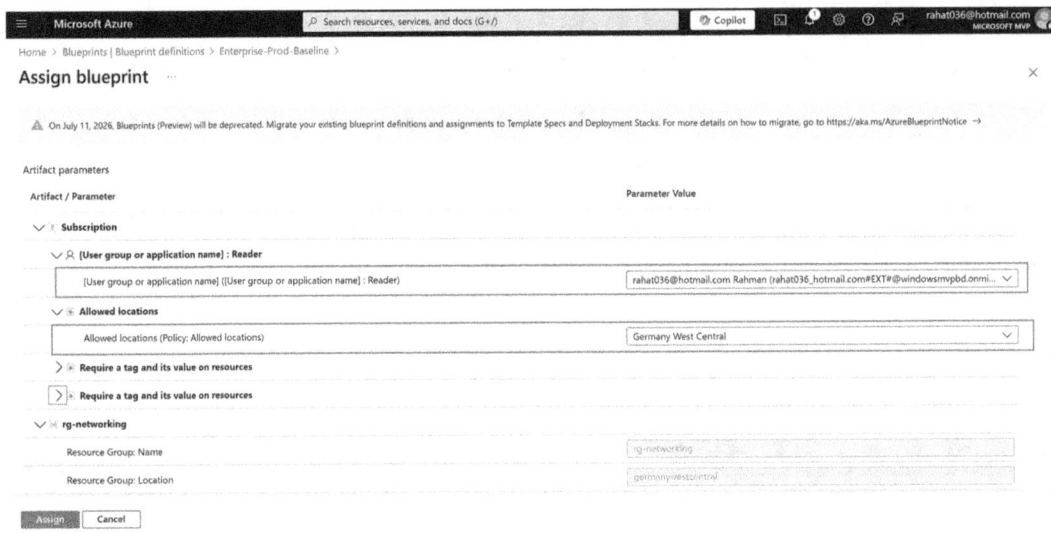

Figure 7-22. Choosing the required parameters

8. After configuring all settings, click Assign.

This is all about assigning blueprints.

Parameterization and Dynamic Assignment

Parameterization is one of the core strengths of Azure Blueprints. It allows blueprint definitions to remain static and reusable while enabling deployment-time flexibility through dynamic assignment. This separation of blueprint logic from environment-specific input is what makes Blueprints scalable across enterprise subscriptions, teams, and geographies.

Within a blueprint, parameters can be defined at the top level and then referenced across any artifact—whether it's a policy assignment, ARM template, role assignment, or resource group. These parameters support types such as **string**, **int**, **bool**, **array**, and **object** and can include optional metadata like descriptions, default values, and allowed value lists.

When constructing the blueprint, the author can choose to supply static values directly in the artifact (often for globally consistent configurations) or to defer the value to **assignment time**, marking it as a dynamic input. For example, while a policy requiring the tag **Environment** might always enforce the same **tagName**, the **tagValue** can vary by environment—**Dev**, **QA**, **Production**—and be passed in during assignment. Similarly, the principal IDs for role assignments or workspace names in ARM templates can be parameterized, allowing the same blueprint to apply different access models or infrastructure identifiers without modifying its core definition.

Dynamic assignment comes into effect when the blueprint is deployed to a subscription. The Azure Portal, PowerShell, or REST API surface all parameterized values as required inputs at assignment time. This offers precise control without compromising governance with intent. If default values or allowed values were defined during authoring, these help guide the assignee and reduce the risk of incorrect or inconsistent values.

From an architectural standpoint, well-parameterized blueprints become governance templates that scale horizontally. Instead of creating unique blueprints per department, region, or environment, organizations define a single versioned standard and parameterize only what must vary. To ensure success

- Blueprint authors should document each parameter clearly using **metadata.description** fields.
- Use **allowedValues** to prevent incorrect inputs.
- Keep parameters minimal and meaningful; too many configurable options can undermine standardization.
- Avoid hardcoding sensitive data. Use Key Vault references or secure deployment methods when parameters involve secrets or identities.

Ultimately, parameterization enables Blueprints to bridge the gap between centralized control and decentralized flexibility. A single governance model can adapt to the dynamic needs of multiple teams, environments, and projects—without rewriting code or redefining structure.

Blueprint Assignment Modes: Locking Options (ReadOnly, DoNotDelete, Don't Lock)

Azure Blueprints provide an additional layer of control through assignment-level resource locks, allowing governance teams to enforce operational boundaries automatically at deployment time. These locks—already discussed in the "Assigning Blueprint to Subscriptions" section—can be set to either allow full flexibility, prevent deletions, or entirely block modifications post-deployment.

While the locking modes themselves are straightforward in concept, their operational consequences can be significant. In practice, these locks translate into Azure Resource Manager–level protections that apply directly to deployed resources, depending on their scope in the blueprint assignment. However, overly restrictive locking—such as using `DoNotDelete` or `ReadOnly` across broad scopes—can lead to operational bottlenecks. For example, administrators may be unable to make critical updates or decommission obsolete resources without first modifying or removing the blueprint assignment. This can delay incident response, complicate DevOps workflows, and create friction during regular maintenance. It's important to balance governance needs with operational flexibility, applying locks only where necessary and documenting exceptions.

Why Locking Matters

Locking adds a nonnegotiable control boundary. When combined with RBAC, it prevents even high-privilege users from bypassing governance policies unintentionally. Resource locks cannot be overridden by Owners nor removed independently—they are bound to the blueprint assignment. The only way to remove them is to delete or reassign the blueprint.

This mechanism is particularly useful in regulated environments or when infrastructure must be protected from well-intentioned but potentially harmful changes introduced by automation, DevOps teams, or even service principals.

Strategic Use of Locking in Blueprints

Rather than defining what each lock does (covered in the "Assigning Blueprint to Subscriptions" section), let's focus on when and why each should be used.

ReadOnly (Strictest Control)

This mode is ideal for shared resources that must remain unchanged under any circumstances—such as

- Hub network infrastructure in a shared services model
- Central DNS zones or custom policy definitions
- Organizational root-level tagging enforcement

Use this mode sparingly, as it blocks all PUT, PATCH, and DELETE operations—even from automation pipelines.

DoNotDelete (Balanced Control)

This is the most recommended mode for most production assignments. It allows teams to update resources (e.g., configure App Service settings or change diagnostic retention) but protects the resource from deletion—either accidental or malicious. Apply this to

- Monitoring infrastructure like Log Analytics
- Key Vaults storing secrets or certificates
- Core platform services like shared storage accounts

Don't Lock (Flexible Control)

This mode should be used when you are building

- Environments intended for experimentation or learning
- Blueprints used for "starter templates" rather than compliance enforcement
- CI/CD-heavy environments where frequent, automated changes are expected

Troubleshooting Assignment Failures

Even with careful planning and design, blueprint assignments can occasionally fail—either during the initial assignment process or during the deployment of one or more artifacts. Understanding how to diagnose and resolve these failures is essential for maintaining operational reliability, especially in environments where compliance and automation are tightly integrated.

This section outlines the most common causes of assignment failures in Azure Blueprints, how to investigate them, and the best practices for preventing or mitigating issues in production environments.

Common Causes of Assignment Failures

Here are some common causes of assignment failures:

- **Invalid or Missing Parameter Values**

    Blueprints that rely on dynamic parameterization require accurate input at assignment time. If required parameters are left blank, malformed, or violate constraints (e.g., **allowedValues**), the assignment will fail.

Note Always validate parameters locally before assignment. Use consistent naming and type definitions across artifacts.

- **Insufficient Permissions for Managed Identity**

    When assigning a blueprint, Azure uses a managed identity (system assigned or user assigned) to deploy artifacts. If this identity lacks permissions—such as Contributor access at the subscription or resource group level—artifact deployment will fail.

Note Confirm that the identity has the **Microsoft.Blueprint/ blueprintAssignments/write** permission and role-based access to deploy each artifact (e.g., policy, resource, role).

- **Resource Conflicts**

    Assignments may fail if the blueprint attempts to deploy or configure resources that already exist with conflicting configurations—for example:

CHAPTER 7   SCALING GOVERNANCE WITH AZURE BLUEPRINTS

- Resource groups already exist with different locations.
- Policies with the same name are already assigned at the same scope.
- Role assignment conflicts with an existing one.

Note   Azure Blueprints are not idempotent in the same way as ARM templates—conflicts must be manually resolved before reassignment.

- **Policy Violations During Deployment**

    Policies included in the blueprint (e.g., allowed locations, naming conventions) may inadvertently block the deployment of the blueprint's own ARM templates or resources. This is especially common when initiative definitions enforce policies with **Deny** or **DeployIfNotExists** effects.

Note   Test policy artifacts separately before embedding them in Blueprints. Use **Audit** mode initially during development.

- **ARM Template Failures**

    ARM template artifacts can fail due to

    - Missing or incorrect parameter mappings
    - Unsupported API versions or incorrect resource syntax
    - Unmet resource dependencies (e.g., trying to deploy a VM without first creating the VNet)

Note   Use **Test-AzResourceGroupDeployment** with the same parameters outside the blueprint to validate the template in isolation.

Table 7-9 shows the ways to diagnose assignment failures.

Table 7-9. Ways to diagnose assignment failures

Tool	Use
Activity Log	Check for blueprint assignment errors, authorization failures, or denied operations
Blueprint Assignment Blade	Review assignment status, artifact execution results, and failed resources
Resource Health	Confirm the operational status of targeted resource groups or services
Azure Policy Compliance Blade	Identify policies that caused failed deployments or deny effects
Azure Monitor Logs	Use custom queries to track deployment and lock-related operations

Lifecycle Management of Blueprints

Creating and assigning a blueprint is only part of the story. To truly support long-term governance at scale, organizations must manage how blueprints evolve over time—how they're versioned, updated, deprecated, and reassigned. This section explores the full lifecycle of a blueprint, from draft to decommission, and how to maintain control as your governance standards mature.

Understanding the Blueprint Lifecycle

Azure Blueprints are not static artifacts; they are version-controlled governance templates designed to evolve alongside your cloud strategy. As governance standards shift—whether due to organizational growth, regulatory changes, or architectural adjustments—so must the blueprints that enforce them. Managing this change effectively requires a clear understanding of the Azure Blueprint lifecycle.

The lifecycle of a blueprint consists of four core stages: **Draft**, **Published**, **Assigned**, and **Updated**. Each phase has a distinct purpose and sets of behaviors within the Azure management plan. This section provides a detailed explanation of how these stages function and how they interact with your versioning and deployment strategy.

Figure 7-23 shows the lifecycle management of blueprints.

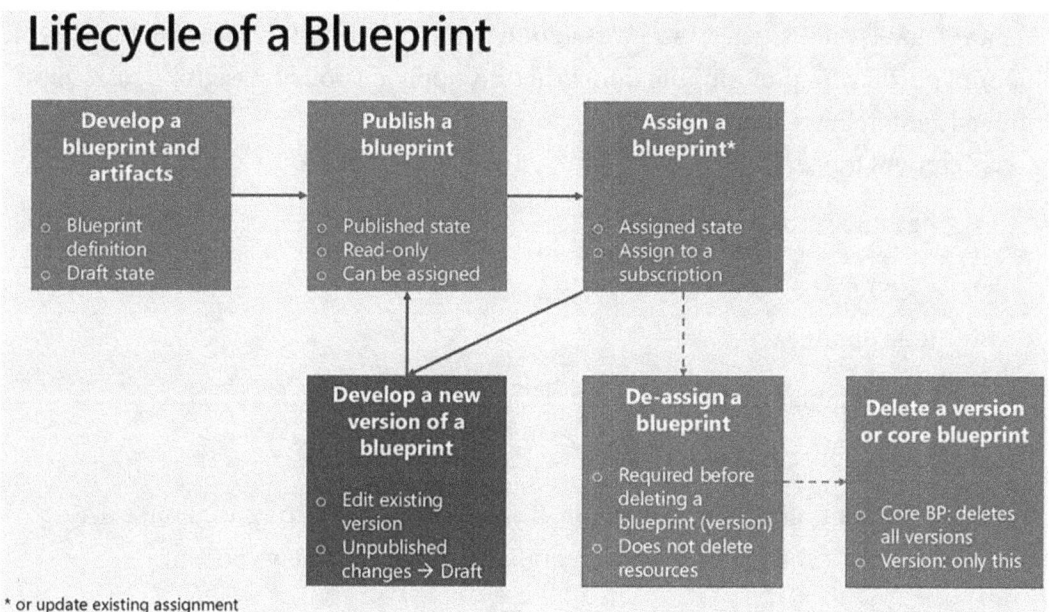

Figure 7-23. Lifecycle management of blueprints (Image: Microsoft)

Blueprint Lifecycle Stages

Draft

When a blueprint is first created, it enters the **Draft** state. In this phase, the blueprint is editable—you can add, modify, or remove artifacts (e.g., policies, RBAC assignments, ARM templates, resource groups). You can also define or adjust blueprint-level parameters.

Blueprints in draft form **cannot be assigned**. They are strictly for design, iteration, and internal review.

Published

Once a draft is complete and validated, it is **published**. Publishing locks the blueprint definition and creates a **versioned, immutable snapshot**. This version can now be assigned to one or more subscriptions.

You can publish multiple versions of the same blueprint over time. Each version is preserved, enabling traceability and rollback if needed.

Assigned

After a version is published, it can be **assigned** to a subscription. This action deploys the blueprint's artifacts—provisioning infrastructure, applying policy, assigning roles, and optionally enforcing resource locks.

Assignment triggers

- Resource group creation
- Policy and initiative assignment
- Role bindings
- ARM template deployment
- Lock application (if selected)

The assignments are **version specific**. If you later publish a new version, existing assignments do not change unless you manually reassign the new version.

Updated/Deprecated

Governance evolves and so do blueprints. To change an existing blueprint

- Return to the draft state (Azure maintains a single editable draft per blueprint)
- Modify artifacts, parameters, or metadata
- Publish a new version (e.g., moving from **1.0.0** to **1.1.0** or **2.0.0**)
- Reassign the new version to appropriate subscriptions

Old versions remain available but should be deprecated through documentation or internal lifecycle management processes.

Note   Azure Blueprints does not support explicit deprecation or expiration of published versions; you must manage version hygiene through process and policy.

Updating Blueprints Without Impacting Assignments

In large-scale environments, blueprints are often assigned to dozens—or even hundreds—of subscriptions. Making changes to a blueprint, therefore, must be done with precision to avoid disrupting existing workloads or violating operational expectations. Fortunately, Azure Blueprints provides a mechanism to **update blueprint definitions without affecting active assignments**—as long as the blueprint version remains unchanged.

This section focuses on how to make controlled updates to a blueprint **safely and predictably**, without unintentionally triggering changes in previously assigned environments.

Understanding the Version-Assignment Decoupling

Each time you publish a new version, that version becomes immutable. When you assign a specific version, it applies once and only once, meaning

- Future edits to the blueprint draft have no effect on that assignment.
- Assignments are tied to the version, not the draft.

This architectural design allows you to iterate on governance models safely, without retroactively changing what's already deployed in production.

Key Point Updating a blueprint draft or even publishing a new version does not impact any existing assignments unless you explicitly reassign them to the updated version.

To safely update a blueprint, follow the steps:

1. Each blueprint maintains a single draft. To update this, go to the Azure portal ➤ Blueprint ➤ Blueprint definitions. Select the existing blueprint. In this case, I am selecting the blueprint that we created before.

CHAPTER 7 SCALING GOVERNANCE WITH AZURE BLUEPRINTS

2. Click Edit Blueprint from the top menu. Make the necessary changes, such as

   a. Add or remove artifacts

   b. Update parameter metadata

   c. Modify default values or scopes

   Refer to Figure 7-24.

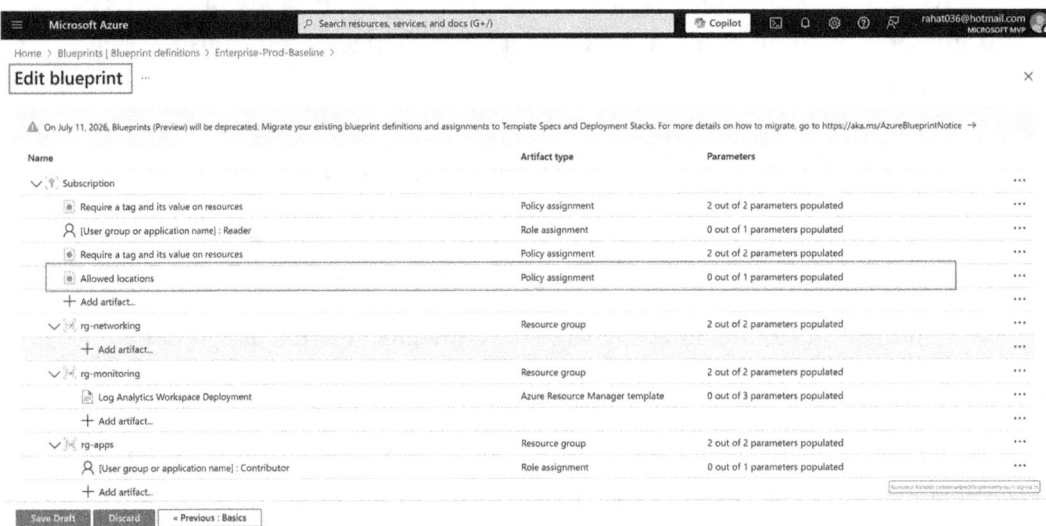

Figure 7-24. *Selecting allowed location to edit the blueprint*

3. Click Save Draft. Before publishing, test the updated blueprint draft in a test environment. Ensure parameters, artifacts, locks, and templates behave as expected.

4. Once validated, publish the updated draft by clicking Publish blueprint, with a new version number and change note, as shown in Figure 7-25.

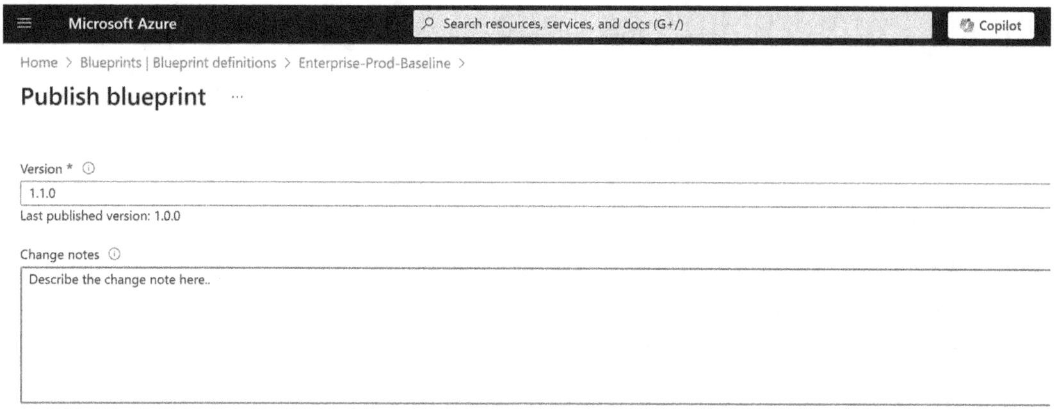

CHAPTER 7 SCALING GOVERNANCE WITH AZURE BLUEPRINTS

Figure 7-25. Publishing the updated and new version of blueprint

5. After publishing, assign the blueprint as we did before.

   What You Should Not Do

   - Don't expect assignments to **auto-upgrade** when a new version is published.

   - Don't modify artifacts in the published version; they are immutable.

   - Don't try to "edit around" a live assignment. Always create and test a new version instead.

Infrastructure As Code (IaC) with ARM Templates

While Azure Blueprints provide the framework for governance and compliance, **Infrastructure as Code (IaC)** defines how the actual infrastructure is deployed and managed in a repeatable, controlled manner. Azure Resource Manager (ARM) templates are the native IaC solution in Azure, offering a declarative way to deploy, configure, and update Azure resources on a scale.

This section provides a deep technical overview of using ARM templates in the context of Blueprints and broader governance models, focusing on best practices for maintainability, versioning, modularity, and integration.

What Is Infrastructure As Code in Azure?

Infrastructure as Code (IaC) is a modern, automation-centric approach to infrastructure management where the entire configuration of cloud resources is defined and maintained in machine-readable files. Instead of provisioning infrastructure manually through GUIs or one-off scripts, IaC enables engineers to describe Azure environments declaratively, using version-controlled templates that can be deployed consistently across subscriptions, environments, and regions.

In Azure, the IaC paradigm is implemented primarily through tools like **Azure Resource Manager (ARM) templates**, **Bicep**, and third-party orchestrators such as **Terraform** and **Pulumi**. ARM and Bicep are Microsoft's native solutions, fully integrated with the Azure control plane and supporting first-class governance, policy enforcement, and lifecycle automation.

IaC Core Principles

Infrastructure as Code in Azure adheres to several key principles:

- **Declarative Definitions**: You describe the intended end state, and Azure ensures the infrastructure matches it.

- **Idempotency**: Reapplying the same template will not cause duplication or configuration drift.

- **Versioning**: Infrastructure changes are tracked just like application code—supporting rollback, branching, and peer review.

- **Testability**: Templates can be validated and tested before deployment, ensuring predictability.

- **Automation**: Infrastructure can be integrated into CI/CD pipelines for continuous deployment of environments.

Why IaC Matters in Azure Governance

Without IaC, cloud environments can become unmanageable, inconsistent, and non-compliant, especially in multi-team or multi-region deployments. Infrastructure as Code

- Enforces standardization across all Azure subscriptions

- Supports policy-aligned provisioning (e.g., enforced regions, tag compliance)

- Reduces human error by automating complex resource creation

- Integrates seamlessly into DevOps workflows, enabling self-service with governance baked in

When used alongside **Azure Blueprints**, IaC becomes a foundational element of **Compliance as Code**, delivering governed infrastructure without sacrificing speed or developer autonomy.

Native IaC Tools in Azure

Table 7-10 shows the native IaC tools available in Azure.

Table 7-10. List of native IaC tools available in Azure

Tool	Description	Use Case
ARM Templates	JSON-based declarative language	Enterprise-scale templates, tightly coupled with Azure Policy and Blueprints
Bicep	DSL (Domain-Specific Language) that compiles to ARM	Modern syntax, modular IaC for engineers, good for inner-loop development
Terraform	HashiCorp tool with Azure provider	Cross-cloud environments, supports open source IaC tooling
Pulumi	Code-based IaC using general-purpose languages	Developer-centric, dynamic provisioning patterns

Infrastructure as Code is not just a tooling choice, it's an architectural model that defines how modern cloud platforms are built, governed, and scaled. In Azure, IaC provides the declarative foundation for building repeatable, policy-compliant, and audit-friendly environments. Whether authored in ARM, Bicep, or third-party DSLs, IaC enables your infrastructure to evolve like software—through automation, version control, and continuous integration.

Core Concepts of ARM Template Design

Designing robust and reusable ARM (Azure Resource Manager) templates is foundational to implementing Infrastructure as Code (IaC) in Azure. These templates define the declarative logic that translates governance intent into real infrastructure deployments. When authored correctly, ARM templates deliver consistent environments across subscriptions, resource groups, and environments—regardless of who runs them.

Here, I introduce the core components of ARM templates, explain their interrelationships, and outline principles that support secure, maintainable, and scalable IaC practices.

Structure of an ARM Template

An ARM template is a JSON document that conforms to the Azure Resource Manager schema and includes the top-level sections shown in Table 7-11.

Table 7-11. Structure of an ARM template

Section	Purpose
`$schema`	Identifies the JSON schema version to validate the template structure
`contentVersion`	A user-defined version of the template, for tracking and compatibility
`parameters`	Defines inputs that can be passed at runtime to customize deployment
`variables`	Internal values derived from parameters or expressions for reuse
`resources`	The Azure resources to be created or updated
`outputs`	Values returned after deployment (e.g., resource IDs, connection strings)

Here is an example skeleton:

```
{
  "$schema": "https://schema.management.azure.com/schemas/2025-05-12/
  deploymentTemplate.json#",
  "contentVersion": "1.0.0.0",
  "parameters": {},
  "variables": {},
  "resources": [],
  "outputs": {}
}
```

Core Design Concepts

At the heart of ARM template architecture are a few foundational design principles that ensure reliability, reusability, and governance alignment.

1. **Declarative Definition**

    ARM templates describe *what* to deploy, not *how*. Azure ensures the infrastructure reaches the declared state. This includes

    - Creating missing resources
    - Updating changed configurations
    - Ignoring unchanged elements

2. **Parameterization**

    Use parameters to inject dynamic values at deployment time. Parameters allow the same template to deploy across environments without modification.

    Each parameter can include

    - **type** (e.g., **string, int, bool, array, object**)
    - **defaultValue**
    - **allowedValues**
    - **metadata.description**

    Here is the example of JSON:

    ```
    "parameters": {
      "location": {
        "type": "string",
        "defaultValue": "East US",
        "metadata": {
          "description": "Region where resources will be deployed"
        }
      }
    }
    ```

3. **Variables**

   Variables simplify template logic and reduce repetition. They can be used to construct resource names, create standard tags, or group calculated values.

   Here is the example:

   ```
   "variables": {
     "storageAccountName": "[toLower(concat('st',
     uniqueString(resourceGroup().id)))]"
   }
   ```

4. **Resource Definitions**

   The resource block is the core of any ARM template. Each resource is declared with

   - **type** (e.g., **Microsoft.Compute/virtualMachines**)
   - **apiVersion** (ensure it's current and regionally supported)
   - **name**, **location**, **properties**, **dependsOn**

   Here is the code example:

   ```
   {
     "type": "Microsoft.Storage/storageAccounts",
     "apiVersion": "2025-05-12",
     "name": "[parameters('storageAccountName')]",
     "location": "[parameters('location')]",
     "sku": {
       "name": "Standard_LRS"
     },
     "kind": "StorageV2",
     "properties": {}
   }
   ```

CHAPTER 7 SCALING GOVERNANCE WITH AZURE BLUEPRINTS

5. **Expressions and Functions**

   ARM templates support rich expressions using built-in functions for string manipulation, math, logic, and referencing Azure metadata.

   Examples:

   - `[resourceGroup().location]`
   - `[concat(parameters('prefix'), '-vm')]`
   - `[if(equals(parameters('env'), 'prod'), 'P1', 'B1')]`

6. **Outputs**

   Outputs return information from the deployment that can be used by downstream processes or referenced in nested deployments.

   ```
   "outputs": {
     "storageAccountId": {
       "type": "string",
       "value": "[resourceId('Microsoft.Storage/storageAccounts',
       parameters('storageAccountName'))]"
     }
   }
   ```

Template and Parameter Files

In ARM-based deployments, separating your **template** from its **parameter file** is not just a stylistic choice, it's a core design pattern that facilitates **modular, reusable, and auditable Infrastructure-as-Code (IaC)** workflows. This separation allows a single deployment definition (template) to be reused across environments by passing different parameter files for configuration variance.

Here, we will explore the technical design of both files, the schema formats required by Azure Resource Manager, and how parameter injection works during execution.

Template File: Declarative Infrastructure Definition

An ARM **template file** (commonly `.json`) defines what Azure resources should exist, along with their configurations, relationships, and metadata. This is the **authoritative source of truth** for your infrastructure layout.

Here is a sample code for the ARM template file:

```json
{
  "$schema": "https://schema.management.azure.com/schemas/2019-04-01/deploymentTemplate.json#",
  "contentVersion": "1.0.0.0",
  "parameters": {
    "location": {
      "type": "string",
      "defaultValue": "eastus",
      "allowedValues": [ "eastus", "westus2", "westeurope" ],
      "metadata": {
        "description": "The Azure region to deploy resources into."
      }
    }
  },
  "variables": {},
  "resources": [],
  "outputs": {}
}
```

Table 7-12 shows the description of the fields that I used in the code.

Table 7-12. Description of the field that I used in the code

Field	Description
$schema	Defines which template schema version to validate against. Always use the latest compatible version
contentVersion	Used internally for tracking template versions; not validated by Azure
parameters	Defines dynamic values expected at deployment time
variables	Intermediate expressions computed from parameters
resources	Main body: list of resource declarations to be deployed
outputs	Optional values returned post-deployment (e.g., IDs, connection strings)

> **Note** Every resource block must include a valid **type**, **apiVersion**, and **name**. Failing to declare a correct **apiVersion** or parameter-reference syntax results in runtime errors or silent failures.

Parameter File: Deployment-Time Configuration

The **parameter file** supplies values to the template's parameters section during deployment. It allows for strict input typing and easy reusability across subscriptions and environments.

Here is a sample code for a parameter file:

```
{
  "$schema": "https://schema.management.azure.com/schemas/2019-04-01/
  deploymentParameters.json#",
  "contentVersion": "1.0.0.0",
  "parameters": {
    "location": {
      "value": "westeurope"
    },
    "storageAccountName": {
      "value": "prodlogs01"
    }
  }
}
```

Linked and Nested Templates

As Azure environments grow in complexity, maintaining large, monolithic ARM templates becomes difficult and counterproductive. To manage this scale, ARM templates support a modular architecture through **linked** and **nested** templates. These features allow you to **break down complex deployments into smaller, reusable components**, improving readability, manageability, and CI/CD integration.

This section focuses on the differences between linked and nested templates, when to use each, and how they enable scalable infrastructure composition in large Azure deployments.

Why Modular Templates Matter

Monolithic templates are difficult to test, version, and reuse. Modularization solves this by

- Separating responsibilities (e.g., networking, identity, monitoring)
- Enabling team-level ownership over specific domains
- Reducing cognitive load by limiting each template's scope
- Allowing incremental deployment, testing, and rollback

Both linked and nested templates allow templates to **call other templates**, but they differ in execution model and use cases.

Linked Templates

Linked templates are **external templates** referenced via a URI—usually pointing to an Azure Storage Blob or GitHub location. This enables **separation of files**, reducing duplication and supporting better reuse across teams and pipelines.

When to Use

- You want to **reuse a template across projects or teams**.
- You need to manage **template versions independently**.
- Your pipeline or automation can fetch templates via URI (e.g., GitHub or Azure Blob with SAS token).

Here is a sample JSON code for a linked template:

```
{
  "type": "Microsoft.Resources/deployments",
  "apiVersion": "2025-05-12",
  "name": "linkedTemplateDeployment",
  "properties": {
    "mode": "Incremental",
    "templateLink": {
      "uri": "https://mystorage.blob.core.windows.net/templates/vnet.json",
      "contentVersion": "1.0.0.0"
    },
```

```
    "parameters": {
      "vnetName": { "value": "core-vnet" }
    }
  }
}
```

> **Security Note** Linked templates must be accessible from Azure's backend. Private links require **SAS tokens** or publicly accessible endpoints.

Nested Templates

Nested templates are embedded within a parent ARM template using the **Microsoft.Resources/deployments** resource type. The full content of the child template is included **inline** or stored as a local file in the same deployment package.

When to Use

- You want to **reuse logic internally** across sections of the same template.
- You're building **blueprint artifacts** that must include everything in a single file.
- You're deploying using **local tooling**, like PowerShell or Azure CLI.

Here is a sample JSON code for a nested template:

```
{
  "type": "Microsoft.Resources/deployments",
  "apiVersion": "2021-04-01",
  "name": "nestedStorageDeployment",
  "properties": {
    "mode": "Incremental",
    "template": {
      "$schema": "...",
      "contentVersion": "1.0.0.0",
      "parameters": {},
```

```
    "resources": [
      {
        "type": "Microsoft.Storage/storageAccounts",
        "apiVersion": "2022-09-01",
        "name": "[parameters('storageAccountName')]",
        "location": "[parameters('location')]",
        "sku": { "name": "Standard_LRS" },
        "kind": "StorageV2",
        "properties": {}
      }
    ]
  }
 }
}
```

Note Use nested templates inside **Azure Blueprints**, as blueprints do not support external links to secured resources.

Table 7-13 shows the key differences between nested and linked templates.

Table 7-13. *Key differences between nested and linked templates*

Feature	Nested Template	Linked Template
Location	Inline (same file or same deployment)	External URI (e.g., Azure Blob, GitHub)
Network dependency	None	Requires public or SAS-accessible endpoint
Use in Blueprints	Fully supported	Not supported (unless public)
CI/CD suitability	Moderate	High (decoupled versioning)
Deployment structure	Single ARM deployment	Multi-file, orchestrated deployment

Template Functions and Expressions

ARM templates are more than static configuration files—they support a rich expression language and set of built-in functions that allow you to dynamically generate values, perform conditional logic, and reference Azure-specific runtime metadata. This capability makes your templates **more flexible**, **less repetitive**, and **environment-aware**, supporting scalable deployments across environments and regions.

Let's explore the most commonly used functions and expression patterns in ARM templates, along with guidance on secure and efficient use.

Expression Syntax in ARM Templates

ARM templates use the syntax **[functionName(parameters)]** to denote an expression. These expressions can appear in any field that supports dynamic evaluation—such as **name**, **location**, **dependsOn**, **sku**, or **properties**.

For example:

`"name": "[concat(parameters('namePrefix'), '-storage')]"`

You can **nest expressions**, **combine functions**, and use both **parameters** and **variables** within functions.

Commonly Used ARM Functions

Table 7-14 shows the commonly used ARM template functions.

Table 7-14. List of commonly used ARM template functions

Category	Function	Purpose	Example
String Functions	concat()	Joins strings together	[concat('web', uniqueString(resourceGroup().id))]
	toLower()/toUpper()	Converts string case	[toLower(parameters('env'))]
	substring()	Extracts part of a string	[substring(parameters('name'), 0, 8)]
Resource and Metadata Functions	resourceGroup()	Returns current resource group metadata	[resourceGroup().location]
	subscription()	Returns subscription details	[subscription().subscriptionId]
	deployment()	Gets deployment metadata	[deployment().name]
Math and Logic Functions	add(), sub(), mul(), div()	Basic arithmetic operations	[add(parameters('base'), 5)]
	if()	Conditional expression	[if(equals(parameters('env'), 'prod'), 'Standard', 'Basic')]
	equals(), not(), and(), or()	Logical comparisons	[equals(parameters('tier'), 'prod')]
Unique and Deterministic Functions	uniqueString()	Generates consistent hash from seed input	[uniqueString(resourceGroup().id)]
	guid()	Generates deterministic GUID from input values	[guid(resourceGroup().id, parameters('suffix'))]

Best Practice Patterns

When authoring ARM templates, using expressions effectively is not just about syntax—it's about applying repeatable patterns that enhance **readability, security, reusability,** and **automation friendliness.** Below are key best practice patterns that leverage built-in functions to make templates more dynamic, modular, and scalable across Azure environments:

1. **Name Construction (Dynamic Resource Naming)**

   Dynamically generate globally unique or environment-specific names for resources using concatenation and hash functions.

   Pattern:

   ```
   "name": "[concat(parameters('namePrefix'), '-',
   uniqueString(resourceGroup().id))]"
   ```

2. **Conditional Logic with if() and equals()**

   Conditionally select values or properties based on parameter input.

   Pattern:

   ```
   "sku": {
   "name": "[if(equals(parameters('env'), 'prod'), 'Premium',
   'Standard')]"
   }
   ```

Note Too many `if()` chains reduce readability. For complex logic, consider using Bicep or modular templates.

---

3. **Modular Deployment with Indexing (Using copyIndex())**

   Deploy multiple instances of a resource (e.g., VMs, NICs, subnets) using an indexed array and loop.

   Pattern:

```
"variables": {
  "vmNames": [ "vm-app1", "vm-app2", "vm-app3" ]
},
"resources": [
  {
    "type": "Microsoft.Compute/virtualMachines",
    "name": "[variables('vmNames')[copyIndex()]]",
    "copy": {
      "name": "vmLoop",
      "count": "[length(variables('vmNames'))]"
    },
    ...
  }
]
```

4. **Metadata Referencing for Environment Awareness**

   Use built-in metadata functions to make deployments self-aware of their context.

   Pattern:

   ```
   "location": "[resourceGroup().location]"
   ```

Note Avoid duplicating the location parameter across every resource—use `resourceGroup().location` when possible.

---

5. **Deterministic Naming with guid()**

   Generate repeatable but unique GUIDs for secure resources or naming within automation workflows.

   Pattern:

   ```
   "name": "[guid(resourceGroup().id, parameters('applicationId'))]"
   ```

Validation and Testing of ARM Templates

The quality of any Infrastructure-as-Code strategy depends on confidence that the code will behave as expected—every time. With Azure Resource Manager (ARM) templates, validation and testing are essential to ensure correctness, compliance, and stability before deployment. Especially in enterprise environments, where templates are embedded in pipelines or Blueprints, even a minor misconfiguration can lead to failed rollouts, policy violations, or security gaps.

Azure provides several mechanisms to validate and test ARM templates both structurally and functionally, from schema validation to dry-run execution and policy-aware auditing.

Validating Templates Before Deployment

Before any deployment, templates should be statically validated to confirm they adhere to ARM's schema structure and syntax. This can be done using tools such as the Azure CLI or PowerShell.

For example, using the Azure CLI (minimum required version: **v2.60**), a simple validation command would be

```
az deployment group validate \
  --resource-group myRG \
  --template-file azuredeploy.json \
  --parameters @azuredeploy.parameters.json
```

This validation checks not just the template's structure but also whether required parameters are present, values are of the correct type, and all referenced resource types and API versions are valid in the target subscription and region. This is an essential gate before integrating the template into a production deployment pipeline or a governance mechanism like Azure Blueprints.

Testing in Context: Policy and Role Impacts

Validation becomes even more critical when templates are used in regulated environments where Azure Policy is actively enforced. A template that attempts to deploy a resource in an unapproved region or without mandatory tags will pass schema validation but still fail at deployment time due to policy evaluation.

Templates should be tested in a non-production environment with active policies enabled to reveal such conflicts early. This includes

- Required tags and naming policies
- Restrictions on SKU or location
- Mandatory diagnostic settings
- Role assignment policies tied to tenant or group membership

Dry-run deployments help expose these policy-related failures under real-world conditions.

Using Static Analysis Tools

Beyond functional testing, Microsoft provides the ARM Template Toolkit (ARM-TTK), a PowerShell-based static analysis tool that validates best practices, such as

- Avoiding hardcoded values
- Using secureString for sensitive parameters
- Ensuring parameters have metadata descriptions
- Ensuring use of consistent API versions

Running ARM-TTK against templates during pull requests or as part of CI/CD workflows adds an additional quality gate before release.

Parameter Set Testing and Input Variation

Templates become more powerful when decoupled from hardcoded values through parameterization. However, this introduces another source of potential error: mismatched or invalid inputs.

Every environment (e.g., **dev**, **test**, **prod**) should have its own tested parameter file. Templates should include validation logic—like **allowedValues**, **minLength**, and **defaultValue**—to enforce acceptable input ranges.

Functional testing involves deploying the template with each parameter file to a sandbox subscription. This validates not only syntax but also how the template behaves with different inputs and whether it delivers consistent infrastructure outputs across environments.

Deployment Simulation Through Sandbox Environments

Finally, the best validation is deployment. Use a dedicated test subscription to simulate full deployments, observe output, monitor policy compliance, and verify that created resources match expectations.

This includes

- Verifying resource names and locations are correct
- Checking if dependent resources are created in the right order
- Ensuring role assignments and diagnostic settings are applied correctly
- Capturing and validating outputs (such as resource IDs or connection strings)

Only after a successful test deployment should a template be promoted to production or embedded in a blueprint.

Integration with Source Control Systems

IaC succeeds not just through automation, but through **discipline, collaboration, and traceability**. These qualities are unlocked when ARM templates—and the parameter files, modules, and metadata that support them—are integrated into **source control systems** such as Git. By versioning templates just like application code, organizations gain the ability to safely test, review, deploy, and audit infrastructure changes at scale.

Let's explore how source control supports governance, quality, and agility across the infrastructure lifecycle and how to structure repositories to enable DevOps workflows around ARM templates.

Why Source Control Matters for ARM Templates

When ARM templates are managed outside of source control, they are prone to

- Drift and inconsistency between environments
- Lack of review, approvals, or rollback
- Poor traceability of changes
- Manual, error-prone deployments

Storing templates in a Git-based system like **GitHub**, **Azure Repos**, or **GitLab** introduces structured change management:

- Templates are committed, reviewed, and merged through pull requests.
- CI/CD pipelines validate, lint, and test templates before deployment.
- Changes are tracked with author, timestamp, diff, and justification.

Note Treat infrastructure like code—use branching, tagging, and peer reviews to enforce organizational standards.

Recommended Repository Structure

For enterprise-scale environments, the repository should reflect a **modular, domain-aligned, and environment-aware** design. Each template module should be isolated to a specific functional domain, and parameter sets should be segmented per environment.

```
repo-root/
├── templates/
│   ├── compute/
│   │   └── vm.template.json
│   ├── network/
│   │   └── vnet.template.json
│   ├── security/
│   │   └── keyvault.template.json
│   ├── diagnostics/
│   │   └── loganalytics.template.json
│   └── shared/
│       ├── tagging.template.json
│       └── naming.template.json
├── parameters/
│   ├── dev/
│   │   ├── vm.parameters.json
│   │   └── vnet.parameters.json
```

```
│   ├── prod/
│   │   ├── vm.parameters.json
│   │   └── vnet.parameters.json
│   └── staging/
│       └── keyvault.parameters.json
├── pipeline/
│   ├── azure-pipelines.yml
│   └── template-validation.yml
└── docs/
    └── README.md
```

This layout enables teams to

- Deploy each module independently
- Maintain versioned parameters for each environment
- Build and test each template in isolation

Refer to Microsoft official documentation to learn more about Azure pipeline library:

https://learn.microsoft.com/en-us/azure/devops/pipelines/library/.

https://learn.microsoft.com/en-us/azure/devops/pipelines/library/.

Table 7-15 shows the purpose of the folders used in the repository structure.

Table 7-15. Purpose of the folders used in the repository structure

Folder/File	Purpose
templates/	Domain-specific ARM templates grouped by resource type or business function
parameters/	Environment-specific parameter sets aligned with deployment contexts
pipeline/	YAML pipeline definitions for validation and deployment automation
docs/	Internal usage guidance, naming standards, and module descriptions

Security Tip Do **not** store secrets in parameter files. Use **secureString** and integrate with Azure Key Vault via CI/CD variable injection or linked parameters.

CHAPTER 7   SCALING GOVERNANCE WITH AZURE BLUEPRINTS

CI/CD Integration: Automating Validation and Deployment

To ensure ARM templates remain reliable and compliant as they evolve, you should connect your source control system to a CI/CD pipeline that performs

1. **Template validation** (schema and parameter conformity)

2. **Static analysis using ARM-TTK**

3. **Policy enforcement checks** (e.g., tag compliance, location constraints)

4. **Deployment to sandbox environments**

5. **Promotion to staging or production** (optionally gated by approvals)

Here is the sample yaml code of Azure DevOps workflow:

```yaml
trigger:
  branches:
    include:
      - main

jobs:
- job: ValidateAndTest
  pool:
    vmImage: 'ubuntu-latest'
  steps:
    - task: AzureCLI@2
      inputs:
        azureSubscription: 'My-Connection'
        scriptType: bash
        scriptLocation: inlineScript
        inlineScript: |
          az deployment group validate \
            --resource-group test-rg \
            --template-file templates/network/vnet.template.json \
            --parameters @parameters/dev/vnet.parameters.json
```

```
- task: PowerShell@2
  inputs:
    targetType: 'inline'
    script: |
      Invoke-ARMTemplate -TemplatePath 'templates/network/vnet.
      template.json'
```

> **Note** Store pipeline templates in a **/pipeline** directory and reuse them across modules via includes or templates to reduce maintenance overhead.

Refer to Microsoft official documentation to learn more about Azure pipeline library: https://learn.microsoft.com/en-us/azure/devops/pipelines/library/.

Real-World Scenarios: Automating Environment Deployments

In real-world enterprise environments, infrastructure needs to be deployed repeatedly, across many subscriptions, and with full consistency. ARM templates, integrated into CI/CD pipelines, allow this to happen automatically—without sacrificing governance or flexibility.

Below is a practical scenario showing how organizations use ARM templates to automate full-stack environment provisioning through pipelines.

Scenario: Provisioning a Development Environment via Azure DevOps Pipeline

The goal is to automate the deployment of a development environment, including networking, compute, and monitoring resources.

The foundational components required to enable automated deployment through a pipeline include templates, parameters, and service connections.

- **Templates stored in Git** (e.g., **templates/network/vnet.template.json, templates/compute/vm.template.json**)
- **Parameter files stored per environment** (e.g., **parameters/dev/**)

- **Azure Pipelines** configured for CI/CD
- **Service connection** with `Contributor` rights on target subscription

The step-by-step execution flow is triggered by a commit, ensuring validation, compliance, and deployment to the target environment.

1. On commit or pull request to the **dev** branch, the pipeline triggers.
2. The pipeline performs
   - Template validation (`az deployment group validate`)
   - Static analysis via ARM-TTK
   - Deployment to a sandbox resource group
3. Parameter values (e.g., VM size, region, tags) are injected from environment-specific files.

The operational advantages gained by automating deployments using ARM templates and CI/CD pipelines in a controlled, repeatable manner include the following:

- Each environment is reproducible and version-controlled.
- Teams can deploy and update their own infra modules without manual portal access.
- Governance is enforced through peer review, pre-approved templates, and consistent policy application.

Best Practice Capture all outputs (e.g., resource IDs, connection strings) as pipeline artifacts to feed into downstream deployment stages.

Summary

In this chapter, we explored how to scale governance across complex, distributed environments using Azure Blueprints. We examined how Blueprints enable organizations to define and enforce security, compliance, and operational standards by packaging role-based access controls, resource templates, Azure Policy assignments, and ARM templates into reusable, version-controlled artifacts. We discussed how Blueprints can be assigned at the subscription or management group level to ensure consistency across environments and how integration with Azure DevOps pipelines enables continuous compliance as part of Infrastructure-as-Code deployments. By leveraging Blueprints, organizations can move from reactive enforcement to proactive, automated governance, ensuring that every resource deployed adheres to predefined organizational standards from day one.

In Chapter 8, we shift our focus from governance to cloud-native security operations with Microsoft Sentinel, Azure's scalable SIEM and SOAR platform. You'll learn how Sentinel ingests and correlates data from Defender for Cloud and other sources to detect complex threats, how to create detection rules, run threat-hunting queries, investigate incidents, and automate responses using playbooks. This chapter will guide you in building a modern, intelligent SOC capability in the cloud—one that is deeply integrated with the Microsoft security ecosystem and powered by analytics, automation, and intelligence.

CHAPTER 8

Azure Sentinel: Next-Generation SIEM

In the previous chapter, we explored how to scale governance across large cloud estates using Azure Blueprints and DevOps automation. You learned how to enforce standardized configurations, role assignments, policies, and compliance baselines at scale, ensuring that all deployed resources align with your organization's governance framework. Now that we have a robust governance structure in place, it's time to shift our focus toward real-time threat detection, investigation, and response.

In this chapter, we dive into Microsoft Sentinel, Microsoft's next-generation cloud-native SIEM and SOAR platform. You will learn how Sentinel helps security teams detect advanced threats, correlate signals across services, automate incident responses, and conduct proactive threat hunting across multi-cloud and hybrid environments. With built-in machine learning, behavioral analytics, and deep integration into the broader Microsoft security ecosystem, Sentinel enables you to build an intelligent and responsive Security Operations Center (SOC) in the cloud.

Introduction to Azure Sentinel

As organizations adopt cloud-first strategies and hybrid environments become the norm, security teams face the urgent challenge of gaining visibility and control across a growing, complex attack surface. Azure Sentinel is Microsoft's response to this challenge—a scalable, cloud-native SIEM and SOAR platform designed to collect, detect, investigate, and respond to threats across your entire digital estate.

CHAPTER 8   AZURE SENTINEL: NEXT-GENERATION SIEM

What Is Azure Sentinel?

Azure Sentinel is Microsoft's cloud-native Security Information and Event Management (SIEM) and Security Orchestration, Automation, and Response (SOAR) platform. It is built from the ground up to help security operations teams detect, investigate, and respond to threats across the modern enterprise—whether those threats originate in the cloud, on-premises, or across hybrid environments.

At its core, the Azure Sentinel functions as a centralized command and control platform. It aggregates security-related data from a wide variety of sources—including Azure resources, Microsoft 365 services, AWS, firewalls, routers, identity providers, endpoints, and third-party applications. Once data is ingested into Sentinel, it is normalized and stored in an Azure Log Analytics Workspace, where it becomes searchable using Kusto Query Language (KQL).

But Sentinel goes far beyond simple log collection. It enables security teams to

- **Analyze data at cloud scale**, using Microsoft's global infrastructure
- **Detect advanced threats** using machine learning models, anomaly detection, and Microsoft's proprietary threat intelligence feeds
- **Correlate events across diverse systems** to surface high-fidelity security incidents
- **Investigate incidents efficiently** using timeline views, entity mapping, and embedded investigation tools
- **Respond to incidents automatically** using **playbooks** powered by Azure Logic Apps

Because Sentinel is cloud native, there is no need for provisioning servers, managing storage, or performing updates. This removes the operational burden commonly associated with traditional SIEM platforms and allows organizations to focus purely on detection, investigation, and response.

Azure Sentinel supports multiple security use cases, including

- **Centralized threat detection and monitoring** across multi-cloud and hybrid systems
- **Insider threat detection** using User and Entity Behavior Analytics (UEBA)

CHAPTER 8   AZURE SENTINEL: NEXT-GENERATION SIEM

- **Real-time alerting and correlation** using customizable analytics rules
- **Automated incident response** using rule-triggered playbooks
- **Threat hunting and hypothesis testing** using custom KQL queries and interactive notebooks

Sentinels are also modular and extensible. It comes with over 100 out-of-the-box data connectors for Microsoft and non-Microsoft platforms. In addition, organizations can build custom connectors using REST APIs or Azure Functions, enabling ingestion of virtually any telemetry source.

Because Sentinel is deeply embedded in the **Microsoft Intelligent Security Graph**, it benefits from trillions of daily signals collected across Microsoft services like Windows, Azure, Xbox, and Office 365. This rich threat intelligence enhances Sentinel's ability to detect sophisticated and previously unknown attack techniques.

Why Cloud-Native SIEM?

As organizations continue moving to the cloud and expanding across hybrid environments, security teams are being asked to do more with less—monitor more systems, respond to more threats, and manage more complexity, often with limited resources. This shift has exposed the limitations of traditional SIEM systems, many of which were designed for static, on-premises infrastructures.

That's where cloud-native SIEM solutions like Azure Sentinel come in.

Unlike traditional SIEMs that require you to install software, manage servers, and manually scale resources, Azure Sentinel runs entirely in the cloud. You don't have to worry about provisioning infrastructure or planning storage—you simply connect your data sources and start analyzing.

Let's explore why being cloud-native makes such a difference.

Scale Without Limits

With a traditional SIEM, scaling up to handle more data often means buying new hardware, configuring storage, and planning for future growth. It's slow, expensive, and resource intensive. Azure Sentinel, by contrast, automatically scales based on your needs. Whether you're collecting a few gigabytes or several terabytes of data per day, Sentinel adjusts in the background—no manual intervention required.

See Everything, Everywhere

Modern IT environments are rarely confined to a single data center. Most organizations use a mix of services from Azure, Microsoft 365, Amazon Web Services, and even on-premises infrastructure. Azure Sentinel is designed to meet this reality head-on. It offers built-in connectors for Microsoft services, supports third-party integrations, and lets you collect data from virtually any source. This means you can monitor your entire environment—from the cloud to your local data center—all in one place.

Smarter, Not Just Louder

One of the biggest complaints about legacy SIEMs is that they generate too many alerts—many of which turn out to be noise. Sentinel improves this by using machine learning and Microsoft's global threat intelligence to prioritize the alerts that matter most. It can correlate related events across systems, identify patterns of suspicious behavior, and even surface threats that would otherwise go unnoticed. This makes your investigations faster and your decisions more accurate.

No Maintenance Headaches

Because Azure Sentinel is a fully managed service, there's nothing to install or maintain. You don't have to worry about patching operating systems, managing databases, or monitoring disk usage. Microsoft handles all of that behind the scenes, so your team can focus on what really matters—protecting your organization.

Fast to Deploy, Easy to Start

Getting started with Sentinel is refreshingly simple. Within hours, you can connect your data sources, start collecting logs, and begin running analytics. Microsoft provides prebuilt workbooks, queries, rules, and templates, so you're not starting from scratch. It's designed to help you start seeing value on day one.

Built for Automation

Lastly, Sentinel includes built-in support for automated response actions. You can create playbooks that run automatically when certain types of incidents occur. For example, if a user account shows signs of compromise, Sentinel can automatically disable the account, send an alert, and create a ticket in your ITSM system. This kind of automation not only saves time but also helps ensure that nothing slips through the cracks.

Comparison: Traditional SIEM vs. Azure Sentinel

Over the years, SIEM solutions have played a crucial role in helping security teams monitor and respond to threats. But the environments they were built to protect have changed. What once worked well in centralized, on-premises data centers now struggle to keep up with the demands of cloud services, remote workforces, and constantly shifting attack surfaces. Azure Sentinel was developed to meet these modern needs—replacing hardware-heavy deployments with a flexible, cloud-native platform that's smarter, faster, and easier to manage. Table 8-1 shows how Azure Sentinel compares to traditional SIEM systems across key dimensions.

Table 8-1. Comparison between traditional SIEM and Azure Sentinel

Category	Traditional SIEM	Azure Sentinel (Cloud-Native SIEM)
Deployment Model	On-premises or self-hosted virtual machines	Fully managed SaaS (built on Azure Monitor and Log Analytics)
Scalability	Manual scaling required (hardware upgrades, storage planning)	Autoscales based on ingestion and query load; no infrastructure to manage
Setup Time	Weeks to months; involves sizing, provisioning, and tuning	Hours to deploy; onboarding through built-in connectors and templates
Data Ingestion Sources	Often limited to network and endpoint logs; cloud support via plugins or agents	100+ built-in connectors including Azure, Microsoft 365, AWS, GCP, and more
Cost Model	High upfront CapEx; ongoing maintenance and license costs	Pay-as-you-go (based on data volume and retention); predictable and elastic
Threat Detection	Static rule-based correlation; high alert fatigue	AI-driven analytics, ML models, UEBA, and Fusion for correlated high-fidelity alerts

(continued)

Table 8-1. (*continued*)

Category	Traditional SIEM	Azure Sentinel (Cloud-Native SIEM)
Response Capabilities	Manual or third-party integrated response workflows	Native SOAR (Security Orchestration, Automation, and Response) via Logic Apps
Maintenance	Requires patching, upgrades, backups, and hardware lifecycle management	Zero infrastructure management; handled entirely by Microsoft
Visibility	Fragmented across different platforms; complex multi-cloud support	Unified visibility across cloud, hybrid, and on-prem with single-pane-of-glass
User Experience	Often outdated UI; difficult integration with other tools	Modern, intuitive Azure portal experience; seamless Microsoft ecosystem integration
Extensibility	Custom integrations require professional services or third-party tools	Open APIs, REST interfaces, custom connectors, Jupyter notebooks supported
Compliance and Regulations	Requires manual configuration for regulatory compliance reporting	Built-in templates and dashboards for SOC 2, ISO 27001, GDPR, etc.
Threat Intelligence	Optional or third-party feeds; often expensive	Integrated Microsoft Threat Intelligence and global security signals
Time to Value	Long ramp-up period; difficult to achieve ROI quickly	Rapid deployment and detection with out-of-the-box rules and content

Positioning Sentinel Within Microsoft Security Ecosystem

Azure Sentinel is not a standalone tool—it is a central component of Microsoft's broader security ecosystem. Microsoft has built a layered, interconnected set of security solutions that cover everything from identity protection to endpoint defense, email filtering, data governance, and cloud workload security. Sentinel sits at the heart of this architecture as the **central hub for security analytics, threat correlation, and response orchestration**.

CHAPTER 8   AZURE SENTINEL: NEXT-GENERATION SIEM

The Nerve Center for Microsoft Security Signals

Microsoft's ecosystem generates a vast amount of security telemetry. Every day, Microsoft processes over **65 trillion threat signals**, collected from services like

- **Microsoft 365** (Exchange, Teams, SharePoint)
- **Microsoft Defender for Endpoint**
- **Microsoft Defender for Identity**
- **Microsoft Defender for Cloud Apps**
- **Microsoft Entra ID** (formerly Azure Active Directory)
- **Microsoft Defender for Cloud**

Azure Sentinel acts as the **aggregator and analyzer** of these signals. It not only collects and visualizes them in a unified interface but also applies correlation logic and threat detection models to find patterns that may indicate an attack in progress.

Seamless Integration with Defender XDR

One of the strongest advantages of using Azure Sentinel is its **tight integration with Microsoft Defender XDR**. While Defender XDR is designed for **deep detection and response across Microsoft workloads**, Sentinel provides the **cross-platform, cloud-scale SIEM and SOAR capabilities** to bring those insights into a broader security strategy.

- Defender XDR can feed rich telemetry into Sentinel for further correlation.
- Incidents identified by Defender can be investigated, enriched, and responded to through Sentinel's automation and investigation tools.
- Sentinel enhances the data with third-party sources and contextual signals from beyond the Microsoft stack.

This creates a **complementary relationship** where Defender handles deep telemetry and real-time protection, while Sentinel enables **strategic visibility and coordinated response** across the enterprise.

A Platform, Not Just a Product

Sentinel is also part of the **Microsoft Intelligent Security Association (MISA)**, which brings together over 300 partner solutions that extend Sentinel's capabilities. Through open APIs, custom connectors, and Logic Apps integration, Sentinel becomes a **security platform** that adapts to the unique needs of every organization.

Microsoft also regularly publishes **solution content** for specific industries (e.g., financial services, healthcare) and threat categories (e.g., ransomware, insider threats), helping SOCs deploy effective detection frameworks faster.

SOC (Security Operations Center)   A SOC is a dedicated team, often within an enterprise or service provider, responsible for continuously monitoring, detecting, analyzing, and responding to cybersecurity incidents. SOC analysts use tools like Azure Sentinel to gain visibility across systems, investigate alerts, and coordinate automated or manual responses to threats in real time.

Key Features and Benefits of Azure Sentinel

Azure Sentinel is more than just a SIEM—it's a comprehensive security operations platform built to handle the scale, complexity, and speed of modern threats. In this section, I tried to discuss the deep technical dive into the key features and benefits that set Sentinel apart, with real-world relevance to how they are used in practice.

Scalability and Cloud-Native Architecture

Azure Sentinel is architected as a fully cloud-native solution built on top of **Azure Monitor** and **Log Analytics**, which means it leverages the scalability, reliability, and global distribution of Microsoft Azure. Unlike traditional SIEMs that require careful resource planning, manual scaling, and hardware procurement, Sentinel automatically adjusts to the volume and velocity of data it receives.

Architectural Insights

- **Data Ingestion Scalability**

  Sentinel can handle log ingestion at petabyte scale. Data is collected into a **Log Analytics Workspace**, which can ingest millions of records per minute without user-side tuning. This workspace serves as the foundation for query execution, incident correlation, and retention.

- **Automatic Scaling**

  The underlying Azure services (like Azure Monitor) elastically scale compute, ingestion throughput, and storage based on usage. For instance, if you onboard 20 new data connectors or if a spike in telemetry occurs during a live attack, the Sentinel will scale ingestion and compute capacity behind the scenes.

- **Global Redundancy**

  Log Analytics Workspaces can be provisioned in any Azure region. Sentinel uses Azure's **geo-redundant architecture** for high availability and disaster recovery. Additionally, **multi-region deployments** support geographically distributed compliance and sovereignty requirements.

- **No Infrastructure Footprint**

  Unlike legacy SIEMs that require provisioning of storage, log shippers, indexers, and collectors, Azure Sentinel requires no local agent infrastructure when using native connectors. Management overhead is drastically reduced.

- **Retention and Archiving**

  Sentinel supports flexible data retention policies—from 30 days (free) up to 730 days (chargeable)—and **cold storage archiving** via Azure Data Explorer or Azure Blob Storage for long-term compliance storage.

CHAPTER 8 AZURE SENTINEL: NEXT-GENERATION SIEM

Native Integration with Microsoft 365, Defender, and Other Services

One of the standout capabilities of Azure Sentinel is its **seamless integration across Microsoft's security, identity, and productivity ecosystem**. Because Microsoft owns the underlying cloud infrastructure, productivity suite, identity platform, and security tooling, Sentinel is uniquely positioned to ingest and correlate telemetry with **minimal configuration and no third-party overhead**.

Architectural Insights

- **Built-In Data Connectors**

    Azure Sentinel includes over **100 built-in connectors**, with out-of-the-box support for Microsoft-native services such as

    - Microsoft 365 Defender
    - **Microsoft Entra ID** (formerly Azure Active Directory)
    - Microsoft Defender for Cloud Apps
    - Microsoft Defender for Endpoint
    - Microsoft Defender for Identity
    - Microsoft Intune
    - Microsoft Purview Compliance Suite

- **Connector Configuration**

    These connectors are **natively integrated into the Azure Sentinel UI**. Configuring them requires just a few clicks—authentication is handled via Azure RBAC and consent-based permissions. No agent installation or custom parsing is necessary.

- **Security Signal Enrichment**

    Ingested data includes enriched telemetry like

    - Sign-in risk levels (from Entra ID's risk-based conditional access)
    - Endpoint detection data (from Defender for Endpoint)

- Shadow IT discovery (from Defender for Cloud Apps)

- Email compromise patterns (from Microsoft Defender for Office 365)

- Compliance alerts (from Purview DLP and Insider Risk)

- **Cross-Solution Incident Correlation**: Sentinel can correlate multiple security events across services into a **single incident**. For example:

  - A suspicious login to Microsoft 365

  - Followed by privilege escalation in Microsoft Entra ID

  - And suspicious downloads via OneDrive

These events can be automatically **fused** into one high-confidence incident using **Fusion analytics rules**, reducing alert fatigue and focusing analyst attention where it matters most.

- **Entra ID Integration**

  Sentinel can query Entra ID logs for sign-in anomalies, conditional access policy outcomes, token misuse, legacy authentication attempts, and risky user detections—making it possible to detect identity-based attacks such as **MFA fatigue**, **pass-the-cookie**, and **token replay**.

- **Microsoft Defender XDR Pipeline**

  Sentinel complements Microsoft Defender XDR by pulling XDR incidents into Sentinel's SIEM layer. Sentinel provides long-term log retention, advanced query capabilities (KQL), and the ability to **enrich Defender alerts with third-party data** (e.g., firewall logs or threat intel feeds).

Machine Learning and AI for Threat Detection

Azure Sentinel integrates **machine learning (ML), artificial intelligence (AI), and behavioral analytics** directly into its detection and correlation engine. These capabilities allow Sentinel to move beyond traditional rule-based alerts and surface threats that would otherwise go undetected in high-noise environments.

CHAPTER 8   AZURE SENTINEL: NEXT-GENERATION SIEM

Architectural Insights

- **Fusion Correlation Engine**

    Fusion is Sentinel's built-in AI model that correlates related alerts across data sources like Entra ID, Microsoft Defender, and Cloud Apps. It detects multi-stage attacks—such as a risky sign-in followed by lateral movement—and aggregates these into a **single high-confidence incident**, reducing alert noise and triage time.

    Unlike standard analytics rules that depend on predefined logic and thresholds, Fusion uses machine learning to dynamically correlate signals that may seem benign in isolation but indicate a threat when viewed collectively. This approach enables earlier detection of complex attack patterns with minimal manual rule tuning, enhancing both detection accuracy and operational efficiency.

- **UEBA (User and Entity Behavior Analytics)**

    Sentinel continuously builds behavioral baselines for users and devices. It flags anomalies such as

    - Impossible travel
    - Sudden privilege elevation
    - Atypical data access or sign-in patterns

    UEBA operates in the background, requiring no manual configuration or tuning.

- **Anomaly-Based Analytics Rules**

    Sentinel includes ML-powered analytics rules to detect statistically rare activities, such as unusual PowerShell usage or unexpected network destinations. These use **unsupervised models**, ideal for discovering new or evolving threats.

- **Custom ML with Jupyter Notebooks**

    Analysts can create and run custom ML models using integrated Jupyter notebooks. These support Python and allow access to Sentinel logs via API. Use cases include clustering rare IPs, detecting beaconing patterns, and classifying phishing indicators.

For example, a notebook can apply K-Means clustering to group login attempts based on geolocation and time of access, revealing suspicious behavior patterns. The classification model can highlight anomalies, such as logins from uncommon countries during non-business hours, helping prioritize investigations.

- **Global Intelligence Integration**

  Sentinel leverages Microsoft's global threat intelligence—derived from over **65 trillion daily signals**—to continuously improve detection models and match behaviors with known attack techniques and actor patterns.

Integration with MITRE ATT&CK Framework

Azure Sentinel integrates natively with the **MITRE ATT&CK framework**, allowing security teams to align their threat detection and investigation strategies with a globally recognized knowledge base of adversary tactics and techniques. This mapping improves both **threat coverage visibility** and **analyst response workflows**.

Architectural Insights

- **Built-In Mapping for Analytics Rules**

  Sentinel analytics rules are mapped to specific **ATT&CK techniques and sub-techniques**. For example, an alert for PowerShell abuse may be linked to `T1059.001 - PowerShell`, while suspicious cloud credential access may align with `T1078 - Valid Accounts`. This tagging helps analysts understand the attack stage and method being used.

- **Workbooks for Coverage Visualization**

  Microsoft provides a **MITRE ATT&CK Workbook** that visualizes current rule coverage across ATT&CK tactics like

  - Initial Access
  - Persistence
  - Privilege Escalation

- Lateral Movement
- Exfiltration

SOC (Security Operations Center) teams can use this to identify gaps in detection and prioritize new rule development.

- **Hunting Queries and Playbooks Aligned to ATT&CK**

  Sentinel's threat hunting library includes prebuilt KQL queries organized by ATT&CK techniques. For instance, a hunting query under `T1021.002 - SMB/Windows Admin Shares` might identify lateral movement via admin shares.

- **Integration with Microsoft Threat Intelligence**

  Sentinel enriches alerts and incidents with MITRE-based threat actor references when relevant. For example, a series of actions resembling techniques used by **APT29** may be tagged accordingly in the incident record.

Benefit to the SOC

Aligning with MITRE ATT&CK enables structured investigation workflows, standardized reporting, and improved red team/blue team exercises—especially in enterprises following **NIST**, **ISO 27001**, or **MITRE D3FEND** frameworks.

Custom Workbooks and Dashboards

Azure Sentinel includes a robust visualization layer built on **Azure Monitor Workbooks**, allowing SOC analysts and engineers to create interactive dashboards for real-time monitoring, threat tracking, and operational reporting. These workbooks are fully customizable and enable a wide range of use cases, from executive summaries to deep-dive threat analysis.

Architectural Insights

- **Workbook Architecture**

    Workbooks are composed of **query-driven visualizations** powered by **Kusto Query Language (KQL)**. Each component (chart, table, metric, or markdown block) is tied to a specific Log Analytics query and can be configured using dynamic parameters, filters, and time ranges.

- **Prebuilt Templates**

    Azure Sentinel offers dozens of **prebuilt workbooks** for common services and scenarios, including

    - Microsoft 365 Defender Overview
    - Microsoft Entra ID Sign-In Analysis
    - AWS CloudTrail Log Insights
    - Microsoft Defender for Endpoint Risk Summary
    - Threat Intelligence Report View

    These templates serve as starting points and can be cloned, modified, or extended.

- **Custom Visualization Capabilities**

    Workbooks support

    - Line, bar, pie, donut, and area charts
    - Time-series and heatmap visualizations
    - Geolocation mapping (e.g., sign-in locations)
    - Markdown for narrative context or analyst notes
    - Conditional formatting for threshold-based visual alerts

- **Drill-Through and Interactivity**

    Analysts can build **drill-through experiences** by linking workbook elements to other Sentinel views, such as incidents, hunting queries, or entity profiles. This enables rapid pivoting from a high-level chart to the raw data driving it.

- **Role-Based Access Control (RBAC)**

  Workbooks honor Azure RBAC, allowing different teams to see dashboards relevant to their responsibilities—for example, a network security team may have access to firewall telemetry workbooks, while an identity team views Entra ID sign-in anomalies.

- **Refresh and Sharing**

  Workbooks are refreshed automatically and can be shared across teams, exported to PDF, or embedded in other Azure dashboards. They can also be included in incident response runbooks for reporting purposes.

Example Use Case

A SOC manager creates a workbook showing

- Failed sign-in attempts by country
- Active incidents by MITRE technique
- Top ten alert-generating hosts in the past 24 hours
- Summary of high-risk users with UEBA flags

This workbook becomes a **real-time SOC dashboard**, updated every few minutes and used during daily stand-ups and executive reviews.

Deploying and Configuring Azure Sentinel

Deploying Azure Sentinel is a straightforward yet strategic process. While enabling the service itself takes only a few clicks, its effectiveness depends on thoughtful configuration—selecting the right workspace, connecting relevant data sources, setting access controls, and tuning ingestion settings for performance and cost optimization. This section walks through the practical steps required to deploy Sentinel in a secure, scalable, and production-ready manner, ensuring your environment is prepared to monitor, detect, and respond from day one.

CHAPTER 8   AZURE SENTINEL: NEXT-GENERATION SIEM

Prerequisites and Initial Planning

Before deploying Azure Sentinel, it's essential to lay a solid foundation. Although Sentinel itself is easy to enable, its architecture is tightly coupled with Azure Monitor Logs, Log Analytics Workspaces, and role-based access controls. Misconfigurations in these early steps can lead to security gaps, performance bottlenecks, or unmanageable costs.

Below are the key prerequisites and planning considerations:

1. **Azure Subscription**

   You must have an active **Azure subscription** where Sentinel resources will reside. Users deploying Sentinel must have sufficient privileges—typically Owner or Contributor at the subscription or resource group level.

2. **Log Analytics Workspace (LAW)**

   Azure Sentinel runs on top of a Log Analytics Workspace. This workspace acts as the central data store for all logs ingested into Sentinel and supports

   - Kusto Query Language (KQL) for queries and detections
   - Data retention and access controls
   - Dashboards, workbooks, and notebooks
   - Analytics rule correlation and case management

   Each Sentinel instance is tied to a single workspace. For multi-region or multi-department environments, consider deploying **multiple workspaces** and managing them via **Azure Lighthouse** or **cross-workspace queries**.

3. **Workspace Region Selection**

   Choosing the correct region for your Log Analytics Workspace is critical. Ideally, this should

   - Be geographically close to your primary data sources
   - Aligning with compliance or data residency requirements
   - Match the region of Microsoft 365 logs if integrating Entra ID or M365 Defender

> **Note** Log Analytics ingestion and query performance is sensitive to region mismatch. It's recommended to avoid cross-region data collection unless explicitly required.

4. **Role-Based Access Control (RBAC)**

    Azure Sentinel relies on Azure RBAC to manage access to workspaces and Sentinel components. Recommended roles include

    - **Azure Sentinel Contributor**: Create and manage analytics rules, incidents, hunting queries, and workbooks
    - **Log Analytics Reader**: Query data, view dashboards, and run KQL queries
    - **Reader**: View-only access to Sentinel blades, without query or configuration rights
    - **Security Reader (Microsoft Defender Integration)**: Required for reading Defender data and incidents

> **Note** Always follow the principle of least privilege and use Microsoft Entra ID Privileged Identity Management (PIM) to enforce just-in-time access for administrative roles.

5. **Data Retention Strategy**

    Sentinel provides the first **31 days of data retention for free**. Additional retention is billed per GB per month. You can configure

    - Default retention (31–730 days)
    - Custom retention by table
    - Archival export to Azure Storage or Azure Data Explorer

    Plan retention policies early, especially for organizations with **compliance mandates (e.g., GDPR, HIPAA, SOX)** or long forensic investigation cycles.

CHAPTER 8   AZURE SENTINEL: NEXT-GENERATION SIEM

Step by Step: Onboarding Azure Sentinel

Once the prerequisites are in place—namely, a Log Analytics Workspace and appropriate permissions—enabling Azure Sentinel is a direct and guided process via the Azure Portal. This section shows the exact steps required to onboard Sentinel and prepare it for data collection and operational use.

1. In the Azure portal, use the global search bar or browse through the Microsoft Sentinel in the "All Services" blade. Click to open the Sentinel dashboard as shown in Figure 8-1.

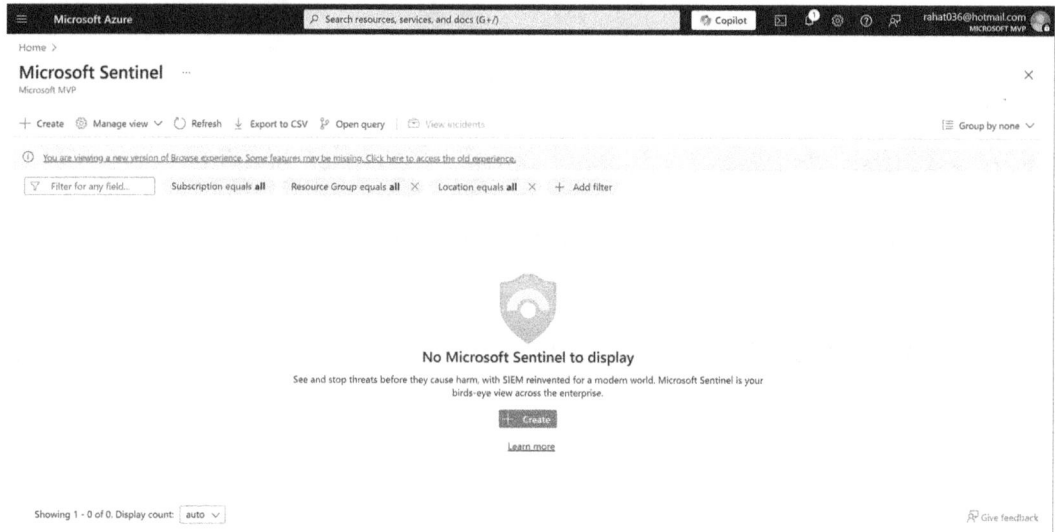

Figure 8-1. *Microsoft Sentinel dashboard*

2. You will be prompted to select an existing Log Analytics Workspace, or you can create a new one. To create a new workspace, click Create and you will be redirected to a new page as shown in Figure 8-2.

357

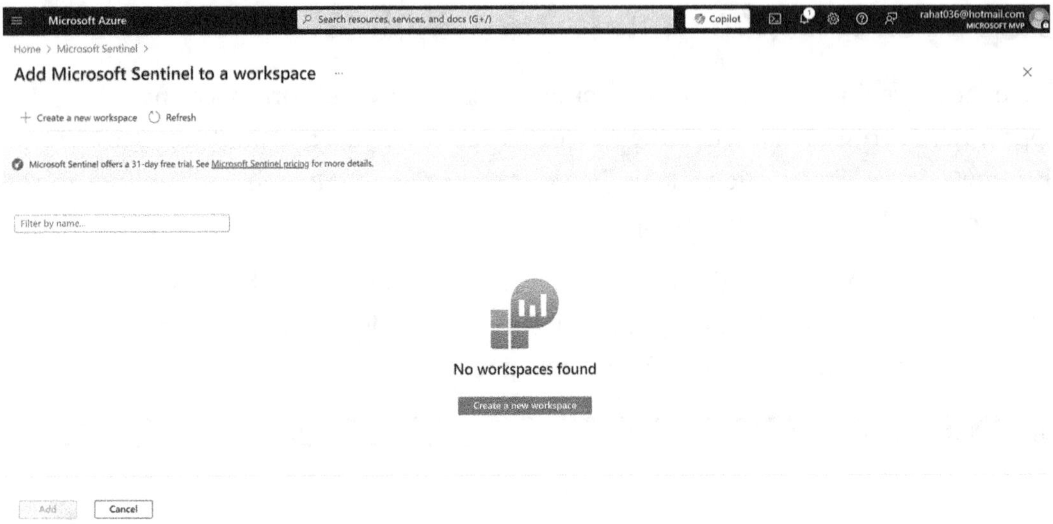
Microsoft Azure
Search resources, services, and docs (G+/)
Copilot
rahat036@hotmail.com
MICROSOFT MVP
Home > Microsoft Sentinel >
Add Microsoft Sentinel to a workspace
Create a new workspace
Refresh
Microsoft Sentinel offers a 31-day free trial. See Microsoft Sentinel pricing for more details.
Filter by name...
No workspaces found
Create a new workspace
Add
Cancel

Figure 8-2. *Creation page of a new workspace in Microsoft Sentinel*

3. Click Create a new workspace, and it will open a new window as shown in Figure 8-3.

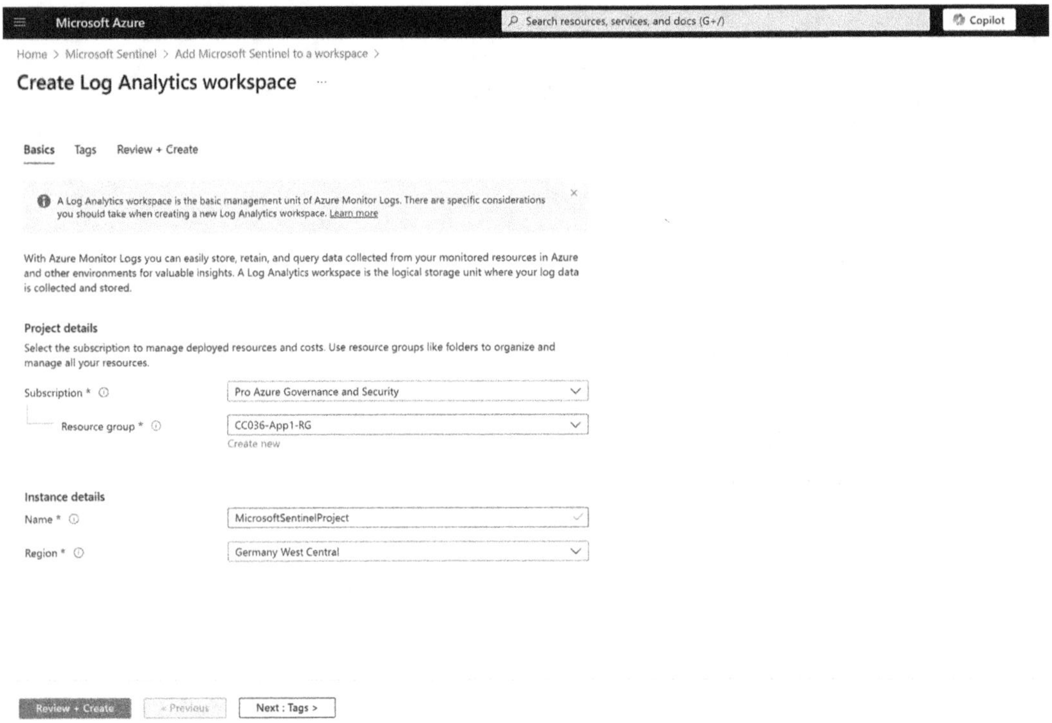
Microsoft Azure
Search resources, services, and docs (G+/)
Copilot
Home > Microsoft Sentinel > Add Microsoft Sentinel to a workspace >
Create Log Analytics workspace
Basics
Tags
Review + Create
A Log Analytics workspace is the basic management unit of Azure Monitor Logs. There are specific considerations you should take when creating a new Log Analytics workspace. Learn more
With Azure Monitor Logs you can easily store, retain, and query data collected from your monitored resources in Azure and other environments for valuable insights. A Log Analytics workspace is the logical storage unit where your log data is collected and stored.
Project details
Select the subscription to manage deployed resources and costs. Use resource groups like folders to organize and manage all your resources.
Subscription *
Pro Azure Governance and Security
Resource group *
CC036-App1-RG
Create new
Instance details
Name *
MicrosoftSentinelProject
Region *
Germany West Central
Review + Create
< Previous
Next : Tags >

Figure 8-3. *Creating a new Log Analytics workspace*

4. Fill out the necessary information. Please note that you must choose the same region as your primary data sources. Then click Review + Create. It will create the Log Analytics Workspace as shown in Figure 8-4.

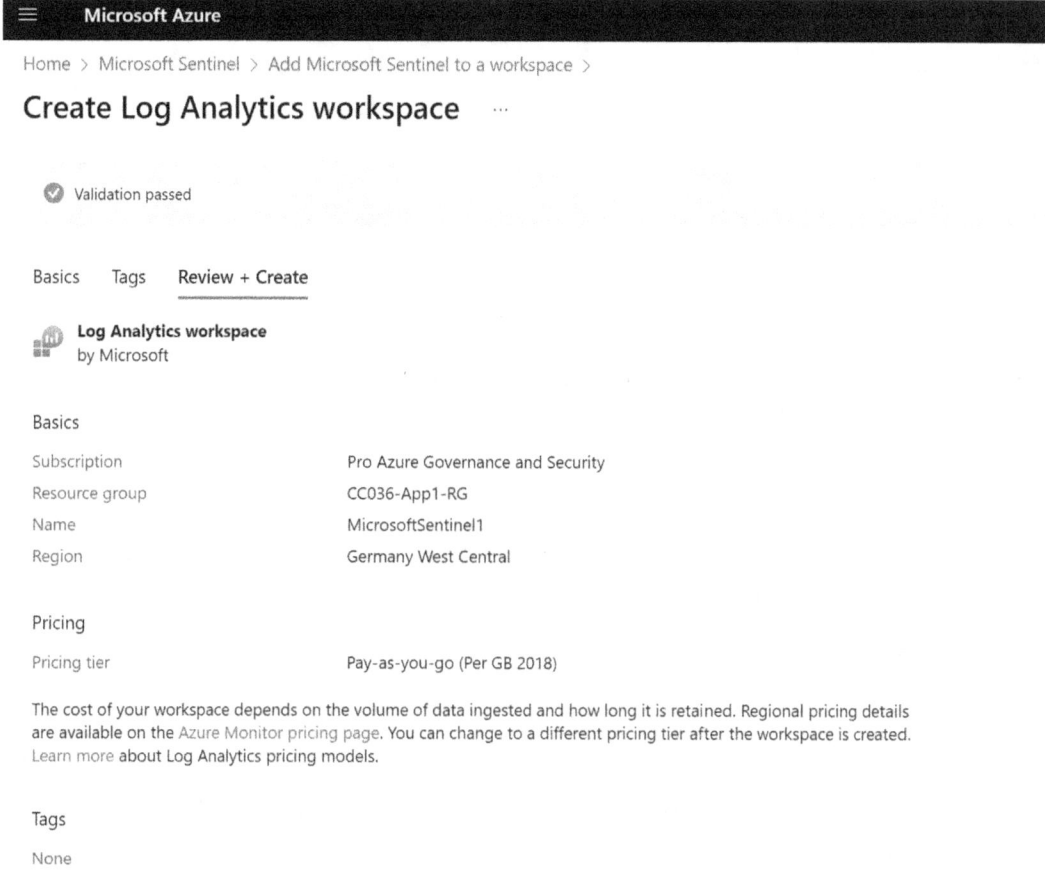

Figure 8-4. Validating the new workspace

Note Create separate workspaces for production, staging, and testing to avoid noisy data overlapping and to support RBAC isolation.

---

5. Once the workspace is selected, click *"Add"* to attach Microsoft Sentinel to the workspace as shown in Figure 8-5.

CHAPTER 8 AZURE SENTINEL: NEXT-GENERATION SIEM

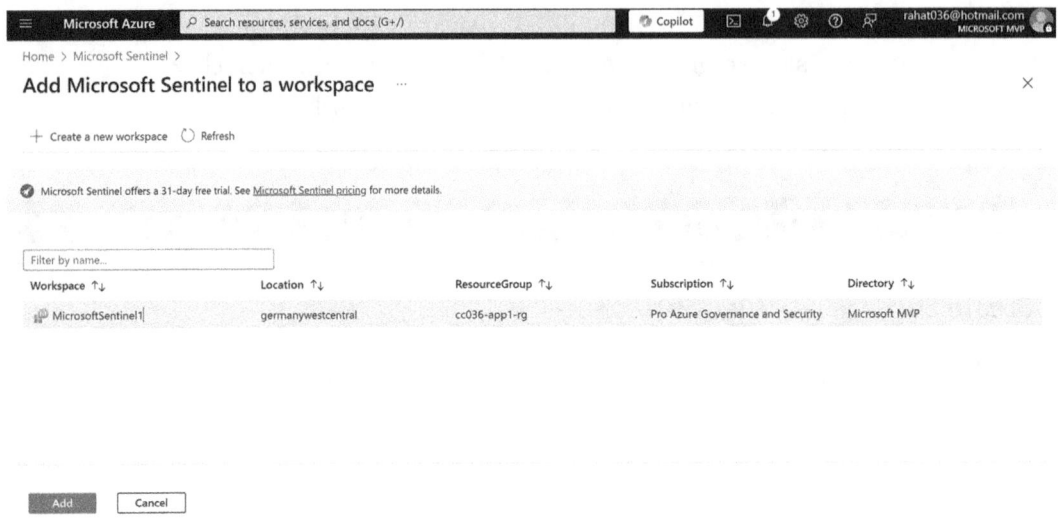

Figure 8-5. *Verifying the newly created workspace is showing in the Microsoft Sentinel*

Note Behind the scenes, this activation registers the Sentinel solution on the workspace and allows for additional security content to be deployed via Content hubs.

---

6. After enabling Sentinel, it's recommended to

   a. Assign users to appropriate Sentinel roles (**Contributor**, **Reader**, **Playbook Operator**, etc.)

   b. Configure basic workspace settings, including **retention policies** and **data access permissions**

   c. Create a **resource group** structure that logically separates Sentinel resources from production workloads

7. Navigate the **Sentinel Overview** blade. A correctly configured deployment should show

   a. Sentinel is enabled for the selected workspace.

   b. The "Connect data sources" option is visible.

CHAPTER 8   AZURE SENTINEL: NEXT-GENERATION SIEM

c. Usage metrics (once logs start flowing) and incident counts are displayed.

Figure 8-6 shows the Sentinel Overview.

Figure 8-6. *Overview of Microsoft Sentinel*

At this point, Azure Sentinel is onboarded and operational. However, no data will appear until data connectors are configured, which is covered in the next section.

Connecting Data Sources

After onboarding Azure Sentinel, the next critical step is to connect your data sources. Sentinel's detection and analytics capabilities rely entirely on the quality and breadth of the data ingested into its underlying **Log Analytics Workspace**. Microsoft Sentinel offers an extensive library of **built-in data connectors** designed to simplify integration across Microsoft, Azure, and third-party platforms.

Data Connector Overview

Azure Sentinel provides over **100 built-in data connectors**, grouped into the following categories:

Microsoft Cloud Services

- Microsoft 365 Defender (including Defender for Endpoint, Identity, and Cloud Apps)
- Microsoft Entra ID (formerly Azure Active Directory)
- Microsoft Defender for Office 365
- Microsoft Intune
- Azure Resource and Activity Logs

Azure Infrastructure

- Azure Firewall
- Azure Key Vault
- Azure DDoS Protection
- NSG Flow Logs (via Network Watcher)

Third-Party Platforms

- AWS CloudTrail
- Google Cloud Platform (GCP)
- Cisco ASA, Palo Alto, Fortinet, and Check Point Firewalls
- Okta, Duo, Zscaler, Symantec, and more

Syslog and CEF Sources

Sentinel supports ingesting logs using **Syslog**, **Common Event Format (CEF)**, or **custom log formats** via

- Log Analytics Agent (legacy)
- Azure Monitor Agent (AMA—recommended)

Connecting Microsoft Data Sources

For Microsoft-native services, integration is typically OAuth based and agentless.

CHAPTER 8   AZURE SENTINEL: NEXT-GENERATION SIEM

Example: Entra ID (Azure AD) Sign-In Logs

1. In the Sentinel portal, go to **Data connectors** under **Configuration** and click **Get these data connectors**, as shown in Figure 8-7.

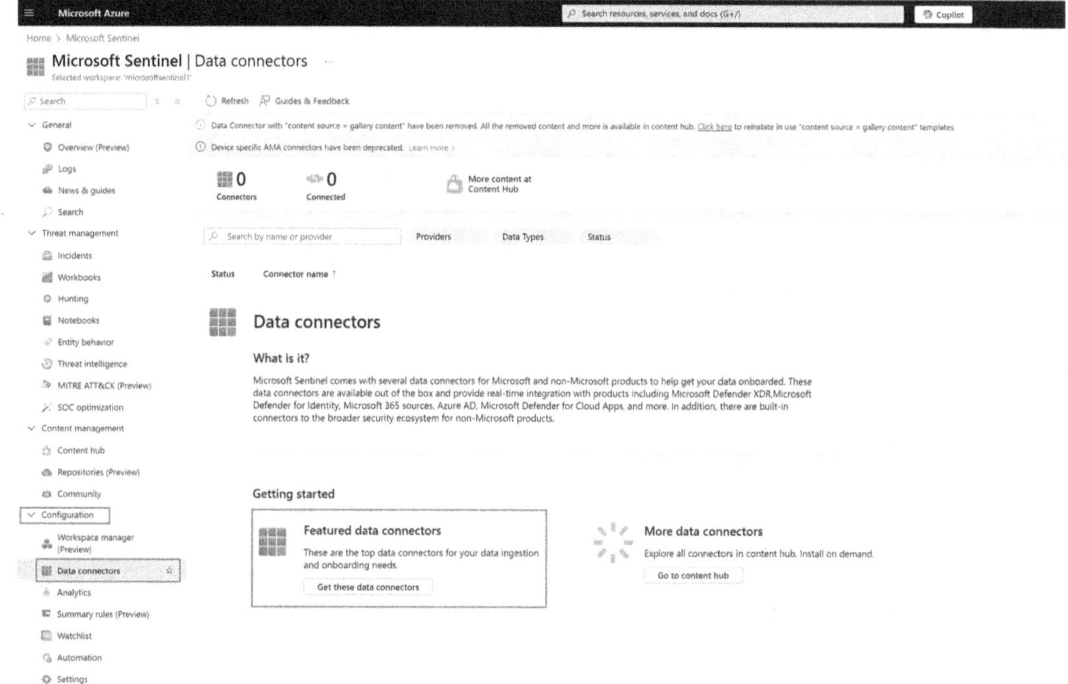

Figure 8-7. *Data connector page of Microsoft Sentinel*

2. Find or search Microsoft Entra ID and install it as shown in Figure 8-8.

363

CHAPTER 8   AZURE SENTINEL: NEXT-GENERATION SIEM

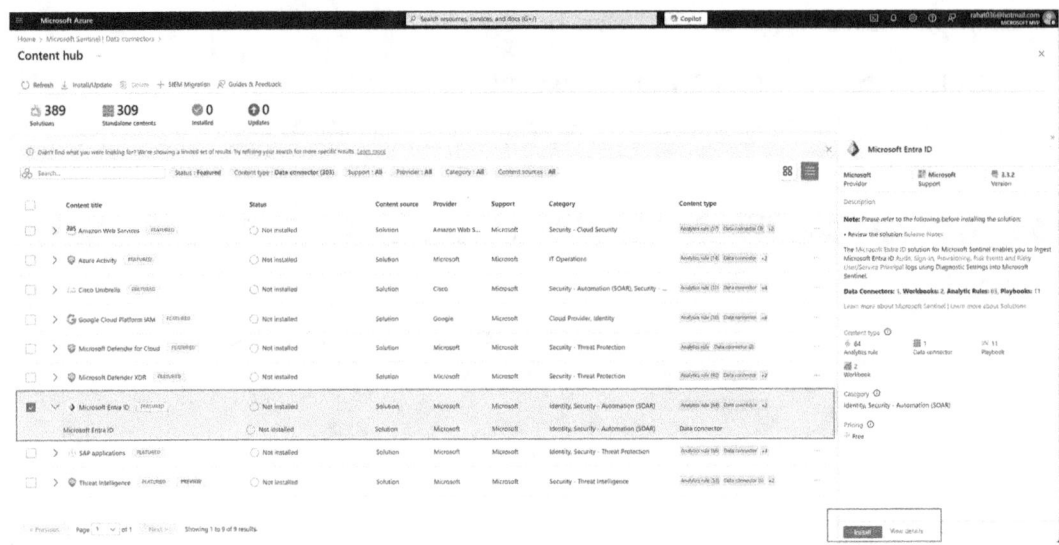

Figure 8-8. *Adding a connector from the Content hub*

3. After installing the connector, you can see the connector is available on the Data Connectors page. Select the connector and click Open connector page as shown in Figure 8-9.

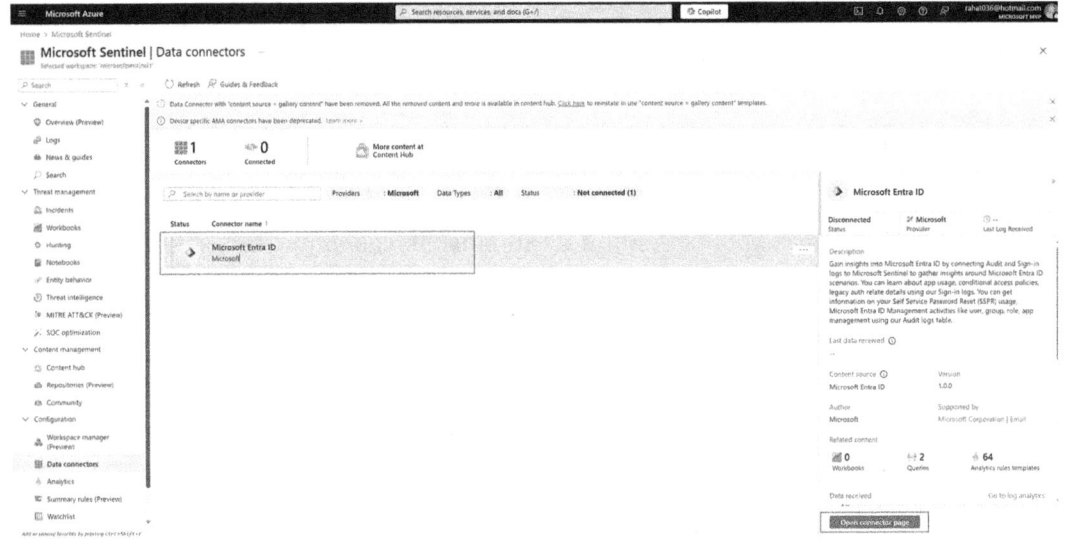

Figure 8-9. *Search Microsoft Entra ID and add it as a connector*

CHAPTER 8   AZURE SENTINEL: NEXT-GENERATION SIEM

4. From the connector page, enable the Sign-In Logs and Audit Logs and click Apply Changes as shown in Figure 8-10.

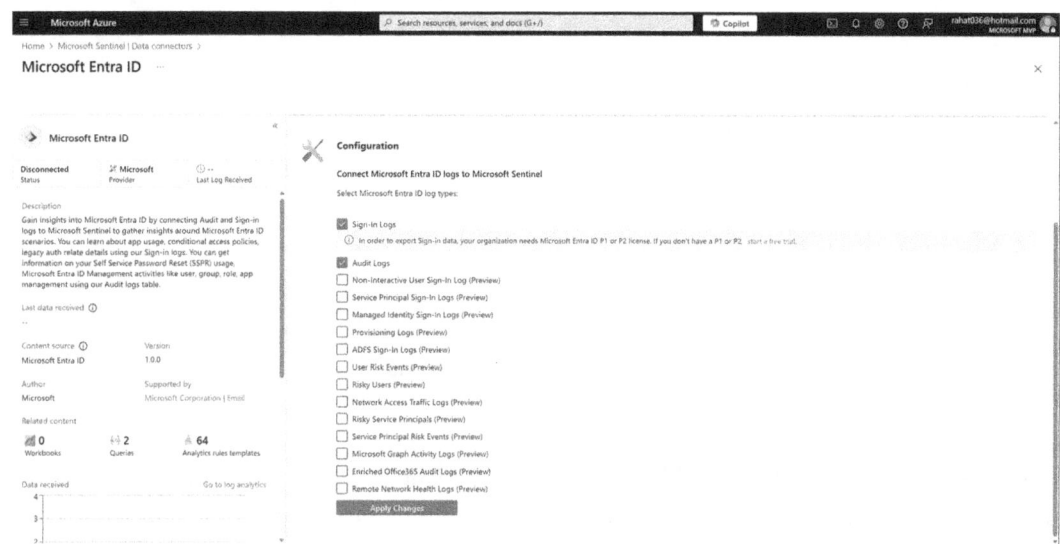

Figure 8-10. *Configuring the Microsoft Entra ID connector*

5. The data begins flowing into the Log Analytics Workspace within a few minutes and can be queried using built-in KQL samples.

To learn more about connecting data with Microsoft Sentinel, follow the official Microsoft documentation: https://learn.microsoft.com/en-us/azure/sentinel/configure-data-connector?tabs=defender-portal%2Cdefender-portal-1.

Cost Considerations

While Azure Sentinel is feature-rich and operationally flexible, it's also important to understand how it impacts your organization's budget. Sentinel follows a consumption-based pricing model, meaning you are billed based on the volume of data ingested into your Log Analytics Workspace and how long you retain it. Proper planning and ongoing optimization are essential to avoid unexpected cost spikes, especially in large-scale or data-heavy environments.

1. Data Ingestion Costs

Sentinel charges based on the **amount of data ingested per day**, measured in gigabytes (GB). There are two pricing options:

Pay-As-You-Go
Default model
Billed per GB of ingested data
Ideal for unpredictable or small-volume environments

Commitment Tiers
Pre-purchase a fixed amount of data ingestion per day (e.g., 100 GB, 500 GB, etc.)
Receive a discount on ingestion cost
Recommended for stable, high-volume environments

Example Ingesting 100 GB/day under a commitment tier is significantly cheaper per GB than under pay-as-you-go. If you exceed your tier temporarily, you're billed the overage at standard rates.

---

2. Data Retention and Archival

By default, Azure Sentinel includes **31 days of data retention at no cost**. After that period, retention is billed monthly per GB.

You have several options:

- **Extended Retention in Sentinel**
    - Configure the Log Analytics Workspace to retain logs for up to **730 days**
    - Useful for regulatory compliance, historical analysis, or long-term hunting
- **Archived Storage**
    - Export older data to **Azure Blob Storage** or **Azure Data Explorer**
    - Much lower cost than hot retention
    - Support cold-querying through solutions like Azure Data Explorer or Sentinel Data Archive Analytics

- **Table-Level Retention Policies**
  - Set different retention periods for specific log tables
  - For example, retain high-value tables (like **SecurityAlert**) for 180 days and low-value tables (like **Heartbeat**) for only 30 days

3. Additional Cost Factors

- **Automation (Logic Apps)**
  - Sentinel's SOAR playbooks run on **Azure Logic Apps**, which are billed per action and trigger.
  - Complex or high-frequency playbooks (e.g., integrations with ServiceNow or Slack) can incur moderate costs.
- **Notebook Execution**
  - Notebooks run on compute resources; costs depend on the underlying **Azure Machine Learning workspace**.
  - This is typically minimal unless performing large-scale or scheduled analysis.
- **Data Export and APIs**
  - Exporting logs to storage or streaming to other platforms may generate **egress costs** or **additional storage charges**.

4. Monitoring and Optimization

Azure Sentinel includes built-in tools to help monitor usage and optimize cost:

- **Usage and Estimated Costs Workbook**

    Visualize daily ingestion by table, workspace, or connector

    Identify top contributors to ingestion volume

- **Diagnostic Settings Review**

    Adjust the volume of logs collected from Azure resources by tweaking diagnostic settings (e.g., reduce verbose metrics)

- **Sampling and Filtering**

    Use **Data Collection Rules (DCRs)** with Azure Monitor Agent to filter out unwanted log noise at the source—saving ingestion volume

---

Note Set up alerting on ingestion thresholds and daily burn rate to stay ahead of your Sentinel billing.

Automating Incident Response with Playbooks

As security operations teams face an overwhelming volume of alerts, the ability to respond quickly and consistently becomes a critical requirement. Microsoft Sentinel addresses this challenge by enabling automation through **playbooks**, which are essentially workflows powered by **Azure Logic Apps**. These playbooks can automatically take actions such as sending notifications, isolating compromised users, or integrating with ticketing systems like ServiceNow or Jira. By automating repetitive and time-sensitive response actions, organizations can reduce response time, minimize human error, and improve their overall security posture. This section explores how playbooks work, how to design them effectively, and how they fit into a modern Security Orchestration, Automation, and Response (SOAR) strategy within Sentinel.

What Are Playbooks (Based on Logic Apps)?

In Microsoft Sentinel, a **playbook** is an automated workflow designed to respond to security incidents or alerts. These playbooks are built using **Azure Logic Apps**, a serverless automation service that enables you to create workflows by chaining together various triggers, conditions, and actions—without writing code.

Each playbook in Sentinel starts with a **trigger**, typically based on an event such as

- A new incident being created in Sentinel
- A specific alert or analytics rule firing
- A manual invocation by an analyst

Once triggered, the playbook can perform a wide range of **automated response actions**, such as

- Sending email or Teams notifications
- Blocking an IP address using Microsoft Defender for Endpoint
- Disabling a user account in Microsoft Entra ID
- Opening or updating a ticket in ServiceNow
- Posting to a Slack channel or triggering a webhook

Because playbooks are built on **Azure Logic Apps**, they benefit from deep integration with over **600 connectors**, including both Microsoft services and third-party platforms. These connectors make it possible to automate virtually any task—from containment to case enrichment to workflow documentation—across a wide security stack.

Common Use Cases: Email Alerts, Ticketing Integration, Containment

Azure Sentinel playbooks are designed to automate incident response tasks that would otherwise require manual, repetitive effort from security analysts. Below are three of the most common and practical use cases, each addressing a key aspect of modern SOC workflows: communication, process management, and threat containment.

1. Email Alerts and Notifications

Playbooks can be configured to automatically notify stakeholders or response teams when specific types of incidents occur. Using the **Office 365 Outlook** or **SendGrid** connector, you can craft emails that include

- Incident title, severity, and status
- Entities involved (e.g., IP address, username, host)
- Direct links to the incident in the Sentinel portal
- Suggested response steps or runbook references

> **Example** When a high-severity incident involving credential compromise is created, a playbook automatically sends an email to the SOC lead and escalates to the CISO if the user has privileged roles.

These alerts can also be routed to **Microsoft Teams**, **Slack**, or **SMS**, depending on organizational preferences and urgency levels.

2. Ticketing System Integration

Playbooks can automate the creation or updating of tickets in IT service management (ITSM) systems, ensuring that every actionable incident is logged and tracked. Using built-in connectors, you can integrate with

- **ServiceNow**
- **Jira**
- **Zendesk**
- **Freshservice**
- **BMC Remedy**

Playbooks typically

- Create new incidents with contextual data
- Update ticket status when Sentinel incidents change
- Add comments or analyst notes to tickets
- Tag tickets based on MITRE ATT&CK techniques or data classifications

> **Example** When a malware detection alert from Defender for Endpoint is ingested into Sentinel, a playbook creates a ServiceNow incident prefilled with user information, device name, and severity, reducing manual triage time.

This not only accelerates response but ensures **compliance and audit readiness** by maintaining a full case history.

3. Threat Containment and Remediation

Perhaps the most powerful application of playbooks is their ability to **take immediate containment actions** in response to a threat, minimizing dwell time and reducing attack impact. These actions often involve

- **Disabling user accounts in Entra ID**
- **Isolating compromised devices in Defender for Endpoint**
- **Blocking IPs in network firewalls or Azure NSGs**
- **Revoking tokens and sessions for cloud apps**
- **Forcing password resets via Graph API**

Example   When Sentinel detects a sign-in from an unfamiliar location followed by risky behavior, a playbook disables the account in Entra ID, isolates the device, revokes tokens, and notifies the user and SOC—all within seconds.

These containment playbooks are often paired with logic that checks for conditions before acting (e.g., account is not already disabled, device is still active), reducing the risk of false positives triggering disruptive actions.

Creating Playbooks from Templates

To accelerate deployment and reduce development effort, Microsoft Sentinel provides a wide array of **prebuilt playbook templates**. These templates are designed around common incident response scenarios and are built using **Azure Logic Apps**. Each template includes preconfigured actions and connectors, allowing you to quickly customize and deploy them without starting from scratch.

1. Accessing Templates via Content Hub

The **Content hub** in Microsoft Sentinel serves as a centralized catalog of official and community-contributed solutions. Playbooks are often bundled as part of these solutions and can be deployed in just a few clicks.

To deploy a playbook from a template

1. Navigate to **Microsoft Sentinel ➤ Content hub**.

2. Filter by **Solution type: Automation** or browse a full solution pack (e.g., "ServiceNow Integration" or "Email Notification Templates") as shown in Figure 8-11.

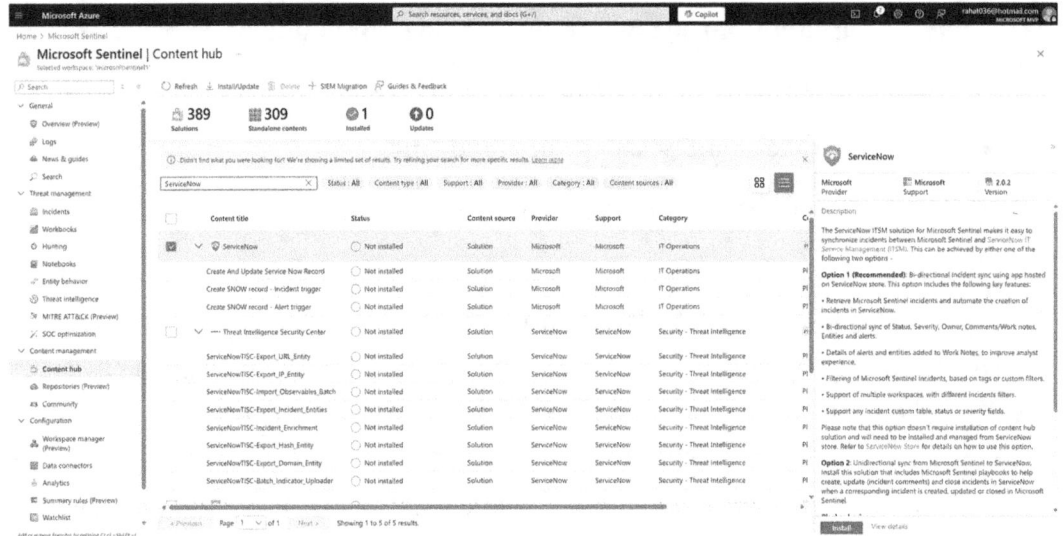

Figure 8-11. Searching ServiceNow from the Content hub

3. Select a solution and click **Install**.

4. Once installed, go to **Automation** under Configuration and select **Playbooks** to review or modify the logic app.

These templates follow best practices for error handling, API throttling, and secure credential management using **Azure Key Vault**.

2. Using Logic App Designer for Customization

After deploying a template, you can open it in the **Logic App Designer**, a visual editor that allows drag-and-drop modification of the workflow.

Common customizations include

- Changing the recipient list or email content for alert notifications
- Mapping Sentinel incident fields to ITSM ticket fields
- Adding conditional logic (e.g., "only run if severity = High")
- Inserting approval steps before executing remediation

Example A template that isolates a device in Defender for Endpoint can be enhanced with an approval step that requires a Tier 2 analyst to validate the alert before proceeding with containment.

3. Trigger Types and Automation Rules

Each playbook is triggered by a **Logic App trigger**, typically one of the following:

- **When a Sentinel alert is created**
- **When a Sentinel incident is created**
- **Manually triggered from an incident**
- **Triggered via automation rule with specific conditions**

You can configure **Automation Rules** in Sentinel to determine when and how a playbook runs:

- Automatically for all incidents
- Only for incidents with specific severity, tags, or entities
- Based on analytics rule names or alert sources

Note *Playbooks and automation rules are complementary. While playbooks define the workflow, automation rules control when they're executed.*

CHAPTER 8 AZURE SENTINEL: NEXT-GENERATION SIEM

Triggering Playbooks via Analytics Rules

While playbooks define the workflow for responding to incidents, **analytics rules** are responsible for detecting threats and triggering those responses. In Microsoft Sentinel, you can link playbooks directly to analytics rules so that when specific alerts fire, an automated response is launched in real time. This connection forms the backbone of **automated incident response** and is central to implementing a scalable SOAR strategy.

1. Linking Playbooks to Analytics Rules

When creating or editing an analytics rule in Sentinel, you can define one or more **automated responses**. These responses can be configured to run

- **Immediately upon alert creation**
- **After incident creation**
- **Conditionally, based on alert details (severity, entities, tactics)**

To attach a playbook to an analytics rule

1. Go to **Microsoft Sentinel ➤ Configuration ➤ Analytics**.
2. Click **+ Create** to build a new Schedule query rule, as shown in Figure 8-12, or edit the existing rule.

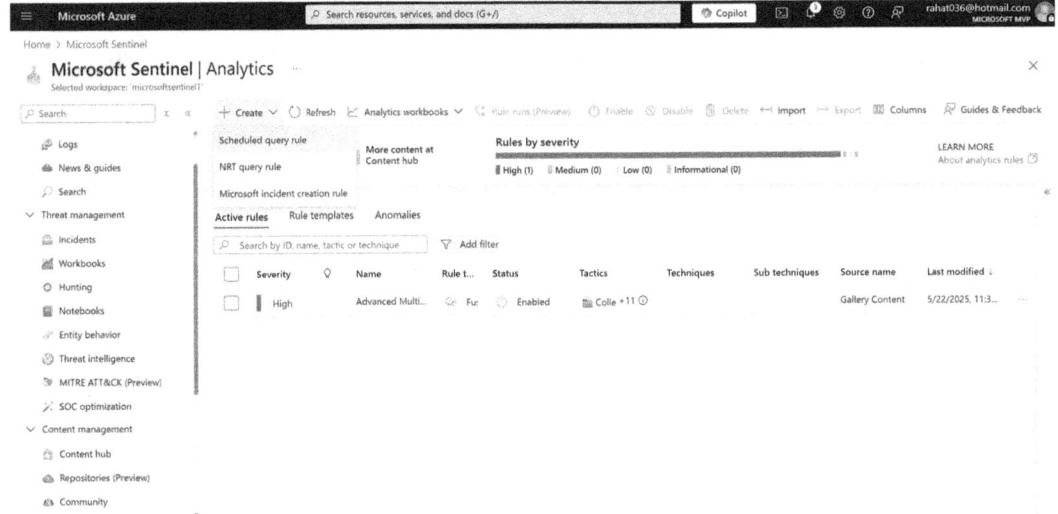

Figure 8-12. *Creating new schedule query rule*

3. Next, you will be redirected to a multi-tab wizard as shown in Figure 8-13.

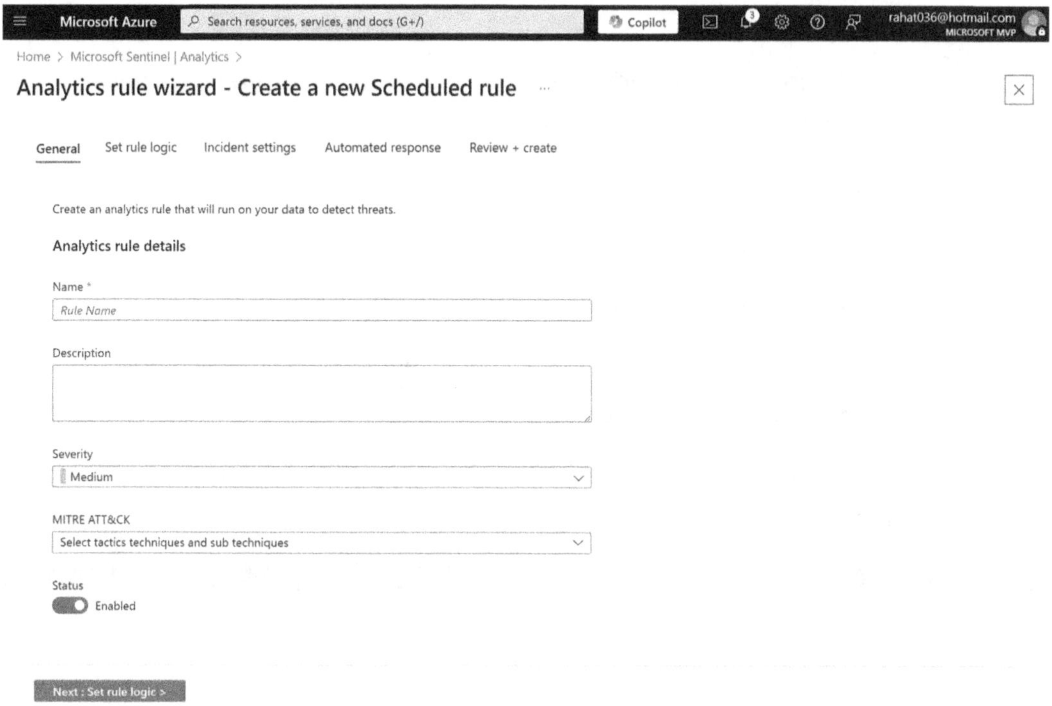

Figure 8-13. *Analytics rule wizard to create a new schedule rule*

Add the following information:

General

- Set a rule name (e.g., Detect Multiple Failed Logins)
- Optionally assign tags or MITRE ATT&CK tactics

Set Rule Logic

- Enter your **KQL query** (e.g., check failed logins from same IP)

```
SigninLogs
| where ResultType != 0 // Failed sign-ins only
| where TimeGenerated > ago(30m)
| summarize FailedAttempts = count() by IPAddress,
  UserPrincipalName
```

CHAPTER 8 AZURE SENTINEL: NEXT-GENERATION SIEM

```
| where FailedAttempts > 5
| extend timestamp = now(), AccountCustomEntity =
  UserPrincipalName, IPCustomEntity = IPAddress
```

- Configure **query schedule** (e.g., every 5 mins) and **lookup period** (e.g., past 30 mins)

- Define thresholds for alert generation

Incident Settings

- Decide how alerts are grouped into incidents

- Choose grouping options (e.g., by user, IP address, or rule name)

4. On the **Automated response** tab

    - Click + Add new to create new automation rules as shown in Figure 8-14.

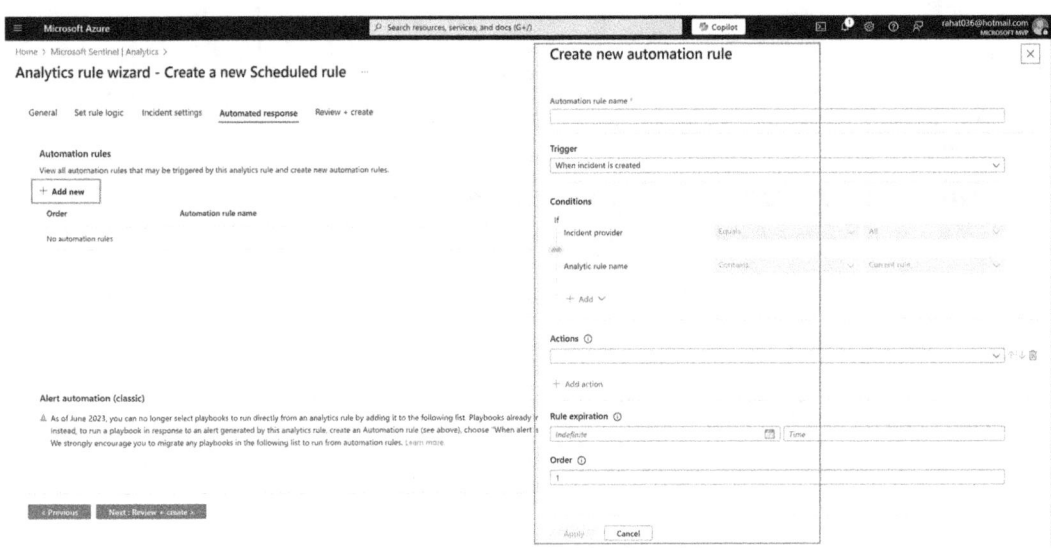

Figure 8-14. *Creating a new automation rule*

- A new slide will open to create the automation rule. Provide the following information:

    1. Name: Add your automation name

    2. Under Trigger, select one of the following:

376

a. When an incident is created (recommended for incident-level response)

b. When alert is created (recommended for individual alert, use carefully to avoid duplication)—**I am selecting this one for our demo. I'll explain some important announcements from Microsoft at the end of this demo.**

3. Under conditions, optionally add filters:

   a. Filter by name, severity, product name, entity type, etc.

   b. For example, "Only run when severity = High and Alert Name contains "Failed Login"

4. Under Actions, click + Add action.

   a. Select Run Playbook.

   b. Choose the playbook name from the drop-down.

   c. If needed, click Authorize to allow Sentinel to use the playbook.

5. Figure 8-15 shows the actual slide.

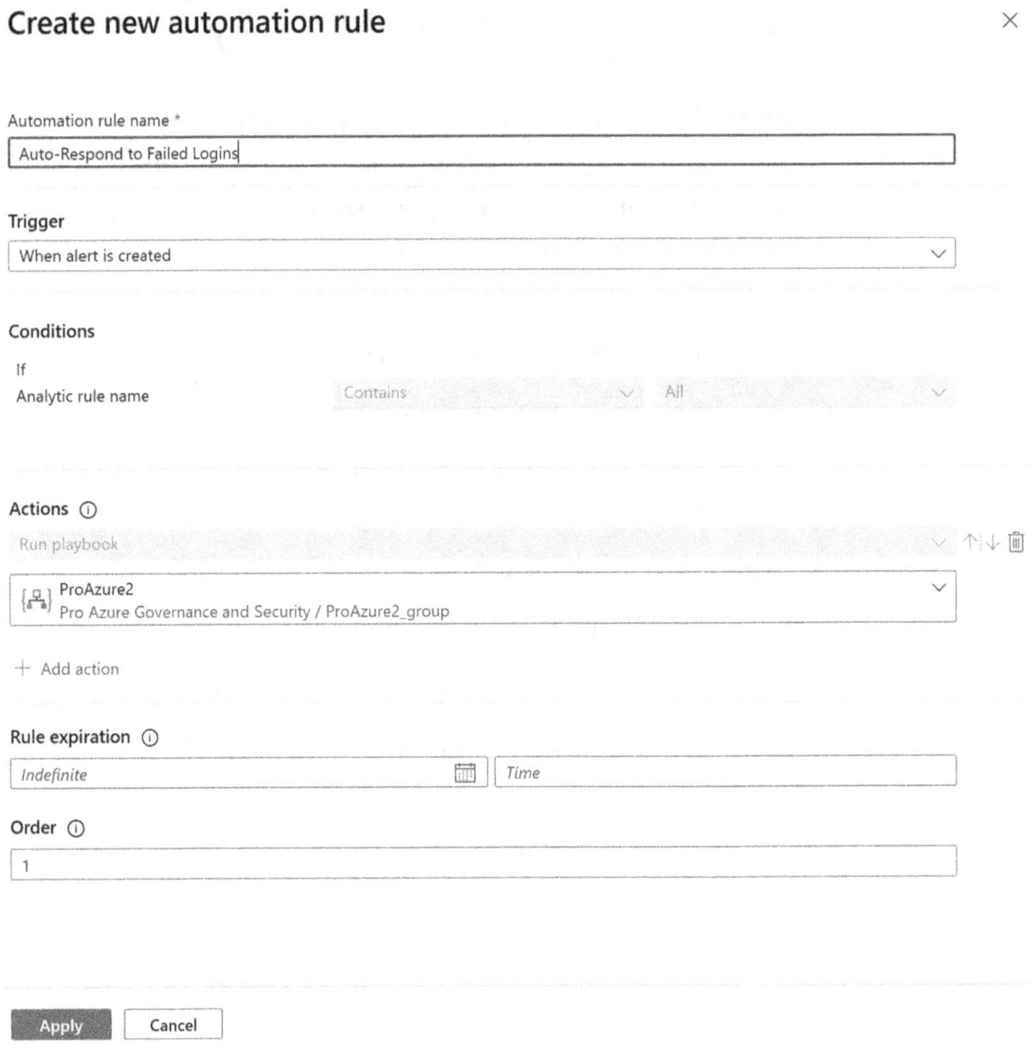

CHAPTER 8   AZURE SENTINEL: NEXT-GENERATION SIEM

Figure 8-15. Adding the required information to create a new automation rule

- Click Apply to save the automation rule.

5. Click Review + Create. It will start validating the automation rule. After passing the rule, click Save as shown in Figure 8-16.

CHAPTER 8   AZURE SENTINEL: NEXT-GENERATION SIEM

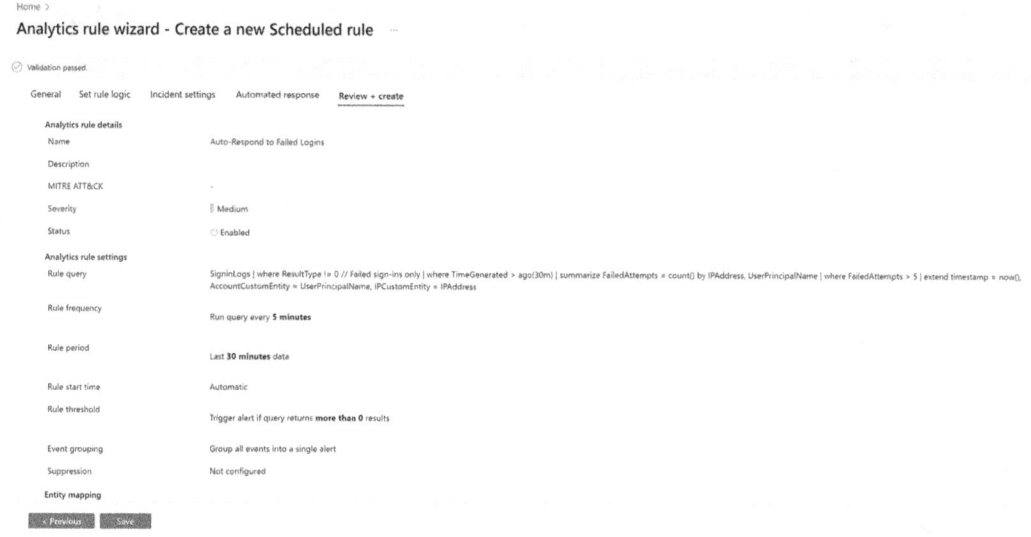

Figure 8-16. *Validating the new schedule rule*

6. Your automation rule is now active and will execute the playbook automatically when the specified conditions are met.

   If you go back to the Overview of Microsoft Sentinel, you can see now the active automation rule, analytics, and data as shown in Figure 8-17.

CHAPTER 8   AZURE SENTINEL: NEXT-GENERATION SIEM

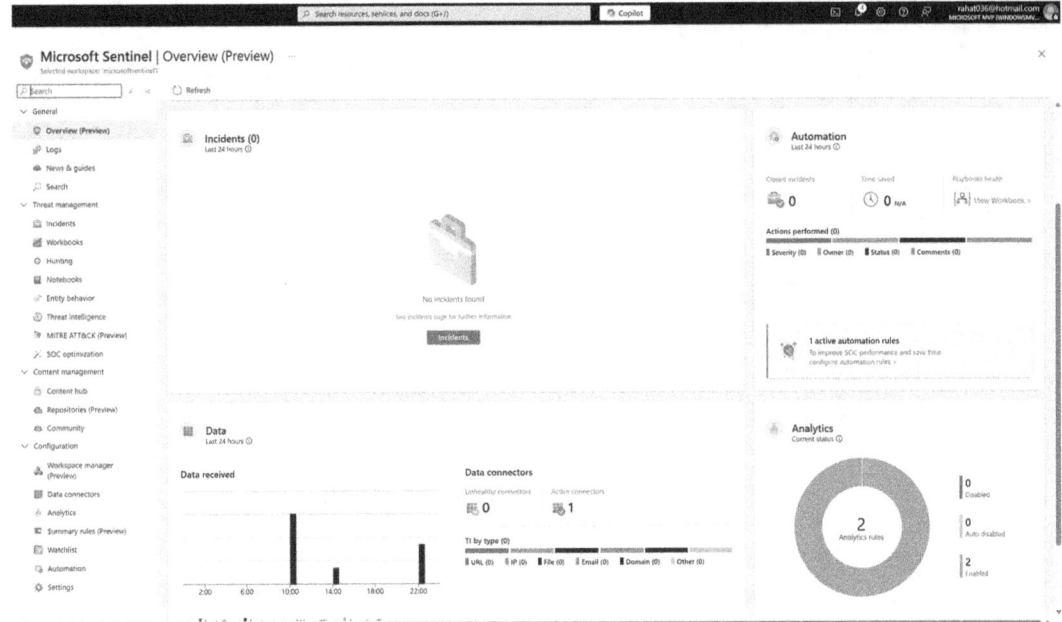

Figure 8-17. *Validating the newly created automation rule from Microsoft Sentinel*

IMPORTANT ANNOUNCEMENTS FROM MICROSOFT

This is a message from Microsoft:

As of June 2023, you can no longer select playbooks to run directly from an analytics rule by adding it to the following list. Playbooks already in the list will continue to run until **March 2026**, *when this method will be deprecated. Instead, to run a playbook in response to an alert generated by this analytics rule, create an Automation rule, choose "When alert is created" as the rule's trigger, and add the playbook to the rule's Actions list. We strongly encourage you to migrate any playbooks in the following list to run from automation rules.*

That means directly linking playbooks within analytics rules is now deprecated. Instead, Microsoft requires using automation rules—configured to trigger when an alert or incident is created—to run playbooks as part of the response workflow.

Mandatory Tips

If you cannot find the logic app or playbook in the run playbook drop-down, please ensure

- Your **playbook** (Logic App) has the correct **trigger**:
  - When a response to an **Azure Sentinel incident** is triggered
  - When a response to an **Azure Sentinel alert** is triggered
- The playbook is in the **same region and resource group** as your Sentinel workspace.
- The playbook is **saved and published**.

Advanced Threat Hunting Techniques

In modern security operations, not all threats can be detected through predefined rules or automated alerts. Adversaries often use stealthy, low-and-slow tactics that bypass standard detection mechanisms. Microsoft Sentinel empowers security analysts to proactively discover these threats through advanced threat hunting capabilities. By leveraging **Kusto Query Language (KQL)**, analysts can sift through raw log data, search for subtle anomalies, and correlate behaviors across environments. Sentinel also supports **hunting bookmarks and annotations** to organize findings, as well as **custom detection rules** to operationalize successful hunts. This section will walk through practical techniques for conducting advanced hunts, annotating and converting discoveries into actionable detections, and managing investigations through Sentinel's built-in **case management workflow**.

What Is Threat Hunting?

Threat hunting is a proactive cybersecurity practice where analysts search through systems and telemetry data to identify signs of malicious activity that automated tools may have missed. Unlike alerts that rely on predefined rules or signatures, threat hunting is often **hypothesis driven**, based on patterns, behaviors, or weak signals observed across environments.

Threat hunting in Microsoft Sentinel empowers defenders to investigate raw data from cloud services, identities, endpoints, and infrastructure using the powerful **Kusto Query Language (KQL)**. Instead of waiting for alerts, hunters formulate questions like

"Has anyone disabled a governance policy?"

"Did a user escalate privileges after logging in from an unusual location?"

These proactive queries uncover **policy evasion**, **identity misuse**, or **configuration drift**—core concerns in a governance and security-focused Azure environment.

Importance of Threat Hunting in Azure Governance

In a cloud-first organization with multiple teams, environments, and self-service capabilities, **governance drift and shadow IT are inevitable**. Threat hunting allows you to

- Detect **unauthorized changes** to subscriptions, resource groups, or policies
- Identify users operating **outside of role boundaries**
- Uncover suspicious admin actions across shared services
- Reveal **identity threats** like token replay or location anomalies
- Validate if resource deployments align with governance baselines

Automated alerts may miss these subtleties—but targeted hunting queries won't.

Demo: Use Threat Hunting Query in Microsoft Sentinel

Let's walk through a practical threat hunting scenario using **Microsoft Sentinel**, focusing on detecting privileged role abuse, a key governance concern.

1. Open the Microsoft Sentinel portal.
2. Navigate to Threat Management ➤ Hunting as shown in Figure 8-18.

CHAPTER 8   AZURE SENTINEL: NEXT-GENERATION SIEM

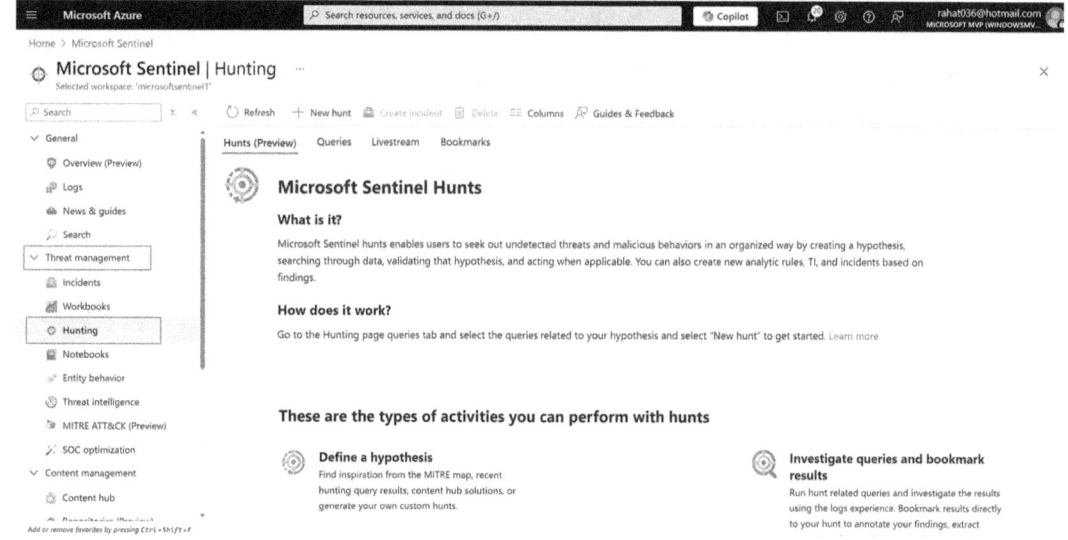

Figure 8-18. *Hunting page in Microsoft Sentinel*

3. Select **Queries** from the top section and click **+ New query** as shown in Figure 8-19.

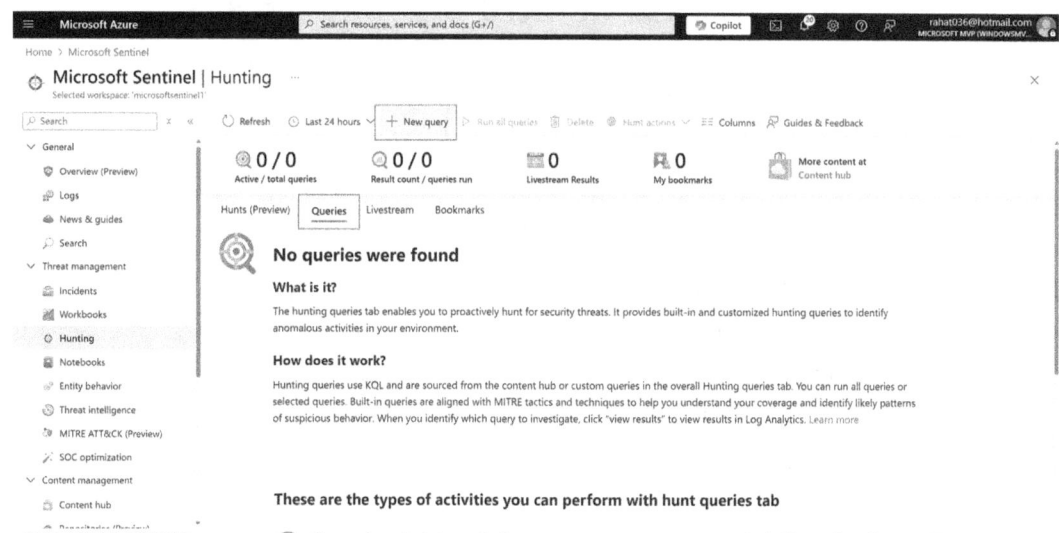

Figure 8-19. *Selecting the query and creating a new query from the hunting page*

383

4. Provide the following information on the new query page:

    - **Name**: Provide a name for the query, for example, **Sensitive Azure Resource Changes**.

    - **Description**: Provide a description of this query.

    - **Query**: Add the following KQL code in the query section.

        ```
        AzureActivity
        | where TimeGenerated > ago(7d)
        | where ActivityStatusValue == "Succeeded"
        | where OperationNameValue has_any (
            "Create or Update Virtual Machine",
            "Delete Virtual Machine",
            "Create or Update Network Security Group",
            "Create or Update Storage Account",
            "Delete Storage Account",
            "Update Key Vault"
        )
        | extend InitiatedBy = Caller,
                 Action = OperationNameValue,
                 Resource = ResourceGroup,
                 Subscription = SubscriptionId
        | project TimeGenerated, InitiatedBy, Action, Resource, Subscription
        ```

    This query will filter Azure Activity Logs for successful actions in the last seven days. Also, it will focus on critical governance-impacting operations, such as VM provisioning or deletion, NSG or storage account changes, or key vault modifications. It will also project who did what, when, and where.

    - Click +Add new entity and add the following:

        1. Account ➤ **FullName** ➤ InitiatedBy

        2. Azure resource ➤ **ResourceID** ➤ Resource

        3. Azure resource ➤ **ResourceID** ➤ Subscription

- In the Tactic and Technique part, choose the following:

  1. **Tactic**: Choose Defense Evasion
  2. **Technique**: `T1562.001 - Disable or Modify Tools`

5. Figure 8-20 shows the actual settings.

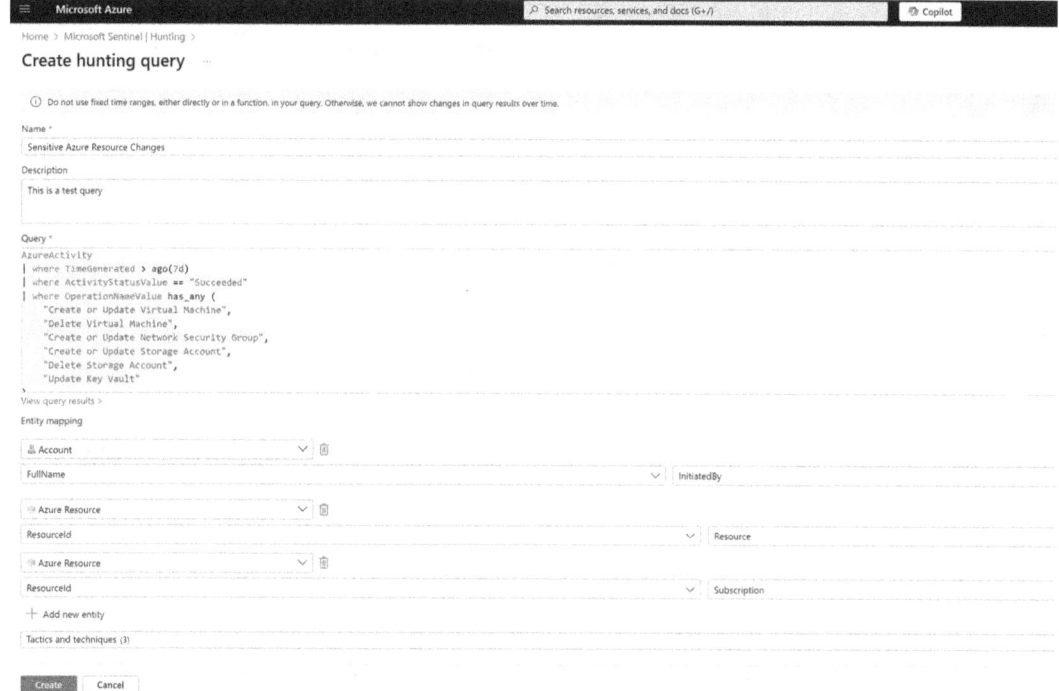

Figure 8-20. *Creating a hunting query page with all the required information*

6. Save and run the query to see anything unusual. If you find anything unusual, you can bookmark that. Bookmarks help you to track suspicious activity and investigate later using the Investigation graph.

Using Hunting Bookmarks and Annotations

As discussed, Microsoft Sentinel allows analysts to create **bookmarks** to preserve the queries, results, observations, and findings during threat hunting sessions. Bookmarks facilitate collaboration and provide a structured approach to investigations. To create a bookmark

1. Navigate to Microsoft Sentinel ➤ Threat Management ➤ Hunting.

2. Select a hunting query and run it.

3. In the query results, select the relevant events.

4. Click Add bookmark, provide necessary details, and save.

Bookmarks can be annotated with comments, linked to incidents, and visualized in the investigation graph, enhancing the collaborative investigation experience. To learn more about bookmarks, refer to the Microsoft official documentation here: https://learn.microsoft.com/en-us/azure/sentinel/bookmarks.

Leveraging Machine Learning in Azure Sentinel

In the previous sections, we explored how proactive techniques like KQL-driven threat hunting and custom detection rules empower analysts to find threats beyond what traditional alerts can catch. But as environment scale and threat actors grow more sophisticated, even well-tuned rules can fall short. This is where **machine learning (ML) and artificial intelligence (AI)** become critical components of modern cloud-native security.

Microsoft Sentinel integrates **intelligent analytics** at multiple levels—combining behavioral baselines, graph-based correlation, anomaly detection, and global threat intelligence to detect attacks that would be virtually impossible to uncover with static rules alone. These ML capabilities are designed not just to reduce noise but to surface meaningful incidents that may otherwise go unnoticed.

In this section, we'll explore how Microsoft Sentinel uses **User and Entity Behavior Analytics (UEBA)** to identify anomalous identity activity, how **Fusion rules** use graph correlation to link seemingly unrelated alerts into high-confidence incidents, and how the **Microsoft Security Graph** powers Sentinel's ML models with global telemetry from across the Microsoft ecosystem. Finally, we'll look at how advanced teams can build **custom machine learning models** using Azure ML and integrate them directly into Sentinel through **Jupyter notebooks**.

Together, these capabilities enable organizations to move from reactive alert handling to **predictive and adaptive defense**, aligning with the evolving needs of secure and governed cloud operations.

UEBA (User and Entity Behavior Analytics)

User and Entity Behavior Analytics (UEBA) in Microsoft Sentinel is a built-in machine learning capability that helps detect insider threats, compromised identities, and privilege misuse by establishing behavior baselines for users and devices. Instead of relying on static rule conditions (e.g., five failed logins), UEBA analyzes patterns over time—such as when and where users typically sign in, what resources they access, and how frequently they perform certain actions. When someone behaves outside of their usual pattern, Sentinel flags that behavior as anomalous.

How UEBA Works in Microsoft Sentinel

Microsoft Sentinel's UEBA engine operates by continuously learning from user and device behaviors using data from connected sources. The process includes **data ingestion**, **behavior profiling**, **anomaly detection**, and **risk scoring**—all powered by machine learning.

Table 8-2 shows the Data Sources for UEBA Analysis. All of these data connectors must be enabled for UEBA to deliver full insight.

Table 8-2. Data sources for UEBA analysis

Source	What It Provides
Microsoft Entra ID (Azure AD)	Sign-in activity, role changes, conditional access, MFA patterns
Microsoft Defender for Endpoint	Device process launches, lateral movement behavior, file access patterns
Microsoft Defender for Cloud Apps	Cloud service access logs, app usage trends
AuditLogs	Administrative operations like user creation, policy updates
SigninLogs	Login attempts, geolocation data, client app info

Table 8-3 shows the machine learning capabilities applied by UEBA. This enables Sentinel to flag unusual behavior without relying on static detection rules, ideal for discovering stealthy insider threats or zero-day tactics.

CHAPTER 8 AZURE SENTINEL: NEXT-GENERATION SIEM

Table 8-3. *Machine learning capabilities applied by UEBA*

Capability	Description
Behavior Profiling	Learns each user's or device's normal activity over time, including location, time of day, and access patterns
Anomaly Detection	Detects statistically significant deviations from learned baselines
Entity Correlation	Links user and device activities to identify multi-stage attack paths
Dynamic Risk Scoring	Continuously updates risk levels (Low, Medium, High) for each entity based on real-time activity and deviations

How to Enable and Use UEBA

UEBA is **enabled by default** in Microsoft Sentinel, but you need to connect the right data sources for it to work effectively.

1. Go to Microsoft Sentinel ➤ Configuration ➤ Settings ➤ Settings tab, expand Entity behavior analytics, and select Set UEBA as shown in Figure 8-21.

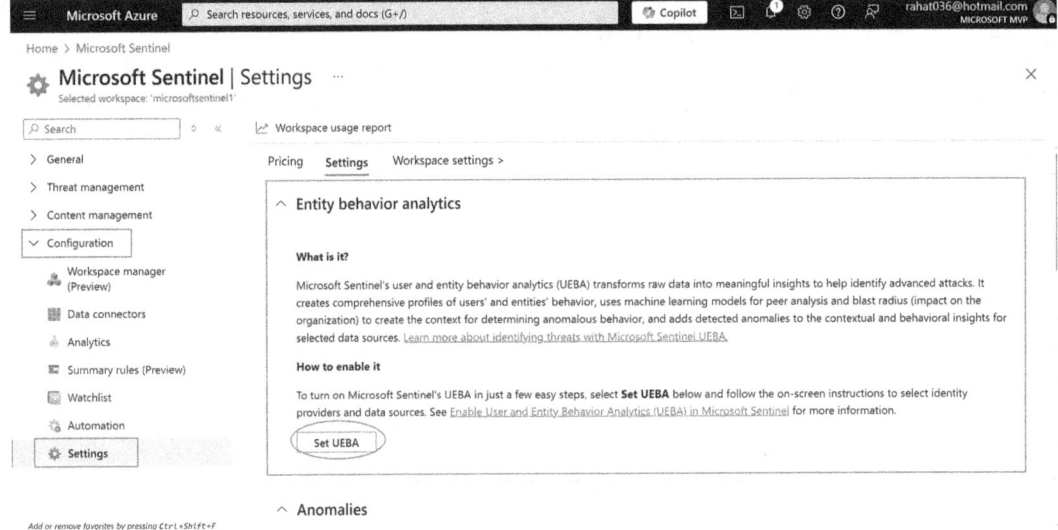

Figure 8-21. *Setting UEBA from Microsoft Sentinel settings*

CHAPTER 8 AZURE SENTINEL: NEXT-GENERATION SIEM

2. A new section will open as shown in Figure 8-22.

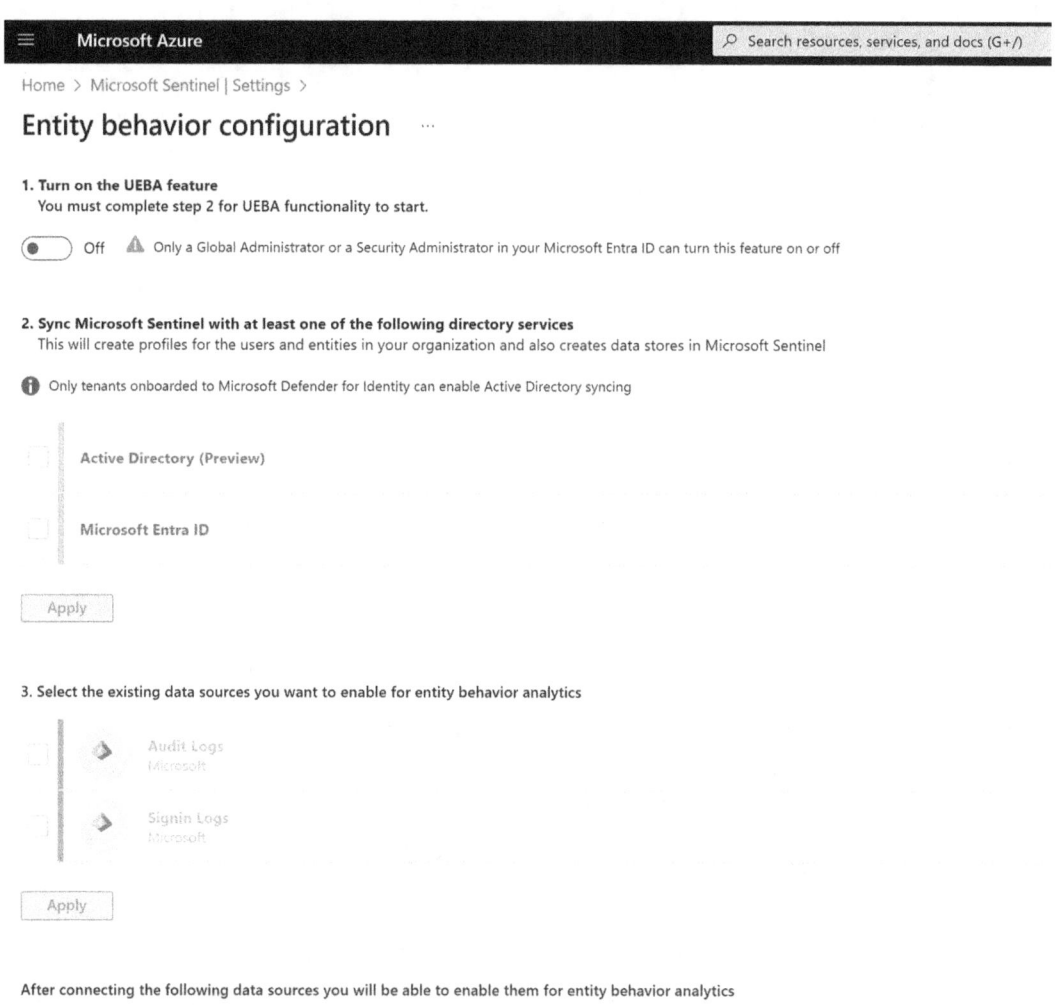

Figure 8-22. Entity behavior configuration page of UEBA

3. Turn on the UEBA feature. Sync Microsoft Sentinel with at least one Microsoft directory service. Then select the data source that you want to enable for entity behavior analytics as shown in Figure 8-23.

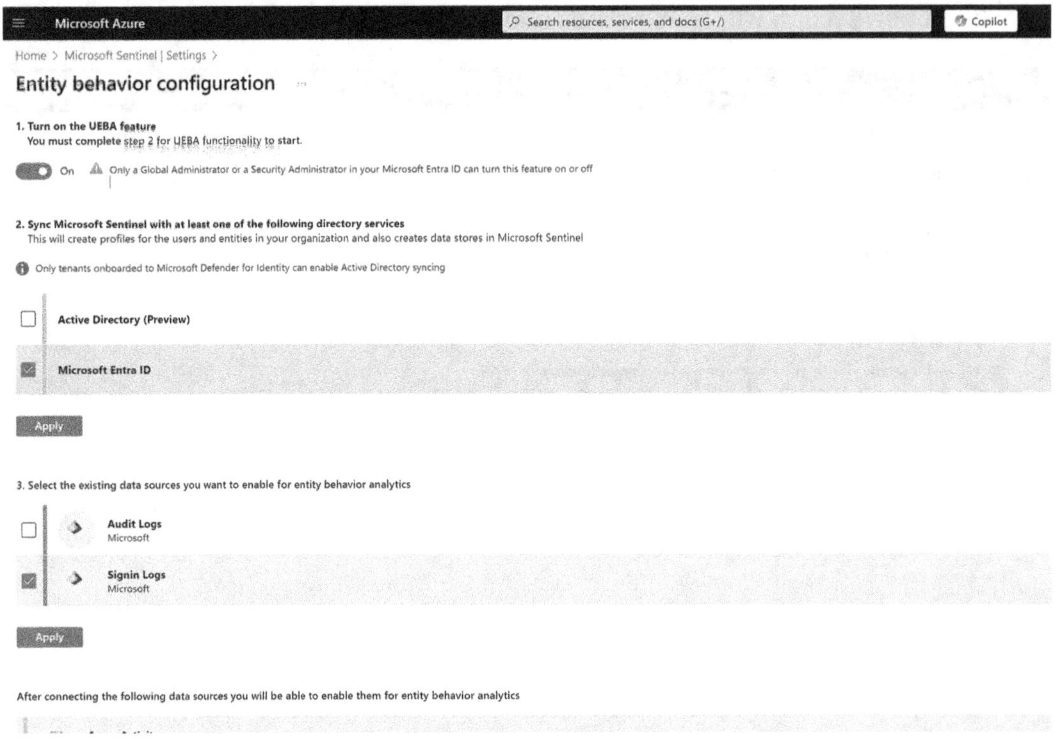

Figure 8-23. Turning on UEBA and selecting directory services

4. Save the settings. You do not need to create or configure UEBA manually, you just need to connect the required data sources for it to begin functioning effectively.

UEBA adds a crucial layer of intelligent detection in Microsoft Sentinel by profiling user and device behavior to uncover subtle anomalies. For governance-focused environments, it helps identify threats that static rules might miss—like insider activity or policy evasion. With the right data sources connected, it runs automatically and integrates seamlessly with advanced features like Fusion, which I explained in the next.

Fusion Rules and Correlation

Cyberattacks in enterprise environments are often complex and gradual, involving various users, devices, and services. Microsoft Sentinel's **Fusion** engine uses machine learning and graph-based correlation to link related signals from the Microsoft security ecosystem, identifying multi-stage attacks. Fusion combines subtle clues from different events into a single, high-confidence incident, without needing manual adjustments or custom rules.

How Fusion Works?

Fusion uses advanced machine learning models, developed by Microsoft and trained on massive volumes of global threat data to recognize patterns that indicate real attacks.

- **Understands Relationships**: Fusion builds a map (graph) that links together users, devices, IP addresses, and alerts. If the same user signs in from a risky location and then a device linked to that user runs suspicious code, Fusion connects these dots.

- **Identifies Attack Sequences**: Rather than treating each event in isolation, Fusion looks at the order of events. For example, a suspicious sign-in followed by privilege escalation and then data access could indicate a multi-stage attack.

- **Surfaces High-Confidence Incidents**: Fusion filters out the noise by only creating incidents when there's a strong connection between events. This helps your team focus on the alerts that really matter—reducing false positives and alert overload.

How to Use Fusion in Microsoft Sentinel

Fusion is **enabled by default**. You don't need to configure rules manually—just ensure the necessary Microsoft data connectors are active and sending data.

To unlock the full power of Fusion, make sure the following connectors are connected and healthy:

- **Microsoft Defender for Endpoint**: Provides endpoint detection and response (EDR) signals, such as malware activity, lateral movement, and exploit attempts

- **Microsoft Defender for Identity**: Offers insights into suspicious behavior on domain controllers, like pass-the-ticket or reconnaissance

- **Microsoft Defender for Cloud Apps (MCAS)**: Captures user activity across SaaS and cloud applications, useful for detecting data exfiltration and shadow IT

- **Microsoft 365 Defender (Office 365 Security)**: Surfaces anomalies in Exchange, Teams, and SharePoint, such as inbox rule abuse or anomalous file access

- **Azure Active Directory (Entra ID) Sign-In and Audit Logs**: Tracks authentication events, role assignments, risky sign-ins, and token behavior

Once these connectors are enabled and ingesting data, **Fusion automatically begins analyzing and correlating alerts across these sources**, surfacing only the most contextually relevant and strategically linked incidents to reduce noise and accelerate response.

Configure Fusion Rules in Microsoft Sentinel

While Microsoft Sentinel's **Fusion engine** is largely automated and enabled by default, you still can **manage and configure Fusion rules** to suit your environment. This includes enabling or disabling specific rule templates, viewing the rule logic, and understanding which data connectors are required for each correlation scenario. Fine-tuning Fusion helps align it with your organization's detection priorities—particularly useful in environments where strict governance and compliance controls are in place.

What Are Fusion Rule Templates?

Fusion rules are based on predefined **rule templates** maintained by Microsoft. These templates define the logic that links multiple alerts across services (e.g., Defender for Endpoint + Entra ID + Sentinel analytics). You can view these templates under the **Analytics blade** in Sentinel.

Fusion rule templates are

- **Non-editable** in logic (you can't customize KQL)
- **Toggleable** (you can enable or disable them)
- **Continuously updated** by Microsoft with new detection scenarios

To configure Fusion rules, follow the steps below:

1. In the Azure portal, navigate to Microsoft Sentinel ➤ Configuration ➤ Analytics.

2. Click Add filter, and choose Fusion as shown in Figure 8-24.

CHAPTER 8   AZURE SENTINEL: NEXT-GENERATION SIEM

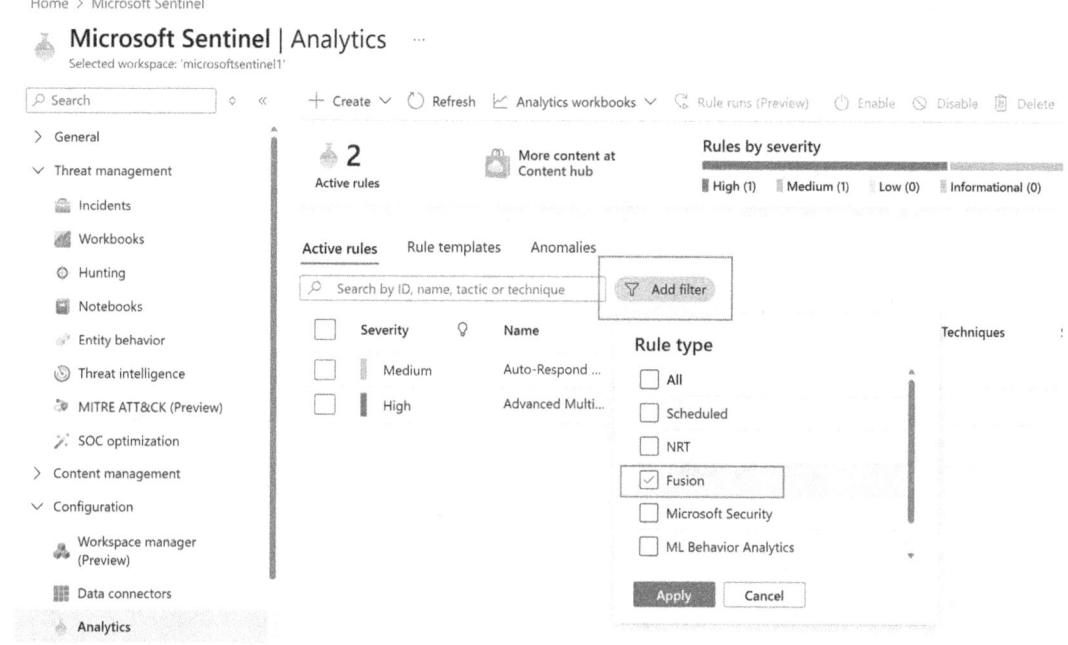

Figure 8-24. Choosing Fusion from filter

3. After selecting the rule type, it will filter only the fusion rules as shown in Figure 8-25.

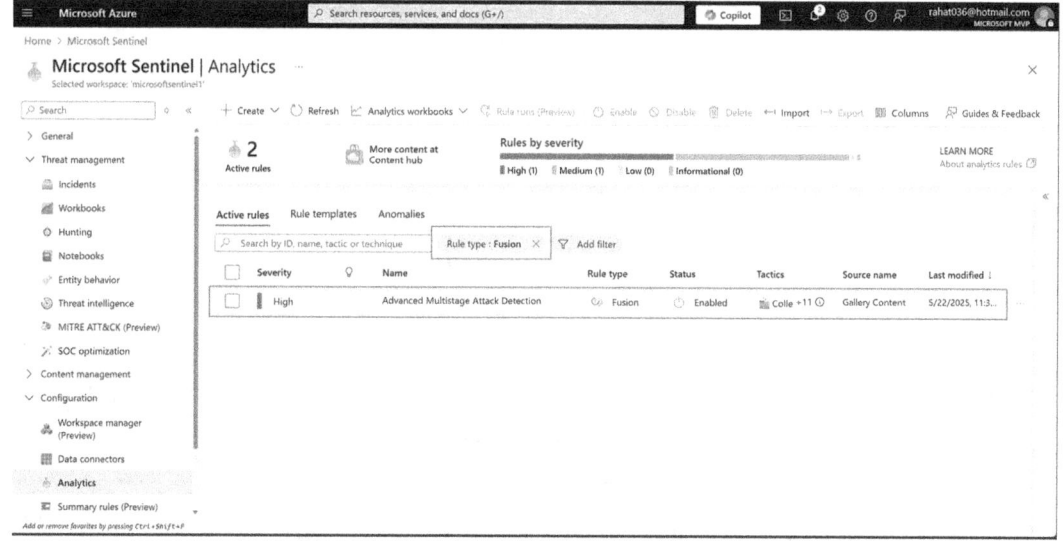

Figure 8-25. Filtering only fusion rules

393

CHAPTER 8 AZURE SENTINEL: NEXT-GENERATION SIEM

4. Select the rule and click edit.

5. In the **General** tab of the **Analytics rule wizard**, note the status (Enabled/Disabled), or change it if you want.

6. Next, in *Configure Fusion*, under *Configure source signals for Fusion detection*, I recommend you include all the listed source signals, with all severity levels, for the best result. By default, they are already all included, but you have the option to make changes. Refer to Figure 8-26.

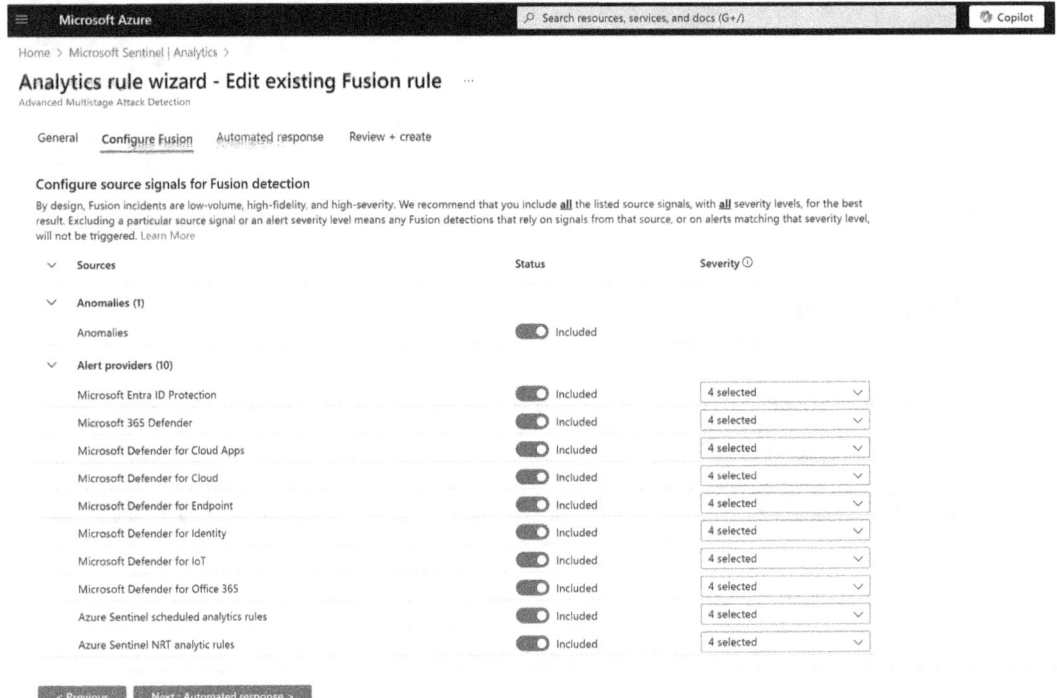

Figure 8-26. Editing and configuring Fusion rule

Note Fusion rules are lightweight to enable—you don't need to define queries, just verify that required connectors are available.

For more information, you can visit the official Microsoft documentation: https://learn.microsoft.com/en-us/azure/sentinel/configure-fusion-rules.

Fusion for Ransomware Detection

Ransomware attacks are complex, multi-stage operations that often generate various low- and medium-severity alerts—many of which, if viewed in isolation, might not be treated as critical. Microsoft Sentinel's **Fusion engine** is uniquely equipped to detect such attacks by correlating disparate signals across multiple Microsoft security platforms into a single **high-confidence ransomware incident**.

Fusion for ransomware is designed to detect **multiple alert types that indicate suspicious behavior associated with ransomware execution and defense evasion**, even when those alerts originate from different tools and carry different severities.

Data Sources Monitored for Ransomware Correlation

To enable this functionality, Fusion automatically ingests and analyzes alerts from the following connected data sources:

- **Microsoft Defender for Endpoint**
- **Microsoft Defender for Cloud**
- **Microsoft Defender for Identity**
- **Microsoft Defender for Cloud Apps**
- **Microsoft Sentinel Scheduled Analytics Rules**

Note Fusion will only consider Sentinel analytics rules that are mapped to MITRE ATT&CK tactics (e.g., Execution, Defense Evasion) and include valid entity mapping.

Let's look at how Fusion detects ransomware using cross-signal logic. Imagine the alerts are generated on the **same host** within a short time window, as shown in Table 8-4.

Table 8-4. Example of some alert that Fusion detects

Alert	Source	Severity
Windows Error and Warning Events	Microsoft Sentinel (Analytics Rule)	Informational
"GandCrab" ransomware was prevented	Microsoft Defender for Cloud	Medium
"Emotet" malware was detected	Microsoft Defender for Endpoint	Informational
"Tofsee" backdoor was detected	Microsoft Defender for Cloud	Low
"Parite" malware was detected	Microsoft Defender for Endpoint	Informational

Individually, none of these alerts might trigger an urgent response. But when they occur together on the same host, within the same time frame, **Fusion correlates them** and automatically generates a new incident titled

"Multiple alerts possibly related to Ransomware activity detected"

This incident is tagged with MITRE tactics such as

- **Execution (TA0002):** Running malware or payloads
- **Defense Evasion (TA0005):** Obfuscating or bypassing security tools

Microsoft Security Graph

Microsoft Sentinel's advanced detection capabilities, including UEBA and Fusion, rely heavily on data intelligence provided by the **Microsoft Intelligent Security Graph**. This is Microsoft's global, cloud-powered threat intelligence backbone, aggregating trillions of security signals each day from across the Microsoft ecosystem and beyond. By integrating with this graph, Sentinel gains access to **real-time global threat indicators, behavioral patterns, and known attack signatures**, which significantly enhances its machine learning–driven analytics.

What Is the Microsoft Security Graph?

The Microsoft Security Graph, also called **Microsoft Intelligent Security Graph (ISG)**, is a vast cloud-based knowledge base that

- Ingests signals from **Microsoft Defender XDR**, **Microsoft 365**, **Azure**, **Edge**, and **Bing**

CHAPTER 8   AZURE SENTINEL: NEXT-GENERATION SIEM

- Includes data from **partners**, **threat intelligence feeds**, and **customer telemetry**

- Is continuously updated and curated by Microsoft's security research teams

This graph is the foundation for features like **threat intelligence enrichment**, **global anomaly baselines**, **entity reputation scoring**, and **correlation across tenants**—all of which directly benefit Sentinel's ML models.

How Does Microsoft Sentinel Uses Microsoft Security Graph?

When data enters your Sentinel workspace, Microsoft Security Graph helps through the use cases shown in Table 8-5.

Table 8-5. How Microsoft Sentinel uses Microsoft Security Graph

Use Case	How the Graph Enhances It
Alert correlation (Fusion)	Provides global context to link alerts across services
UEBA risk scoring	Uses crowd-based behavior modeling to detect outliers
IP/Domain reputation	Flags communication with known malicious infrastructure
Threat intelligence enrichment	Augments detections with global threat actor indicators
Cloud-based threat detection	Detects activity matching campaigns seen in other environments

The result is smarter detection—not just within your tenant, but in the context of what Microsoft sees globally.

Building Custom ML Models with Azure ML and Notebooks

While Microsoft Sentinel provides powerful out-of-the-box machine learning capabilities—such as UEBA and Fusion—advanced security teams can take detection even further by building and integrating their own **custom ML models** using **Azure Machine Learning** and **Jupyter notebooks**. This approach is ideal for

CHAPTER 8   AZURE SENTINEL: NEXT-GENERATION SIEM

scenarios where organizations require bespoke anomaly detection logic, compliance-specific patterns, or deeper statistical modeling that goes beyond what's available in prebuilt rules.

Preconfigured analytics work well for common attack patterns, but they may not capture

- Organization-specific threat behavior (e.g., abnormal access to internal legacy systems)
- Domain-specific fraud patterns
- Advanced statistical anomalies across resource usage, subscription drift, or admin access

Custom ML models allow you to define **what's abnormal in your environment**, train models on your historical telemetry, and output detections directly into Sentinel.

Demo: Anomaly Detection with Azure ML and Sentinel

Let's start a basic walk-through of creating a notebook that detects anomalies in sign-in frequency per user:

1. Go to Microsoft Azure portal ➤ Microsoft Sentinel. Choose the Sentinel and click Logs from the left panel as shown in Figure 8-27.

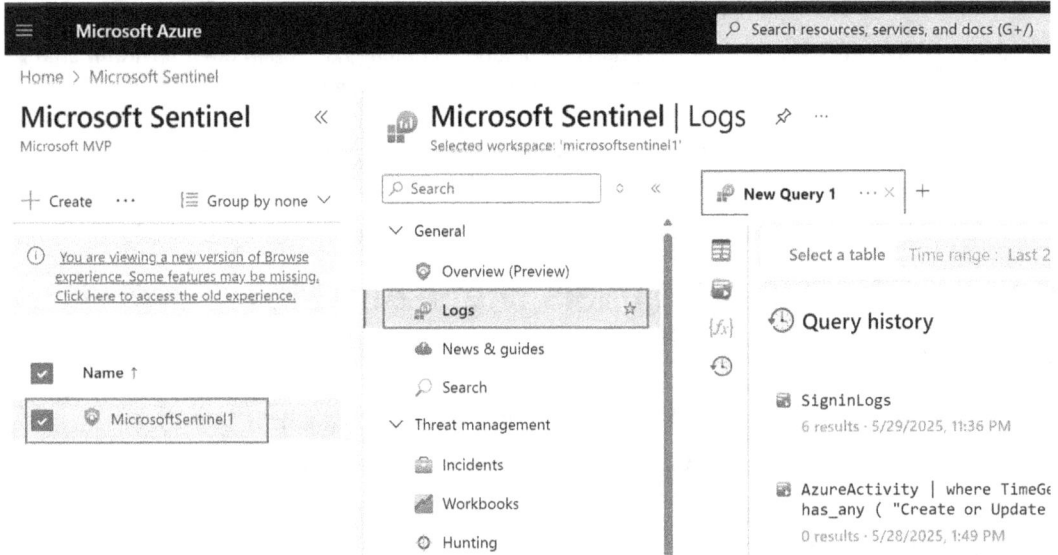

Figure 8-27. *Logs option in Microsoft Sentinel*

398

CHAPTER 8   AZURE SENTINEL: NEXT-GENERATION SIEM

2. Click Select a table from the New Query section as shown in Figure 8-28.

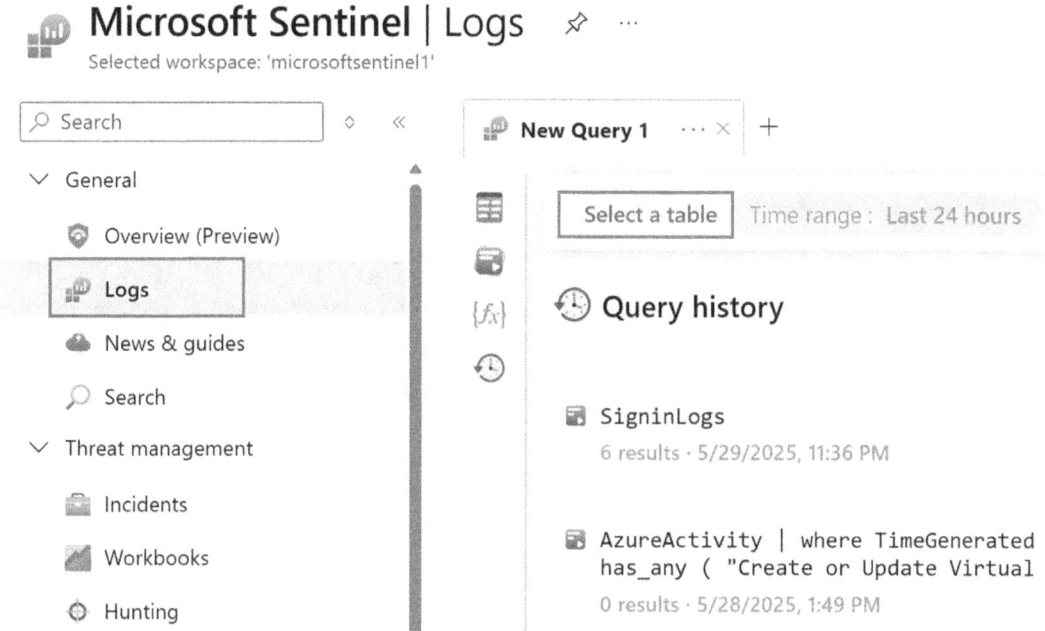

Figure 8-28. *Adding new query to get log information*

3. Choose SigninLogs under LogManagement as shown in Figure 8-29.

399

CHAPTER 8   AZURE SENTINEL: NEXT-GENERATION SIEM

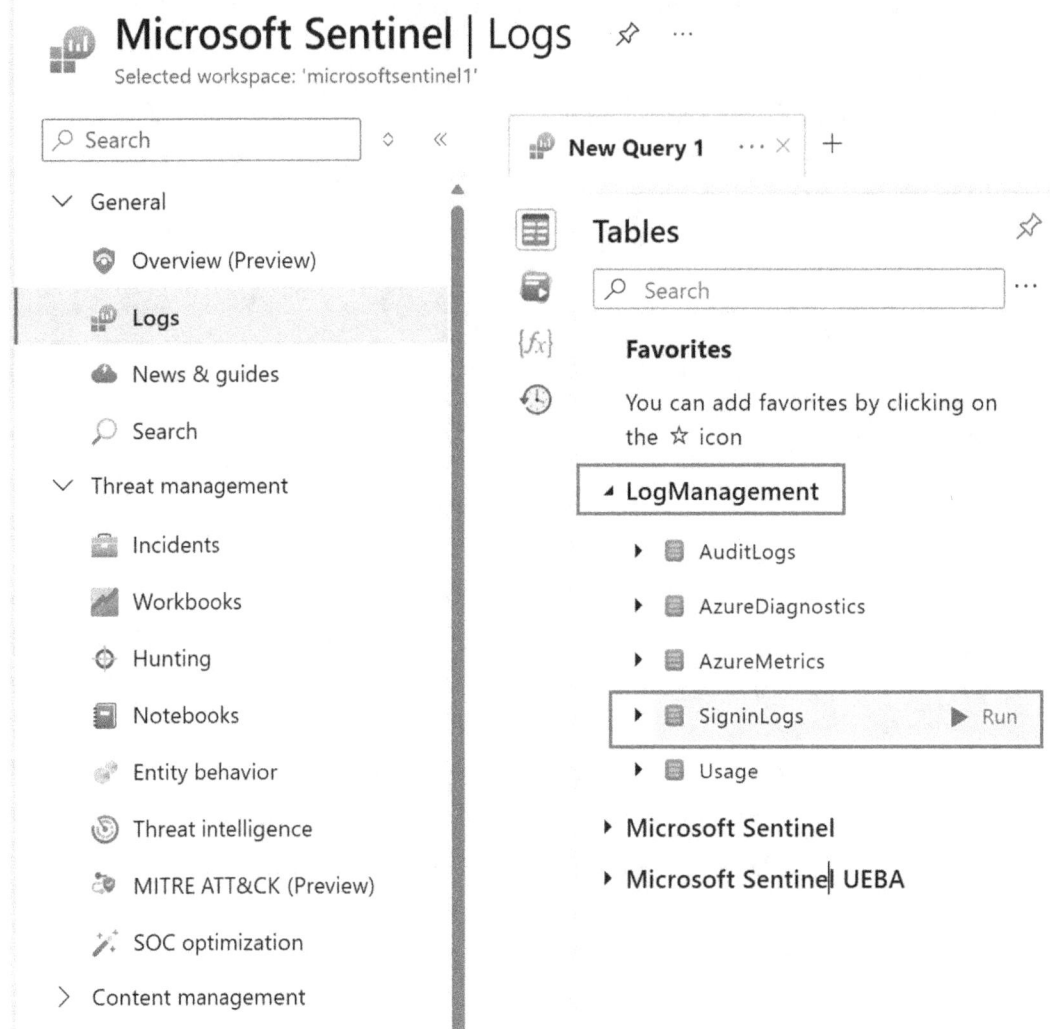

Figure 8-29. *Choosing the SigninLogs table under the LogManagement section*

4. You can see the list of data in the result section as shown in Figure 8-30. Choose seven days' time range.

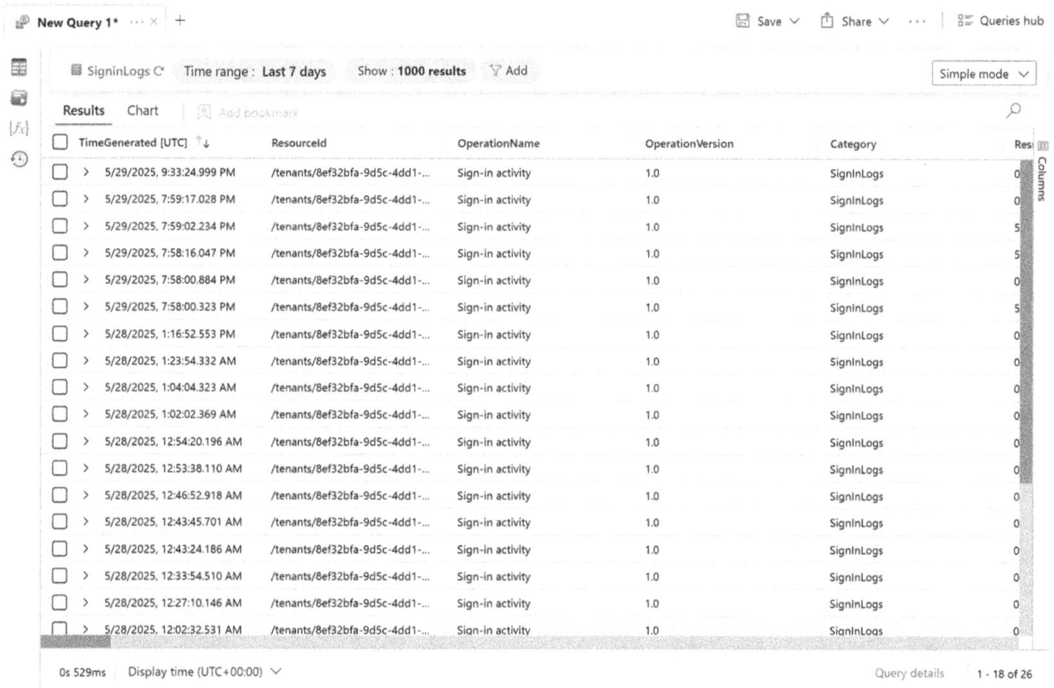

CHAPTER 8 AZURE SENTINEL: NEXT-GENERATION SIEM

Figure 8-30. *Query result that shows the SigninLogs for the last seven days*

5. Click Share from the top menu and export the file as CSV (all columns) as shown in Figure 8-31.

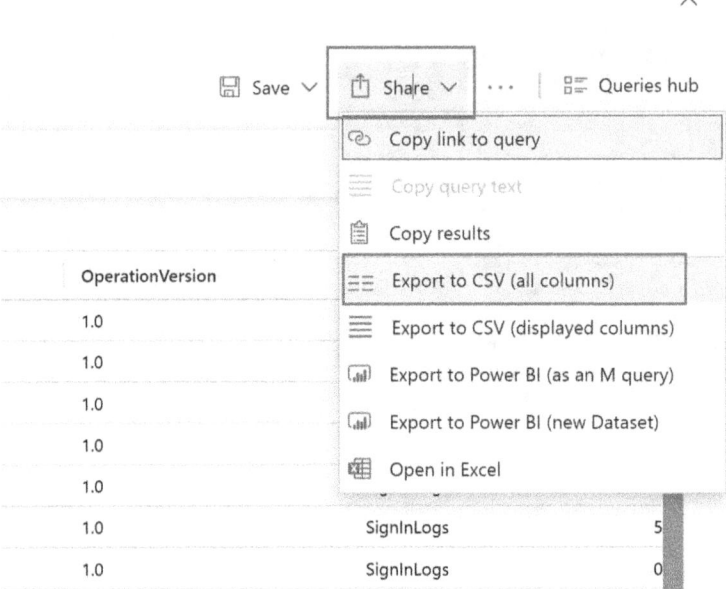

Figure 8-31. Exporting the file in CSV format

6. Now it's time to play with Azure Machine Learning. Open Azure Machine Learning Studio from `https://ml.azure.com/`. Log in with the credentials where you have the Azure subscription. You will see the page as shown in Figure 8-32.

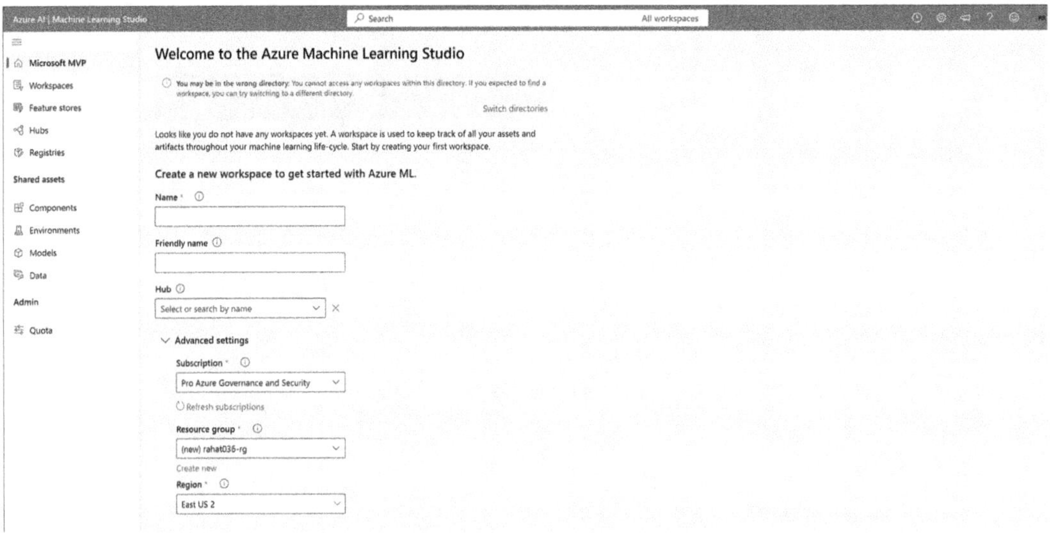

Figure 8-32. Azure Machine Learning Studio page

CHAPTER 8   AZURE SENTINEL: NEXT-GENERATION SIEM

7. Create or open an Azure ML workspace.

8. Select the workspace; go to Data ➤ + Create. A new panel will open as shown in Figure 8-33.

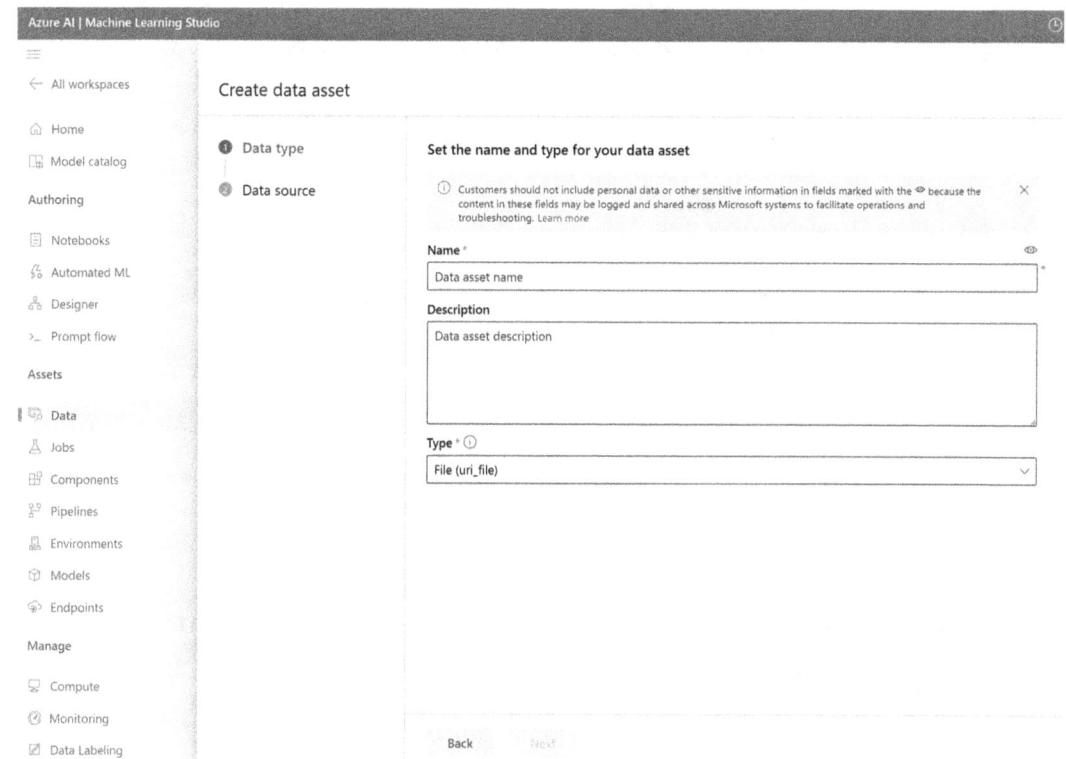

Figure 8-33. *Creating data asset in Azure ML Studio*

9. Provide a name of the data asset and file type, and go next.

10. Choose the file and upload it as shown in Figure 8-34.

CHAPTER 8   AZURE SENTINEL: NEXT-GENERATION SIEM

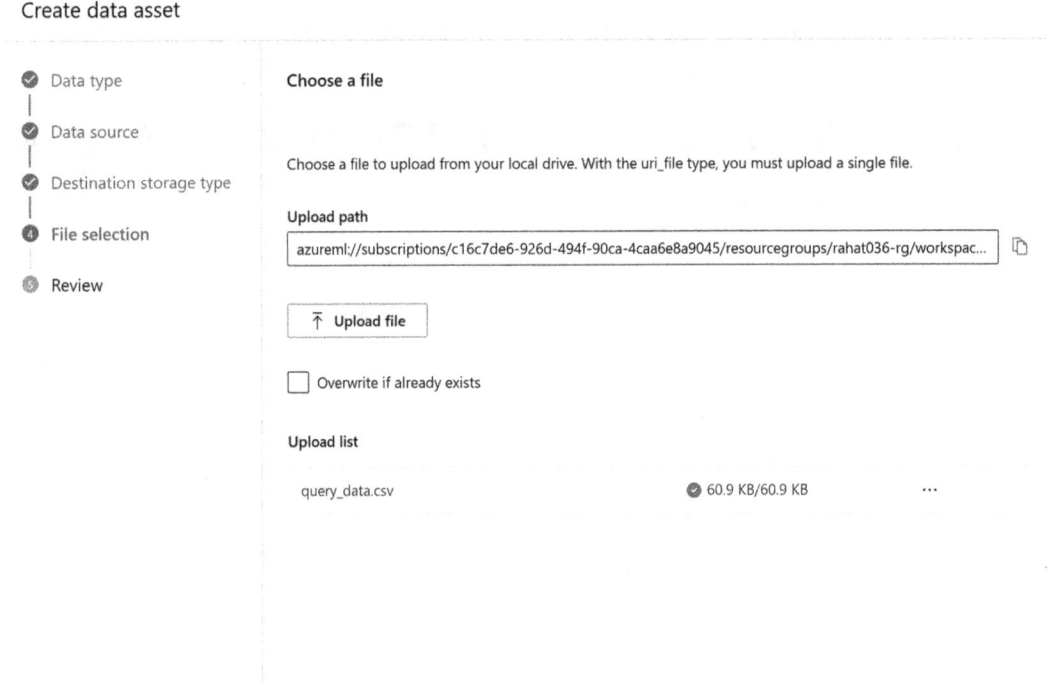

Figure 8-34. *Selecting and uploading the data file that we downloaded as csv.*

11. Click Next. Review and then click Create. It will create the data asset, which you can see as shown in Figure 8-35.

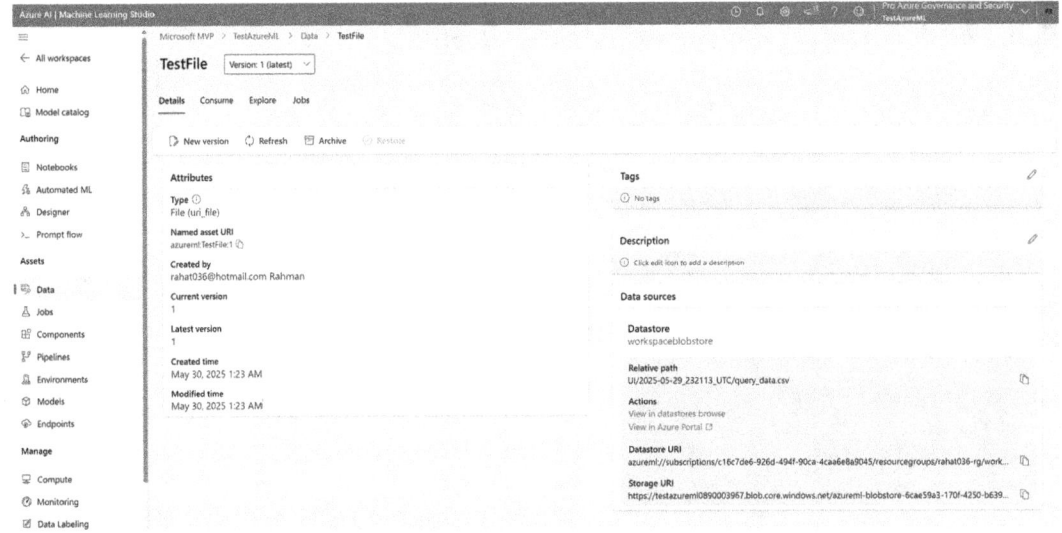

Figure 8-35. *Data file overview page with the URI and other details*

CHAPTER 8   AZURE SENTINEL: NEXT-GENERATION SIEM

12. Go to the Notebook under the Authoring section. Click + Files and select Create new file as shown in Figure 8-36.

Notebooks is your space to add, browse, and edit files.

You can add files of any type, including Jupyter Notebooks (.ipynb). The files you see here are stored in the workspace file share, and are accessible and shared within the workspace.

In order to run notebooks and scripts, you must connect to an Azure Machine Learning compute resource. Once a notebook or terminal is connected, you can access all workspace assets including experiment details, data, models, and more. Learn more ⬈

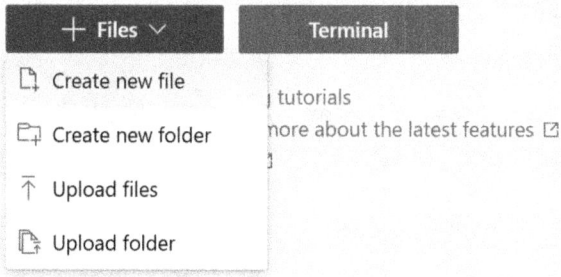

Figure 8-36. *Creating a new notebook file*

13. Name the file `SigninAnomalyDetection.ipynb` as shown in Figure 8-37.

405

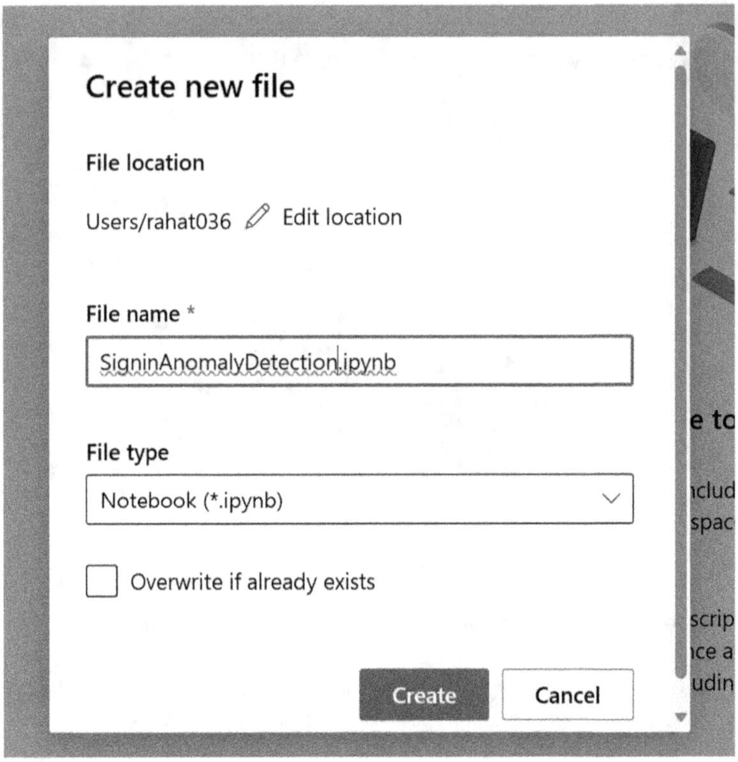

CHAPTER 8   AZURE SENTINEL: NEXT-GENERATION SIEM

Figure 8-37. Creating a .ipynb file

14. Paste the following code into the code cell:

```
from sklearn.ensemble import IsolationForest
import pandas as pd

# Load dataset from local file or Azure ML dataset
df = pd.read_csv("TestFile.csv")

# Prepare data (optional: group by user if analyzing per-
user trend)
df["SigninCount"] = df["SigninCount"].astype(float)

# Train Isolation Forest
model = IsolationForest(contamination=0.05, random_state=42)
df["anomaly"] = model.fit_predict(df[["SigninCount"]])
```

```
# Filter out anomalies
anomalies = df[df["anomaly"] == -1]

# Show anomalies
print(anomalies)
```

This model labels data points as

- 1 = normal
- −1 = anomaly (unusual sign-in pattern)

15. Now we need the Workspace ID and Primary Key (Shared Key) to get connected with Microsoft Sentinel. To get the Workspace ID and Primary Key, follow the steps:

    a. Go to Azure portal ➤ Microsoft Sentinel, then select the Sentinel ➤ Settings ➤ Agents. There you can find the Workspace ID and Primary Key as shown in Figure 8-38.

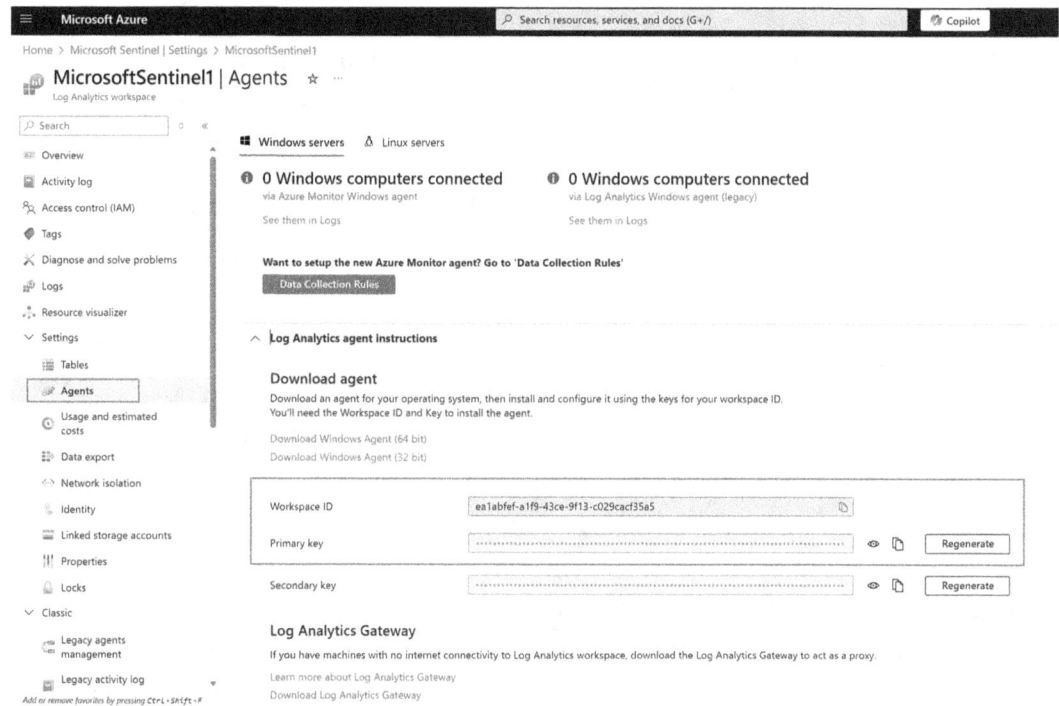

Figure 8-38. *Getting the Workspace ID and Primary Key from Microsoft Sentinel*

16. Add a new Python code cell in Azure ML workspace and add the following code:

```python
import hashlib, hmac, base64
import requests, json
from datetime import datetime

def build_signature(workspace_id, shared_key, date, content_length, method, content_type, resource):
    x_headers = 'x-ms-date:' + date
    string_to_hash = f"{method}\n{content_length}\n{content_type}\n{x_headers}\n{resource}"
    bytes_to_hash = bytes(string_to_hash, encoding="utf-8")
    decoded_key = base64.b64decode(shared_key)
    encoded_hash = base64.b64encode(hmac.new(decoded_key, bytes_to_hash, digestmod=hashlib.sha256).digest()).decode()
    return f"SharedKey {workspace_id}:{encoded_hash}"
```

17. Add the Workspace ID and Primary Key and run the Python code in Azure ML Studio. Now it will detect anomalies in sign-in frequency per user.

That's it! In the next chapter, we will see how AI and machine learning work in cloud security.

Summary

In this chapter, we explored Microsoft Sentinel, Microsoft's cloud-native SIEM (Security Information and Event Management) and SOAR (Security Orchestration, Automation, and Response) solutions. You learned how Sentinel ingests and analyzes telemetry across cloud, hybrid, and on-premises environments, correlating signals into high-fidelity alerts and enabling real-time threat detection. We walked through setting up data connectors, building analytic rules, and conducting investigations using the MITRE ATT&CK framework. You also gained hands-on experience with Kusto Query Language (KQL) for advanced threat hunting and saw how Sentinel integrates with Logic Apps to orchestrate automated responses using security playbooks. Together, these capabilities empower organizations to operationalize security, reduce response time, and scale their Security Operations Center (SOC) with intelligence and agility.

In Chapter 9, we shift gears to focus on AI and machine learning in cloud security. While Sentinel gives us tools to monitor and react to threats, artificial intelligence pushes us into the realm of proactive, predictive defense. You'll learn how Microsoft leverages AI across Defender for Cloud, Entra ID, and Sentinel to identify previously unseen threats, reduce false positives, and assign dynamic risk scores. We'll also walk through building custom ML models using Azure Machine Learning to classify suspicious activities, automate triage, and even forecast future threats. By the end of this chapter, you'll see how intelligent models and predictive analytics are reshaping the future of cloud security—from incident response to prevention.

CHAPTER 9

AI and Machine Learning in Cloud Security

In the previous chapter, we explored how **Microsoft Sentinel** empowers security teams with centralized visibility, automated response, and advanced threat detection through its powerful SIEM and SOAR capabilities. We examined how to ingest and correlate data from diverse sources, build analytic rules, investigate incidents using the MITRE ATT&CK framework, and automate workflows using Logic Apps. These capabilities are essential for modern Security Operations Centers—but as threats evolve in speed and sophistication, reactive security operations alone are no longer sufficient.

In this chapter, we shift focus toward the **next frontier of cloud security: artificial intelligence and machine learning.** You will learn how Microsoft Defender for Cloud, Entra ID, and Sentinel embed AI-driven models to enhance detection accuracy, identify unknown threats, and reduce false positives. We'll also explore how you can build and train your own machine learning models using **Azure Machine Learning**, with real-world use cases for predictive security. This chapter will help you understand how to move from rule-based detection to **intelligent, adaptive, and proactive defense**—laying the foundation for future-ready security architectures.

AI and ML for Threat Detection

As cloud environments grow in complexity and scale, traditional security approaches—centered on static rules, manual correlation, and perimeter-based thinking—are no longer sufficient. In today's threat landscape, adversaries use sophisticated tactics that blend into normal behavior, making them difficult to detect using signature-based or rule-driven methods alone. Microsoft has responded to this challenge by embedding artificial intelligence (AI) and machine learning (ML) into its cloud-native security tools to enable real-time, adaptive, and intelligent threat detection.

AI and ML now form the core of modern threat detection systems such as Microsoft Defender for Cloud, Microsoft Sentinel, and Microsoft Entra. These systems move beyond traditional SIEM logic by ingesting vast volumes of telemetry data—spanning authentication events, resource access, configuration changes, and behavioral signals—from both Microsoft and non-Microsoft platforms. Through advanced analytics, including unsupervised learning and graph-based modeling, these tools detect previously unseen attack patterns, predict emerging threats, and prioritize alerts based on real-world context.

One of the key innovations Microsoft has introduced is **probabilistic risk scoring through graph-based telemetry**. This approach evaluates the relationships between users, devices, resources, and actions across hybrid and multi-cloud environments, assigning dynamic risk scores that adjust in real time. For example, Microsoft Sentinel's Fusion technology uses AI to correlate signals from disparate sources and identify complex, multi-stage attacks such as credential compromise followed by lateral movement.

Additionally, AI is used to **reduce false positives** by analyzing alert history, tuning models automatically, and suppressing redundant or low-confidence detections—enabling security teams to focus on true threats. Microsoft also emphasizes **cross-cloud visibility** with native support for AWS CloudTrail and GCP logs in Microsoft Sentinel, allowing organizations to detect threats spanning Azure, AWS, and Google Cloud from a unified, AI-augmented analytics layer.

According to Microsoft, these AI-driven capabilities continue to evolve, with ongoing investments in deep learning models, natural language threat hunting (e.g., Copilot in Microsoft Defender XDR), and integrated security graph APIs to power next-generation detection engines.

Gaps in Rule-Based Detection: Why Custom ML Is Now Necessary

Modern cloud environments generate an immense volume of telemetry—sign-ins, role assignments, resource access, configuration changes, and network connections—on a continuous basis. Traditionally, security operations have relied on **rule-based detection systems** to monitor this activity and raise alerts when something suspicious occurs.

A rule-based approach typically uses deterministic logic like

"If more than five failed login attempts occur within 10 minutes, trigger a brute-force alert."

While this type of logic is easy to understand and quick to implement, it has significant limitations in today's threat landscape. These limitations are especially pronounced in dynamic, distributed, and hybrid environments such as Microsoft Azure.

Static Rules Don't Detect Unknown Threats

Rule-based systems are only effective when you know what to look for. They require security teams to **manually define thresholds, keywords, or behavior patterns** in advance. This makes them incapable of detecting **new, subtle, or evolving attack techniques** that don't match any existing rule.

For instance, if an attacker gains access using valid credentials but behaves slightly differently—perhaps logging in at unusual times, from uncommon devices, or pivoting laterally within short time windows—a rule-based system may not flag this behavior as suspicious at all.

For example, a rule-based system might not flag multiple failed login attempts spread across different user accounts (a password spray attack), as each attempt looks benign in isolation. However, a machine learning model can recognize the unusual login pattern across accounts and detect it as an anomaly.

By contrast, machine learning models trained on historical behavior can identify **outliers** and **anomalies** that go unnoticed by fixed logic.

Rule Correlation Is Shallow and Non-contextual

Most security information and event management (SIEM) systems, including Microsoft Sentinel, allow basic correlation between signals (e.g., failed logins + conditional access failures). However, these rules are often **shallow and context blind**. They lack the ability to evaluate **temporal relationships**, user behavior baselines, or cross-entity movement.

Custom ML models, on the other hand, can consider a wide range of inputs—user type, access history, resource sensitivity, and geographic profile—and assign a risk score based on statistical and behavioral patterns.

Excessive False Positives and Alert Fatigue

Rule-based systems produce binary outcomes: either the condition matches or it doesn't. As a result, they often generate **too many alerts**, many of which are **false positives**. Security analysts waste time chasing alerts that don't require action, leading to fatigue and burnout.

Machine learning introduces **probabilistic reasoning**. Instead of simply flagging events, it assigns a **confidence score** or **threat probability**, helping SOC teams prioritize what matters most.

Rules Require Manual Tuning and Don't Learn

Static rules are rigid. They must be constantly updated to reflect new attack techniques, updated business logic, or changing user behavior. They do not improve over time, and they do not adapt based on analyst feedback or changing environments.

In contrast, machine learning models can be **retrained periodically** using real incident data, automatically adapting to changing patterns. This makes them far more sustainable and scalable in large, complex environments.

Using Azure Machine Learning to Classify Suspicious Logins or Resource Changes

As organizations scale their cloud infrastructure, the volume and variety of sign-in and resource access data increases dramatically. Microsoft Sentinel and Entra ID (formerly Azure Active Directory) provide powerful telemetry, but extracting actionable intelligence from that data—especially for dynamic or nuanced threats—requires more than simple rules. This is where **Azure Machine Learning (Azure ML)** offers a significant advantage.

By building custom ML models tailored to your environment, you can classify sign-in attempts or resource changes as **suspicious or benign** based on historical behavior, risk factors, and contextual attributes. These models are especially useful for detecting **behavioral anomalies**, **low-and-slow attacks**, and **unusual access chains** that are hard to define using static rules.

Problem Framing: Binary Classification

At the core of this task is a **binary classification problem:** given a set of attributes related to a login event or resource modification, determine whether the event is

- **0** = Legitimate (normal behavior)
- **1** = Suspicious (anomalous or high-risk behavior)

To achieve this, you can train a supervised ML model using historical telemetry labeled by your SOC—that is, known good vs. confirmed incidents. Once trained and validated, the model can be deployed as a real-time scoring service.

While binary classification is effective for distinguishing between benign and malicious activities, **multi-class classification** can be used when the objective is to assign events to multiple categories—such as brute-force attack, phishing, insider threat, or normal activity. This adds more context to the alert and can guide more targeted incident response.

Key Data Sources and Features

Azure provides rich telemetry through several services. Table 9-1 shows some of the most relevant attributes that can be used as **input features**.

Table 9-1. Feature-purpose mapping of Entra ID and Defender telemetry for threat detection

Telemetry Source	Feature Name	Purpose
Entra ID/Sign-in Logs	UserPrincipalName	Identify the user identity
	IPAddress/Location	Detect geographic anomalies
	Sign-in time (hour, weekday)	Identify time-based outliers
	Device type	Flag unusual or unmanaged devices
	MFA result/Conditional Access	Evaluate access controls applied
	Application accessed	Assess app-specific risk or misuse
	Risk level (Microsoft risk engine)	Leverage Microsoft's internal risk scoring
Activity Logs/ Defender/Policy	Resource type	Identify sensitivity and type of asset
	Initiator identity	Determine if user, service principal, or script
	Operation (create/update/delete)	Understand scope and impact
	Time of action	Detect off-hours changes
	Previous vs. new config	Spot misconfigurations or escalation attempts
	Tags/Policy compliance states	Enrich with compliance context

Model Development with Azure ML

Azure Machine Learning enables you to build, train, and deploy models entirely within the Azure ecosystem. Let's make a demo, classifying suspicious login events using Azure Machine Learning:

1. First, we need the Sign-in Logs to start the demo. To get the Sign-in Logs, go to **Microsoft Azure portal ➤ Microsoft Sentinel ➤ Select the Sentinel ➤ Logs** and export the Sign-in Logs as csv format. Refer to Chapter 8, where I discussed this in detail.

2. Go to the Azure ML Studio (https://ml.azure.com/), create new workspace, and load the csv file.

3. In the data section, upload the .csv file as we uploaded in Chapter 8.

4. In the Notebook section, create a new Python file named DataPreparation.py, and add the following code there:

```python
import pandas as pd
import numpy as np
from sklearn.model_selection import train_test_split
from sklearn.ensemble import RandomForestClassifier
from sklearn.metrics import classification_report
import joblib

# Replace with your actual CSV file path or blob mount

df = pd.read_csv('azureml://subscriptions/
c16c7de6-926d-494f-90ca-4caa6e8a9045/resourcegroups/
rahat036-rg/workspaces/SignInLogs/datastores/workspaceblobstore/
paths/UI/2025-05-31_094745_UTC/signin_data.csv')

# Step 3: Label suspicious logins (based on location logic)
# For demo purposes, label all non-Germany/Austria locations as
suspicious

df['Suspicious'] = df['Location'].apply(lambda x: 1 if x not in
['Germany', 'Austria'] else 0)
```

```
# Step 4: One-hot encode categorical variables (AppDisplayName, 
Location)

df = pd.get_dummies(df, columns=['Location', 'AppDisplayName'])

# Step 5: Drop unnecessary string-based identifiers (e.g., 
usernames, GUIDs)

# Keep only numeric features for the model
X = df.drop(['UserPrincipalName', 'Suspicious'], axis=1, 
errors='ignore')
X = X.select_dtypes(include=[np.number])

# Step 6: Define target variable

y = df['Suspicious']

# Step 7: Split the dataset into training and testing sets

X_train, X_test, y_train, y_test = train_test_split(
    X, y, test_size=0.3, random_state=42
)

# Step 8: Train a Random Forest classifier

model = RandomForestClassifier(n_estimators=100, random_state=42)
model.fit(X_train, y_train)

# Step 9: Evaluate the model on test data

y_pred = model.predict(X_test)
print("Classification Report:")
print(classification_report(y_test, y_pred))

# Step 10: Save the trained model to a file for deployment

joblib.dump(model, 'login_classifier.pkl')
print("Model saved as 'login_classifier.pkl'")
```

Figure 9-1 shows the actual code in Python.

CHAPTER 9   AI AND MACHINE LEARNING IN CLOUD SECURITY

Figure 9-1. *Python code provided above in the Azure ML Studio page*

Here I already give the comments on the code for your better understanding.

5. If you run the code, you will get the output as shown in Figure 9-2.

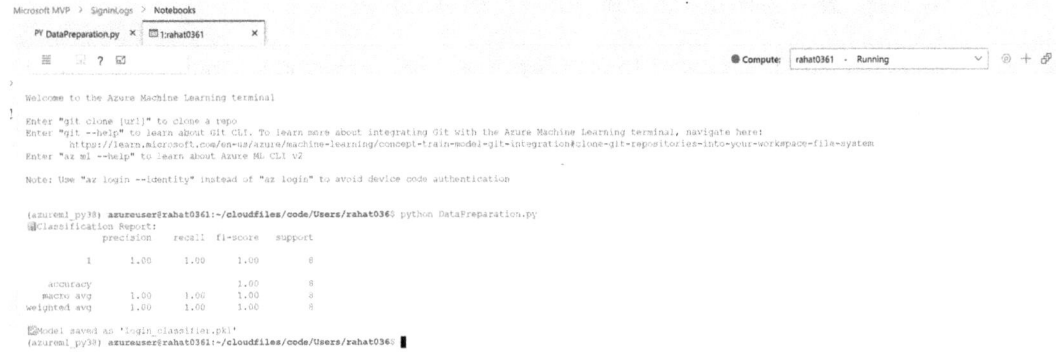

Figure 9-2. *Output of the Python code*

6. Now, create a new Python code file named score.py and add the following code:

```
import joblib
import json
```

418

CHAPTER 9   AI AND MACHINE LEARNING IN CLOUD SECURITY

```
import numpy as np
import os

def init():
    global model
    model_path = os.path.join(os.getenv('AZUREML_MODEL_DIR'),
    'login_classifier.pkl')
    model = joblib.load(model_path)

def run(raw_data):
    try:
        data = json.loads(raw_data)
        features = np.array(data['features']).reshape(1, -1)
        prediction = model.predict(features)
        return {"prediction": int(prediction[0])}
    except Exception as e:
        return {"error": str(e)}
```

Figure 9-3 shows the code in score.py file.

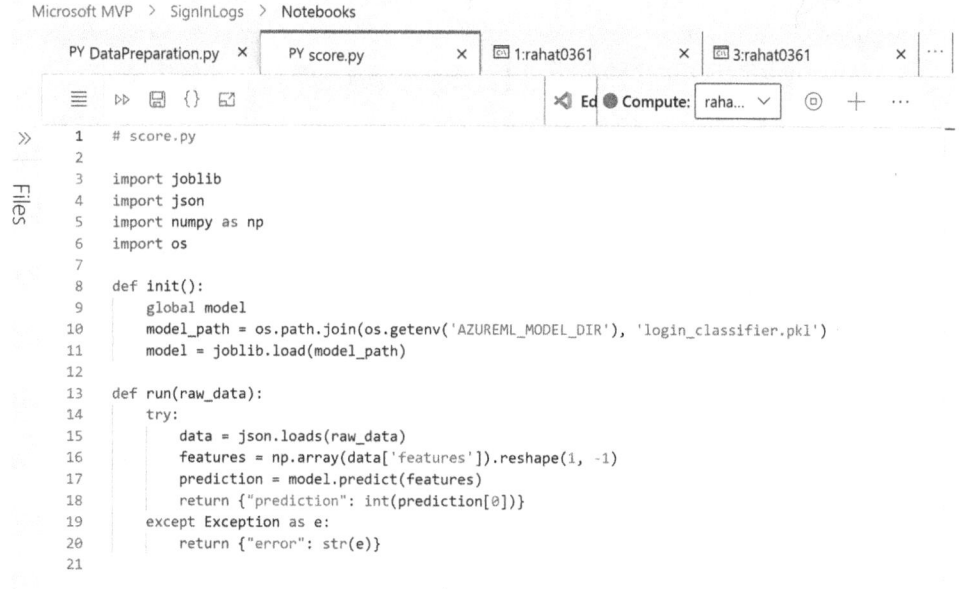

Figure 9-3. Python code added in scopre.py file

419

CHAPTER 9   AI AND MACHINE LEARNING IN CLOUD SECURITY

7. After creating the scpre.py file and adding the code there, add the following code in the DataPreparation.py:

```python
from azureml.core import Workspace, Model, Environment
from azureml.core.model import InferenceConfig
from azureml.core.webservice import AciWebservice, Webservice
from azureml.exceptions import WebserviceException
import json
import requests

# Step 1: Connect to Azure ML workspace
print("Connecting to Azure ML Workspace...")
ws = Workspace.from_config()
print(f"Connected to workspace: {ws.name} in region: {ws.location}")

# Step 2: Define web service name
service_name = "loginclassifierv2"
# Must be lowercase, alphanumeric or dashes, 3-32 chars

# Step 3: Try deleting existing webservice (if any)
try:
    print(f"Checking for existing service '{service_name}'...")
    old_service = Webservice(workspace=ws, name=service_name)
    old_service.delete()
    print(f" Old service '{service_name}' deleted successfully.")
except WebserviceException:
    print(f" No existing service named '{service_name}' to delete.")

# Step 4: Register the trained model (skip if already registered)
print(" Registering model...")
model = Model.register(
    workspace=ws,
    model_path="login_classifier.pkl",  # Update path if needed
    model_name="LoginClassifier"
)
```

```python
# Step 5: Create inference environment
print(" Creating inference environment...")
env = Environment(name="sklearn-env")
env.python.conda_dependencies.add_pip_package("scikit-learn")
env.python.conda_dependencies.add_pip_package("numpy")
env.python.conda_dependencies.add_pip_package("joblib")

# Step 6: Create inference config using score.py
print(" Creating inference config...")
inference_config = InferenceConfig(entry_script="score.py",
environment=env)

# Step 7: Configure deployment (ACI)
print(" Configuring ACI deployment...")
deployment_config = AciWebservice.deploy_configuration(
    cpu_cores=1,
    memory_gb=1,
    auth_enabled=True
)

# Step 8: Deploy model as web service
print(f" Deploying model as '{service_name}'...")
service = Model.deploy(
    workspace=ws,
    name=service_name,
    models=[model],
    inference_config=inference_config,
    deployment_config=deployment_config
)

# Step 9: Wait for deployment to complete
service.wait_for_deployment(show_output=True)

# Step 10: Display endpoint details
print(" Deployment Complete!")
print(" Endpoint URI:", service.scoring_uri)
print(" Auth Enabled:", service.auth_enabled)
```

```python
# Step 11: Get the authentication key
token = service.get_keys()[0]

# Step 12: Send a test request to the model
headers = {
    "Content-Type": "application/json",
    "Authorization": f"Bearer {token}"
}

from sklearn.impute import SimpleImputer
from sklearn.pipeline import Pipeline
from sklearn.ensemble import RandomForestClassifier

pipeline = Pipeline([
    ('imputer', SimpleImputer(strategy='mean')),
    # or 'most_frequent'
    ('model', RandomForestClassifier(n_estimators=100,
    random_state=42))
])

pipeline.fit(X_train, y_train)

# Replace with a real input vector matching your model's feature
size and order
data = {
    "features": [1.0, 50074.0, 0.0, 0.0, 4.0, 0.0, 0.0, 0.0,
                 206.0, 0.0,
                 0.0, 0.0, 0.0, 0.0, 0.0, 0.0, 0.0, 0.0, 0.0, 0.0,
                 0.0, 0.0, 0.0, 0.0, 0.0, 0.0, 1.0, 0.0, 0.0]
}

response = requests.post(
    url=service.scoring_uri,
    headers=headers,
    data=json.dumps(data)
)

print("💬 Prediction Response:", response.json())
```

CHAPTER 9   AI AND MACHINE LEARNING IN CLOUD SECURITY

Figure 9-4 shows the code in DataPreparation.py file.

```
Microsoft MVP > SignInLogs > Notebooks
 PY *DataPreparation.py      PY score.py      1:rahat0361
                                        Edit in VS Code    Compute:  rahat0361  -  Running

45   from azureml.core import Workspace, Model, Environment
46   from azureml.core.model import InferenceConfig
47   from azureml.core.webservice import AciWebservice, Webservice
48   from azureml.exceptions import WebserviceException
49   import json
50   import requests
51
52   # Step 1: Connect to Azure ML workspace
53   print("Connecting to Azure ML Workspace...")
54   ws = Workspace.from_config()
55   print(f"Connected to workspace: {ws.name} in region: {ws.location}")
56
57   # Step 2: Define web service name
58   service_name = "loginclassifierv2"  # Must be lowercase, alphanumeric or dashes, 3-32 chars
59
60   # Step 3: Try deleting existing webservice (if any)
61   try:
62       print(f"Checking for existing service '{service_name}'...")
63       old_service = Webservice(workspace=ws, name=service_name)
64       old_service.delete()
65       print(f" Old service '{service_name}' deleted successfully.")
66   except WebserviceException:
67       print(f"ℹ No existing service named '{service_name}' to delete.")
68
69   # Step 4: Register the trained model (skip if already registered)
70   print(" Registering model...")
71   model = Model.register(
72       workspace=ws,
73       model_path="login_classifier.pkl",  # Update path if needed
74       model_name="LoginClassifier"
75   )
76
77   # Step 5: Create inference environment
78   print(" Creating inference environment...")
79   env = Environment(name="sklearn-env")
```

Figure 9-4. *Python code added in DataPreparation.py file*

8. If you run the final code, you will get the response. If you get prediction: 1, then the model detected the login behavior as suspicious. For prediction: 0, the model considered the login is non-suspicious (normal). Figure 9-5 shows the preview of the code of our demo.

Figure 9-5. Successful output of the final code

Creating Custom Models with Historical Incident Labels (True/False Positive)

Security teams often struggle to distinguish meaningful alerts from false positives in massive log streams. Custom machine learning models trained on **historical incident triage labels**—such as "true positive" or "false positive"—can dramatically improve this process.

Instead of relying solely on fixed rule engines, you can **teach a model to learn your SOC's decision patterns**, using labeled security alerts as training data.

Let's say your SOC analysts manually close incidents with comments like

- **True Positive:** Confirmed malicious
- **False Positive:** Benign anomaly, user error, and misconfiguration

These triage outcomes can be extracted from Microsoft Sentinel's incident comments or tags or used to train a supervised ML model to **predict whether a new alert is worth escalating**.

Let's have a quick demo of training a Classifier using past alert labels.

1. We will simulate this with sample data. You can later replace it with your own Sentinel exports. Table 9-2 shows a sample incident .csv file.

Table 9-2. Sample incident.csv file

Alert Name	Entity Count	TTP Match	Source IP Risk	Duration	Label
Unusual login	3	1	0.8	10	TruePositive
Mass file delete	5	1	0.4	3	FalsePositive
Impossible travel	2	0	0.6	8	TruePositive
Password spray	6	1	0.9	12	TruePositive
New admin role	1	1	0.7	6	TruePositive
Unusual login	2	0	0.5	4	TruePositive
Unknown process	4	1	0.3	7	TruePositive
High data egress	5	1	0.9	5	TruePositive
Malware alert	3	1	0.7	9	TruePositive
Brute force	7	1	0.6	2	TruePositive
Unusual login	3	0	0.6	6	FalsePositive

2. Go to the Azure ML Studio (https://ml.azure.com/), create new workspace, and load the .csv file.

3. In the data section, upload the .csv file.

CHAPTER 9   AI AND MACHINE LEARNING IN CLOUD SECURITY

4. In the Notebook section, create a new Python file named incident. py, and add the following code there:

```python
import pandas as pd
from sklearn.ensemble import RandomForestClassifier
from sklearn.model_selection import train_test_split
from sklearn.metrics import classification_report
import joblib

# Load labeled incident dataset
df = pd.read_csv("azureml://subscriptions/
c16c7de6-926d-494f-90ca-4caa6e8a9045/resourcegroups/rahat036-
rg/workspaces/SignInLogs/datastores/workspaceblobstore/paths/
UI/2025-05-31_202651_UTC/incident.csv")
# Replace with your actual path

# Encode the label column (target)
df['Label'] = df['Label'].map({'TruePositive': 1,
'FalsePositive': 0})

# Convert categorical columns (e.g., AlertName) to dummy variables
df = pd.get_dummies(df)

# Separate features and target
X = df.drop('Label', axis=1)
y = df['Label']

# Train/test split
X_train, X_test, y_train, y_test = train_test_split(
    X, y, test_size=0.3, stratify=y, random_state=42
)

# Train the model
model = RandomForestClassifier(n_estimators=100, random_state=42)
model.fit(X_train, y_train)

# Evaluate performance
y_pred = model.predict(X_test)
print(classification_report(y_test, y_pred))
```

```
# Save model and columns
joblib.dump(model, 'incident_triage_model.pkl')
joblib.dump(X.columns.tolist(), 'incident_feature_columns.pkl')

print("Model and feature columns saved.")
```

Figure 9-6 shows the code of incident.py.

```
import pandas as pd
from sklearn.ensemble import RandomForestClassifier
from sklearn.model_selection import train_test_split
from sklearn.metrics import classification_report
import joblib

# Load labeled incident dataset
df = pd.read_csv("azureml://subscriptions/c16c7de6-926d-494f-90ca-4caa6e8a9045/resourcegroups/rahat036-rg/workspaces/SignInLogs/datastores/workspaceblobstore/paths/UI/2025-05-31_202651_UTC/incident.csv")  # Replace with your actual path

# Encode the label column (target)
df['Label'] = df['Label'].map({'TruePositive': 1, 'FalsePositive': 0})

# Convert categorical columns (e.g., AlertName) to dummy variables
df = pd.get_dummies(df)

# Separate features and target
X = df.drop('Label', axis=1)
y = df['Label']

# Train/test split
X_train, X_test, y_train, y_test = train_test_split(
    X, y, test_size=0.3, stratify=y, random_state=42
)

# Train the model
model = RandomForestClassifier(n_estimators=100, random_state=42)
model.fit(X_train, y_train)

# Evaluate performance
y_pred = model.predict(X_test)
print(classification_report(y_test, y_pred))

# Save model and columns
joblib.dump(model, 'incident_triage_model.pkl')
joblib.dump(X.columns.tolist(), 'incident_feature_columns.pkl')
print("Model and feature columns saved.")
```

Figure 9-6. *Python code in incident.py file*

5. Create another Python code file named score.py and add the following code:

```
probs = model.predict_proba(input_df)
return {
    "prediction": int(prediction[0]),
    "confidence": float(probs[0][1])
# likelihood of true positive
}
```

Figure 9-7 shows the code of score.py.

CHAPTER 9 AI AND MACHINE LEARNING IN CLOUD SECURITY

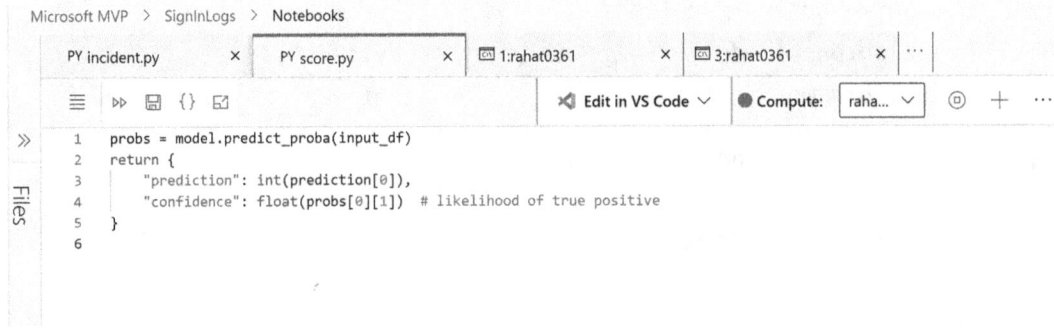

Figure 9-7. Python code of scope.py file

6. Run the script, and you will get the result as shown in Figure 9-8.

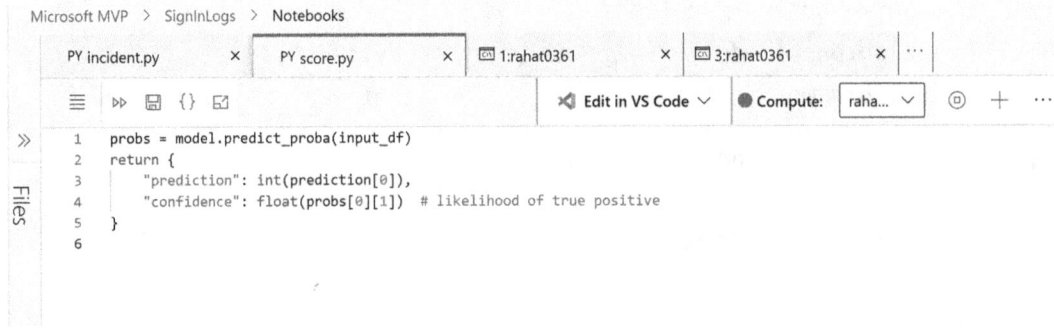

Figure 9-8. Outcome of the final script

You can see now the model is successfully trained, evaluated correctly, and saved the necessary files for deployment. You can see in the demo that

- **Accuracy: 0.50**—the model got three out of six correct in the test set.

- Not great performance yet, but totally fine for a **demo/PoC** model.

- It will improve once you add more historical data over time.

CHAPTER 9   AI AND MACHINE LEARNING IN CLOUD SECURITY

Automating Security Responses

As threats become faster and more sophisticated, traditional manual response processes can no longer keep up with the pace of modern attacks. Automating incident response workflows not only reduces mean time to respond (MTTR) but also improves consistency and scalability in cloud security operations. By integrating machine learning models into Azure Logic Apps or Microsoft Sentinel playbooks, organizations can move beyond static thresholds and adopt AI-driven decision logic that adapts to real-world context. Instead of triggering remediation based on simple conditions, security teams can now configure workflows to act only when a model predicts high-risk behaviors—for example, isolating a device if the ML-predicted threat probability exceeds 75%. This convergence of intelligent detection and automated response marks a shift from reactive to proactive, precision-guided defense, built on live telemetry and model-informed confidence.

AI-Driven Decision Logic in Playbooks: Confidence-Based Branching in Logic Apps

Traditional playbooks in Microsoft Sentinel or Azure Logic Apps often rely on fixed triggers such as "**if alert severity is high**" or "**if risk level is elevated**." While useful, these rule-based conditions lack nuance and can result in over-triggering or under-responding. With the integration of machine learning, however, you can design **adaptive workflows** that react based on dynamic confidence scores from predictive models.

Let's say your trained ML model returns a classification result along with a **probability score**. This probability can now be parsed by a Logic App or Sentinel playbook and used to make branching decisions.

1. We will continue with the demo which we did "Creating custom models with historical incident labels (true/false positive)".

2. Create a new folder named "incident_model_bundle" and move the incident_feature_columns.pkl and incident_triage_model.pkl files in the folder.

3. Now, we will create a total of four Python code files named train_model.py, score.py, deploy_model.py, and predict_incident.py.

CHAPTER 9 AI AND MACHINE LEARNING IN CLOUD SECURITY

4. In the train_model.py file, add the following code:

```python
# train_model.py
import pandas as pd
from sklearn.ensemble import RandomForestClassifier
import joblib

# Minimal sample dataset
data = pd.DataFrame({
    'feature1': [0, 1, 1, 0],
    'feature2': [1, 0, 1, 0],
    'label': [1, 0, 1, 0]
})

X = data[['feature1', 'feature2']]
y = data['label']

model = RandomForestClassifier()
model.fit(X, y)

# Save model
joblib.dump(model, 'incident_model.pkl')
print("Model saved as incident_model.pkl")
```

Figure 9-9 shows the train_model.py code file.

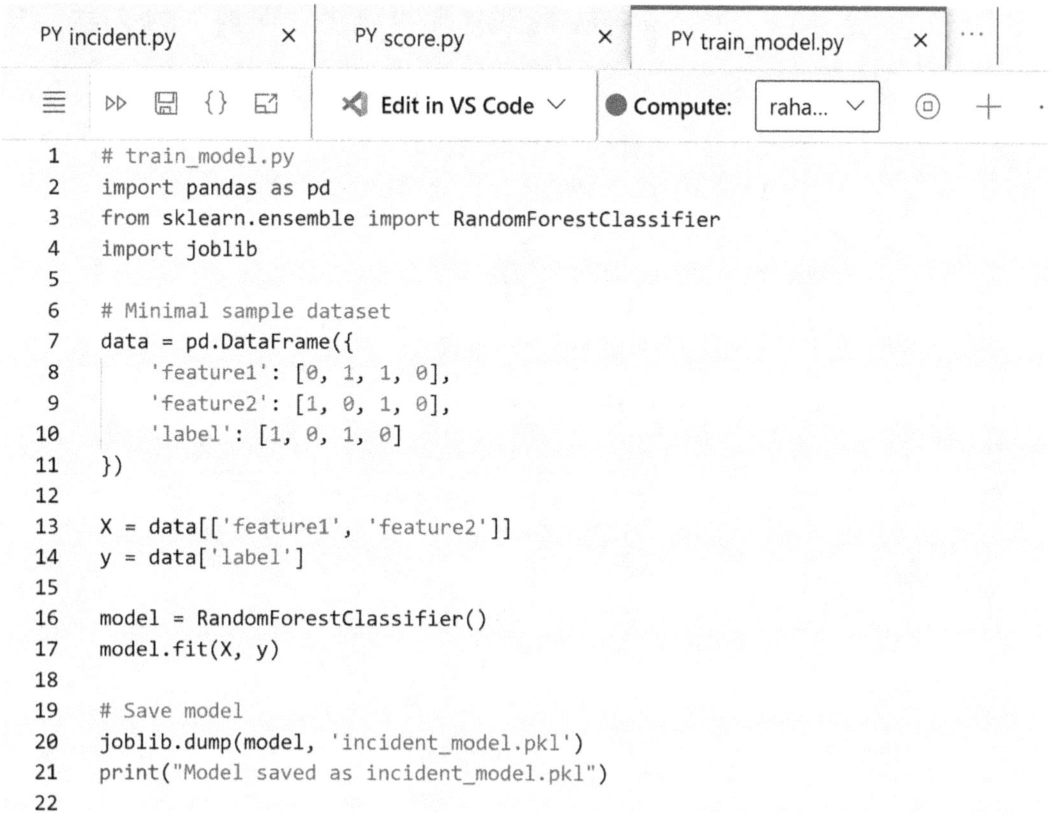

CHAPTER 9   AI AND MACHINE LEARNING IN CLOUD SECURITY

```
1   # train_model.py
2   import pandas as pd
3   from sklearn.ensemble import RandomForestClassifier
4   import joblib
5
6   # Minimal sample dataset
7   data = pd.DataFrame({
8       'feature1': [0, 1, 1, 0],
9       'feature2': [1, 0, 1, 0],
10      'label': [1, 0, 1, 0]
11  })
12
13  X = data[['feature1', 'feature2']]
14  y = data['label']
15
16  model = RandomForestClassifier()
17  model.fit(X, y)
18
19  # Save model
20  joblib.dump(model, 'incident_model.pkl')
21  print("Model saved as incident_model.pkl")
22
```

Figure 9-9. Python code of train_model.py code file

5. Add the following code in score.py file:

```
import json
import joblib
import numpy as np
import os

def init():
    global model
    model_path = os.path.join(os.getenv("AZUREML_MODEL_DIR"), "incident_model.pkl")
    model = joblib.load(model_path)

def run(raw_data):
    try:
```

```
            data = json.loads(raw_data)["data"]  # Should be list
of lists
            data_np = np.array(data)   # Ensure it's a 2D NumPy array
            prediction = model.predict(data_np)
            return {"prediction": int(prediction[0])}
        except Exception as e:
            return {"error": str(e)}
```

Figure 9-10 shows the code file of score.py.

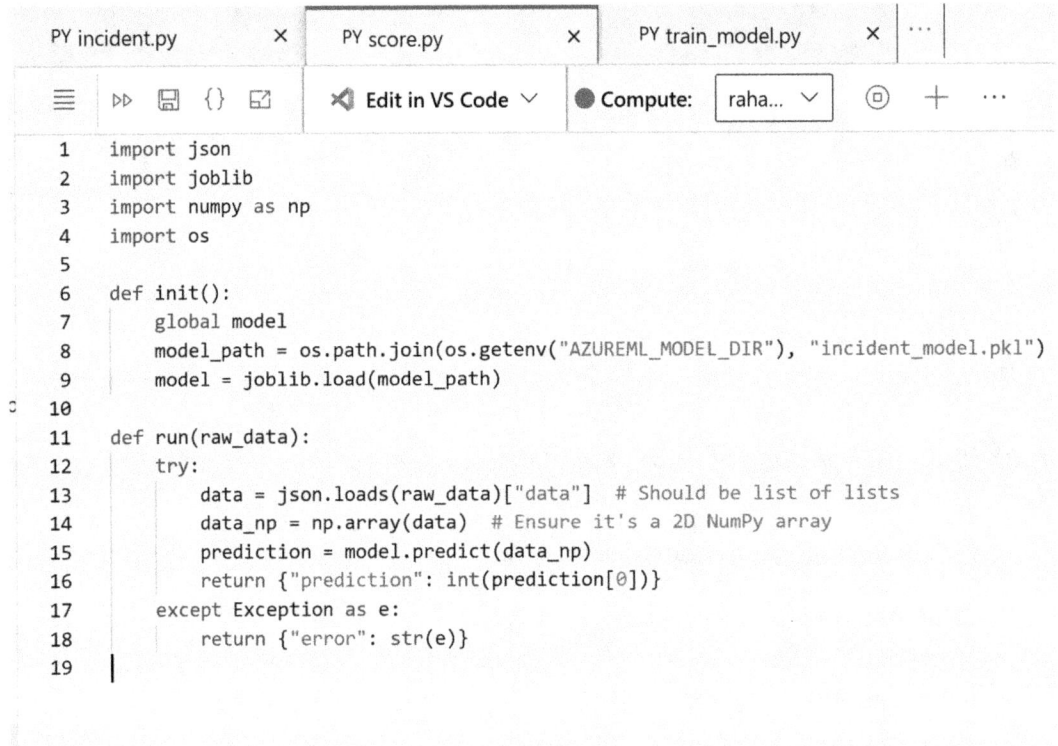

Figure 9-10. Python code of score.py code file

6. In the deploy_mode.py file, add the following code:

```
# deploy_model.py
from azureml.core import Workspace, Model, Environment
from azureml.core.model import InferenceConfig
from azureml.core.webservice import AciWebservice
```

```python
ws = Workspace.from_config()

# Register model
model = Model.register(
    workspace=ws,
    model_path="incident_model.pkl",
    model_name="IncidentModel"
)

# Define environment
env = Environment(name="incident-env")
env.python.conda_dependencies.add_pip_package("scikit-learn")
env.python.conda_dependencies.add_pip_package("joblib")

# Define inference config
inference_config = InferenceConfig(entry_script="score.py", environment=env)

# Deployment config
deployment_config = AciWebservice.deploy_configuration(cpu_cores=1, memory_gb=1)

# Deploy
service = Model.deploy(
    workspace=ws,
    name="incident-triage-apiv2",
    models=[model],
    inference_config=inference_config,
    deployment_config=deployment_config
)

service.wait_for_deployment(show_output=True)
print("Endpoint:", service.scoring_uri)

from azureml.core import Workspace
from azureml.core.webservice import Webservice

# Connect to your Azure ML workspace
ws = Workspace.from_config()
```

CHAPTER 9   AI AND MACHINE LEARNING IN CLOUD SECURITY

```
# Load your deployed service by name
service = Webservice(name="incident-triage-api", workspace=ws)

# Get the authentication keys
keys = service.get_keys()

# The primary key is:
api_key = keys[0]

print("API Key:", api_key)
```

Figure 9-11 shows the code file of deploy_model.py.

Figure 9-11. *Screenshot of the deploy_model.py code file*

7. Now run the deploy_model.py file, and you will get the Endpoint URL and API key as shown in Figure 9-12.

CHAPTER 9   AI AND MACHINE LEARNING IN CLOUD SECURITY

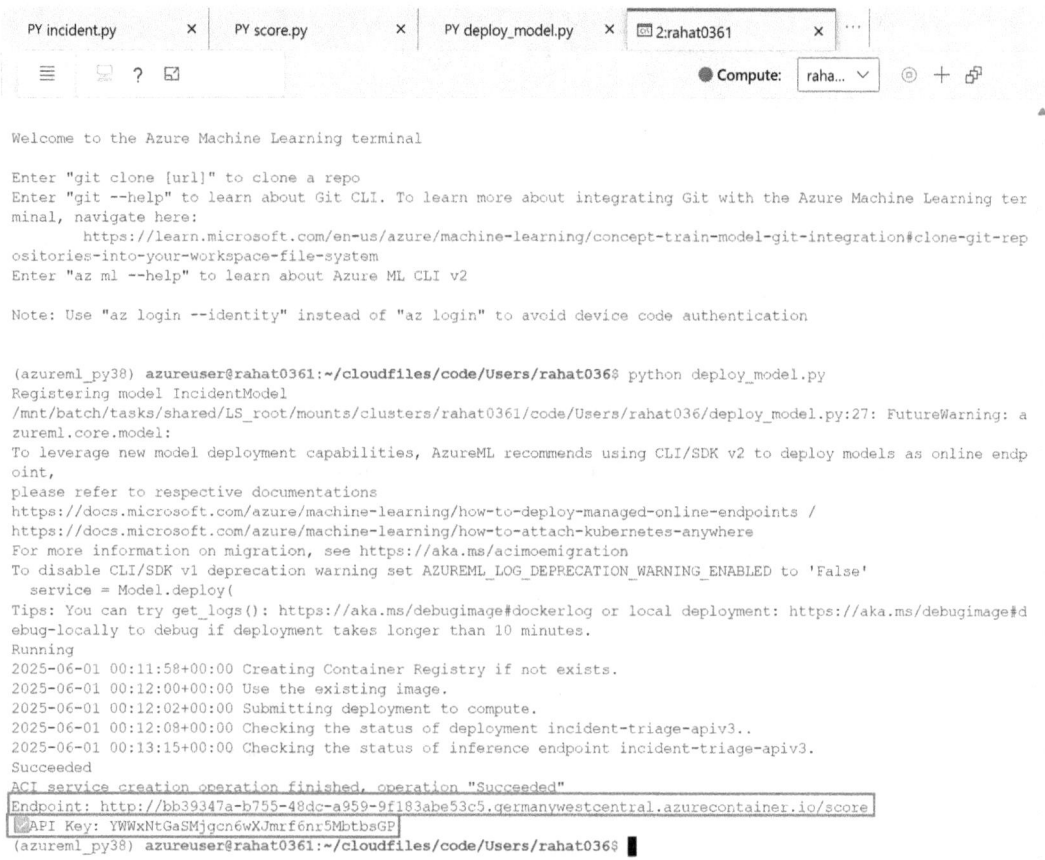

Figure 9-12. *Getting the Endpoint URL and API key*

8. Copy the Endpoint URI and API key, and store it in a secure place.

9. Open the predict_incident.py file and paste the following code:

```
import requests
import json

# Replace with your actual scoring URI and API key
# Replace with your actual deployed service URL
url = "<PASTE YOUR ENDPOINT URL>"

# Replace with your actual API key
api_key = "PASTE YOUR API KEY"
```

```python
    headers = {
        "Content-Type": "application/json",
        "Authorization": f"Bearer {api_key}"
    }

    # Replace with your actual 29 input features
    data = {
        "data": [
            0.1, 1.0
        ]
    }
    response = requests.post(url, headers=headers, data=json.dumps(data))
    print("Prediction Response:", response.json())
```

Figure 9-13 shows the code in predict_incident.py file.

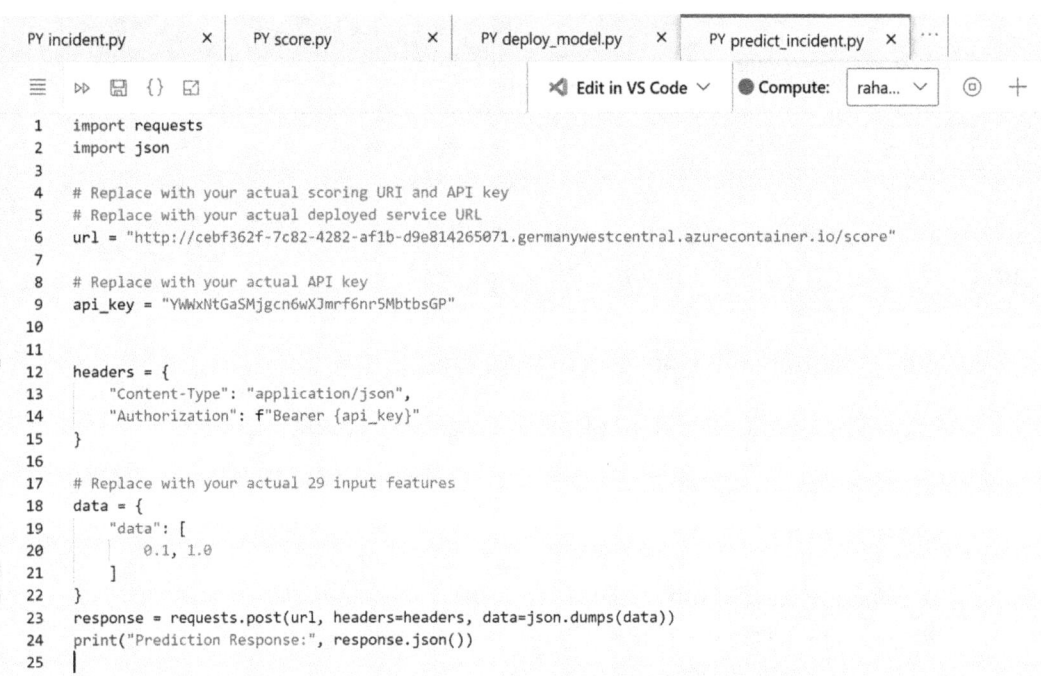

Figure 9-13. *Python code in predict_incident.py file*

CHAPTER 9   AI AND MACHINE LEARNING IN CLOUD SECURITY

10. Run the code and you will get the result as shown in Figure 9-14.

Figure 9-14. *Prediction result after running the final code*

11. If you get response 1, then the model thinks it's a threat or suspicious. And if you get 0, then the model thinks it's safe. In our demo, it's showing 1, so the model thinks it's suspicious.

Using Enrichment Data to Escalate, Isolate, or Log

In modern security operations, automation alone is not enough—actions must be context-aware. This is where **AI-enriched telemetry** such as **predicted severity scores**, **user risk levels**, or **attack paths** become critical in deciding whether to **escalate**, **isolate**, or **log** a security event.

What Is Enrichment?

Enrichment is the process of enhancing raw telemetry—such as alerts, logs, or security events—with meaningful, context-rich data that improves understanding and response. Instead of acting on isolated events, security systems incorporate *AI-generated metadata* to derive insight and prioritize response.

Common enrichment attributes include

- **ML-predicted threat severity** (e.g., Low, Medium, High)

- **User risk score** (e.g., derived from Identity Protection or behavioral analytics)

- **Predicted attack impact** (based on historical data or simulated outcomes)
- **Lateral movement paths or privilege escalation potential**

These enrichments transform basic security signals into **actionable intelligence**. They provide context that is essential for effective, scalable, and targeted automation in a modern Security Operations Center (SOC).

Applying AI-Powered Enrichment in Automated Security Workflows

Modern security operations go beyond simple alerting—they leverage AI-enriched context to drive **precise and adaptive responses**. Enrichment empowers automation systems to make smarter decisions based on dynamic indicators such as risk scores, threat probability, and behavioral anomalies. Below are the three most common strategies organizations implement based on enrichment insights.

Escalation to the Security Operations Center (SOC)

If the enriched metadata reveals a **high-severity threat** or flags a **user account with elevated risk**, the situation warrants human oversight. Instead of relying solely on automation, critical incidents must be surfaced to the SOC for expert analysis and response.

For example, this is the sample conditional logic:

```
IF predicted_severity == "High" OR user_risk_score == "High"
THEN escalate to SOC
```

This logic ensures that any incident flagged by the AI as *severe*, or involving a user with elevated risk, is brought to the attention of the SOC for immediate handling.

Once triggered, the response workflow initiates a series of automated actions to immediately notify and engage the Security Operations Center (SOC) team. First, a new incident is created in Microsoft Sentinel, enriched with AI-generated metadata such as predicted severity, user behavior analytics, and asset risk scores—allowing analysts to quickly assess and prioritize the threat. Simultaneously, a real-time notification is dispatched to the designated SOC Microsoft Teams channel using adaptive cards or structured messages, ensuring that the right personnel are alerted without delay.

Additionally, a formal case is logged in ServiceNow (or another ITSM platform), providing a centralized ticket that includes all relevant contexts to support thorough investigation and resolution tracking by the security team.

Isolation of Compromised Users or Devices

Isolation is a critical containment strategy that must be executed decisively when the system detects indicators of high-risk compromise. This step becomes essential when both of the following conditions are met: the AI model predicts a threat with a probability greater than 90%, and the affected user or endpoint is flagged as high risk. These dual indicators point to credible and urgent security incidents such as potential privilege escalation, malware propagation, or unauthorized data access—that must be halted to prevent further spread within the environment.

Here is an example of conditional logic:

```
IF threat_probability > 0.90 AND user_risk_score == "High"
THEN isolate endpoint or suspend user
```

This logic ensures that containment is triggered only when AI-driven assessments confirm a high-confidence threat and the user or asset is already operating in a risk-prone context.

By integrating these isolation responses, organizations can swiftly contain threats before they spread across the network. The automation playbook can trigger Microsoft Defender for Endpoint to isolate a compromised device, effectively severing its connection from the network while preserving admin control for remediation. Simultaneously, Microsoft Graph Security API can be leveraged to suspend the user's session, disable the Microsoft Entra ID account, or enforce multi-factor authentication, thereby neutralizing account-based risks. Additionally, Microsoft Entra ID Conditional Access policies can be dynamically modified to block further access from high-risk locations or devices, ensuring that the affected user or endpoint is fully contained. These coordinated actions help prevent lateral movement, privilege escalation, and data exfiltration in real time, forming a proactive defense layer powered by AI-enriched telemetry.

Logging and Monitoring Low-Risk Events

Logging and Monitoring Low-Risk Events is a vital part of a balanced, scalable security strategy. Not every anomaly or alert necessitates an immediate escalation or containment response. When AI-enriched telemetry determines that an event carries low severity—based on predicted threat level, user behavior, or contextual risk factors—the most appropriate action is to document the occurrence for future audit, trend analysis, or correlation with other signals. This ensures that security operations remain focused on high-impact threats without neglecting the long tail of low-risk data that may inform future attacks.

Once the condition `IF predicted_severity == "Low"` is met, the workflow can trigger a set of passives but meaningful logging actions. For instance, enriched events can be stored in **Azure Log Analytics** workspaces, where they contribute to ongoing threat intelligence and compliance tracking. For long-term retention and cost-effective storage, the data can be archived in **Azure Blob Storage**, ensuring it is available for digital forensics or retrospective analysis. Security analysts can later **query and visualize** this telemetry using **Kusto Query Language (KQL)** within **Microsoft Sentinel**, enabling the detection of recurring low-severity behaviors that might signal emerging threats.

Figure 9-15 shows how Microsoft integrates threat intelligence into its AI pipeline. By correlating alerts, incidents, and entity relationships, the system enhances the accuracy of ML predictions and prioritizes risk scoring.

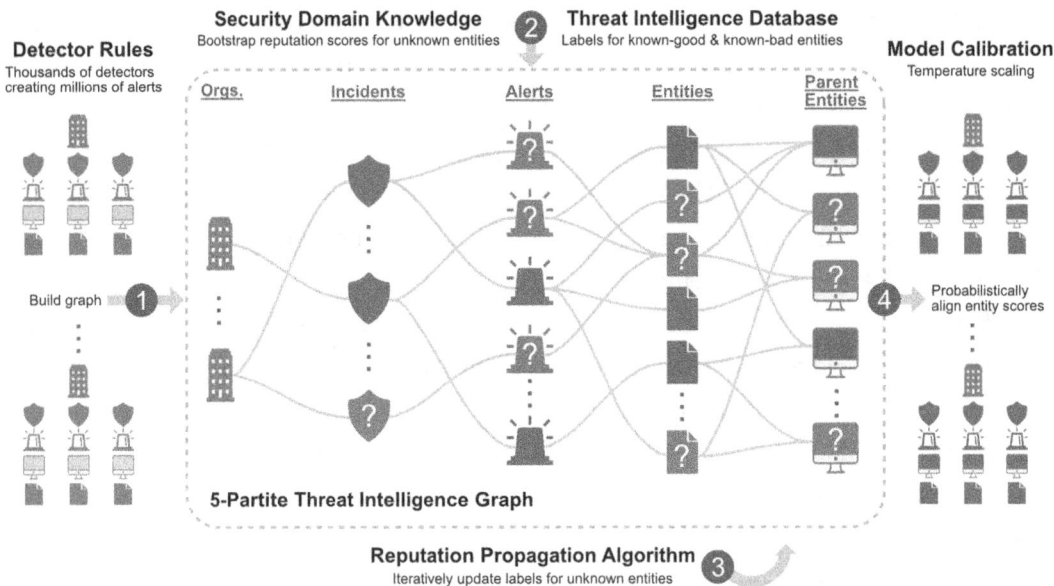

Figure 9-15. *Microsoft's threat intelligence engine uses a 5-partite graph model combining security rules, domain knowledge, and threat intel databases. Reputation scores are propagated across entities to probabilistically align alerts and assess severity using AI Models (Image: Microsoft).*

Predictive Analytics for Security

As security threats grow in speed and sophistication, reactive defense mechanisms are no longer sufficient. Modern security operations must shift from responding to incidents **after** they occur to anticipating them **before** they cause harm. This is the foundation of **predictive security**—an approach that leverages historical telemetry, behavioral trends, and machine learning models to forecast where future threats are most likely to occur. By combining tools like **Microsoft Sentinel** and **Azure Machine Learning** and enriched identity or device data from services such as **Entra ID Protection** or **Microsoft Defender**, security teams can build intelligent models that highlight high-risk users, devices, or workloads ahead of time. These predictive insights empower organizations to prioritize remediation, allocate SOC resources more effectively, and ultimately reduce the window of exposure—turning cybersecurity into a proactive, intelligence-driven discipline.

What Is Predictive Security?

Predictive security is an advanced cybersecurity approach that uses machine learning, behavioral analytics, and historical telemetry to **anticipate potential threats before they materialize**. Instead of relying solely on static rules or post-incident alerts, predictive security analyzes patterns—such as repeated login failures, privilege escalations, or abnormal access behaviors—to **forecast which users, devices, or assets are most likely to be compromised**.

By leveraging data from services like Microsoft Sentinel, Azure Machine Learning, Microsoft Defender, and Entra ID Protection, predictive models assign **risk scores** or **breach probabilities** to entities across the environment. These scores are not just reactive, they enable **forward-looking decisions**, allowing security teams to proactively isolate vulnerable assets, enhance monitoring, or implement conditional access policies before an actual breach occurs.

Predictive security shifts the operational mindset from *"respond when it happens"* to *"intervene before it does."* This helps reduce response times, prevent lateral movement, and significantly lower the attack surface in modern cloud and hybrid environments.

CHAPTER 9   AI AND MACHINE LEARNING IN CLOUD SECURITY

Predictive Security in Cybersecurity

Predictive analytics empowers security teams to shift from reactive to proactive defense strategies. By anticipating potential breaches, unusual user behavior, or targeted assets, organizations can prioritize risks before they escalate. This forward-looking approach enables faster incident prevention, reduces alert fatigue, and enhances resource allocation by focusing attention on the most probable threats. Rather than waiting for attacks to happen, predictive models guide decision-makers to act on signals that indicate what's likely to occur next—improving resilience and operational efficiency.

Forecasting Future Threats

Cybersecurity is increasingly shifting from reactive defense to proactive protection—and at the heart of this evolution lies forecasting. Forecasting future threats refers to the ability of security teams to anticipate and identify potential security incidents before they occur by analyzing behavioral trends and historical telemetry. Instead of only responding to alerts once an attack has begun, forecasting enables preemptive action based on probabilistic indicators.

Security telemetry—such as failed login attempts, lateral movement signals, privilege escalation, or anomalous authentication patterns—often contains subtle cues that precede a security breach. These cues may not individually trigger alerts, but when aggregated over time and analyzed using time-series or classification models, they can uncover emerging risks. For example, a sudden spike in login failures from a specific IP range or multiple access attempts outside business hours might point toward a brute-force attack or credential stuffing attempt in progress.

Using machine learning, especially time-series models like ARIMA or LSTM, or classification models like Random Forests, organizations can train systems on past incident data to recognize precursors to compromise. These models can predict

- Which users or devices are most likely to be targeted soon
- When a surge in specific attack vectors might occur (e.g., phishing, ransomware, brute-force login attempts)
- What attack paths may become viable due to current misconfigurations or behavioral changes

The ability to forecast such threats empowers defenders to act early. For instance, high-risk users can be prompted for multi-factor authentication (MFA), privileged accounts can be temporarily restricted, and vulnerable endpoints can be isolated or patched. This proactive strategy reduces the mean time to detect (MTTD) and mean time to respond (MTTR) while simultaneously lowering the organization's overall exposure.

In practice, predictive forecasting is implemented using Azure Machine Learning services for model training and Microsoft Sentinel for operational response. Forecast outputs can be integrated into Sentinel playbooks or dashboards to automatically escalate high-risk cases, enabling the security team to focus on potential threats rather than combing through logs post incident.

Forecasting transforms cybersecurity into a strategic function. It enables threat anticipation, smarter allocation of defensive resources, and a meaningful reduction in response latency—key elements in a resilient security posture.

Prioritizing Risks with AI Models

Security teams often struggle with alert fatiguing thousands of alerts flood their dashboards daily, but only a few represent genuine high-risk threats. Prioritizing which alerts to investigate first is critical to maintaining effective security operations. This is where AI-powered risk models provide strategic value: they allow teams to **focus their attention on the threats that matter most**.

What Is Risk Prioritization?

Risk prioritization with AI involves assigning a **probability-based risk score** to alerts or users, helping defenders sort and respond based on **potential impact** rather than just the order of arrival. These scores are typically enriched using contextual data, such as

- **User risk level** from Microsoft Entra ID Protection
- **Asset criticality** (e.g., domain controllers vs. kiosks)
- **Behavioral deviations** (e.g., rare time of access and abnormal volume)
- **Historical alert correlation** (e.g., has this alert been a precursor to previous breaches?)

Proactive Responses Based on Predictions

Proactive cybersecurity is no longer a visionary concept. It is now a practical necessity. As threats become faster and more elusive, security teams must shift from reactive defense toward predictive action. This is where machine learning plays a pivotal role: enabling organizations to forecast potential breaches based on behavioral patterns, enrichment data, and probabilistic threat modeling. The objective is simple yet powerful act **before the attacker does**.

Instead of waiting for an incident to escalate, predictive models help identify high-risk users, devices, or behaviors in real time. These models analyze telemetry—such as failed logins, login anomalies, lateral movement signals, or token misuse—and assign a **breach probability score** or **risk tier** to each observed entity. When these scores exceed defined thresholds, automated workflows can be triggered to mitigate the risk, notify analysts, or initiate access control actions—all without waiting for a confirmed breach.

When a predictive model determines that a user or device exhibits suspicious behavior—say, an 89% likelihood of credential compromise—this insight can serve as the basis for automation, for example,

- **If** the model predicts `risk_score > 0.75`
- **Then** initiate a sequence of automated actions before damage occurs

When predictive logic identifies a potential security threat, it initiates a series of automated responses designed to minimize risk and accelerate remediation. First, an incident is automatically created in Microsoft Sentinel, enriched with contextual metadata such as the predicted severity score, user behavior anomalies, geographic indicators, and device sensitivity. This context helps security analysts prioritize the alert and understand its potential impact at a glance. Simultaneously, access control policies in Azure Active Directory can be dynamically adjusted. For instance, if the model predicts a high likelihood of compromise, it may trigger the enforcement of stricter Conditional Access rules—blocking access, requiring multi-factor authentication (MFA), or even suspending the user session via the Microsoft Graph API.

To ensure rapid human oversight, the system also pushes real-time notifications to the Security Operations Center (SOC) using Microsoft Teams. These messages are delivered as adaptive cards, enabling SOC analysts to view key incident details and act without switching platforms. Additionally, integration with IT service management (ITSM) platforms like ServiceNow or Jira allows for automated ticket creation. These tickets contain predictive insights and recommended response steps, facilitating a seamless handoff to response teams and maintaining a clear audit trail. Together, these automated interventions enable organizations to respond proactively, reducing time to containment and elevating their overall security posture.

This predictive approach drastically improves **mean time to respond (MTTR)**, reduces false positives, and allows SOC analysts to focus on events that matter most. By intervening before exploitation, organizations can **contain threats early**, reduce lateral movement opportunities, and maintain operational continuity even during high-risk situations.

Real-World Applications and Case Studies

While predictive security concepts are powerful in theory, their true value is best demonstrated through practical implementation. This section explores how organizations across industries are applying AI and machine learning models to address real-world cybersecurity challenges. From reducing alert fatigue in large enterprises to detecting cross-cloud threats, these use cases highlight the operational impact of predictive analytics. By leveraging enrichment data, supervised learning, and historical patterns, security teams are not only reacting to incidents faster—but also forecasting and preventing them more intelligently. Each case study below illustrates a distinct scenario where machine learning enhances detection accuracy, improves triage, and drives automation across the security lifecycle.

Enterprise Use Case: Reducing Alert Fatigue Using Supervised ML to Rank Alerts

In large enterprise environments, security operations centers (SOCs) are often overwhelmed by thousands of alerts generated daily by SIEM and XDR systems. Many of these alerts are redundant, low priority, or false positives. Analysts must manually sift through noise to identify truly actionable threats—resulting in fatigue, slower response times, and, in some cases, missed critical incidents.

To address this, one enterprise implemented a supervised machine learning model designed specifically to rank alerts by their likelihood of being true security incidents. The team first labeled historical alerts based on previous analyst investigations—indicating which ones led to confirmed breaches and which did not. Features such as anomaly type, user risk score, alert source, and asset sensitivity were extracted and fed into a classification model (e.g., Random Forest or XGBoost).

Once trained, the model was integrated with Microsoft Sentinel as a scoring layer. When new alerts arrived, the model assigned a predicted incident probability between 0 and 1. Alerts with high scores (e.g., > 0.8) were automatically escalated for immediate review, while lower-scoring alerts were either logged for context or deprioritized.

This intelligent ranking mechanism significantly reduced the noise-to-signal ratio and improved analyst focus. Instead of treating all alerts equally, the SOC could triage based on actual risk. Over time, the feedback loop—where analyst decisions fed back into model training—further improved prediction accuracy. This enterprise case demonstrates how even basic supervised learning, when applied strategically, can transform alert management and enhance overall SOC efficiency.

Cross-Cloud Risk Detection: Azure ML Model Consuming AWS IAM and Microsoft Entra ID Login Anomalies

As enterprises increasingly operate in hybrid or multi-cloud environments, detecting cross-cloud identity threats has become a growing challenge. Traditional security tools often operate in silos—AWS CloudTrail and IAM logs are analyzed separately from Microsoft Entra ID sign-in events—leading to fragmented threat visibility and missed correlations. To overcome this, one organization developed a custom Azure Machine learning model capable of ingesting login anomalies from both AWS IAM and Azure Active Directory to detect potential credential misuse across cloud boundaries.

The solution involved building a unified telemetry pipeline using Azure Data Factory and AWS Lambda functions. These services extracted login events, including failed and anomalous sign-ins, from AWS CloudTrail and Microsoft Entra ID sign-in logs, respectively. Key metadata such as source IP, user agent, login time, geolocation, and identity type (human vs. service principal) were standardized and pushed into a centralized Azure Data Lake.

A time-series enriched dataset was then constructed, allowing the organization to model not only individual anomalies but also cross-cloud patterns—such as the same user failing to authenticate in Azure and then attempting access in AWS minutes later from a new location. The machine learning model—based on a multi-class classification algorithm—learned to identify these cross-environment threat indicators and assign a unified risk score.

The model was deployed as a real-time scoring endpoint in Azure. Sentinel playbooks were configured to trigger when specific cross-cloud patterns were detected, allowing analysts to intervene early in potentially orchestrated account compromise scenarios.

By bridging visibility gaps between Azure and AWS, the organization dramatically improved its detection of federated identity attacks, credential reuse, and lateral movement attempts across cloud providers. This case study demonstrates the power of AI in modern, cloud-native threat detection that transcends traditional platform boundaries.

Financial Sector: Predicting Fraudulent Resource Creation Using Correlation Graphs

In the highly regulated and risk-sensitive financial sector, cybercriminals often attempt to exploit cloud services for fraudulent activities, such as spinning up virtual machines for cryptomining or deploying storage resources for data exfiltration. A leading financial institution tackled this threat by building a graph-based AI model in Azure Machine Learning that could predict fraudulent resource creation before damage occurred.

Rather than relying solely on individual anomalies (e.g., a sudden burst of VM creation), the organization focused on correlations between entities: users, subscriptions, IP addresses, resource types, and time of day. They transformed raw Azure Activity Logs and Resource Graph queries into a rich knowledge graph, where nodes represented identities, assets, and operations, and edges captured interactions between them.

This graph was then fed into an Azure ML pipeline where GraphSAGE (a graph neural network technique) was used to train on known historical fraud incidents. The model learned to identify subtle relational patterns—such as an external IP previously associated with dormant accounts, or users who rarely created storage suddenly provisioning multiple resources in a short burst. These relationships were weighted and analyzed contextually rather than in isolation.

The model's predictions were then exposed through a REST API endpoint. A custom Logic App in Sentinel regularly queried recent resource creation events, enriched them with graph-based risk scores, and triggered preemptive actions. For instance, if a newly created VM scored high on the fraud probability scale, it was immediately quarantined, and an alert was sent to the Security Operations Center.

This approach reduced false positives by over 60%, significantly improved incident response time, and ensured regulatory compliance through proactive, intelligence-driven monitoring. The case exemplifies how financial organizations can harness the power of graph machine learning and Azure cloud telemetry to stay ahead of sophisticated fraud vectors in real time.

Summary

In this chapter, we focused on how Artificial Intelligence (AI) and Machine Learning (ML) are transforming cloud security from reactive defense to proactive protection. We looked at how Microsoft integrates AI-driven detection and behavioral analytics into Defender for Cloud, Microsoft Sentinel, and Entra ID to enhance threat detection, minimize false positives, and surface previously undetected attack patterns. The chapter also introduced the use of Azure Machine Learning to build custom models for predicting security events, classifying anomalies, and automating incident response. These intelligent capabilities help security teams stay ahead of evolving threats by continuously learning from data and adapting to new attack vectors.

In Chapter 10, the focus shifts to building a resilient and secure cloud architecture based on the principles of Zero Trust. You'll learn how to apply a "never trust, always verify" approach across identities, devices, applications, and networks. Using Azure-native tools such as Conditional Access, Private Endpoints, Microsoft Defender for Identity, and Privileged Identity Management (PIM), we will walk through practical strategies for enforcing least-privileged access, validating trust dynamically, and protecting assets in hybrid and multi-cloud environments.

CHAPTER 10

Implementing Zero Trust Architecture in Azure

In Chapter 9, we explored how Artificial Intelligence and Machine Learning are reshaping cloud security by enabling predictive insights, dynamic risk scoring, and automated responses. We saw how Microsoft's security tools—such as Defender for Cloud, Sentinel, and Entra ID—leverage AI to detect threats more accurately and respond faster to emerging attack patterns. This shift toward intelligent, data-driven defense empowers organizations to stay ahead of sophisticated adversaries.

Building on that momentum, this chapter introduces the Zero Trust security model, a foundational approach for securing cloud-native, hybrid, and remote-first environments. Instead of assuming trust within a perimeter, Zero Trust enforces continuous verification of users, devices, applications, and workload, regardless of their network location. In this chapter, you'll learn how to implement Zero Trust principles using native Azure capabilities like Conditional Access, Privileged Identity Management (PIM), Microsoft Defender for Identity, and Private Endpoints. We'll explore how to apply least-privileged access, segment networks, monitor authentication signals, and enforce adaptive policies that align with the "assume breach" mindset—ensuring stronger, more resilient security by design.

Principles of Zero Trust

The security landscape has changed drastically with the rise of mobile workforces, cloud adoption, and increasingly sophisticated cyber threats. To meet these challenges, Microsoft advocates a Zero Trust security model—one that treats every access attempt as potentially hostile until proven otherwise. Rather than relying on implicit trust within network boundaries, Zero Trust enforces explicit verification of every identity, device, and access request. As outlined in Microsoft's Zero Trust guidance, the model is built

CHAPTER 10   IMPLEMENTING ZERO TRUST ARCHITECTURE IN AZURE

around three key principles: verify explicitly, use least-privileged access, and assume breach. These principles serve as the foundation for modern security architectures in Azure and other cloud platforms. In the following subsections, we will examine the rationale behind this model and how it contrasts with traditional perimeter-based approaches.

What Is Zero Trust?

Zero Trust is a comprehensive security strategy that assumes breach and requires strict verification for every access request, regardless of where it originates or what resource it targets. As defined by Microsoft, "***Zero Trust is a security strategy that eliminates implicit trust and continuously validates every stage of a digital interaction***". The model shifts away from the legacy notion of trusted internal networks and untrusted external ones. Instead, trust is never granted by default—even to users or devices inside the corporate network.

This approach requires that every request is authenticated, authorized, and encrypted before access is granted. Whether the user is working remotely on a personal device or operating within a corporate environment, Zero Trust ensures that no implicit trust is assumed. It leverages signals from identity, endpoint health, location, and behavior to make adaptive access decisions. In cloud-centric platforms like Azure, this means integrating identity and access control, endpoint compliance, data classification, and monitoring into a unified security posture.

By decoupling security from physical network boundaries, Zero Trust enables organizations to secure hybrid and remote workforces, embrace Bring Your Own Device (BYOD) policies, and protect sensitive resources distributed across on-premises and cloud environments.

Core Tenets of Zero Trust

Zero Trust is not a product or a discrete security feature—it is an integrated architectural strategy that redefines how trust is established and maintained in digital systems. Microsoft frames Zero Trust as both a response to the failure of traditional perimeter defenses and as a proactive model for securing dynamic, cloud-first, hybrid environments. In this model, no entity—whether internal or external or human or machine—is trusted by default. Every interaction must be continuously verified against identity, device, and contextual signals.

The first and most essential principle—**verify explicitly**—requires that access decisions be based on real-time evaluation of all available context signals. This includes user identity, group membership, device health and compliance status, geolocation, network metadata, and the sensitivity of the data being accessed. Within the Azure ecosystem, this principle is realized through Entra ID Conditional Access engine, which enforces policy-based decisions grounded in multi-factor risk analytics. This moves authentication and authorization away from static models based on IP ranges or network segmentation and toward adaptive, intelligence-driven enforcement.

The second principle—**least-privileged access**—demands a systemic shift in how permissions are granted across infrastructure and workloads. Every access grant, whether for human users or service principals, must be tightly scoped and time bound. Entra ID Privileged Identity Management (PIM) and Azure Role-Based Access Control (RBAC) operationalize this principle by enabling just-in-time (JIT) elevation, approval workflows, and time-limited role assignments. From a governance perspective, this principle is further reinforced through automated access reviews and entitlement management processes that ensure stale permissions are regularly pruned, reducing attack surface and mitigating insider risk.

Finally, the principle of **assume breach** reframes the security strategy from prevention focused to detection and containment oriented. In this model, trust boundaries are eliminated in favor of deep instrumentation, continuous monitoring, and rapid response. Azure-native services such as Microsoft Defender for Cloud and Microsoft Sentinel enable telemetry aggregation, anomaly detection, and automated incident response using behavioral analytics and threat intelligence from Microsoft's global security graph. Zero Trust architectures presume that every system, user, and device are potentially compromised, and they are designed to contain and isolate blast radio through network segmentation, endpoint hardening, and real-time threat mitigation.

Figure 10-1 shows the principles of Zero Trust.

Figure 10-1. *Principles of Zero Trust (Image: Microsoft)*

Microsoft's leadership in Zero Trust implementation reflects its own transformation. As reported in the 2021 blog post, Microsoft had already applied to Zero Trust across its enterprise by protecting more than 475,000 employees and partners with Conditional Access using telemetry from over 181 million devices and 335 million user accounts. This scale of deployment exemplifies how the core tenets—verify explicitly, use least-privileged access, and assume breach—are not simply design ideals but operational realities that form the backbone of global cyber resilience.

Why Zero Trust in the Cloud Era

The shift to cloud-first architecture, hybrid work, and platform decentralization has rendered traditional perimeter-based security models obsolete. In legacy IT environments, network boundaries functioned as the primary control plane—access was granted based on whether a user or device was "inside" the trusted corporate network. However, in the modern cloud era, users access resources from unmanaged endpoints, across distributed locations, and through a multitude of SaaS, PaaS, and IaaS environments. Trust anchored to location or network topology can no longer be assumed.

Microsoft's architectural response to this paradigm shift is the Zero Trust model, which repositions identity, policy, and continuous risk assessment as the new control plane. In Microsoft Azure, this manifests as a convergence of identity-centric access control (via Microsoft Entra ID), real-time enforcement (via Conditional Access and Microsoft Defender for Cloud), and telemetry-driven decision-making (via Microsoft Sentinel and the Microsoft Security Graph). These components work cohesively to validate every request dynamically, regardless of whether the user is on a corporate laptop in an office or using a personal mobile device from a public network.

From an architectural standpoint, Zero Trust in Azure ensures that every layer—identity, endpoint, network, application, infrastructure, and data—is protected under the assumption that it may already be compromised. This aligns with Microsoft's principle of "assume breach," which drives the need for segmentation, least privilege, and continuous monitoring. As modern workloads span on-premises, multi-cloud, and edge environments, a unified security model that eliminates implicit trust is essential to maintain governance and enforce compliance across these domains.

Microsoft's own enterprise journey underscores this reality. As detailed in their global Zero Trust deployment, the company implemented policy-based access across over 90% of its internal resources, removed VPN dependencies, and adopted strong authentications for all users—including employees, vendors, and contractors. These changes were not merely operational but strategic responses to the cloud-native threat landscape.

Furthermore, modern attacks increasingly exploit identity and privilege misuse, not firewall misconfigurations or network intrusions. According to Microsoft threat intelligence, more than 98% of cyberattacks involve identity compromise. This reinforces why Zero Trust starts with identity as the first perimeter, enforcing authentication and authorization based on comprehensive telemetry—not on presumed location.

Ultimately, Zero Trust is not just compatible with cloudy it is required by it. In Azure, this requirement is met through an architecture that embraces dynamic access policies, integrated threat detection, and centralized security governance. As organizations modernize their digital estates, Zero Trust provides the only scalable, resilient model for protecting identities, applications, and data in a borderless, hyperconnected world.

Zero Trust vs. Traditional Perimeter Security Models

Traditional perimeter-based security models were built on the foundational assumption that anything inside the network could be trusted. Once authenticated through VPN or corporate firewall, users and devices were granted broad access with minimal internal restrictions. This approach was effective in tightly controlled, on-premises environments but is fundamentally incompatible with the distributed, cloud-native architectures of today.

In contrast, the Zero Trust model eliminates implicit trust and treats every access request as untrusted until verified. It decouples trust from location, shifting control from the network perimeter to identity, device compliance, and telemetry signals.

For example, in the 2020 SolarWinds cyberattack, adversaries gained access to internal systems by compromising trusted update mechanisms. Once inside the network perimeter, they moved laterally with minimal resistance, exploiting the flat network and implicit trust model. This breach highlighted a critical flaw in traditional perimeter-based defenses—trusting users and services solely based on their location within the network.

A Zero Trust model would have reduced the blast radius by requiring continuous identity verification, device health checks, and real-time policy evaluation for each access request—even for internal actors.

Microsoft characterizes this transition as moving from a **"castle-and-moat" model** to a **"contextual access plane**,*"* where each access decision is governed by dynamic policy evaluation. The architectural implication is profound: in Azure, organizations must replace reliance on traditional VPNs and flat network designs with granular, policy-driven enforcement using Conditional Access, Just-In-Time (JIT) elevation, micro-segmentation, and real-time analytics.

Table 10-1 illustrates the architectural and operational differences between traditional perimeter security and the Zero Trust model as implemented in Microsoft Azure.

Table 10-1. *Architectural and operational differences between traditional perimeter security and the Zero Trust model*

Dimension	Traditional Perimeter Model	Zero Trust Model (Azure)
Trust Boundary	Network perimeter (IP range, VLANs)	Identity, device posture, session risk, and real-time signals
Access Control	Role-based, broad internal access after login	Conditional Access, least privilege, risk-based adaptive policies
Network Architecture	Flat, centralized, VPN based	Segmented, micro-segmented, Internet first with secure access
Assumptions	Internal = trusted, external = untrusted	Assume breach, validate everything continuously
Authentication Model	One-time login, static credentials	Continuous validation, MFA, risk-based re-authentication
Monitoring and Response	Perimeter firewall logs, periodic audits	Continuous monitoring with Microsoft Sentinel and Defender for Cloud
Device Trust	Implicit if on internal network	Evaluated per session via Intune and Defender for Endpoint
Application Access	Internal access without segmentation	Proxy-based isolation via Azure Entra ID App Proxy or Private Link

Zero Trust Model in Azure

Transitioning to a Zero Trust architecture in Azure requires more than isolated configurations—it demands a cohesive, policy-driven design that spans identity, devices, applications, data, networks, and infrastructure. Microsoft's Zero Trust framework provides a comprehensive approach for embedding security controls across each of these pillars using native Azure services. By treating identity as the primary control plane and enforcing least-privileged access and continuous validation, Azure enables organizations to operationalize Zero Trust as a scalable and adaptable security foundation for cloud-native and hybrid environments.

Zero Trust Architecture for Microsoft Azure

At the center of the Zero Trust model is **policy-based access control**, enforced dynamically through Azure Entra ID using **Conditional Access** and **Multi-Factor Authentication (MFA)**. This control plane evaluates identity signals (such as sign-in risk), device posture (such as compliance status via Microsoft Intune), and session context to determine whether to grant or deny access in real time.

Surrounding this control plane are six security domains—**identities, endpoints, data, applications, infrastructure, and networks**—each fortified with Azure-native services and governed through coordinated security policies:

- **Identities** are authenticated using Microsoft Entra ID and continuously monitored for compromise through Microsoft Defender for Identity.

- **Devices** are assessed for compliance using Microsoft Intune and Defender for Endpoint, which feed device health signals into Conditional Access decisions.

- **Applications** are secured through Microsoft Entra ID Application Proxy, Microsoft Defender for Cloud Apps, and runtime controls such as Azure App Gateway WAF.

- **Data** is classified, labeled, and encrypted using Microsoft Purview, Azure Information Protection, and Key Vault.

- **Infrastructure** is governed using Azure Policy and monitored through Microsoft Defender for Cloud, which ensures workloads adhere to security baselines and detect misconfigurations.

- **Networks** are segmented and isolated using Azure Firewall, Network Security Groups, Application Security Groups, and Private Link.

Table 10-2 shows the six security domains of Zero Trust with their objectives and key Azure services.

Table 10-2. *Six security domains of Zero Trust with their objectives and key Azure services*

Zero Trust Pillar	Objective	Key Azure Services
Identity	Authenticate and authorize every identity	Microsoft Entra ID, Conditional Access, MFA, PIM
Devices	Ensure device health and compliance	Microsoft Intune, Defender for Endpoint, Microsoft Entra ID Join
Applications	Secure access to apps and APIs	Microsoft Entra ID App Proxy, Microsoft Defender for Cloud Apps, Azure API Management
Data	Protect data at rest and in transit	Microsoft Purview, Azure Information Protection, Azure Key Vault
Infrastructure	Secure cloud and hybrid infrastructure	Azure Policy, Defender for Cloud, Azure Arc
Networks	Micro-segment networks and verify traffic	Azure Firewall, Network Security Groups (NSGs), Azure Private Link, Azure Virtual WAN

Security Policy Enforcement as the Architectural Core

Security policy enforcement acts as the **architectural nucleus**. Microsoft Entra ID Conditional Access policies serve as the real-time decision engine, ingesting inputs such as the following:

- User risk (calculated via Identity Protection)
- Sign-in risk and session controls
- Device compliance status
- Geolocation and network metadata
- Application sensitivity

These signals enable adaptive access controls that align user and workload behavior with enterprise security posture. For instance, access to a sensitive Azure SQL Database might require a compliant, corporate-managed device, verified identity with MFA, and a valid justification through Microsoft Entra ID Privileged Identity Management (PIM).

Threat Intelligence and Automated Remediation

Microsoft's Zero Trust architecture is powered by **threat intelligence and detection capabilities** provided by Microsoft Defender XDR and Microsoft Sentinel. These tools aggregate telemetry across domains, apply machine learning to detect anomalies, and trigger automated playbooks via Logic Apps and Sentinel SOAR capabilities. For example, a user showing signs of credential theft might be automatically blocked, their session revoked, and an investigation launched—all in real time.

Figure 10-2 shows the logical flow of Microsoft Zero Trust architecture.

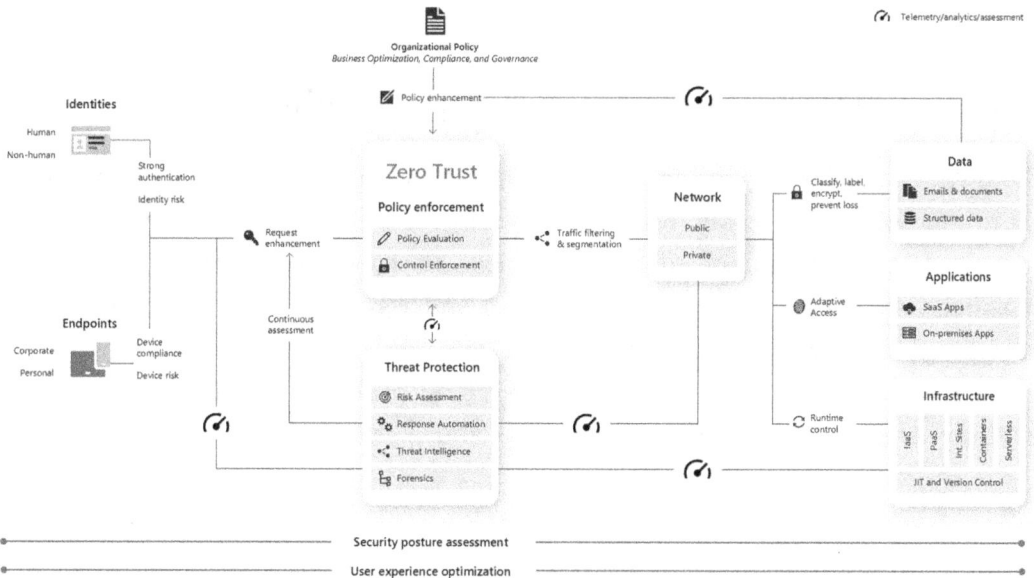

Figure 10-2. *Diagram that illustrates how identities, devices, applications, data, infrastructure, and networks are enforced through a central policy engine in Azure, supported by continuous threat intelligence*

Deployment Strategy: From Components to Initiatives

While Microsoft provides **step-by-step configuration guides** for deploying Zero Trust across each component, the **Rapid Modernization Plan (RaMP)** accelerates implementation by aligning technical deployment with business objectives. Rather than focusing solely on tool configuration, RaMP breaks down Zero Trust into **deployment initiatives** such as the following:

- Protecting sensitive data from exfiltration
- Ensuring secure remote access
- Preventing credential compromise
- Enforcing compliance across cloud workloads

Each initiative bundles together relevant technologies and tasks—making Zero Trust both achievable and measurable through defined outcomes and milestones.

Mapping Zero Trust Pillars to Azure Services

A Zero Trust model is only as effective as its implementation across each foundational security domain. In Azure, Microsoft provides purpose-built services to support every pillar of the Zero Trust architecture. Each service is designed to enforce the principles of **explicit verification**, **least-privileged access**, and **assume breach**—forming a coordinated security mesh across your cloud estate.

Table 10-3 shows the maps of Microsoft's six foundational Zero Trust pillars to the key Azure services and capabilities that enforce and operationalize them.

Table 10-3. The maps of Microsoft's six foundational Zero Trust pillars to the key Azure services and capabilities

Zero Trust Pillar	Purpose	Core Azure Services and Capabilities
Identity	Verify user and workload identities; enforce strong authentication and access policies	**Azure Entra ID** for centralized identity **Conditional Access** for real-time policy enforcement **Multi-Factor Authentication (MFA) Microsoft Entra ID Identity Protection** for user risk scoring **Privileged Identity Management (PIM)** for JIT and role-based access
Devices	Ensure device health and compliance before granting access	**Microsoft Intune** for device configuration and compliance **Microsoft Defender for Endpoint** for EDR and threat detection **Microsoft Entra ID Join** and **Hybrid Join** for identity-aware devices
Applications	Secure SaaS and line-of-business apps with identity-aware access and monitoring	**Microsoft Entra ID Application Proxy** for secure app publishing **Microsoft Defender for Cloud Apps (MCAS)** for app discovery, control, and session monitoring **Azure API Management** for secure, authenticated API exposure
Data	Protect data based on classification, sensitivity, and context	**Microsoft Purview** for data discovery and classification **Azure Information Protection (AIP)** for sensitivity labels and encryption **Azure Key Vault** for secure key and secret management

(continued)

Table 10-3. (*continued*)

Zero Trust Pillar	Purpose	Core Azure Services and Capabilities
Infrastructure	Enforce secure configurations and monitor for drift, threats, and misconfiguration	**Azure Policy** for compliance enforcement and automation
		Microsoft Defender for Cloud for threat detection, CSPM, and workload protection
		Azure Resource Graph for configuration assessment
		Azure Arc to extend Zero Trust to on-prem and multi-cloud resources
Network	Segment networks and isolate sensitive workloads; monitor and control traffic	**Azure Firewall Premium** for intelligent traffic filtering
		Network Security Groups (NSGs) and **Application Security Groups (ASGs)** for Layer 3–4 control
		Azure Private Link and **Service Endpoints** for private network access
		Azure Virtual WAN for centralized hub-and-spoke topologies and secure remote connectivity

CHAPTER 10 IMPLEMENTING ZERO TRUST ARCHITECTURE IN AZURE

Figure 10-3 shows the architectural overview of Zero Trust pillars.

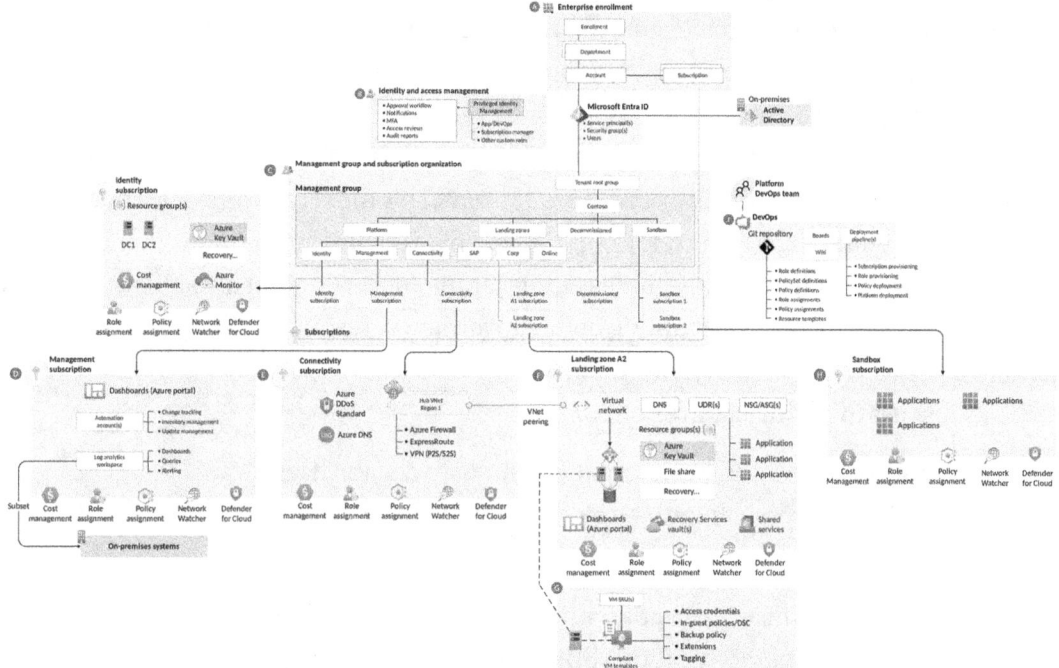

Figure 10-3. *Architectural overview of Zero Trust pillars (Image: Microsoft)*

In Azure, the power of Zero Trust lies in layering signals from these services to inform access decisions, for example,

- A user identity authenticated via Microsoft Entra ID triggers **Conditional Access**, which evaluates device compliance (from Intune), user risk (from Identity Protection), and app sensitivity (from Defender for Cloud Apps).

- If the access request meets all criteria, the user is allowed access— but only for the scope and time defined by **PIM** and RBAC.

- Meanwhile, **Microsoft Sentinel** continuously ingests logs from these services to detect anomalies and launch automated remediation workflows if necessary.

This **multi-layered enforcement model** ensures that no single failure in identity, endpoint, or network control can compromise the system. Every layer is both a checkpoint and a telemetry source, enabling adaptive, intelligent defense at cloud scale.

Zero Trust Maturity Model (Basic to Optimal)

Implementing a Zero Trust architecture in Azure is not a binary process—it is an evolutionary journey. To support this, Microsoft has developed a **Zero Trust Maturity Model** that defines progressive capability levels across six security pillars. Each pillar—identity, device, applications, data, infrastructure, and networks—has defined outcomes for **three** maturity stages: **Traditional**, **Advanced**, and **Optimal**. This model enables organizations to assess their current state, set strategic priorities, and plan incremental improvements.

The maturity model not only guides control implementation but also aligns business risks with security readiness, enabling better governance, resource allocation, and compliance posture in Azure environments.

Let's discuss this with example.

- **Traditional**: A mid-sized organization uses a static username/password approach for user sign-ins and lacks centralized identity management.

- **Advanced**: The organization implements Azure Active Directory with multi-factor authentication (MFA), conditional access policies, and limited identity lifecycle automation.

- **Optimal**: All users and devices are governed by adaptive access policies, Just-In-Time (JIT) access is enforced, and full identity governance (including entitlement management, risk-based sign-in, and lifecycle workflows) is automated via Microsoft Entra ID Premium and Microsoft Entra.

Table 10-4 shows the maturity levels with appropriate descriptions.

Table 10-4. Zero Trust maturity levels with appropriate descriptions

Level	Description
Traditional	Security controls are fragmented or perimeter based. Trust is implicitly granted based on network location or role. Reactive monitoring is minimal.
Advanced	Key controls are in place such as MFA, Conditional Access, segmentation, and continuous monitoring. Trust decisions are adaptive but not unified.
Optimal	Security is fully integrated across domains with centralized, risk-based, and automated responses. Trust is continuous, and posture is proactive.

Also, Table 10-5 shows the Zero Trust maturity by pillar.

Table 10-5. Zero Trust maturity by pillar

Zero Trust Pillar	Traditional	Advanced	Optimal
Identity	Password-based access; static roles	MFA and Conditional Access; basic identity protection	Risk-based Conditional Access; continuous access evaluation; PIM with just-in-time access
Devices	Unmanaged, unmonitored endpoints	Devices enrolled in Intune; compliance policies enforced	Continuous monitoring with Defender for Endpoint; device risk signals integrated into access decisions
Applications	Uncontrolled access to apps; no app discovery	Centralized authentication via Microsoft Entra ID; App Proxy; MCAS for visibility and session control	Real-time app governance; data-aware access policies; app isolation and conditional session enforcement
Data	No classification or protection; ad-hoc data controls	Sensitivity labels with AIP; data discovery via Purview	End-to-end data lifecycle protection; auto-labeling; adaptive DLP and encryption based on context
Infrastructure	Manual configurations; no baseline enforcement; reactive monitoring	Azure Policy for compliance; Defender for Cloud for threat protection	Automated remediation; Infrastructure-as-Code (IaC) governance; unified telemetry with Microsoft Sentinel
Network	Flat network; perimeter firewall; static IP allow lists	NSGs and ASGs for segmentation; VPN and basic inspection	Zero Trust segmentation with Private Link, Azure Firewall Premium, and adaptive micro-segmentation

CHAPTER 10 IMPLEMENTING ZERO TRUST ARCHITECTURE IN AZURE

Identity and Access Management

In a Zero Trust architecture, identity is the first and most critical control plane—serving as the core enabler of access decisions across users, applications, services, and devices. Microsoft's approach to Identity and Access Management (IAM) in Azure is rooted in the principle of **explicit verification**, where trust is continuously assessed and enforced based on the real-time context of the identity involved. Microsoft Entra ID provides the backbone of this identity platform, integrating **strong authentication**, **Conditional Access**, **identity protection**, and **privileged access governance** into a single policy-driven engine. Rather than relying on static roles or trusted network locations, Azure's IAM framework enforces **risk-based, least-privileged, and just-in-time access** by correlating signals across the user lifecycle, device health, location metadata, and behavioral anomalies. This identity-centric approach not only minimizes the attack surface but also enables granular governance across hybrid and multi-cloud environments, ensuring that only the right entity, under the right conditions, has access to the right resource at the right time.

Microsoft Entra ID as the Identity Control Plane

Microsoft Entra ID serves as the **central control plane for authentication, authorization, and access governance.** It replaces traditional, perimeter-based identity assumptions with **continuous, risk-informed policy enforcement** that is identity centric and cloud native. Every access request in Entra ID is evaluated in real time using **Conditional Access policies, user and sign-in risk signals**, and **contextual telemetry**, ensuring that trust is never assumed based on network location or static credentials.

As the foundation of Microsoft's Zero Trust identity pillar, Entra ID provides **federated authentication, Single Sign-On (SSO), Multi-Factor Authentication (MFA)**, and **role-based access control (RBAC)** across Microsoft 365, Azure, and thousands of integrated third-party applications. It is tightly integrated with **Microsoft Defender for Identity** and **Microsoft Entra ID Protection**, enabling it to detect compromised accounts, anomalous sign-in behavior, and lateral movement attempts in hybrid environments.

Table 10-6 shows the key capabilities of Entra ID in Zero Trust.

Table 10-6. *Key capabilities of Microsoft Entra ID in Zero Trust*

Capability	Purpose in Zero Trust	Entra ID Feature
Authentication and SSO	Centralizes identity and access across cloud and hybrid environments	SAML, OIDC, WS-Fed, OAuth2 support with SSO
Conditional Access	Enforces access policies based on real-time risk, location, device, and app context	Conditional Access policies with integrations to Intune and Defender for Endpoint
Multi-factor Authentication	Adds a second layer of identity verification to prevent credential-based attacks	Azure MFA with support for FIDO2, Authenticator app, SMS, and passwordless sign-in
Privileged Identity Management	Limits standing access, enables just-in-time elevation and role assignments	Entra ID PIM with approval workflows, notifications, and time-bound access
Identity Protection	Uses machine learning to detect risky users and sign-ins, enabling automated remediation	Entra ID Identity Protection (User Risk and Sign-In Risk), risk-based Conditional Access
Workload Identity Management	Secures service principals, managed identities, and app registrations used by workloads	Managed Identities for Azure resources, service principal governance, certificate and secret lifecycle
Access Reviews and Governance	Automates periodic access review and entitlement lifecycle management for regulatory compliance	Access Reviews, Entitlement Management, group and app lifecycle policies

Privileged Identity Management (PIM)

In Zero Trust architecture, one of the most critical objectives is to **minimize the attack surface posed by standing administrative privileges**. Microsoft's **Entra ID Privileged Identity Management (PIM)** provides a cloud-native governance solution that enforces just-in-time (JIT) access, approval workflows, role-based elevation, and auditing for privileged accounts. As part of the Microsoft Entra product family, PIM helps organizations implement the least-privileged principle in a controlled, auditable, and scalable manner.

Traditional identity systems often suffer from privilege sprawl—where users accumulate permanent rights that exceed what is needed, exposing the environment to insider threats and lateral movement in case of credential compromise. PIM addresses this challenge by dynamically assigning and revoking privileged roles only when required, with policy-based constraints such as time limits, approval requirements, and MFA.

Table 10-7 shows the key features of PIM with the purpose in Zero Trust architecture.

Table 10-7. Key features of PIM with the purpose in Zero Trust architecture

Capability	Purpose in Zero Trust Architecture	Microsoft Entra ID PIM Feature
Just-in-Time Role Activation	Reduces attack surface by ensuring admin privileges are time bound	Users activate roles only when needed, with automatic expiration
Approval-Based Access	Adds oversight and governance for sensitive role assignments	Requires one or more approvers to authorize elevation requests
Multi-factor Authentication	Enforces stronger controls for privilege escalation	Role activation can require MFA, regardless of session authentication
Audit Logging and Alerts	Ensure visibility into when and why privileged access was granted	Integrated with Microsoft Entra ID logs, Microsoft Sentinel, and Defender for Identity
Time-Limited Role Assignments	Prevents accumulation of dormant admin rights	Assignments can expire after a defined time or be revoked upon inactivity
Justification and Ticket Integration	Ensures accountability and ties access to support processes	Requires users to provide reason codes or reference tickets when activating roles
PIM for Azure Resources	Extends privilege control beyond Microsoft Entra ID to resource-level RBAC (subscriptions, VMs, etc.)	Governance of built-in Azure roles across subscriptions, management groups, and resources

Role Activation Workflow Using Microsoft Entra ID PIM

Here I am explaining how Microsoft Entra ID Privileged Identity Management (PIM) enables secure, time-limited activation of privileged roles via group-based assignment. Figure 10-4 shows a typical **Privileged Identity Management (PIM)** workflow in Microsoft Entra ID, where users request **time-bound elevated access** by joining

role-assignable groups. This process supports Zero Trust principles by ensuring that **privileged access is not persistent** but governed by approval policies, conditional access, and automatic revocation.

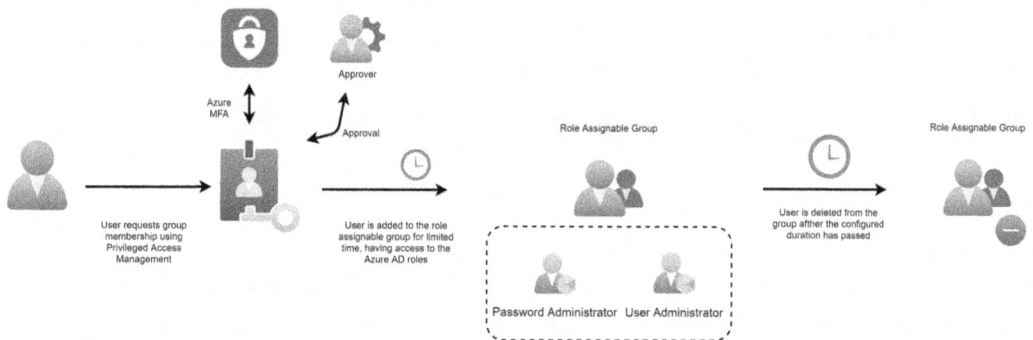

Figure 10-4. Privileged Identity Management (PIM) workflow in Microsoft Entra ID (Image: Microsoft)

Below is a step-by-step breakdown of the flow:

- **User Request Initiation**: A user initiates a role activation request through Microsoft Entra ID PIM by requesting to join a role-assignable group. This request is typically triggered via the Azure portal.

- **MFA Enforcement**: Upon submission, Microsoft Entra ID enforces **Multi-Factor Authentication (MFA)** to verify the requester's identity. This security checkpoint ensures that the elevation request comes from a legitimate and authenticated user.

- **Approval Workflow**: If the group is configured to require approval, the request is routed to one or more designated **approvers**. These approvers can approve or deny the request based on business context and justification (such as ticket numbers). All decisions are logged for auditability.

- **Temporary Group Membership**: Upon approval, the user is automatically **added to the role-assignable group** for a **limited duration**. The group is already associated with one or more **Microsoft Entra ID roles**, such as *Password Administrator* or *User Administrator*, enabling the user to perform specific administrative actions.

- **Auto-Revocation of Access**: After the configured access period elapses, **Microsoft Entra ID PIM automatically removes the user** from the group. This revokes their elevated privileges, ensuring that standing administrative access does not persist beyond the operational need.

Entitlement Management and Access Reviews

In a Zero Trust model, managing "who has access to what" is not a one-time configuration, but a **continuous governance process**. As organizations scale in complexity, onboarding new users, partners, and workload manually managing access rights becomes error-prone, time-consuming, and risky. **Microsoft Entra ID Governance** addresses this with two complementary features: **Entitlement Management** and **Access Reviews**. Together, they ensure that access to resources is not only controlled at the time of assignment but also validated, reviewed, and expired as needed—enforcing **least-privileged access**, **access lifecycle automation**, and **policy-driven controls**.

Entitlement Management

Entitlement Management is a **policy-based identity governance system** that automates **access package creation**, **approval workflows**, and **time-bound assignments** for internal users, guest users (B2B), and third-party collaborators. Table 10-8 shows the core concept of entitlement management.

Table 10-8. *The core concept of entitlement management*

Component	Description
Access Package	A bundle of access rights (e.g., groups, apps, SharePoint sites, Teams) bundled into one offering
Policy	Defines who can request the package, approval requirements, and assignment duration
Approval Workflow	Multi-step process to validate access requests before provisioning
Connected Organizations	External tenant configurations to onboard partners or vendors securely
Assignment Expiration	Access is automatically revoked after a defined period or based on inactivity

Access Reviews

Access Reviews provide a **systematic way to validate and clean up existing access** across identities and resources. They help organizations enforce governance for **Microsoft Entra ID roles, group memberships, app assignments**, and **entitlement packages**—ensuring users still require the access they were previously granted. Table 10-9 shows the key features of access reviews.

Table 10-9. The key features of access reviews

Capability	Purpose
Automated Reviews	Scheduled and recurring reviews of access to resources
Reviewer Assignment	Reviews can be performed by managers, group owners, app owners, or delegated reviewers
Recommendations Engine	AI-powered insights that suggest who no longer needs access
Self-Review Option	Allows users to certify their own access (common in BYOD or B2B scenarios)
Auto-remediation	Access is removed automatically if the user fails review or is unresponsive
Integration with PIM	Review privileged roles (Global Admin, User Admin, etc.) with time-bound enforcement

I tried to make a comparison between Entitlement Management vs. Access Reviews, which are shown in Table 10-10.

Table 10-10. Comparison between Entitlement Management vs. Access Reviews

Aspect	Entitlement Management	Access Reviews
Focus	Automating access requests and provisioning	Periodically validating existing access
Trigger	Initiated by user or policy	Initiated by admin or recurring schedule
Applies to	Groups, Teams, apps, SharePoint, external users	Groups, roles, access packages, privileged roles
Approval Required	Optional, defined in access package policy	Optional; review decision can be delegated
Auto-expiration	Yes	Yes (removal on review failure or inactivity)
Governance Use Case	Onboarding/offboarding, external collaboration	Attestation, audit readiness, privilege clean-up

Entitlement Management automates how users request and receive access to resources such as groups, apps, Teams, and SharePoint. It's ideal for onboarding scenarios, external collaboration, and managing access through time-bound packages with optional approvals. In contrast, **Access Reviews** focus on ensuring that existing access remains valid over time. They allow managers, app owners, or users themselves to periodically certify or remove access to roles, groups, and apps. While Entitlement Management governs how access is granted, Access Reviews govern whether access should still be retained—together enabling lifecycle governance in a Zero Trust model.

Let's make a demo here. The scenario is your organization wants to securely onboard a guest vendor to collaborate on a project. The guest needs access to the Microsoft Teams workspace, a SharePoint site, and group email alias. You will use Entitlement Management to automate this onboarding and then configure Access Reviews to periodically validate that the guest still requires access.

Before starting this demo, ensure you meet the necessary prerequisites. You must have an active **Entra ID Premium P2 license**, as both **Entitlement Management** and **Access Reviews** are part of Microsoft Entra ID Governance, which requires P2 features. Additionally, you need **admin-level access** to the **Microsoft Entra portal** to create access packages, approve requests, and configure reviews. Lastly, prepare a **guest test**

user, such as an external Gmail or Outlook account, which will be used to simulate the experience of an external collaborator requesting and receiving access. So, let's start.

1. Log in to the Microsoft Entra Admin Center from `https://entra.microsoft.com`.

2. Navigate to **Identity Governance** ➤ **Entitlement Management** ➤ **Access packages** ➤ **Access New Packages** as shown in Figure 10-5.

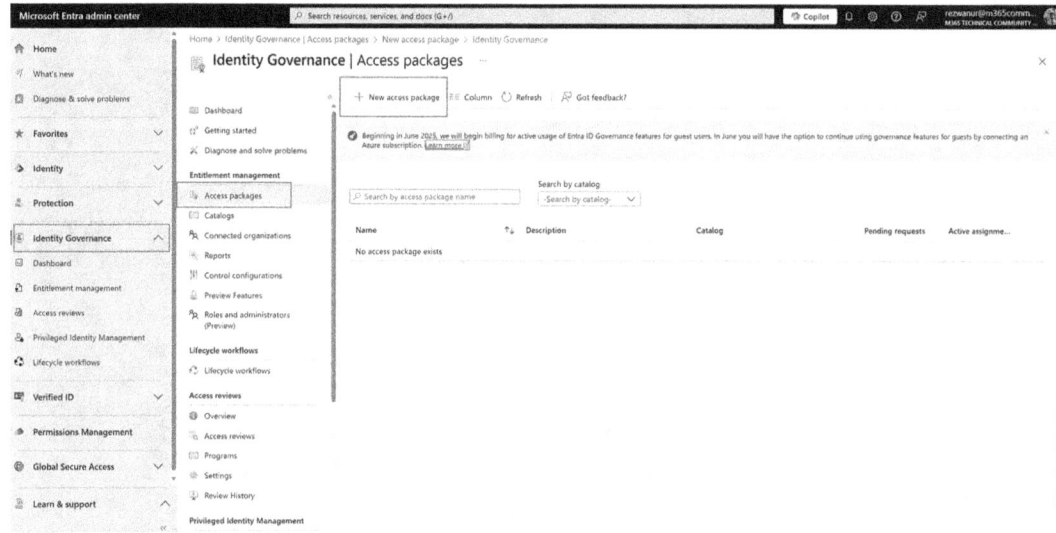

Figure 10-5. *Creating new access package from Identity Governance of Microsoft Entra ID Admin Center*

3. In the Basic tab, provide a name, description, and catalog as shown in Figure 10-6.

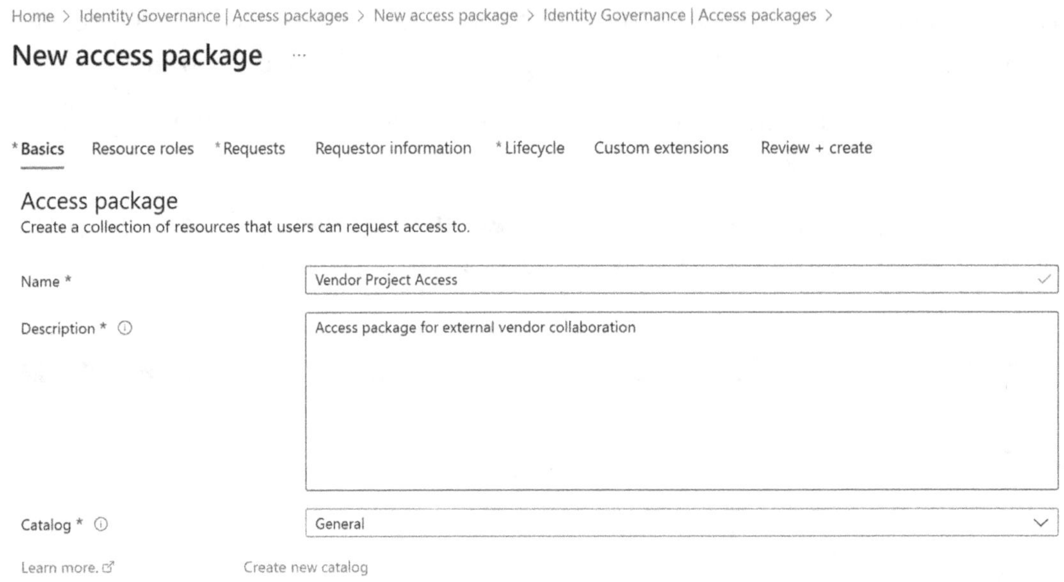

CHAPTER 10   IMPLEMENTING ZERO TRUST ARCHITECTURE IN AZURE

Figure 10-6. Providing new access package information

4. Click Next ➤ Resource roles. Here you can add different resources to these access packages. For example, I am adding Github Team from Group and Team section, set the role as Member, and added Samsung Email from the application section, set the role as Default access, as shown in Figure 10-7.

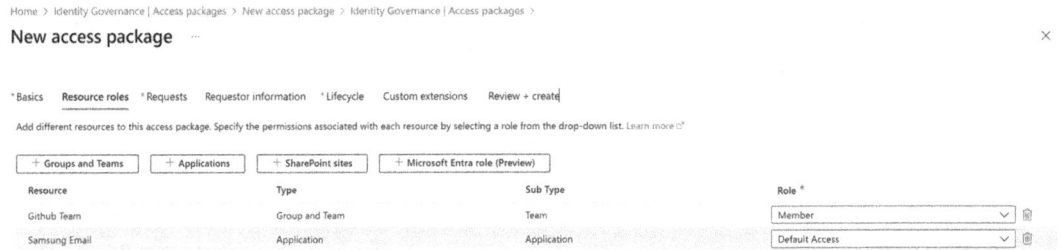

Figure 10-7. Selecting the resource roles

5. Click Next ➤ Requests. Here you can manage the settings of access. Check the following:

   a. **User who can request access:** *For users not in your directory* (which can allow users in connected organizations to request this access package).

   b. **Require approval:** *Yes.*

CHAPTER 10   IMPLEMENTING ZERO TRUST ARCHITECTURE IN AZURE

c. **How many stages:** Select the stages from 1, 2, or 3. For this demo, I choose 1.

d. **First Approver:** Select specific approver, and in the next page, choose the approver or your name.

e. **Require approver justification:** *Yes*.

f. Check the additional settings as well.

Figure 10-8 shows the actual settings of Request page.

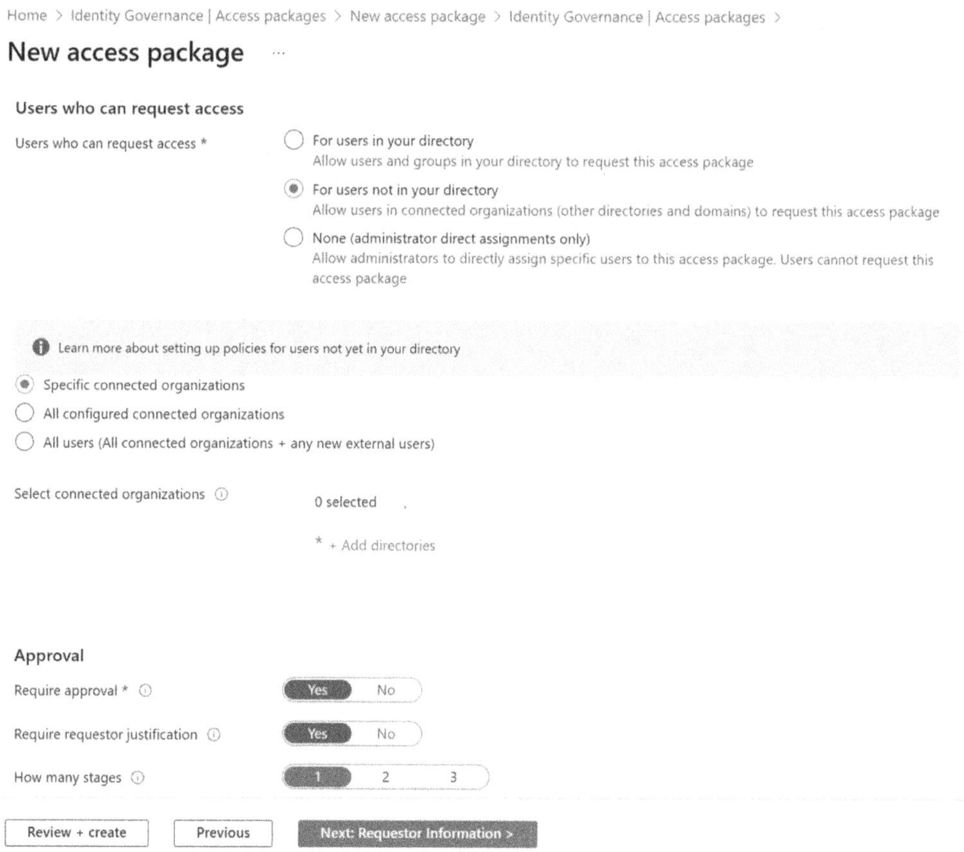

Figure 10-8. Request page settings for new access package

6. Go to the Lifecycle tab, and set the following settings:

    a. **Access package assignment expire:** Number of days

    b. **Assignments expire after (number of days):** 30

    c. **Users can request specific timeline:** Yes

    d. **Require access reviews:** Yes

        i. **Starting on:** Set the starting date.

        ii. **Review frequency:** Set the review frequency. In this demo, I set it to Quarterly.

        iii. **Duration (in days):** 25

        iv. **Reviewers:** Specific reviewers (select the reviewer).

    Figure 10-9 shows the settings of the lifecycle page.

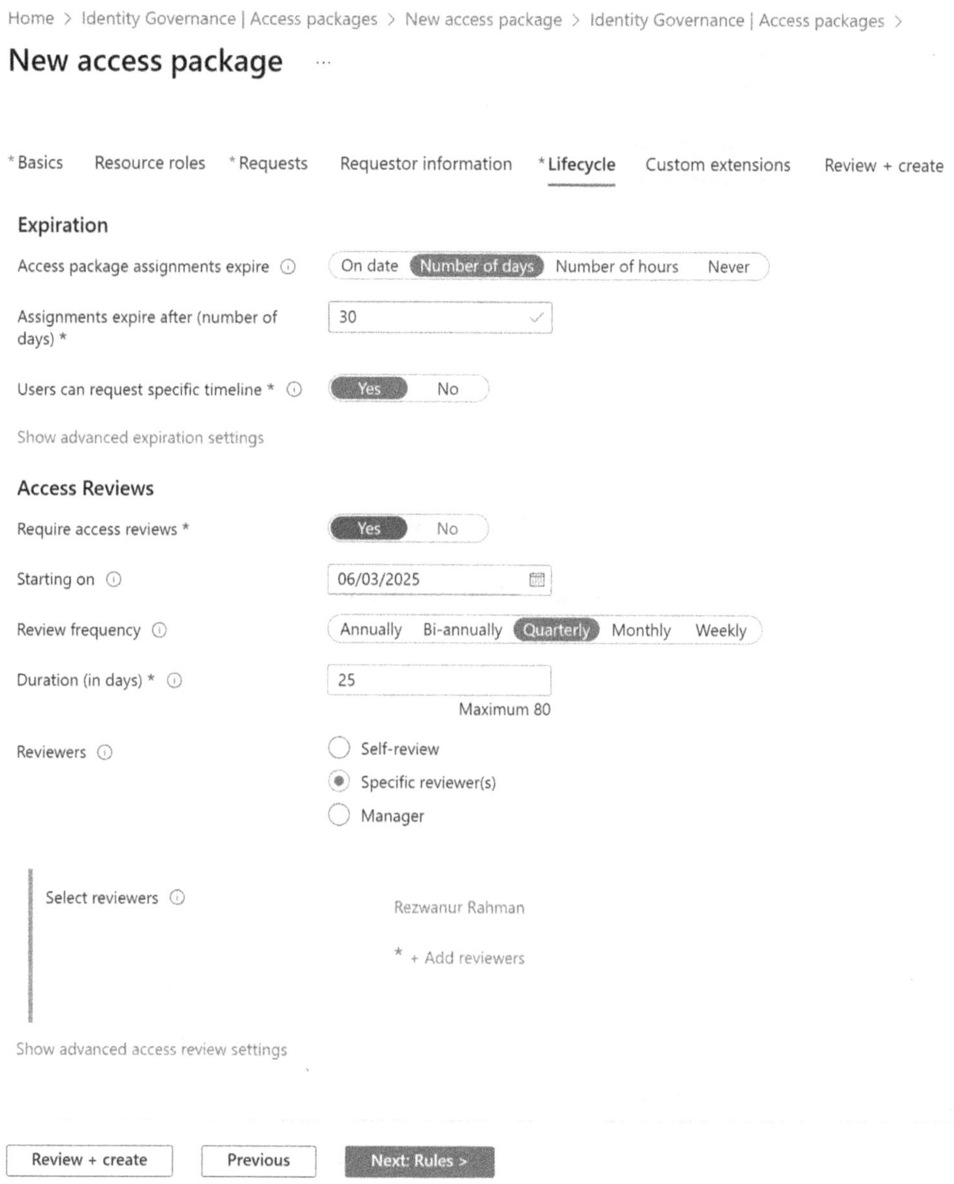

CHAPTER 10   IMPLEMENTING ZERO TRUST ARCHITECTURE IN AZURE

Home > Identity Governance | Access packages > New access package > Identity Governance | Access packages >

New access package

Figure 10-9. Lifecycle settings for new access package

7. Select **Review + create**. You can see the access page is created as shown in Figure 10-10.

475

CHAPTER 10 IMPLEMENTING ZERO TRUST ARCHITECTURE IN AZURE

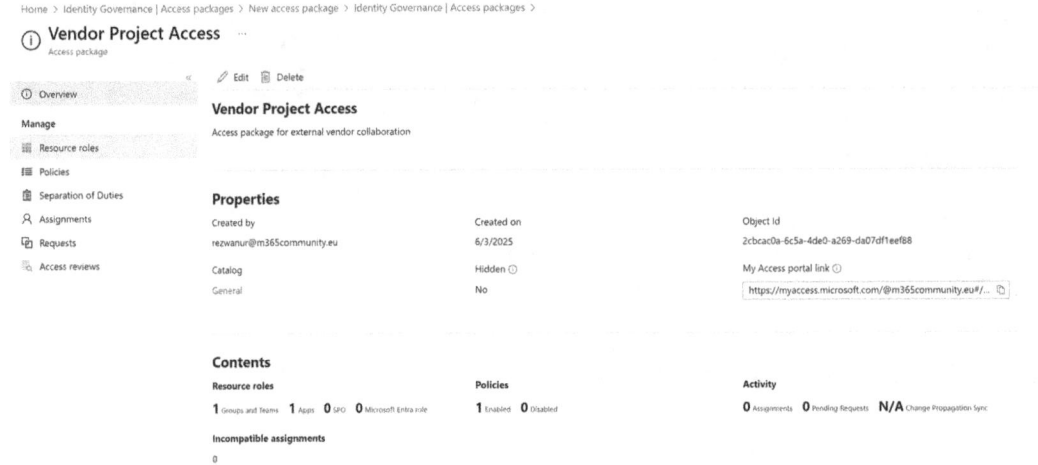

Figure 10-10. *Newly created access package page*

    8. Copy the My Access portal link as shown in Figure 10-11.

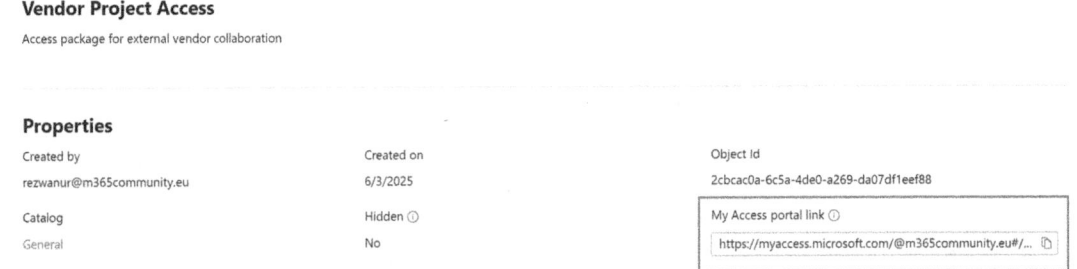

Figure 10-11. *My Access portal link option*

    9. Now, open an Incognito browser window (or private browser).

    10. Paste the link in the browser.

    11. Log in with a guest email (like your Hotmail/Gmail/Outlook account).

    12. After login, you will see a page as shown in Figure 10-12.

CHAPTER 10 IMPLEMENTING ZERO TRUST ARCHITECTURE IN AZURE

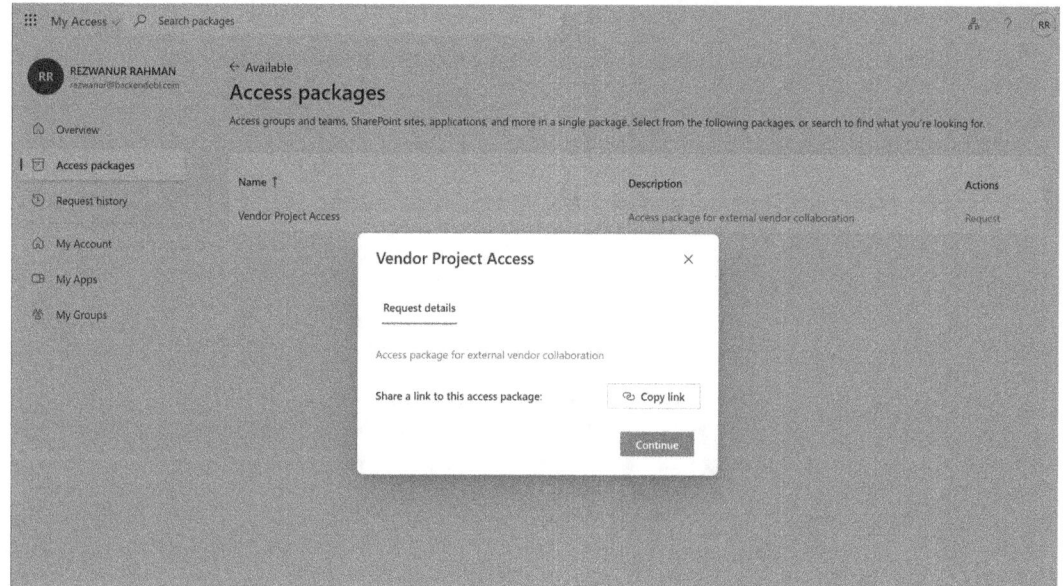

Figure 10-12. Requesting from a demo account using InPrivate browser

13. Click Continue. Fill the justification form and click Continue as shown in Figure 10-13.

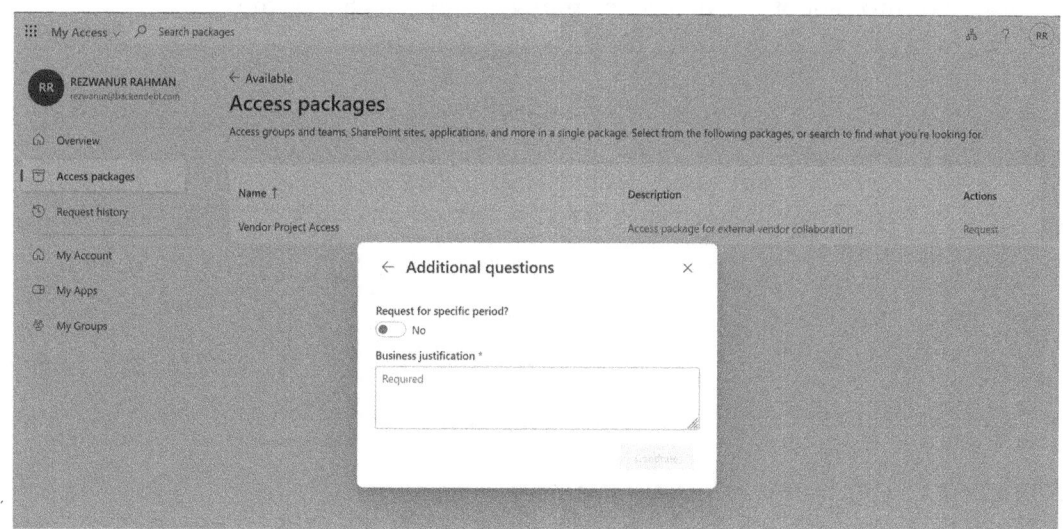

Figure 10-13. Business justification description option

14. Go back to the Entra Admin Center ➤ **Identity Governance** ➤ **Entitlement Management** ➤ **Access packages** ➤ **Select the package** ➤ **Requests** and you can see the new pending request there as shown in Figure 10-14.

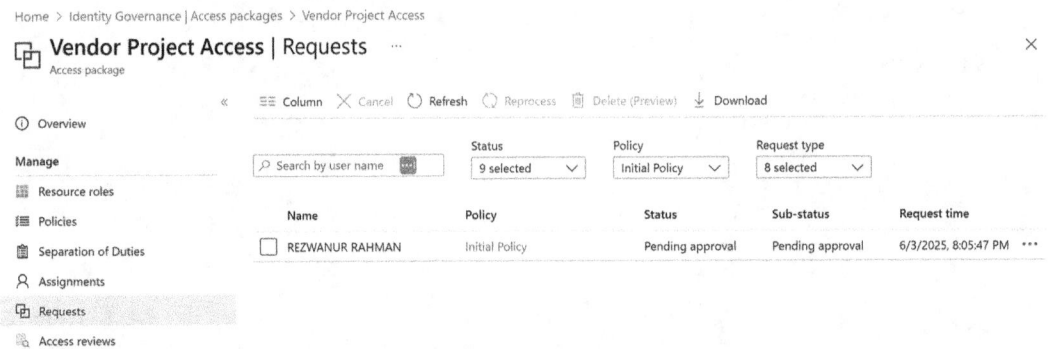

Figure 10-14. *Requests list from access package dashboard*

15. From here, you can only see the request. But to approve the request, you need to go to the My Access portal as an admin.

16. Paste the URL that you copied from My Access portal with the admin credential. Then go to approval, and you will see the pending request there as shown in Figure 10-15.

Figure 10-15. *Approving the user to access*

17. Select the profile and approve it.

CHAPTER 10   IMPLEMENTING ZERO TRUST ARCHITECTURE IN AZURE

18. Now it's time to configure an access review. To do this, go to Entra Admin Center ➤ **Identity Governance** ➤ **Access Reviews** ➤ **New Access Review** as shown in Figure 10-16.

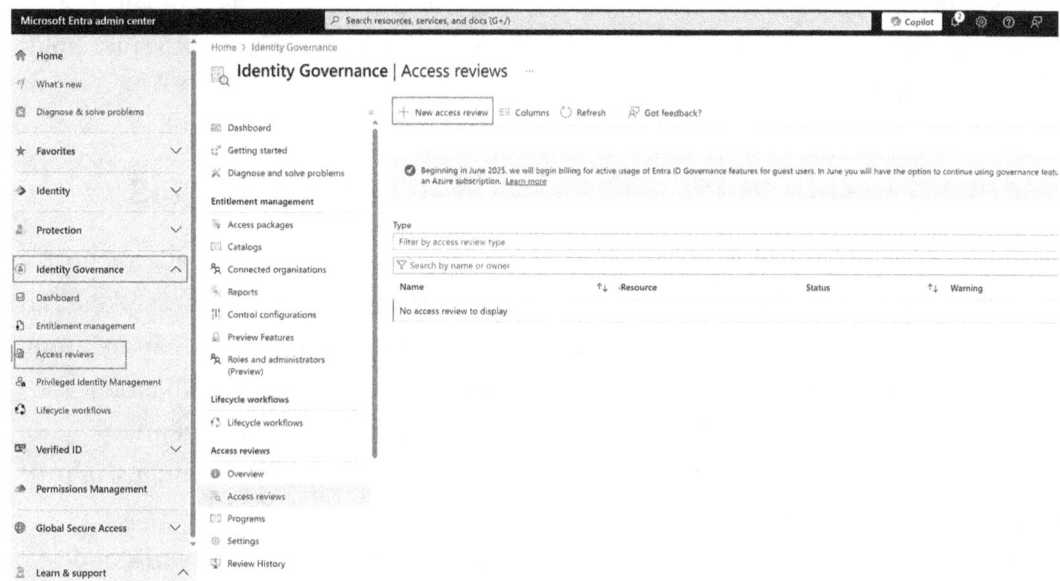

Figure 10-16. *Creating new access review option from Entra ID*

19. Select the following:

    a. **Review Type:** Teams + Groups or Applications: Choose the group or application.

    b. **Review Settings:**

    　　i. **Reviewers:** Group owners or yourself

    　　ii. **Recurrence:** Monthly

    　　iii. **Duration:** 7 days

20. That's it!

Once the access package is configured and the guest user submits a request, the onboarding process becomes fully automated through self-service and governed by predefined policies. Upon approval, access is automatically provisioned to the assigned Microsoft Teams workspace and SharePoint site without further administrative intervention. The guest's access is time bound, with a lifecycle expiration set to 30 days by default—ensuring that permissions are not retained indefinitely. To further enforce governance, Access Reviews are configured to periodically evaluate whether the guest still requires access. If the guest is found to be inactive or if no action is taken during the review period, their access is automatically revoked, aligning with Zero Trust principles of least privilege and continuous validation.

Securing Machine Identities and Service Principals

As cloud-native architectures evolve, applications and automated workloads are no longer passive actors—they are active participants that authenticate, request tokens, and access sensitive resources across distributed environments. In Azure, these **non-human identities**, such as service principals and managed identities, form a foundational layer of inter-service security. Yet, despite their critical role, they are frequently underprotected, often configured with excessive permissions, static credentials, or no visibility into their usage.

Microsoft's Zero Trust model asserts that **every identity—human or workload—must be explicitly verified, least privileged, and continuously governed**. This includes the identities used by CI/CD pipelines, automation scripts, microservices, and serverless applications. Azure addresses this challenge with robust mechanisms like **service principals**, **managed identities**, and **federated credentials**, each designed to eliminate credential sprawl and enforce policy-bound authentication.

Understanding the Identity Types

In Azure's identity system, not all identities belong to human users. Applications, scripts, automation pipelines, and cloud-native services also need identities to securely access APIs, secrets, and infrastructure components. These are known as **workload identities**, and they primarily take the form of **service principals** and **managed identities**. Understanding the distinctions between them is key to applying Zero Trust controls on a scale.

Service Principals

A **service principal** is the identity abstraction Azure creates when an application is registered in Microsoft Entra ID. It allows the application—or script, daemon, or backend service—to authenticate and obtain tokens to access Azure resources via role-based access control (RBAC) or Microsoft Graph.

Service principals support multiple credential types:

- **Client secrets** (password-like strings, often stored in key vaults or pipelines)
- **X.509 certificates** for stronger authentication
- **Federated identity credentials**, such as those used in **GitHub Actions**, which eliminate secrets entirely by issuing tokens from a trusted identity provider

Given their ability to run unattended and continuously, service principals can be **high-risk entities** if not carefully governed. Poor secret hygiene, overprivileged roles, and lack of visibility can turn them into silent backdoors for attackers.

Managed Identities

Managed identities are a cloud-native alternative designed to eliminate the need for manually managing credentials. These identities are provisioned and rotated automatically by Azure and can be used by services like Azure VMs, App Services, Functions, Logic Apps, and more to securely authenticate to other Azure resources.

There are two flavors:

- **System-assigned managed identity** is automatically tied to the lifecycle of a specific Azure resource. When the resource is deleted, the identity is also purged.
- **User-assigned managed identity** is a standalone identity object that can be assigned to one or more resources and managed independently.

Managed identities offer seamless integration with services like **Azure Key Vault**, **Azure SQL**, and **Storage Accounts**, enabling secure, token-based access without ever exposing secrets in code or configuration files.

Network Segmentation and Micro-segmentation

Traditional network security models that rely on perimeter defenses are no longer sufficient in cloud environments where workloads are dynamic, distributed, and Internet exposed by design. Azure addresses this challenge by enabling organizations to enforce network segmentation at multiple layers—from virtual networks and subnets down to individual workloads and application tiers. Through services like Network Security Groups (NSGs), Application Security Groups (ASGs), Azure Firewall, and Private Endpoints, administrators can isolate traffic, restrict east-west movement, and apply granular access policies between services. This approach extends further into micro-segmentation, where workloads are not only protected at the subnet level but are also grouped and filtered based on application roles and security posture. Together, these capabilities allow teams to design resilient, policy-enforced networks that are aligned with Zero Trust principles—minimizing implicit trust, enforcing traffic verification, and enabling telemetry-driven control.

The Role of Network Isolation in Zero Trust

Network isolation plays a foundational role in securing modern cloud environments by reducing the attack surface and limiting lateral movement between resources. Rather than trusting all traffic inside a corporate network, Azure's security framework emphasizes **explicitly permitted communication paths**, enforced through **logical segmentation**, **resource-based access controls**, and **boundary-aware inspection**. At the most basic level, **Virtual Networks (VNets)** act as private communication spaces in the Azure cloud, where workloads are grouped and traffic is restricted through **subnet-level policies**. Isolation can be further enhanced using **user-defined route tables**, **NSGs**, and **ASGs** to tightly control traffic flows both between and within subnets.

For critical systems and regulated workloads, Azure enables **multitier network isolation**, such as separating frontend, middleware, and backend services into distinct subnets—each with its own security posture and access rules. These boundaries are enforced not only by IP or port filtering but also through **identity-aware access** (e.g., Conditional Access or application-layer firewalls), **threat detection**, and **real-time policy enforcement**.

Table 10-11 shows the benefits of network isolation in Azure.

Table 10-11. Benefits of network isolation in Azure

Security Objective	How Azure Implements It
Minimize Lateral Movement	Use NSGs and ASGs to isolate VM workloads by role, zone, or function
Protect Against External Threats	Deploy Azure Firewall and DDoS Protection to control and monitor ingress/egress traffic
Restrict Public Exposure	Route traffic through Private Endpoints and Service Endpoints instead of public IPs
Aligning with Tiered Architecture	Separate workloads across subnets with specific policies per application tier
Enhance Compliance	Use segmentation to enforce data sovereignty, PCI, HIPAA, and other regulatory boundaries

Hub-and-Spoke Network Topology in Azure

The **hub-and-spoke** network topology is a well-established architectural pattern in Azure that enables centralized control of shared services while isolating workloads in logically segmented environments. This model mirrors an enterprise-grade approach to network governance and is especially relevant for large-scale deployments that require **multi-subscription management**, **centralized inspection**, and **controlled east-west and north-south traffic flows**. Figure 10-17 shows the architecture of hub-and-spoke network topology.

CHAPTER 10   IMPLEMENTING ZERO TRUST ARCHITECTURE IN AZURE

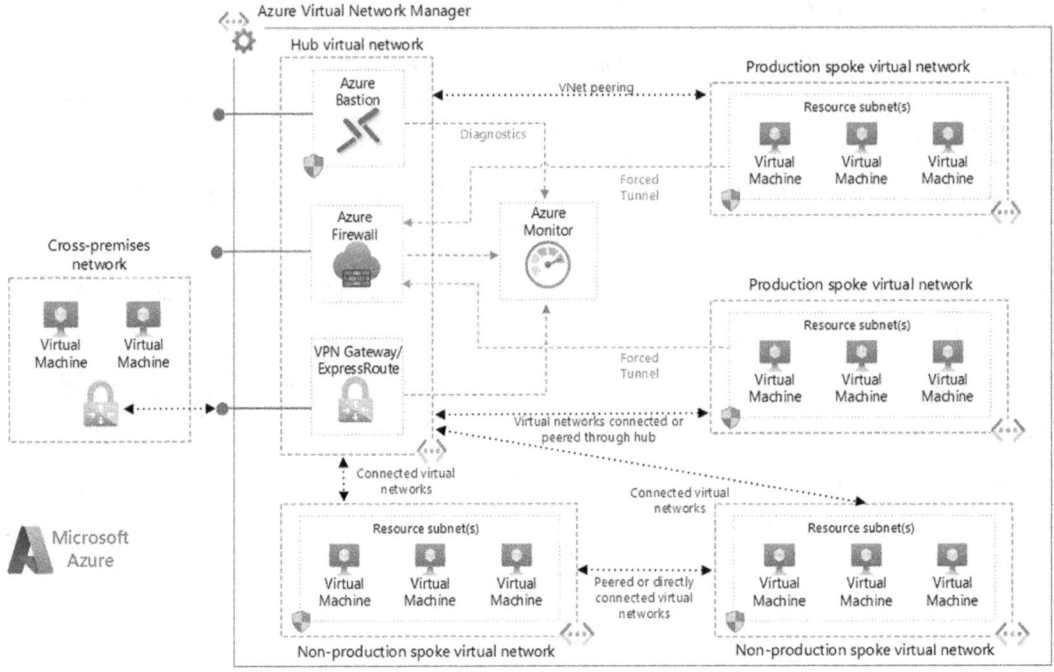

Figure 10-17. *Architecture of hub-and-spoke network topology (Image: Microsoft)*

The hub-and-spoke network topology in Azure centralizes shared connectivity and security services in a **Hub Virtual Network** while isolating workloads across multiple **Spoke Virtual Networks**. Connectivity from on-premises environments is established through a **VPN Gateway or ExpressRoute** located in the hub, acting as the single ingress and egress point for hybrid traffic. The hub hosts critical services such as **Azure Firewall**, **Azure Bastion**, and **Azure Monitor**, which provide packet inspection, secure access to virtual machines and centralized logging and diagnostics. Each spoke network, whether for production or non-production workload, contains its own subnets and virtual machines and is connected to the hub via **VNet peering**. All inter-VNet and outbound traffic from the spokes is **force tunneled through the hub**, enabling consistent inspection and governance through the Azure Firewall. Traffic flows are controlled with **User-Defined Routes (UDRs)** to ensure that spokes cannot bypass the centralized security controls. Azure Monitor collects logs from across the topology, feeding them into security and compliance systems like **Microsoft Sentinel**. This design not only enforces **network isolation** and **the least-privileged traffic paths** but also supports scalability, multi-environment separation, and full observability across enterprise-grade Azure deployments.

484

NSGs, ASGs, and Route Tables

Effective network segmentation in Azure is enforced through a combination of **Network Security Groups (NSGs)**, **Application Security Groups (ASGs)**, and **User-Defined Route Tables (UDRs)**. These tools provide layered control over traffic at the **subnet** and **network interface** levels, enabling organizations to isolate workloads, regulate east-west traffic, and route packets through inspection points like firewalls or network appliances.

Together, these components form the backbone of **network-layer enforcement** under a Zero Trust model—ensuring that no traffic flows without explicit permission and that all routing paths are policy-driven and observable.

Network Security Groups (NSGs)

NSGs are the primary enforcement mechanism for **allowing or denying traffic** at the subnet or NIC (Network Interface Card) level. Each NSG contains **inbound and outbound security rules**, defined by

- Source/destination IP or tag (e.g., Internet, Virtual Network)
- Port range (e.g., TCP 443, 22)
- Protocol (TCP, UDP, or any)
- Priority (lower value = higher priority)
- Action (Allow or Deny)

NSGs are **stateful**, meaning if an inbound rule allows traffic in, the return traffic is automatically permitted.

Application Security Groups (ASGs)

ASGs allow you to group virtual machines **logically by application role** rather than hardcoding IP addresses into NSG rules. This enables dynamic and scalable network policies, especially useful in microservices or autoscaling environments.

- VMs are assigned to ASGs during NIC configuration.
- NSG rules can reference ASGs as source or destination.
- Policies stay valid even as IPs change or VMs are re-provisioned.

User-Defined Route Tables (UDRs)

UDRs give administrators control over how packets are routed between subnets, VNets, and the Internet. By default, Azure uses system routes, but UDRs allow

- **Forced tunneling** through Azure Firewall or NVA
- Routing between isolated subnets
- Isolation of internal services

Each route in a UDR includes

- **Address prefix** (e.g., 10.10.0.0/16)
- **Next hop type** (Virtual Appliance, VNet peering, Internet)
- **Next hop IP address** (for appliances like firewalls)

Table 10-12 shows the feature comparison of NSGs, ASGs, and UDRs.

Table 10-12. Feature comparison of NSGs, ASGs, and UDRs

Feature	Purpose	Granularity	Zero Trust Role
NSGs	Filter traffic by IP, port, protocol	Subnet/NIC	Allow/Deny rules for east-west and north-south access
ASGs	Logical VM grouping for NSG rules	Application layer	Dynamic traffic filtering across app tiers
UDRs (Route Tables)	Override default Azure routing	Subnet level	Enforce inspection paths (e.g., firewall tunneling)

Private Endpoints and Service Endpoints

Securing access to platform services such as Azure Storage, SQL Database, and Key Vault is a key network isolation strategy. Azure provides two powerful mechanisms to achieve this—**Private Endpoints** and **Service Endpoints**—each offering different levels of isolation, security, and operational control.

Private Endpoints enable private and secure connectivity from virtual networks to Azure PaaS services over the Microsoft backbone network. When a private endpoint is configured, it maps a specific instance of a PaaS resource to an NIC (network interface) inside a VNet, effectively giving it a private IP address. This prevents the service from being exposed to the public Internet entirely. DNS resolution is also automatically handled via Azure Private DNS Zones, redirecting traffic internally. This mechanism is especially critical in Zero Trust architecture where minimizing public surface area is a core goal.

Service Endpoints, by contrast, extend the virtual network identity to the Azure service's public endpoint. Traffic remains on the Azure backbone network and is not exposed to the open Internet, but the service itself still retains its public endpoint. Service Endpoints are simpler to implement and can restrict access to specific subnet identities using built-in firewall rules.

Table 10-13 shows the comparison of Private Endpoint vs. Service Endpoint.

Table 10-13. Comparison of Private Endpoint vs. Service Endpoint

Feature	Private Endpoint	Service Endpoint
Exposure to public Internet	Fully private; no public IP	Uses public endpoint; secured via VNet/subnet identity
IP Resolution	Private IP in VNet via NIC	Public IP (service DNS)
DNS Dependency	Requires Azure Private DNS	Standard Azure DNS resolution
Supported Services	Azure Storage, SQL, Key Vault, Web Apps, etc.	Broader support but limited control
VNet Integration	True VNet binding	Extended identity to public service
Cost and Complexity	Higher (per endpoint); more secure	Lower; faster to configure

Let's make a quick demo! We will configure a Private Endpoint for Azure Storage account. The objective is to securely connect a Storage Account to a virtual network using a Private Endpoint—ensuring traffic stays within Azure's private backbone and does **not traverse the public Internet**.

Before getting started by configuring a Private Endpoint for an Azure Storage Account, make sure you have the necessary prerequisites in place. You will need an active Azure subscription where you have sufficient permission, ideally the Contributor or Owner role—to create and manage resources. Additionally, you should either have an existing Azure Storage Account or be prepared to create one as part of the process.

CHAPTER 10   IMPLEMENTING ZERO TRUST ARCHITECTURE IN AZURE

It's also essential to have a Virtual Network (VNet) already configured with at least one subnet, which will be used to associate the Private Endpoint and route traffic securely within the Azure backbone network. So, let's start!

1. Go to **Azure portal** ➤ search for **Virtual networks** ➤ **+ Create** as shown in Figure 10-18.

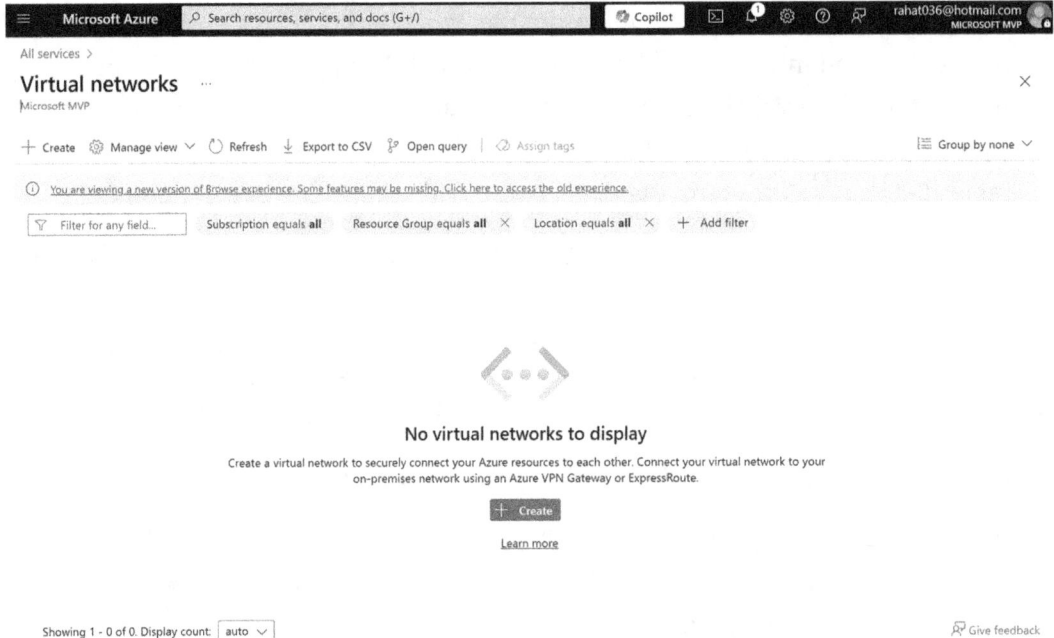

Figure 10-18. *Virtual Networks page in Microsoft Azure*

2. Select the subscription and resource group. Enter a name of the VN, like Demo-VNet as shown in Figure 10-19.

488

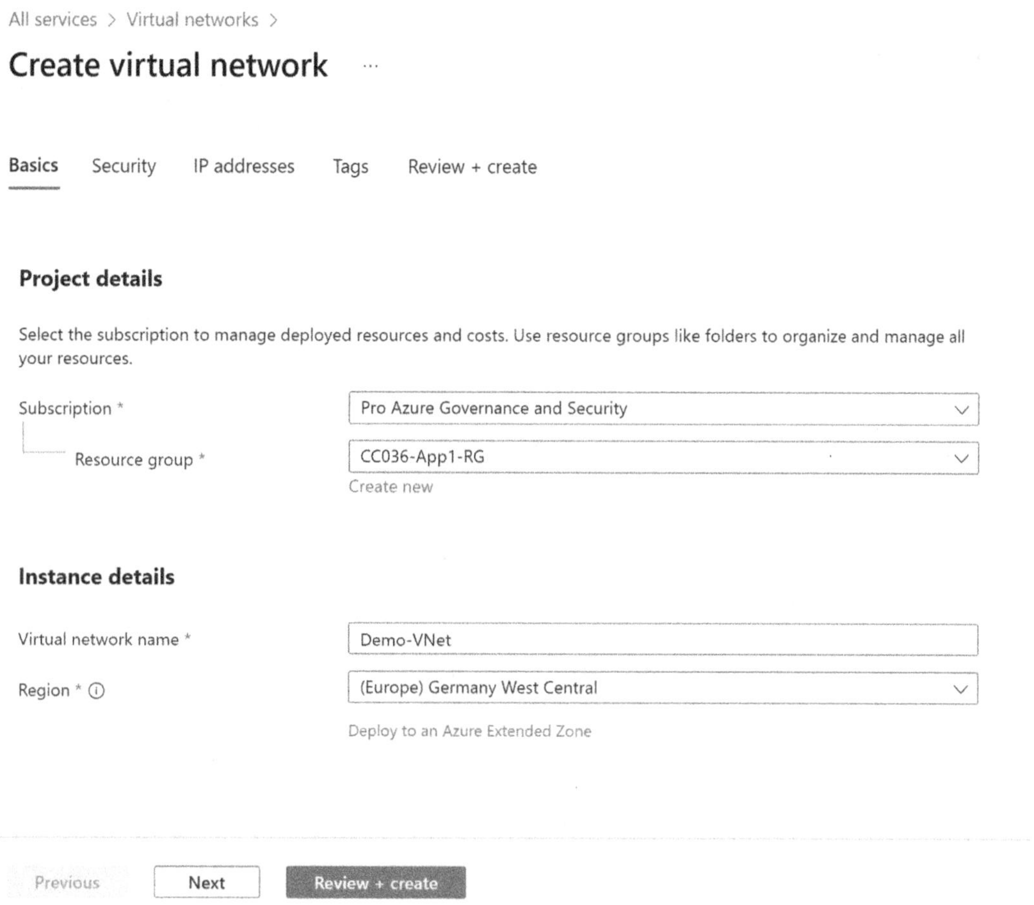

CHAPTER 10 IMPLEMENTING ZERO TRUST ARCHITECTURE IN AZURE

Figure 10-19. Creating new virtual network

3. Set the region the same as your storage account. If you don't have any storage account, I will show you how to make it.

4. Go to the IP addresses tab and click Add a subnet as shown in Figure 10-20.

CHAPTER 10   IMPLEMENTING ZERO TRUST ARCHITECTURE IN AZURE

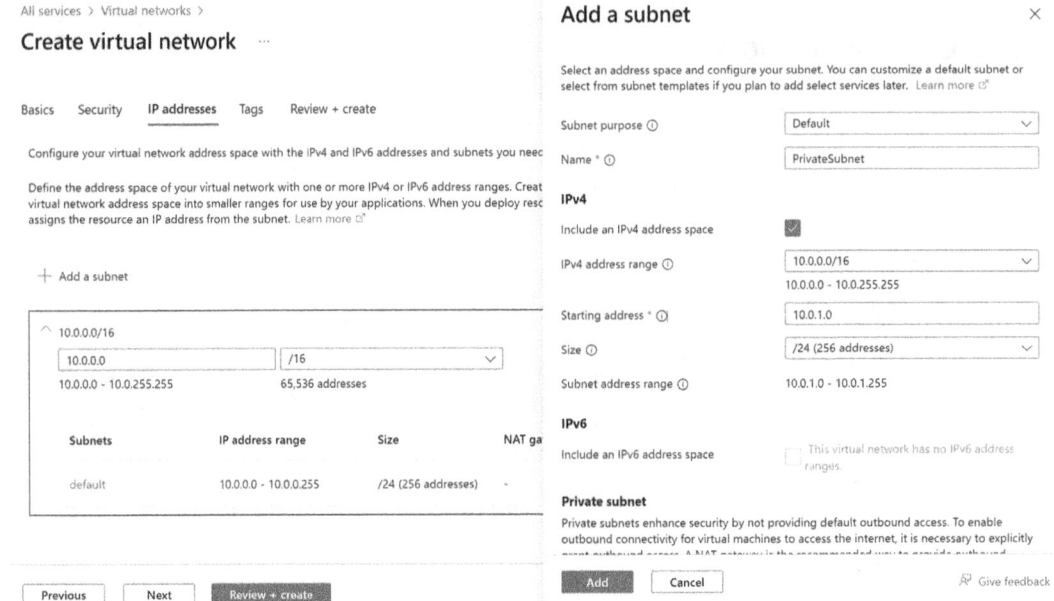

Figure 10-20. *Adding subnet for the virtual network*

5. Click **Review + create**, and then create it.

6. Now, search for **Storage Account ➤ + Create**.

7. Choose the same region and resource group as your VNet as shown in Figure 10-21.

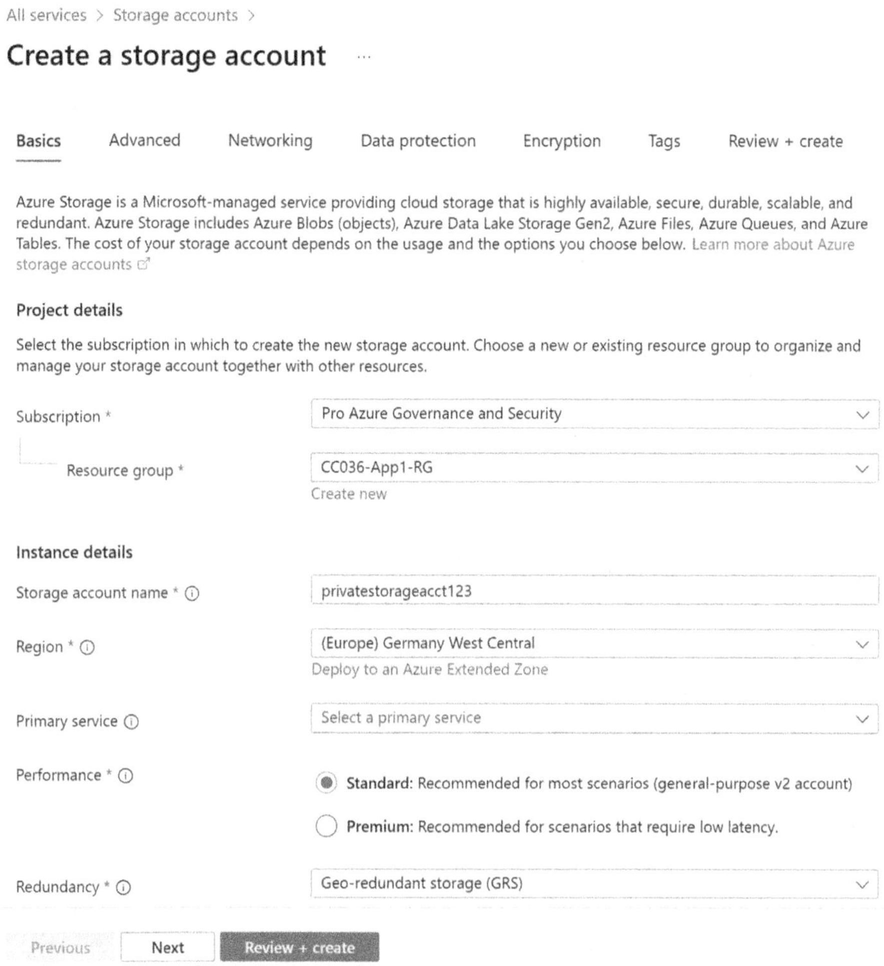

CHAPTER 10   IMPLEMENTING ZERO TRUST ARCHITECTURE IN AZURE

All services > Storage accounts >

Create a storage account

Basics   Advanced   Networking   Data protection   Encryption   Tags   Review + create

Azure Storage is a Microsoft-managed service providing cloud storage that is highly available, secure, durable, scalable, and redundant. Azure Storage includes Azure Blobs (objects), Azure Data Lake Storage Gen2, Azure Files, Azure Queues, and Azure Tables. The cost of your storage account depends on the usage and the options you choose below. Learn more about Azure storage accounts

Project details

Select the subscription in which to create the new storage account. Choose a new or existing resource group to organize and manage your storage account together with other resources.

Subscription *	Pro Azure Governance and Security
Resource group *	CC036-App1-RG
	Create new

Instance details

Storage account name *	privatestorageacct123
Region *	(Europe) Germany West Central
	Deploy to an Azure Extended Zone
Primary service	Select a primary service
Performance *	● Standard: Recommended for most scenarios (general-purpose v2 account)
	○ Premium: Recommended for scenarios that require low latency.
Redundancy *	Geo-redundant storage (GRS)

Previous   Next   **Review + create**

Figure 10-21. Creating a new storage account in the same resource group and region where we created the new Virtual Network

8. Leave other settings default.

9. Click Review + Create, and then click Create.

10. Now, let's create a Private DNS zone. Search for Private DNS Zones and click + Create.

11. Name it according to the service. For blob storage, use privatelink.blob.core.windows.net. Click **Create**.

12. Lastly, we need to create a Private Endpoint. Go to the **Private Link Center ➤ Private endpoint ➤ + Create** as shown in Figure 10-22.

491

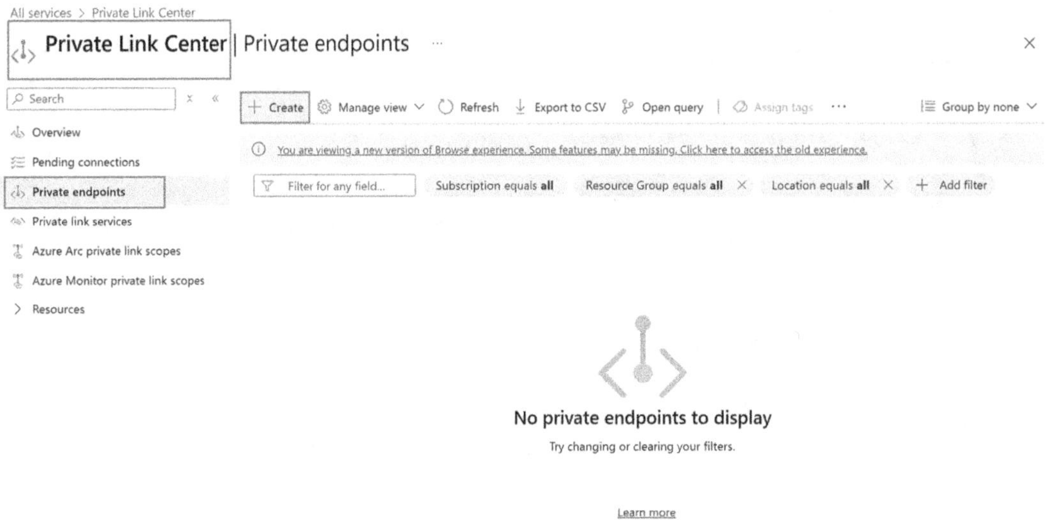

CHAPTER 10   IMPLEMENTING ZERO TRUST ARCHITECTURE IN AZURE

Figure 10-22. Creating new private endpoint

13. Select the same resource group and region. Give it a name as shown in Figure 10-23.

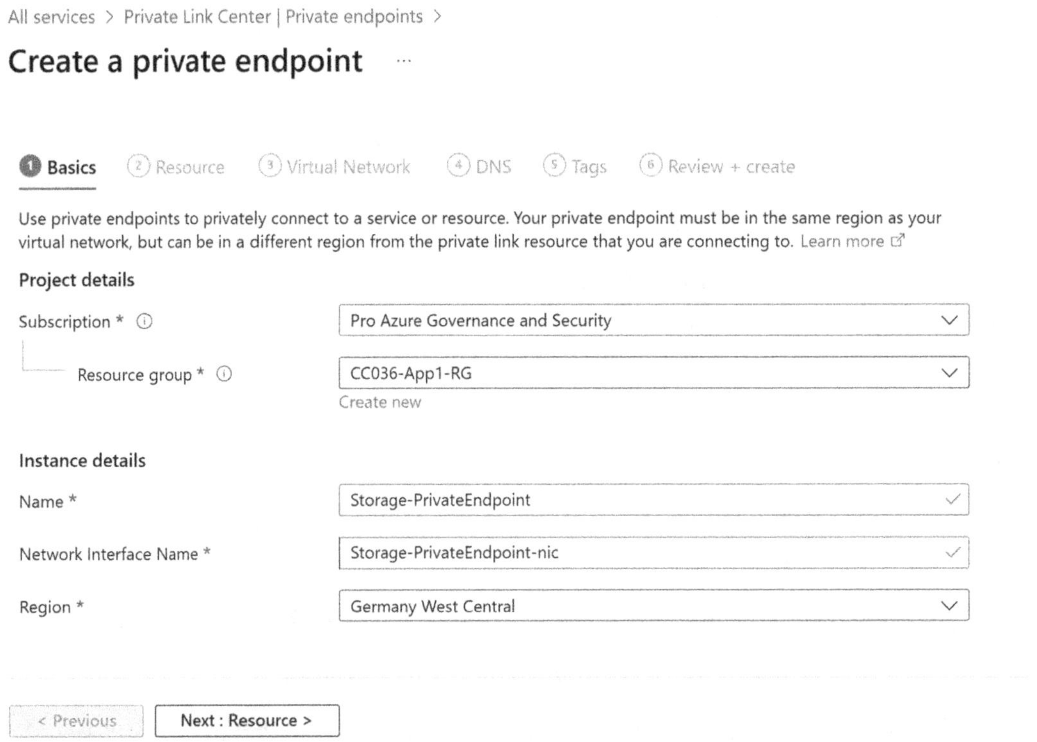

Figure 10-23. Filling the required information for the private endpoint

CHAPTER 10 IMPLEMENTING ZERO TRUST ARCHITECTURE IN AZURE

14. Click Next. Under **Resource** section, choose

    a. **Resource type:** *Microsoft.Storage/storageAccounts*

    b. **Resource:** Select the storage account.

    c. **Target sub-resource:** blob

    Figure 10-24 shows the resource page.

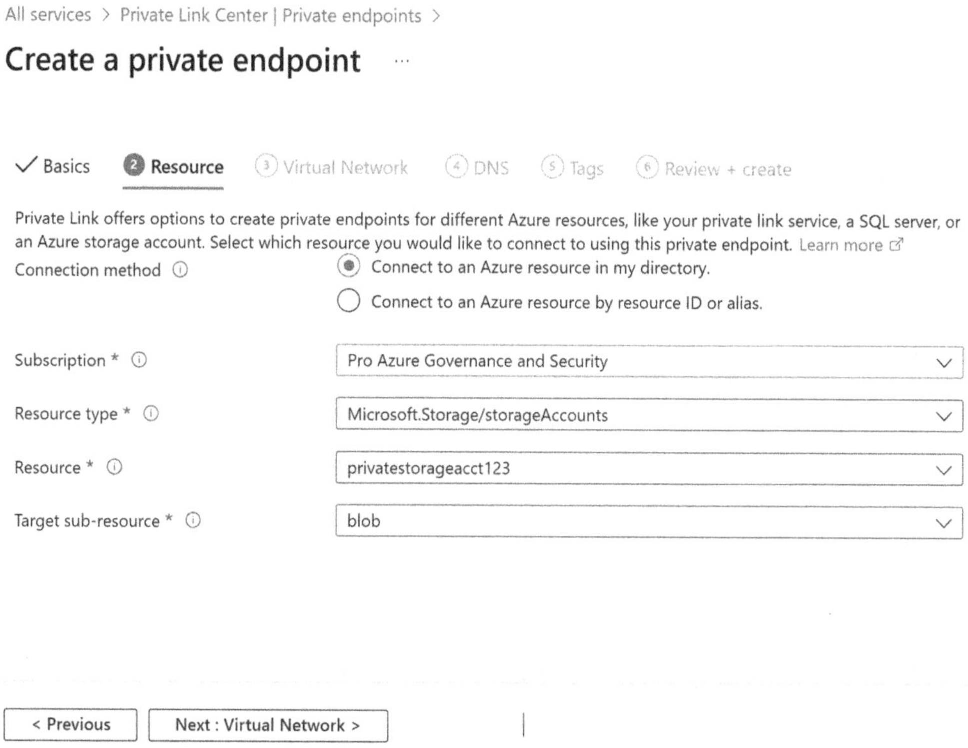

Figure 10-24. Selecting the subscription, resource type, resource, and target sub-resource for the private endpoint

15. In the Virtual Network, choose

    a. **Virtual Network**: Demo-VNet

    b. **Subnet**: PrivateSubnet

    As shown in Figure 10-25.

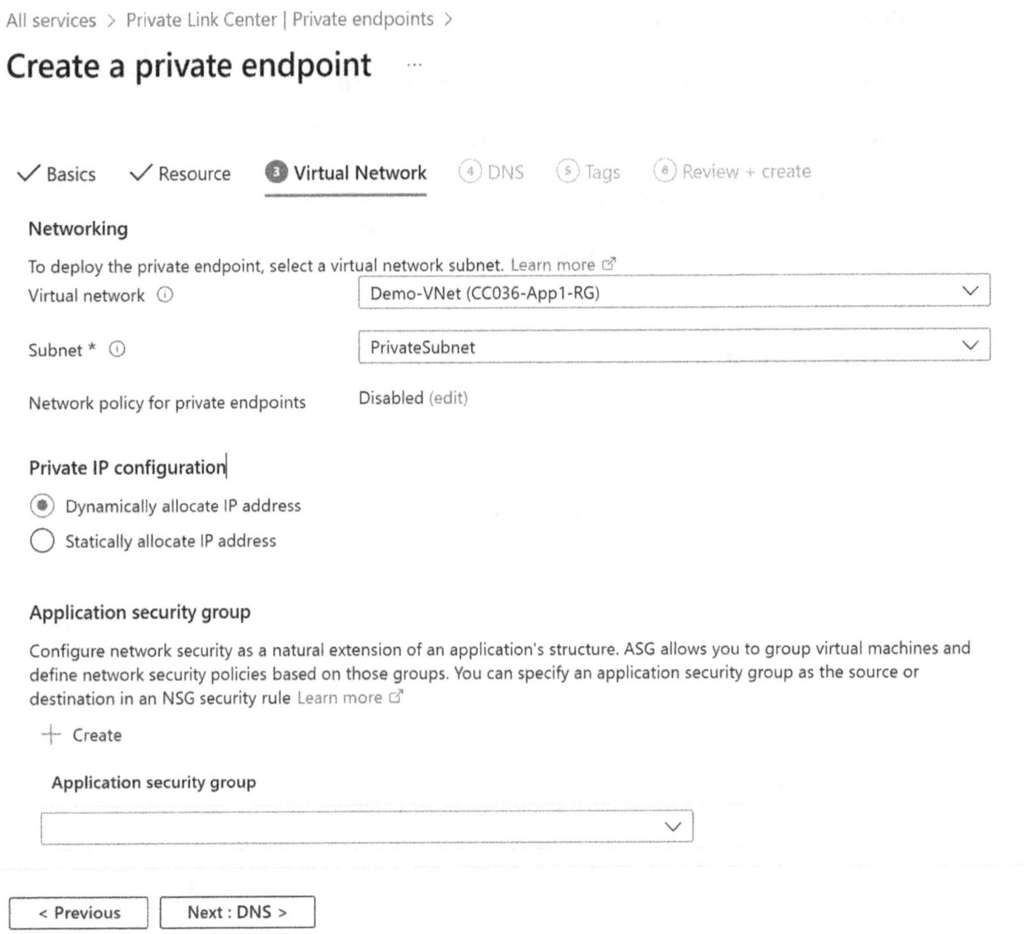

CHAPTER 10 IMPLEMENTING ZERO TRUST ARCHITECTURE IN AZURE

All services > Private Link Center | Private endpoints >

Create a private endpoint

✓ Basics   ✓ Resource   ③ Virtual Network   ④ DNS   ⑤ Tags   ⑥ Review + create

Networking

To deploy the private endpoint, select a virtual network subnet. Learn more

Virtual network ⓘ   Demo-VNet (CC036-App1-RG)

Subnet * ⓘ   PrivateSubnet

Network policy for private endpoints   Disabled (edit)

Private IP configuration

● Dynamically allocate IP address
○ Statically allocate IP address

Application security group

Configure network security as a natural extension of an application's structure. ASG allows you to group virtual machines and define network security policies based on those groups. You can specify an application security group as the source or destination in an NSG security rule Learn more

+ Create

Application security group

[< Previous]   [Next : DNS >]

Figure 10-25. *Selecting the virtual network that we created before*

16. Under **DNS Integration**, link to the Private DNS Zone created earlier.

17. Click **Review + Create ➤ Create**.

18. We are done! Let's test the private connectivity.

19. Create a test VM inside the Demo-VNet. Log in the VM and open a browser or terminal.

20. Try accessing the storage account endpoint by using the following cmdl:

    `nslookup <yourstorage>.blob.core.windows.net`

21. You should see the private IP address as shown in Figure 10-26.

```
Rezwanur@TestVM:~$ nslookup privatestorageacct123.blob.core.windows.net
Server:         127.0.0.53
Address:        127.0.0.53#53

Non-authoritative answer:
privatestorageacct123.blob.core.windows.net     canonical name = privatestorageacct123.privatelink.blob.core.windows.net.
privatestorageacct123.privatelink.blob.core.windows.net canonical name = blob.fra22prdstr04a.store.core.windows.net.
Name:   blob.fra22prdstr04a.store.core.windows.net
Address: 20.150.125.193

Rezwanur@TestVM:~$
```

Figure 10-26. Accessing the storage account by cmdl to check the private IP address

With this configuration in place, your Azure Storage Account is now securely accessible only from within the private network, effectively eliminating any exposure to the public Internet. All communication to the storage account is routed through the Azure backbone network using a Private Endpoint. Additionally, DNS resolution is seamlessly managed by the Azure Private DNS Zone, which ensures that name resolution occurs securely and internally within the connected Virtual Network. This setup provides a strong foundation for enforcing Zero Trust principles by tightly controlling and monitoring access paths to storage resources.

Micro-segmentation with Azure Application Gateway and WAF

In complex cloud environments, network boundaries are no longer just about virtual network edges—they are about **application-level visibility and control**. This is where Azure Application Gateway, coupled with the Web Application Firewall (WAF), plays a crucial role in achieving micro-segmentation. Unlike traditional segmentation techniques that isolate network traffic at the subnet or VLAN level, micro-segmentation with Application Gateway inspects and controls traffic at Layer 7, the application layer, enabling more granular policy enforcement.

Azure Application Gateway supports routing decisions based on HTTP attributes such as URI path and host headers, allowing fine-grained segmentation between microservices, frontend and backend components, or APIs within the same virtual network. By applying **WAF policies at the gateway**, organizations can enforce OWASP rule sets, mitigate common web vulnerabilities, and integrate with Azure DDoS Protection plans. The WAF is stateful, TLS terminated, and fully managed, enabling inspection of both inbound and outbound traffic without placing burdens on developers or infrastructure teams.

With features like **Custom WAF rules**, **Geo-blocking**, **Bot protection**, and **IP restriction policies**, Azure Application Gateway extends micro-segmentation by embedding logic into each HTTP/S request. Moreover, it integrates with Azure Policy and Defender for Cloud to ensure compliance and threat protection are embedded into the traffic inspection pipeline. Real-time telemetry and diagnostic logging feed into tools like **Azure Monitor**, **Microsoft Sentinel**, or **Log Analytics**, allowing centralized visibility into segmented flows and potential attack surfaces.

Note Layer 7 refers to the application layer in the OSI model, which is responsible for handling communication between user-facing applications and network services. It supports protocols such as HTTP/S, DNS, FTP, and SMTP. In security contexts, Layer 7 enables deep inspection of application-level data, allowing firewalls like Azure Web Application Firewall (WAF) to enforce granular policies based on URI paths, HTTP headers, cookies, and other request attributes. This provides more precise, context-aware control compared to traditional network-layer filtering, making Layer 7 segmentation essential for modern microservice architectures and Zero Trust implementations.

Summary

In this chapter, we focused on implementing the Zero Trust security model in Microsoft Azure, a critical framework for securing modern, cloud-native environments. We discussed how the traditional perimeter-based approach to security is no longer sufficient and how Zero Trust enforces strict access controls, continuous verification, and least-privileged principles across identities, devices, networks, applications, and data. You learned how to design and deploy Zero Trust strategies using Azure-native tools such as Conditional Access, Privileged Identity Management (PIM), Microsoft Defender for Identity, and Private Endpoints. These technologies collectively enable organizations to protect against internal and external threats by verifying every request as though it originated from an untrusted network.

In Chapter 11, we expand our security and governance lens to a multi-cloud environment, where organizations leverage services from multiple cloud providers such as Azure, AWS, and Google Cloud. While this approach provides flexibility and resilience, it introduces significant complexity in governance, visibility, and cost control. In the next chapter, you will learn how to define consistent policies, implement cross-cloud monitoring, and enforce security and compliance at scale using tools like Azure Arc, Azure Policy, and Cost Management. We'll also explore naming conventions, tagging strategies, and integration approaches that help maintain control over distributed cloud workloads while avoiding vendor lock-in.

CHAPTER 11

Multi-Cloud Environment

In the last chapter, we explored how to implement Zero Trust architecture in Azure, emphasizing identity-centric access, continuous verification, and policy-driven security using tools like Conditional Access, PIM, and Microsoft Defender. This approach helps secure cloud-native and hybrid environments—but it primarily focuses on a single cloud platform.

Now, in Chapter 11, we expand our view to **multi-cloud environments**, where organizations operate across Azure, AWS, and GCP. While this strategy offers flexibility and resilience, it introduces new governance challenges: fragmented visibility, inconsistent policies, and complex cost management.

In this chapter, you'll learn how to address these challenges with tools like **the Azure Arc**, unified tagging strategies, and cross-cloud policy enforcement. We'll also explore practical demos to track and manage costs in Azure and Google Cloud.

Let's explore how to bring clarity, control, and consistency to the complexities of multi-cloud governance.

Governance Challenges in Multi-cloud Environments

As enterprises increasingly embrace multi-cloud strategies—distributing workloads across platforms like **Microsoft Azure, Amazon Web Services (AWS)**, and **Google Cloud Platform (GCP)**—they are confronted with new layers of governance complexity. While this approach offers flexibility, resilience, and access to best-in-class services, it also challenges traditional governance models. From inconsistent policy enforcement and fragmented visibility to varying compliance standards and billing practices, managing a secure and cost-effective multi-cloud environment demands a deliberate and unified governance framework. Microsoft emphasizes that without a standardized approach, organizations risk increased operational overhead, security vulnerabilities, and misaligned regulatory compliance efforts.

These emerging governance challenges in multi-cloud environments include inconsistent policy enforcement, limited cross-platform visibility, fragmented compliance standards, and rising operational complexity. Without a unified governance model, organizations are more likely to encounter security vulnerabilities, regulatory misalignment, and cost inefficiencies.

What Is Multi-cloud?

Multi-cloud is a strategic approach where an organization utilizes cloud services from multiple providers such as **Microsoft Azure**, **Amazon Web Services (AWS)**, and **Google Cloud Platform (GCP)**—to optimize workload performance, enhance flexibility, and mitigate risks associated with vendor lock-in. By distributing workloads across various cloud platforms, businesses can leverage the unique strengths and specialized services of each provider to meet specific operational requirements.

For instance, a company might choose Azure for its robust enterprise solutions, AWS for its extensive machine learning capabilities, and GCP for its advanced data analytics tools. This diversified approach allows organizations to tailor their cloud infrastructure to best fit their needs, ensuring that each workload operates in the most suitable environment.

Adopting a multi-cloud strategy also enhances resilience and availability. By not relying on a single cloud provider, organizations can reduce the impact of potential outages or service disruptions, as workloads can fail over to alternative platforms if necessary. Moreover, this approach can aid in compliance with data residency requirements by allowing data to be stored in specific geographic locations offered by different providers.

However, managing a multi-cloud environment introduces complexities in governance, security, and cost management. Organizations must implement comprehensive strategies to maintain consistent policies, ensure security across platforms, and monitor expenditures effectively. Tools like Azure Arc can assist in providing unified management experience across diverse cloud environments.

Why Companies Use More Than One Cloud

In modern enterprise IT architecture, the use of multiple cloud service providers, commonly known as **multi-cloud adoption**, has become a deliberate and strategic choice rather than a side effect of organic growth. This approach addresses specific operational and technical needs, offering more than just flexibility—it offers precision control over performance, availability, compliance, and cost.

1. **Avoiding Vendor Lock-In Through Platform Decoupling**
   Cloud-native architecture often relies heavily on platform-specific services (e.g., Azure Functions, AWS Lambda, GCP Cloud Run). However, deep integration with one provider can lead to **vendor lock-in**, making future migration or integration costly and complex. By designing workloads to be **provider agnostic** (e.g., using containers with Kubernetes or Infrastructure as Code with Terraform), organizations can deploy the same application stack across Azure, AWS, or GCP—maximizing portability and strategic flexibility.

2. **Selecting Cloud-Native Services by Technical Strength**
   Each cloud provider innovates differently. Microsoft Azure leads in hybrid services and enterprise integrations (e.g., Azure Arc and Microsoft Entra ID), AWS dominates in scalable compute and developer tooling, while GCP offers advanced capabilities in data analytics and machine learning. By embracing a multi-cloud model, companies can **bind each workload to the most technically advantageous environment**, avoiding suboptimal performance or tooling compromises.

3. **Improving High Availability and Disaster Recovery (DR) Models**
   Multi-cloud architectures support **cross-cloud redundancy**, which is a step beyond zonal or regional redundancy within a single provider. For example, critical data or compute functions may be replicated between Azure and AWS to prevent downtime in case of a regional failure or vendor-specific service degradation. This is often implemented using **geo-redundant storage**, **DNS failover routing**, or **multi-cloud load balancing**.

4. **Meeting Regulatory and Data Sovereignty Requirements**
   Cloud regions and data residency laws vary significantly. A single provider might not operate in all required jurisdictions. Multi-cloud architectures allow enterprises to **pin sensitive workloads**

to a specific geography (e.g., storing healthcare data in Azure Germany while running analytics in GCP US). Microsoft provides detailed regional compliance coverage through services like **Microsoft Compliance Manager** and **Azure Policy**, but some mandates require using multiple clouds to stay compliant.

5. **Latency Optimization for Distributed Applications**
   Multi-cloud deployment allows businesses to **reduce network round-trip latency** by deploying compute and services near end users. For example, a retail company might serve European customers from Azure West Europe, US users from AWS Oregon, and Asian users from GCP Tokyo. Combining **Azure Front Door**, **Cloud CDN**, or **Route 53 latency routing** ensures global responsiveness for mission-critical apps.

6. **Cost Efficiency Through Dynamic Workload Placement**
   Cloud providers frequently update their pricing and introduce new discounts (e.g., Azure Reserved Instances and AWS Savings Plans). Multi-cloud architectures enable **cost-aware workload scheduling**, where workloads can shift between providers based on real-time pricing, resource availability, or even sustainability metrics like carbon intensity. Tools like **Azure Cost Management + Billing** and **FinOps platforms** help visualize and optimize cloud economics on scale.

Common Problems in Multi-cloud: Visibility, Control, and Costs

Multi-cloud environments are like a high-performance engine made of parts from different manufacturers. While powerful, such complexity often leads to misalignment and inefficiencies. Here's a technical dissection of the three most persistent problems enterprises face: visibility, control, and cost—and why these are more than just operational headaches.

Visibility Challenges

One of the primary governance issues in a multi-cloud setup is the fragmented visibility of resources. Each cloud provider offers its own native monitoring, logging, and alerting tools—such as Azure Monitor, AWS CloudWatch, or Google Cloud Operations Suite—but these tools do not provide a unified view by default. This makes it difficult for security and operations teams to track activities, detect anomalies, or respond to incidents consistently across environments. Without centralized visibility, blind spots are inevitable, increasing the risk of undetected misconfigurations or policy violations.

Control Inconsistencies

Governance policies such as resource tagging, identity access control, and compliance rules are implemented differently across providers. Azure uses Azure Policy and Azure RBAC, while AWS relies on IAM and SCPs, and GCP uses its own resource hierarchy and policy framework. This inconsistency leads to uneven control enforcement, where the same policy might be applied differently—or not at all—depending on the cloud platform. Managing policy drift becomes increasingly difficult when organizations lack a common governance baseline or cross-cloud policy engine.

Cost Management Complexity

Each cloud provider has its own billing system, pricing model, and cost optimization tools. This creates challenges in consolidating expenses, forecasting budgets, and identifying unnecessary spending across providers. Azure offers Cost Management + Billing with multi-cloud support (including AWS via connectors), but real-time insights across all clouds remain limited unless external tools or FinOps platforms are integrated. Without centralized cost governance, organizations may overlook underutilized resources, redundant services, or high-cost consumption patterns spread across platforms.

Real-World Example: Inconsistent Tagging Across Clouds

Imagine a global enterprise that runs workloads across Azure, AWS, and GCP. The operations team has decided to enforce a standard tagging structure to organize resources by environment, cost center, and application owner. The intended format includes tags like `environment=production`, `costcenter=FIN123`, and `owner=rezwanur@m365community.eu`.

On Azure, the governance team uses Azure Policy to audit and enforce tags across all resources. It works well—Azure supports up to 50 tags per resource, and the team applies policies to flag any deployments that miss the required tags. But when the same standards are applied in AWS, problems start to emerge.

In AWS, tag keys and values are case-sensitive. So, `Environment=Production` and `environment=production` are treated as two different tags—something Azure would treat as the same. Suddenly, when trying to generate a cost report in AWS, resources appear under inconsistent categories due to causing mismatches introduced by different deployment pipelines.

In GCP, the challenge shifts. GCP supports "labels," which are like tags but have stricter character limits—63 characters for both keys and values—and must match a specific format (lowercase letters, numbers, underscores, and dashes). The previously used email-based `owner` tag (e.g., `john.doe@company.com`) becomes invalid, breaking downstream automation that depends on that label for access reviews.

These inconsistencies lead to a situation where

- A unified cost report across Azure, AWS, and GCP is nearly impossible without data normalization.
- Automation scripts that rely on specific tag values fail unpredictably.
- Compliance reports show missing metadata in one cloud while appearing complete in another.

From a governance perspective, this small example—just a few tags—creates a ripple effect that impacts cost management, access control, and resource lifecycle automation. Microsoft recommends adopting a **tagging taxonomy** that is both cloud agnostic and enforced through automation. Tools like **Azure Arc** can help bridge this gap by enabling policy enforcement across connected AWS and GCP resources, but consistent design from the start remains critical.

The key takeaway: **tags are not just labels—they are governance metadata**. Without a normalized tagging strategy across cloud platforms, visibility and control begin to degrade the moment your environment scales.

Tools and Strategies for Multi-cloud Governance

As companies manage resources across Azure, AWS, and GCP, keeping everything organized and under control becomes more difficult. To solve this, Microsoft offers tools like Azure Policy, Azure Arc, and Cost Management that help apply consistent rules, track spending, and enforce security—no matter which cloud is being used. This section introduces practical strategies and tools to build strong, unified governance in a multi-cloud environment.

Introduction to Governance Tools

Effective governance plays a critical role in managing resources, enforcing compliance, and controlling costs across multiple cloud platforms. To support these needs, leading cloud providers—Microsoft Azure, Amazon Web Services (AWS), and Google Cloud Platform (GCP)—offer specialized governance tools that enable organizations to apply consistent policies, monitor usage, and maintain security across their environments.

Microsoft Azure Governance Tools

- **Azure Policy**: Enables the creation and enforcement of rules to ensure resources comply with organizational standards. It allows for automatic remediation of non-compliant resources and provides a comprehensive compliance dashboard.

- **Azure Management Groups**: Facilitate the organization of subscriptions into a hierarchy, enabling the application of governance conditions at scale. This structure supports the implementation of policies and access controls across multiple subscriptions.

- **Azure Cost Management and Billing**: Provides tools to monitor, allocate, and optimize cloud spending across Azure and other cloud platforms, helping organizations manage budgets and forecast expenditures effectively.

Amazon Web Services (AWS) Governance Tools

- **AWS Organizations**: Allows for the management of multiple AWS accounts under a single organization, enabling centralized governance and policy enforcement using Service Control Policies (SCPs).

- **AWS Identity and Access Management (IAM)**: Provides fine-grained access control across AWS services, allowing administrators to manage permissions for users and resources securely.

- **AWS Config**: Offers continuous monitoring and assessment of AWS resource configurations to ensure compliance with desired settings. It enables the detection of configuration changes and evaluation against defined rules.

Google Cloud Platform (GCP) Governance Tools

- **Resource Manager**: Allows for the hierarchical organization of GCP resources using organizations, folders, and projects, facilitating centralized management and policy application.

- **Identity and Access Management (IAM)**: Provides unified access control for GCP services, enabling administrators to define who can take what action on specific resources, ensuring secure and compliant access management.

- **Cloud Billing**: Offers tools to monitor, analyze, and optimize cloud expenditures, helping organizations manage costs effectively across their GCP resources.

Organizing Resources with Tags and Naming Rules

Organizing cloud resources effectively is crucial for maintaining clarity, ensuring compliance, and optimizing costs. Implementing standardized naming conventions and tagging strategies across Microsoft Azure, Amazon Web Services (AWS), and Google Cloud Platform (GCP) facilitates better resource management and governance.

Microsoft Azure: Naming and Tagging Best Practices

Organizing Azure resources effectively is foundational for governance, automation, cost tracking, and access control. Microsoft recommends adopting a standardized approach to **naming conventions** and **tagging strategies** to maintain clarity and consistency across cloud environments.

Naming Conventions in Azure

A consistent naming convention helps identify resource purpose, ownership, location, and environment briefly. Microsoft recommends that each resource name includes a combination of the following components shown in Table 11-1.

Table 11-1. Naming conventions in Azure with an example

Element	Description	Example
Resource Type	Abbreviated form of the Azure resource	**vm**
Environment	Usage context like production or dev	**prod**
Region	Azure region abbreviation	**eus**
App/Project ID	Application or workload identifier	**webapp01**
Instance	Optional numeric or alpha suffix	**001**

For example, **vm-prod-eus-webapp01-001**, this name indicates a production virtual machine deployed in East US for the "webapp01" application.

Table 11-2 shows the standard abbreviations for common resource types.

Table 11-2. Standard abbreviation for common azure resource types

Resource Type	Abbreviation
Virtual Machine	`vm`
Resource Group	`rg`
Storage Account	`st`
Network Interface	`nic`
Virtual Network	`vnet`
Public IP Address	`pip`

You can learn more about naming and tagging strategy for Azure resources from official Microsoft documentation: https://learn.microsoft.com/en-us/azure/cloud-adoption-framework/ready/azure-best-practices/naming-and-tagging.

Tagging Strategy in Azure

Tags in Azure are metadata elements applied to resources in key-value format. They are used for classification, automation, compliance, billing, and operational management.

The primary purpose of tagging in Azure is to enhance operational efficiency and governance by attaching meaningful metadata to cloud resources. Tags play a crucial role in **cost management**, enabling organizations to attribute spending to specific departments, projects, or cost centers for accurate chargeback and budgeting. They also support **automation workflows**, such as triggering automatic shutdowns, backups, or vulnerability scans based on tag values. In the realm of **access control**, tags can be used in conjunction with Azure Policy or Blueprints to scope role-based access dynamically, ensuring only authorized users can interact with tagged resources. Additionally, tags are essential for **compliance reporting**, helping teams identify resources that meet regulatory requirements or flag those missing critical metadata during audits. Table 11-3 shows the tag format and limits for Microsoft Azure.

Table 11-3. Tag format and limits for Microsoft Azure

Constraint	Limit
Max tags per resource	50
Max key length	512 characters (256 for some)
Max value length	256 characters
Case Sensitivity	Keys: Not case-sensitiveValues: Case-sensitive

Table 11-4 shows the common tags used in enterprise environments.

Table 11-4. List of common tags used in enterprise environments

Tag Key	Value Examples	Purpose
Environment	Production, Development	Identify the lifecycle environment
CostCenter	FIN1234, MKT5678	Enables chargeback and cost reporting
Owner	Rahat036@hotmail.com	Assigns responsibility to individuals
Department	Finance, Marketing	Groups resources by business unit
Project	AppModernization, CRM2025	Links to initiative or budget line
Compliance	HIPAA, ISO27001, GDPR	Flags compliance-relevant resources

To ensure consistency, organizations should define a centralized tagging taxonomy approved by IT, security, and finance. Naming conventions must be unique and easy to interpret. Use Azure Policy and Blueprints to enforce standards, and automate tag application during deployments with ARM, Bicep, or Terraform.

Amazon Web Services (AWS): Tagging Best Practices

Tagging in AWS is essential for organizing resources, tracking costs, enabling automation, and supporting security and compliance efforts. Tags are applied as **case-sensitive key-value pairs** and can be attached to most AWS resource types, including EC2 instances, S3 buckets, Lambda functions, IAM roles, and more.

Tagging Strategy in AWS

Each tag consists of a **key** and an optional **value**, both of which are case-sensitive strings. AWS supports up to **50 tags per resource**, and tag keys can be up to **128 characters**, while values can be up to **256 characters**, for example:

- Key: **Environment** | Value: **production**
- Key: **Owner** | Value: **jane.doe@company.com**
- Key: **CostCenter** | Value: **CC5678**

You can learn more about tagging in AWS from official AWS documentation: https://docs.aws.amazon.com/tag-editor/latest/userguide/tagging.html.

Table 11-5 shows the common tags and use cases in AWS environment.

Table 11-5. *List of common tags and use cases in AWS environment*

Tag Key	Example Value	Purpose
Environment	production, development, test	Segments workloads by lifecycle stage
Owner	Rahat036@hotmail.com	Assigns accountability for the resource
CostCenter	CC5678	Supports chargeback, showback, and budgeting
Application	CRM-System	Identify the workload or project
Compliance	PCI, HIPAA	Flags resources for audit or regulation scope

To establish effective tag governance in AWS, organizations should start by enforcing consistency across accounts with standardized tag keys and values, ideally using lowercase, hyphenated formats for clarity and automation. Tagging should be embedded into Infrastructure-as-Code workflows using tools like AWS CloudFormation, Terraform, or the AWS CDK, ensuring tags are applied automatically during deployment. Governance can be strengthened with AWS Organizations and Service Control Policies (SCPs), while **Tag Policies** help define approved tag keys and enforce value formats across accounts. For auditing and visibility, AWS provides tools such as the Resource Groups Tagging API, Cost Explorer, and AWS Config to monitor compliance and support cost allocation.

Google Cloud Platform (GCP): Labels and Tags

GCP provides two primary mechanisms for resource metadata management and governance: **Labels** and **Tags**. Though often used interchangeably, they serve distinct purposes—**Labels** are primarily for organization, billing, and filtering, while **Tags** (Resource Manager tags) are used for **fine-grained access control and conditional policy enforcement**.

Labels in GCP

Labels in GCP are structured as key-value pairs and are applied to resources to help with organization, cost tracking, and filtering. Both keys and values must be lowercase, no longer than 63 characters, and must start with a letter. They can include numbers, underscores, and dashes. These rules ensure label consistency and compatibility across GCP services. Labels in GCP are structured as key-value pairs and are applied to resources to help with organization, cost tracking, and filtering. Both keys and **values must be lowercase**, **no longer than 63 characters**, and **must start with a letter**. They can include numbers, underscores, and dashes. These rules ensure label consistency and compatibility across GCP services.

For more information, check the official documentation of Google Cloud at https://cloud.google.com/resource-manager/docs/creating-managing-labels.

Table 11-6 shows the common labels of Google Cloud.

Table 11-6. List of common labels of Google Cloud

Label Key	Example Values	Purpose
Environment	prod, dev, test	Indicates stage of workload lifecycle
Owner	Rahat036@hotmail.com	Assigns responsibility to users
cost-center	CC9012	Enables billing and financial tracking
application	ecommerce, crm	Groups related resources

To use labels effectively in GCP, organizations should follow key best practices. First, establish a consistent labeling taxonomy by defining approved label keys and value formats, documented centrally to ensure organization-wide standardization. Labels should be applied programmatically using Infrastructure-as-Code (IaC) tools like Terraform, Deployment Manager, or the gcloud CLI, which reduces manual errors and ensures consistency during resource provisioning. From a governance perspective, labels enable powerful filtering and reporting in Google Cloud Console, Billing Reports, Cloud Asset Inventory, and Cloud Monitoring. They also support label-based IAM conditions, enabling more precise and secure access control policies.

GCP Tags (Resource Manager Tags)

In Google Cloud Platform, **Resource Manager tags** serve a more advanced function than labels. While labels are used primarily for organization and cost management, **tags are designed for governance**, specifically enabling **attribute-based access control (ABAC)** and **conditional IAM policies**. This makes them ideal for large-scale environments where access needs to be managed dynamically based on resource attributes.

Tags are centrally managed at the organization level. Administrators can define **tag keys**—such as env—and assign **tag values** like dev or prod. Once defined, these tags are **attached to resources** using a mechanism called **tag bindings**, which link the tag to specific GCP resources like Compute Engine instances, projects, or folders.

What makes GCP tags powerful is their integration with IAM. You can write conditional policies that allow or restrict access to resources **based on the presence of specific tags**. For example, to limit DevOps access to only non-production workloads, you could define a tag env=dev, bind it to all relevant development resources, and create an IAM condition that grants permissions only if that tag is present.

The general workflow for using GCP tags involves four steps:

1. **Define a tag key** at the organization level using Cloud Console or the gcloud CLI.

2. **Create values** under that key (e.g., dev, prod, qa).

3. **Bind tags** to specific resources, effectively labeling them with governance metadata.

4. **Write IAM conditions** that reference those tags for precise, context-aware access control.

This approach allows organizations to decouple access permissions from static roles or project structures and instead use flexible, tag-driven policies that scale with the environment. Learn tag overviews of Google Cloud from the official documentation at https://cloud.google.com/resource-manager/docs/tags/tags-overview.

Tracking Cloud Costs with Microsoft Cost Management + GCP Billing

Tracking and optimizing cloud costs across Microsoft Azure and Google Cloud Platform (GCP) is essential for effective financial governance in multi-cloud environments. Here's a technical overview of the tools and strategies provided by both platforms to manage and control cloud expenditures.

In addition to native tools from Microsoft and GCP, organizations can also leverage **third-party platforms** such as **CloudHealth** and **Apptio** for more comprehensive, multi-cloud financial management. These tools offer advanced capabilities like cross-platform cost analytics, forecasting, and automated budget controls, enabling centralized visibility and governance across diverse cloud environments.

Microsoft Azure: Cost Management + Billing

Microsoft Cost Management + Billing offers a comprehensive suite of tools to monitor, allocate, and optimize Azure spending.

Let's discuss some key features of cost management in Microsoft Azure:

- **Cost Analysis**: Provides detailed insights into resource consumption and spending patterns. Users can filter costs by subscription, resource group, service, or tag to identify spending trends and anomalies

- **Budgets and Alerts**: Allows setting up budgets for different scopes (e.g., subscription, resource group) and configuring alerts to notify stakeholders when spending approaches or exceeds defined thresholds

- **Recommendations**: Offers actionable suggestions to optimize costs, such as rightsizing or shutting down underutilized resources

- **Integration with Power BI**: Enables exporting cost data to Power BI for advanced analytics and custom reporting

- **Cost Allocation**: Supports splitting shared costs across departments or projects using tags and cost allocation rules

Learn how cost management + billing work in Microsoft Azure from the official documentation at `https://learn.microsoft.com/en-us/azure/cost-management-billing/`.

Google Cloud Platform: Cloud Billing

Google Cloud's Cloud Billing provides tools to understand, control, and optimize GCP spending.

Here are some key features of cloud billing in Google Cloud Platform:

- **Billing Reports**: Visual dashboards that display cost trends over time, allowing grouping by project, service, or SKU to identify cost drivers

- **Budgets and Alerts**: Enables setting budgets at various levels (e.g., project, billing account) and configuring alerts to notify when spending exceeds predefined thresholds

CHAPTER 11   MULTI-CLOUD ENVIRONMENT

- **Export to BigQuery**: Facilitates exporting detailed billing data to BigQuery for custom analysis and integration with tools like Looker Studio

- **Committed Use Discounts (CUDs)**: Offers discounts for committing to use specific resources (e.g., Compute Engine) over a set period, leading to significant cost savings

Learn the Google billing from the official Google documentation at https://cloud.google.com/billing/docs.

Let's have two demos of tracking cloud costs in Microsoft Azure and Google Cloud Platform.

Demo: Tracking Cloud Costs in Azure with Microsoft Cost Management

Let's set up a cost analysis view and budget alert for a subscription in Azure. To do this, you will need an Azure subscription with the Owner or Cost Management Reader role. Also, you need at least one deployed resource, like VM, or WebApp. Now, let's start.

1. Go to Azure portal and search for Cost Management + Billing.

2. Select the Subscriptions under the Billing section as shown in Figure 11-1.

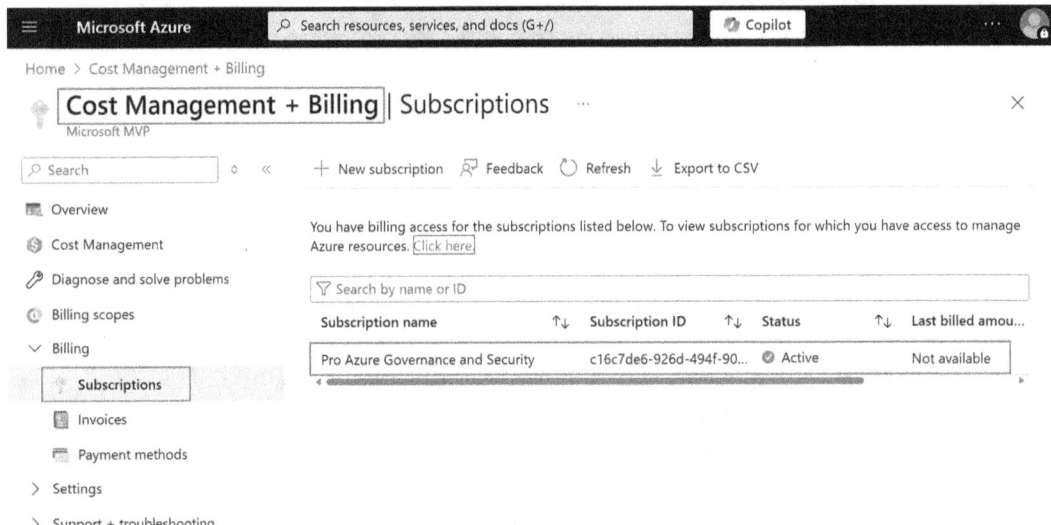

Figure 11-1. *Cost management + Billing section in Microsoft Azure*

CHAPTER 11 MULTI-CLOUD ENVIRONMENT

3. Select your subscription.

4. Navigate to Cost analysis under Cost Management section as shown in Figure 11-2.

Figure 11-2. *Cost analysis section of Microsoft Azure*

5. By default, the subscription scope is applied. However, you can select a specific resource group if you want to view costs at the resource group level.

6. You can analyze spending in this part.

7. Now, we will set a budget alert. To do this, go to Budget under the Cost Management, and click +Add.

8. Give a name of the budget, set the creation and expiration date, and select the budget amount as shown in Figure 11-3.

515

Figure 11-3. *Creating budget in Microsoft Azure cost management*

9. Click next, and you will see the option to set alert. Add the alert conditions, alert recipient, and language preference as shown in Figure 11-4.

Figure 11-4. *Setting alert and condition in budget*

CHAPTER 11 MULTI-CLOUD ENVIRONMENT

10. Click Create.

11. You can now track Azure costs. When your spending exceeds 50% of the set budget, you'll receive both an email and a notification alert.

Demo: Tracking Costs in Google Cloud Platform with Cloud Billing

Let's create budget alerts and analyze GCP costs. To get started with tracking costs in GCP, you need to have the **Billing Account Administrator** role, which allows you to configure budgets and export settings. Additionally, you must have at least one **GCP project linked to the billing account** with active resource usage, ensuring there's meaningful cost data available for analysis.

1. Go to Google Cloud Console from `https://console.cloud.google.com/`.

2. Navigate to Billing and choose your billing account.

3. Click Budgets & alerts under Cost management section as shown in Figure 11-5.

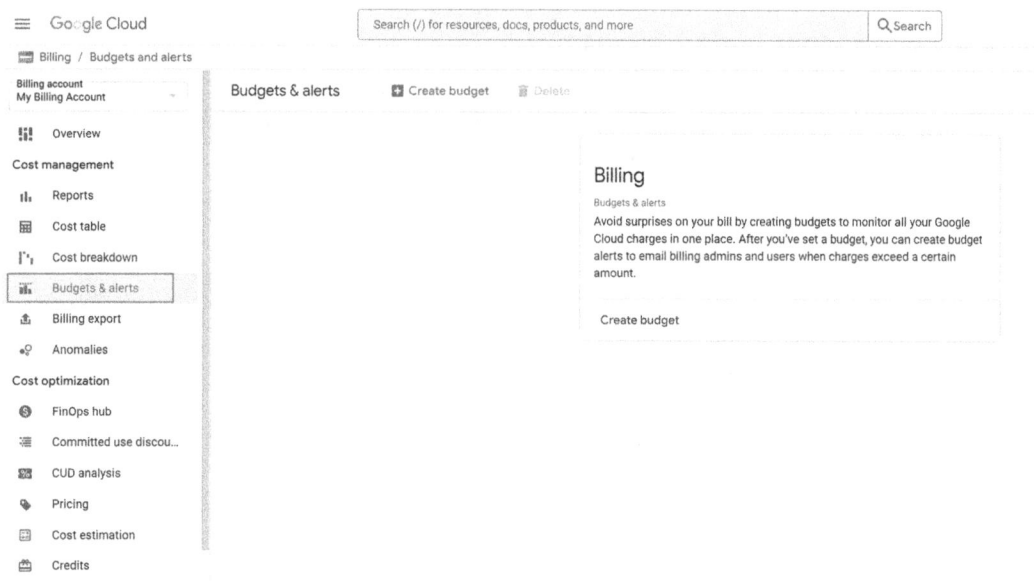

Figure 11-5. *Budgets & alerts option in Google Cloud*

4. Click Create Budget.

CHAPTER 11 MULTI-CLOUD ENVIRONMENT

5. Give a name of the scope. Set the time range, project, and services as shown in Figure 11-6.

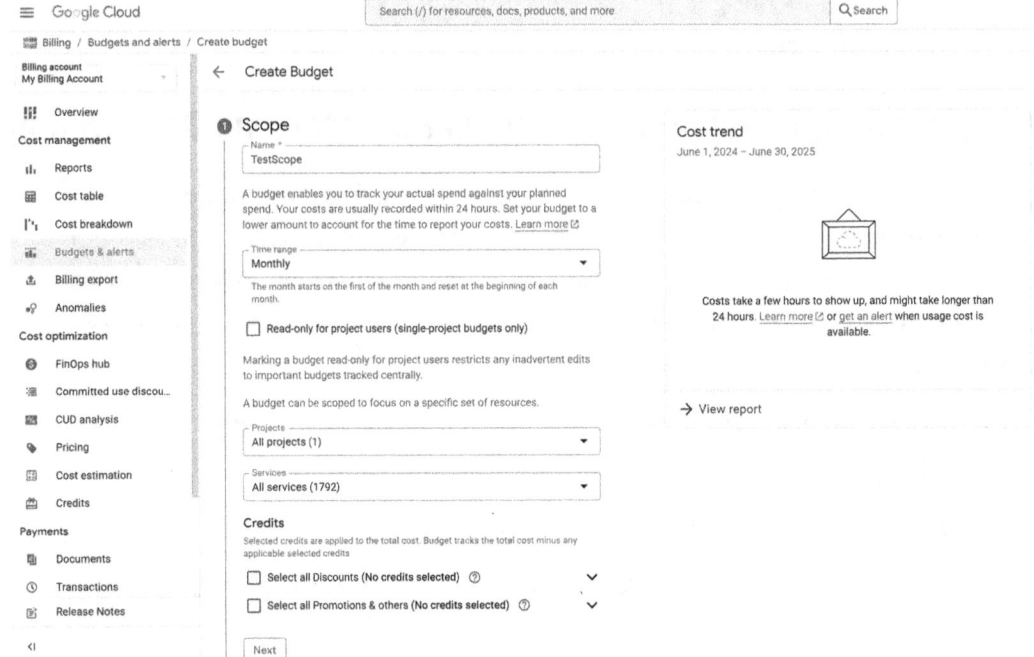

***Figure 11-6.** Creating budget in Google Cloud*

6. Click Next to set the amount. Set your budget type and target amount as shown in Figure 11-7.

CHAPTER 11 MULTI-CLOUD ENVIRONMENT

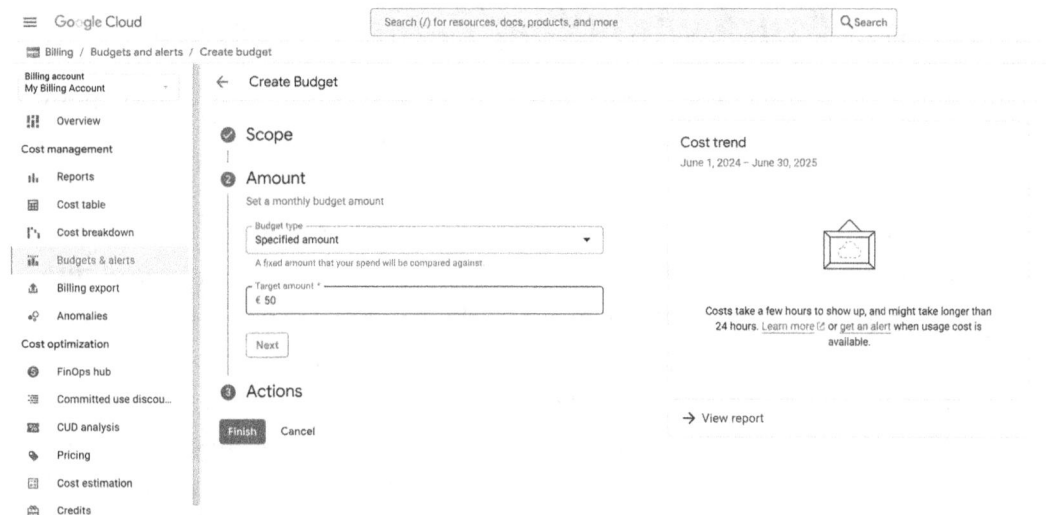

Figure 11-7. *Setting up the budget type and target amount for Google Cloud*

7. Click Next to set the account. Google Cloud automatically set some actions as shown in Figure 11-8.

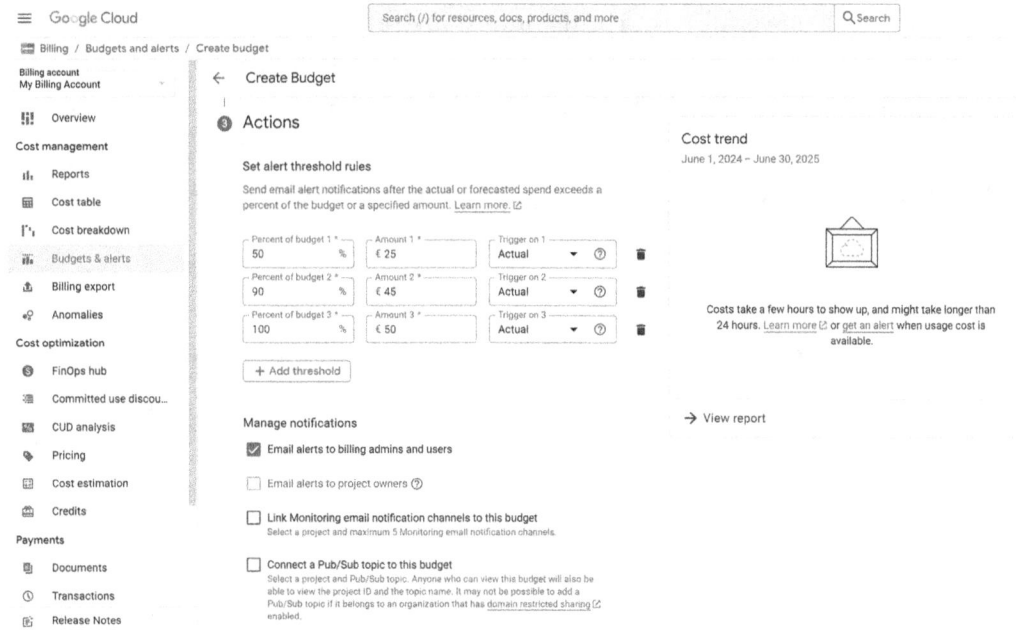

Figure 11-8. *Adding conditions and actions*

8. Click Finish.

Now, you will be notified once the budget exceeds.

519

Integrating Azure with Other Cloud Providers

Integrating Azure with other cloud providers is increasingly essential as organizations adopt multi-cloud strategies to optimize performance, ensure resiliency, and avoid vendor lock-in. Microsoft Azure facilitates this through services like **Azure Arc**, which enables centralized governance and management of external resources—such as AWS EC2 instances and GCP virtual machines—directly from Azure Portal. By using **Azure Policy with Azure Arc**, organizations can extend Azure's governance capabilities across all cloud resources, applying tagging rules, compliance checks, and auditing uniformly. In addition, cloud-native dashboards and monitoring tools like Azure Monitor and Log Analytics can aggregate telemetry data from multiple providers, creating a single pane of glass for operational oversight. These integrations support consistent policy enforcement, cost tracking, and identity management across platforms—without the need for hybrid or on-prem infrastructure setups.

Connecting Azure and AWS Using Azure Arc

Azure Arc provides a powerful way to bring **non-Azure infrastructure**, such as **AWS EC2 instances**, under **Azure Resource Manager (ARM)** control. Once connected, these AWS resources become **Azure Arc-enabled servers**, allowing organizations to manage them centrally through the Azure Portal alongside native Azure resources.

Azure Arc works by deploying a lightweight **Connected Machine Agent** onto the AWS EC2 instance. This agent

- Registers the machine in Azure as a **hybrid resource**
- Enables **Azure Policy**, **Azure Monitor**, and **Defender for Cloud**
- Communicates securely over **HTTPS (port 443)**—no need for VPN or ExpressRoute

Let's proceed with a demonstration of the step-by-step process for onboarding an AWS EC2 instance into Azure Arc.

1. Go to AWS console from `https://aws.amazon.com/`, log in with your billing account, and create an EC2 Instance with the following requirements. You can use your own instance as well. I am creating this instance just for this demo!

CHAPTER 11 MULTI-CLOUD ENVIRONMENT

   a. OS supported: Windows Server 2012 R2+, Ubuntu 16.04+, RHEL 7+, Amazon Linux 2+.

   b. Open outbound port 443.

   c. Set a unique hostname and ensure time sync.

2. Make sure the outbound port 443 is open.

3. Now, go back to Microsoft Azure portal. Go to Azure Arc ➤ All Azure Arc Resources. Click Add and select Add infrastructure as shown in Figure 11-9.

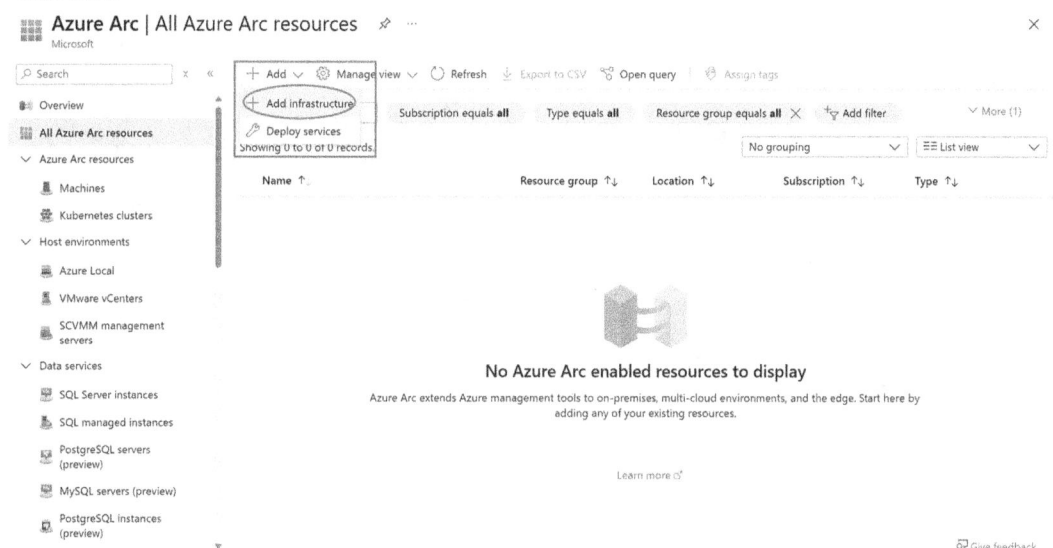

Figure 11-9. *Adding Azure Arc infrastructure in Azure Arc portal*

4. Click Add a machine as shown in Figure 11-10.

521

CHAPTER 11   MULTI-CLOUD ENVIRONMENT

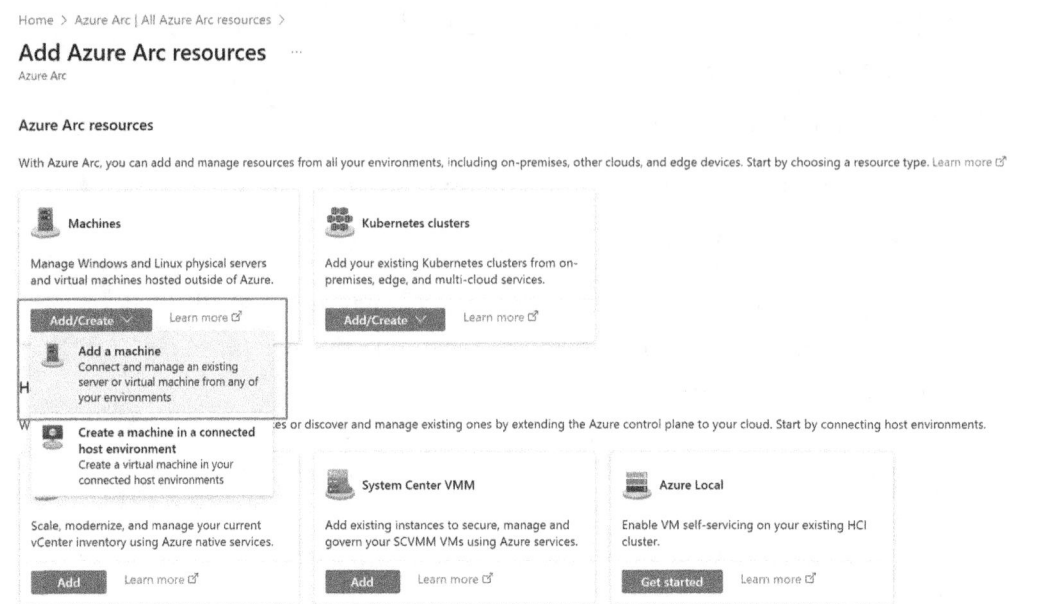

Figure 11-10. Adding virtual or physical machine as Azure Arc resource

5. Select Add a single server as shown in Figure 11-11.

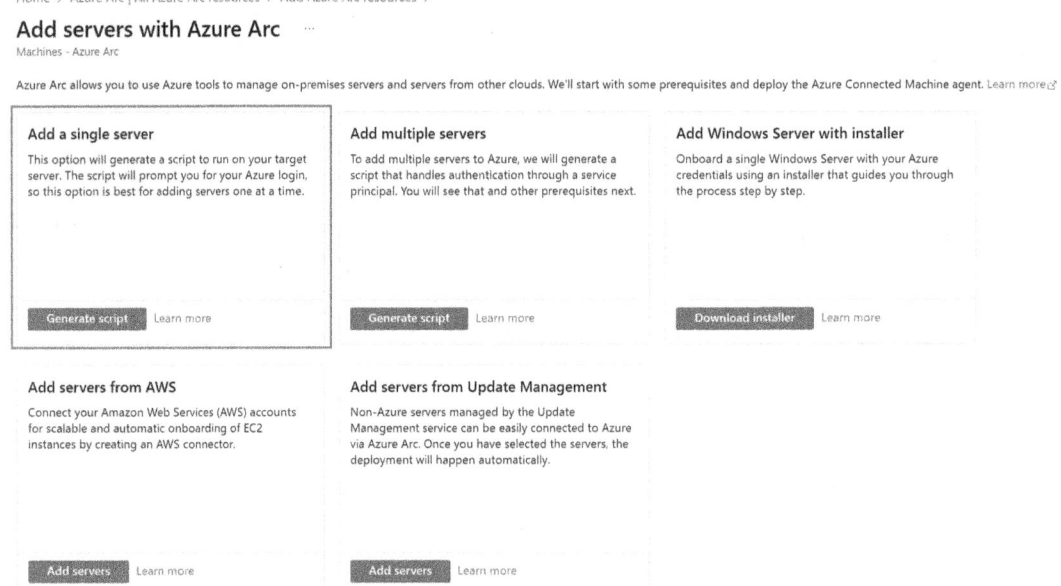

Figure 11-11. Generating script to add the resource in Azure Arc

CHAPTER 11 MULTI-CLOUD ENVIRONMENT

6. Click Generate script.

7. Fill the project details, server details, and connectivity method (public endpoint) and click Download and run script as shown in Figure 11-12.

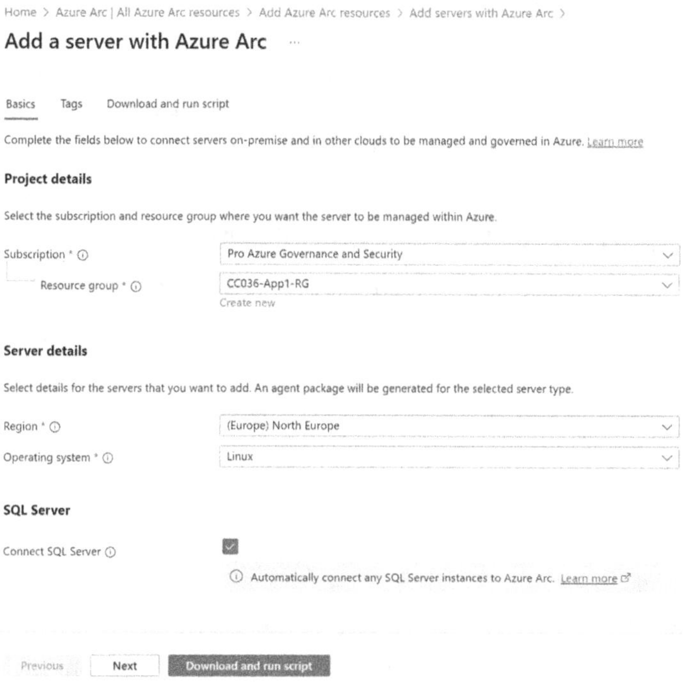

Figure 11-12. Providing server information, connectivity method, and project details

8. You will get a script like the following:

```
export subscriptionId="c16c7de6-926d-494f-90ca-4caa6e8a9045";
export resourceGroup="CC036-App1-RG";
export tenantId="8ef32bfa-9d5c-4dd1-b081-1ab2e78e94c0";
export location="northeurope";
export authType="token";
export correlationId="4ebc850b-b65b-4309-9c38-8159fca32d97";
export cloud="AzureCloud";
```

523

```
# Download the installation package
LINUX_INSTALL_SCRIPT="/tmp/install_linux_azcmagent.sh"
if [ -f "$LINUX_INSTALL_SCRIPT" ]; then rm -f
"$LINUX_INSTALL_SCRIPT"; fi;
output=$(wget https://gbl.his.arc.azure.com/azcmagent-linux -O
"$LINUX_INSTALL_SCRIPT" 2>&1);
if [ $? != 0 ]; then wget -qO- --method=PUT --body-data="{\"subscr
iptionId\":\"$subscriptionId\",\"resourceGroup\":\"$resourceGroup\
",\"tenantId\":\"$tenantId\",\"location\":\"$location\",\"correlat
ionId\":\"$correlationId\",\"authType\":\"$authType\",\"operation\
":\"onboarding\",\"messageType\":\"DownloadScriptFailed\",\"messag
e\":\"$output\"}" "https://gbl.his.arc.azure.com/log" &> /dev/null
|| true; fi;
echo "$output";

# Install the hybrid agent
bash "$LINUX_INSTALL_SCRIPT";
sleep 5;

# Run connect command
sudo azcmagent connect --resource-group "$resourceGroup"
--tenant-id "$tenantId" --location "$location" --subscription-
id "$subscriptionId" --cloud "$cloud" --correlation-id
"$correlationId";
```

9. You will get the page as shown in Figure 11-13.

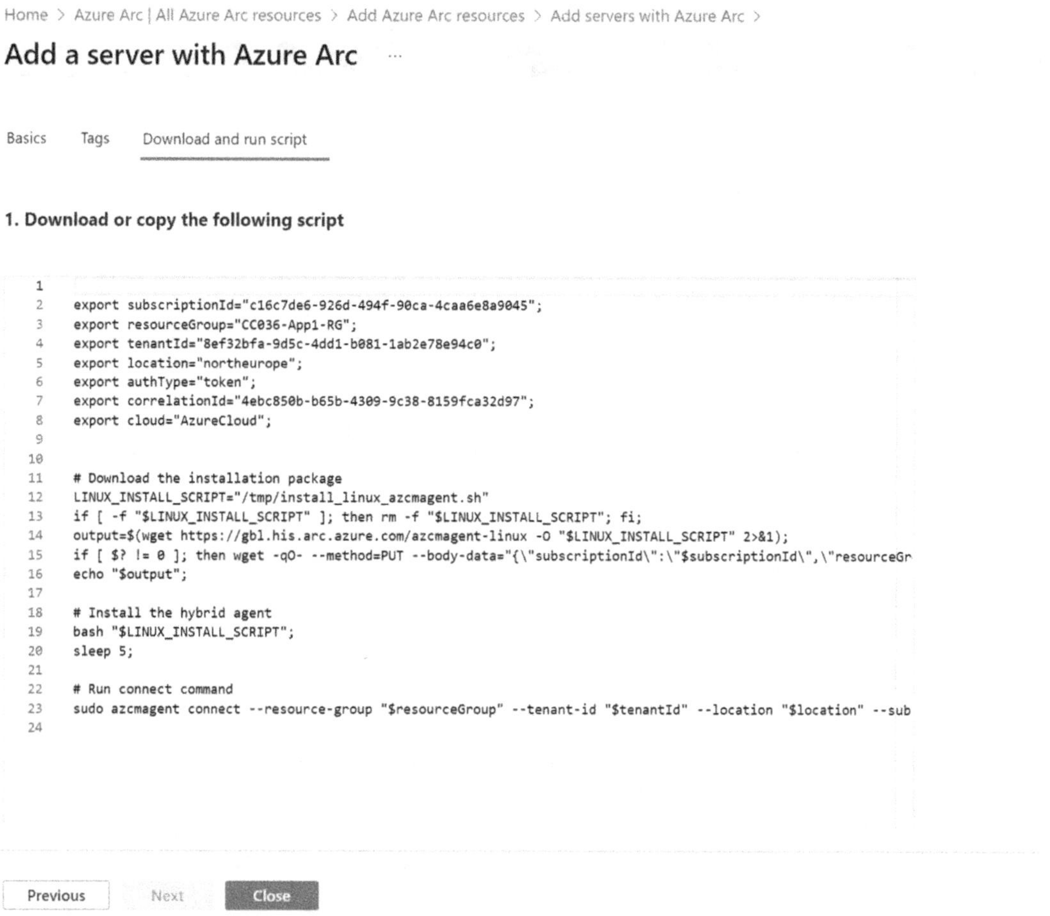

CHAPTER 11　MULTI-CLOUD ENVIRONMENT

Home > Azure Arc | All Azure Arc resources > Add Azure Arc resources > Add servers with Azure Arc >

Add a server with Azure Arc

Basics　Tags　Download and run script

1. Download or copy the following script

```
export subscriptionId="c16c7de6-926d-494f-90ca-4caa6e8a9045";
export resourceGroup="CC036-App1-RG";
export tenantId="8ef32bfa-9d5c-4dd1-b081-1ab2e78e94c0";
export location="northeurope";
export authType="token";
export correlationId="4ebc850b-b65b-4309-9c38-8159fca32d97";
export cloud="AzureCloud";

# Download the installation package
LINUX_INSTALL_SCRIPT="/tmp/install_linux_azcmagent.sh"
if [ -f "$LINUX_INSTALL_SCRIPT" ]; then rm -f "$LINUX_INSTALL_SCRIPT"; fi
output=$(wget https://gbl.his.arc.azure.com/azcmagent-linux -O "$LINUX_INSTALL_SCRIPT" 2>&1);
if [ $? != 0 ]; then wget -qO- --method=PUT --body-data="{\"subscriptionId\":\"$subscriptionId\",\"resourceGr
echo "$output";

# Install the hybrid agent
bash "$LINUX_INSTALL_SCRIPT";
sleep 5;

# Run connect command
sudo azcmagent connect --resource-group "$resourceGroup" --tenant-id "$tenantId" --location "$location" --sub
```

Previous　Next　Close

Figure 11-13. *Downloading or copying script to add the resource in Azure Arc*

10. Now, connect your EC2 instance via SSH or RDP as shown in Figure 11-14.

CHAPTER 11 MULTI-CLOUD ENVIRONMENT

***Figure 11-14.** CloudShell of AWS EC2 instance*

11. Paste and run the script. This installs the **Connected Machine Agent** and registers the instance with Azure.

12. After a few seconds, you can see the registration is completed successfully as shown in Figure 11-15.

CHAPTER 11 MULTI-CLOUD ENVIRONMENT

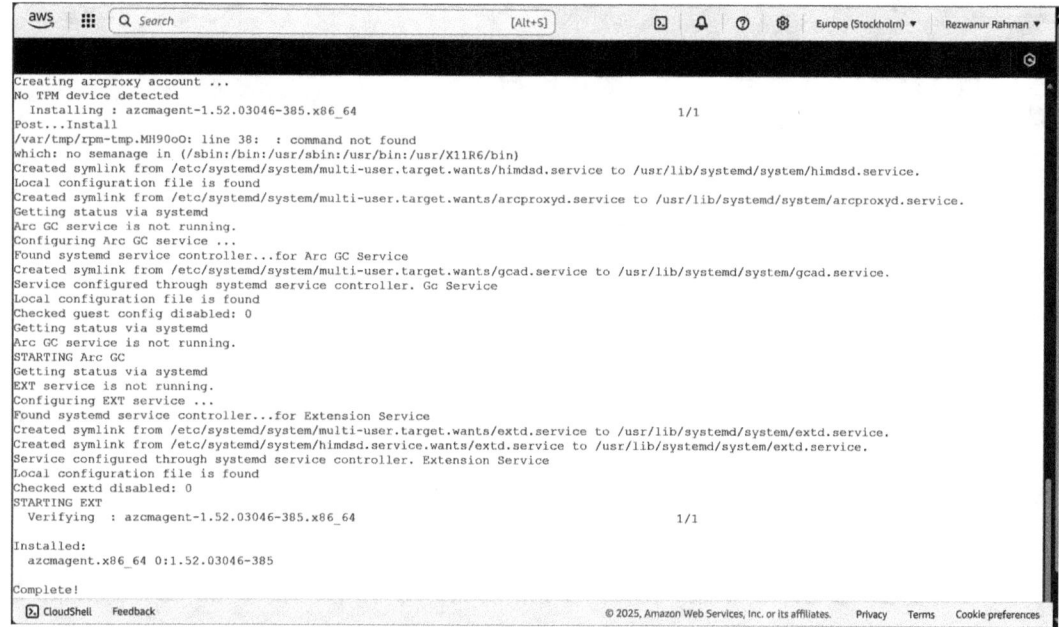

***Figure 11-15.** Running the script in CloudShell in AWS*

13. It will show a verification code that you have to provide through https://microsoft.com/devicelogin.

14. Add the code and it will be completed as shown in Figure 11-16.

CHAPTER 11   MULTI-CLOUD ENVIRONMENT

Figure 11-16. *Logs that confirming the successful integration of the AWS VM with Azure Arc*

15. Now, go back to Azure Arc dashboard; you can see the VM that you just added as shown in Figure 11-17.

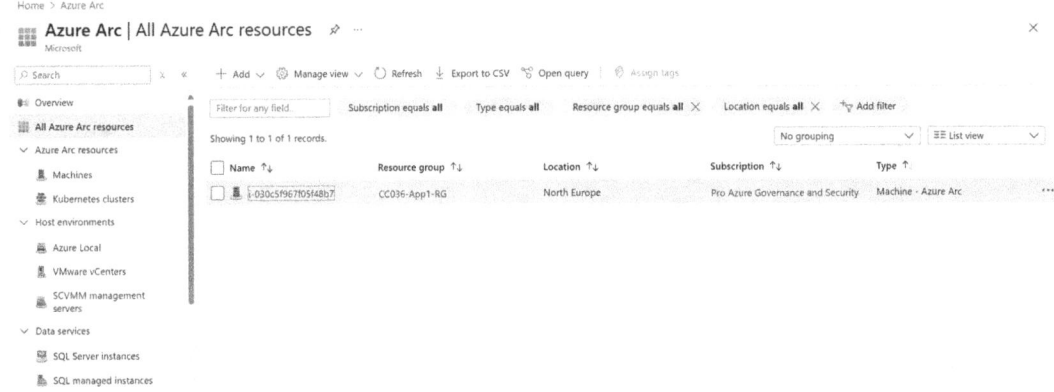

Figure 11-17. *AWS machine in Azure Arc dashboard*

16. To verify this, click the resource, and you will see all the information including the cloud provider and manufacturer as shown in Figure 11-18.

CHAPTER 11   MULTI-CLOUD ENVIRONMENT

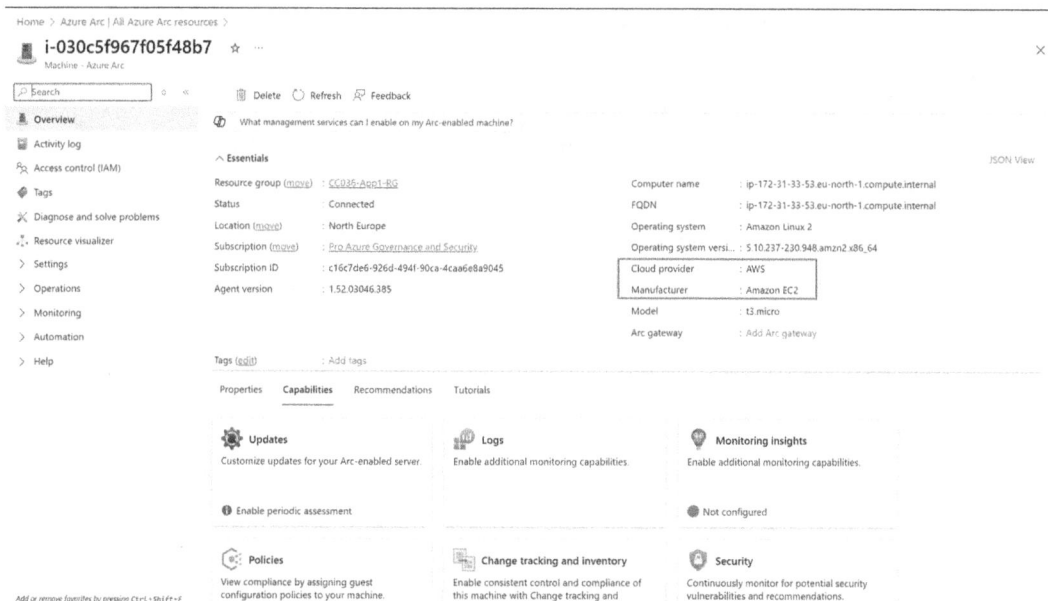

Figure 11-18. Verifying the cloud provider of the VM

Once your AWS VM is Azure Arc enabled, it becomes manageable as a native Azure resource, unlocking a range of governance and operational capabilities. You can apply Azure tags for cost tracking and inventory classification, ensuring consistent metadata across clouds. Azure Policy can be used to audit configurations or enforce compliance rules directly on the AWS VM. Monitoring becomes seamless by installing the Log Analytics agent (either AMA or MMA), which enables telemetry collection and log analysis within Azure Monitor. For update lifecycle management, Azure Automation allows you to schedule, deploy, and report on system updates. Lastly, integrating the instance with Microsoft Defender for Cloud enhances its security posture by providing threat detection, vulnerability assessment, and security recommendations—all from within the Azure Portal.

Summary

In this chapter, we explored the governance challenges that arise when organizations operate in **multi-cloud environments** spanning Azure, AWS, and GCP. As cloud strategies become more distributed, the complexity of maintaining consistent policies, unified cost management, and clear visibility across platforms increases significantly.

We looked at how tools such as **Azure Arc**, **AWS Organizations**, and **GCP Labels** can help bridge these gaps by enabling centralized control and consistent policy enforcement. Through real-world scenarios and hands-on demos, we saw how unified tagging, cross-cloud cost tracking, and automation can bring order to fragmented environments.

Ultimately, this chapter highlighted the importance of having a **coherent multi-cloud governance strategy** to ensure compliance, operational efficiency, and security across all platforms.

CHAPTER 12

Future Directions in Cloud Governance and Security

In the previous chapter, we addressed the growing challenges of managing governance across **multi-cloud environments**. We explored how organizations can maintain consistency, compliance, and control using tools like **Azure Arc**, unified tagging strategies, and cross-cloud cost tracking. These practices help ensure governance doesn't break down when working across multiple cloud providers.

In this chapter, we shift our focus to what lies ahead. As cloud technologies evolve, so do the approaches to governance and security. We'll explore **emerging trends** such as AI-driven automation, confidential computing, decentralized identity, and sustainability governance. These forward-looking topics aim to prepare you for the next wave of innovation and complexity in cloud environments.

Let's explore the future of cloud governance and security—and how to stay ahead of the curve.

Emerging Trends and Technologies

As cloud environments grow more complex, governance and security strategies must evolve to keep pace with emerging technologies. This section explores the latest trends shaping the future of cloud governance—from the expansion of Zero Trust into AI, IoT, and edge computing to the growing role of cloud-native tools and multi-cloud management platforms. These developments are redefining how organizations enforce policy, ensure compliance, and build resilient, intelligent governance across increasingly distributed systems.

The Expansion of Zero Trust into AI, IoT, and Edge Workloads

In Chapter 10, I introduced the foundational principles and architectural patterns of Zero Trust within Azure, focusing on how Microsoft implements identity-driven, policy-enforced, and continuously verified access control. That discussion addressed the six core pillars of Zero Trust—identity, devices, applications, data, infrastructure, and networks—and highlighted Azure-native tools like Microsoft Entra ID, Conditional Access, Azure Policy, and Defender for Cloud.

Here, we take that conversation a step further. As cloud environments evolve to include intelligent applications, connected sensors, and distributed edge computing platforms, the Zero Trust model must also evolve. Traditional enforcement mechanisms—based on human identities, corporate networks, or centralized workloads—are insufficient in these decentralized, automated, and occasionally offline environments. In this section, I explore how Microsoft is expanding Zero Trust principles to secure AI workloads, IoT ecosystems, and edge infrastructure, turning the model into a universal framework for modern cloud-native security.

Securing AI Workloads with Zero Trust

AI models and pipelines are increasingly integrated into business-critical applications hosted across Azure and hybrid environments. These workloads often operate autonomously, driven by APIs or automation services, making them susceptible to unauthorized access, model theft, or data leakage.

To enforce Zero Trust in AI, Microsoft provides the following capabilities:

- **Access Control via Azure Machine Learning RBAC**: Permissions to workspaces, datasets, pipelines, and model registries are tightly scoped using role-based access control, ensuring that only authorized users or services can interact with specific AI assets.

- **Token-Based Inference Authentication**: Deployed model endpoints in Azure Machine Learning are protected with OAuth2 tokens or Managed Identity authentication, which eliminates hardcoded secrets and ensures secure, auditable access.

- **Data Governance Integration**: Microsoft Purview helps classify and track the datasets used for training and inference. Sensitivity labels, encryption, and access policies enforce compliance with internal governance and external regulations.

- **Secure Deployment Pipelines**: GitHub Actions and Azure DevOps pipelines can use Federated Identity Credentials to access Azure ML without storing secrets, aligning with Zero Trust's principle of minimizing implicit trust.

These safeguards ensure that every API call, training job, and deployment are subject to continuous validation and that trust decisions are context aware and telemetry driven.

Zero Trust for IoT Devices

Internet of Things (IoT) devices introduce a different set of risks—long lifecycles, physical exposure, weak default configurations, and limited processing capacity. Many IoT systems lack human intervention and operate over public or semi-trusted networks, making Zero Trust principles essential but challenging to enforce.

Microsoft Defender for IoT and Azure IoT Hub implement key Zero Trust strategies for this environment:

- **Per-Device Identity and Authentication**: Devices register through Azure Device Provisioning Service (DPS) and authenticate using X.509 certificates, symmetric keys, or Trusted Platform Modules (TPMs). This ensures each device has a unique, verifiable identity.

- **Device Isolation and Segmentation**: Using Application Security Groups (ASGs), Virtual Networks, and Network Security Groups (NSGs), IoT devices are isolated based on function, location, or sensitivity. Lateral movement is minimized, and communication is explicitly allowed based on need.

- **Behavioral Monitoring**: Microsoft Defender for IoT profiles expected device behavior and alerts administrators to deviations—such as unusual protocols, excessive connections, or changes in traffic patterns.

- **Update Control and Policy Enforcement**: Devices can be assigned update rings, compliance policies, and firmware governance policies that ensure ongoing alignment with the organization's security baseline.

These Zero Trust strategies are particularly valuable in high-risk, high-scale environments such as **smart factories**, where IoT sensors control robotic arms and machinery; **healthcare systems**, where connected devices monitor patient vitals; and **energy grids**, where IoT endpoints manage real-time distribution and load balancing. In each of these scenarios, enforcing device identity, segmentation, and behavioral monitoring is critical to ensuring operational security and continuity.

These measures bring Zero Trust into environments previously thought too constrained to benefit from modern security architecture, enabling visibility and control over billions of edge-connected sensors and smart devices.

Edge Computing and Zero Trust with Azure Stack and Azure Arc

Edge computing platforms, such as **Azure Stack Edge**, **Azure Stack HCI**, and **Azure Arc-enabled servers**, introduce a hybrid architecture where compute resources are physically close to data sources but logically part of the cloud. These platforms must operate securely even when disconnected from Azure's control plane, requiring local policy enforcement and secure synchronization when connectivity resumes.

Microsoft enables Zero Trust at the edge through the following strategies:

- **Identity Federation and Conditional Access**: Azure Stack can federate with Entra ID to apply authentication, authorization, and Conditional Access policies. Cached tokens ensure continuity even during outages.

- **Privileged Access Management**: Administrator access to edge devices is controlled through Microsoft Entra ID Privileged Identity Management (PIM), allowing time-bound elevation and audit trails. This prevents persistent privileges on sensitive devices.

- **Secure Configuration and Monitoring via Azure Arc**: Azure Arc enables centralized visibility and configuration compliance across edge environments. Policies applied in Azure (e.g., Azure Policy) extend to registered Arc-enabled resources, enforcing configuration drift detection and governance at scale.

- **Telemetry and Threat Protection**: Even at the edge, devices can send logs and telemetry to Microsoft Defender for Cloud or Microsoft Sentinel (when connected), allowing anomalies to be captured and remediated centrally.

This unified model aligns disconnected or bandwidth-constrained environments with the same Zero Trust principles that govern cloud-native applications, ensuring policy consistency and security coherence.

Rise of AI-Powered Governance and Security Tools

The integration of artificial intelligence (AI) into governance and cybersecurity has moved from theory to practice, redefining how organizations manage threats, enforce policy, and achieve compliance at scale. Microsoft has been at the forefront of this transformation, embedding machine learning (ML), large language models (LLMs), and generative AI into its security and governance ecosystem. AI is no longer simply a tool for data science teams—it now acts as an intelligent layer within the operational fabric of Microsoft Azure, Entra, Defender, and Sentinel. Let's explore how AI-powered tools are enhancing cloud governance and security, automating complex workflows, identifying threats proactively, and reducing operational burden through intelligent insights.

While these AI-powered capabilities offer significant benefits, it's important to recognize their current limitations—such as potential false positives, model bias, or overreliance on automated decisions without human oversight. Incorporating AI responsibly requires continuous tuning, validation, and human-in-the-loop governance.

Microsoft Security Copilot: AI for Threat Detection and Response

Launched as part of Microsoft's unified security vision, **Microsoft Security Copilot** is a generative AI assistant built on OpenAI's GPT foundation and fine-tuned with Microsoft's global threat intelligence. Integrated with tools like **Microsoft Sentinel**, **Defender XDR**, and **Entra ID**, Security Copilot helps security professionals understand, investigate, and respond to incidents faster. Here are some key features of Microsoft Security Copilot.

Natural Language Incident Summarization

Security Copilot uses Microsoft's fine-tuned large language models to automatically interpret and summarize alert data ingested from Microsoft 365 Defender and Microsoft Sentinel. These summaries are generated by analyzing entities involved (user, IP, file hash, hostname), timestamped actions, and correlated threat intelligence. Let's see how it works:

- Parses alert metadata and threat analytics using data from Microsoft Graph Security API

- Identifies MITRE ATT&CK techniques (e.g., Credential Access— T1003) present in alert context

- Structures the alert into an easy-to-read timeline or summary

For example:

"User rezwanur@m365community.eu authenticated from IP 203.0.113.14 via RDP outside business hours. Lateral movement was attempted via SMB to dc01.m365community.eu Suspicious PowerShell execution was detected (PID 4423, Script: Invoke-Mimikatz.ps1)."

This reduces the time needed to comprehend complex multi-alert incidents.

Automated Playbook Generation

When a threat is detected, Copilot can suggest a customized remediation playbook. These workflows may include isolating a device in Microsoft Defender for Endpoint, revoking a user's session in Entra ID, or triggering alerts via Logic Apps.

Rather than starting from scratch, SOC teams are presented with ready-to-deploy responses aligned with Microsoft Sentinel's SOAR framework.

Threat Hunting with Natural Language

Instead of manually crafting **Kusto Query Language (KQL)** queries, analysts can use plain language to instruct Copilot to run complex log searches across Microsoft Sentinel data, for example:

"Show me all lateral movement attempts from the compromised user in the last 72 hours"

KQL Output:

```
DeviceNetworkEvents
| where ActionType == "RemoteDesktopProtocol"
| where InitiatingProcessAccountName == "compromised_user"
| where Timestamp > ago(72h)
```

Copilot interprets the question, builds the correct query, runs it against Sentinel logs, and displays the results—making threat hunting accessible to non-KQL experts.

Context-Aware Recommendations

Copilot correlates real-time signals from Microsoft 365 Defender, Entra ID, Intune, and Microsoft Purview to provide **situation-specific mitigation recommendations**. These suggestions are tailored based on the following:

- **User risk level** (via Entra Identity Protection)
- **Endpoint posture** (via Microsoft Intune and Defender for Endpoint)
- **App and data sensitivity** (via Microsoft Purview classification)
- **Threat confidence score** (from Microsoft Threat Intelligence Graph)

Copilot not only recommends actions but can also provide the technical steps or even generate a ready-to-use Logic App to implement them. In the next chapter, I discussed the Azure Copilot and Azure AI briefly with configuration and demo.

AI-Enhanced Policy Recommendations in Microsoft Defender for Cloud

Microsoft Defender for Cloud now incorporates AI-driven logic to go beyond traditional rule-based misconfiguration alerts. Instead of simply flagging non-compliance, it applies graph-based analysis, behavioral modeling, and context-aware prioritization to help security teams focus on the most critical risks—those that are both **exploitable** and **exposed**. Let's discuss some key capabilities of AI in Microsoft Defender for Cloud:

- **Attack Path Analysis:** Uses graph-based AI to identify exposed attack paths, for example, a public VM linked to an over-permissioned identity and a sensitive storage account

- **Contextual Risk Scoring:** Determines risk levels based on exploitability, not just misconfiguration frequency

- **Automated Remediation:** Suggests and sometimes auto-applies remediations such as NSG rules or RBAC pruning

Copilot for Microsoft Entra: Governance and Identity Insights

Microsoft Entra Copilot, currently in preview, brings AI into **identity governance**, helping organizations manage access rights, analyze role assignments, and streamline compliance reviews. Some governance use cases are the following:

- **Explain Role Assignments**: Understand why a user has access to a resource—through direct assignment, group inheritance, or entitlement package.

- **Automate Access Review Decisions**: AI can assist reviewers by surfacing activity logs and recommending decisions based on user behavior and compliance context.

- **Just-in-Time Insights**: Ask Entra Copilot to show access risk by department, project, or location in natural language.

Table 12-1 shows some sample prompts based on categories.

Table 12-1. Sample Copilot prompt based on the governance category

Category	Sample Prompt
Privileged Access and Roles	"List all users with Global Administrator roles and their last sign-in date."
	"Show all users who were assigned privileged roles but haven't signed in during the last 45 days."
	"Which users have active PIM (Just-in-Time) roles in the past 7 days?"

(continued)

Table 12-1. (*continued*)

Category	Sample Prompt
Guest and External Users	"Which guest users still have access to Teams shared channels and haven't been active in 30 days?"
	"List external users who are part of any security group with write permissions in production tenants."
	"Show all B2B users with access to sensitive applications."
Role Justification and Mapping	"Why does rezwanur@m365community.eu have access to the HR system?"
	"Map the access path of user rezwanur@m365community.eu, including direct and group-based permissions."
	"What access package assignments grant roles to contractor@partner.com?"
Risk and Compliance Monitoring	"Identify users with high-risk sign-ins who still hold privileged roles."
	"Which users with GDPR-labeled data access are using unmanaged devices?"
	"Show all admin role assignments that have not been reviewed in over 90 days."
Access Review Optimization	"Suggest access removal for users with no activity in the last 60 days."
	"List departments with the highest number of inactive privileged accounts."
	"Who approved the last five role elevation requests in the 'Finance Admin' group?"

Microsoft Purview and AI-Powered Data Governance

Governance is not limited to security—it also encompasses **data discovery, classification, retention, and lifecycle control**. Microsoft Purview now integrates AI for

- **Auto-classification** of sensitive data (e.g., credit card numbers, GDPR-regulated content).

- **AI-Driven Data Mapping** across cloud and hybrid environments, helping organizations understand data movement.

- **Adaptive DLP Policies**: AI adapts enforcement based on real-time context (e.g., preventing export of sensitive data over unmanaged devices).

Shift Toward Multi-cloud Governance Standards

As enterprises expand their digital footprint across multiple cloud providers—Microsoft Azure, Amazon Web Services (AWS), Google Cloud Platform (GCP), and beyond—the need for unified governance becomes critical. A fragmented governance model introduces operational inefficiencies, compliance gaps, and increased security risk. To address this, Microsoft and industry partners are aligning around **multi-cloud governance standards** that promote consistent visibility, policy enforcement, and compliance across heterogeneous environments. These tools support alignment with widely adopted compliance frameworks such as **ISO 27001**, **SOC 2**, **HIPAA**, and **FedRAMP**, which are recognized across major cloud platforms including AWS and GCP.

Microsoft has responded to this shift through **Microsoft Defender for Cloud**, **Azure Arc**, and **Azure Policy for multi-cloud**, enabling governance at scale without forcing lock-in or vendor-specific tooling.

Microsoft's Approach to Multi-cloud Governance

To help organizations govern diverse environments consistently, Microsoft delivers a cloud-native yet cloud-agnostic governance model that extends well beyond Azure. With services like Microsoft Defender for Cloud, Azure Arc, and Azure Policy, enterprises can manage compliance, enforce controls, and secure resources across Azure, AWS, GCP, and even on-premises data centers—all from a single control plane.

Microsoft Defender for Cloud: Multi-cloud Security Posture Management

Defender for Cloud supports not just Azure, but also AWS and Google Cloud environments. It connects to these platforms through built-in API connectors and Azure Arc, allowing you to onboard external resources in minutes.

Once connected, Defender applies security assessments using well-known frameworks like **CIS**, **NIST**, and **ISO 27001**. It then consolidates findings into a unified **Secure Score** that reflects your overall risk posture across all clouds.

Azure Arc: Unifying Governance Across Platforms

Azure Arc plays a key role in bringing **non-Azure resources**—like on-prem servers, AWS EC2 instances, Kubernetes clusters, and SQL databases—into Azure's governance framework. Once registered with Arc, these resources behave like native Azure objects, meaning you can apply **Azure Policy**, enable **Defender for Servers**, and manage updates centrally.

Azure Policy and Azure Monitor for Multi-cloud Environments

Through Azure Arc, you can assign governance policies to resources outside Azure. This includes enforcing naming conventions, tagging standards, VM sizing restrictions, and cost controls—no matter which cloud your resource lives in.

In addition, **Azure Monitor** and **Log Analytics** can collect performance and security logs from virtual machines, containers, and Kubernetes clusters across all environments. These logs can be used for auditing, alerting, and reporting.

The Role of Quantum Computing in Cloud Security

Quantum computing is no longer a theoretical concept—it is rapidly progressing toward real-world applications that could significantly disrupt modern cryptographic systems. While today's quantum machines are still in their early stages, the eventual arrival of large-scale quantum computers poses a serious challenge to classical encryption algorithms that secure our data in the cloud. RSA, ECC, and other widely used public key cryptosystems rely on mathematical problems that quantum algorithms, such as Shor's algorithm, could solve exponentially faster than classical counterparts. This has profound implications for cloud security, where identity, communication, and data protection are built on these cryptographic foundations. In this section, I will walk you through the risks introduced by quantum computing, the emerging discipline of post-quantum cryptography (PQC), and how Microsoft is preparing Azure and its ecosystem to remain resilient in a post-quantum world.

Understanding Post-Quantum Cryptography (PQC)

Post-Quantum Cryptography (PQC) refers to a new class of cryptographic algorithms designed to withstand attacks from large-scale quantum computers. While current encryption schemes such as RSA, ECC (Elliptic Curve Cryptography), and DH (Diffie-Hellman) provide adequate protection today, they are based on problems—like integer factorization and discrete logarithms—that quantum computers could break using **Shor's algorithm**. Once such quantum capabilities are realized, these algorithms will become obsolete, putting all encrypted data at risk of future decryption—also known as **"harvest now, decrypt later."**

To proactively address this risk, Microsoft and the broader security community are adopting **quantum-resistant algorithms**, guided by the **NIST Post-Quantum Cryptography Standardization Project**. The goal is to transition cloud platforms and dependent systems toward **quantum-safe cryptography** before quantum adversaries can break the existing protections. Table 12-2 shows the key concepts of PQC.

Table 12-2. Key concepts of PQC

Term	Description
Quantum-Safe Algorithms	Cryptographic algorithms resistant to both classical and quantum attacks
Shor's Algorithm	Quantum algorithm that breaks RSA, DSA, and ECC by factoring large numbers quickly
Lattice-Based Cryptography	A leading PQC approach using hard lattice problems—used in NIST finalist schemes
Hybrid Cryptography	Combines classical and post-quantum algorithms for transitional deployments
Harvest Now, Decrypt Later	Threat model where encrypted traffic is stored and decrypted when quantum tech matures

Table 12-3 shows how PQC differs from classical cryptography.

Table 12-3. Difference between classical cryptography and PQC

Characteristic	Classical Cryptography (RSA/ECC)	Post-Quantum Cryptography (PQC)
Mathematical Foundation	Factorization, discrete log	Lattice problems, code based, hash based, etc.
Quantum Resistance	Vulnerable to Shor's algorithm	Designed to resist both classical and quantum
Key Size	Smaller (256–4096 bits)	Larger (often > 1 KB, depending on scheme)
Standardization	Widely adopted (TLS, VPNs, PGP, etc.)	Still being standardized (NIST, IETF in progress)
Performance Impact	Optimized, hardware accelerated	Slightly slower, ongoing optimization underway

How Microsoft Is Preparing

Microsoft is working closely with international standards bodies like **National Institute of Standards and Technology (NIST)** to help choose and test the best quantum-safe algorithms. Microsoft is also updating products like the following:

- **Windows 11**: Supports hybrid encryption (classical + quantum safe)
- **Azure Key Vault**: Being upgraded to support post-quantum key exchanges
- **TLS (used in HTTPS)**: Now being tested with a mix of traditional and post-quantum encryption (e.g., X25519 + Kyber)

In 2023, Microsoft began deploying hybrid PQC handshakes in **Windows Insider builds** and released tools to help developers begin migrating.

How to Prepare Your Cloud Environment for PQC

To prepare for the transition to post-quantum cryptography, organizations should begin by conducting a comprehensive inventory of their encryption tools, libraries, and protocols, especially those involved in long-term data protection, identity management, and key exchange. Understanding where classical algorithms like RSA and ECC are used is essential for planning future upgrades. Next, organizations should prioritize crypto-agility—the ability to switch from one cryptographic algorithm to another without re-architecting entire systems. This means adopting modular cryptographic libraries, flexible TLS stacks, and updatable certificate infrastructures. Finally, it's critical to stay aligned with Microsoft's ongoing PQC developments across Azure, Microsoft 365, Windows, and related services. Microsoft continues to release tools, previews, and technical guidance to help customers make a smooth and secure transition toward quantum-safe cryptography.

Quantum Threat Modeling for Cloud Systems

As quantum computing advances, it introduces an entirely new class of threats—ones that cannot be adequately addressed by classical cryptographic assumptions. Traditional threat modeling focuses on attack vectors such as privilege escalation, lateral movement, or malware injection. **Quantum threat modeling**, on the other hand, evaluates long-term confidentiality risks, cryptographic durability, and future adversary capabilities.

The purpose of quantum threat modeling is to identify and prioritize **cloud systems, services, and data flows** that would be vulnerable if current cryptographic protections (like RSA, ECC, or ECDSA) were rendered obsolete by a quantum-capable adversary. This helps organizations take preemptive steps—such as crypto inventory, system hardening, and PQC adoption—before the threat becomes practical.

Why Quantum Threat Modeling Is Needed

Unlike zero-day threats, quantum attacks are **not imminent but inevitable**. This requires a **long-view security mindset**, where systems must remain secure even if the encryption methods used today are broken in 10–20 years. Table 12-4 shows the core elements of quantum threat modeling.

Table 12-4. *List of core elements of quantum threat modeling*

Modeling Dimension	Description
Cryptographic Inventory	Identify all uses of asymmetric encryption and digital signatures
Data Longevity Risk	Classify data by how long it must remain confidential (e.g., 5, 10, 20+ years)
Algorithmic Vulnerability	Flag algorithms like RSA, DH, and ECDSA that are quantum vulnerable
Trust Boundary Mapping	Understand which internal/external systems rely on non-quantum-safe keys
Control Evaluation	Assess whether systems support crypto-agility, hybrid PQC adoption, or key rotation

Microsoft recommends using the **STRIDE** methodology extended for post-quantum risk evaluation. While STRIDE typically focuses on Spoofing, Tampering, Repudiation, Information Disclosure, Denial of Service, and Elevation of Privilege, it can be augmented to include

- **Quantum-resilient authentication (QRA)**
- **Post-quantum integrity assurance (PQIA)**
- **Long-term confidentiality assurance (LTCA)**

Microsoft's internal threat modeling tools (e.g., Threat Modeling Tool in Azure DevOps or SDL Toolkit) can be customized to include these PQC parameters. To learn more, check out the official Microsoft documentation at https://learn.microsoft.com/en-us/azure/security/develop/threat-modeling-tool.

Quantum-Resistant Key Management in Azure

Key management is at the heart of cloud security. Every encrypted communication, protected file, or authenticated session relies on the confidentiality and integrity of cryptographic keys. With the rise of quantum computing, traditional key management practices—especially those based on **RSA** and **ECC**—are at risk. To address this,

CHAPTER 12   FUTURE DIRECTIONS IN CLOUD GOVERNANCE AND SECURITY

Microsoft Azure is evolving its **key lifecycle management** to support **quantum-resistant cryptographic algorithms**, particularly in **Azure Key Vault, Azure Key Vault Managed HSM**, and **Azure confidential computing** workloads.

Azure's post-quantum strategy centers around **crypto-agility, hybrid key exchange support**, and the ability to **safely rotate, store, and use PQC keys** without compromising existing systems.

Quantum computers could eventually

- Recover private keys from public certificates (e.g., RSA-2048 or ECDSA)
- Forge digital signatures
- Break key exchange protocols like TLS and SSH
- Compromise long-term secrets stored in vaults

How Azure Supports Quantum-Resistant Key Management

Azure has begun integrating quantum-resilient cryptography into various services, particularly through the adoption of **Kyber**, a NIST-selected lattice-based key encapsulation mechanism (KEM). The current approach focuses on **hybrid modes**, which combine classical algorithms like **X25519** with Kyber to ensure backward compatibility and enhanced security. Table 12-5 shows Azure components and their post-quantum cryptography (PQC) readiness.

Table 12-5. Azure components with PQC readiness

Component	PQC Readiness
Azure Key Vault	Can store and manage PQC-compatible keys; hybrid TLS support in preview
Azure Key Vault Managed HSM	Supports BYOK (Bring Your Own Key) models with future support for PQC formats
Azure TLS Stack (Windows and Linux)	Hybrid key exchange supported (X25519 + Kyber) via OpenSSL in latest builds
Azure Confidential Ledger	Designed for long-term data integrity, with upcoming support for PQC hash schemes

Microsoft is currently testing **hybrid TLS** handshakes using **X25519 + Kyber**. This means the client and server exchange keys using **both algorithms** in parallel. If a quantum adversary breaks X25519 in the future, Kyber ensures the session remains secure.

Table 12-6 shows the future-proof key scenarios in Azure.

Table 12-6. Future-proof key scenarios in Azure with PQC readiness

Use Case	Post-Quantum Readiness
TLS Handshake (Web Apps)	X25519 + Kyber hybrid mode available (TLS 1.3)
Client/Server Certificates	PQC support under development for PKI and Azure-managed certificates
Database Encryption (TDE)	AES based—already quantum resistant (with 256-bit key)
Signing API Calls (JWT, OAuth)	Signature schemes like **Dilithium** and **SPHINCS+** under evaluation
Azure Storage Encryption	AES-256 by default—secure against quantum threats

Quantum-resistant key management is critical to ensuring cloud security in the post-quantum era. Microsoft Azure is enabling this transition through hybrid cryptographic support, secure key lifecycle automation, and a roadmap aligned with global cryptographic standards. By adopting Azure's PQC-ready features today, organizations can protect their data, credentials, and systems for the challenges of tomorrow.

Microsoft's Quantum Initiatives in Cloud Security

Microsoft plays a dual role in the quantum era: as both a **pioneer in building scalable quantum computers** and a **leader in preparing the cloud ecosystem for post-quantum threats**. While the long-term goal is to deliver fault-tolerant quantum computing through the Azure Quantum platform, Microsoft is already taking concrete steps to ensure its cloud security infrastructure is ready for the cryptographic challenges that quantum computing introduces. To learn more about Microsoft Quantum, refer to the official Microsoft docs at https://learn.microsoft.com/en-us/azure/quantum/.

These initiatives span research, standardization, implementation of post-quantum cryptography (PQC), and integration into Azure services—providing customers with quantum-safe capabilities well ahead of the threat horizon. Table 12-7 shows the key focus areas of Microsoft's Quantum Security Strategy.

Table 12-7. List of key focus areas of Microsoft Quantum Security Strategy

Initiative	Purpose
Post-Quantum Cryptography (PQC)	Integrate quantum-resistant cryptographic algorithms into TLS, identity, and key management
Crypto-Agility Engineering	Enable services to quickly switch cryptographic algorithms without architectural redesigns
Quantum-Resilient TLS (Hybrid)	Support hybrid key exchange using X25519 + Kyber in Windows, Azure, and OpenSSL stacks
Secure Key Lifecycle Management	Update Azure Key Vault and HSMs to handle PQC key formats, including rotation and audit
Standardization Participation	Active contributions to NIST PQC, IETF, ISO, and ETSI working groups

Azure Quantum and Cryptography Research

Microsoft has begun rolling out **post-quantum cryptographic support** across multiple services. Highlights include the following:

- **Windows 11 and Windows Server**: Preview support for hybrid TLS (X25519 + Kyber) via updated Schannel and OpenSSL libraries

- **Microsoft Edge**: Experimental PQC cipher suite negotiation during HTTPS sessions

- **Azure Key Vault**: Ongoing support for PQC-ready key storage, crypto-agile APIs, and reduced key validity cycles

- **Azure TLS Gateway and App Services**: Planned rollout of PQC hybrid handshakes for TLS 1.3 endpoints by late 2025

These updates are designed to be transparent to applications but critical for future-proofing secure communications.

CHAPTER 12 FUTURE DIRECTIONS IN CLOUD GOVERNANCE AND SECURITY

Microsoft's Role in Global PQC Standardization

Microsoft is actively engaged in international standard-setting bodies that are shaping the future of quantum-safe security. Table 12-8 shows the contributions of Microsoft to the organizations.

Table 12-8. *Contributions of Microsoft to the international standard-setting organizations*

Organization	Microsoft's Contribution
NIST	Provided PQC algorithm proposals (e.g., FrodoKEM), feedback on performance models
IETF	Drafted TLS working group extensions for hybrid key exchange (RFC 9180—HPKE)
ETSI/ISO	Participates in the development of global PQC compliance and interoperability profiles

These engagements ensure Azure and Microsoft 365 services remain aligned with upcoming regulations and industry's best practices.

Microsoft also empowers customers to prepare for post-quantum transition via the following:

- **Cryptography Next Generation (CNG) APIs**: Crypto-agile APIs in .NET and Windows

- **Quantum Safe Cryptography documentation**: Developer guides, threat modeling templates, and migration toolkits

- **Azure Security Benchmark**: Recommendations updated to address crypto-agility and PQC planning

Interested to learn more about Quantum Safe Cryptography, check the official Microsoft documentation here: https://learn.microsoft.com/en-us/security/quantum-safe.

Enhanced Compliance and Regulatory Requirements

In this technically advanced world, regulatory compliance has evolved from a checkbox exercise into a dynamic, high-stakes priority that directly impacts cloud architecture, data governance, and security strategy. Global data protection regulations—like the **EU GDPR**, **US HIPAA**, **India's DPDP Act**, and **Brazil's LGPD**—are continuously evolving, and new mandates around AI governance, digital sovereignty, and sustainability are emerging across regions and industries. Cloud providers must now offer not just secure infrastructure but **transparent, auditable, and policy-driven controls** that help organizations demonstrate compliance in real time.

Microsoft Azure addresses this challenge through a combination of **regulatory mapping**, **automated compliance tools**, and **industry-specific frameworks** such as the **Microsoft Cloud for Healthcare** and **Azure Confidential Computing**. In this section, we'll explore how Azure helps customers navigate tightening compliance landscapes—by anticipating legal changes, automating audits, and building adaptive frameworks that scale across geographies and sectors.

Anticipating Changes in Global Data Privacy Laws

As cloud adoption accelerates and data volumes explode, governments around the world are updating privacy laws to protect individuals' digital rights. For cloud architects, compliance officers, and IT leaders, staying ahead of these changes is not just about avoiding fines—it's essential to maintaining customer trust, enabling cross-border operations, and designing cloud systems that are privacy-resilient by default.

Microsoft recognizes this complexity and helps organizations navigate it through its **Compliance Manager**, **Microsoft Purview**, **Azure Policy**, and **regional cloud services** (e.g., Azure EU Data Boundary). These tools and practices allow enterprises to align with current laws and prepare for new ones as they emerge.

Table 12-9 shows an overview of current and emerging global data protection laws.

Table 12-9. Overview of current and emerging global data protection laws

Region	Law	Key Focus	Enforcement Status
EU	GDPR (Regulation EU 2016/679)	Consent, data minimization, cross-border data flow	In effect since 2018
USA	CCPA/CPRA (California), ADPPA (draft federal bill)	Consumer rights, opt-out, data sales limitation	Varies by state
India	DPDP Act 2023	Consent, purpose limitation, digital sovereignty	Enacted, in implementation
China	PIPL (2021)	Localization, cross-border transfer, user rights	In effect
Brazil	LGPD (Law 13.709/2018)	Lawful use, transparency, individual control	In effect since 2020
Canada	Bill C-27 (proposed CPPA)	Consumer privacy, algorithmic transparency	Under parliamentary review
EU (upcoming)	AI Act	Trustworthy AI, risk classification, algorithmic bias	Expected in 2025–2026

Table 12-10 shows how Microsoft supports privacy-ready cloud operations.

Table 12-10. Capabilities of Microsoft to support privacy-ready cloud operations

Microsoft Capability	Use Case
Microsoft Purview Compliance Manager	Assess compliance posture and map controls to 360+ regulations globally
Microsoft Purview Data Map	Discover, classify, and govern sensitive data across hybrid and multi-cloud environments
Azure Policy + Azure Blueprints	Enforce regulatory-aligned configurations across cloud resources (e.g., ISO 27001, GDPR)
EU Data Boundary (2023+)	Keeps all customer data processing and storage within the EU for selected Microsoft services
Customer Lockbox	Requires explicit customer approval for Microsoft engineer access to content during support
Data Residency Transparency	Microsoft provides clear geolocation insights for data storage, backup, and processing

Preparing for Regulatory Change—Microsoft's Guidance

Organizations should take the following steps to stay updated with regulatory changes:

1. **Assess Legal Exposure**: Identify which jurisdictions and laws apply based on user location, industry, and data type.

2. **Map Data Flows**: Understand how personal data moves across regions, systems, and cloud services.

3. **Operationalize User Rights**: Implement workflows to handle data subject requests (DSRs) using tools like Microsoft Purview.

4. **Deploy Encryption and Retention Policies**: Ensure sensitive data is encrypted (at rest, in transit) and retained only as long as needed.

5. **Stay Informed**: Subscribe to Microsoft regulatory updates, product roadmap blogs, and compliance manager insights.

Industry-Specific Compliance Trends

While global privacy regulations like GDPR and CCPA define general data protection principles, many industries operate under **specialized compliance regimes** that impose sector-specific rules for data storage, security, auditability, and reporting. In highly regulated industries such as **healthcare, financial services, energy,** and **public sector**, cloud governance frameworks must integrate domain-specific controls to maintain both **regulatory compliance** and **industry certification**.

Microsoft Azure supports these needs through dedicated compliance offerings such as **Microsoft Cloud for Healthcare**, **Microsoft Cloud for Financial Services**, and **Azure Blueprints** tailored to standards like **HIPAA, PCI DSS,** and **FedRAMP**.

Healthcare Compliance Trends

Healthcare providers and life sciences organizations must comply with strict data confidentiality and auditability rules, especially regarding **Protected Health Information (PHI)**.

Table 12-11 provides an overview of key healthcare compliance standards across different regions, highlighting their core requirements.

Table 12-11. Key healthcare compliance standards by region

Standard	Region	Key Requirements
HIPAA (Health Insurance Portability and Accountability Act)	United States	Administrative safeguards, access control, audit logs, breach notification
HITRUST CSF	Global	Harmonized certification framework built on HIPAA, NIST, ISO
GDPR Article 9	EU	Prohibits processing of health data unless under strict lawful basis

Microsoft Cloud for Healthcare provides preconfigured policy packs, audit trails, and encrypted data flows for services like Azure API for FHIR, Microsoft Defender for Cloud, and Microsoft Purview.

Financial Services Compliance Trends

Financial institutions are governed by a mix of national laws and industry consortia that emphasize **fraud prevention**, **transactional integrity**, and **data residency**. Table 12-12 presents a comparison of key financial compliance standards and guidelines across various regions, with a focus on data security, outsourcing, and risk management.

Table 12-12. Financial compliance standards and guidelines by region

Standard/Guideline	Region	Focus Areas
PCI DSS v4.0	Global	Secure processing and storage of credit card data (applies to all merchants)
GLBA (Gramm-Leach-Bliley Act)	US	Financial privacy rule, safeguards rule
EBA/ECB Guidelines	EU	Cloud outsourcing, operational resilience, and third-party risk
FINMA Circular 2018/3	Switzerland	IT outsourcing risk, cloud control framework

Microsoft Cloud for Financial Services enables secure data environments for core banking, capital markets, and compliance reporting—with built-in support for multi-region data residency and audit compliance.

Government and Defense Compliance Trends

Government agencies and defense contractors operate under some of the most stringent cloud compliance requirements globally, focusing on **classified data handling**, **access control**, and **supply chain security**. These requirements often mandate physically and logically isolated cloud environments, strict incident response procedures, and region-specific data sovereignty. Table 12-13 outlines key government and defense compliance frameworks, focusing on data protection requirements for secure systems and sensitive information handling.

Table 12-13. Government and defense compliance standards

Standard/ Framework	Region	Key Requirements
FedRAMP High/ Moderate	United States	Standardized approach to security assessment, authorization, and monitoring
DoD Impact Levels (IL4/IL5/IL6)	US Department of Defense	Secure hosting of Controlled Unclassified Information (CUI) and classified workloads
CJIS Security Policy	US (FBI)	Protects criminal justice information with specific access, encryption, and audit rules
ITAR/EAR	Global/US	Regulates storage and transfer of defense-related technical data

Azure Government Cloud and **Azure Government Secret** are isolated sovereign environments that meet FedRAMP High, DoD IL5/6, and ITAR compliance. Features like **Customer Lockbox**, **Just-in-Time (JIT) access**, and **Azure Blueprints for DoD** help enforce zero-trust and least-privileged models.

Energy and Utilities Compliance Trends

Energy and critical infrastructure providers face unique risks due to the potential for **cyber-physical attacks** on SCADA systems and industrial control systems (ICS). Regulations focus on **grid reliability**, **resilience**, and **incident response**. Table 12-14 highlights key compliance standards and guidelines in the energy and utilities sector, focusing on cybersecurity, asset management, and operational resilience.

Table 12-14. Energy and utilities sector compliance standards

Standard/Guideline	Region	Focus Areas
NERC CIP (v5+)	North America	Cybersecurity for bulk electric systems: asset inventory, access control, audit
ISO 55001/IEC 62443	Global	Asset lifecycle management, industrial automation security
US Department of Energy Cybersecurity Capability Maturity Model (C2M2)	US	Risk management maturity for utilities and energy providers

Azure Security Center for IoT, **Azure Defender for IoT**, and **Azure Arc for OT networks** provide protection, monitoring, and compliance for hybrid ICS environments. Azure Policy helps enforce SCADA network segmentation, encryption, and patch management baselines across hybrid assets.

Education Sector Compliance Trends

Education institutions manage high volumes of **student personal data**, including behavioral, biometric, and academic records. Laws emphasize **data protection for minors**, **consent management**, and **restricted profiling**. Table 12-15 summarizes key data privacy regulations and standards relevant to educational institutions and child data protection, with a focus on access control, consent, and cloud privacy.

Table 12-15. Privacy regulations in education and child data protection

Regulation/Law	Region	Key Requirements
FERPA (Family Educational Rights and Privacy Act)	US	Access, amendment, and consent for student records
COPPA (Children's Online Privacy Protection Act)	US	Restrictions on collecting data from children under 13
ISO/IEC 27018	Global	Privacy controls for personally identifiable information (PII) in the cloud

Microsoft 365 and Azure services for education offer **FERPA-compliant configurations**, role-based access control (RBAC), and identity federation with **Microsoft Entra ID**. **Microsoft Purview** adds classification and retention controls for student records across SharePoint, OneDrive, Teams, and email.

The Future of Cloud Governance Frameworks

Cloud governance is rapidly evolving from a static, policy-bound discipline into a dynamic, integrated strategy that supports agility, decentralization, and sustainability. As cloud architecture becomes more distributed, modular, and automated, organizations must move beyond traditional governance models like static templates or manual reviews. Microsoft Azure is at the forefront of this shift, introducing tools such as **Azure Landing Zones 3.0**, **Policy as Code**, and **Microsoft Entra–based decentralized identity governance**. These capabilities reflect a broader move toward **automated**, **identity-aware**, and **outcome-driven governance frameworks**, built to scale with global enterprises. Additionally, environmental, social, and governance (ESG) factors are becoming central to cloud governance strategies, prompting the need to integrate sustainability metrics and carbon-aware computing into enterprise policy design. This section explores how governance is shifting from rigid guardrails to adaptive control planes—capable of responding to compliance, operational, and environmental changes in real time.

From Blueprints to Azure Landing Zones 3.0

As enterprise cloud adoption matures, organizations require governance that can scale, evolve, and integrate seamlessly with modern DevOps practices. Microsoft's early governance approach—**Azure Blueprints**—offered a way to package policies, RBAC, and ARM templates. However, as Infrastructure-as-Code (IaC) practices advanced, Blueprints became restrictive and were officially **retired in 2023**.

Replacing them is a more powerful and flexible model: **Azure Landing Zones 3.0**, part of the **Microsoft Cloud Adoption Framework (CAF)**. Landing Zones are not a service but a **modular, IaC-based architecture** that enables organizations to deploy secure, scalable, and policy-compliant Azure environments—ready for production workloads.

What Is an Azure Landing Zone?

An Azure Landing Zone provides a **preconfigured cloud foundation** aligned to Microsoft's best practices. It establishes the core building blocks—identity, network, policy, security, and operations—that are **required before hosting workloads**. Unlike Blueprints, Landing Zones are **infrastructure agnostic** and can be deployed via **Terraform, Bicep, or ARM**, integrated into **CI/CD pipelines**, and extended for **multi-cloud or hybrid use cases**.

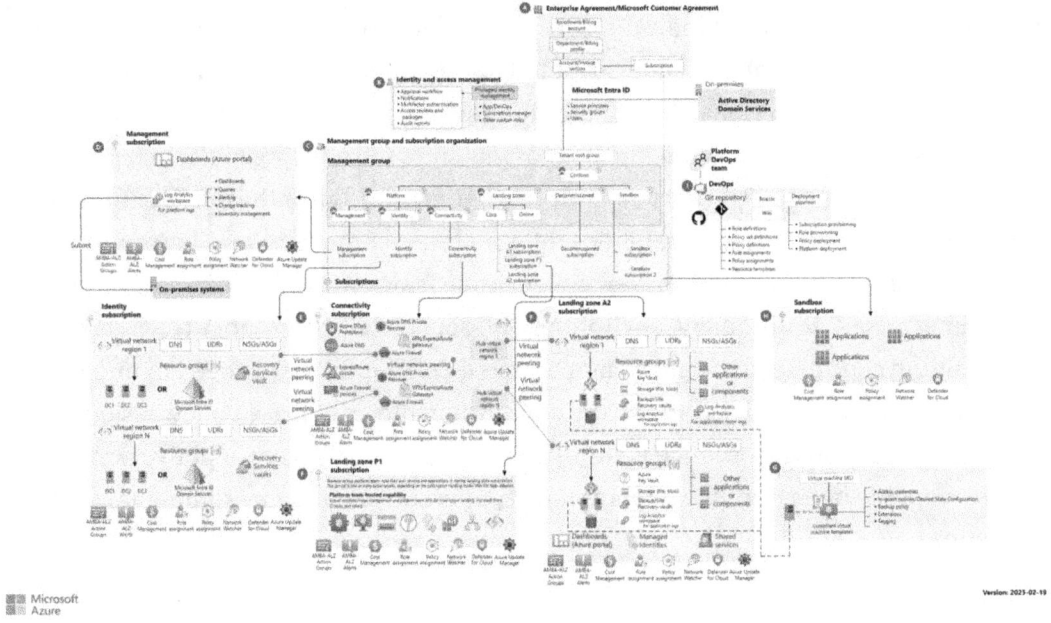

Figure 12-1. Azure landing zone conceptual architecture (Image: Microsoft)

Technical Architecture Overview: Azure Landing Zone Building Blocks

The Azure Landing Zone architecture is structured into modular pillars, labeled A through I in the reference model. Each component plays a critical role in delivering a secure, governed, and scalable foundation for hosting cloud workloads across enterprise environments. Together, they form a cohesive control plane that enforces governance, automates operations, and ensures continuous compliance from day one.

A. **Identity and Access Management**

This layer establishes centralized identity control using **Microsoft Entra ID** (formerly Azure AD). It provides foundational services like **Role-Based Access Control (RBAC), Conditional Access**, and **Privileged Identity Management (PIM)**. These capabilities enforce least-privileged access, enable just-in-time role elevation, and secure privileged operations across subscriptions and workloads.

B. **Resource Organization**

Underpinning the structure of Azure governance, this component defines the **management group and subscription hierarchy**. It enables organizations to segment environments (e.g., Dev, Test, Prod) or business units, apply scope-based policies, and track resource ownership using consistent **naming conventions** and **tagging strategies** for automation, billing, and lifecycle management.

C. **Network Topology and Connectivity**

Networking is built using scalable patterns such as **hub-and-spoke** or **mesh topologies**, ensuring secure communication between workloads, shared services, and external endpoints. It includes **Virtual Networks (VNets), Azure Firewall, Network Security Groups (NSGs), VPN/ExpressRoute Gateways**, and **Private Endpoints**. This segment also supports hybrid integration through encrypted tunnels and peering across regions or tenants.

D. **Security, Governance, and Compliance**

This pillar anchors security and policy enforcement using **Azure Policy, Defender for Cloud**, and **Microsoft Sentinel**. Organizations define policy initiatives to enforce configuration baselines (e.g., disk encryption, region restrictions), map security controls to frameworks like NIST and ISO 27001, and surface compliance gaps through secure score dashboards and alerts.

E. **Monitoring and Management**

Operational visibility is provided by **Azure Monitor**, **Log Analytics**, and **Service Health**, which collect and centralize metrics, logs, and platform events. Teams can configure alerts, dashboards, and analytics to track resource health, performance, and incident response across all layers of the environment—from infrastructure to apps.

F. **Platform Automation**

To reduce manual overhead and ensure consistent operations, this component includes services like **Azure Automation**, **Update Management**, **Change Tracking**, and **Backup**. These tools help enforce patch compliance, manage configurations, automate routine tasks, and support operational governance aligned with DevSecOps models.

G. **DevOps and Infrastructure-as-Code Integration**

Landing Zones are designed for infrastructure automation through modern CI/CD pipelines. DevOps integration includes support for **GitHub Actions**, **Azure DevOps**, **Terraform**, and **Bicep**, enabling continuous delivery of compliant infrastructure. Policy as Code, version control, and environment promotion are fully supported, aligning governance with agile delivery.

H. **Workload Zones**

These are the **landing zones where applications are deployed**—including environments for production, staging, testing, or development. Each inherits baseline controls, networking, identity, and policy from the shared services layer. Workload zones may have custom policies or monitoring profiles based on business criticality or compliance needs.

I. **Hybrid and Multi-cloud Governance**

Modern enterprises often operate beyond Azure. This component enables **hybrid and multi-cloud governance** using **Azure Arc**, **Azure Lighthouse**, and **Private Link**. It allows consistent policy deployment, inventory, monitoring, and automation across on-premises infrastructure, AWS, GCP, and edge environments—extending Azure's control plane globally.

From Blueprints to Code-Based Governance

Azure's shift from Blueprints to Landing Zones 3.0 marks a fundamental change in how governance is delivered and scaled. While Blueprints served as prepackaged templates combining policies, role assignments, and ARM artifacts, they were largely **manual**, **portal centric**, and **limited in extensibility**. This made them suitable for small-scale or one-time deployments, but insufficient for large-scale, DevOps-driven organizations.

In contrast, **Landing Zones 3.0**, aligned with the **Cloud Adoption Framework (CAF)**, are fully modular and **Infrastructure as Code (IaC) first**. They support deployment via **Terraform**, **Bicep**, or **ARM templates** and integrate seamlessly with **GitOps**, **CI/CD pipelines**, and **version control systems**. Rather than defining policies statically, Landing Zones enforce governance through **Policy as Code**, enabling dynamic updates, branching strategies, and pull-request-based validations.

Most importantly, Landing Zones are designed to scale across **multiple regions, tenants, and cloud platforms**, thanks to built-in support for **Azure Arc** and hybrid resource governance. This makes them not only a replacement for Blueprints, but a major step forward—transforming governance from a static toolset into a **living, codified system** that evolves with the business.

Sustainability and ESG Integration in Governance Strategies

As environmental, social, and governance (ESG) goals become central to enterprise strategy, cloud governance must evolve to embed **sustainability metrics and controls** into architectural and operational decisions. Microsoft Azure is at the forefront of this shift, offering native tooling, APIs, and frameworks that help organizations track, reduce, and govern their cloud-related carbon emissions while aligning with ESG compliance and reporting requirements.

Why Sustainability Matters in Cloud Governance

Traditionally, cloud governance focused on cost, security, and compliance. Today, it must also consider **environmental impact** and **resource efficiency**. CIOs and sustainability officers are being asked to

- Report on **Scope 1-3 emissions**, including those generated by cloud workloads
- Ensure workloads are **optimized for carbon and energy efficiency**
- Align cloud operations with frameworks like **CDP**, **GRI**, **SBTi**, and **CSRD**
- Embed sustainability KPIs into IT governance scorecards

Microsoft Azure enables these goals through integrated services that bring **measurable ESG insights** directly into cloud governance workflows.

Azure Tools for ESG-Aware Governance

To help organizations align their cloud operations with environmental, social, and governance (ESG) goals, Microsoft Azure offers a growing suite of built-in tools and services designed specifically for **measuring, managing, and governing sustainability outcomes**. These tools integrate directly into the Azure control plane and support both **strategic ESG reporting** and **tactical workload optimization**. Whether you're looking to monitor carbon emissions, enforce green policies, or automate carbon-aware scheduling, Azure provides a comprehensive governance framework to support your ESG ambitions. Table 12-16 showcases Microsoft tools and services that support enterprise sustainability strategies, particularly in tracking, optimizing, and enforcing carbon-aware operations.

Table 12-16. Microsoft sustainability tools and services

Tool/Service	Purpose in Sustainability Strategy
Microsoft Sustainability Manager	Track ESG KPIs, emissions, water, and energy usage across enterprise systems
Emissions Impact Dashboard for Azure	Provides real-time and historical carbon emissions data for Azure subscriptions
Azure Advisor (Sustainability Pillar)	Recommends VM resizing, idle resource cleanup, and storage optimization for carbon reduction
Azure Policy	Enforce green governance—for example, restrict to carbon-aware regions or SKUs
Azure Carbon Optimization API (Preview)	Automate carbon-aware workload scheduling and reporting
Microsoft Cloud for Sustainability	Integrate sustainability data across cloud, ERP, and on-prem systems

Looking Ahead: A Cloud Governance Vision for 2030

As enterprises race toward digital sovereignty, AI integration, and climate accountability, the nature of cloud governance is set to evolve radically by 2030. Governance will no longer be a set of manual processes or reactive controls—it will become an **intelligent, policy-driven digital nervous system** that adapts continuously to operational, ethical, and regulatory demands.

Microsoft's roadmap—through technologies like **Entra**, **Defender for Cloud**, **Purview**, and **Sustainability Manager**—points toward a future where **governance is autonomous, proactive, and deeply embedded into every layer of the cloud stack**. This future vision is defined by five transformative shifts.

AI-First Governance Engines

By 2030, **AI will drive the enforcement, tuning, and interpretation of policies** in real time. Instead of predefining static rules, cloud governance systems will use **predictive analytics and reinforcement learning** to

- Detect patterns of risk before violations occur
- Adjust access permissions based on behavior and context
- Auto-generate policy definitions using natural language inputs (e.g., via Copilot for Governance)

Decentralized and Self-Sovereign Identities

The adoption of **Decentralized Identity (DID)** standards, supported by Microsoft Entra Verified ID, will empower users, devices, and services to control their own credentials. Cross-organization collaboration will no longer require directory synchronization or federation—instead, trust will be **established cryptographically** via verifiable credentials and smart contracts.

- Verified digital identities will replace legacy B2B accounts.
- Machine-to-machine trust will be managed via decentralized proofs.
- Zero-trust models will extend across ecosystems using blockchain-backed governance claims.

ESG-Aware Governance as a Default

Governance frameworks will **integrate environmental and ethical metrics** natively:

- Policies will enforce **carbon-aware workload scheduling** based on regional grid intensity.
- Governance dashboards will include **Scope 1–3 emissions, water use, and digital waste**.
- AI models used in business processes will require **governance declarations for fairness and transparency**, enforced by cloud policy.

Microsoft's **Cloud for Sustainability** and **Emissions Impact APIs** lays the foundation for this shift.

Unified Multi-cloud and Edge Governance

By 2030, most enterprises will span multiple public clouds, private data centers, edge clusters, and satellite systems. Governance platforms like **Azure Arc**, **Entra Permissions Management**, and **Purview Data Map** will evolve into **cross-cloud policy engines**, enabling

- Policy replication and compliance scoring across Azure, AWS, GCP, and on-prem
- Real-time telemetry aggregation from edge sensors and IoT fleets
- Uniform tagging, classification, and encryption enforcement regardless of location

Trust-Centric and Ethically Aligned Governance

Beyond security and compliance, governance will enforce **ethical use** of AI, data, and automation. This includes

- Mandatory **AI transparency declarations** for enterprise models
- Automated checks for **bias mitigation** and **model explainability**
- **Digital ethics Policy as Code** implemented alongside traditional IT controls

Microsoft's responsible AI principles and integration of **Copilot compliance guardrails** offer early examples of this trajectory.

Table 12-17 shows the five transformative shifts in Cloud Governance by 2030.

Table 12-17. Five transformative shifts in Cloud Governance by 2030

Trend	Key Characteristics
AI-First Governance Engines	Predictive, adaptive policy enforcement using AI, reinforcement learning, and NLP
Decentralized and Self-Sovereign Identity	Verifiable credentials, DID standards, blockchain-based trust across ecosystems
ESG-Aware Governance by Default	Carbon-aware scheduling, ethical metrics, AI fairness declarations
Unified Multi-cloud and Edge Governance	Cross-cloud compliance scoring, telemetry aggregation, uniform policy enforcement
Trust-Centric and Ethically Aligned Governance	AI transparency, bias checks, digital ethics as code embedded into operations

By 2030, cloud governance will resemble a **living organism**—aware, adaptive, and embedded into every transaction and deployment. Organizations will no longer ask "Is this compliant?" but instead rely on **self-auditing, AI-assisted systems** that continuously align infrastructure with regulatory, ethical, and business standards.

This transformation will not only reduce operational overheads, but it will also **build trust**, **enable innovation at scale**, and **ensure that digital transformation is sustainable and responsible**.

Summary

In this chapter, we explored the **future directions of cloud governance and security**, identifying key trends that will shape the next generation of cloud practices. Topics such as **AI-driven automation**, **decentralized identity**, **confidential computing**, and **sustainability governance** highlighted how innovation continues to redefine both risks and opportunities in the cloud landscape. The chapter emphasized the need for organizations to remain agile, forward-thinking, and proactive in adapting their governance strategies to stay resilient and compliant in an ever-evolving digital environment.

CHAPTER 12 FUTURE DIRECTIONS IN CLOUD GOVERNANCE AND SECURITY

Now, in the next chapter, we take that vision a step further by focusing on how **Azure AI and Microsoft Copilot** can be actively leveraged to enhance governance and security practices. You'll discover how AI can streamline compliance checks, automate threat detection, and assist with policy creation—while Copilot transforms the way cloud teams interact with governance tools. Through practical examples, you'll see how intelligence can be embedded directly into your governance workflows.

Let's now explore how to make governance **smarter and more adaptive** with the power of Azure AI and Copilot.

CHAPTER 13

Harnessing Azure AI and Copilot for Governance and Security

In the previous chapter, we explored the **future directions** of cloud governance and security, highlighting how emerging technologies like **AI-driven automation**, **confidential computing**, and **decentralized identity systems** are shaping the next generation of cloud strategy. We discussed why staying ahead of these trends is essential for building resilient, adaptive, and forward-compatible governance frameworks.

Now, in this chapter, we shift from foresight to **practical innovation** by exploring how **Azure AI and Microsoft Copilot** can be used today to enhance governance and security operations. As organizations face increasing complexity in managing cloud environments, intelligent tools are becoming essential—not just for analysis, but for decision-making, automation, and continuous compliance.

In this chapter, you'll learn how Azure AI services and Copilot can simplify policy creation, detect anomalies, generate security insights, and support administrative tasks through natural language interaction. With real-world use cases and demos, we'll uncover how AI is not just a futuristic concept but a present-day enabler of **smart governance**.

Let's explore how to bring intelligence and automation to the core of your governance and security practices.

Overview of Azure AI Capabilities

As artificial intelligence becomes an increasingly integral part of modern enterprise IT strategies, Microsoft Azure has emerged as a comprehensive platform for building, deploying, and scaling AI-powered solutions. Azure AI is not a single product but a broad portfolio of cloud-based services, tools, and frameworks that span machine learning, natural language processing, computer vision, and generative AI. Through services like **Azure Machine Learning, Cognitive Services,** and **Azure OpenAI Service,** Azure empowers organizations to automate processes, enhance decision-making, and secure digital environments with intelligent automation. These capabilities are deeply integrated into other Azure services, enabling seamless implementation of AI across governance, compliance, and security use cases. With Microsoft's commitment to responsible AI principles, Azure AI ensures that enterprise AI adoption remains ethical, secure, and enterprise-grade by design.

Evolution of AI in Microsoft Azure

The evolution of AI in Microsoft Azure reflects a shift from isolated machine learning experimentation to enterprise-grade, integrated AI services capable of powering mission-critical workloads. Microsoft has consistently expanded Azure's AI capabilities across three core pillars: prebuilt AI, custom machine learning, and responsible AI governance—all unified through a scalable and secure cloud platform.

Table 13-1 shows the key milestones in Azure AI evolution.

Table 13-1. *Key milestones in Azure AI evolution*

Year	Milestone/Service	Technical Description
2010	**Launch of Windows Azure**	Initial Platform-as-a-Service (PaaS) offering hosting ASP.NET apps, storage, and SQL Azure. No native AI or ML capabilities yet
2013	**Rebrand to Microsoft Azure**	Signaled the transition to a broader cloud platform supporting Linux, Java, Python, and open source frameworks
2014	**Azure Machine Learning (Classic Preview)**	Drag-and-drop browser-based ML tool (ML Studio) for building and deploying predictive models. Limited versioning, no SDKs or CI/CD

(*continued*)

Table 13-1. (*continued*)

Year	Milestone/Service	Technical Description
2015–2018	Launch of Cognitive Services and Applied AI	Release of prebuilt REST APIs for Computer Vision, Face Detection, Speech-to-Text, Text Analytics, Translator, and Language Understanding (LUIS). Enabled quick integration of AI into applications
2017–2019	Azure Machine Learning Service (SDK)	Introduction of Python SDK (azureml.core), managed compute clusters, model tracking, MLOps support, and deployment via AKS/ACI
2020	Azure AI Supercomputing	Microsoft builds one of the top five publicly known supercomputers in partnership with OpenAI, deployed on Azure with thousands of NVIDIA A100 GPUs
2021	Azure OpenAI Service (Private Preview)	Enterprise-secured access to GPT-3 and Codex with content moderation, rate limiting, and user-level telemetry. Emphasis on responsible AI
2023	GA of Azure OpenAI and Launch of Azure AI Studio	General availability of GPT-3.5/4, Codex, DALL·E, Whisper. Azure AI Studio offers Prompt Flow, RAG pipelines, vector store integration, and no-code orchestration
2024	Copilot Integration into Azure and Microsoft Stack	Copilot stack launched across Microsoft 365, GitHub, Azure Portal. Powered by Azure OpenAI; used for automation, governance, security tasks via natural language
2025	Azure AI Foundry (projected)	Unified SDK and platform for building custom copilots, training/fine-tuning domain-specific models, integrating with GitHub Copilot, Visual Studio, and Azure DevOps. Offers design-to-deployment governance pipelines

Key Azure AI Services

As artificial intelligence moves from research to production, Microsoft Azure offers a comprehensive portfolio of cloud-native AI services designed to support developers, data scientists, and enterprises at scale. These services fall into **three** primary categories: **Azure Cognitive Services**, which provides pretrained APIs for common AI tasks; the

Azure OpenAI Service, offering access to cutting-edge large language models (LLMs); and **Azure Machine Learning (AML)**, a full-fledged platform for building, training, and deploying custom machine learning models.

Together, these services form a layered AI ecosystem within Azure, supporting a wide range of use cases—from customer engagement and document intelligence to MLOps pipelines and enterprise-grade generative AI applications. What makes Azure unique is the native integration of **governance**, **responsibility**, **security**, and **compliance tooling** across the entire stack.

Azure Cognitive Services

Azure Cognitive Services is a cloud-based suite of **prebuilt, AI-powered REST APIs and SDKs** that enable developers to integrate intelligence into applications without building or training machine learning models. These services abstract the complexity of machine learning by providing **ready-to-use AI models** for vision, speech, language, decision-making, and document processing. They're ideal for organizations seeking to enhance apps with intelligent features quickly and reliably.

Microsoft designed Cognitive Services with scalability, modularity, and simplicity in mind. These services follow a "plug-and-play" approach, meaning developers can call a single API endpoint with minimal configuration and receive an intelligent response. The key features of Azure Cognitive Services are the following:

1. **Vision**

    Vision enables apps to interpret and understand visual content. Table 13-2 provides a brief overview of Azure Vision services, highlighting their capabilities in interpreting and processing visual content.

Table 13-2. *Overview of Azure Vision services*

Sub-service	Description
Computer Vision	Extracts information from images and videos: OCR, object detection, image tagging, brand/logo detection
Custom Vision	Allows users to train custom image classifiers using their own labeled datasets
Face API	Detects faces in images, identify facial features, age/gender estimation, and face recognition
OCR	Optical character recognition to extract printed and handwritten text from documents and images

2. **Speech**

    Speech facilitates conversion between spoken and written language. Table 13-3 provides an overview of Azure Speech services, which enable seamless interaction between spoken and written language through advanced AI capabilities.

Table 13-3. *Overview of Azure Speech services*

Sub-service	Description
Speech-to-Text	Convert audio streams or files to readable text in multiple languages
Text-to-Speech	Synthesizes human-like voice output using neural TTS technology
Speech Translation	Real-time multilingual speech translation with support for dozens of languages
Speaker Recognition	Identifies or verifies individuals based on unique voice signatures

3. **Language**

    Language enables natural language processing tasks. Table 13-4 outlines Azure Language services that support natural language processing tasks such as text analysis, translation, and intent recognition.

Table 13-4. *Overview of Azure Language services*

Sub-service	Description
Text Analytics	Extracts sentiment, key phrases, named entities, and language detection
Entity Recognition	Extracts names, organizations, locations, dates, and custom entities
Translator	Supports real-time text translation between over 100 languages
Language Understanding (LUIS)	Natural language intent recognition for custom domain models (retired in favor of Azure Language service)

4. **Decision**

   Decision uses pretrained AI to make intelligent recommendations. Table 13-5 highlights Azure Decision services that leverage pretrained AI models to detect anomalies and deliver personalized, context-aware recommendations.

Table 13-5. *Overview of Azure Decision services*

Sub-service	Description
Anomaly Detector	Detects anomalies in time-series data for use cases like system health monitoring and fraud detection
Personalizer	Delivers contextual user recommendations using reinforcement learning (e.g., dynamic UI personalization)

5. **Document Intelligence (formerly Form Recognizer)**

   Document Intelligence extracts structured information from scanned documents, PDFs, and forms. Table 13-6 presents the core capabilities of Azure Document Intelligence, which enables automated extraction of structured data from documents, PDFs, and forms.

Table 13-6. *Features of Azure Document Intelligence*

Feature	Description
Layout Extraction	Identifies tables, checkboxes, lines, and paragraphs from images or PDFs
Key-Value Pair Extraction	Pulls metadata like invoice number, date, total from structured and unstructured forms
Custom Models	Allows training on specific document types with as few as five labeled samples

Azure OpenAI Services

Azure OpenAI Service is Microsoft's enterprise-grade, cloud-hosted offering that provides secure, governed, and scalable access to OpenAI's most advanced foundation models, including **GPT-4**, **GPT-4o**, **Codex**, **DALL·E 2**, and **Whisper**. Hosted entirely within the Microsoft Azure infrastructure, this service allows organizations to build intelligent applications such as **AI copilots**, **automated assistants**, **document processors**, **semantic search systems**, and **generative content tools**—all under **compliance-ready controls** for data privacy, access management, and usage accountability.

Unlike OpenAI's public API, Azure OpenAI enforces enterprise-grade data handling policies, allowing customers to control model usage via **Azure policies**, **RBAC**, **Private Endpoints**, and **auditing mechanisms**. Table 13-7 briefly shows an overview of Azure OpenAI Service capabilities.

Table 13-7. Overview of Azure OpenAI Service capabilities

Feature	Model	Core Capabilities	Enterprise Use Cases
Text Generation and Chat	GPT-3.5GPT-4GPT-4o	Natural language understandingAnswering questions, summarizing, drafting contentRole-based dialogue with the **ChatCompletion** API	Customer support copilotsKnowledge assistantsAutomated documentation
Code Generation	Codex	Code generation from natural languageAuto-suggest logic/functions across multiple languagesInfra-as-Code templates	GitHub Copilot–like assistantsScripting and automationARM/Bicep provisioning
Image Generation	DALL·E 2	Text-to-image conversionImage editing via inpainting	Marketing visual generationUI prototypingCampaign content creation
Speech Transcription	Whisper	Multilingual audio transcriptionTimestamps, punctuation, diarization	Customer service call logsVoice-to-text appsAccessibility enhancement
Embeddings API	text-embedding-ada-002	Semantic vector representationHigh-dimensional indexing for similarity and relevance	Semantic search systemsIntelligent recommendationsRetrieval-Augmented Generation (RAG)

Azure Machine Learning (AML)

Azure Machine Learning (AML) is Microsoft's fully managed cloud-native platform designed for **developing, training, deploying, and managing machine learning (ML) models** at scale. It supports both **low-code** and **code-first** development approaches, making it accessible to data scientists, ML engineers, and even citizen developers through visual interfaces like AML Studio and automation tools like AutoML.

AML simplifies the complete ML lifecycle—from data ingestion and preprocessing to model development, orchestration, deployment, and governance—underpinned by strong **security**, **compliance**, and **responsible AI** (RAI) tooling.

Table 13-8 provides a comprehensive breakdown of Azure Machine Learning components, highlighting their key features and typical use cases across the ML lifecycle.

Table 13-8. Core components of Azure Machine Learning

Component	Key Features	Purpose/Use Cases
Authoring and Dev	Python SDKs (azureml-core, etc.)AML Studio (low-code)Jupyter integration	Design experiments, managing workspaces, developing models with open source frameworks
Training Infrastructure	Distributed training (MPI, Horovod)GPU compute (NDv5 H100)Docker/Conda environments	Train large models at scale, manage compute clusters, ensure reproducibility
AutoML	Automated classification, regression, forecastingHyperparameter tuningSHAP reports	Rapid model development without writing code; interpret results
Pipelines and MLOps	Modular steps (data ➤ training ➤ deployment)CI/CD with GitHub, DevOps, MLflowLineage	Automate workflows, integrate with DevOps, track and version ML assets
Model Registry and Deploy	Central model storeDeploy to AKS, IoT Edge, or batchCanary/blue-green support	Productionize models with flexible targets and safe rollout strategies
Monitoring and RAI	Drift detectionSHAP, LIMEFairlearnRAI dashboard	Ensure fairness, interpretability, and compliance with Responsible AI standards

Role of AI in Enterprise Governance and Security

Artificial intelligence has become a central component of modern enterprise transformation, not only driving innovation but also reshaping how organizations manage security, compliance, and operational governance. Microsoft Azure integrates AI deeply into its governance and security architecture, ensuring that intelligent solutions are both powerful and controlled, transparent, and compliant by design.

Azure treats governance and security as foundational to AI development—not as afterthoughts. Services like Azure Machine Learning, Azure OpenAI Service, and Cognitive Services come with built-in mechanisms to address risks such as data misuse, prompt injection, unauthorized access, and bias. This makes Azure AI suitable for sensitive and regulated industries, including healthcare, finance, and the public sector.

From an access control perspective, Azure uses Entra ID and Role-Based Access Control (RBAC) to strictly govern who can access models, data, and compute resources. This includes human users and non-human identities such as automated agents and copilots. Every action within an AI workspace—from training a model to invoking an API—is governed, auditable, and enforceable through Azure Policy and logging systems.

Security is also embedded at the network and compute layer. Organizations can isolate AI resources using Virtual Networks and Private Endpoints, preventing public Internet exposure. When sensitive data is involved, models can be trained and run within Confidential Compute environments that encrypt data even while it is being processed. This architecture ensures zero-trust principles are upheld throughout the AI lifecycle.

On the responsible AI front, Azure Machine Learning includes tools for fairness, explainability, and transparency. With SHAP and LIME, developers can interpret model predictions. With Fairlearn, teams can measure and mitigate bias across attributes like gender or ethnicity. The Responsible AI dashboard aggregates these insights into a single view, allowing for informed decision-making before deploying models.

Threat detection is also enhanced by AI itself. For example, Microsoft Defender for Cloud and Microsoft Sentinel use machine learning models to identify anomalies, intrusions, and misuse patterns across cloud resources. Within the Azure OpenAI Service, content filters actively prevent prompt abuse, malicious output, or harmful language generation. These protections are backed by human-in-the-loop reviews and ongoing red-team evaluations of model behavior.

Azure AI services are fully aligned with global compliance standards, including ISO/IEC 27001, HIPAA, GDPR, SOC 2, and FedRAMP. Tools like Microsoft Purview and Compliance Manager help organizations track data lineage, enforce policies, and prepare for audits. All training data, model artifacts, and user activities are logged, ensuring full traceability and accountability.

Implementing Azure AI for Security and Compliance

As the volume, velocity, and sophistication of cyber threats increase, organizations must rethink how they protect digital assets, maintain compliance, and respond to evolving risks. Traditional, rule-based security systems often fall short in detecting subtle anomalies or adapting to new attack patterns. Microsoft Azure addresses this challenge by embedding artificial intelligence into its security and compliance ecosystem—transforming reactive defenses into intelligent, proactive strategies.

Azure AI enhances detection accuracy, speeds up incident response, and automates regulatory reporting. By integrating AI with services such as Microsoft Defender for Cloud, Azure Sentinel, and Azure Monitor, organizations gain real-time threat insights, pattern recognition capabilities, and automated compliance workflows. In this section, we explore how Azure AI empowers security teams to not only protect their environment more effectively but also meet complex compliance requirements with greater efficiency and confidence.

AI-Driven Threat Detection with Microsoft Defender for Cloud

In Chapter 5, I provided an in-depth explanation of Microsoft Defender for Cloud's architecture, policy framework, threat detection logic, and integration into enterprise workloads. In this section, I will go beyond the product fundamentals and focus specifically on how artificial intelligence (AI) amplifies its threat detection capabilities, especially when integrated with broader Microsoft security services such as Microsoft Sentinel, Microsoft Defender XDR, and Microsoft Security Copilot.

Modern cloud-native environments generate millions of low-fidelity signals every day, many of which, when examined in isolation, do not indicate a breach. AI changes this by providing pattern recognition, behavioral baselining, and signal correlation at scale. Defender for Cloud is integrated with Microsoft's threat intelligence graph and uses machine learning algorithms trained on over 65 trillion security signals collected daily from Microsoft's global infrastructure. These models are used not only to detect abnormal activities but to contextualize and correlate them with other suspicious signals across the Microsoft ecosystem.

One of the core AI-enhanced capabilities is found in **Microsoft Sentinel**, which works alongside Defender for Cloud. Sentinel's **Fusion engine** employs graph-based machine learning to connect isolated anomalies—such as abnormal sign-in attempts, suspicious script execution, and resource tampering—into a unified, high-confidence incident. For example, when Defender for Cloud raises an alert about a public-facing VM with an open RDP port, and Sentinel detects repeated brute-force login attempts followed by a token misuse event, the AI engine can automatically stitch these signals into a kill chain that resembles a credential compromise leading to lateral movement.

Another example of AI-assisted detection is identity compromise. Microsoft Entra ID logs, when analyzed by anomaly detection models, can identify a user suddenly authenticating from a foreign IP range and accessing resources never touched before. While these events may not immediately trip traditional alarms, AI-driven baselines—developed over time for each user, service principal, and managed identity—allow Defender and Sentinel to detect and prioritize such anomalies.

These detections become even more powerful when integrated with **Microsoft Defender for Endpoint**, which contributes telemetry from the operating system levels such as kernel calls, process injections, or ransomware behavior. AI models analyze these patterns in real time, scoring them against known malware families and attack frameworks like MITRE ATT&CK. Once correlated with cloud-level events in Defender for Cloud, they offer a complete, AI-driven view of the threat landscape—spanning identity, infrastructure, and endpoint.

The introduction of **Microsoft Security Copilot**, built on Azure OpenAI Service, adds another layer of AI reasoning. Security analysts can use natural language to ask questions like, "What caused the last elevated privilege change in the subscription?" or "Show me all lateral movement indicators for this compromised user." Behind the scenes, Copilot uses GPT-based models to parse signals from Defender for Cloud, Sentinel, and Entra ID, formulate queries, and return interpreted results. This not only reduces investigation time but also enhances the precision of human response decisions.

What makes Azure AI distinct in this context is that it doesn't just flag anomalies—it **understands context**. For instance, an AI model will treat a PowerShell execution on a domain controller differently than the same execution on a developer's sandbox machine. The signal scoring engine adapts threat severity based on operational roles, behavioral norms, and environmental baselines.

In short, AI transforms Microsoft Defender for Cloud from a static alerting engine into an intelligent, self-adaptive detection system. It allows security teams to shift from triaging thousands of disconnected alerts to focusing on high-confidence, AI-prioritized incidents. Combined with its integration across the Microsoft security stack, Defender for Cloud becomes a cornerstone in delivering proactive, real-time, and predictive threat defense at cloud scale.

Using AI in Risk Analysis and Regulatory Compliance

As regulatory demands expand and data landscapes grow more complex, traditional governance and compliance methods—often manual, siloed, and reactive—are no longer sufficient. Microsoft Azure addresses this challenge by embedding artificial intelligence into its governance, risk, and compliance (GRC) stack. AI now plays a vital role in helping organizations evaluate risk posture, detect policy violations, and automate compliance reporting across dynamic cloud environments.

Azure's compliance and risk management ecosystem is powered by services like **Microsoft Purview**, **Compliance Manager**, and **Azure Policy**. These tools incorporate AI models for tasks such as classification, prioritization, and automated enforcement. Together, they form an adaptive, intelligent framework that continuously evolves alongside organizational and regulatory needs.

AI in Microsoft Compliance Manager

Microsoft Purview Compliance Manager provides a centralized dashboard for managing regulatory requirements across frameworks like NIST 800-53, ISO/IEC 27001, GDPR, and PCI DSS. AI enhances this system by automatically assessing control implementation across Azure, Microsoft 365, and hybrid environments. It performs real-time mapping of your configurations to regulatory standards, identifying gaps and generating risk-adjusted improvement actions.

For example, if a virtual machine lacks endpoint protection or encryption, Compliance Manager uses scoring algorithms to determine its potential compliance impact, then prioritizes remediation steps accordingly. These insights are enriched by Microsoft's global threat intelligence and updated regularly to reflect changes in regulatory interpretations or threat activity.

CHAPTER 13   HARNESSING AZURE AI AND COPILOT FOR GOVERNANCE AND SECURITY

AI-Driven Compliance Scoring in Microsoft Defender for Cloud

Microsoft Defender for Cloud calculates a compliance score based on how your resources align with selected benchmarks. The AI models analyze telemetry from services like Azure Monitor and Activity Logs to detect misconfigurations, risky behavior, and policy drift.

What makes this capability powerful is its predictive nature. Instead of merely flagging violations, AI models forecast potential non-compliance trends by evaluating how resource changes may introduce future risks. These models support both reactive detection and proactive governance, enabling real-time enforcement through integration with Azure Policy, Defender for Cloud Recommendations, and automation via Azure Logic Apps.

Automated Classification with Microsoft Purview

Microsoft Purview's Information Protection features leverage AI to classify and label data across Microsoft 365, Azure Storage, Synapse Analytics, and more. It uses pretrained classifiers (e.g., for GDPR, HIPAA, financial data, source code) and allows organizations to create custom ML models for domain-specific labeling.

AI automatically scans data at rest and in motion—tagging files, emails, and structured records with sensitivity labels. These labels can then enforce encryption, access restrictions, and DLP (Data Loss Prevention) policies. For instance, if a document containing personal health information is uploaded to OneDrive, AI can instantly label it "Confidential – Health" and restrict external sharing, in accordance with compliance policy.

Purview's Data Security Posture Management (DSPM)—announced in 2024—extends this capability to Copilot prompts and AI-generated content, ensuring that sensitive data is governed even in generative AI use cases.

AI-Powered Policy Enforcement and Drift Detection

Azure Policy uses AI to monitor thousands of configuration parameters across subscriptions, comparing them against compliance definitions. It supports policy initiatives that group controls by standard (e.g., ISO, NIST) and integrates with resource graph queries to analyze historical compliance posture.

AI models detect drift over time using change tracking and anomaly detection. For example, if encryption at rest is disabled for a new database deployment in a subscription previously aligned with ISO standards, the system will automatically flag the deviation and can trigger auto-remediation workflows.

Demo: Automating Compliance Reports with AI

Generating compliance reports in large cloud environments has traditionally been a resource-intensive task involving manual evidence collection, Excel-based tracking, and static documentation. As regulatory requirements become more dynamic and granular—especially with frameworks like ISO 27001, NIST 800-53, GDPR, and the EU AI Act—organizations need scalable, real-time reporting mechanisms. Microsoft Azure addresses this challenge through **AI-enabled compliance tools** integrated across services like **Microsoft Purview**, **Defender for Cloud**, **Azure Policy**, and **Microsoft Compliance Manager**.

Artificial intelligence is applied across the compliance reporting pipeline in three keyways:

1. **Automated Evidence Collection**: AI analyzes configuration states, usage logs, and data classifications across Azure and Microsoft 365 to extract audit-relevant telemetry.

2. **Prioritization and Scoring**: ML models assign risk-adjusted compliance scores based on how far current implementations deviate from a baseline or regulatory control set.

3. **Language Generation**: Using Azure OpenAI or Copilot integration, AI can generate human-readable compliance summaries tailored to stakeholders such as CISOs, auditors, or board reviewers.

Together, these AI-enhanced capabilities reduce the time required to generate evidence-backed compliance reports from weeks to hours—while improving accuracy and consistency across audits.

Let's make a short demo. I will show you how Microsoft Compliance Manager uses AI to automatically generate a basic compliance report.

CHAPTER 13   HARNESSING AZURE AI AND COPILOT FOR GOVERNANCE AND SECURITY

1. Go to the new Microsoft Purview center from https://purview.microsoft.com/.

2. Sign in using your Microsoft 365 account with Compliance Manager access (usually part of Microsoft 365 E5 or Microsoft Purview license).

3. On the left-hand menu, click Compliance Manager as shown in Figure 13-1.

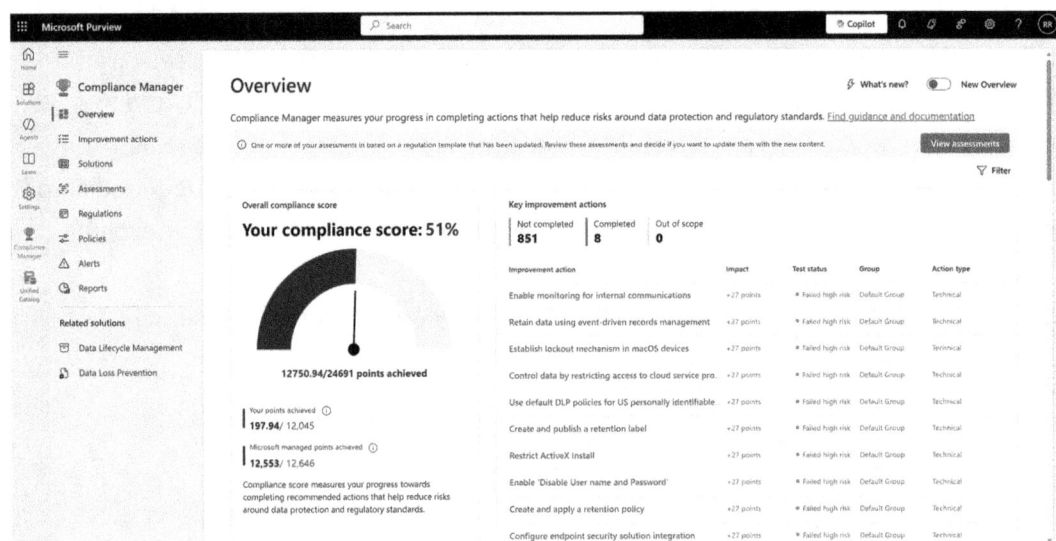

Figure 13-1. *Compliance Manager dashboard of Microsoft Purview*

4. Click Assessments and select Add Assessment as shown in Figure 13-2.

CHAPTER 13   HARNESSING AZURE AI AND COPILOT FOR GOVERNANCE AND SECURITY

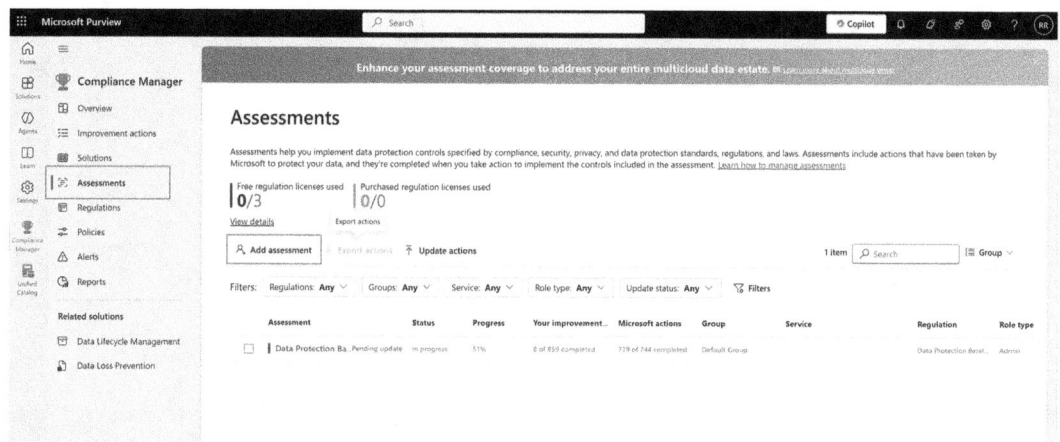

Figure 13-2. *Adding assessment in Compliance Manager*

5. Click "Select regulation" in the regulation section, and search GDPR as shown in Figure 13-3.

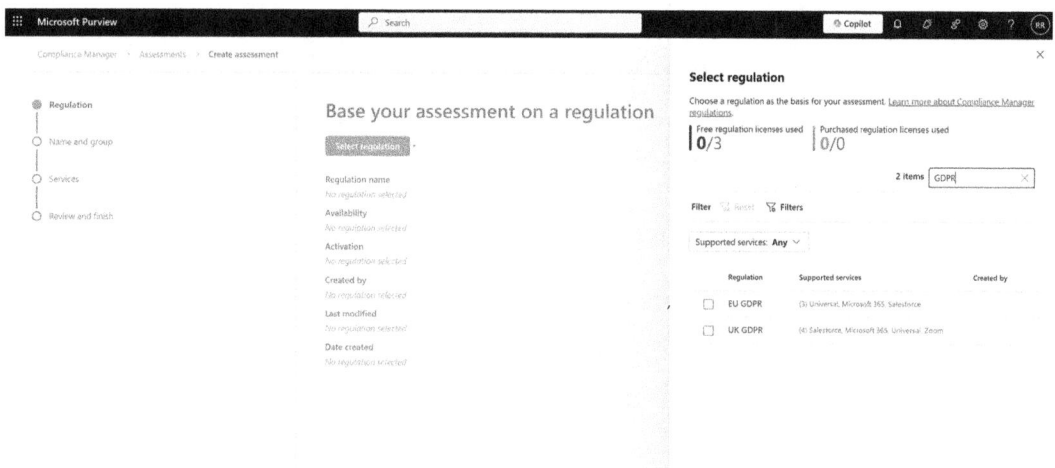

Figure 13-3. *Selecting regulation in assessment*

6. Select the EU GDPR.

7. Add an assignment name and choose an assignment group.

8. Review and create the assignment. Microsoft will now start analyzing the environment against GDPR controls. You will see the page as shown in Figure 13-4.

CHAPTER 13   HARNESSING AZURE AI AND COPILOT FOR GOVERNANCE AND SECURITY

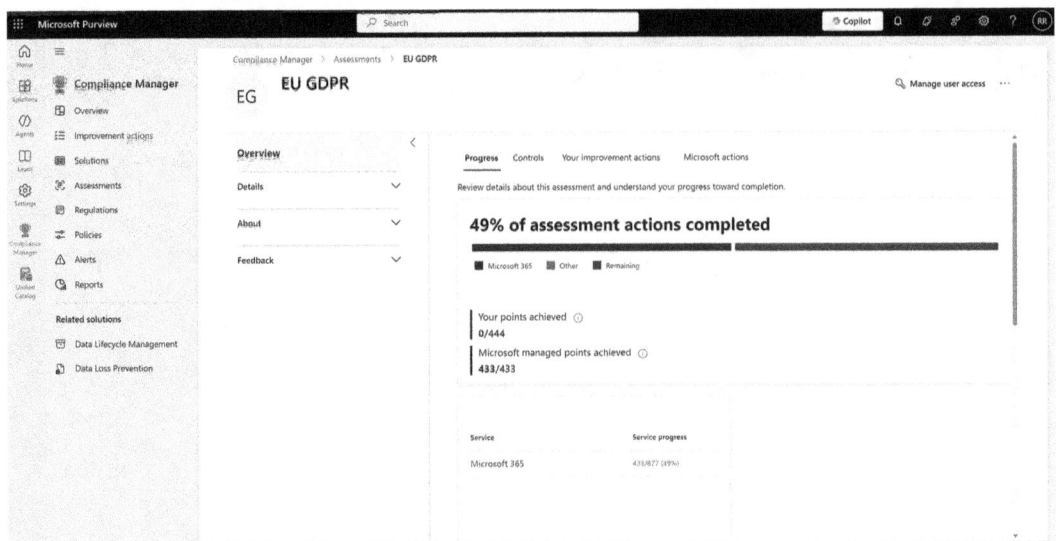

Figure 13-4. Assessment overview page

9. Once the assessment loads, it shows the compliance score (out of 100%), improvement actions, and implementation status.

10. Click Your improvement actions; choose any action to see

    a. What the control is

    b. What Microsoft has already implemented for you

    c. What you will need to do

11. Let's export the compliance report to see the current score, passed vs. failed controls, and action steps to improve compliance. To export the compliance report, click the three dots, and choose the Download as report, as shown in Figure 13-5.

CHAPTER 13   HARNESSING AZURE AI AND COPILOT FOR GOVERNANCE AND SECURITY

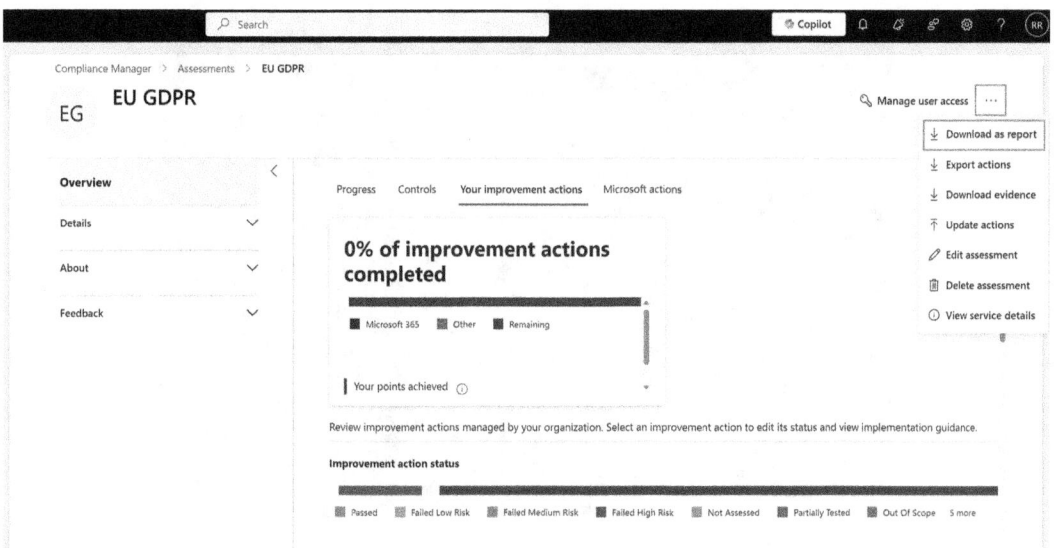

Figure 13-5. Downloading improvement report

12. After downloading the report, you will see the report as PDF format as shown in Figure 13-6.

Figure 13-6. *PDF copy of the assessment report*

13. You can see the summary of the report as shown in Figure 13-7.

CHAPTER 13　HARNESSING AZURE AI AND COPILOT FOR GOVERNANCE AND SECURITY

> **EU GDPR Assessment Report**　　2025-06-12 10:27:20 AM UTC
>
> # Microsoft Compliance Manager Sections Summary
>
> The following is a summary status for each of the sections of the Microsoft cloud security benchmark. For each section, you will find the overall number of passing and failing controls, based on automated assessments run by Microsoft Compliance Manager.
>
> A failing control indicates that at least one Microsoft Compliance Manager assessment associated with this control failed. A passing control indicates that all the Microsoft Compliance Manager assessments associated with this control passed. Note that status is shown only for supported controls, i.e. controls that have relevant Microsoft Compliance Manager assessments associated with them.
>
> ## Control Category Summary : Microsoft 365
>
> The control status for each of these areas can be either passed or failed. The Compliance Posture report provides a summary of the control status for your cloud environment, as well as any recommendations for improving compliance.
>
> | Control Family | Passed Controls | Failed Controls | |
> | --- | --- | --- | --- |
> | Controller and Processor | 26 | 4 | 86% |
> | Principles | 10 | 7 | 58% |
> | Rights of the Data Subject | 10 | 20 | 33% |
> | Transfers of Personal Data to Third Countries or International Organizations | 1 | 8 | 11% |
> | Provisions Relating to Specific Processing Situations | 0 | 1 | 0% |
>
> ## Control Summary : Microsoft 365
>
> The following is a summary status for each supported control of the EU GDPR Assessment. For each control, you will find the overall number of passed and total actions associated with that control.

Figure 13-7. *Microsoft compliance score summary*

By following these simple steps, you've successfully created a GDPR compliance report using Microsoft's AI-powered Compliance Manager. The entire process required no coding or advanced configuration, making it accessible for both technical and nontechnical users. The resulting report is automatically generated based on Microsoft's regulatory templates and real-time analysis of your environment. It provides a clear overview of your compliance posture, including improvement actions and scoring and is ready to be shared with stakeholders, auditors, or IT administrators for further review or evidence submission.

Introduction to Azure Copilot

The evolution of cloud management is entering a new phase, driven by the integration of generative AI into core platform services. Microsoft's vision of transforming user interaction with cloud infrastructure has led to the introduction of **Azure Copilot**, a generative AI assistant integrated directly into the Azure Portal experience. While the specific functionality of Azure Copilot will be detailed in the next section, this chapter focuses on how AI-driven copilots are reshaping cloud operations, governance, and development workflows.

Azure Copilot is part of a broader family of AI copilots—each tailored for a different domain within the Microsoft ecosystem, such as Microsoft 365, GitHub, and Security. These systems leverage large language models hosted in Azure and grounded in enterprise data to deliver conversational interfaces, contextual insights, and automation. In the case of Azure Copilot, its integration into the control plane introduces new opportunities to streamline tasks like resource deployment, diagnostics, policy analysis, and code generationally through natural language input.

In this section, we will discuss the architectural foundations of Azure Copilot, explain how it fits into enterprise environments, and compare it with other Copilot offerings across Microsoft's cloud platforms. Rather than replacing traditional tools, Azure Copilot is designed to augment existing workflows by making cloud operations more intelligent, accessible, and secure.

What Is Azure Copilot?

Azure Copilot (also known as *Microsoft Copilot in Azure*) is an AI-powered assistant integrated directly into the Azure Portal. It enables users, whether administrators, developers, or data professionals, to interact with Azure using **conversational natural language**, powered by large language models (LLMs) hosted on Azure OpenAI.

Rather than navigating through complex UI elements or writing manual scripts, users can ask Copilot to perform tasks like

- `Show me all VMs with less than 10% CPU usage deployed in the last hour in West Europe.`
- `Generate a Bicep template for a storage account with encryption enabled.`
- `Summarize the current network topology and potential security risks.`

Copilot interprets the user's intent, translates it into the appropriate Azure resource graph queries or ARM command structure, and executes the request in-context—while fully respecting the user's Microsoft Entra ID permissions and policy boundaries.

It supports operations such as resource analysis, configuration diagnostics, infrastructure deployment, cost estimation, and security posture checks—all available through both the Azure Portal UI and the Azure mobile app. Additionally, it integrates with tools like **Azure CLI**, **Azure Resource Graph**, **ARM APIs**, and **Azure Monitor**, meaning the AI assistant is not a standalone chatbot—it is a deeply embedded orchestration interface within the Azure control plane.

Architecture and Deployment Overview

Azure Copilot is built on a layered architecture that combines a natural language interface with Azure-native services and AI-powered orchestration. It is designed to help users interact with Azure using everyday language while ensuring all actions are secure, permission-aware, and grounded in real-time context.

At a high level, the architecture consists of three core layers:

1. **Copilot Frontend**: This is the user interface you see in the Azure Portal. It includes the chat experience, context awareness (like which subscription you're in), and dynamic components like forms or suggestions. It's also responsible for handling user input and displaying intelligent, interactive responses.

2. **Orchestration Layer**: This is where the AI engine interprets your request, grounds it in Azure-specific context, filters the prompt for safety, and selects the right plugin (e.g., for cost analysis, KQL generation, or documentation). It ensures the AI output is relevant, accurate, and policy compliant.

3. **AI Infrastructure**: Powered by Azure OpenAI Service, this layer runs large language models like GPT-4 to understand user intent and generate useful responses. It is stateless, secure, and governed by your existing Azure permissions.

Figure 13-8 shows the architectural overview of Copilot for Azure.

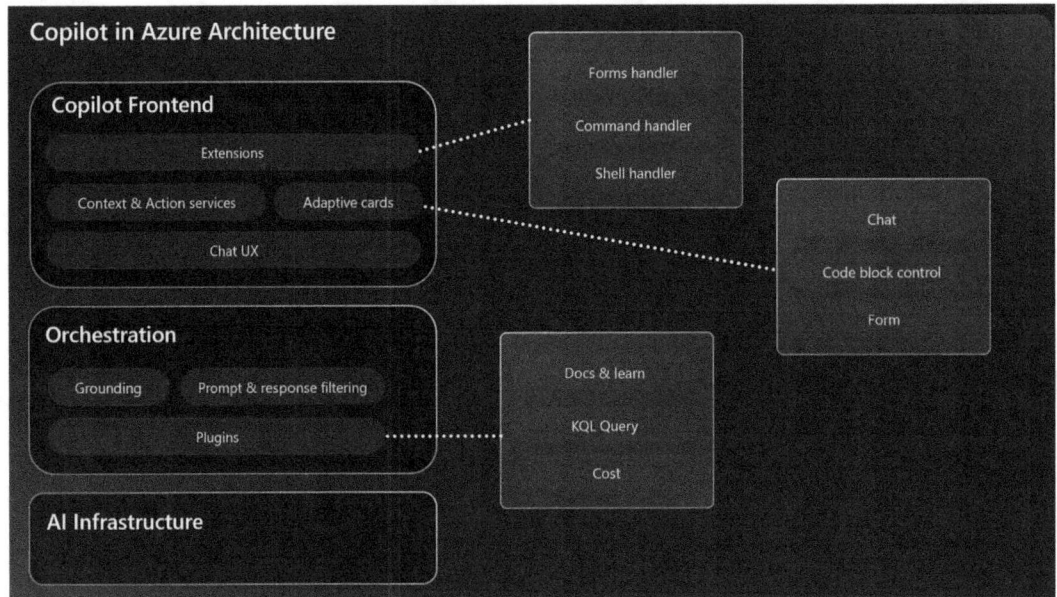

Figure 13-8. *Microsoft Copilot for Azure architectural overview*

Behind the scenes, Copilot connects to services like Azure Resource Graph, ARM, and Microsoft documentation and can generate queries, scripts, or deployment templates—always scoped to what the user is allowed to do.

There's no need to install or deploy anything separately. Azure Copilot runs natively inside the Azure Portal and enforces all existing security, RBAC, and compliance boundaries automatically.

Comparison with Other Microsoft Copilots

Azure Copilot is part of Microsoft's broader family of AI-powered assistants, each designed for a specific domain—ranging from cloud operations to productivity, development, and security. While they all rely on large language models and enterprise data grounding, their focus, integrations, and use cases vary significantly.

Azure Copilot is built to support infrastructure and cloud operations within the Azure Portal. It allows users to query resources, generate Bicep templates, analyze cost and performance, and troubleshoot configurations using natural language. It integrates deeply with Azure Resource Graph, ARM, and Azure Monitor and respects all Azure RBAC permissions.

Microsoft 365 Copilot operates within apps like Word, Excel, Outlook, and Teams. It enhances productivity by summarizing emails, drafting documents, analyzing spreadsheets, and assisting with meeting follow-ups. It leverages Microsoft Graph to access content such as documents, chats, calendars, and emails, all under the user's existing M365 permissions.

GitHub Copilot is focused on developer productivity. Integrated into IDEs like Visual Studio Code, it suggests code, explains functions, and helps generate unit tests in real time. It uses code context from the current file or project and is optimized for common programming languages and frameworks. GitHub Copilot for Business includes privacy controls and telemetry restrictions.

Microsoft Security Copilot serves security analysts by integrating with Microsoft Sentinel, Defender XDR, and other SOC tools. It helps investigate incidents, correlate threat signals, generate KQL queries, and summarize alerts. It's grounded in real-time security data and threat intelligence, with strong policy enforcement and audit logging.

Despite their differences, all Microsoft Copilots are powered by Azure OpenAI Service, adhere to enterprise-grade data governance, and are designed with responsible AI principles—including non-persistence of prompts and outputs, secure access controls, and full compliance alignment.

CHAPTER 13 HARNESSING AZURE AI AND COPILOT FOR GOVERNANCE AND SECURITY

Table 13-9 shows a clear comparison highlighting the primary domain, use cases, and integrations of each Copilot.

Table 13-9. Overview of Microsoft Copilot variants

Copilot	Primary Domain	Key Use Cases	Integrated With
Azure Copilot	Cloud Infrastructure	Resource queries, deployment, diagnostics	Azure Portal, ARM, Azure Monitor, ARG
M365 Copilot	Productivity Apps	Drafting, summarization, meeting insights	Microsoft 365 (Word, Excel, Outlook, Teams)
GitHub Copilot	Software Development	Code suggestions, debugging, test generation	Visual Studio Code, GitHub
Security Copilot	Security Operations	Incident analysis, threat hunting, KQL generation	Microsoft Sentinel, Defender, Entra

Let's check how Azure Copilot works. I will use Azure Copilot to summarize the current network topology and potential security risks.

1. Go to the Azure portal.

2. Click the Copilot button on the top command bar or left menu.
   The Copilot chat will open as shown in Figure 13-9.

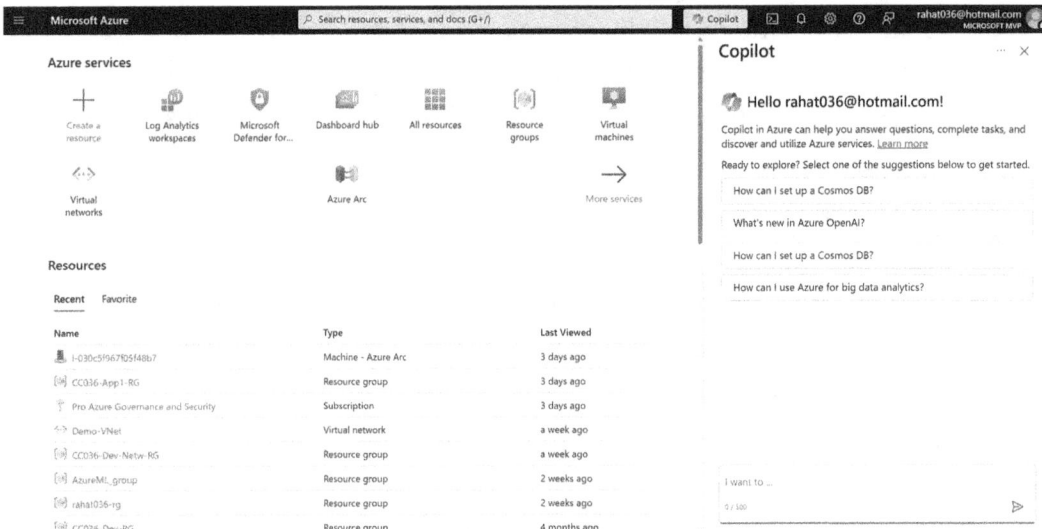

Figure 13-9. Microsoft Copilot chat in Azure portal

CHAPTER 13   HARNESSING AZURE AI AND COPILOT FOR GOVERNANCE AND SECURITY

3. Type the following prompt to the chatbox and hit enter:

    Summarize the current network topology and potential security risks

4. Copilot will generate the response as shown in Figure 13-10.

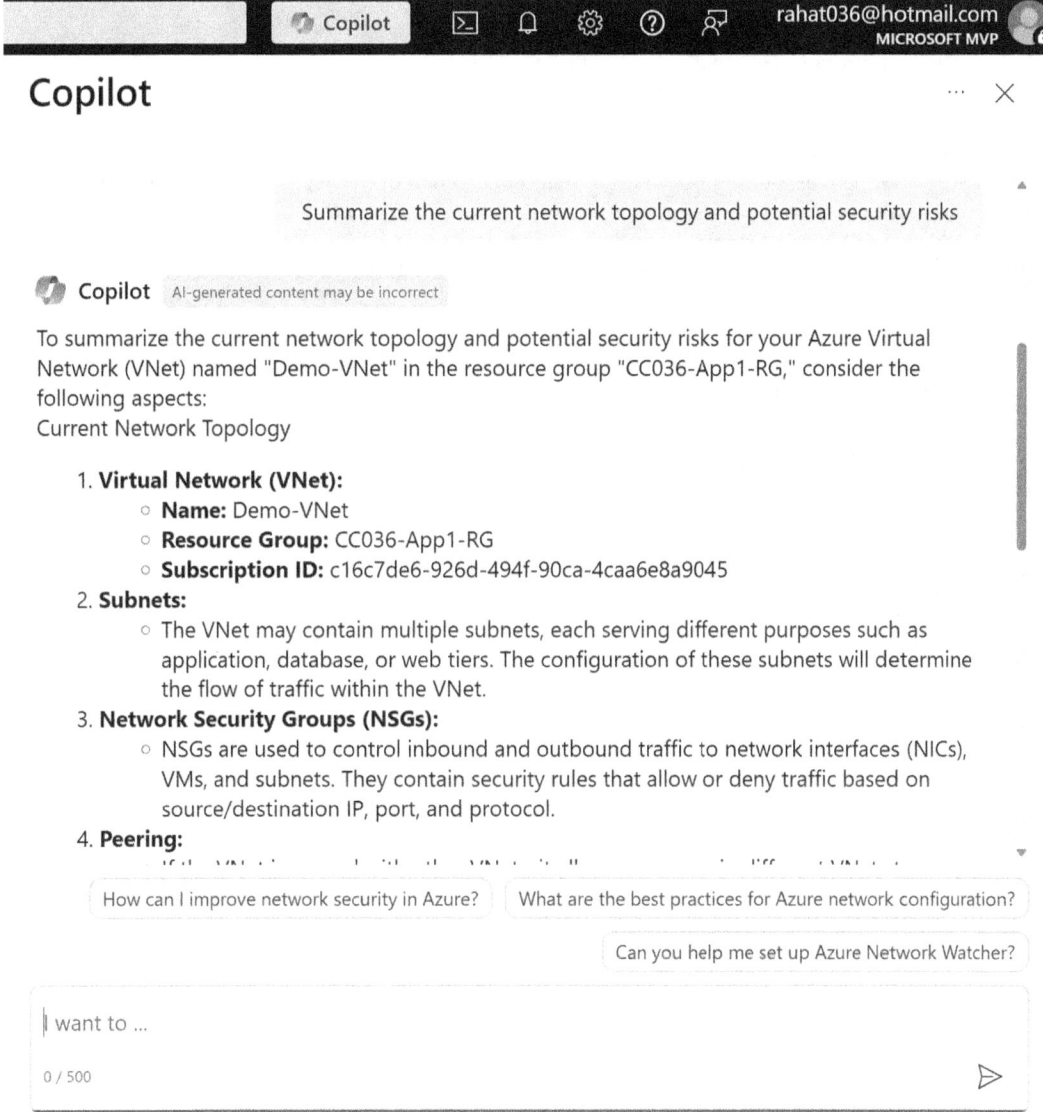

Figure 13-10. Copilot prompt to summarize the current network topology and security risks

CHAPTER 13   HARNESSING AZURE AI AND COPILOT FOR GOVERNANCE AND SECURITY

5. It also shows the potential security risks as well as shown in Figure 13-11.

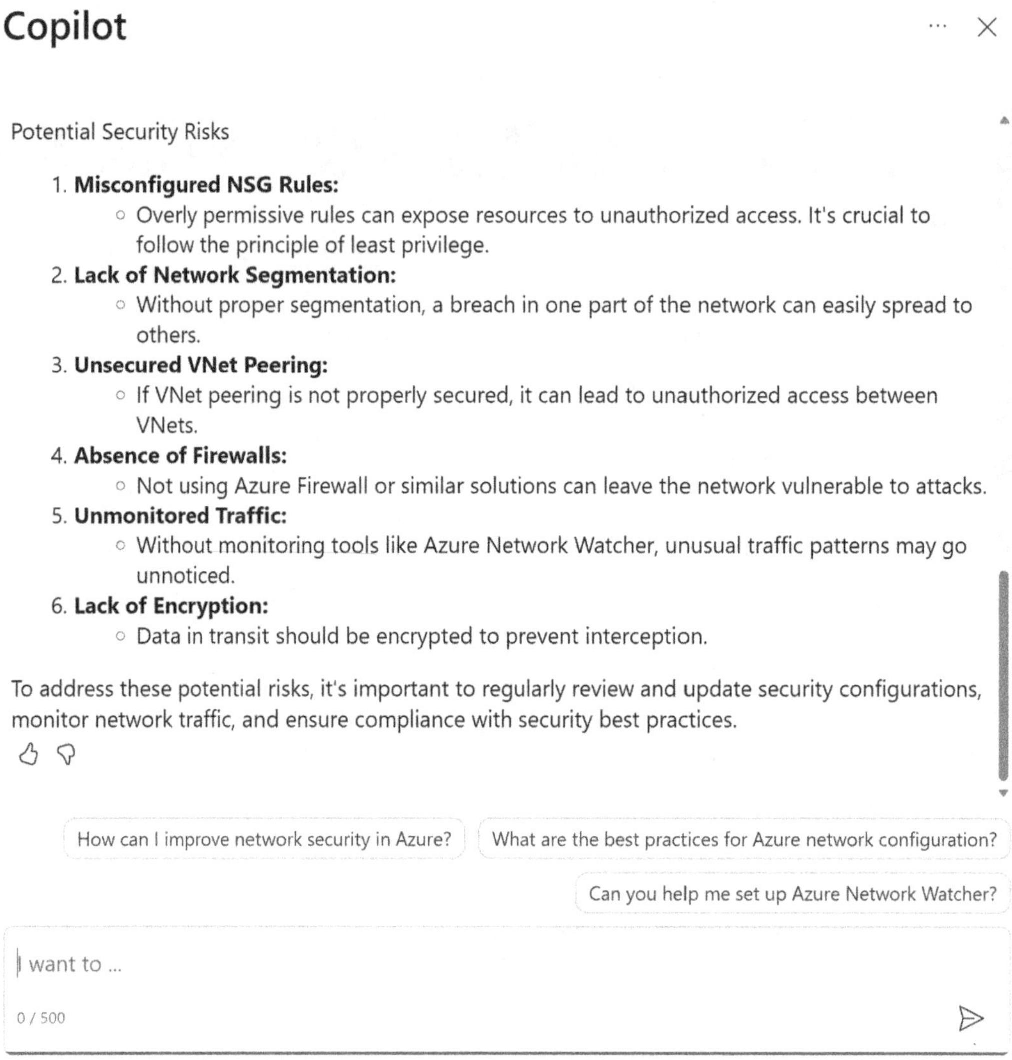

Copilot

Potential Security Risks

1. **Misconfigured NSG Rules:**
   - Overly permissive rules can expose resources to unauthorized access. It's crucial to follow the principle of least privilege.
2. **Lack of Network Segmentation:**
   - Without proper segmentation, a breach in one part of the network can easily spread to others.
3. **Unsecured VNet Peering:**
   - If VNet peering is not properly secured, it can lead to unauthorized access between VNets.
4. **Absence of Firewalls:**
   - Not using Azure Firewall or similar solutions can leave the network vulnerable to attacks.
5. **Unmonitored Traffic:**
   - Without monitoring tools like Azure Network Watcher, unusual traffic patterns may go unnoticed.
6. **Lack of Encryption:**
   - Data in transit should be encrypted to prevent interception.

To address these potential risks, it's important to regularly review and update security configurations, monitor network traffic, and ensure compliance with security best practices.

[How can I improve network security in Azure?]   [What are the best practices for Azure network configuration?]

[Can you help me set up Azure Network Watcher?]

I want to ...

0 / 500

Figure 13-11. Response from Copilot about network topology summary and potential security risks

6. It also shows some related recommendations so that you do not need to write the prompt again.

CHAPTER 13   HARNESSING AZURE AI AND COPILOT FOR GOVERNANCE AND SECURITY

Using Copilot for Governance and Automation

Modern cloud governance involves managing resources at scale while ensuring compliance, cost efficiency, security, and operational consistency. Traditionally, this has required navigating complex tools, writing Infrastructure-as-Code templates, or building policy rule sets manually. With the introduction of **Azure Copilot**, Microsoft brings the power of generative AI directly into the governance and automation layer of the Azure ecosystem. Copilot enables users to interact with Azure governance services—such as **Azure Policy**, **Role-Based Access Control (RBAC)**, **Cost Management**, and **Resource Graph**—using natural language prompts.

Azure Copilot doesn't just surface information; it interprets governance intent and translates it into actionable infrastructure queries, policy definitions, role assignment recommendations, and cost optimization actions. Whether you need to define tagging policies, automate audit rule creation, set budgets, or forecast spending patterns, Copilot can generate Bicep templates, recommend policies based on compliance benchmarks, and simulate enforcement scope—all while maintaining security boundaries defined by Azure RBAC and identity context.

While Azure Copilot simplifies governance tasks through natural language input, it is not immune to prompt misinterpretation, contextual ambiguity, or incomplete automation for complex policies. Users must still validate generated output, especially when configuring security-sensitive rules or budget thresholds. Additionally, Copilot currently relies on predefined schemas and policy models, which may not fully capture edge cases or highly customized governance requirements.

This section explores how Copilot can be used to automate and enhance governance operations across four key areas: **resource governance**, **policy management**, **cost control**, and **access reviews**. Through AI-assisted reasoning and context-aware automation, Copilot reduces the complexity of managing governance at scale—transforming tasks that once took hours of scripting into guided, compliant, and secure actions initiated by a simple prompt.

Copilot Scenarios for Resource Governance

Azure Copilot isn't just a chat interface—it can automate and simplify many core governance tasks through natural language prompts. Here are a few **real-world scenarios** where Copilot enhances resource governance:

CHAPTER 13 HARNESSING AZURE AI AND COPILOT FOR GOVERNANCE AND SECURITY

1. **Tag Management and Enforcement**: Without writing a single line of Bicep or KQL, you can prompt Copilot to generate or apply Azure Policy definitions for tagging, such as

   ```
   Create a policy to enforce 'CostCenter' and 'Environment' tags on all resource groups using the modify effect.
   ```

   Copilot understands your intent, generates the correct policy code, and links it to your scope—grounded in Microsoft documentation on policy structure. Figure 13-12 shows the outcome of the prompt.

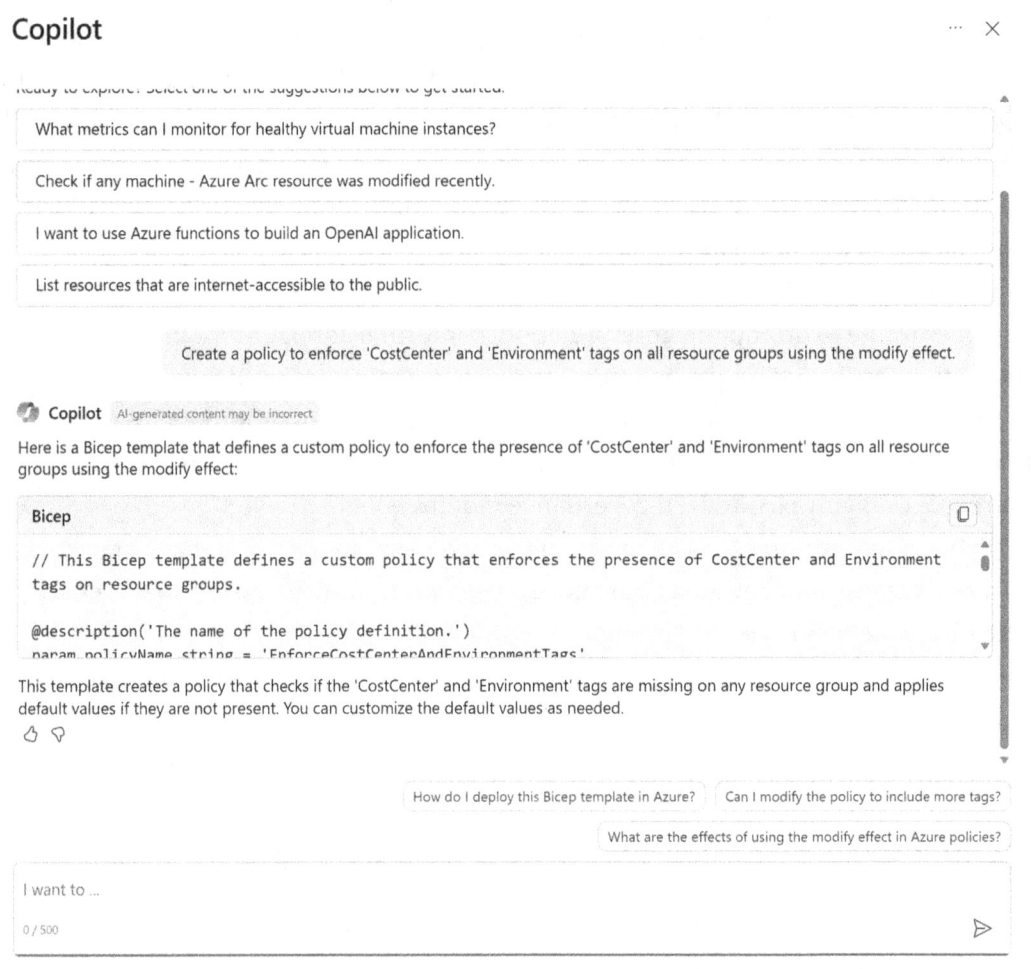

Figure 13-12. *Creating a Bicep template to define a custom policy that enforces the presence of CostCenter and Environment tags on resource groups*

CHAPTER 13   HARNESSING AZURE AI AND COPILOT FOR GOVERNANCE AND SECURITY

2. **Governance Drifts and Remediation:** You can ask Copilot to highlight resource groups or subscriptions deviating from tag policies or encryption rules. It will run Resource Graph queries such as

   ```
   Which virtual machines across all subscriptions do not have encrypted OS disks?
   ```

   Copilot then suggests Bicep or Azure CLI commands to remediate or generate a deploy-if-not-exists policy. Figure 13-13 shows the outcome of the prompt.

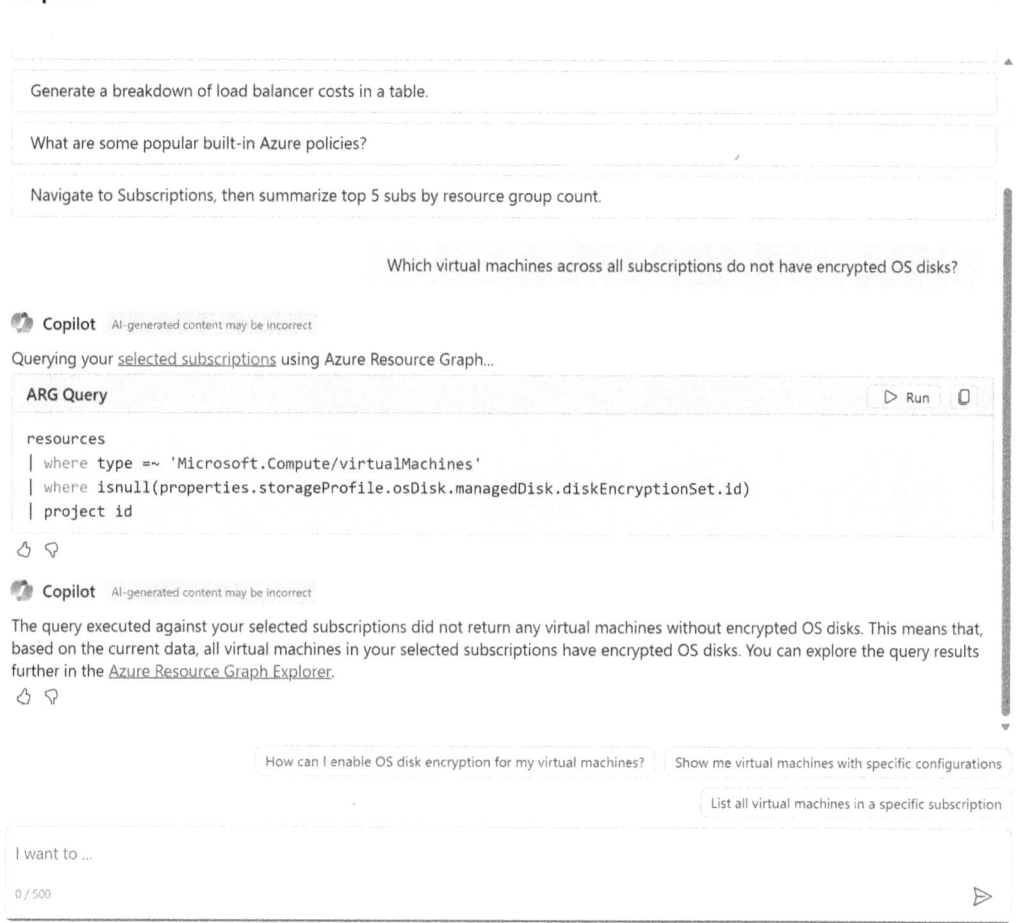

Figure 13-13. *Prompt to get the VM across all subscriptions that do not have any encrypted OS disks*

You can see Copilot composed the ARG query, which you can run directly in Azure Resource Graph Explorer.

3. **Naming Standards Enforcement**: Copilot helps with resource naming governance by crafting policies that enforce naming conventions:

```
Generate a naming policy for storage accounts that
ensures they start with company code and end with region
abbreviation.
```

It produces sample Azure Policy definitions and shows how to test them in your current environment. Figure 13-14 shows the outcome of the prompt.

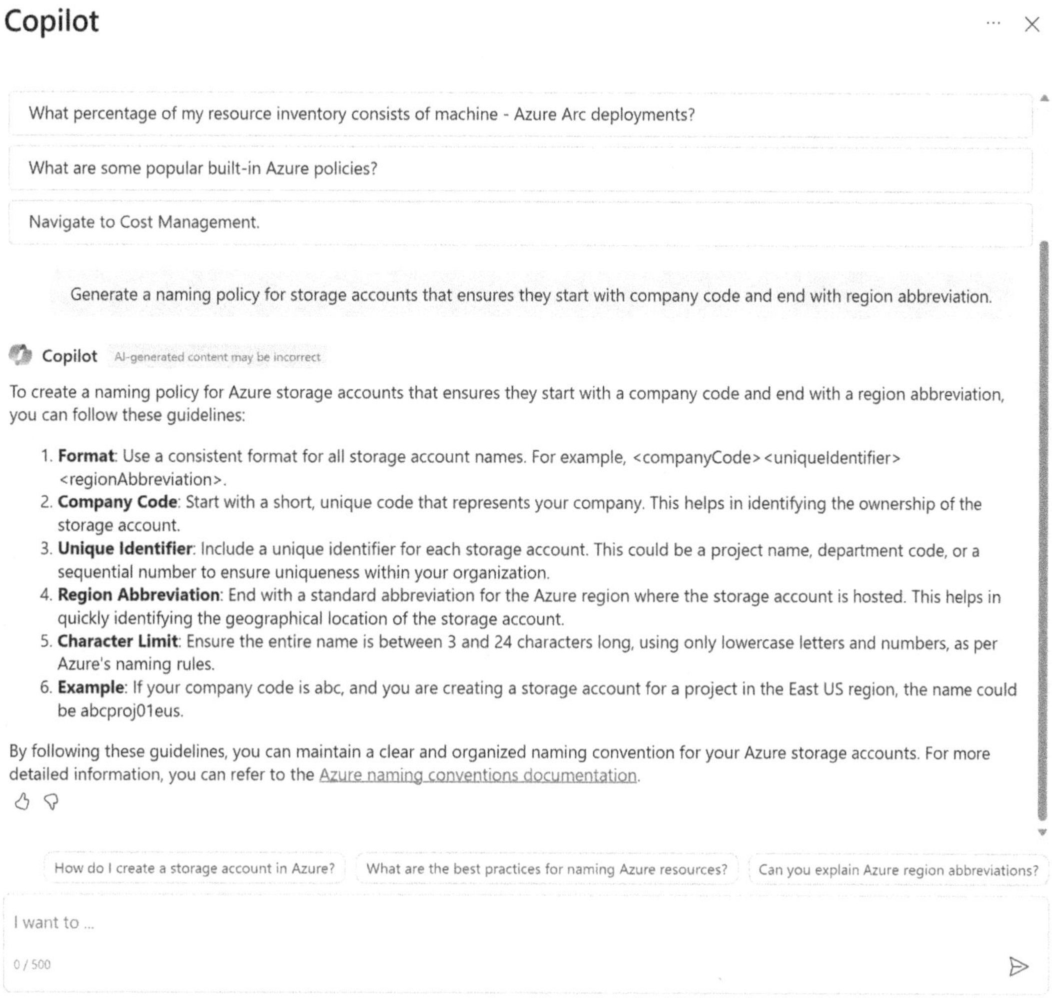

CHAPTER 13   HARNESSING AZURE AI AND COPILOT FOR GOVERNANCE AND SECURITY

Figure 13-14. *Prompt to generate a naming policy for storage accounts that enforces a prefix with the company code and a suffix with the regional abbreviation*

4. **Security and Compliance Overlays:** You can combine governance with security posture by prompting Copilot:

   ```
   List all resource groups without Azure Defender enabled
   and create a remediation plan.
   ```

   Copilot runs diagnostic queries, surfaces the results, and generates scripts or policy recommendations to onboard resources to Defender for Cloud. Figure 13-15 shows the prompt outcome.

601

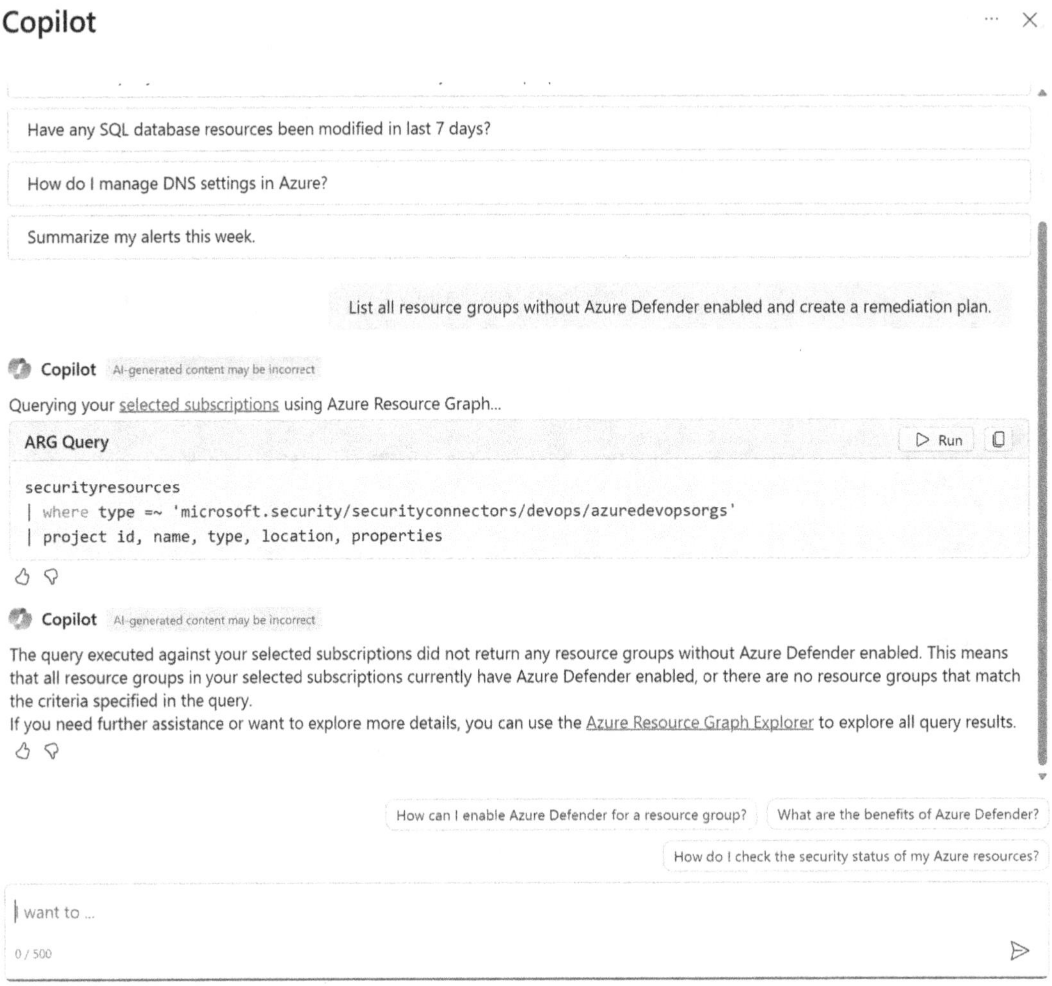

CHAPTER 13 HARNESSING AZURE AI AND COPILOT FOR GOVERNANCE AND SECURITY

Figure 13-15. Prompt to list all the resource groups without Azure Defender enabled and create the remediation plan

Automating Azure Policy Creation and Management with Copilot

Creating and managing Azure Policy has historically involved writing JSON definitions, assigning policies via Azure CLI or ARM templates, and using the portal to monitor compliance. While powerful, this process is time-consuming and requires deep familiarity with policy structure, effects, and scoping. Azure Copilot now introduces a

CHAPTER 13   HARNESSING AZURE AI AND COPILOT FOR GOVERNANCE AND SECURITY

faster, AI-assisted approach by enabling users to define, deploy, and validate policies using simple, natural language prompts—while still generating enterprise-grade governance artifacts.

At its core, Copilot serves as a bridge between intent and implementation. When a user types a prompt like *"Create a policy to enforce the* `'CostCenter'` *tag on all resource groups using the modify effect,"* Copilot generates a complete Azure Policy definition in JSON, as shown in Figure 13-16.

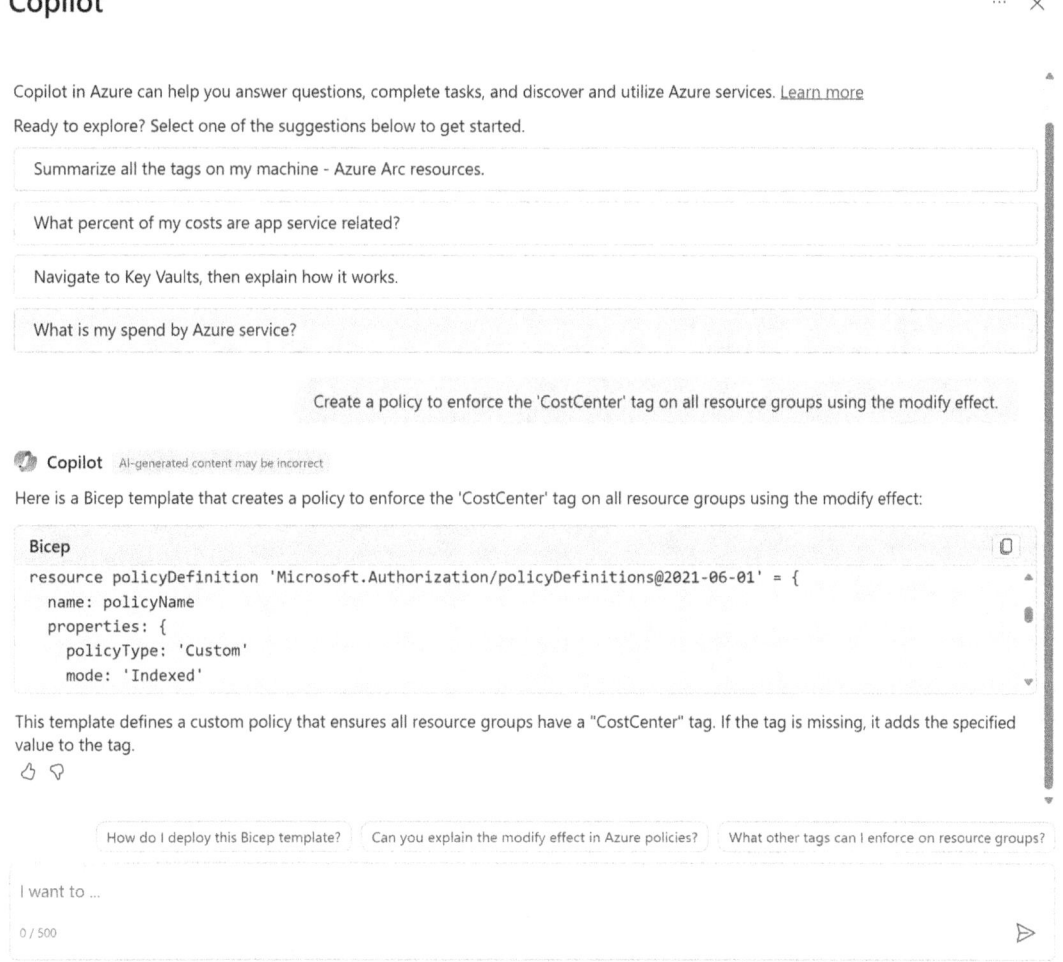

Figure 13-16. *Prompt to generate a policy to enforce the CostCenter tag on all resource groups using the modify effect*

This definition includes the correct policy structure, effect type (such as modify, audit, or deny), and parameterization, all aligned with Microsoft's policy schema. The user can then refine the scope, confirm the logic, and deploy the policy through a guided interface—without needing to open the Azure Policy authoring blade or write code manually.

Copilot also supports initiative management. For example, if a user asks, "*Group our resource tagging, location restrictions, and SKU limitations into a single initiative*," Copilot responds with an ARM-based policy set definition, bundled with individual policies and ready for assignment, as shown in Figure 13-17.

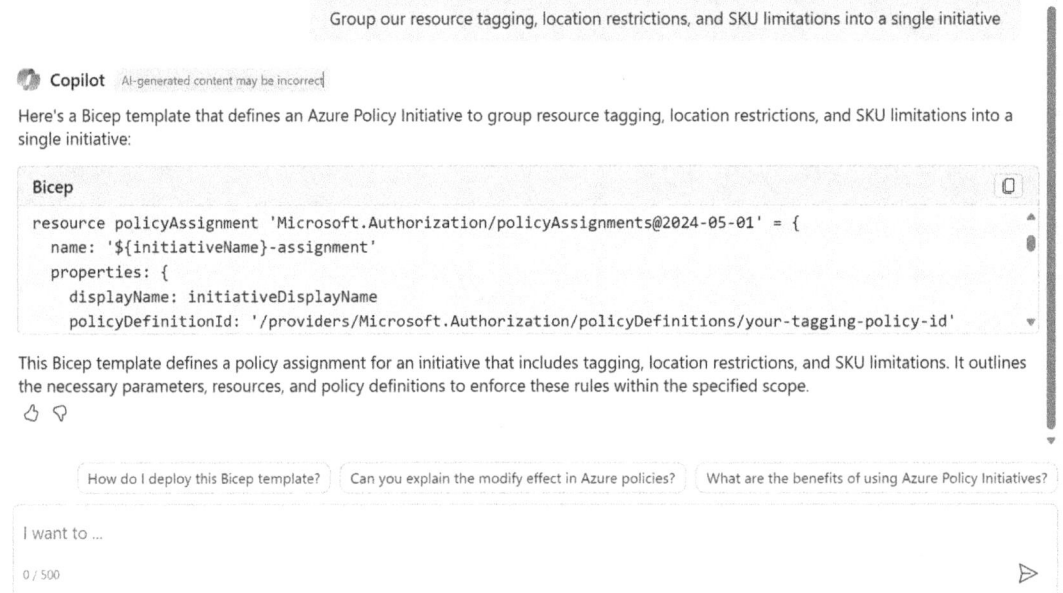

Figure 13-17. *Using Copilot to generate a Bicep template for grouping Azure Policy Initiatives*

This reduces complexity in large environments, where dozens of policies must be grouped for compliance with frameworks like ISO 27001 or NIST 800-53.

One of the key advantages is context awareness. Copilot automatically scopes recommendations to the user's current subscription, resource group, or management group. If the prompt implies assignment or remediation (e.g., "*Apply this policy to our dev subscriptions and fix noncompliant resources*"), Copilot suggests deploying the policy using a managed identity and `deployIfNotExists` logic.

Once the policy is applied, users can ask Copilot to monitor and report on its effect. A prompt like *"What is the compliance state of our mandatory tag policy?"* returns a summary from Azure Policy insights, highlighting compliant vs. non-compliant resources and surfacing remediation suggestions if needed.

Enhancing Cost Management and Budget Forecasting

Azure Copilot is integrated tightly with **Microsoft Cost Management**, enabling users to analyze, forecast, and optimize expenses using simple conversational prompts—eliminating the need to navigate multiple dashboards or write KQL queries.

Real-Time Cost Analysis with Copilot

You can ask Copilot questions like

- `Summarize my cost for the last 6 months.`
- `What were my top five cost drivers last month?`
- `Why is spending higher in West Europe?`

Copilot pulls the current billing scope from **Cost Management**, analyzes usage and pricing data, and responds with clear summaries, graphical breakdowns, and even cost per resource group or service. This makes tracking spending across environments quick and insightful.

Figure 13-18 shows an example of a cost analysis prompt with Copilot.

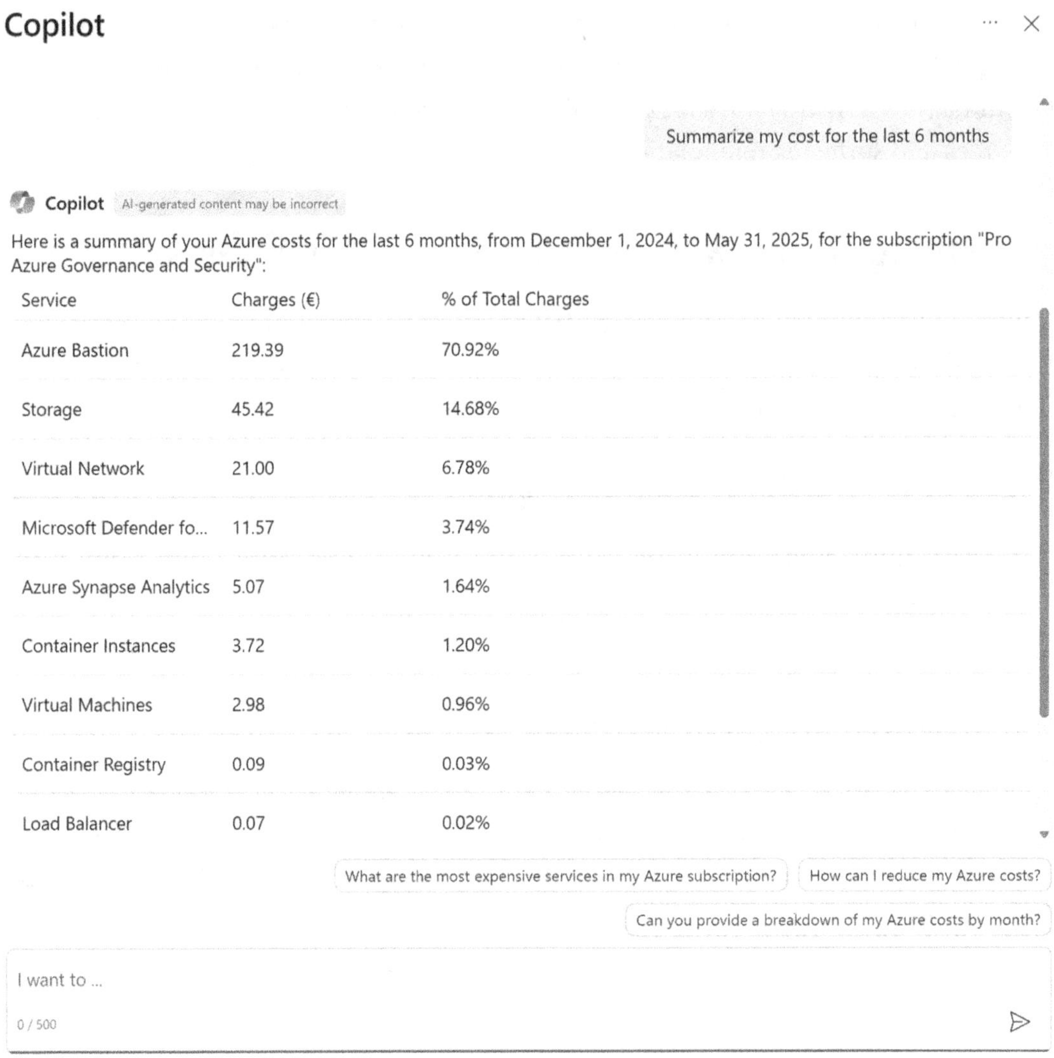

CHAPTER 13   HARNESSING AZURE AI AND COPILOT FOR GOVERNANCE AND SECURITY

Figure 13-18. Azure cost summary generated by Copilot for the last six months

Forecasting and "What If" Models

For planning purposes, Copilot can generate forward-looking cost estimates:

- `Estimate my expenses for the next 3 months.`
- `What if compute usage increases by 20%?`

Leveraging Cost Management's forecasting engine, which uses historical billing trends and simulation models, Copilot generates month-by-month projections. For tokenized services like Azure OpenAI, it can model usage shifts and forecast costs accordingly. These insights allow both technical and finance teams to plan capacity and budget proactively.

Figure 13-19 shows the example of cost estimation with Azure Copilot prompt.

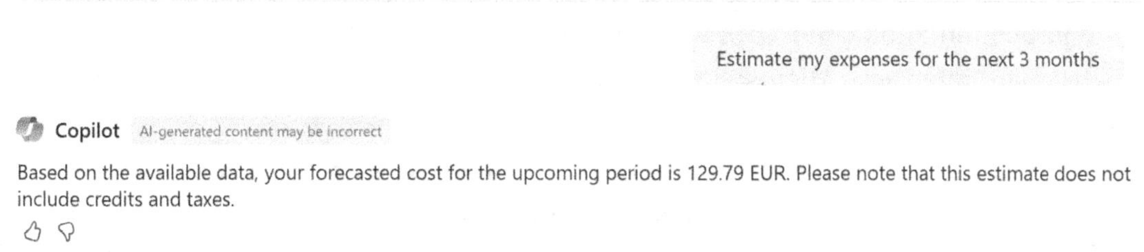

> Estimate my expenses for the next 3 months

Copilot AI-generated content may be incorrect

Based on the available data, your forecasted cost for the upcoming period is 129.79 EUR. Please note that this estimate does not include credits and taxes.

Figure 13-19. *Azure expense forecast generated by Copilot*

AI-Powered Cost Optimization Recommendations

When prompted, Copilot can suggest specific cost-saving actions:

- Resize or deallocate idle VMs
- Purchase reserved instances or savings plans
- Re-architect underutilized services
- Identify unused disk storage or underutilized licenses

Each recommendation includes estimated savings and links to purchase options, such as **Azure Savings Plans** or **Reserved Instance** guides.

Real-World Use Cases and Best Practices

As organizations increasingly adopt AI-driven tools across their cloud environments, practical implementation becomes just as important as innovation. Microsoft's Azure Copilot and Copilot Studio are no longer experimental technologies—they are being deployed across industries to automate governance, accelerate compliance, and improve security operations in real time. This section explores real-world scenarios where Azure AI and Copilot technologies are already adding measurable value: from enforcing policies across thousands of resources to enabling conversational incident response within Zero Trust architectures. It concludes with lessons learned and key principles that can guide secure, scalable, and responsible adoption of Copilot capabilities in enterprise settings.

AI for Large-Scale Policy Enforcement

Azure Policy, combined with AI-driven automation, is critical for enforcing organizational standards at scale across cloud environments. One noteworthy real-world implementation comes from **Maersk**, the global shipping and logistics leader, which collaborated with Microsoft to deploy automated compliance policies across its extensive Azure footprint.

According to a Microsoft customer case study, Maersk faced the challenge of maintaining consistent governance across **thousands of resources and multiple subscriptions** worldwide. To address this, the company implemented the following high-impact strategies:

- **Auto-remediation Using** `modify` **and** `deployIfNotExists` **Effects**: Maersk applied policies that automatically enabled disk encryption, enforced network security group rules, and added mandatory tags (like CostCenter and Environment) to ensure consistent inventory and cost tracking.

- **Continuous Compliance at Scale**: With policy definitions assigned at the management group level, any new or updated resource was instantly evaluated. Non-compliant resources triggered auto-remediation workflows, eliminating drift across over 20,000 virtual machines and storage accounts.

- **Development Pipeline Integration**: Maersk incorporated Azure Policy checks into CI/CD workflows using Policy as Code. Any deployment pipelines detected policy violations and were blocked or provided with guided corrections, accelerating governance and reducing manual review efforts

Copilot for Incident Response in Zero Trust Architectures

Implementing Copilot within a Zero Trust framework significantly enhances incident response capabilities by enabling real-time investigation, triage, and automated remediation—all while enforcing strict identity and access controls.

As part of Microsoft's early-access program for Security Copilot, **AustralianSuper,** the largest superannuation fund in Australia, integrated Copilot for Security to enhance incident response and reinforce their Zero Trust architecture, in alignment with the Australian Signals Directorate's (ASD) cybersecurity framework.

This integration resulted in significant gains in operational efficiency and response accuracy, including

- After adopting Security Copilot, the **AustralianSuper** cyber team achieved a **22% faster response time** and **7% more accurate investigation outcomes**, according to independent research.

- Copilot's generative AI assists SOC analysts by correlating alerts, generating Kusto Query Language (KQL) scripts, and summarizing incidents in minutes—replacing what previously took hours of manual investigation.

- Through Zero Trust alignment, all Copilot interactions were executed under least-privileged Entra ID identities, with secure device compliance and role assignment policies enforced before any sensitive investigation task could begin.

Lessons from Early Adopters

Early adopters of Microsoft Copilot technologies provide valuable insight into both the opportunities and the practical challenges of integrating generative AI into enterprise operations. Among them, **Avanade**, a joint venture between Microsoft and Accenture, stands out as a leader in applying Security Copilot for intelligent incident response across its global security operations centers.

As a preview customer, **Avanade** deployed Security Copilot to assist SOC analysts with real-time threat investigation, Kusto Query Language (KQL) generation, and alert triage. According to Microsoft's official report, Avanade observed **up to 40% faster investigation times**, with junior analysts using Copilot to generate complex queries, summarize multi-signal attacks, and draft incident reports. More importantly, this enabled experienced analysts to shift their focus to threat modeling and proactive defense strategies.

This experience surfaced several key lessons:

- **Start with High-Impact, Narrow Use Cases**: Avanade began by applying Copilot to routine triage scenarios—such as phishing and identity alerts—before expanding its use to threat hunting. This limited scope allowed for faster training and higher trust in early outputs.

- **Integrate with Existing Security Workflows**: Rather than replacing SIEM/SOAR tools, Copilot was embedded into existing Microsoft Sentinel environments, using RBAC and Microsoft Entra ID to maintain control boundaries. This minimizes operational disruption while enhancing context.

- **Balance Autonomy with Human Oversight**: Copilot provided fast recommendations, but decisions—especially on response actions—were left to human analysts. This ensured compliance with internal policies and regulatory obligations.

- **Iterative Feedback Loop Improves Performance**: Teams continuously refined prompts and flagged inaccurate suggestions, which improved Copilot performance over time through adaptive learning.

Copilot technologies are most successful when introduced thoughtfully embedded within trusted systems, focused on real problems, and governed by secure identities and processes.

Ethical Considerations and Data Residency Concerns

The integration of AI-powered copilots into enterprise environments demands careful attention to ethical use and data residency. While technologies like Microsoft 365 Copilot, Azure Copilot, and Security Copilot offer significant productivity and governance gains, their deployment must align with organizational responsibilities around privacy, transparency, and regulatory compliance.

Microsoft has committed to responsible AI principles by ensuring that prompts, responses, and user-accessed content in Copilot interactions are not used to train foundation models. Instead, all generative interactions occur within secure, customer-controlled boundaries. For example, Microsoft 365 Copilot only accesses data that a user is already authorized to view in Microsoft Graph, respecting existing permissions in SharePoint, OneDrive, and Teams. This safeguards against data overexposure and ensures that Copilot operates within each organization's Zero Trust policies.

At the same time, the need for transparency and human oversight remains critical. AI-generated outputs, whether in code, policy summaries, or incident responses, must be reviewed for factual accuracy, bias, and relevance. Enterprises are advised to educate users about the risks of entering sensitive information—such as personal identifiers, health data, or financial records—into prompts and to establish internal usage guidelines to reinforce this behavior.

From a compliance and residency perspective, Microsoft enables organizations to meet national and regional regulatory standards through offerings like the EU Data Boundary and Advanced Data Residency (ADR). These controls ensure that Copilot data—such as interaction history, chat content, and log—remains stored in customer-designated geographic regions. For European customers, Microsoft guarantees that data stays within the EU by default. In addition, Copilot activities are fully auditable through services like Microsoft Purview and Azure Monitor, allowing compliance officers to track access, usage, and retention policies.

Ethical Copilot use is not just about how data is processed but also how decisions are made. Security Copilot, for instance, may recommend remediation steps for threats, but the final decisions remain with analysts. This human-in-the-loop design reinforces accountability and limits overreliance on AI suggestions. Additionally, administrators have full control over whether Copilot logs are retained, deleted, or shared for service improvement.

Recent public debates—such as those around the Windows "Recall" feature—highlight growing sensitivity around AI-enabled data recall and context tracking. Microsoft responded by making such features opt in, encrypted, and admin controlled, reinforcing that ethical defaults matter. For enterprises adopting Copilot technologies, the lesson is clear: ethics, governance, and compliance must be built-in, not bolted on.

Summary

In this chapter, we explored how **Azure AI and Microsoft Copilot** can be leveraged to enhance governance and security operations. We saw how these tools enable smarter decision-making, automate routine tasks, and simplify complex processes through natural language interaction. By integrating AI into cloud management, organizations can boost efficiency, reduce risk, and improve responsiveness—all while maintaining policy alignment and compliance. Through hands-on examples and use cases, we learned how intelligent tools are no longer optional but essential components of modern governance.

In the next chapter, we shift our focus from technology to people. This chapter explores how to **elevate individual and team skills** in Azure governance and security. You'll learn about key certifications, training resources, role-based learning paths, and community engagement strategies that can help professionals stay current and effective in a rapidly evolving cloud landscape. As tools evolve, so must the capabilities of those using them—and this chapter equips you to bridge that gap. Let's now turn to the human side of cloud governance and security—and explore how to build the expertise needed to lead with confidence.

CHAPTER 14

Elevating skills in Azure Governance and Security

In the previous chapter, we explored how **Azure AI and Microsoft Copilot** are transforming cloud governance and security—enabling automation, proactive insights, and intelligent assistance across policy management and threat detection. These advancements highlight an important truth: while technology is advancing rapidly, it is the **skills and expertise** of professionals that bring these tools to life.

As we arrive at the final chapter of this book, the focus shifts from systems to people. Governance and security are not just about policies or platforms, they are also about the **capabilities, awareness, and continuous growth** of those who manage them. In this chapter, we'll explore how to elevate your skills in Azure governance and security through **certifications, hands-on labs, role-based learning paths, and community engagement**. Whether you're an architect, administrator, or strategist, developing the right skills is essential to lead confidently in an evolving cloud landscape.

Let's conclude our journey by focusing on the most critical asset in any governance strategy—**you**.

Evolving As a Governance and Security Practitioner

Cloud governance is no longer just about setting policies; it's about keeping up with constant change. As Azure services grow and evolve, so must the skills and mindset of those managing them. A successful practitioner embraces continuous learning, automation, and proactive thinking. This shift means moving from manual, reactive operations to a model where policy, security, and compliance are built into every layer—at scale. Reactive governance pitfalls often include delayed response to misconfigurations, inconsistent policy enforcement across environments, and security breaches that go unnoticed until audit time. For instance, relying solely on manual monitoring can lead to missed alerts or slow mitigation of compliance violations, introducing business risk and regulatory exposure. With tools like Azure Policy, Defender for Cloud, and the Cloud Adoption Framework, Microsoft provides the foundation. The rest depends on how we adapt.

The Mindset of Lifelong Learning in the Azure Ecosystem

Working in the Azure ecosystem means accepting that change is the only constant. Microsoft releases hundreds of services updated each month, including new governance tools, identity features, security controls, and architectural patterns. To stay relevant, Azure governance and security practitioners must adopt a **lifelong learning mindset**—one that goes beyond certification and embraces continuous, structured, and hands-on learning.

Microsoft officially promotes this mindset through its **Microsoft Learn** platform and **Cloud Adoption Framework**, emphasizing role-based skill development aligned with real-world responsibilities. For example, **administrators** may focus on operational tasks like policy enforcement, monitoring, and automation—making the **Azure Governance Fundamentals** and **Microsoft Defender for Cloud** learning paths more relevant. In contrast, **cloud architects** typically engage in designing scalable governance models, hybrid integrations, and compliance strategies and might prioritize **Azure Arc**, **Entra Permissions Management**, and **Azure Policy authoring** tracks.

Whether you are managing policies, securing resources, or integrating hybrid workloads with Azure Arc, staying updated is a critical responsibility. Table 14-1 shows the recommended Microsoft Learning paths focused on Microsoft Azure Governance and Security.

Table 14-1. Learning resources and certification paths for Azure governance and security

Role/Skill Focus	Learning Path/ Certification	URL
Azure Governance Fundamentals	Azure governance strategy and implementation	https://learn.microsoft.com/en-us/azure/governance/
Azure Security Engineer (Intermediate/ Advanced)	**SC-200**, **AZ-500** certification paths	https://learn.microsoft.com/en-us/credentials/certifications/azure-security-engineer/?practice-assessment-type=certification
Azure Policy and Blueprints	Automate governance using Policy, Blueprints, and RBAC	https://learn.microsoft.com/en-us/azure/governance/blueprints/overview
Defender for Cloud/ Secure Score	Secure resources with Microsoft Defender for Cloud	https://learn.microsoft.com/en-us/azure/defender-for-cloud/
Azure Arc and Hybrid Governance	Manage multi-cloud and on-prem with Azure Arc	https://learn.microsoft.com/en-us/azure/azure-arc/
Microsoft Cloud Adoption Framework	End-to-end strategy and governance maturity	https://learn.microsoft.com/en-us/azure/cloud-adoption-framework/

Tips and Tricks for Lifelong Learning in Azure

To make lifelong learning in Azure effective, it's essential to combine structured training with hands-on practice, community engagement, and regular exposure to service updates. Below are some practical tips and tricks to help you stay current and build expertise over time:

- **Follow Azure Updates Weekly**: Stay updated with new governance and security capabilities: https://azure.microsoft.com/updates/.

- **Use Azure Sandbox Environments**: Many Microsoft Learn modules include free sandbox subscriptions where you can practice with Azure Policy, RBAC, Defender, and more—without needing your own subscription. Learn more about activating sandbox, visit the official Microsoft documentation: https://learn.microsoft.com/en-us/azure/architecture/guide/azure-sandbox/azure-sandbox.

- **Set Learning Goals with Microsoft Certifications**: Break down learning by role: start with fundamentals (e.g., AZ-900), then advance to AZ-500 or SC-100 based on your role in governance or security.

- **Bookmark and Monitor Key Documentation**: Bookmark and monitor regularly the key documentation.

  - Azure governance docs: https://learn.microsoft.com/azure/governance/

  - Azure security docs: https://learn.microsoft.com/azure/security/

  - Microsoft Defender for Cloud: https://learn.microsoft.com/azure/defender-for-cloud/

- **Use GitHub and Azure Architecture Center**: Many real-world governance patterns and security baselines are maintained here.

  - https://github.com/Azure

  - https://learn.microsoft.com/azure/architecture/

Adapting to Continuous Change in Cloud Platforms

The Azure platform evolves rapidly—with hundreds of updates released each month across governance, security, networking, identity, and compliance services. For governance and security practitioners, this means adopting a **change-resilient mindset** and **building routines to track, learn, and adapt** to these changes. Microsoft emphasizes this adaptability in its Well-Architected Framework, which includes *Operational Excellence* and *Reliability* as core pillars that demand continuous alignment with platform changes. Table 14-2 shows the official Microsoft resources for tracking changes in Azure services and governance.

Table 14-2. Official resources for monitoring Azure service and compliance changes

Area of Change Monitoring	Official Resource	URL
Azure Weekly Service Updates	Azure Updates Portal	https://azure.microsoft.com/updates/
Cloud Service Road Maps	Microsoft Learn: Product Road Maps and Deprecation Notices	https://learn.microsoft.com/en-us/lifecycle/products/
Azure Architecture Center	Governance, security, and design patterns	https://learn.microsoft.com/azure/architecture/
Azure Compliance Changes	Microsoft Compliance Manager and Trust Center	https://learn.microsoft.com/microsoft-365/compliance/

Tips and Tricks for Adapting to Azure Changes

To keep pace with Azure's continuous updates, it's essential to build habits that help you monitor, evaluate, and respond to platform changes proactively. Table 14-3 presents practical tips to help you stay aligned with the continuous evolution of Microsoft's cloud ecosystem.

Table 14-3. Proactive tips for tracking Azure changes and governance enhancements

Tip	Description and Action	Resource/Link
Subscribe to RSS or Email Feeds on Azure Updates	Stay current by filtering updates by category such as *Security, Governance,* or *Management*	https://azure.microsoft.com/updates/
Join the Microsoft Tech Community	Engage with product teams, get early insights into previews, and read discussions on feature rollouts	https://techcommunity.microsoft.com/category/Azure
Use Azure Advisor and Defender Secure Score	Azure Advisor gives optimization recommendations, while Secure Score tracks your evolving security posture	https://learn.microsoft.com/en-us/azure/advisor/
Follow Official GitHub Repositories	Monitor Azure sample policies, Bicep templates, and IaC scripts to reflect the latest governance patterns	https://github.com/Azure
Create an "Azure Change Watch" Routine	Block 15–30 minutes weekly to check the Azure Updates feed, run Secure Score, and review advisor insights	Use a task scheduler, Outlook recurring reminder, or Microsoft To Do for routine tracking

The Shift from Reactive Management to Proactive Governance

In traditional IT operations, teams often rely on **reactive management**—responding to incidents, compliance gaps, or configuration drifts after they occur. However, Azure governance tools are designed to help organizations move toward a **proactive governance model**, where policies, role-based access controls, automation, and monitoring are implemented *before* issues arise. Microsoft strongly emphasizes this shift in its Cloud Adoption Framework, highlighting the need to define guardrails and automate enforcement across your Azure estate.

This change is crucial in the cloud era, where agility must be balanced with control. Proactive governance enables you to build secure, compliant, and cost-efficient environments that scale reliably and meet internal or regulatory requirements.

For example, a global healthcare organization used reactive methods to manage access across its hybrid cloud. After a delayed revocation of administrator rights led to a security incident, they adopted Azure Policy and Microsoft Entra Permissions Management for proactive governance. As a result, they achieved a 40% reduction in policy violations and saved over $250,000 annually in audit remediation costs.

Table 14-4 shows the comparison for reactive vs. proactive governance.

Table 14-4. Reactive vs. proactive governance models in Azure

Governance Mode	Reactive Management	Proactive Governance
Approach	Manual, after-the-fact corrections	Automated, preventive controls at deployment
Tools Used	Monitoring dashboards, incident response	Azure Policy, Blueprints, Defender for Cloud, RBAC, Template Specs
Risk Exposure	High—due to late detection	Reduced—issues are prevented or auto-remediated
Example Scenario	Manually removing public IPs from VMs	Azure Policy blocks deployment of VMs with public IPs
Operational Overhead	High—firefighting consumes time	Low—predefined rules and automation improve efficiency

Building a Personal Azure Governance Lab

Creating a personal Azure governance lab is one of the most effective ways to gain hands-on experience with Microsoft's cloud management and security tools. Whether you're preparing for a certification, prototyping enterprise governance strategies, or learning Infrastructure as Code (IaC) with tools like Azure Bicep, a lab environment allows you to test real-world scenarios without affecting production systems.

Microsoft provides multiple **cost-effective** options, including **free-tier subscriptions**, **Azure for Students**, and **sandbox environments** available through Microsoft Learn, enabling safe experimentation with services like Azure Policy, RBAC, Blueprints (now replaced by Template Specs), and Defender for Cloud.

Best Practices for Setting Up a Lab

- Start small: Focus on two to three services like Azure Policy and RBAC before expanding.
- Use naming conventions and tags from the start to simulate real governance structures.
- Enable diagnostic logging and cost analysis to track resource usage and policy impact.
- Document configurations using ARM or Bicep templates for repeatability.

Common Pitfalls to Avoid

- Skipping identity management—test with role-based access control (RBAC) scenarios.
- Ignoring cost alerts—labs can incur charges if services fall outside free-tier limits.
- Not isolating environments—avoid deploying resources into your production tenant or subscription.

Setting Up a Free-Tier or Sandbox Environment Safely

Building a personal governance lab in Azure doesn't require a large budget. Microsoft provides several **free or low-cost options** for learners, developers, and IT professionals to safely explore and test governance configurations. Whether you're experimenting with Azure Policy, RBAC, or security tools like Microsoft Defender for Cloud, you can set up a **sandbox environment** that mimics real-world scenarios without risking unintended costs or policy violations. Table 14-5 shows the options for free-tier or low-cost Azure environments.

CHAPTER 14 ELEVATING SKILLS IN AZURE GOVERNANCE AND SECURITY

Table 14-5. *Free Azure access options for learning and experimentation*

Option	Description	Link
Azure Free Account	Includes 12 months of free services + $200 credit for the first 30 days	https://azure.microsoft.com/free/
Azure for Students	Free $100 credit without needing a credit card (academic email required)	https://azure.microsoft.com/free/students/
Microsoft Learn Sandbox	Temporary environments for training modules on governance, policy, and security (limited use)	https://learn.microsoft.com/training/

Setting Up a Safe Azure Lab Using the Free Account

Let's set up a free Azure account.

1. Visit https://azure.microsoft.com/free. You will get the page as shown in Figure 14-1.

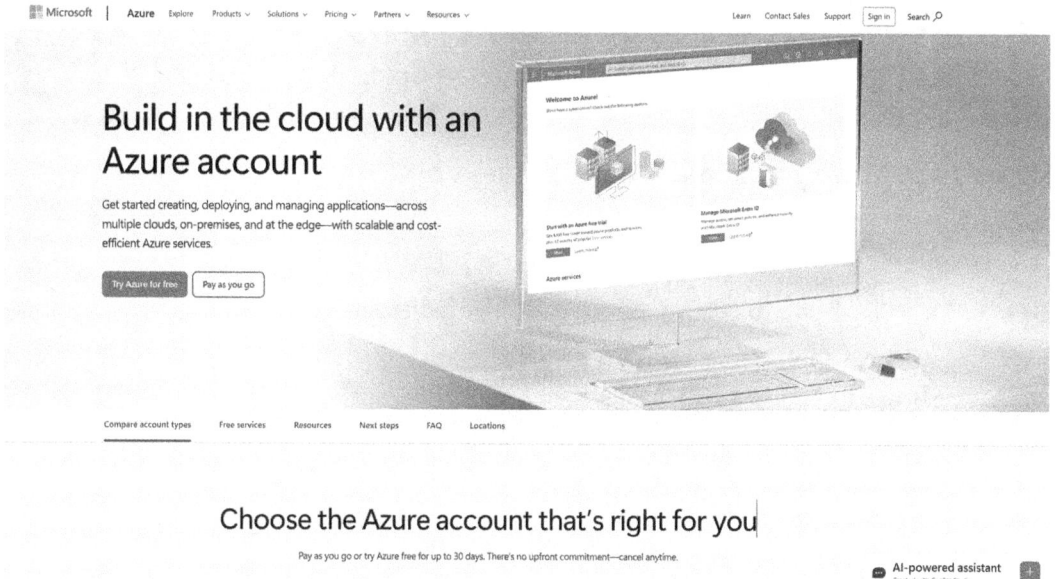

Figure 14-1. *Microsoft Azure account sign-up page*

CHAPTER 14 ELEVATING SKILLS IN AZURE GOVERNANCE AND SECURITY

2. Click Try Azure for free.

3. In the next page, sign in with your Microsoft account. Ensure the account hasn't been used before.

4. After signing in, you will be redirected to Azure sign-up page as shown in Figure 14-2.

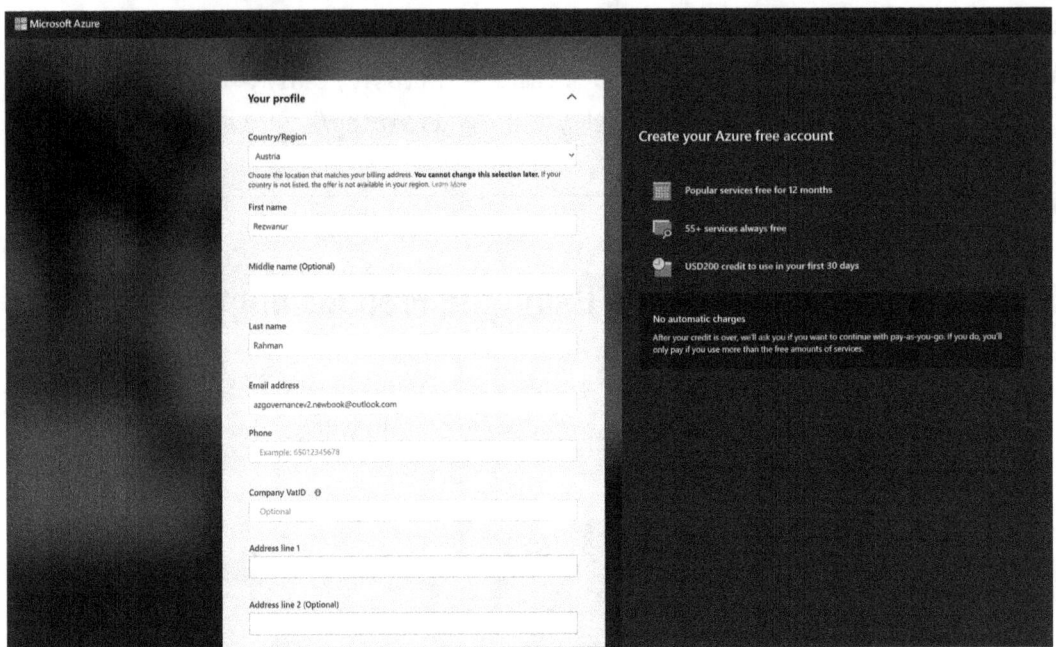

Figure 14-2. Azure free account registration form

5. Fill in the form and click Sign up.

6. It will ask you to verify your identity by credit/debit card. You won't be charged unless you move to pay-as-you-go pricing, as shown in Figure 14-3.

CHAPTER 14 ELEVATING SKILLS IN AZURE GOVERNANCE AND SECURITY

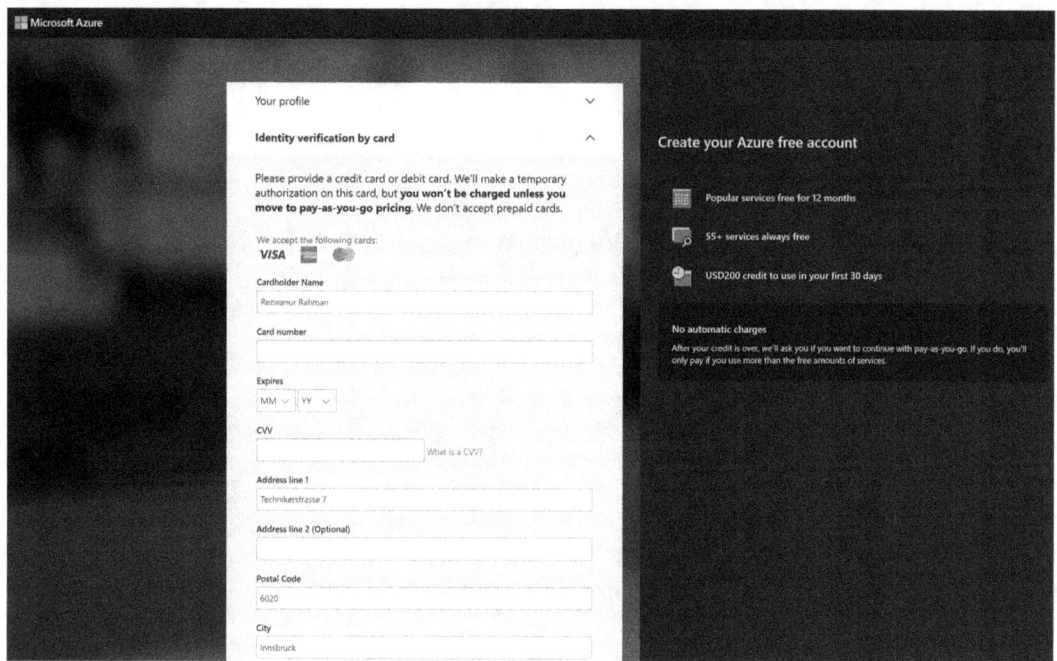

Figure 14-3. *Identity verification by card during Azure account setup*

7. Provide your card details and verify your identity.

8. After successfully signing up, you will see the welcome page as shown in Figure 14-4.

CHAPTER 14   ELEVATING SKILLS IN AZURE GOVERNANCE AND SECURITY

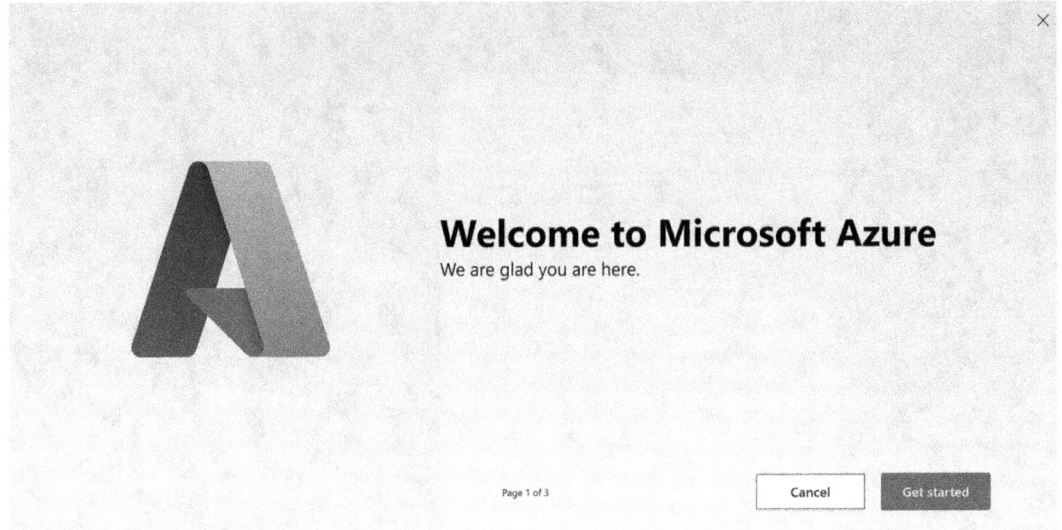

Figure 14-4. *Home page of the Microsoft Azure account*

9. Click Get started. You will be redirected to the Azure portal with $200 free credit for 30 days as shown in Figure 14-5.

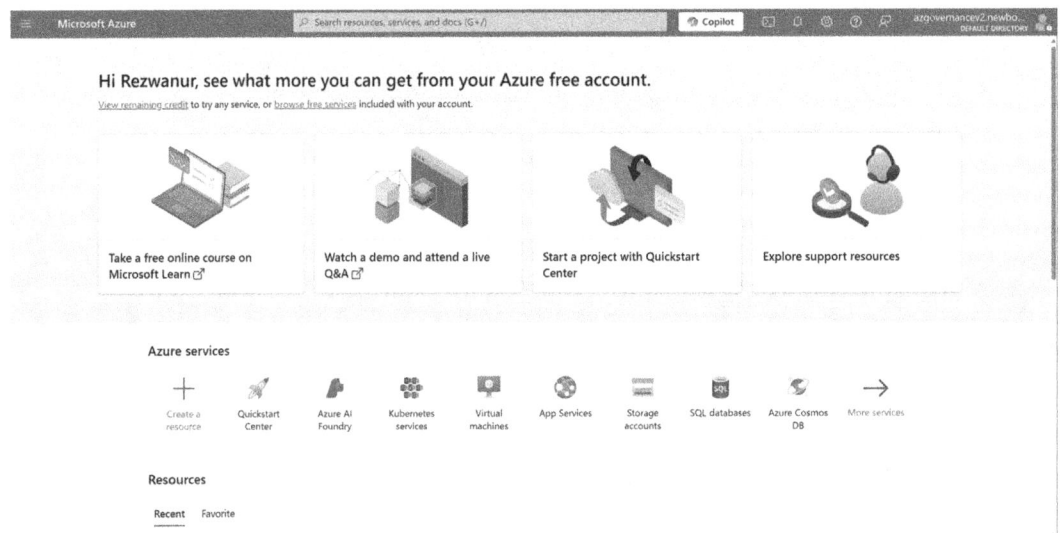

Figure 14-5. *Microsoft Azure portal after signing up for a free account*

By following these steps, you create a **secure, low-cost, and fully functional lab** to test Azure governance capabilities confidently.

Mastering Microsoft Learn for Governance and Security

Microsoft Learn is more than just a documentation platform—it's a structured, role-based learning system that allows practitioners to build real skills through guided modules, interactive sandboxes, and curated learning paths. For Azure governance and security professionals, it offers hands-on experiences that simulate enterprise scenarios like policy enforcement, secure landing zone deployment, and threat monitoring. This section focuses on how to strategically navigate Microsoft Learn to reinforce your technical foundation, align learning with real-world tasks, and continuously build confidence through knowledge checks and applied practice.

Targeted Learning Paths and Modules

Instead of browsing Microsoft Learn at random, Azure professionals should focus on **task-oriented modules and role-specific learning paths** that reflect the real responsibilities of governance and security. These modules are designed around practical scenarios—such as enforcing tagging standards, assigning RBAC roles, or securing workloads with Microsoft Defender—and often include sandbox environments that let you practice without a paid subscription. By targeting content aligned to your goals, you can accelerate skill development while ensuring direct applicability in both test and production environments.

For example, if you're learning how to automate compliance, start with modules on Azure Policy. If you're focused on monitoring threats, follow the Microsoft Sentinel learning path. The key is to build a **progressive learning journey**, where each module builds on what you've previously learned and tested in your governance lab.

Table 14-6 shows the high-impact Microsoft Learn modules for governance and security.

Table 14-6. Microsoft Learn modules for Azure governance and security

Module Title	Focus Area	Link
Introduction to Azure Policy	Learn policy definitions, assignment, effects	https://learn.microsoft.com/en-us/training/modules/intro-to-azure-policy/
Organize policy definitions with initiatives	Create and manage policy sets (initiatives)	https://learn.microsoft.com/en-us/training/modules/sovereignty-policy-initiatives/
AKS governance with Azure Policy	Enforce policies on Azure Kubernetes Service (AKS)	https://learn.microsoft.com/en-us/training/modules/aks-governance-azure-policy/
Introduction to Azure Blueprints *(Legacy Reference)*	Deploy governed environments using blueprints	https://learn.microsoft.com/en-us/training/modules/intro-to-azure-blueprints/
Design Azure Policy-as-Code workflows	Automate governance with Policy as Code	https://learn.microsoft.com/en-us/azure/governance/policy/concepts/policy-as-code
Set up Microsoft Defender for Cloud	Enable Defender and monitor secure score	https://learn.microsoft.com/en-us/training/modules/set-up-microsoft-defender-cloud/
Manage your security posture with Microsoft Defender for Cloud	Interpret recommendations and regulatory compliance	https://learn.microsoft.com/en-us/training/modules/microsoft-defender-cloud-security-posture/
Introduction to Microsoft Sentinel	SIEM overview, data connectors, alerts, and incident handling	https://learn.microsoft.com/en-us/training/modules/intro-to-azure-sentinel/

Maximizing Sandbox Labs and Assessments

Microsoft Learn's **sandbox labs** are one of the most powerful yet underutilized tools for hands-on governance and security training. These labs provide you with **temporary, real Azure environments**—at no cost—so you can safely deploy policies, configure role-based access controls, simulate threats, and test remediation workflows without affecting your own subscription or incurring unexpected charges.

Each sandbox is automatically configured with the required permissions and scope, making it ideal for experimenting with built-in Azure Policy definitions, deploying Bicep templates, or evaluating secure score changes using Microsoft Defender for Cloud. Most governance modules that include sandboxes will guide you step by step, so complex actions like initiative assignment or threat simulation become approachable.

Additionally, **knowledge checks and assessments** at the end of each module allow you to reinforce your understanding. These quizzes are scenario based, testing not just your recall, but your ability to apply concepts in realistic enterprise contexts. When used regularly, they provide valuable feedback loops and help solidify your skills before moving into production scenarios or certification prep.

Here are some tips to get the most from Sandbox labs and assessments:

- **Use a dedicated browser profile** for Learn sandboxes to avoid authentication conflicts with work accounts.

- **Don't skip the CLI/PowerShell steps**—they mimic how governance is managed at scale.

- **Repeat modules with sandboxes periodically**, especially after policy or security updates.

- **Take screenshots** of your results for documentation, review, or training others.

- **Use incorrect answers in quizzes as learning points**—each explanation links back to the documentation for further reading.

Leveraging Open Source and Community Projects

Azure governance and security are no longer limited to internal teams and proprietary tools; much of today's innovation comes from the open source community. Microsoft and its global ecosystem of architects, engineers, and practitioners actively maintain **public GitHub repositories** that include governance frameworks, policy definitions, naming standards, and automation scripts. By tapping into these resources, you can accelerate your own implementation efforts, avoid reinventing the wheel, and contribute back to a shared body of knowledge. This section explores how to identify trusted repositories, adopt reusable assets, and engage with the wider community to stay ahead of governance best practices.

Essential GitHub Repositories Every Architect Should Follow

GitHub hosts a rich ecosystem of Microsoft-backed and community-driven repositories that provide ready-to-use tools, templates, and frameworks for implementing governance, security, and automation on scale. These repositories are not just samples—they often reflect **production-grade patterns** used across enterprises. By bookmarking and regularly exploring these projects, Azure architects can accelerate deployments, ensure compliance, and maintain architectural consistency.

Table 14-7 shows the list of essential repositories, along with their purpose and link.

Table 14-7. Key GitHub repositories for Azure governance and security automation

Repository Name	Description	URL
Azure/azure-policy	Collection of built-in and custom Azure Policy definitions with examples and metadata	`https://github.com/Azure/azure-policy`
Azure/enterprise-scale	Microsoft's reference implementation for landing zones and enterprise-scale architectures	`https://github.com/Azure/enterprise-scale`
Azure/terraform-azurerm-caf-enterprise-scale	Terraform module for deploying the enterprise-scale architecture using Azure CAF standards	`https://github.com/Azure/terraform-azurerm-caf-enterprise-scale`
Azure/azure-quickstart-templates	1,000+ ARM and Bicep templates for deploying various Azure workloads and services	`https://github.com/Azure/azure-quickstart-templates`
Azure/azure-blueprints *(archived)*	Samples of classic Azure Blueprints for standard environments (now mostly replaced by Template Specs)	`https://github.com/Azure/azure-blueprints`
Azure/azure-sdk-for-python	SDK for managing Azure resources programmatically useful for governance automation	`https://github.com/Azure/azure-sdk-for-python`
Azure/Azure-Security-Center	Threat detection queries, policies, and automation scripts for Microsoft Defender for Cloud	`https://github.com/Azure/Microsoft-Defender-for-Cloud`
Azure/ALZ-Bicep	Bicep implementation of Azure Landing Zones for modular, scalable deployments	`https://github.com/Azure/ALZ-Bicep`

These repositories form the **toolkit of a modern Azure architect**—providing Policy as Code, infrastructure templates, and secure-by-default baselines. Staying familiar with them helps you adopt Microsoft's best evolving practices and participate in the broader governance community.

Reusable Templates and Automation Tools

Implementing governance at scale often involves repetitive tasks—assigning policies, configuring access, tagging resources, and deploying secure environments. Rather than starting from scratch, Azure architects can rely on a growing library of **reusable templates and automation tools** provided through GitHub and Microsoft's open source ecosystem. These assets not only save time but also promote consistency, security, and compliance across multiple environments.

The most widely adopted tools follow an **Infrastructure-as-Code (IaC)** model using **Bicep**, **ARM templates**, **Terraform**, and **PowerShell**. These tools enable you to define governance artifacts like **Azure Policy assignments**, **role definitions**, **management groups**, and **landing zones** as code—making them version controlled, testable, and reusable in CI/CD pipelines. Table 14-8 shows some common templates and tools for automating governance tasks in Microsoft Azure.

Table 14-8. Recommended tools and repositories for common Azure governance use cases

Use Case	Recommended Tool/Format	Repository/Resource
Deploying enterprise landing zones	Bicep/Terraform	https://github.com/Azure/ALZ-Bicep https://github.com/Azure/terraform-azurerm-caf-enterprise-scale
Assigning multiple policies and initiatives	ARM template/Bicep	https://github.com/Azure/azure-policy
Auditing and enforcing tags	Azure Policy definitions	https://github.com/Azure/azure-policy/tree/master/samples/Tags
Deploying secure VM workloads	ARM template	https://github.com/Azure/azure-quickstart-templates

Community Contributions and Collaboration

The Azure governance and security community thrives on open collaboration. From individual architects to large enterprise teams, contributors around the world actively share their tools, templates, scripts, and best practices via GitHub, blogs, forums, and social platforms. Engaging with this ecosystem offers more than just access to code—it connects you with **real-world experience**, **emerging patterns**, and **collective innovation** that often move faster than official documentation.

You can participate in several ways. Start by following and watching popular repositories like azure-policy or enterprise-scale. Submit issues or feedback when you identify a bug or improvement. Contribute new policy definitions, templates, or bug fixes via pull requests. You can also share your use cases and success stories on platforms like the Microsoft Tech Community (https://techcommunity.microsoft.com/) or by writing technical blogs that include code samples and architectural guidance.

Microsoft also recognizes and encourages community engagement through programs like the **Azure Heroes badges**, **Microsoft Most Valuable Professional (MVP) award**, and **GitHub contributor highlights**—further motivating architects to share their knowledge.

Contributing to the Azure governance and security community opens the door to continuous learning and recognition. By sharing your work—whether it's a policy template, automation script, or architectural guide—you gain valuable feedback from peers and even Microsoft engineers, helping you refine your approach. It also keeps you closely aligned with the latest tooling and best practices, often ahead of official documentation.

Community involvement strengthens your technical capabilities through real-world problem-solving, collaborative debugging, and open peer review. Over time, consistent contributions build your credibility and visibility within the Azure ecosystem, positioning you as a trusted voice in the field of governance and cloud security.

Certifications for Strategic Advancement

Earning Azure certifications is more than a credentialing exercise—it's a strategic investment in your role as a governance and security professional. Certifications such as **SC-100 (Microsoft Cybersecurity Architect)**, **AZ-500 (Azure Security Engineer Associate)**, and **AZ-305 (Azure Solutions Architect Expert)** validate not only your technical expertise but also your ability to design and secure cloud environments at scale. These credentials are aligned with real-world responsibilities and are widely recognized by employers, making them powerful tools for career growth, credibility, and strategic positioning within enterprise cloud teams. In this section, we explore which certifications are most relevant, how to prepare using Microsoft Learn and hands-on labs, and how to map them to your current or aspiring job role.

CHAPTER 14   ELEVATING SKILLS IN AZURE GOVERNANCE AND SECURITY

SC-100, AZ-500, AZ-305: What to Pursue and Why

When planning your certification journey in Azure governance and security, it's important to choose credentials that reflect your **current responsibilities** and align with your **career trajectory**. Microsoft offers a role-based certification framework, and three certifications stand out as particularly relevant for professionals architecting secure and governed cloud environments.

SC-100: Microsoft Cybersecurity Architect

- **Target Audience**: Senior cloud security architects, CISOs, security consultants

- **Focus Areas**: Zero Trust architecture, hybrid and multi-cloud security, threat protection, regulatory compliance, identity strategy, and governance integration

- **Why Pursue**: SC-100 is an expert-level certification that builds on foundational security knowledge and is ideal for professionals responsible for **end-to-end security strategy across an enterprise**. It validates your ability to design governance and security controls across Microsoft Entra ID, Defender, Sentinel, and Microsoft Purview.

- **Recommended Prerequisites**: AZ-500 or SC-200 (not mandatory but highly advised)

- **More Info**: https://learn.microsoft.com/en-us/credentials/certifications/cybersecurity-architect-expert/

AZ-500: Microsoft Azure Security Engineer Associate

- **Target Audience**: Cloud security engineers, operations analysts, compliance specialists

- **Focus Areas**: Identity and access management, platform protection, data security, security operations, and Defender for Cloud

- **Why Pursue**: AZ-500 is the go-to certification for engineers focused on implementing and managing security controls in Azure. It's hands-on and technical, covering tools like **Azure Policy**, **Key Vault**, **NSGs**, **Defender for Cloud**, **Secure Score**, and more. It's particularly valuable if you're responsible for enforcing governance and security policies in production.

- **Recommended Experience**: 6–12 months hands-on with Azure security tools and configurations

- **More Info**: https://learn.microsoft.com/en-us/credentials/certifications/azure-security-engineer/

AZ-305: Azure Solutions Architect Expert

- **Target Audience**: Cloud architects, lead engineers, enterprise solution designers

- **Focus Areas**: Governance design, workload optimization, identity and access, business continuity, secure landing zones, networking, and cost control

- **Why Pursue**: AZ-305 is essential for anyone architecting scalable, secure, and governed solutions on Azure. It includes governance patterns like **management group design**, **policy assignment**, **naming standards**, and **security-by-design principles**, making it highly relevant for cloud governance roles.

- **Recommended Prerequisites**: Experience with solution design and deployment on Azure, and AZ-104 is suggested but not required.

- **More Info**: https://learn.microsoft.com/en-us/credentials/certifications/azure-solutions-architect/

Each of these certifications supports a **different layer of governance and security responsibility**—from operational defense to architectural planning and strategic oversight. Many professionals pursue **AZ-500 or AZ-305 first**, then move on to **SC-100** to demonstrate broader, cross-domain expertise.

CHAPTER 14   ELEVATING SKILLS IN AZURE GOVERNANCE AND SECURITY

Study Strategies, Labs, and Learn Integration

Preparing for Azure certifications like **SC-100**, **AZ-500**, or **AZ-305** requires more than reading documentation—it demands a structured approach that combines theoretical knowledge, hands-on practice, and regular self-assessment. Microsoft Learn makes this easier by offering **official learning paths**, **sandbox labs**, and **interactive assessments** that are directly aligned with certification objectives.

Let's discuss some effective study strategies.

- **Follow the Official Microsoft Learn Paths**

    Each certification has a dedicated set of learning paths that mirror the exam skills outline. These paths are modular, allowing you to study in 30–60-minute sessions and track your progress with badges and XP.

    - **SC-100 Learning Path**: https://learn.microsoft.com/en-us/credentials/certifications/resources/study-guides/sc-100

    - **AZ-500 Learning Path**: https://learn.microsoft.com/en-us/credentials/certifications/azure-security-engineer/?practice-assessment-type=certification

    - **AZ-305 Learning Path**: https://learn.microsoft.com/en-us/credentials/certifications/exams/az-305/

- **Use Real Azure Environments**

    Create a free-tier Azure subscription or use the Microsoft Learn sandbox to test governance configurations, RBAC, Azure Policy, and Defender features in isolation. Pair each module with tasks in your personal governance lab to reinforce what you've learned.

- **Take Notes in Context**

    Rather than summarizing entire modules, write down key commands, policies, or architecture decisions you practiced. These notes become invaluable during review or on-the-job implementation.

- **Reinforce with Flashcards or Mind Maps**

    Use tools like Anki or XMind to map governance scopes, policy effects, security roles, and landing zone components.

Preparing for Azure certifications presents several common challenges. Many learners struggle with the breadth and depth of the content, finding it difficult to navigate extensive modules across identity, governance, security, and architecture. The lack of hands-on experience can also hinder understanding, especially when dealing with services like Azure Policy, RBAC, and Defender. Some candidates face time management issues, trying to balance study with full-time responsibilities, while others become overwhelmed by isolated theoretical learning that lacks real-world context. Additionally, retaining knowledge for scenario-based or performance-style exam questions can be difficult without repeated practice. To overcome these obstacles, candidates are encouraged to set structured study schedules, use sandbox labs for hands-on experimentation, take contextual notes, and regularly self-assess with quizzes and practice tests that mirror real exam formats.

Mapping Certifications to Job Roles

Microsoft's role-based certification framework is designed to mirror real-world responsibilities in cloud security, governance, and architecture. For Azure professionals, aligning the right certification with your current role—or the role you aspire to—ensures that your learning efforts directly support your career progression. Each certification reflects a different scope of responsibility, from tactical implementation to strategic decision-making.

Table 14-9 shows the mapping of Azure certifications to real-world governance and security roles.

Table 14-9. Azure certifications aligned with governance and security responsibilities

Certification	Ideal Job Roles	Focus Area
AZ-500	Azure Security Engineer, Security Operations Analyst, Cloud Administrator	Tactical security implementation: RBAC, Defender, NSG, logging, incident response
AZ-305	Cloud Architect, Infrastructure Engineer, Solutions Designer	Designing secure, scalable, and governed Azure architectures
SC-100	Security Architect, Chief Information Security Officer (CISO), Security Consultant	Strategic security and compliance planning across hybrid/multi-cloud environments

Let's discuss how to choose the certification based on responsibility level.

- **Hands-On Role? Start with AZ-500**

  If you're directly managing security tools like Microsoft Defender for Cloud, Azure Firewall, or Identity Protection, AZ-500 equips you with the operational knowledge to secure services effectively.

- **Designing Solutions? Go with AZ-305**

  Architects who define infrastructure blueprints, align deployments with governance frameworks, or lead DevSecOps workflows will benefit most from AZ-305.

- **Shaping Enterprise Strategy? Aim for SC-100**

  Professionals guiding the broader security strategy across business units, managing compliance at scale, or implementing Zero Trust principles should pursue SC-100 to formalize their authority.

Staying Current in the Azure Ecosystem

Azure evolves rapidly, with hundreds of updates released each month across governance, security, identity, and infrastructure services. For governance and security practitioners, staying current isn't optional—it's essential for maintaining compliance, protecting workloads, and applying best practices effectively. This section explores how

CHAPTER 14   ELEVATING SKILLS IN AZURE GOVERNANCE AND SECURITY

to track platform changes, leverage Microsoft's communication channels, and develop a personal review rhythm to ensure your governance strategies remain aligned with the latest capabilities and industry standards.

Monitoring Updates, Blogs, and Release Notes

To keep pace with Azure's fast-moving development cycle, it's critical to regularly monitor **official update feeds**, **engineering blogs**, and **product release notes**. Microsoft provides a range of channels where governance and security changes are first announced—often including previews of features, upcoming deprecations, policy enhancements, and new security capabilities.

The most direct way to monitor product changes is the **Azure Updates** page. It allows you to filter by category (e.g., "Security," "Management and Governance") and track services that affect your architecture. For deeper insights and road map context, follow the **Azure Blog** and the **Microsoft Tech Community**, where product teams share announcements, tutorials, and migration strategies.

Additionally, major services like Microsoft Defender for Cloud, Azure Policy, and Microsoft Sentinel maintain their own release notes and GitHub changelogs. Subscribing to these updates ensures that you're aware of **new policy definitions**, **enhanced monitoring capabilities**, and **breaking changes** that may affect your governance baselines.

Table 14-10 shows the key monitoring resources of Microsoft Azure.

Table 14-10. Official and community resources for Azure news and updates

Resource Type	Purpose	URL
Azure Updates Portal	Track service changes and feature releases	https://azure.microsoft.com/en-us/updates/
Azure Blog	Official engineering blog with deep dives and previews	https://azure.microsoft.com/en-us/blog/
Microsoft Tech Community—Azure	Community-driven insights, news, and discussions	https://techcommunity.microsoft.com/category/Azure
Defender for Cloud Release Notes	Monthly updates on security capabilities and policy rules	https://learn.microsoft.com/en-us/azure/defender-for-cloud/release-notes

Tools for Tracking Road Map and Platform Changes

Beyond update announcements and blogs, Microsoft provides several tools to help you anticipate platform evolution and plan governance accordingly. These tools offer insights into **what's coming**, **what's changing**, and **what's being deprecated**, so you can align your policies, controls, and automation strategies with the Azure road map.

The most comprehensive resource is the **Microsoft Azure road map**, which outlines upcoming features across all Azure services. You can filter the road map by product category (e.g., "Management and Governance," "Security," "Hybrid") and track items by their development stage—such as "In Development," "Public Preview," or "Generally Available." This allows governance teams to prepare for new policy features or compliance tools before they are released.

Additionally, GitHub changelogs for repositories like **azure-policy** and **Defender for Cloud** provide detailed version histories, including added policy definitions, deprecated parameters, or security rule changes. These are especially valuable for environments using **Policy as Code** or automated governance pipelines.

To integrate this awareness into your workflow, consider setting up **RSS feeds**, **email alerts**, or **browser bookmarks** for these tools. For larger teams, changes from these sources can be integrated into **internal governance newsletters**, **Change Advisory Boards (CABs)**, or **monthly review meetings**. Table 14-11 shows the tools to track the changes and road map.

Table 14-11. Platforms for monitoring Azure and Microsoft cloud governance changes

Tool/Platform	Purpose	URL
Azure Road Map	Discover upcoming Azure features and updates	`https://azure.microsoft.com/en-us/updates`
Azure Policy GitHub Changelog	Track policy definition updates and rule changes	`https://github.com/Azure/azure-policy/tree/master`
Defender for Cloud GitHub	Review changes in security rules and integrations	`https://github.com/Azure/Microsoft-Defender-for-Cloud`
Microsoft 365 Message Center (if applicable)	Track platform-wide changes across Microsoft cloud (for hybrid governance)	`https://admin.microsoft.com/` (requires admin login)

Summary

In this final chapter, we focused on the most critical element in cloud governance and security: **people**. While previous chapters provided you with tools, frameworks, and automation strategies, this chapter highlighted the importance of **continuous learning, certification, and skill development**. We explored how professionals can elevate their expertise through **role-based learning paths, hands-on labs, community engagement, and Microsoft certifications**, all of which are essential for sustaining secure and well-governed Azure environments.

This chapter reminded us that even the most advanced technologies—AI-driven governance, intelligent automation, and multi-cloud orchestration—are only as effective as the people who design, implement, and manage them. In a rapidly evolving digital world, your commitment to learning is what transforms potential into real-world impact.

As we conclude this book, you are no longer just a reader, you are a practitioner equipped with **end-to-end knowledge** of Azure governance and security. From foundational policies and identity management to threat detection with Sentinel, machine learning, and future-ready cloud architectures, you've built a robust toolkit for navigating and leading in the cloud era.

Now, the responsibility—and the opportunity—rests with you. Whether you're advising an enterprise, securing a startup, or building governance frameworks for tomorrow's innovations, you are ready to lead with confidence, clarity, and purpose.

Let this book be your launchpad—not your landing zone. The cloud evolves daily. So should you.

Happy learning!

Index

A

ABAC, *see* Attribute-based access control (ABAC)
Access management, 8, 36
Activity logs, 223
Adaptive application controls, 159
Adaptive workflows, 429
ADR, *see* Advanced data residency (ADR)
Advanced data residency (ADR), 611
Advanced persistent threats (APTs), 130, 170
Agent-based collection, 157
Agentless scanning, 148
AI, *see* Artificial intelligence (AI)
AKS, *see* Azure Kubernetes Service (AKS)
Alerting
    action group, 250
    aggregation type and threshold, 249
    confirmation email, 255, 256
    creating rule, 247, 248
    creation, 247
    monitor section, 247
    notification, 251, 252
    resource group and instance details, 250, 251
    review page, 255
    rule name and severity, 254
    selecting signal type, 249
    selecting VM, 248
    verifying action group, 252, 253
Amazon Web Services (AWS), 135, 499, 500, 505
    governance tools, 506
    tagging strategy, 509
    tag policies, 510
    tags and use cases, 510
AML, *see* Azure machine learning (AML)
Anomaly-based analytics rules, 350
Anomaly detection, 137
Application logs, 224
Application security groups (ASGs), 485, 486, 533
APTs, *see* Advanced persistent threats (APTs)
Architectural governance, 3
Architectural nucleus, 456
Artifacts
    ARM templates, 288–290
    blueprint context, 286, 287
    definition, 260
    execution and order, 267
    implications, 286
    planning, 270
    policies and initiatives, 286
    RBAC, 290–292
    structuring resource groups, 292, 293
    types, 260, 265–267, 271
Artificial intelligence (AI), 349–351, 386, 411
    cognitive services, 572–574
    compliance reports, 583–590
    data governance, 540
    enrichment, 438–440
    enterprise governance and security, 577, 578

INDEX

Artificial intelligence (AI) (*cont.*)
    evolution, 570, 571
    governance engines, 563
    integration, 535
    limitations, 535
    OpenAI service, 575, 576
    playbooks, 429–437
    policy enforcement, 608
    policy recommendations, 537, 538
    risk analysis and regulatory
        compliance, 581–583
    services, 570
    threat detection and response,
        535–537, 579–581
    threat intelligence engine, 440
    zero trust, 532, 533
ASC, *see* Azure Security Center (ASC)
ASGs, *see* Application security
    groups (ASGs)
Assignment failures, 305–308
Assignment naming conventions, 65, 66
Attribute-based access control
    (ABAC), 511
Auditability, 143
Automatic remediation, 122, 123
Automating tagging, 49
Automation of naming standards
    benefits, 50, 51, 53
    challenges, 50
    enforcement, 50
    methods, 51–53
    multi-region and multi-team
        scenarios, 54
    resources and examples, 55
    virtual machines, 50
Automation workflows, *see* Security
    playbooks
Avanade, 609, 610

AWS, *see* Amazon Web Services (AWS)
Azure Active Directory, 392
Azure Arc, 541
    agent, 520
    AWS machine, 528
    downloading/copying script, 524, 525
    EC2 instance, 525, 526
    generating script, 522
    infrastructure, 521
    running script, 526, 527
    server information, connectivity
        method and project details, 523
    verifying cloud provider, 528, 529
    virtual/physical machine, 521, 522
Azure Copilot
    architecture and deployment, 591, 592
    comparison, 593–596
    concept, 590
    cost optimization, 607
    defined, 590, 591
    ecosystem, 590
    forecasting, 606, 607
    generative AI, 597
    governance tasks, 597
    network topology and security
        risks, 595
    policy creation and
        management, 602–605
    real-time cost analysis, 605
    resource governance, 597–601
    variants, 594
Azure ecosystem
    tracking road map and platform
        changes, 638
    updates, blogs and release notes, 637
Azure Firewall Manager
    comparison, architectures, 208
    defined, 206

INDEX

features, 209, 210
network architecture types, 207
Azure governance planning
   artifacts, 31
   foundational artifacts, 22, 23
   management groups, 28–30
   policy exclusions, 30
   principle, 22
   resource groups, 27
   subscriptions, 24–26
   tenants, 23, 24
Azure governance services
   blueprints, 18, 19
   components, 9
   management groups, 13–16
   resources and resource groups, 16–18
   subscriptions, 11, 12
   tenant, 10, 11
Azure Kubernetes Service (AKS), 129, 222
Azure landing zone
   blueprints, 561
   conceptual architecture, 558
   defined, 558
   technical architecture, 558–561
Azure Logic Apps, 135, 142, 368, 369
Azure Machine Learning (AML), 576, 577
Azure Monitor Agent (AMA), 157, 171
Azure Resource Manager (ARM) templates, 19, 51, 520
   artifact, 260, 267
   best practices, 289, 290
   characteristics, 289
   core design concepts, 317–319
   declarative infrastructure deployment, 263, 264
   defined, 316
   functions and expressions, 325–328
   linked and nested, 321–324

   sequential deployment, 261
   source control systems, 331, 332
   structure, 316
   template and parameter files, 319–321
   validation and testing, 329–331
Azure scaffolding
   comparison, agreement types, 34, 35
   components, 33, 34
   designing, 33, 34
   governance and security best practices, 35–37
   management group strategies, 38–40
   subscription models and scalability, 41, 42
Azure Security Center (ASC), 156
Azure Sentinel
   creation page, 357, 358
   custom workbooks and dashboards, 352–354
   dashboard, 357
   data sources
      built-in connectors, 361, 362
      configuration, 365
      connector page, 363
      content hub, 363, 364
      cost factors, 367
      data ingestion costs, 366
      data retention and archival, 366, 367
      monitoring and optimization, 367, 368
      search entra ID, 364
   defined, 340
   functions, 340
   hunting bookmarks and annotations, 381
   log analytics workspace, 358
   log collection, 340
   MITRE ATT&CK framework, 351, 352

INDEX

Azure Sentinel (*cont.*)
    overview, 361
    prerequisites and planning
        considerations, 355, 356
    scalability and cloud-native
        architecture, 346, 347
    security ecosystem, 344–346
    services, 348, 349
    threat detection, 349–351
    vs. traditional SIEM, 343, 344
    use cases, 340
    validation, 359
    verification, 359, 360

B

Behavioral analytics, 137, 349
Behavioral monitoring, 137
Binary classification problem, 414
Blueprints, 18, 19
    adding name and value
        parameters, 283
    allowed locations policy, 281
    ARM templates *vs.* Azure policy, 265
    artifacts, 260, 265–267,
        278–280, 286–293
    assignment modes, 261, 304, 305
    best practices, embedding policies,
        287, 288
    blank selection, 277
    code-based governance, 561
    creation, 274, 276
    declarative approach, 258
    definition, 258–260
    editing required tag, 282
    elements, 69
    governance artifacts, 258
    governance as code, 259

    governance packaging and lifecycle
        management, 264, 265
    HIPAA/HITRUST compliance, 262, 263
    information review, 295
    lifecycle (*see* Lifecycle management of
        blueprints)
    name and description, 277, 278
    naming standards, 69–74
    overview, 259
    parameterization and dynamic
        assignment, 302, 303
    parameter name and usages, 285
    publishing, 296
    scale challenge, 262
    searching, 274, 275
    selecting, 275, 276
    strategic advantage, 263
    structural design
        artifact planning, 270
        defined, 270
        execution order planning, 273
        infrastructure template, 272
        naming and versioning, 274
        parameterization plan, 273
        policy assignments, 271
        RBAC, 272
        resource group, 271
    subscriptions, 298–302
    tag policy, 282
    template code, 283, 285
    troubleshooting assignment
        failures, 305–308
    use cases, 268, 269
    version and change notes, 72, 73
    versioning, 294–298
Brownfield environments, 268, 269
Business continuity, 3
Business-critical systems, 122

C

Castle-and-moat model, 453
CC036-Engineering-Dev, 60
Certifications
    AZ-305, 633
    AZ-500, 632, 633
    concept, 631
    mapping job roles, 635, 636
    SC-100, 632
    study strategies, labs and learn integration, 634, 635
Change-resilient mindset, 616
CI/CD, *see* Continuous integration and continuous delivery (CI/CD)
Classical cryptography *vs.* PQC, 543
Cloud governance
    Azure landing zones, 557–561
    consumers, 3
    digital transformation, 20, 21
    enforcement tools
        initiatives, 7, 8
        policies, 6–8
        RBAC, 6, 8, 9
    ESG, 562
    evolution, 1
    landscape, 1
    layers, 4
    planning and implementation, 21–31
    principles, 4, 5
    providers, 2
    services (*see* Azure governance services)
    sustainability, 562
    transformation, 269
    transformative shifts, 565, 566
    vision 2030, 563–566
Cloud-native application protection platform (CNAPP), 211
Cloud-native environment, 219
Cloud security
    challenges, 129–131
    defined, 127
    DevOps, 138–140
    shared responsibility, 128, 129
    virtual machine, 127
    workloads, 126
Cloud security posture management (CSPM), 131, 132, 143, 152, 198
Cloud workload protection (CWP), 132, 144, 153–155
CMKs, *see* Customer-managed keys (CMKs)
CNAPP, *see* Cloud-native application protection platform (CNAPP)
Cognitive services, 572–574
Committed use discounts (CUDs), 514
Compliance, 5, 20
    changes, 617
    continuous enforcement policies, 264
    dashboards, 288
    data privacy laws, 550
    data protection regulations, 550
    education sector, 556, 557
    energy and utilities, 555, 556
    financial services, 554
    government and defense trends, 554, 555
    healthcare providers, 553
    HIPAA/HITRUST, 262, 263
    management and reporting, 116–121
    manager, 581, 584, 585
    monitoring and reporting, 140, 141
    and policy enforcement, 134
    predefined templates, 140
    privacy-ready cloud operations, 551, 552

INDEX

Compliance (*cont.*)
   regulatory changes, 552
   reports, 583–590
   role assignments, 239
   score, 589
   tagging, 49
Compliance-by-design model, 263
Conditional IAM policies, 511
Consumption-based pricing model, 365
Context-aware recommendations, 537
Contextual access plane, 453
Continuous integration and continuous delivery (CI/CD), 52, 138, 334, 335
Continuous security monitoring
   components, 198
   hardening network resources, 201–205
   monitoring resource health, 200, 201
   recommendations, 198, 199
CostCenter tag, 49
CSPM, *see* Cloud security posture management (CSPM)
CUDs, *see* Committed use discounts (CUDs)
Customer-managed keys (CMKs), 262
Custom logs, 224
Custom metrics, 221
Custom ML models
   adding new query, 399
   choosing SigninLogs table, LogManagement, 400
   creating data asset, 403
   creating .ipynb file, 406
   creating notebook file, 405
   defined, 397
   exporting CSV format, 402
   log option, 398
   patterns, 398
   query result, 401
   selecting and uploading data file, 404
   studio page, 402
   URI, 404
   workspace ID and primary key, 407, 408
CWP, *see* Cloud workload protection (CWP)
Cyberattacks, 390
Cybersecurity, 140, 442

D

Data collection rules (DCRs), 368
Data exfiltration, 447
Data loss prevention (DLP), 582
Data residency, 610, 611
Data retention strategy, 356
DCRs, *see* Data collection rules (DCRs)
Decentralized identity (DID), 564
Decision services, 574
Declarative deployment, 289
Departmental governance, 3
Dependency management, 289
Device provisioning service (DPS), 533
DevOps, 138–140, 335, 336
DevSecOps, 134
Diagnostic logs, 223
DID, *see* Decentralized identity (DID)
Digital transformation, 20, 21
Disaster recovery (DR), 501
DLP, *see* Data loss prevention (DLP)
Document intelligence, 575
DPS, *see* Device provisioning service (DPS)
DR, *see* Disaster recovery (DR)
Drift detection, 582
Dynamic assignment, 303

INDEX

E

Edge computing, 534, 535
Endpoint detection and response (EDR), 391
EDR, *see* Endpoint detection and response (EDR)
Enrichment
    attributes, 437
    defined, 437
    isolation, 439
    low-risk events, 439, 440
    SOC, 438, 439
Entitlement management *vs.* access reviews, 470
Environment tag, 49
ESG-aware governance, 564
Ethical considerations, 610, 611

F

File integrity monitoring (FIM), 159, 166–168
FIM, *see* File integrity monitoring (FIM)
Finance-RG, 47, 48
Firewall management, 206–211
Forecasting future threats, 442, 443
Fraudulent resource creation, 447, 448
Functional testing, 330
Fusion analytics rules, 349
Fusion engine, 580
    connectors, 391, 392
    correlation, 350
    defined, 390
    patterns, 391
    ransomware detection, 395
    templates
        choosing filter, 393
        defined, 392
        editing and configuration, 394
        filtering, 393

G

GCP, *see* Google Cloud Platform (GCP)
Generative AI, 535
GitHub repositories
    community contributions and collaboration, 630, 631
    governance and security automation, 629
    production-grade patterns, 628
    public, 628
    reusable templates and automation tools, 630
    use cases, 630
Global intelligence integration, 351
Google Cloud Platform (GCP), 135, 499, 500, 505
    adding conditions and actions, 519
    budgets and alerts option, 517
    budget type and target amount, 518, 519
    cloud billing, 513
    creating budget, 518
    governance tools, 506
    labels, 510, 511
    Resource Manager tags, 511, 512
Governance, *See also* Cloud governance
    and compliance, 49
    edge, 565
    elements, 36, 37
    enhancements, 618
    hierarchy, 36, 39
    and identity insights, 538
    integration, 141, 142
    organization, 37

INDEX

Governance (*cont.*)
    reactive management, 618, 619
    sample prompt, 538, 539
    and security best practices, 35–37
    trust-centric and ethically aligned, 565
Graph-based modeling, 412
GraphSAGE, 447
Greenfield deployments, 268

H

HA, *see* High availability (HA)
Hardcoded secrets detection, 139
Hardcoding values, 287
Harvest now, decrypt later, 542
Healthcare systems, 534
High availability (HA), 501
Hub-and-spoke network topology, 483, 484
Hub virtual network, 207
Hybrid environment, 218, 219

I

IaaS, *see* Infrastructure as a service (IaaS)
IaC, *see* Infrastructure as Code (IaC)
IAM, *see* Identity and access management (IAM)
ICS, *see* Industrial control systems (ICS)
Identity and access management (IAM)
    access reviews, 469, 470
    approving user access, 478
    business justification, 477
    creating access package, 471
    demo account, InPrivate browser, 477
    entitlement, 468, 470
    explicit verification, 464
    lifecycle expiration set, 480
    lifecycle settings, 474, 475
    Microsoft Entra ID, 464, 465
    PIM, 465–468
    portal link option, 476
    prerequisites, 470
    providing access package, 472
    request page settings, 473
    requests list, 478
    selecting resource roles, 472
    types, 480, 481
Indicators of compromise (IoCs), 171
Industrial control systems (ICS), 555
Industry-standard regulations, 140
Infrastructure as a service (IaaS), 11, 25, 26
Infrastructure as Code (IaC), 2, 46, 51, 134, 138, 139, 263, 267, 619
    ARM (*see* Azure Resource Manager (ARM))
    automation-centric approach, 314
    defined, 313
    multi-team/multi-region deployments, 314, 315
    principles, 314
    source control systems, 331–335
    tools, 314, 315
Initiatives
    assignment, 69
        definition, 110, 111
        governance rules, 108
        initial page, 109
        organizational needs, 109
        overview page, 112, 113
        selecting parameters value, 111, 112
        selecting scope, 110
    cloud governance, 7
    creation

built-in library, 103
confirmation, 108
definition, 103, 104
location, name and description, 105
parameter as value type, 107, 108
parameters, 106, 107
scope, policies, 104
selecting policy definition, 105, 106
custom category, 67, 68
defined, 102
naming standards, 67, 68
parameters, 102
updation
add additional policies, 114
best practice, 113
remove policies, 114
Internet of Things (IoT), 533, 534
IoCs, *see* Indicators of compromise (IoCs)
IoT, *see* Internet of Things (IoT)
IT service management (ITSM), 370, 444
ITSM, *see* IT service management (ITSM)

J

Jupyter notebooks, 350, 397
Just-in-time (JIT) VM access, 159
advanced protection options, 163
auditing, 166
checking and configuring, recommended ports, 164
classification, 160
customer environments, 160
enabling, 164
initiating request configuration, 165
prerequisites, 161, 162
selecting port, 163, 165
workload protections, 162

K

KEM, *see* Key encapsulation mechanism (KEM)
Key encapsulation mechanism (KEM), 546
KQL, *see* Kusto Query Language (KQL)
Kusto Query Language (KQL), 172, 211, 213, 223, 224, 227, 228, 340, 353, 355, 381, 382, 440, 536, 609
average CPU usage over time, 237
count entries per VM, 236
defined, 234
demo environment
AppAvailabilityResults, 242
calculating success rate percentage, 246
changing mode, 241
default query, 241
filtering, 244
history page, 240
learners, 239
search result, 245
sorting, 243
telemetry, 239
types, 240
filter logs by specific computer, 236
identify failed login attempts, 237
pipeline, 234
query statement, 234, 235
return log entries, 236
selecting specific columns, 236
sort logs by time, 236
syntax elements, 235
use cases
checking virtual machine health and reporting gaps, 238, 239
identifying unauthorized resource deletions, 238

INDEX

Kusto Query Language (KQL) (*cont.*)
    monitoring role assignments, 239
    repeated sign-in failures, 237
    tracking cost-intensive operations over time, 238

L

Landing zone concept, 268
Language services, 574
Large language models (LLMs), 535, 572
Lifecycle management, 17, 31
Lifecycle management of blueprints, 309
    cloud strategy, 308
    stages, 308
        assigned, 310
        draft, 309
        published, 309
        updated/deprecated, 310
    without affecting assignments mechanism, 311
        version-assignment decoupling, 311–313
Lifelong learning mindset
    administrators, 614
    defined, 614
    practical tips and tricks, 615, 616
    resources and certification paths, 614, 615
Linked templates, 322, 324
LLMs, *see* Large language models (LLMs)
Locking
    DoNotDelete (balanced control), 305
    Don't Lock (flexible control), 305
    high-privilege users, 304
    mechanism, 304
    ReadOnly (strictest control), 305
    restrictive, 304

Log analytics workspaces, 223, 224
    adding resources
        destination details, 233
        diagnostic settings, 231, 232
        storage accounts, 231
    Azure Sentinel, 355, 358
    creation, 229, 230
    defined, 227, 228
    functions, 227
    reviewing, 230
    searching, 229
    template, 272
Long-term confidentiality assurance (LTCA), 545
LTCA, *see* Long-term confidentiality assurance (LTCA)

M

Machine learning (ML), 137, 349–351, 386, 411, 535
    cross-cloud risk detection, 446, 447
    historical incident labels, 424–428
    incident.csv file, 425
    rule-based approach, 413–415
    supervised, 445, 446
    suspicious logins/resource changes
        data sources and features, 415
        feature-purpose mapping, 415
        model development, 416–423
        problem framing, 414
        Python code, 418, 419, 423
    UEBA, 387, 388
Managed identities, 481
Management groups
    benefits, 14
    creating structure, 13
    defined, 13, 41

INDEX

hierarchical levels, 61
hierarchy, 41
ID and display name, 62
key points, 13
naming standards, 60–63
organization structure, 13, 14
planning, 28–30
policies, 81
strategies, 38–40
structure, 15
   hierarchy, 61, 62
   planning, 61
subscriptions, 16, 29, 38, 39
syntax, 62
top view, 38
Manual remediation, 122
MCAS, *see* Microsoft Defender for Cloud Apps (MCAS)
MCSB, *see* Microsoft Cloud Security Benchmark (MCSB)
MDE, *see* Microsoft Defender for Endpoint (MDE)
MDTI, *see* Microsoft Defender Threat Intelligence (MDTI)
Mean time to detect (MTTD), 443
Mean time to respond (MTTR), 429, 443, 445
Metadata tags, 83
MFA, *see* Multi-factor authentication (MFA)
Micro-segmentation, 495, 496
Microsoft Azure, 499, 500, 505
   cost analysis, 515
   cost management + billing, 513, 514
   creating budget, 515, 516
   enterprise environments, 509
   governance tools, 505
   naming conventions, 507

resource types, 507
tag format and limits, 508
tagging strategy, 508
Microsoft Azure Security Center, *see* Microsoft Defender for Cloud
Microsoft Cloud Security Benchmark (MCSB), 199
Microsoft 365 Defender, 392
Microsoft Defender for Cloud, 126, 582, *See also* Cloud security
   concept, 126
   dashboard, 131
   data collection
      Azure virtual machines, 157, 158
      non-Azure virtual machines, 158
   defined, 126
   edit environment settings, 151
   editions, 156
   enabling free tier, 147, 148
   enabling paid defender plans, 151–156
   example, 126
   features, 131–136
   inventory dashboard, 201
   overview page, 148
   plans and targeted workloads, 132, 133
   plan settings page, 152
   PowerShell, 148–150
   pricing, 143–146
   searching, 147
   threat intelligence report, 171–179
   tools, 127
Microsoft Defender for Cloud Apps (MCAS), 391
Microsoft Defender for Endpoint (MDE), 167, 391, 580
Microsoft Defender for Identity, 391
Microsoft Defender Threat Intelligence (MDTI), 172

651

INDEX

Microsoft Defender XDR, 345
Microsoft Intelligent Security Association (MISA), 346
Microsoft Intelligent Security Graph, 341, 396, *See also* Microsoft Security Graph
Microsoft Learn
    sandbox labs and assessments, 627
    targeted learning paths and modules, 625, 626
Microsoft Monitoring Agent (MMA), 167
Microsoft Purview, 582
Microsoft Security Copilot, 580
Microsoft security ecosystem, 136
Microsoft Security Graph, 396, 397
Microsoft's global threat intelligence, 137
Microsoft Threat Intelligence Center (MSTIC), 168
Migration program, 18
MISA, *see* Microsoft Intelligent Security Association (MISA)
MITRE ATT&CK framework, 133, 137, 351, 352
ML, *see* Machine learning (ML)
MMA, *see* Microsoft Monitoring Agent (MMA)
Modularization, 322
Monitoring strategy
    alerting and response, 246–255
    comparison, 226
    defined, 214
    elements, 221
    governance-critical questions, 214
    governance focus areas, 215
    hybrid *vs.* cloud-native environment, 218–220
    lifecycle, 216
    logs
        case study, 225
        characteristics, 223
        types, 223, 224
        working, 224, 225
    metrics, 216
        characteristics, 221
        flowchart, 222
        types, 221, 222
        use case, 222
    observability *vs.* alerting, 217, 218
    personas, 215, 216
    workbooks
        characteristics, 226
        use case, 226
MSTIC, *see* Microsoft Threat Intelligence Center (MSTIC)
MTTD, *see* Mean time to detect (MTTD)
MTTR, *see* Mean time to respond (MTTR)
Multi-cloud adoption, 500
Multi-cloud environments
    challenges, 500
    control inconsistencies, 503
    cost management complexity, 503
    cost management + GCP billing, 512–519
    defined, 500
    governance tools, 505, 506
    inconsistent tagging, 503, 504
    operational and technical needs, 501–503
    tags and naming rules, 506–512
    visibility challenges, 503
Multi-cloud governance standards
    compliance frameworks, 540
    environments, 541
    industry partners, 540
    platforms, 541
    posture management, 541

Multi-factor authentication (MFA), 442, 444, 455
Multi-layered enforcement model, 461
Multitier network isolation, 482

N

Naming conventions, 31
  categories, 45, 46
  and labels, 37
  recommendations and standards, 44, 45
  rules, 45
  template-based ARM, 51
  tools, 43
Naming standards
  automation, 50–55
  blueprints, 69–74
  categories, 55
  initiatives, 67, 68
  management groups, 60–63
  policies, 52, 63–66
  resource groups, 59, 60
  subscription, 56–59
  tagging, 47–49
National Institute of Standards and Technology (NIST), 543
Natural language, 536
Nested templates, 323, 324
Network isolation, 482, 483
Network map, 201–203
Network security groups (NSGs), 485, 486, 533
Network topology
  filters, 203
  inbound and outbound traffic option, 206
  map, 202
  resource information, 204
  security recommendation, 205
Nextron systems, 170
NIST, see National Institute of Standards and Technology (NIST)
Non-human identities, 480
NSGs, see Network security groups (NSGs)

O

OpenAI service, 575, 576

P

PaaS, see Platform as a service (PaaS)
Parameter file, 321
Parameterization, 273, 287, 289, 302, 303, 317, 330
Personal Azure governance lab
  best practices, 620
  cost-effective options, 619
  free-tier/sandbox environment experimentation, 621
  free account registration form, 622
  home page, 624
  low-cost options, 620
  setting up, 621–624
  verification card, 623
  pitfalls, 620
PHI, see Protected health information (PHI)
PIM, see Privileged identity management (PIM)
Pipeline-level visibility, 139
Platform as a service (PaaS), 11, 25, 26, 129
Platform logs, 223
Platform metrics, 221

INDEX

Playbooks
  analytics rules
    automated responses, 374
    automation, 376
    creating schedule query, 374
    information requirement, 378
    multi-tab wizard, 375
    validation, 379, 380
  automated generation, 536
  automated response actions, 369
  confidence-based branching, 429–437
  configuring triggers, 195–198
  defined, 368
  email alerts and notifications, 369, 370
  event driven, 142
  incident response procedures, 142
  security, 179, 180
  tasks, 142
  templates
    content hub, 371, 372
    customizations, 373
    trigger types and automation rules, 373
  threat containment and remediation, 371
  ticketing system integration, 370
  trigger, 368
Plug-and-play approach, 572
POC, *see* Proof of concept (POC)
POL, *see* Policy definitions (POL)
Policies, 83, See also Policy definitions (POL)
  assignment, scope and exclusions, 115, 116
  and assignment scope options, 8
  basics, 78–81
  categories, 63

  cloud governance, 6, 7
  continuous enforcement and compliance, 264
  custom category example, 63
  defined, 75
  definition mode, 7
  implementation, 64
  initiatives and scoping, 102–116
  location, 81–83
  management, 141, 142
  names, editing, 65
  naming standards, 52, 63–66
  operations, conditions and fields, 81
  overlaps, 288
  planning, 76
  predefined, 46
  scoping, 288
  and security, 26
  terminology, 76–78
Policy assignment
  artifact, 260, 266
  scope and effect, 271, 272
Policy definitions (POL), 264
  assignment
    changing assignment name and adding description, 93
    changing description and category, 97
    changing name, description and rule, 101
    compliance status, 94
    compliance view, 99
    custom selection, 92
    duplication, 99
    editing description, SKUs information, 98
    editing option, 97
    events, 95

filtering, 91
location, 100
major objective changes, 99–101
minor objective changes, 96–99
option, 90
schedule evaluation, 94
selecting parameters, 93
selecting subscription and resource group, 91
virtual machines, 89
creation
assigning name and description, 87
changing category and effect value, 88
custom verification, 89
duplication, 85, 86
searching and selecting portal, 84
searching and selecting virtual machine size SKUs, 85
selecting blade, 84
selecting location, 86
steps, 83
defined, 83
storage location, 82
Policy effects
AddToNetworkGroup, 117
append, 117, 118
audit, 119
AuditIfNotExists, 119
deny, 120
DenyAction, 120
DeployIfNotExists, 120
disable type, 120, 121
Policy enforcement, 134, 139, 582
Post-quantum cryptography (PQC), 542–544, 546, 547, 549
Post-quantum integrity assurance (PQIA), 545

PowerShell, 52, 148–150
PQC, *see* Post-quantum cryptography (PQC)
PQIA, *see* Post-quantum integrity assurance (PQIA)
Predictive security, 441, 442
Pricing
cost management and estimation tools, 146
free tier, 143, 144
multi-cloud and hybrid billing, 146
paid defender plans, 144, 145
Privacy, 5
Private endpoints, 486, 487, 492, 495
Privileged identity management (PIM), 356, 451, 534
defined, 465
features, 466
policy-based constraints, 466
workflow, 466–468
Proactive cybersecurity, 444, 445
Probabilistic reasoning, 414
Probability score, 429
Production, 96
Prometheus metrics, 222
Proof of concept (POC), 18
Protected health information (PHI), 553

Q

QRA, *see* Quantum-resilient authentication (QRA)
Quantum computing
concept, 541
cryptography research, 548
fault-tolerant, 547
initiatives, 548
key management, 545–547

INDEX

Quantum computing (*cont.*)
    PQC, 542–544, 549
    security, 548
    threat modeling, 544, 545
Quantum-resilient authentication (QRA), 545
Quantum-resistant algorithms, 542
Query-driven visualizations, 353

R

RaMP, *see* Rapid modernization plan (RaMP)
Ransomware attacks, 395, 396
Rapid modernization plan (RaMP), 457
RBAC, *see* Role-based access control (RBAC)
RDP, *see* Remote Desktop Protocol (RDP)
Reactive *vs.* proactive governance models, 619
Real-time policy enforcement, 121–123
Real-time threat protection, 137, 138
Regulation, 5
Relationship structure, 17, 18
Remediation
    automatic, 122, 123
    guidance, 139
    manual, 122
    options, 122
Remote Desktop Protocol (RDP), 127
Resource groups, 17, 40
    architectural principles, 293
    artifacts, 260, 266, 292, 293
    environment and application type, 28
    exclusions, 116
    geographic location, 27
    naming standards, 59, 60
    planning, 27
    structure, 271
    tagging, 47, 48
Resource inventory, 135
Resource logs, 223
Resource management, 21, 34
Resources, 16, 17
Retrofit governance, 268
Risk prioritization, 443
Role assignment artifacts, 260, 266, 267, 269, 290
Role-based access control (RBAC), 3, 8, 9, 36, 39, 42, 228, 266, 272, 354, 356, 451, 481, 578
    best practices, role assignments, 290–292
    blueprint context, 290
    principles, 290
Root management group, 38, 39
Rule-based detection systems, 412–414
Rule-based security systems, 579

S

SaaS, *see* Software as a service (SaaS)
Sandbox environments, 331
Scaling tagging, 49
SCOM, *see* System Center Operations Manager (SCOM)
Scoping, 102
Secure development lifecycle support, 140
Secured virtual hub, 207
Security alert, 137
Security automation, 142
Security information and event management (SIEM), 133, 341–343, 413
Security logs, 224

Security Operations Center (SOC), 346, 352, 354, 438, 439, 444
Security orchestration, automation and response (SOAR), 368
Security playbooks, 135, 179, 180
Security protocols, 3
Self-sovereign identities, 564
Service endpoints, 487
Service principal, 480, 481
Shared responsibility model, 128, 129
SIEM, *see* Security information and event management (SIEM)
Signature-based detection, 137
Simulating attacks, 170, 171
SOAR, *see* Security orchestration, automation and response (SOAR)
SOC, *see* Security Operations Center (SOC)
Software as a service (SaaS), 11, 25
Source control systems
    ARM templates, 331, 332
    CI/CD integration, 334, 335
    repository structure, 332, 333
    versioning, 331
Speech services, 573
Starter templates, 305
Static analysis tools, 330
STRIDE methodology, 545
Subscriptions
    Azure Sentinel, 355
    blueprint assignment, 298–302
    capabilities, 11
    changing, 58
    core cloud service categories, 11
    default names, 56
    elements, 56
    key points, 12
    list, 57
    management groups, 29
    options and link, 25, 26
    planning, 24–26
    policies, 81
    and relationship, 12
    rename option, 57, 58
    and scalability, 41, 42
    search result, 56, 57
    updated name, 59
    usage and departmental ownership, 56
System Center Operations Manager (SCOM), 219

T

Tag bindings, 512
Tagging strategies
    categorization, 47
    governance and compliance, 49
    purpose, 47, 48
    resource groups, 47, 48
    streamline tasks, 47
Template file, 319, 320
Tenants
    concept, 10
    identity and access management system, 10
    key points, 11
    planning, 23, 24
    and relationship, 12
    representation, 10
Testing, governance, 31
Threat detection and response, 168–170
Threat hunting
    bookmarks and annotations, 385, 386
    creation, 385
    defined, 381
    importance, 382

Threat hunting (*cont.*)
    navigation, 382, 383
    selecting query, 383
Threat intelligence correlation, 137
Threat intelligence report
    data access perspective, 172
    defined, 171
    higher-order analysis, 172
    mitigation, 172
    reports, 171, 172
    security alerts
        action page, 176, 177
        changing status, 178
        investigation, 173–175
        management, 173
        responding, 176–179
        viewing, 175
Threat signals, 345
TPMs, *see* Trusted platform modules (TPMs)
Traditional enforcement mechanisms, 532
Transparency, 5
Trigger automated workflows, 138
Trusted platform modules (TPMs), 533

U

UDRs, *see* User-defined routes (UDRs)
UEBA, *see* User and entity behavior analytics (UEBA)
Unified management, 17
Unsupervised learning, 412
Unsupervised models, 350
User and entity behavior analytics (UEBA), 350
    data sources, 387
    defined, 387

directory services, 389, 390
entity behavior configuration page, 389
machine learning capabilities, 387, 388
setting, 388
User-defined routes (UDRs), 484, 486

V

Virtual machines (VM), 50, 55, 89, 127, 157, 158
Virtual networks (VNets), 482, 488–490, 494
Visibility, 143
Vision services, 573
VM, *see* Virtual machines (VM)
VNets, *see* Virtual networks (VNets)

W, X, Y

WAF, *see* Web Application Firewall (WAF)
Web Application Firewall (WAF), 495
Workflow automation, logic apps
    adding, 182
    Azure Resource Manager, 191, 192
    configuring email action, 189, 190
    creation, 184, 185, 194
    dashboard, 181
    designer, 185, 186
    form, 182, 183
    Office 365 Outlook action, 188, 189
    prerequisites, 180, 181
    providing parameters information, 193
    selecting hosting plan, 184
    trigger, 186–188
Workload identities, 480
Workspace region selection, 355

Z

Zero trust architecture
    AI workloads, 532, 533
    cloud era, 452, 453
    core tenets, 450–452
    defined, 450
    deployment strategy, 457, 458
    edge computing, 534, 535
    incident response, 608, 609
    IoT devices, 533, 534
    layering signals, 461
    mapping, 458–460
    maturity model, 462, 463
    overview, 461
    pillars, 532
    policy-based access control, 455
    policy enforcement, 456
    principles, 450, 451
    security domains, 455, 456
    security model, 449
    threat intelligence and automated remediation, 457
    vs. traditional perimeter security models, 453, 454
    transitioning, 454

GPSR Compliance

The European Union's (EU) General Product Safety Regulation (GPSR) is a set of rules that requires consumer products to be safe and our obligations to ensure this.

If you have any concerns about our products, you can contact us on

ProductSafety@springernature.com

In case Publisher is established outside the EU, the EU authorized representative is:

Springer Nature Customer Service Center GmbH
Europaplatz 3
69115 Heidelberg, Germany

www.ingramcontent.com/pod-product-compliance
Lightning Source LLC
LaVergne TN
LVHW080309260326
834688LV00038B/1018